Exploring Chromebook

2025 Edition

Kevin Wilson

elluminet Press

www.elluminetpress.com

Exploring Chromebook: 2025 Edition

Images used with permission under CCASA, Andrew Neel, Luminescent Media / CC-BY-SA-3.0. iStock.com/golibo, PeopleImages, ymgerman. Photo 130859010 © Kaspars Grinvalds - Dreamstime.com. Photo 103557713 © Konstantin Kolosov - Dreamstime.com. Photo 175930931 / Chromebook © Info849943 | Dreamstime.com. Yuri Arcurs via Getty Images, 177549431 © Fizkes | Dreamstime.com

Publisher: Elluminet Press
Director: Kevin Wilson
Lead Editor: Steven Ashmore
Technical Reviewer: Mike Taylor, Robert Ashcroft
Copy Editors: Joanne Taylor, James Marsh
Proof Reader: Mike Taylor
Indexer: James Marsh
Cover Designer: Kevin Wilson

eBook versions and licenses are also available for most titles. Any source code or other supplementary materials referenced by the author in this text is available to readers at www.elluminetpress.com/resources

For detailed information about how to locate your book's resources, go to www.elluminetpress.com/resources

Table of Contents

About the Author

With over 20 years' experience in the computer industry, Kevin Wilson has made a career out of technology and showing others how to use it. After earning a master's degree in computer science, software engineering, and multimedia systems, Kevin has held various positions in the IT industry including graphic & web design, programming, building & managing corporate networks, and IT support.

He serves as senior writer and director at Elluminet Press Ltd, he periodically teaches computer science at college, and works as an IT trainer in England while researching for his PhD. His books have become a valuable resource among the students in England, South Africa, Canada, and in the United States.

Kevin's motto is clear: "If you can't explain something simply, then you haven't understood it well enough." To that end, he has created the Exploring Tech Computing series, in which he breaks down complex technological subjects into smaller, easy-to-follow steps that students and ordinary computer users can put into practice.

Acknowledgements

Thanks to all the staff at Luminescent Media & Elluminet Press for their passion, dedication and hard work in the preparation and production of this book.

To all my friends and family for their continued support and encouragement in all my writing projects.

To all my colleagues, students and testers who took the time to test procedures and offer feedback on the book

Finally thanks to you the reader for choosing this book. I hope it helps you to use your Chromebook with greater understanding.

Have fun!

1

Introducing Chromebook

What is a Chromebook? A Chromebook is a laptop or tablet computer that runs ChromeOS, an operating system developed by Google and first released on June 15, 2011. This operating system is derived from the open-source ChromiumOS project and its primary interface is built around the Google Chrome web browser.

In this chapter, we'll take a look at:

- What's New with Chromebook?

- Chromebook & The Chromebook Plus

- ChromeOS & Cloud Computing

- Gemini & AI

- Anti-virus & Security

To help you understand this section, open your web browser and navigate to the following website.

e l l u m i n e t p r e s s . c o m / chromebook

What's New?

Over the past few years, Chromebooks have undergone various changes, including the addition of some new features.

ChromeOS now supports more versatile window arrangement with snapping and partial splits, making it easier to arrange multiple windows side by side in different ratios.

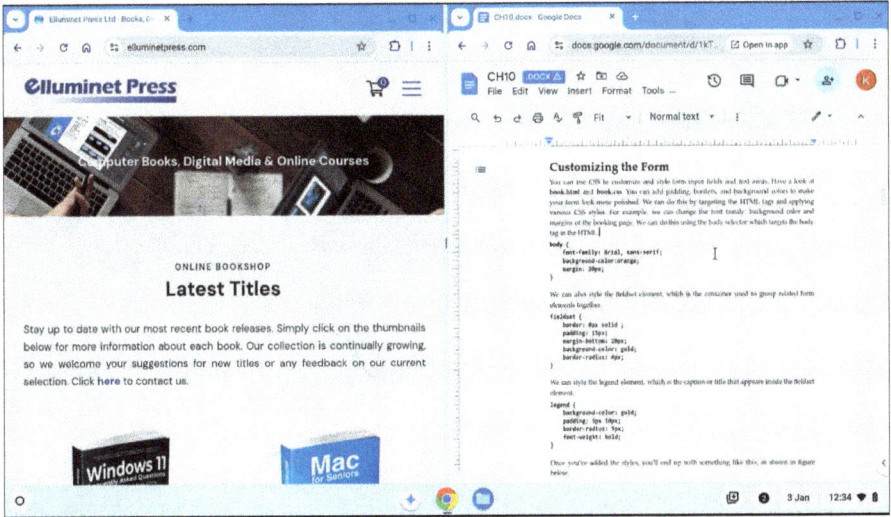

The Virtual Desks feature has been upgraded with new gestures and shortcuts, making it simpler to switch between workspaces and drag apps from one desk to another.

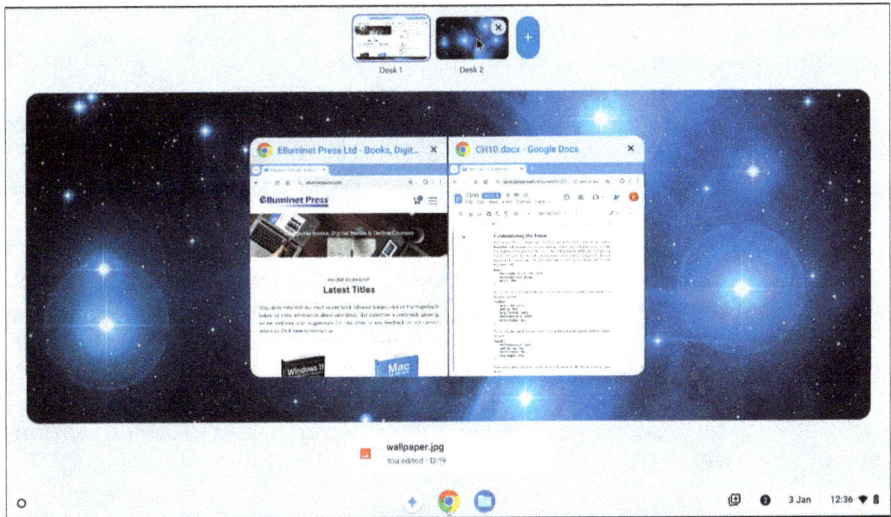

Chapter 1: Introducing Chromebook

A streamlined file manager interface includes faster search, additional sorting options, and tighter integration with Google Drive (and other cloud storage providers).

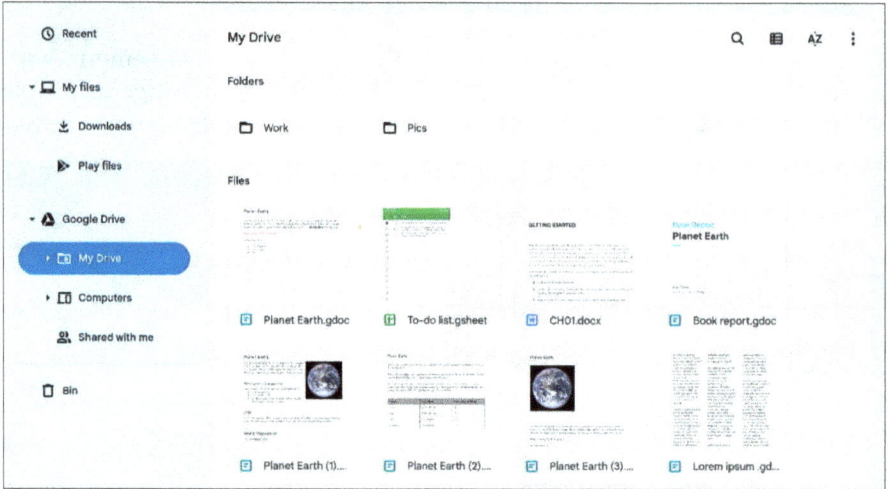

Phone Hub is a built-in feature that allows you to link your Android phone to your Chromebook.

Phone Hub now offers improved controls over your connected Android phone. You can view your phone's notifications on your Chromebook, access recent Chrome tabs from your phone, and send or receive text messages directly on your Chromebook. It also enables instant tethering, allowing your Chromebook to use your phone's mobile data for internet access seamlessly. Additionally, if you misplace your phone nearby, you can use Phone Hub to make it ring, helping you locate it quickly.

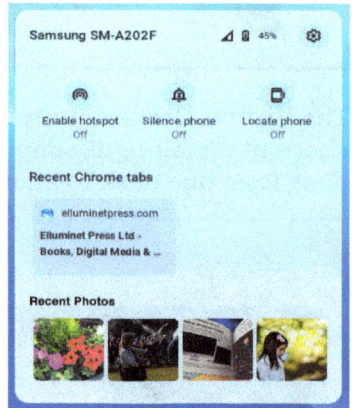

ChromeOS can now automatically adjust webcam and microphone levels in real time to reduce background noise and improve video clarity. System-level background blur and virtual backgrounds are compatible across multiple video-conferencing platforms (Google Meet, Zoom, and others).

Chrome OS has introduced a system-wide light/dark theme option, letting you switch between a brighter or more subdued interface.

google.com/chromebook/whatsnew/

Chromebook and Chromebook Plus

There are two types of Chromebook: The standard Chromebook and Chromebook Plus.

Chromebook

The standard Chromebook is a lightweight, affordable laptop designed to run Google's ChromeOS, including seamless integration with Google Apps such as Gmail, Google Drive, Docs, Sheets, and Slides.

These machines are ideal for web browsing, email, basic productivity such as document editing, video chat, and messaging.

One of the most appealing aspects of Chromebook is its affordability, with prices often starting as low as a few hundred dollars.

They're perfect for students, casual users, or anyone who primarily works online and wants a secure, low-maintenance device.

Chromebook Plus

The Chromebook Plus represents a new tier of Chromebooks that offer more powerful hardware. These machines also run ChromeOS along with Google Apps but are equipped with higher powered processors, such as Intel Core or ARM, typically 8GB of RAM, and at least 128GB of local storage. This makes them better suited for multitasking, more demanding apps, and light creative tasks.

Due to its higher specs and enhanced features, the Chromebook Plus is more expensive, typically starting from the mid-range to premium laptop price points. They also come with exclusive features like enhanced video conferencing, and built-in AI tools.

You'll be able to find more up to date information on Google's website.

google.com/chromebook

ChromeOS & Cloud Computing

ChromeOS is a lightweight, cloud-based operating system developed by Google and is derived from the open-source ChromiumOS project. Designed around the Google Chrome web browser, ChromeOS provides a simple, secure, and fast computing environment. This is the operating system that runs on your Chromebook.

Rather than relying on extensive local storage, files are stored remotely in Google Drive which is hosted on Google's secure servers. This approach—often called saving your files in the cloud—means you can access your files from anywhere with an internet connection, on any device where you're signed in with your Google Account.

These secure servers are managed by Google and are part of a large server farm or data center like the one pictured below.

Google Drive is accessible through its web interface as you can see in the screenshot below.

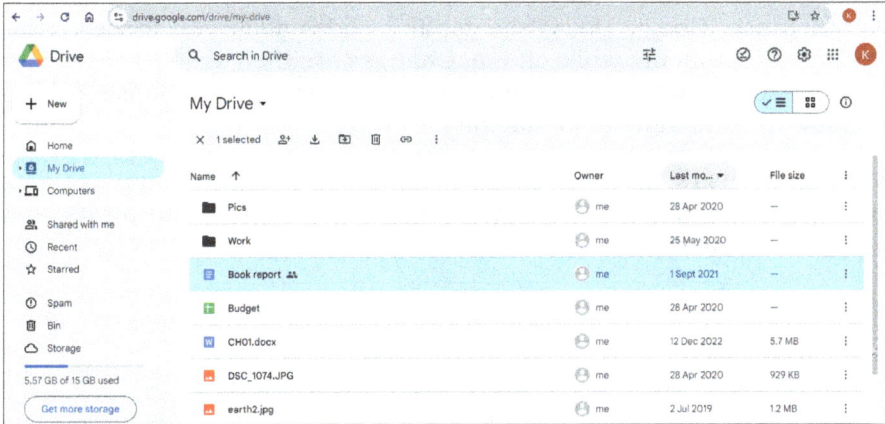

You can also access Google Drive on Android and iOS devices using the App.

An important feature of the service is the Backup and Sync functionality, which automates the backup of folders from devices to the cloud, keeping files up-to-date across all devices. It also integrates with Google Docs, Sheets, Slides, as well as other Google services.

Chapter 1: Introducing Chromebook

While ChromeOS is designed to be is cloud-based, it also provides offline functionality, allowing you to continue working without an internet connection. Many Chromebook apps have offline capabilities. For instance, Google Docs, Sheets, and Slides allow you to view, edit, and save documents while offline. Changes are then synchronized with Google Drive once you reconnect to the internet. Chromebooks also come with local storage for saving files directly to your device.

ChromeOS also seamlessly integrates with Google's suite of applications, which are accessible through both personal Google accounts and Google Workspace accounts.

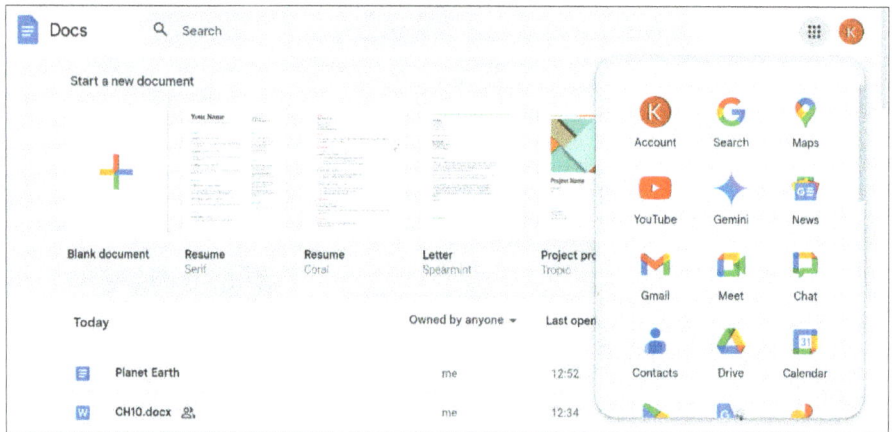

What's the difference between these two account types? A Google Personal account is free and designed for individual use, and provides access to Gmail for email, Google Drive for cloud storage, and productivity tools such as Google Docs, Sheets, and Slides for creating and editing documents, spreadsheets, and presentations. As well as Google Calendar, Photos, YouTube, Google Meet and Google Chat. You get 15 GB of storage on Google Drive for free with the option to purchase more.

A Google Workspace account is part of a paid subscription plan taken out by businesses, educational institutions, non-profits, and other organizations. This allows these organizations to manage users, devices, security settings, and permissions from a centralized administrative console. These accounts offers more professional email addresses using the organization's custom domain name (e.g., you@ yourcompany.com rather than you@gmail.com). Google Workspace provides enhanced versions of Google Meet, and Google Chat with longer meeting durations, meeting recordings, breakout rooms, and live streaming. Storage options are greater, ranging from 30 GB per user to unlimited storage, depending on the chosen plan.

Gemini and AI

Google Gemini is an Artificial Intelligence technology platform developed by Google. It's part of a broader suite of tools and models that use advanced data analytics and machine learning to assist with a variety of every day tasks.

For example, Gemini can write stories, poems, articles, and other text. It can also summarizing text, translate languages, and write code.

You can ask Gemini questions and it will provide answers to your questions on a wide range of topics. However, check with official sources as these AI models can sometimes generate incorrect information.

Gemini can generate images from text descriptions and it can help you edit photos and videos with features like Magic Editor, which allows you to make changes to your photos and videos with just a few taps.

You can find Gemini using this link: `gemini.google.com`

Here, you can type queries into the text field at the bottom of the window.

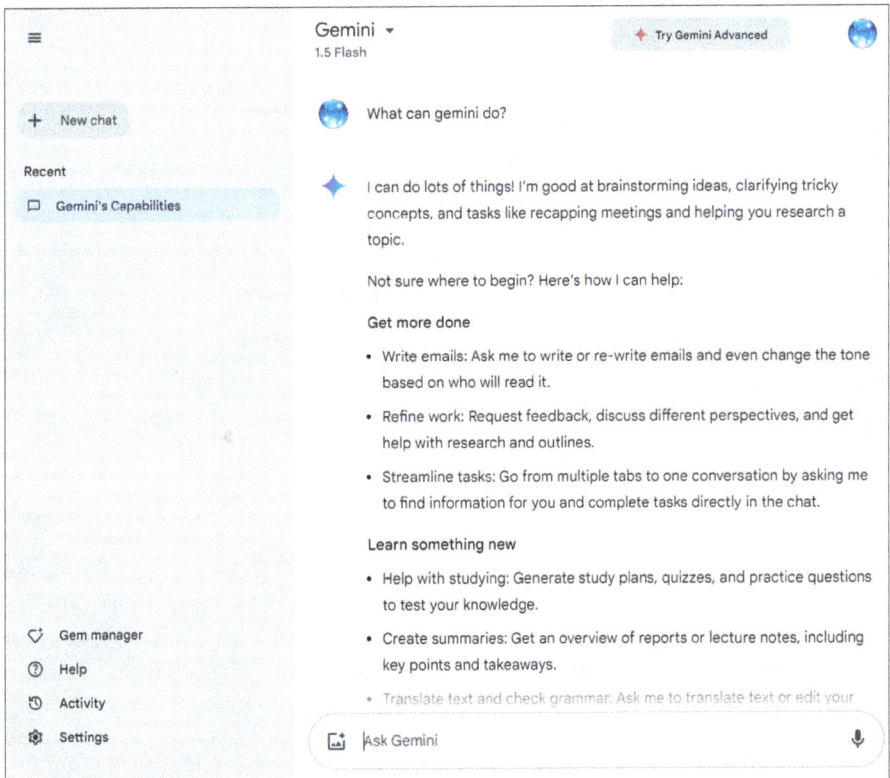

Chapter 1: Introducing Chromebook

Google Gemini offers both free and paid options. The free version includes standard AI capabilities such as basic content generation, simple data analysis, and integration with some Google services such as Gmail and Google Docs.

The paid subscription options enhance the basic functionalities available in the free version. The Gemini Advanced subscription includes more sophisticated AI features, such as larger context windows and advanced language models, designed for both individual professionals and enterprise users. I've included a summary below according to Google's Gemini website.

Feature	Gemini	Gemini Advanced
Availability	Free, widely available	Part of Google One Premium plan
Core Capabilities	• **Text Generation:** Write stories, articles, code, etc • **Translation:** Translate languages accurately and fluently • **Summarization:** Condense long articles, reports, or documents into concise summaries • **Question Answering:** Find answers to your questions from a vast knowledge base • **Creative Content:** Generate ideas for stories, poems, etc • **Basic Coding:** Assist with simple coding tasks and debugging.	• All of Gemini's capabilities with significant enhancements • **Advanced Coding:** Develop complex code, debug intricate programs, and assist with software development. • **In-depth Research:** Conduct thorough research, analyze data, and synthesize information from diverse sources • **Creative Collaboration:** Co-author stories, scripts, and other creative works with unique styles and perspectives • **Complex Problem-Solving:** Tackle challenging puzzles, solve intricate equations, and navigate complex scenarios • **Enhanced Reasoning & Planning:** Demonstrate superior logical reasoning, plan multi-step actions, and make informed decisions
Context Window	32K tokens (approximately 24,000 words)	1 million tokens (approximately 750,000 words) - Allows for processing of significantly longer texts, such as entire books or research papers.
Key Differences	• **Focus:** General-purpose AI assistant for everyday tasks. • **Performance:** Good for basic text generation, translation, and simple tasks. • **Accessibility:** Free and widely available to all users.	• **Focus:** High-performance AI for demanding tasks and professionals • **Performance:** Excels in complex coding, in-depth research, creative projects, and advanced problem-solving • **Accessibility:** Requires a paid Google One Premium subscription.
Additional Benefits	None	• **2 TB of Google Drive Storage:** Ample storage space for your files and documents. • **Premium Google Support:** Priority access to expert support for any Google services. • **Priority Access to New Features:** Early access to the latest AI advancements and exclusive features.

For businesses, Google provides tailored plans like Gemini Business and Gemini Enterprise, which offer additional security, advanced translation capabilities, and enterprise-level tools. These subscriptions are priced per user per month and cater to larger organizations needing comprehensive AI integration across multiple Google Workspace applications.

The "Help Me Read" feature uses artificial intelligence to summarise lengthy documents or web content, providing a condensed version of the material. It also offers an interactive Q&A format, allowing you to ask specific questions about the text, thereby facilitating a better understanding without the need to sift through all the original material yourself.

The "Help Me Write" feature analyzes texts entered by the user and suggests corrections and enhancements in grammar, style, and overall coherence. It can also assist with a variety of writing tasks such as composing emails, crafting reports, or creating content.

Anti-virus and Security

Chromebooks are designed with security in mind and have several built-in features to help protect against malware and viruses.

Each app runs in a restricted environment known as a sandbox. If malware is encountered, it's confined to the sandbox, preventing it from affecting other apps or system files on the Chromebook.

Every time a Chromebook starts up, it checks the integrity of its operating system ChromeOS. If it detects any modifications by malicious software, it can automatically repair itself by reverting to a prior safe state.

For Chromebooks that run Android apps, Google Play Protect continuously scans these apps for malware before and after you install them. This reduces the risk of downloading apps that might be harmful.

Chromebooks automatically update to the latest version of Chrome OS, which includes the latest security features and fixes, ensuring that the system's defences are up-to-date against current threats.

User data is encrypted, which helps protect sensitive information if the device is lost or stolen.

If something goes wrong, Chromebooks have a recovery mode that allows you to restore your operating system to a clean state.

While traditional antivirus software isn't necessary on a Chromebook due to built-in protection features discussed above, it's still important to practice safe browsing habits and be cautious about which apps and extensions you install and what links you click on in emails, as you can still fall victim to scams, phishing and other cyber attacks.

2

Setting up your Chromebook

Chromebooks are very easy to set up. They come pre-installed with Chrome OS. All you need to do is go through the initial setup, sign in with your Google Account and you're pretty much ready to go.

In this chapter, we'll take a look at:

- Creating a Google Account
- Initial Setup
- Personalise your Chromebook
- Transferring Files to Chromebook
- Setting up Printers
- Adding Bluetooth Devices
- Connect your Phone
- Connect to WiFi
- Tethering
- Managing Users
- Parental Controls
- Configuring Other Settings
- Remote Desktop

For this chapter, take a look at the video resources section. Open your browser and navigate to the following website

elluminetpress.com/using-chromebook

Creating a Google Account

If you use Gmail you will already have a Google Account. If this is the case, you don't need to create a new Google Account so you can skip this step.

If you don't have one, you can create one online before you start, if you have another computer by opening your web browser and browsing to the following page

`accounts.google.com/signup`

Fill in your name in the first two fields, then under 'username', type in the name you want to appear in your email address. This can be a nickname or your full name. The name must be unique, so if someone else has already taken the name, you'll need to choose a new one or add a couple of numbers. Google will tell you if the username you entered has already been used.

Enter the password you want to use in the 'password' field, then type it again to confirm it in the 'confirm' field.

Click 'next'.

Initial Setup

When you first turn on your Chromebook, you'll come to the welcome screen. From here, if you need to change your language, click on the default language link at the top of the screen.

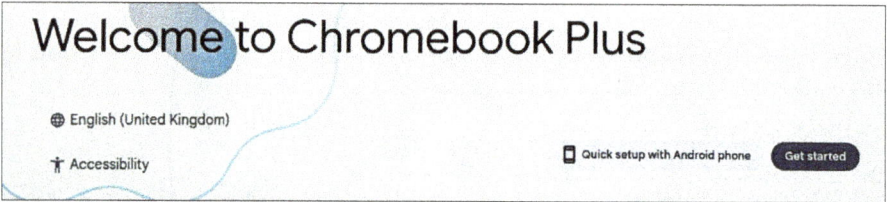

Select your WiFi network, click 'next'. Then enter your WiFi password when prompted. Click 'connect'.

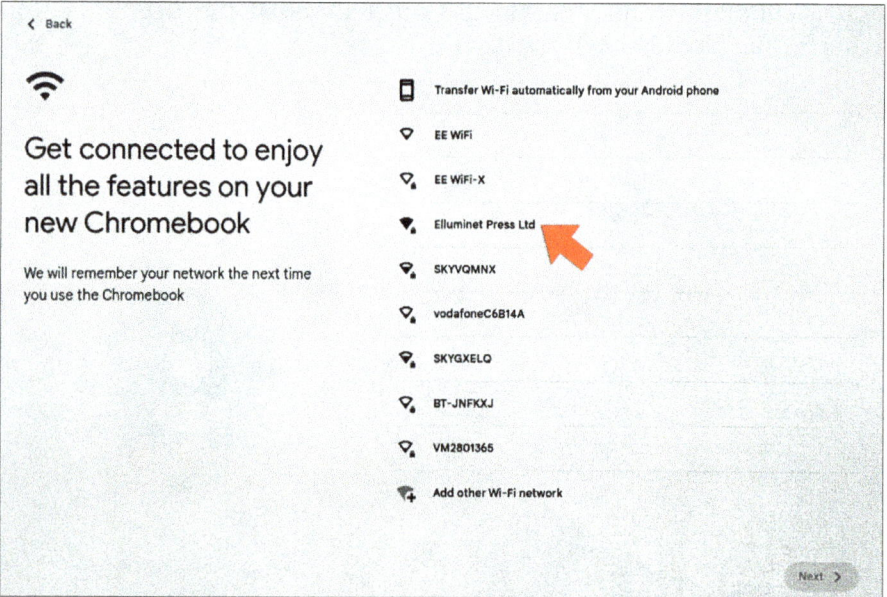

Allow your Chromebook to check for updates.

Choose your Chromebook's setup. To do this, click on one of the three options.

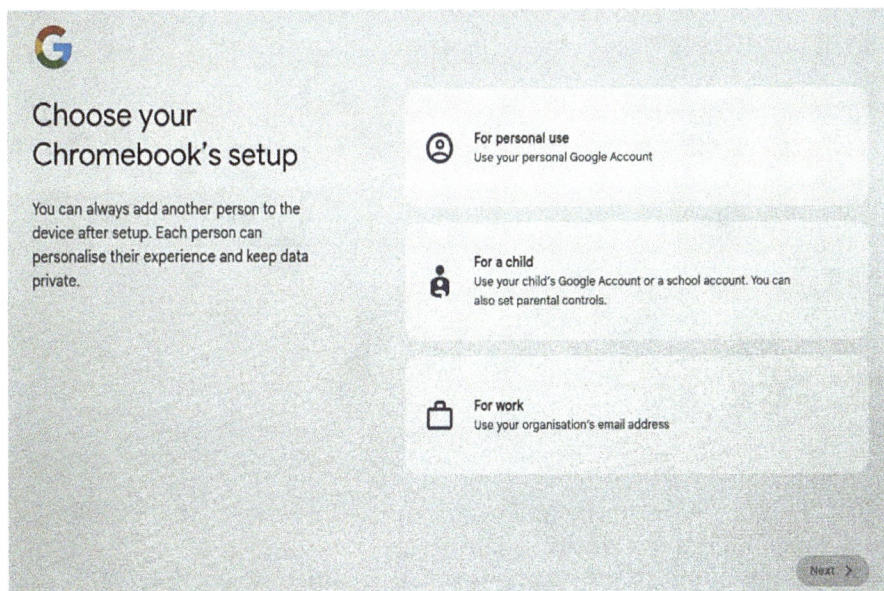

For most home users, select 'for personal use', then click 'next'. The options available are explained below.

For personal use is intended for individuals who want to use the Chromebook with their own personal Google Account. Selecting this path sets up the device for general personal use, enabling features like Gmail, Google Drive, YouTube, and Chrome Sync. You will have full control over settings, apps, and data. It is the standard choice for most home users.

For a child is designed for children under the supervision of a parent or guardian. It requires signing in with the child's Google Account (one managed through Google Family Link). Parents can set content filters, screen time limits, and app restrictions. If the child has a school-issued Google Workspace for Education account, it can also be used here, often with preset admin controls defined by the school.

For work is for employees or users in a managed enterprise or educational environment. It requires signing in with a work-issued email address associated with Google Workspace . Choosing this option enrols the Chromebook into the organization's management system, allowing IT administrators to enforce device policies, push apps, and manage updates remotely. It's suitable for businesses, schools, and other organizations with centralized management needs.

Chapter 2: Setting up your Chromebook

Once you've done this, your Chromebook will install any updates it has found.

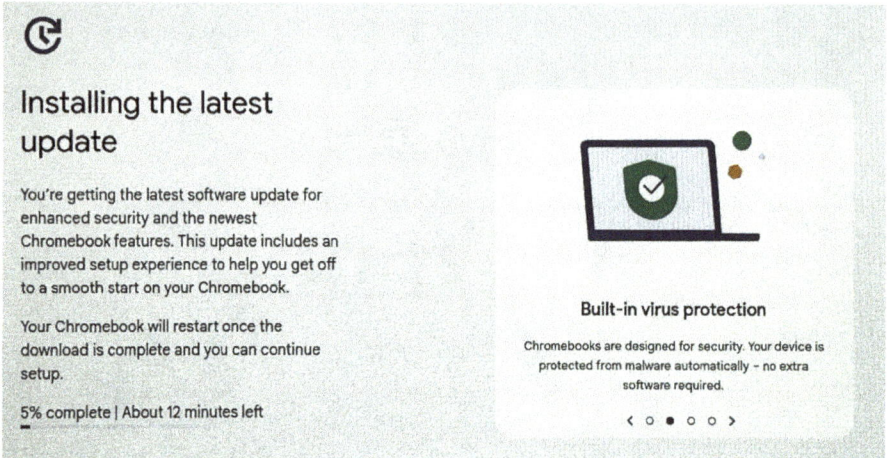

Installing the latest update

You're getting the latest software update for enhanced security and the newest Chromebook features. This update includes an improved setup experience to help you get off to a smooth start on your Chromebook.

Your Chromebook will restart once the download is complete and you can continue setup.

5% complete | About 12 minutes left

Built-in virus protection

Chromebooks are designed for security. Your device is protected from malware automatically – no extra software required.

Next, sign in with your Google Account. There are two ways to do this. You can enter your Google Account and password, or if you use an android phone, you can get your account from Android phone automatically

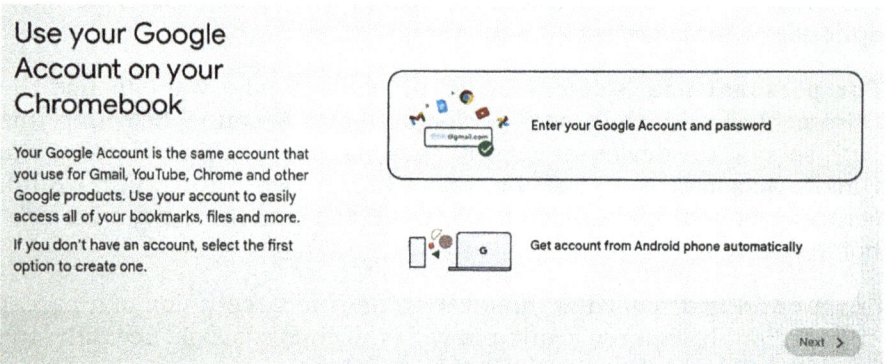

Use your Google Account on your Chromebook

Your Google Account is the same account that you use for Gmail, YouTube, Chrome and other Google products. Use your account to easily access all of your bookmarks, files and more.

If you don't have an account, select the first option to create one.

Enter your Google Account and password

Get account from Android phone automatically

Next >

Enter your Google Account and password allows you to manually sign in by entering your Google Account Gmail address and password. It's the standard method for signing into ChromeOS and links your device to your personal Google services. If you don't yet have a Google Account, this option will also allow you to create one.

Get account from Android phone automatically simplifies the sign-in process by using your nearby Android phone. If the Chromebook and phone are both signed into the same Google Account and have Bluetooth enabled, the phone can transfer your credentials securely to the Chromebook.

Review terms and conditions. Click 'accept and continue'.

Sync your Chromebook apps. Click 'accept and continue'.

Sync your Chromebook apps, settings and more refers to syncing preferences such as installed apps, Wi-Fi networks, accessibility settings, wallpaper, and system configurations.

Sync your Chrome browser bookmarks, passwords, history and more syncs browser-related data including saved passwords, open tabs, bookmarks, extensions, autofill information, and browsing history.

Review sync options following setup allows you to manually review and customize what data gets synced after setup is complete.

Chapter 2: Setting up your Chromebook

Enter a PIN. Instead of entering your full Google Account password each time you sign into the Chromebook, you can create a 6-digit PIN. This PIN will be specific to only this device and is a more convenient way to unlock your Chromebook. The PIN never leaves the device — it's stored and authenticated locally, unlike your Google Account password, which is transmitted and validated over the internet.

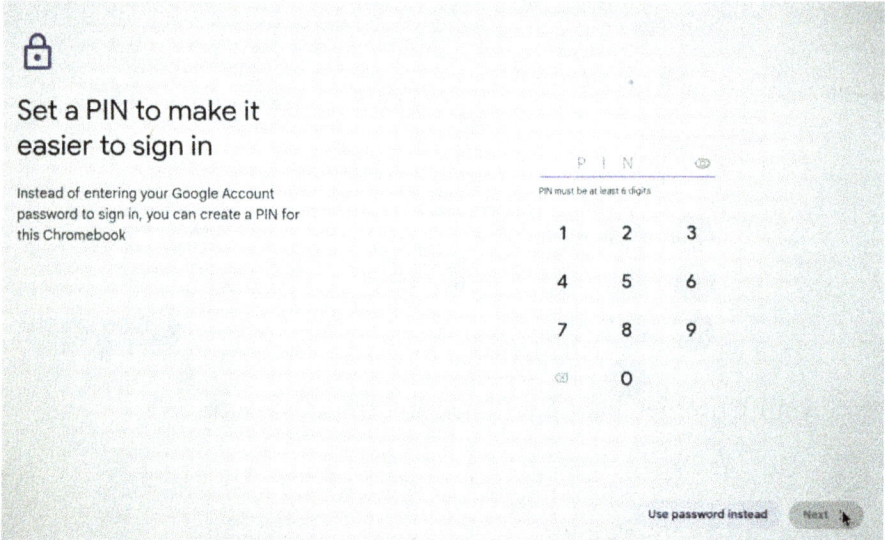

Select what you'll use your Chromebook for. You can select one of the options or click 'skip'.

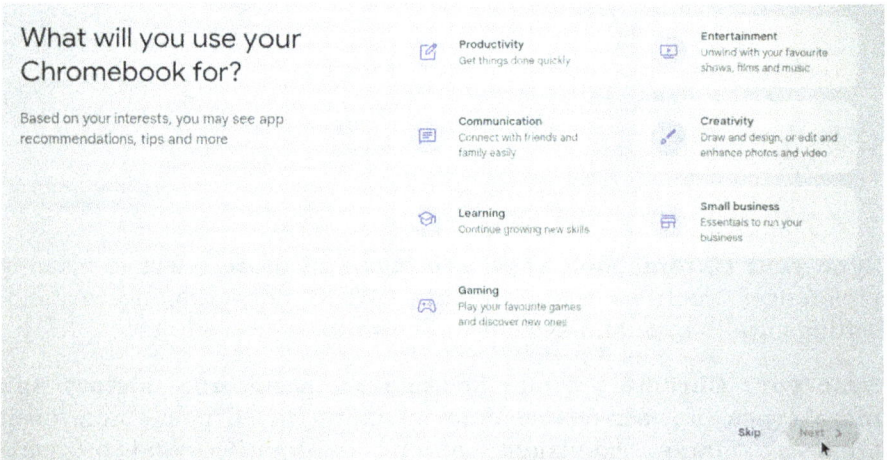

In most cases, it's perfectly fine to skip this step, especially if you already know which apps and tools you'll install yourself. Skipping has no impact on your ability to use any features or install apps later.

Click 'next' through the following screens about Google AI and Chromebook Plus.

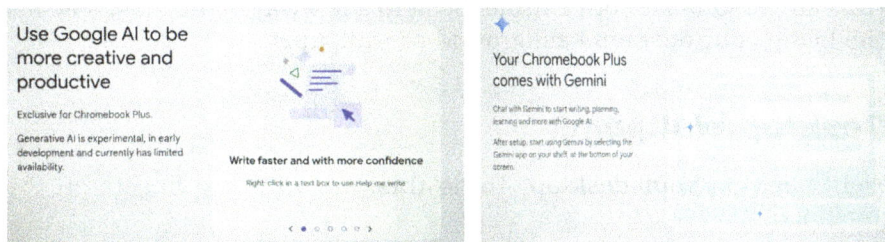

Make some final tweaks. Select any of the four settings to make adjustments.

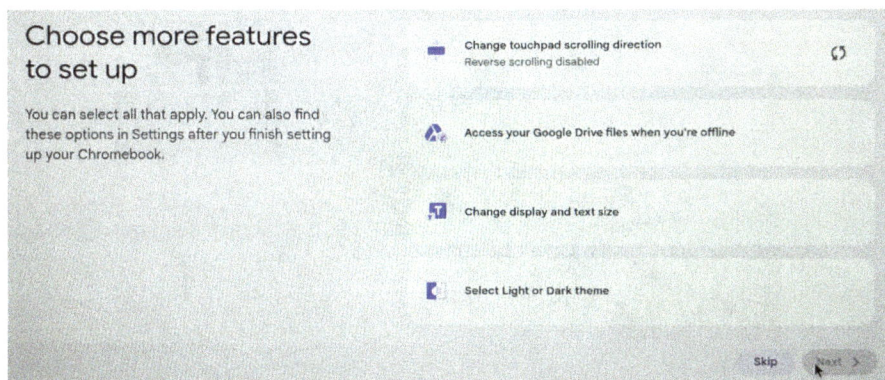

Change touchpad scrolling direction lets you enable or disable reverse scrolling (also called "natural scrolling"). Disabling it means scrolling behaves like traditional desktop mice, where dragging down scrolls down.

Access your Google Drive files when you're offline enables offline access to files stored in Google Drive, allowing you to view and edit documents even when you're not connected to the internet. Changes are synced once you're back online.

Change display and text size allows you to modify scaling and font size for better readability or to fit more content on screen, which can improve accessibility or user comfort.

Select Light or Dark theme lets you choose between light mode, dark mode, or system-based theme appearance for the ChromeOS user interface.

Take a look at "Desktop and the App Shelf" on page 108 for more details on getting around the desktop.

Personalise your Chromebook

You can personalise your Chromebook in a few ways - the most obvious one being your desktop background or wallpaper.

Desktop Wallpaper

Right click on your desktop. To do this, tap with two fingers on the touchpad.

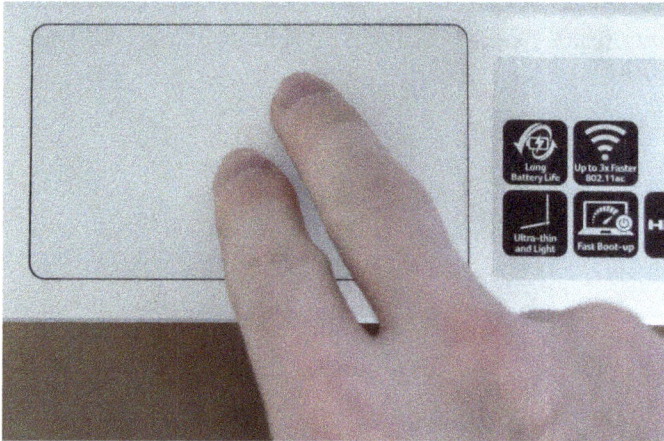

From the popup menu, select 'set wallpaper and style'.

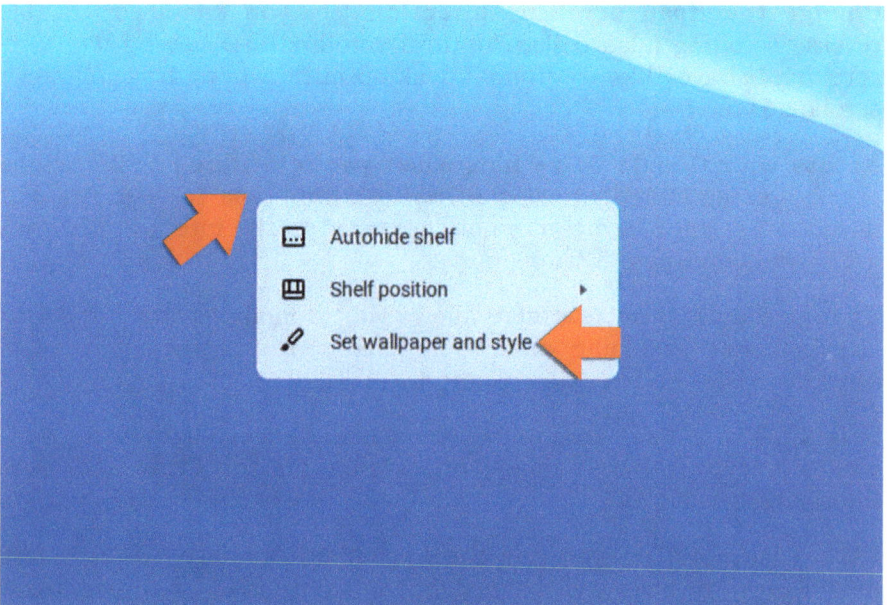

Click on the wallpaper on the left hand side of the window.

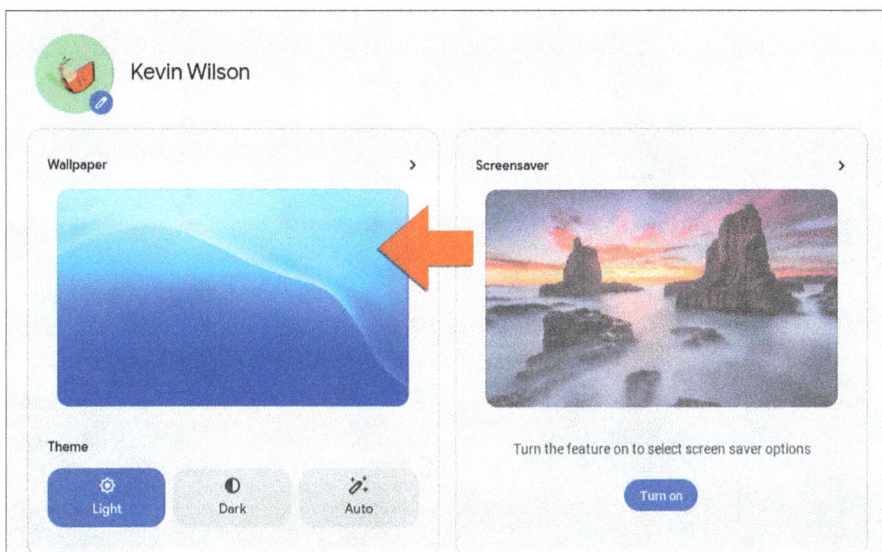

You'll see some folders listed in the window.

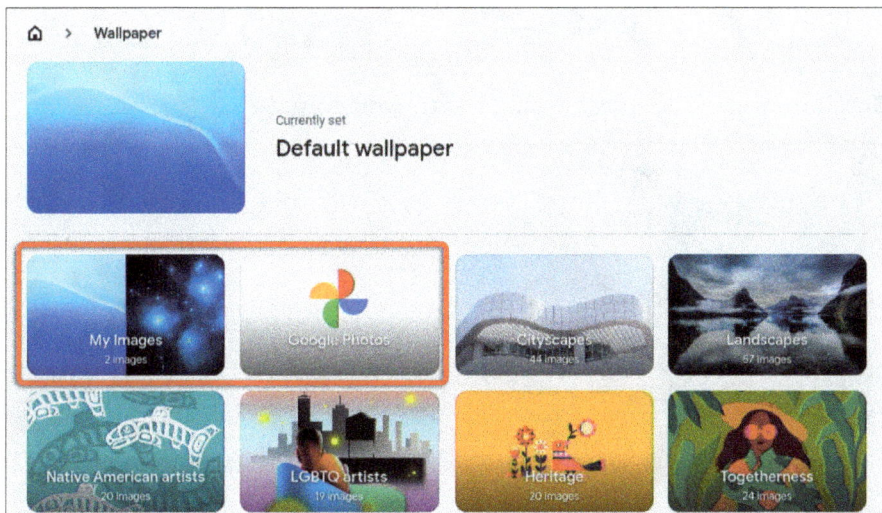

In the 'my images' folder, you'll find any images or photos you've downloaded from the internet. In the 'Google Photos' folder, you'll find photos you've taken with your camera and any photo you've added to the Google Photos app. The remaining folders contain various different types of photos covering a variety of genres.

Browse through these to see if there are any photos you like. Click on one to select it.

Chapter 2: Setting up your Chromebook

In this demo, I'm going to use a photo I have saved in Google Photos. So I'd select 'Google Photos'.

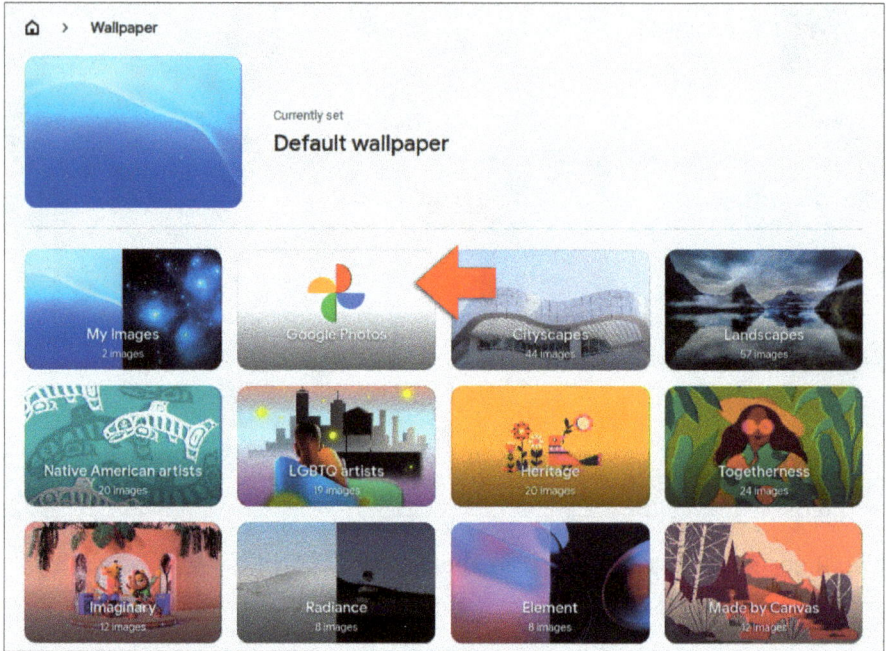

Scroll down and select the photo you want to use

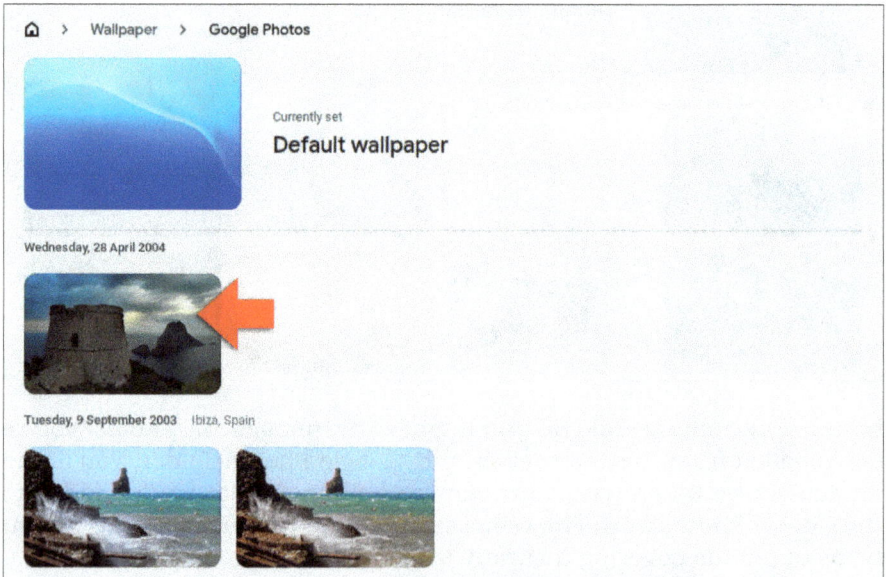

The photo you select will appear on your desktop.

Account Image

This image is commonly known as an avatar. To change it, right click on your desktop, then from the popup menu, select 'set wallpaper and style'.

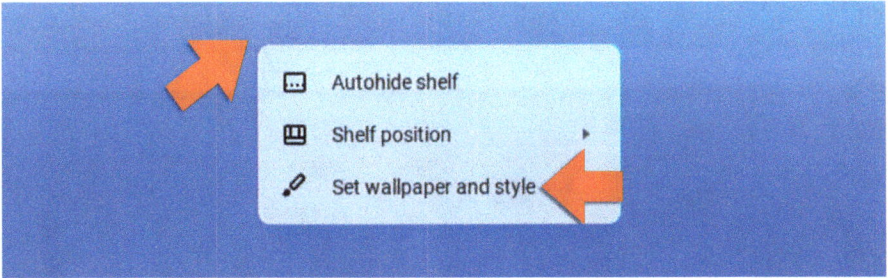

Click on the icon next to your name on the top left hand side of the window.

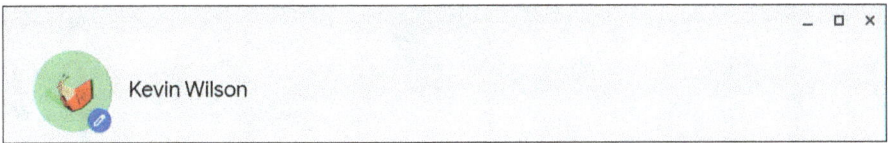

You'll see a whole list of images you can use. Note the first four icons. The first icon allows you to take a photo using your on board camera - so you can take a selfie. The second icon allows you to create a looped video which is a bit like an animation. The third icon along allows you to use a photo you've downloaded to your Chromebook. The fourth icon allows you to use your Google Account profile photo.

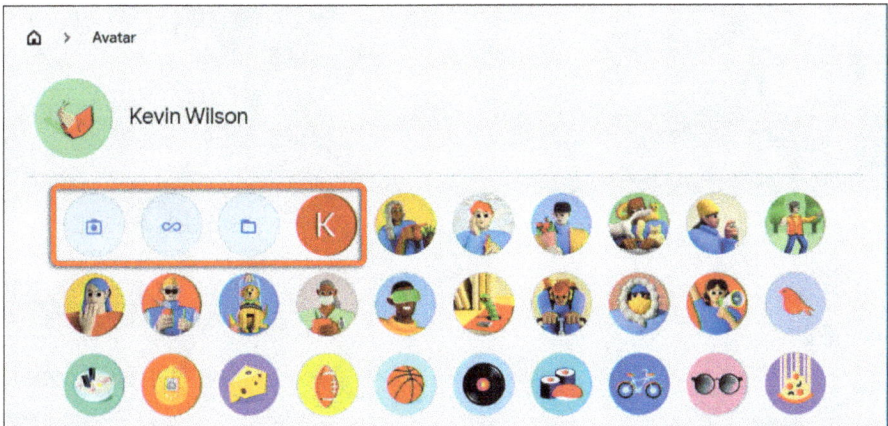

Select an image from the library.

Sync & Google Services

Your Chromebook synchronises data between your machine and the cloud. This keeps your data consistent between all your devices. You can control what data is synchronised.

Click the clock on the bottom right to open the system tray, then click the 'settings' icon.

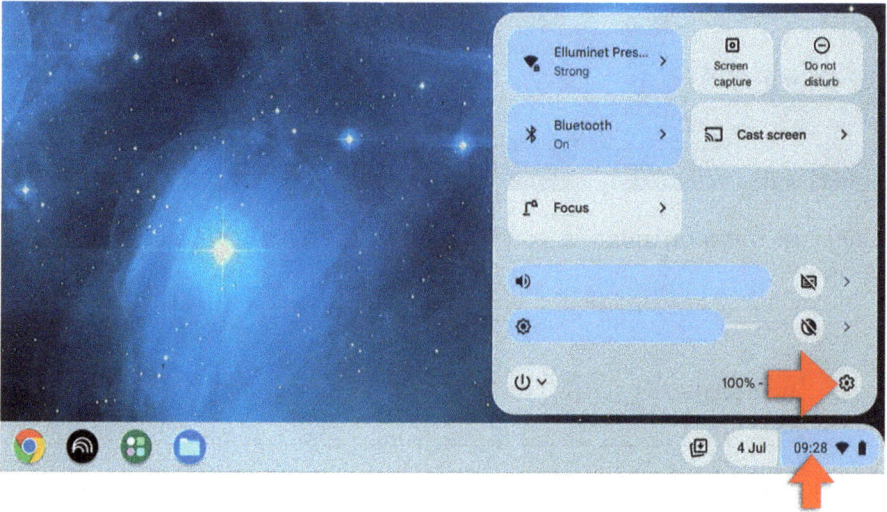

Select 'privacy & security' from the list on the left then click 'Sync and Google services'.

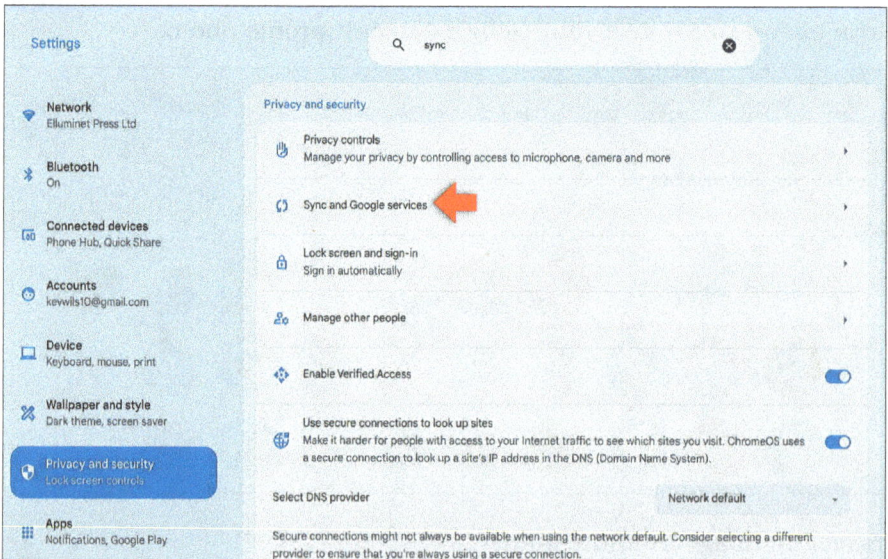

Under the 'sync' section, select 'manage what you sync'.

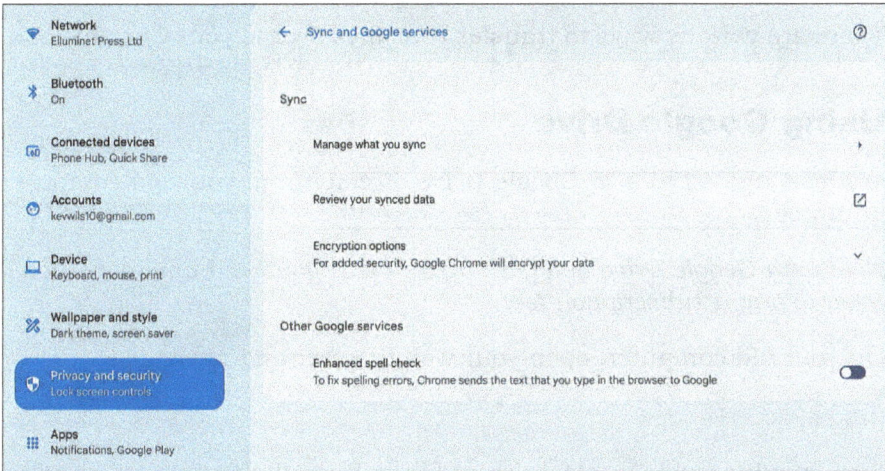

Choose what you want to sync. To sync everything, turn on 'sync everything'.

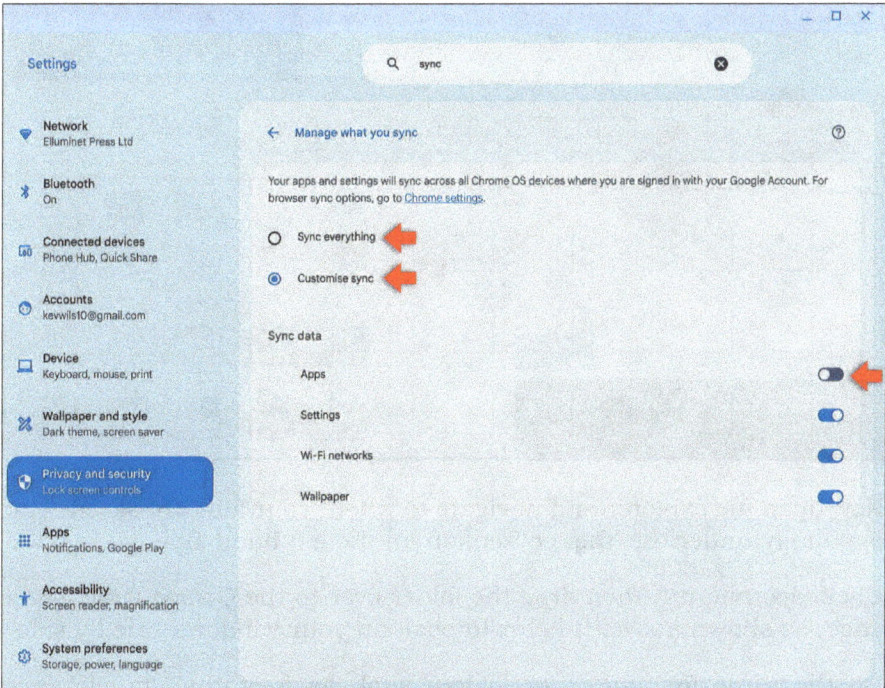

If you only want to sync certain data such as apps, settings, WiFi networks or wallpapers, click 'customise sync', then turn the switches on the data you want to the 'on' position.

Transferring your Files to Chromebook

There are various ways to transfer your files over to your Chromebook.

Using Google Drive

You can upload files to Google Drive directly from your old computer or device.

Note with Google Drive you get 15GB free. If you need any more, you'll need to pay a subscription fee.

On your old computer, open your web browser and navigate to

`drive.google.com`

Sign in with your Google Account, then from the Google Drive home page, click 'my drive' on the left hand side of your browser window.

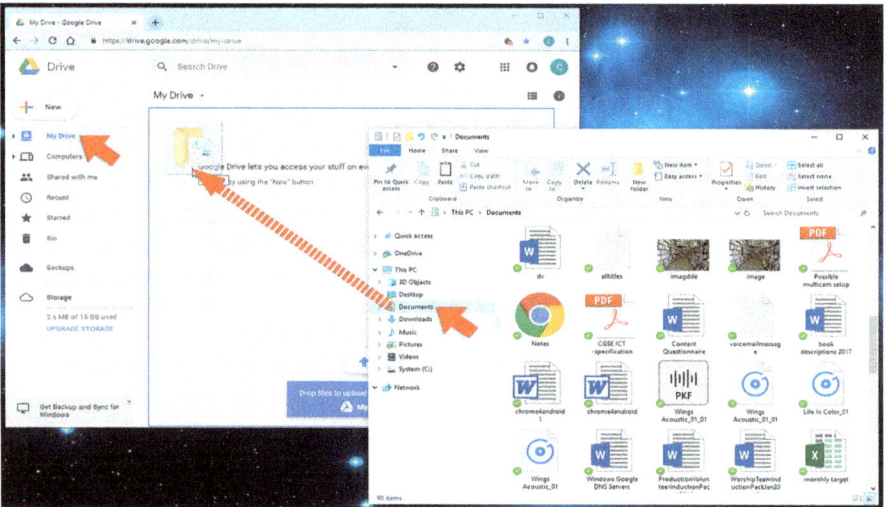

Now open file explorer and navigate to where your files are saved. This is usually under the 'this pc' section on the left hand side.

Click 'documents', then drag the folder over to the Google Drive home page, as shown above. It helps to position your windows side by side.

Do the same for any other folders such as 'pictures', 'music', and 'videos'. Allow the files to upload - it could take a while depending on the speed of your internet connection. Keep in mind that you can only upload 15GB of data. If you need more space you'll need to pay a subscription fee.

Using an External Drive

You can use a flash drive or external hard drive that has enough space to store your data.

Plug the external drive or flash drive into a USB port on your old computer. Then open up file explorer. Your external drive will show up as a USB Drive.

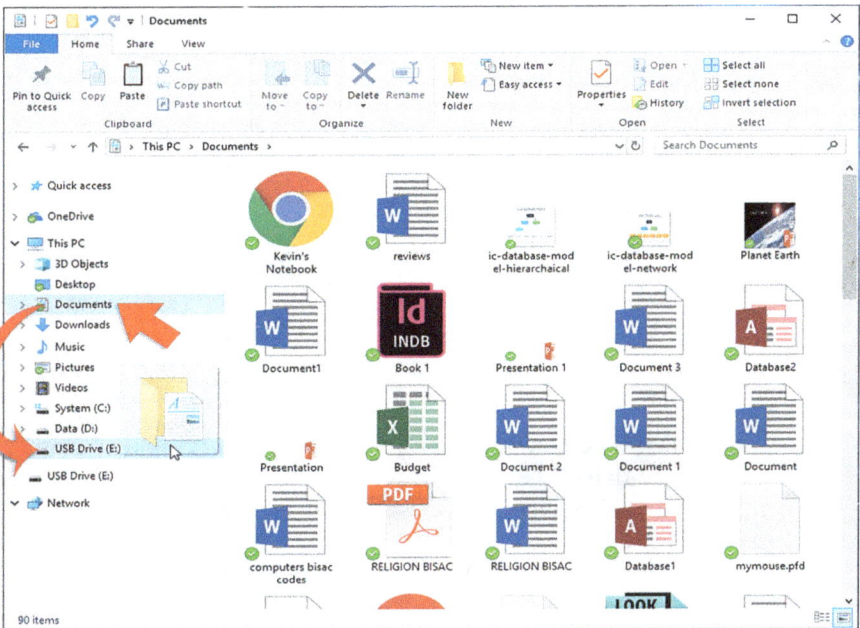

Navigate to where your files are saved. This is usually under the 'this pc' section on the left hand side.

Click 'documents', then drag the folder over to the USB Drive, as shown above. Do the same for any other folders such as 'pictures', 'music', and 'videos'.

Chapter 2: Setting up your Chromebook

Once the files have finished copying, remove the drive from your old computer and plug it into a USB port on your Chromebook.

Now, on your Chromebook, open 'files' from the app shelf. You'll also find it on your launcher.

Select your USB drive from the panel on the left hand side of the window.

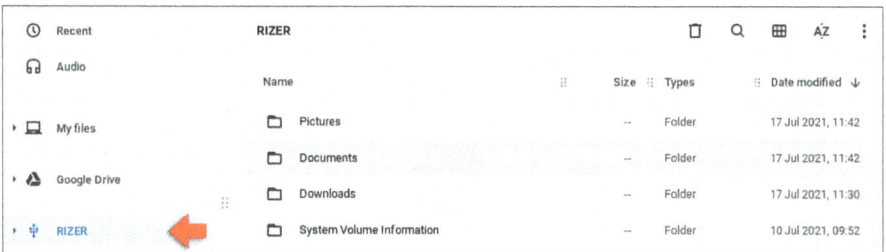

Open Google Drive. Click and drag the 'documents' folder from the USB drive to 'my drive'. Do the same with the rest of the folders you copied from your old device.

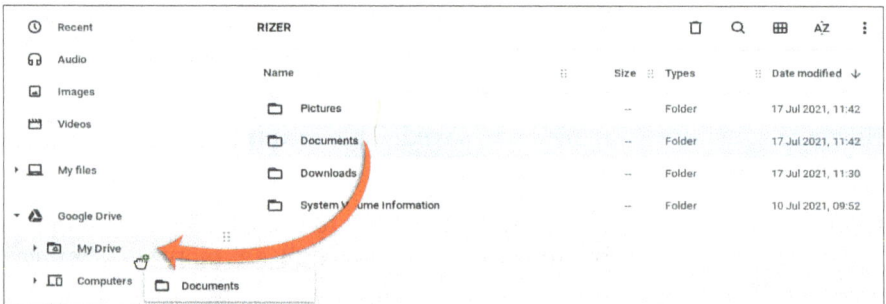

Setting up Printers

Your printer needs to support wireless (Wi-Fi) printing. Most modern printers from brands like HP, Canon, Epson, and Brother support this. You can check compatibility in your printer's documentation.

Wireless Printers

Turn on your printer and ensure it is connected to the same Wi-Fi network as your Chromebook. If you're not sure how to connect your printer to Wi-Fi, refer to the printer's user manual or manufacturer's support website for specific instructions.

On your Chromebook, click the clock on the bottom right to open the system tray, then click the 'settings' icon.

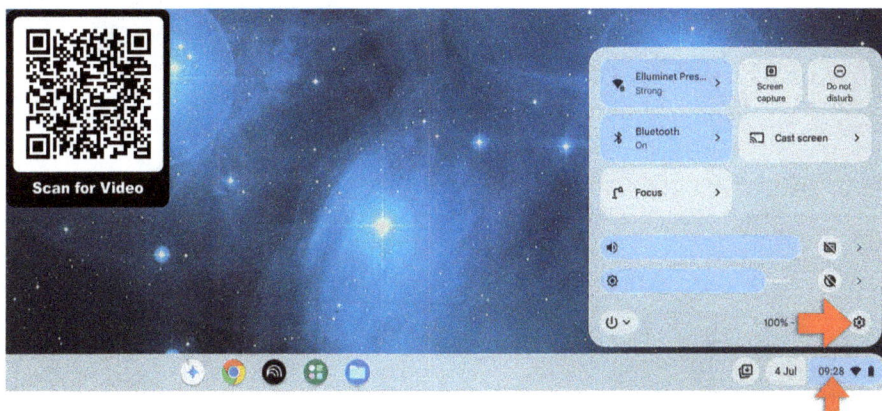

Scroll down to the bottom of the page and click 'device', then select 'print'.

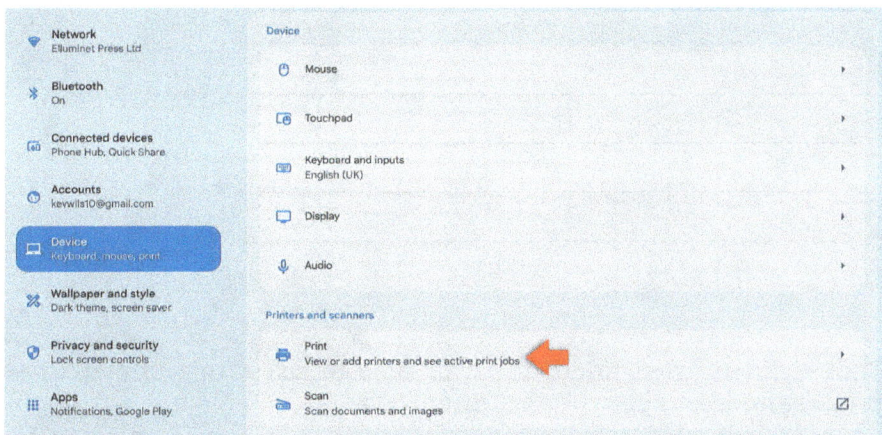

Chapter 2: Setting up your Chromebook

Your Chromebook will detect any compatible printers and list them on this page. Sometimes it takes a while for them to show up. When your printer pops up on the list, click 'save'.

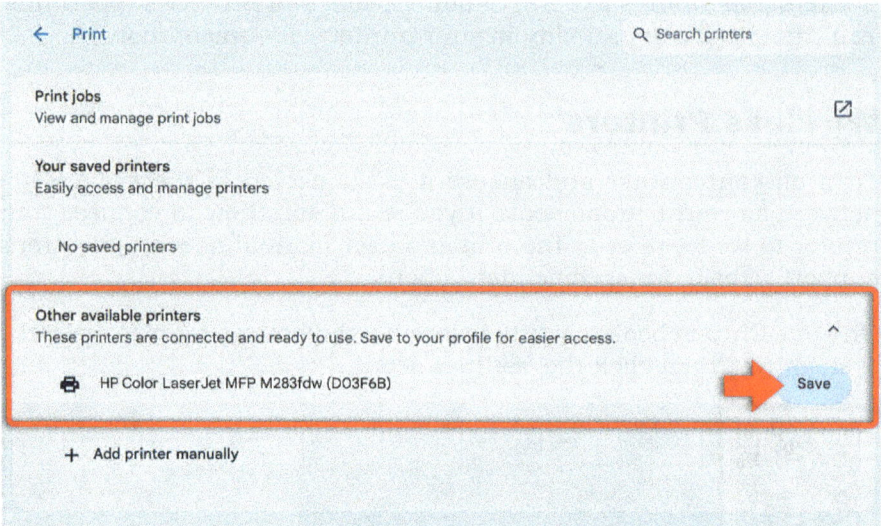

Your printer will be listed under 'your saved printers'.

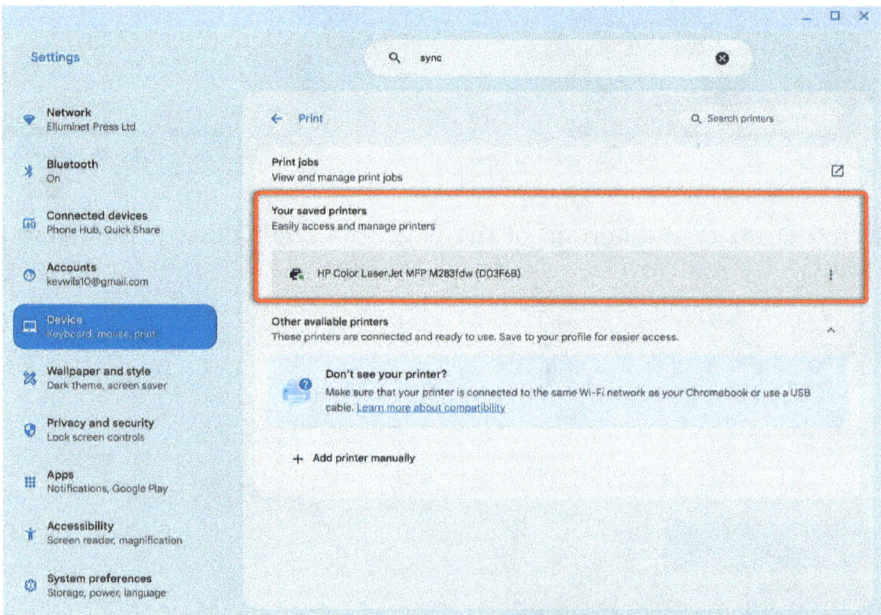

That's all you need to do. You'll be able to select this printer when printing from an app on your Chromebook.

Traditional Printers

If your printer is older and doesn't support wireless printing, you can connect it directly to your Chromebook using a USB cable. This is often the easiest way to use a traditional printer.

First, plug your printer into your Chromebook using a USB cable.

On your Chromebook, click the clock on the bottom right of your screen to open the system tray.

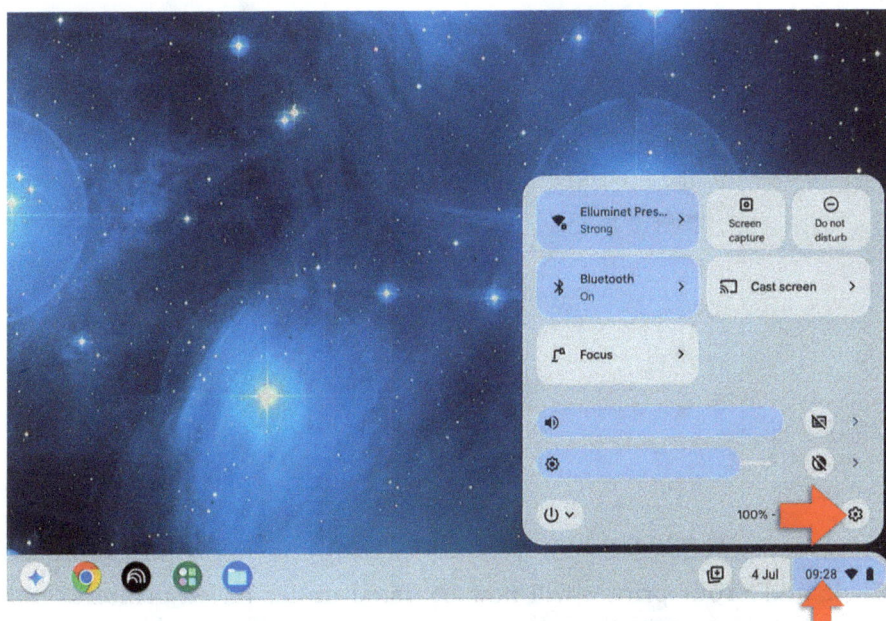

Chapter 2: Setting up your Chromebook

Scroll down and click 'devices', then select 'print'.

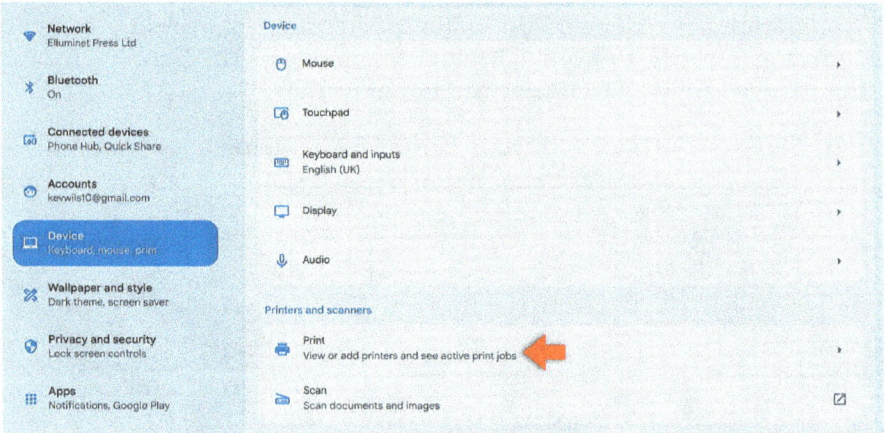

Your Chromebook should automatically detect the connected USB printer. When it appears in the list, click "Set up".

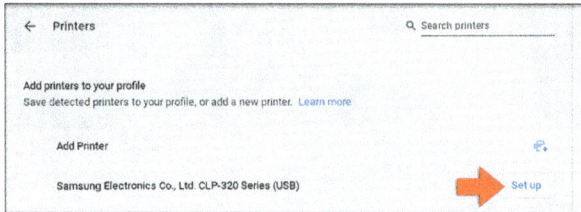

In the setup screen select manufacturer, and model.

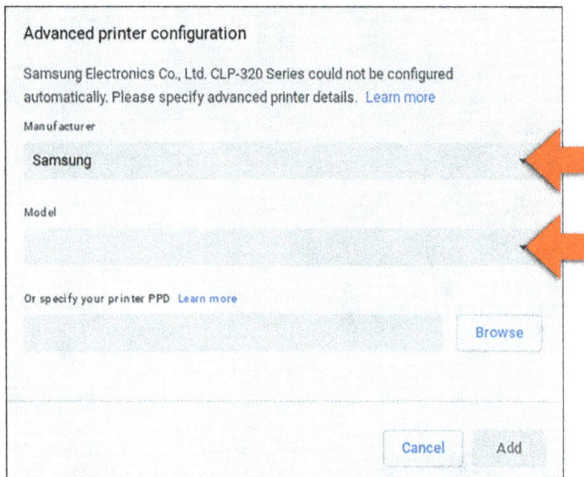

Click 'add'. Your printer will now be listed under Saved printers, and you can select it when printing from apps or the Chrome browser.

44

Adding Bluetooth Devices

You can add bluetooth mice, headphones, keyboards to your Chromebook. This process is called pairing.

To add a bluetooth device, you need to put the device into pairing mode. To do this, press the pairing button on the bottom of the device - you might need to read the device's instructions on how to do this.

In this example, I'm going to add a bluetooth mouse. First power the mouse on and press the pairing button underneath. The light will begin to flash.

Press and hold the pairing button...

Scan for Video

On your Chromebook, click on the clock on the bottom right to open the system tray. Select the bluetooth icon.

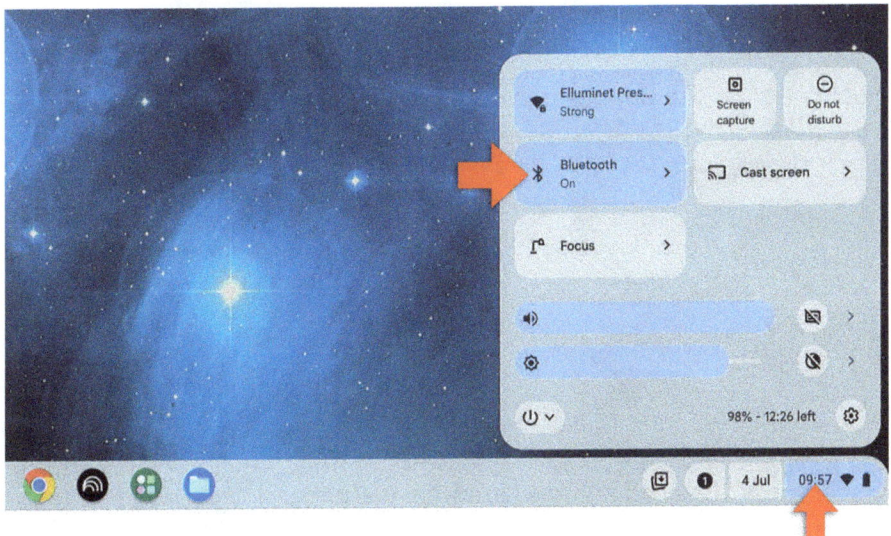

Chapter 2: Setting up your Chromebook

Turn Bluetooth on if it isn't already - the switch should be blue, then select 'pair new device'

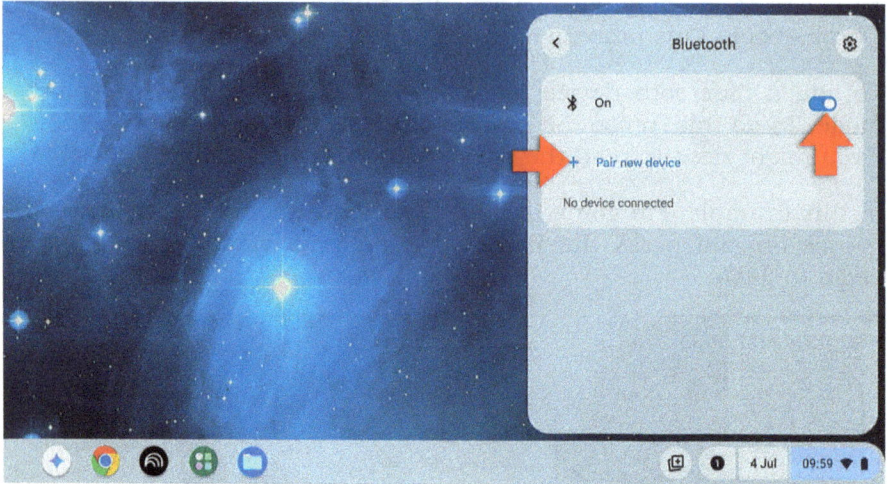

Allow your Chromebook to scan for nearby devices, this will take a minute or two. Once a device has been found, it will appear in the list. Click on the device in the list to connect it.

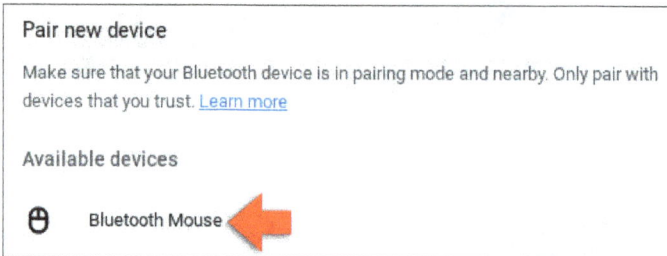

Click 'pair' on the bottom right of the dialog box.

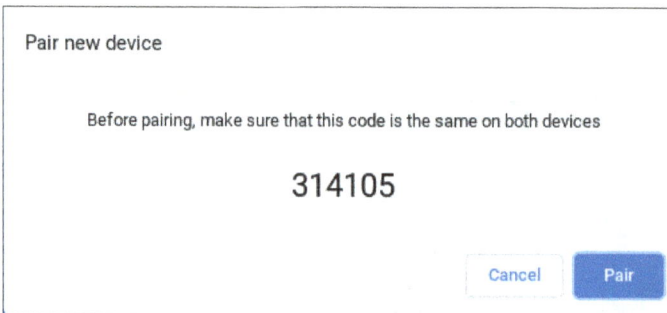

Once your Chromebook has made a connection, you can use your device as normal.

Connect your Phone

You can connect an android phone to your Chromebook. You'll need a Chromebook with ChromeOS 71 or later and an Android phone with Android 8.1 or later. You'll also need to be signed in with the same Google Account on all devices. Also this won't work on an iPhone.

Make sure both your phone is on, then place it next to your Chromebook.

Next, on your Chromebook, click the clock on the bottom right to open the system tray, then click the 'settings' icon.

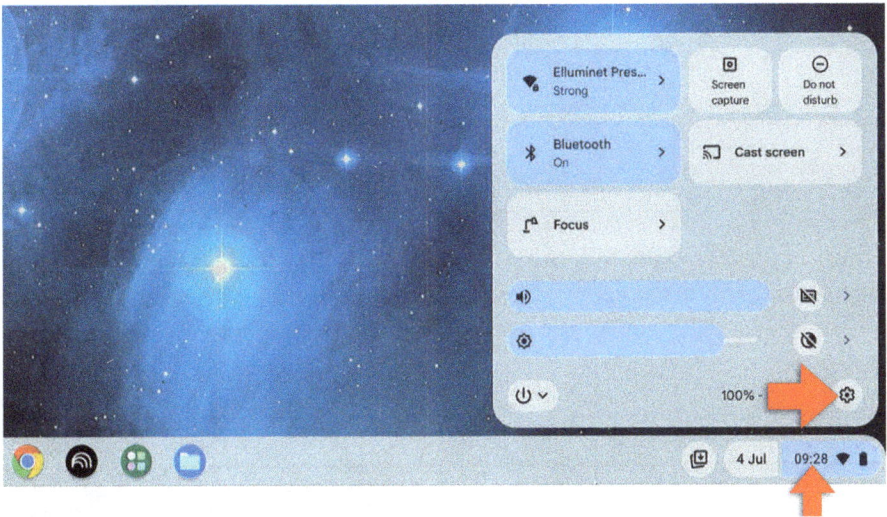

Select 'connected devices' from the list on the left hand side. Next to 'Android phone' select 'set up'.

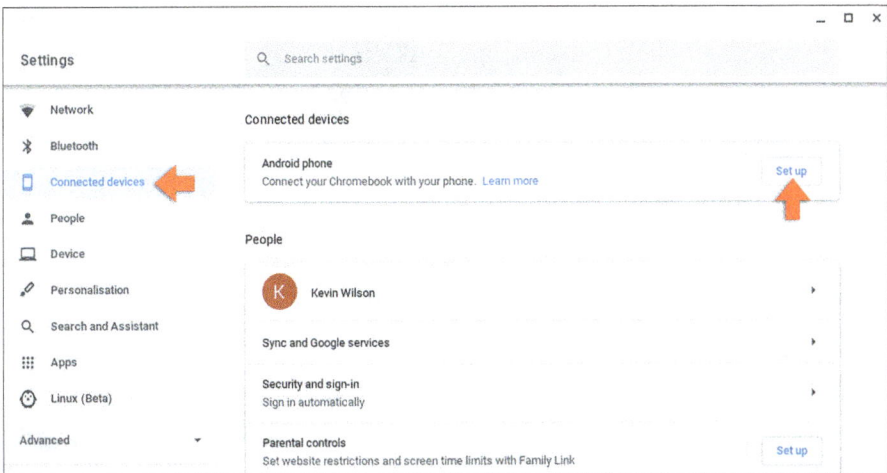

Chapter 2: Setting up your Chromebook

Any detected phones that are eligible will be listed here. If not make sure your phone and Chromebook are signed in with the same Google Account. Click 'accept & continue'.

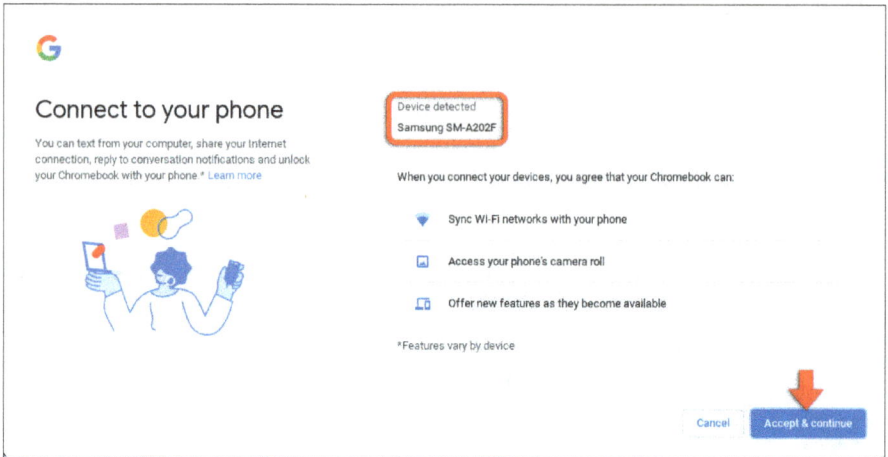

Enter your Google Account email address and password when prompted. Click 'done'.

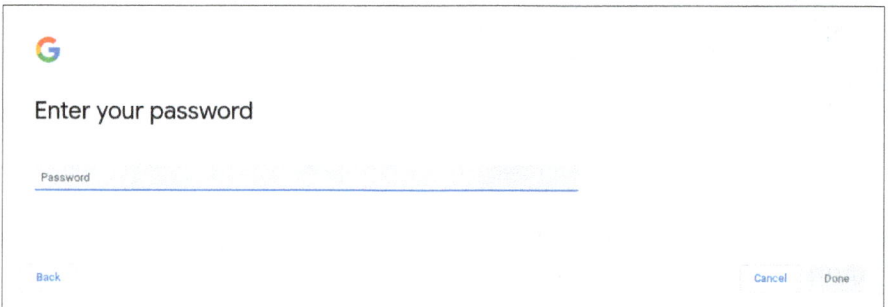

Once confirmed click the 'settings' link on the top left.

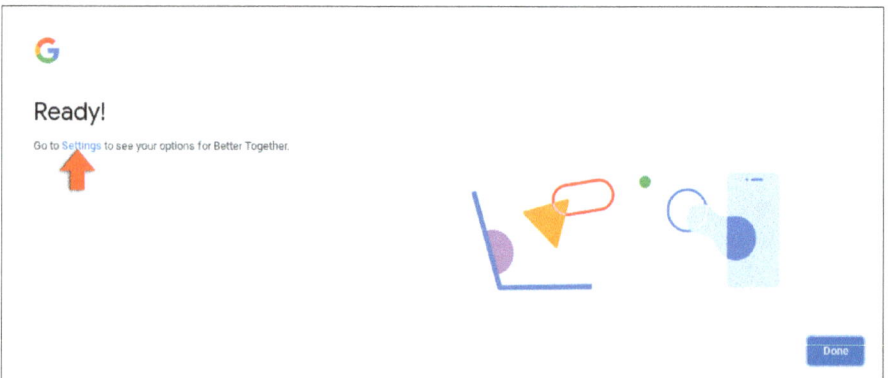

Here you can change various settings for your phone. Just click on the blue switches on the right to enable or disable the feature.

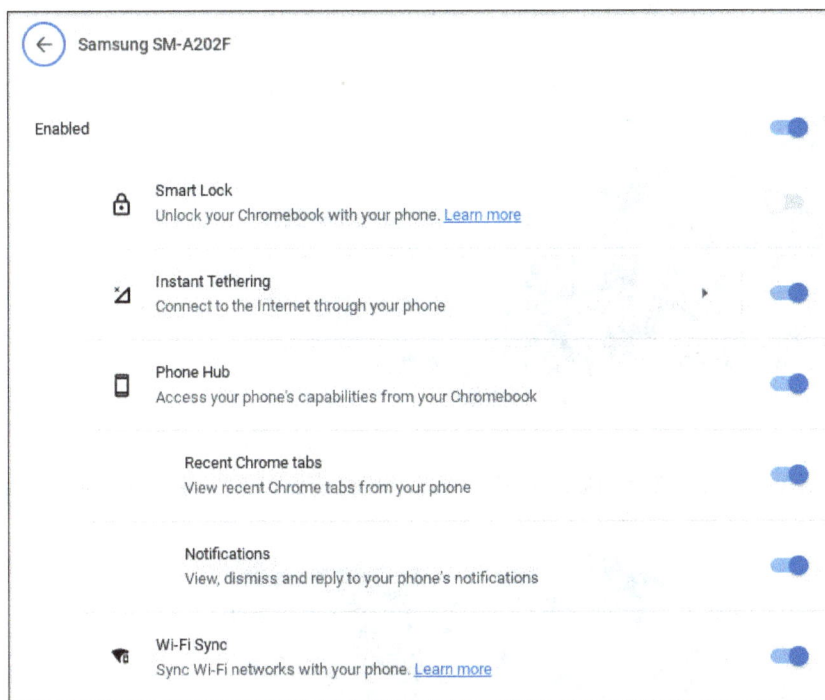

Smart lock allows you to automatically unlock your Chromebook with your phone instead of a password.

Instant tethering allows you to connect to the internet using the mobile data connection on your phone. Useful if you want to use your Chromebook in a location where the WiFi is poor or non-existent.

Phone hub allows you to access features on your phone from your Chromebook. For example, you can check your phone notifications or find open tabs from your phone's chrome browser. Phone hub appears as a small icon on the bottom right of the shelf.

WiFi Sync allows your connected devices to sync your data between various devices connected to the same WiFi network. Don't enable this feature if you're using public WiFi hotspots.

If you need to disconnect your phone, click 'disconnect' next to 'forget phone'.

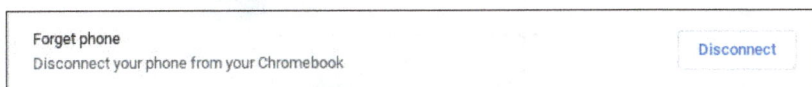

Connect to WiFi

To connect to a WiFi network, click the clock on the bottom right of the screen, then select the WiFi icon.

Turn WiFi on if it isn't already, then select the WiFi network you want to connect to.

Enter the WiFi passcode in the 'password' field.

Click 'connect'.

Tethering

You can use your phone's mobile data to connect your Chromebook to the Internet if WiFi isn't available. This is known as tethering.

Almost every modern smartphone whether it's android or iPhone, is able to broadcast a Wi-Fi hotspot that your Chromebook can connect to just like any Wi-Fi network.

Android Phone

First connect your android phone to your Chromebook as shown on page 47.

Next, click the clock on the bottom right of the screen, then select the WiFi icon.

At the top of the list you'll see a 'mobile data' section. Make sure the small blue switch is turned on, then select your phone from the list.

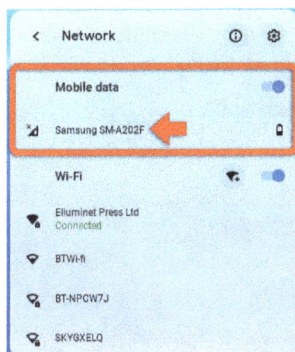

This will use the data connection on your phone to connect to the internet.

Click 'connect' on the 'create new hotspot' dialog box.

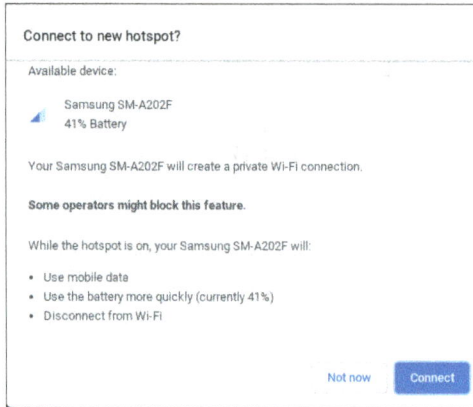

Click 'verify' or 'confirm' on your phone to accept the connection. If you want to turn off the mobile data, click on the clock icon on the bottom right, select the WiFi icon, then click the switch next to 'mobile data' to turn it off.

iPhone

If you're using an iPhone you can tether the data connection to your Chromebook.

First, you need to enable the WiFi hotspot on your iPhone. Open the settings app, then select 'personal hotspot'. Turn on 'allow others to join'.

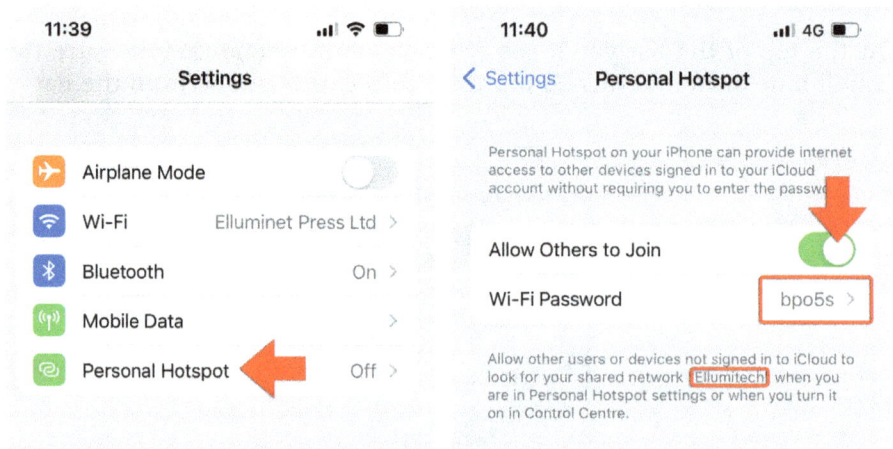

Remember the WiFi password and the name of your phone as shown on the screen.

On your Chromebook, click the clock icon on the bottom right, then select WiFi

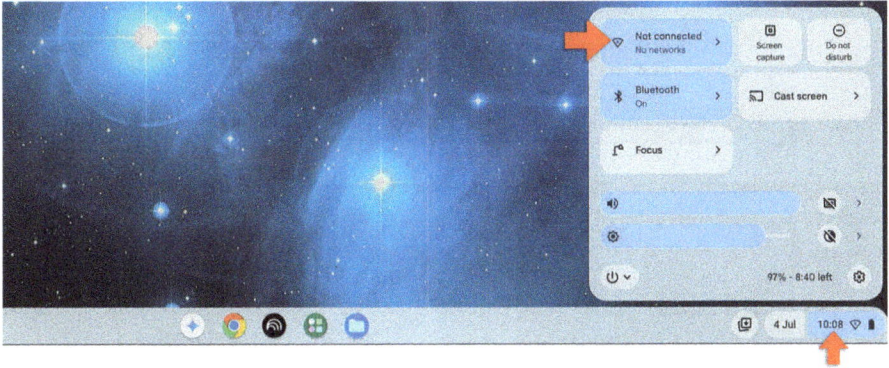

Your iPhone will show up as another network. The name of the network will be the name of your iPhone. In this demo, the name of my iPhone is 'Ellumitech'.

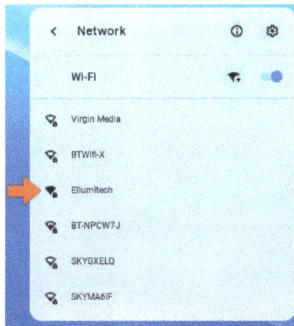

Enter the password you got from your iPhone.

Managing Users

You can add multiple users to your Chromebook. This is useful if more than one person uses your Chromebook and need access to their own email, apps, and files.

You can add two types of users to your Chromebook. The first is a guest. This allows any user to get onto your Chromebook without having to sign in with a Google Account. Guest users do not have access to the Google Play store, Web store or a email, they can pretty much just browse the internet.

The other type, is a user with a Google Account. This is the recommended way to use your Chromebook.

Adding a Standard User

On the login screen click 'add person' on the bottom left of the screen.

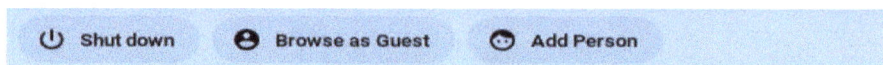

Select the account type you want to add. Select 'you' if you're adding your own account, or one for someone else. Click 'next'.

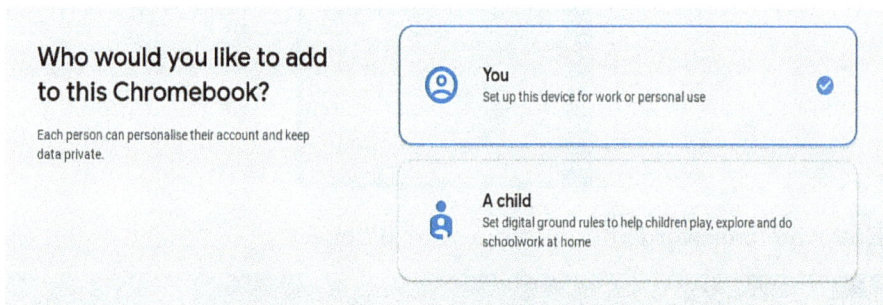

Enter the Google Account email address and password of the account you want to add. Click 'next'.

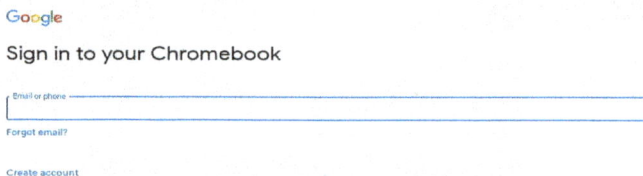

If they haven't got an account, click 'create account' then fill in the details.

Turn off 'send diagnostic and usage data', then click 'accept & continue'.

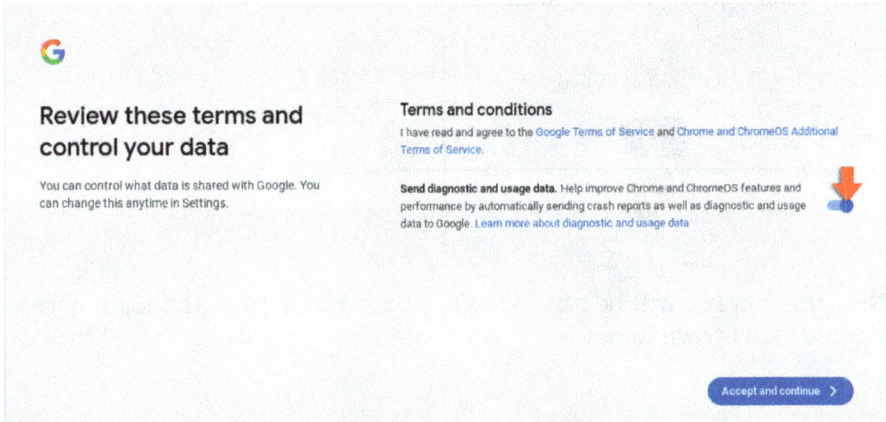

Click 'accept & continue', click 'more' on the 'terms & services' screen, then click 'accept'.

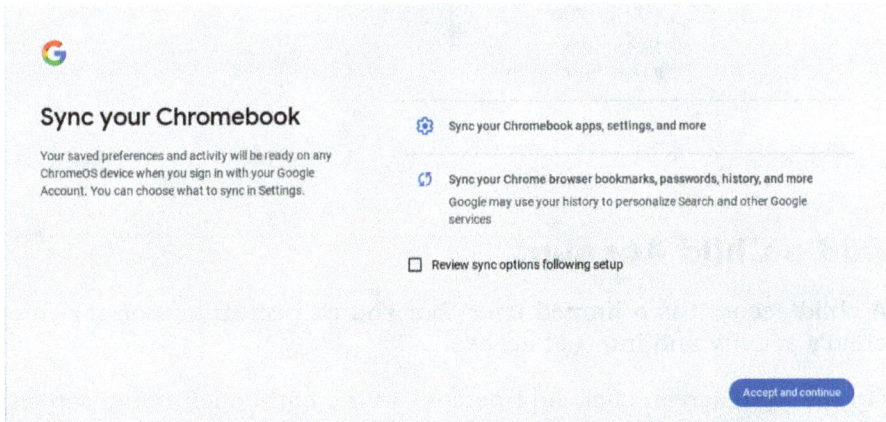

Click 'I agree' on the 'Google assistant' screen and follow the instructions.

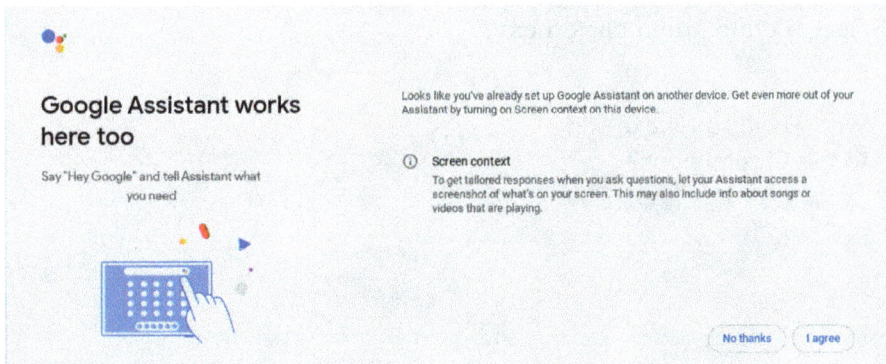

Chapter 2: Setting up your Chromebook

Select your theme: Auto, Light or Dark. If you're not sure, leave it on auto. Click 'next'. On the final screen click 'get started'.

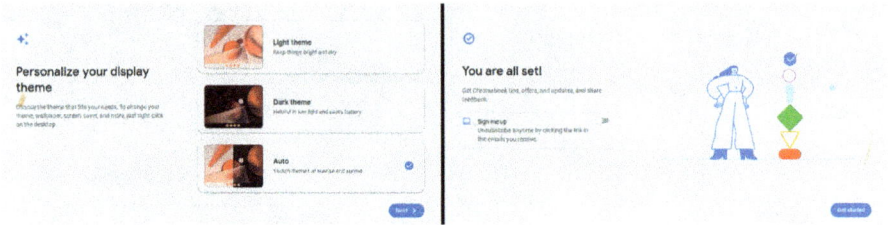

Now this person will be able to select their name from the login screen and use their own account.

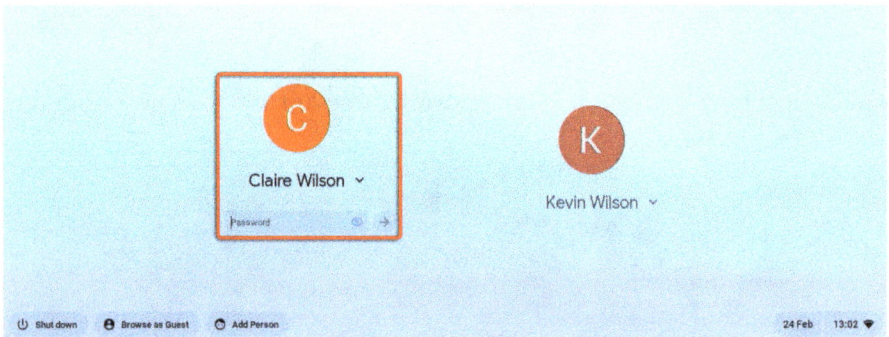

Add a Child Account

A child account is a limited user that you can setup to monitor your child's activity and internet access.

On the login screen click 'add person' on the bottom left of the screen.

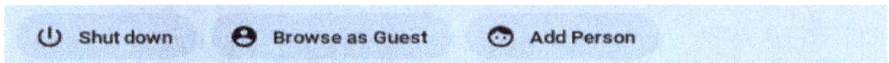

Select 'a child', then click 'next'.

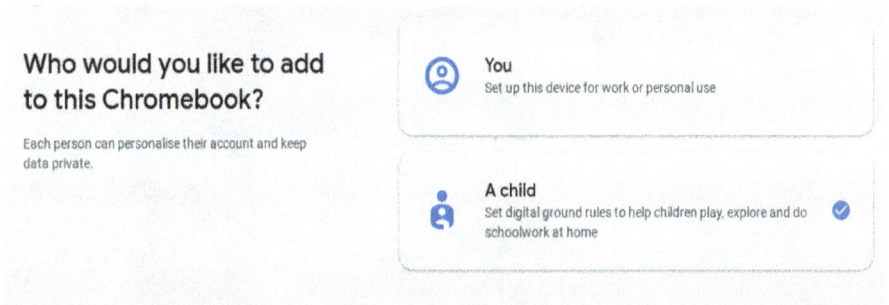

If your child already has a Google Account, click 'sign in with a child's Google Account', then enter the Google Account email address and password. If they don't then click 'create a Google Account for a Child' and fill in their details. In this demo, I'm going to create an account.

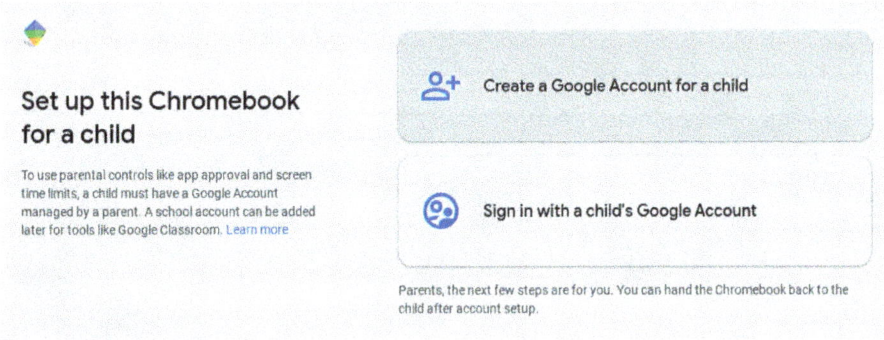

Click 'yes continue'

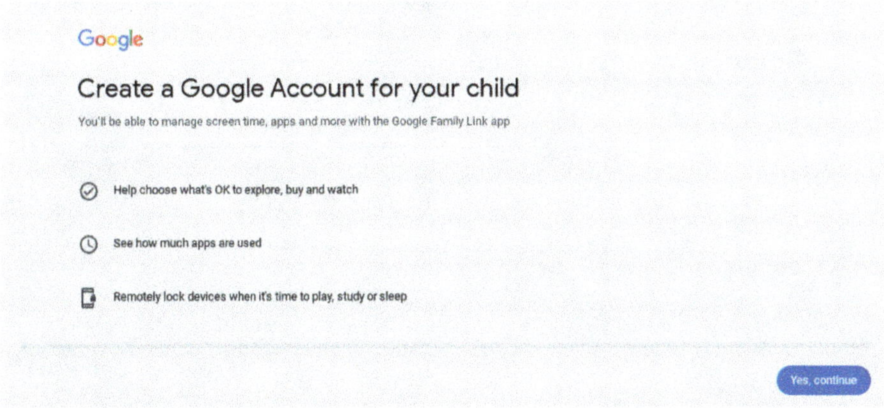

Enter your child's name, click 'next'.

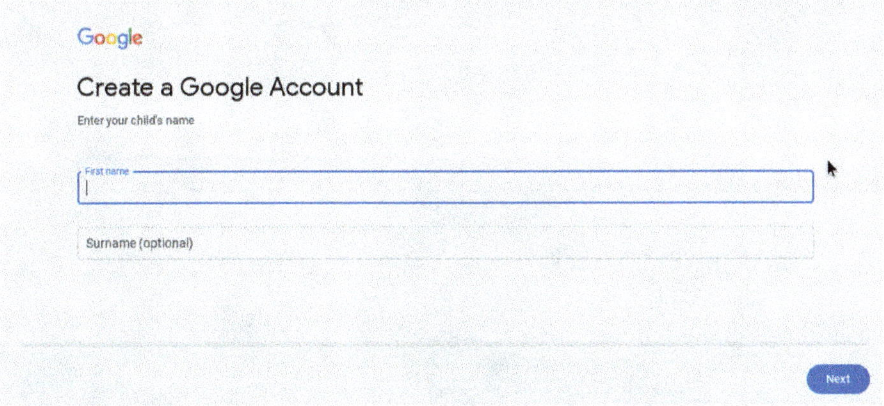

Chapter 2: Setting up your Chromebook

Enter the basic information requested. Click 'next'.

Google

Basic information

Enter Emma's birthday and gender

| Day | Month ▼ | Year |
| Gender | | ▼ |

Next

Now choose a Google Account email address and password. Click 'next'.

Google

Choose how Emma will sign in

She'll use this email to sign in to her Google Account

Username
@gmail.com

You can use letters, numbers and full stops

Next

Enter your phone number to receive the SMS verification message.

Google

Confirm that you're not a robot

Get a verification code sent to your phone

Phone number

Google will verify this number via SMS (charges may apply)

Next

Enter the number you received on your phone.

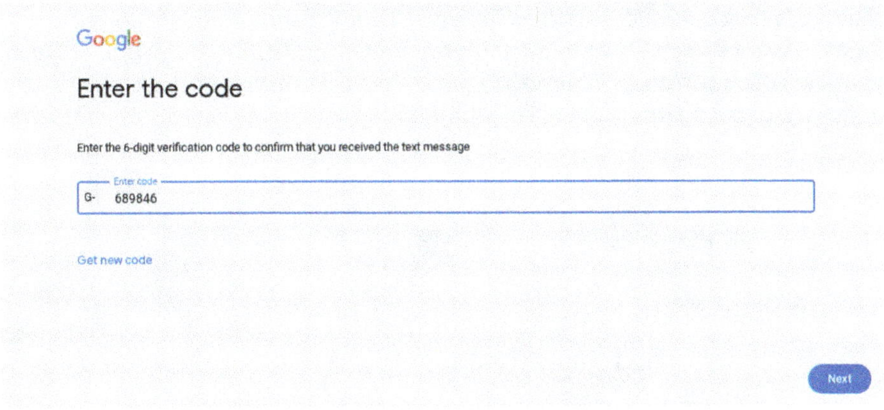

Google

Enter the code

Enter the 6-digit verification code to confirm that you received the text message

Enter code
G- 689846

Get new code

Next

If your child is under 13, enter your Google Account email address and password. Click 'next'.

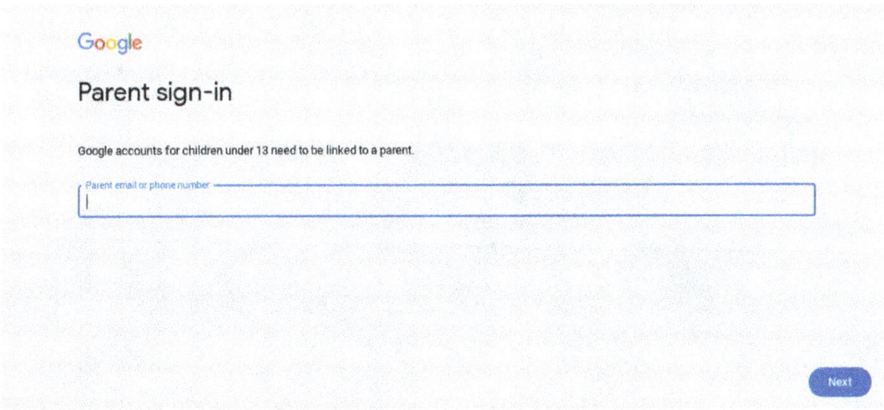

Google

Parent sign-in

Google accounts for children under 13 need to be linked to a parent.

Parent email or phone number

Next

Scroll down, select the two check boxes next to the agreement, then click 'agree'.

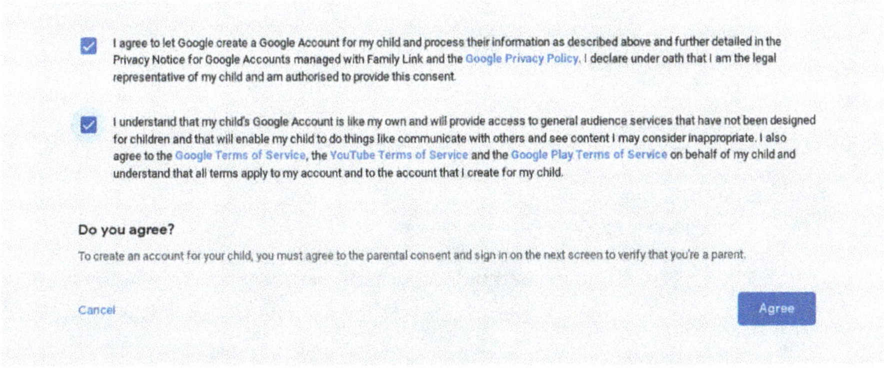

☑ I agree to let Google create a Google Account for my child and process their information as described above and further detailed in the Privacy Notice for Google Accounts managed with Family Link and the Google Privacy Policy. I declare under oath that I am the legal representative of my child and am authorised to provide this consent.

☑ I understand that my child's Google Account is like my own and will provide access to general audience services that have not been designed for children and that will enable my child to do things like communicate with others and see content I may consider inappropriate. I also agree to the Google Terms of Service, the YouTube Terms of Service and the Google Play Terms of Service on behalf of my child and understand that all terms apply to my account and to the account that I create for my child.

Do you agree?

To create an account for your child, you must agree to the parental consent and sign in on the next screen to verify that you're a parent.

Cancel   Agree

Chapter 2: Setting up your Chromebook

Enter the password for your Google Account - not your child's password.

Choose personalised settings for your child. Most of the time you can select 'express personalisation' If you want to manually configure these just select 'manual personalisation.' In this demo, I'm going to use 'express personalisation'. Click 'next'.

Google

Choose personalisation settings for Emma

○ Express personalisation
  Use personalisation settings that deliver tailored content and recommendations to your child.

○ Manual personalisation
  Configure your child's personalisation settings step by step. You decide which settings should be on or off to provide the Google experience that's right for your child.

You can change your child's settings in the Family Link app or at g.co/YourFamily

[Next]

Scroll down, click 'confirm'.

How you can manage Emma's data

In addition to being able to manually delete your child's activity through their account, Web & App Activity older than 18 months and YouTube History older than 36 months will be automatically deleted. You can see your child's data, delete it, change their settings and withdraw your consent by accessing their account at account.google.com.

About cookies and IDs

We rely on cookies and device IDs to remember your child's settings and other preferences across their signed-in devices. We also use cookies and IDs to

- deliver, maintain and improve our services and provide contextual ads
- tailor your child's content based on their activity on Google services and sites (depending on their settings)
- conduct analytics and measurement.

[Back]   [Confirm]

Scroll down, click 'agree'.

- Customising our services to provide your child with a tailored user experience
- Providing contextual advertising, which keeps our services free of charge
- Detecting, preventing or otherwise addressing fraud, abuse, security or technical issues with our services
- Protecting against harm to the rights, property or safety of Google, our users or the public as required or permitted by law, including disclosing information to government authorities
- Performing research that improves our services for our users and benefits the public
- Fulfilling obligations to our partners, like developers and rights holders
- Enforcing legal claims, including investigation of potential violations of applicable Terms of Service

You can change your child's settings in the Family Link app or at g.co/YourFamily

In selecting agree below, I confirm that I am authorised to provide this consent and that I agree to let Google create a Google Account for my child, and process their information as detailed in the aforementioned Privacy Notice and the Google Privacy Policy (https://policies.google.com/privacy).

Cancel   [Agree]

Click 'next' or 'agree' on the remaining screens.

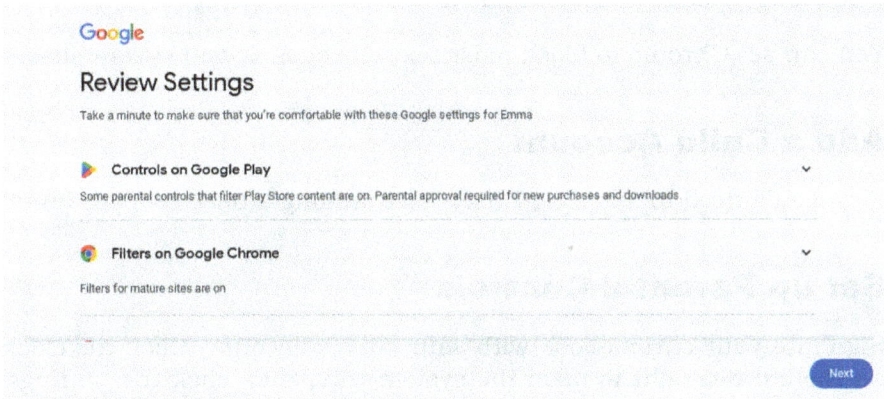

Deleting Users

On the login screen, select the small arrow next to the profile you want to remove.

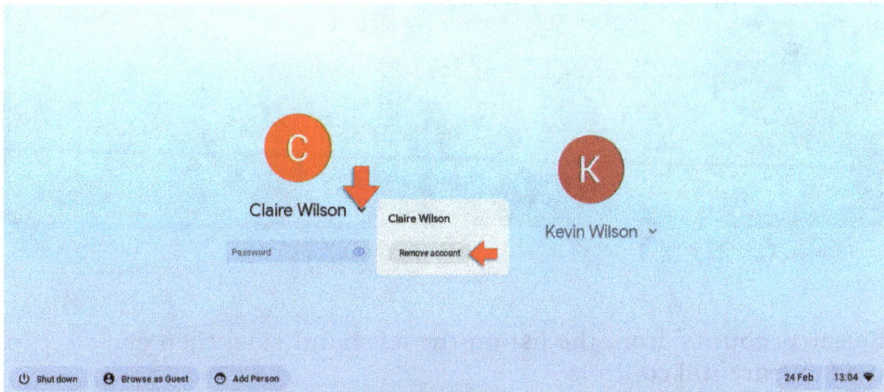

Select 'remove account' from the popup menu. In the confirmation box that appears, select 'remove account'.

This will completely remove the user from your Chromebook.

Parental Controls

You can set up 'child accounts' on your chromebook. This allows you to impose limitations on apps and services they can access as well as monitor web activity.

Chapter 2: Setting up your Chromebook

You will be able to manage which websites your children can visit and block most sexually explicit and violent sites.

You can set Chrome to block most sexually explicit and violent sites.

Add a Child Account

First you'll need to add a new user - see 'adding a user' on page 56.

Set up Parental Controls

Sign into your chromebook with your child's account. Click the clock on the bottom right to open the system tray, then click the 'settings' icon.

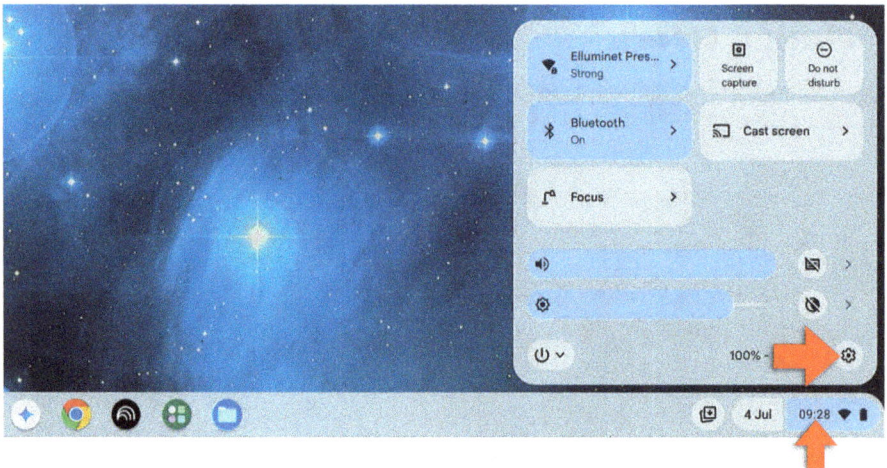

Select 'accounts' from the list on the left hand side, then click 'setup' next to 'parental controls'.

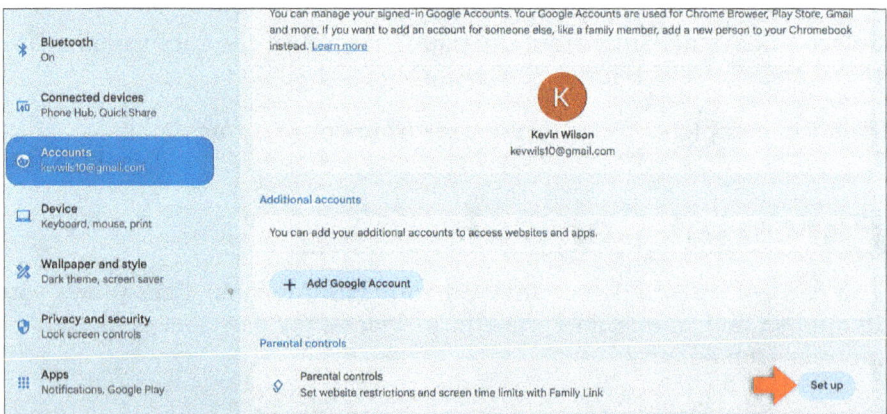

Select 'getting started'.

Set up parental controls

with Google's Family Link

Stay in the loop
Supervise your child's device remotely with the Family Link app for parents

Set digital ground rules
Keep an eye on screen time and set limits as needed

Guide your child to good content
Add restrictions to Google services, like app approvals or content filters on Google Play

Cancel   Getting started >

Click 'next' on the 'how to set up parental controls' screen. Then select 'yes' on the supervisor screen.

Is this the child you want to supervise?

To set up parental controls, your child must be signed in to this device

C **Claire Wilson**
clairewilson977@gmail.com

< Back   No   Yes

Click 'next'.

How parental controls work on Claire's devices

Devices that can be supervised
Parental controls will apply when Claire uses her account on Android and Chrome OS devices. Learn more

Google Intel Apollo Lake Chromebook

TCT (Alcatel) Alcatel 1

< Back   Next >

Chapter 2: Setting up your Chromebook

Now, sign in with your own Google account email and password.

Parent account

Enter the Google account that you'll use to supervise your child.

Email or phone

| |

Forgot email?

Before using this app, you can review Family Link's privacy policy and terms of service.

Next

Scroll down to the bottom of the 'about supervision' page, enter the password for your child's account then click 'agree'.

×

How to start and stop supervision

Once Family Link supervision is set up, either a parent or a child can stop supervision at any time.

If a child stops supervision without parental permission:

- Parents are notified
- Supervised Android devices get locked for 24 hours
- Calls can still be made from a locked mobile device

You can always set up supervision again with Family Link.

Claire, enter your password to agree to supervision

To confirm **Claire (clairewilson988@gmail.com)** and **Kevin (kevwils10@gmail.com)** have both reviewed what supervision means and want to link your accounts, select Agree.

C clairewilson988@gmail.com

Claire, enter your password*   👁

‹ Back   Cancel   Agree

Your accounts will now be linked. Click 'next' on the confirmation screen.

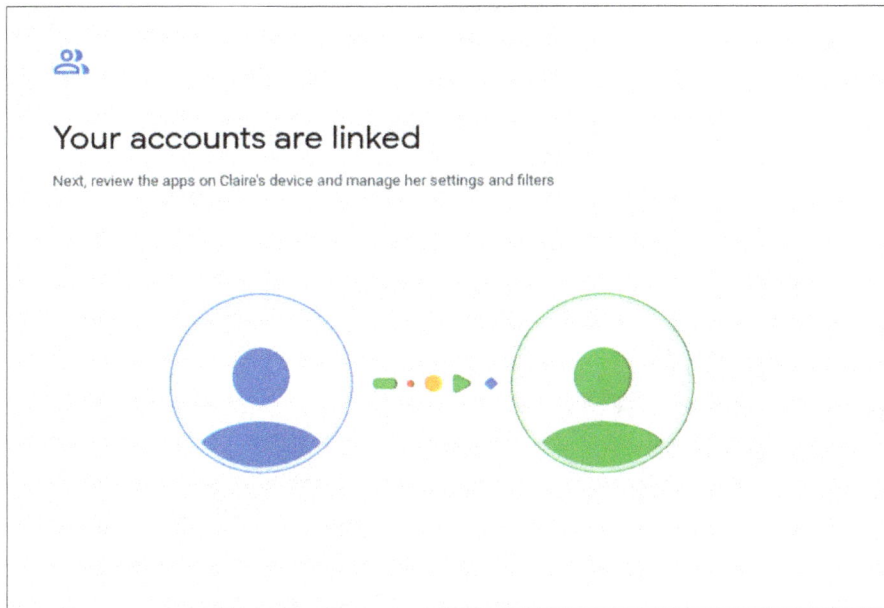

Your accounts are linked

Next, review the apps on Claire's device and manage her settings and filters

Now review the apps, un-select any apps you don't want your child to use. Scroll to the bottom and click 'next'.

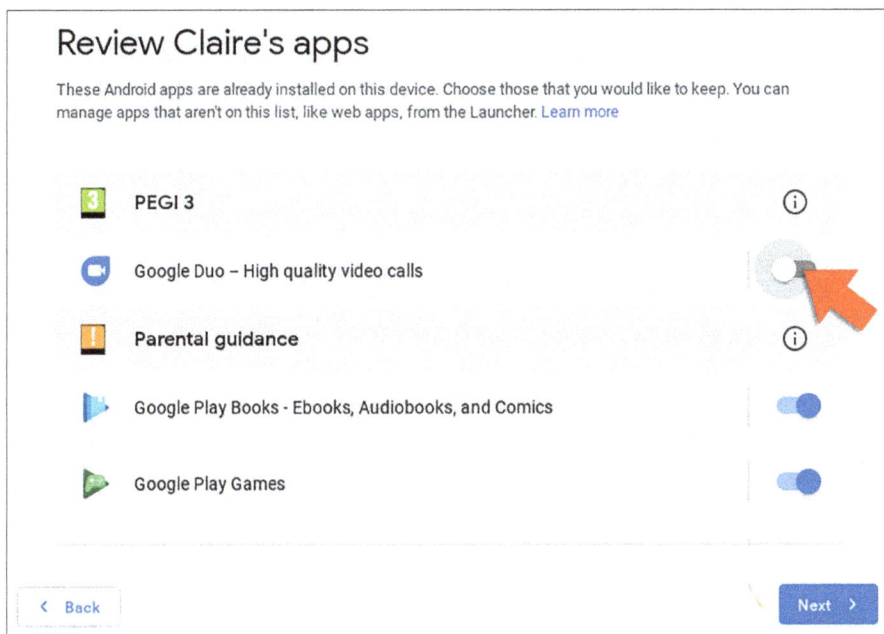

Review Claire's apps

These Android apps are already installed on this device. Choose those that you would like to keep. You can manage apps that aren't on this list, like web apps, from the Launcher. Learn more

3	PEGI 3	ⓘ
	Google Duo – High quality video calls	
!	**Parental guidance**	ⓘ
	Google Play Books - Ebooks, Audiobooks, and Comics	
	Google Play Games	

‹ Back   Next ›

Scroll through the filters, click each one to review the settings. Most of these you can leave on the default settings. Click 'next'.

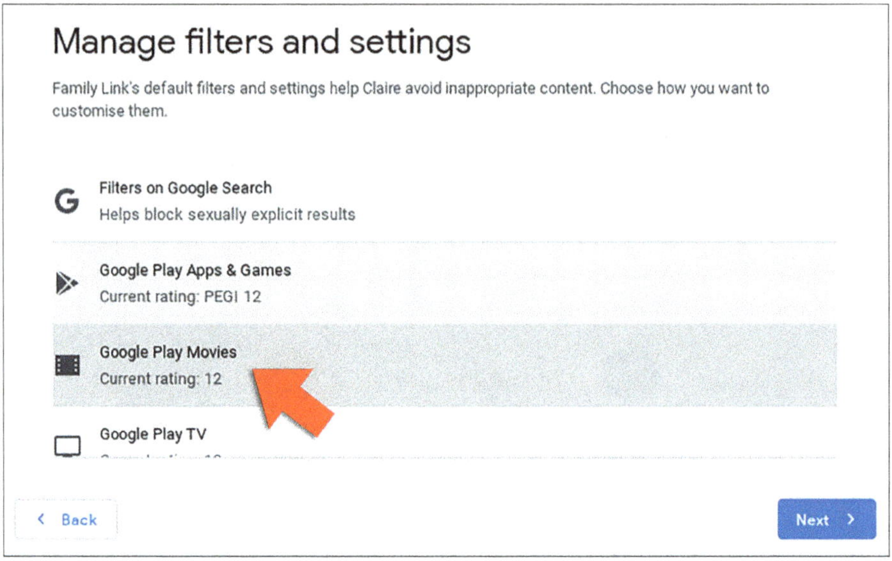

Click 'next' on the 'supervise from personal device' screen. Then select the devices you want to install 'family link' on. This allows you to monitor what your child is doing from your other devices such as your phone. Select them all then click 'install'.

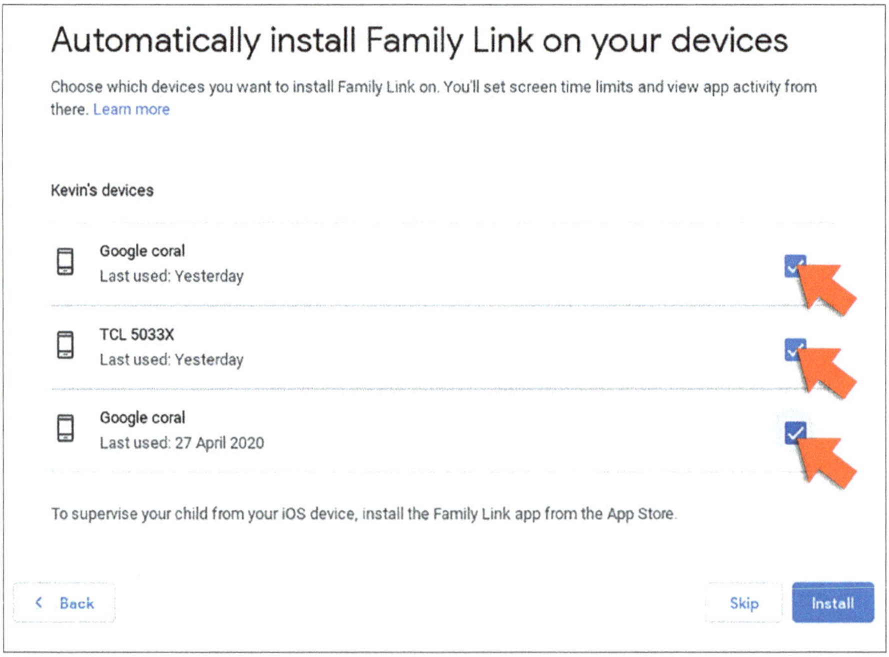

Click 'next', then 'sign out'.

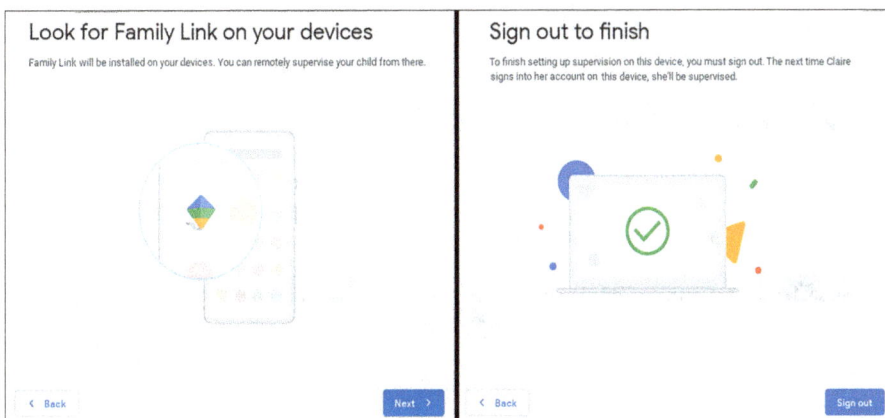

When you sign into your device, the 'family link' app will be installed automatically. You'll find the app on your launcher. If not, go to the Google play store and search for and install 'family link'.

Monitoring Child Accounts with Family Link

Once you have set up your child account and enabled parental controls as discussed in the previous section, you can use family link to monitor your child's online activity. To do this, make sure you're signed in with your own account - not a child's account, then click the circle icon on the bottom left of your screen to open app launcher. Click the 'family link' icon.

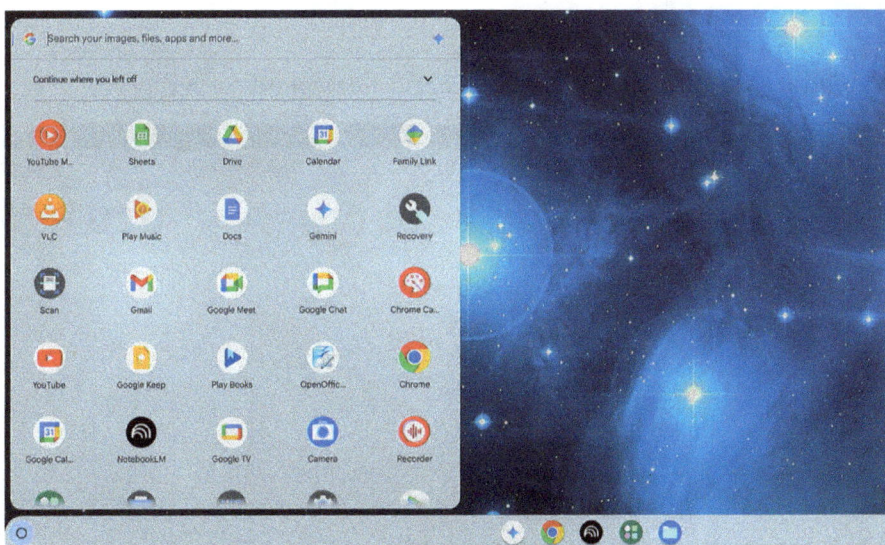

Chapter 2: Setting up your Chromebook

Screen Time

On the main screen, select the hamburger icon on the top left hand side.

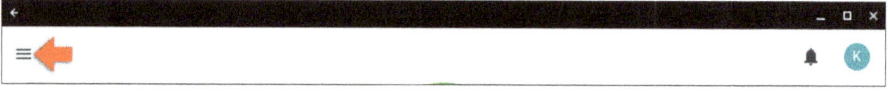

Select your child's name from the list.

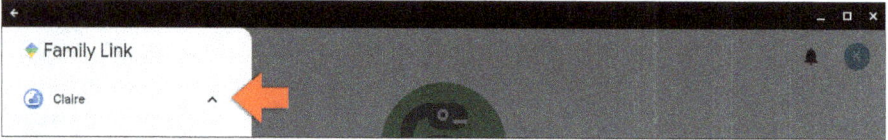

You'll land on the highlights page. Here, you'll see a summary of the amount of time your child has spent on their device. Click on the time to see more details.

You'll be able to see the time your child has spend each day

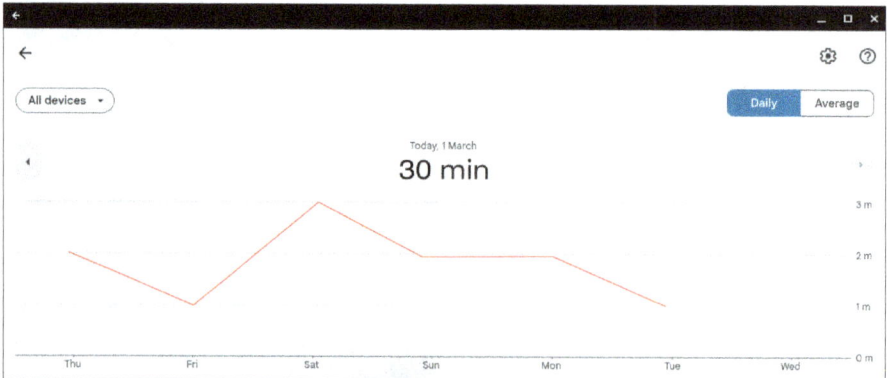

Click the arrow on the top left to go back.

Settings Screen Time Limits

Select 'controls' from the three options along the bottom of the screen.

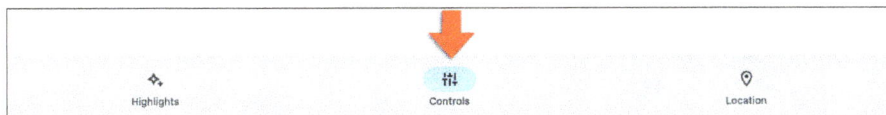

Select 'no limit' on the left

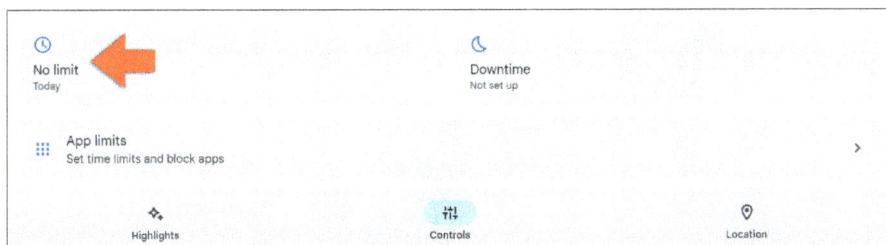

Turn on the 'schedule', then select a day.

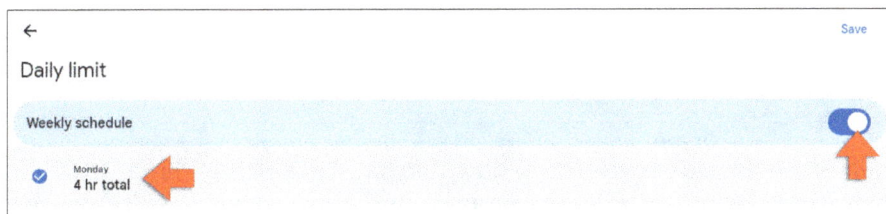

Enter the amount of time for each day you want to allow. Eg: 3 hours and 45 minutes.

Click 'apply to' on the bottom left, then select 'school'. This will apply the time to all week days. Click 'done'.

To edit any other day, just select it from the schedule and enter a time.

Click 'save' on the top right when you're done.

69

Chapter 2: Setting up your Chromebook

Set Downtime

Downtime is the time when you want your child to finish for the night. Select 'controls' from the three options along the bottom of the screen.

Click on 'downtime'.

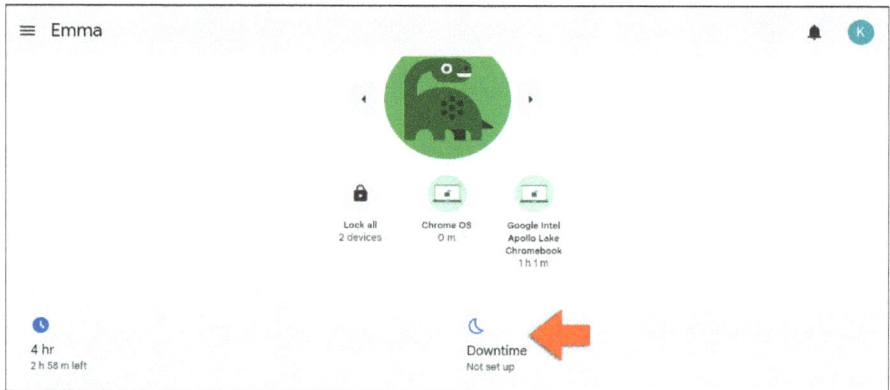

Select the days using the drop down box at the top, then enter the time you want downtime to start and end. In the example below, the device will lock at 21:00 and unlock at 07:00 the next morning.

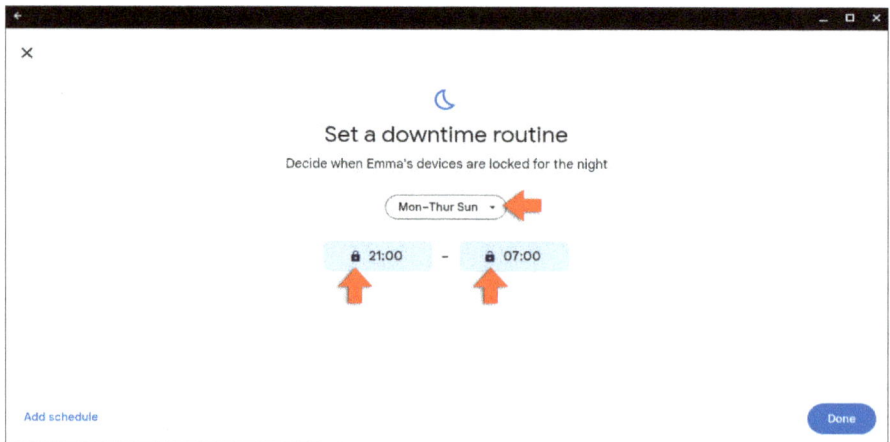

To add another schedule for weekends, click 'add schedule', then enter the times

Click 'done'

70

Manage Apps

Select 'controls' from the three options along the bottom of the screen.

Click on 'app limits'.

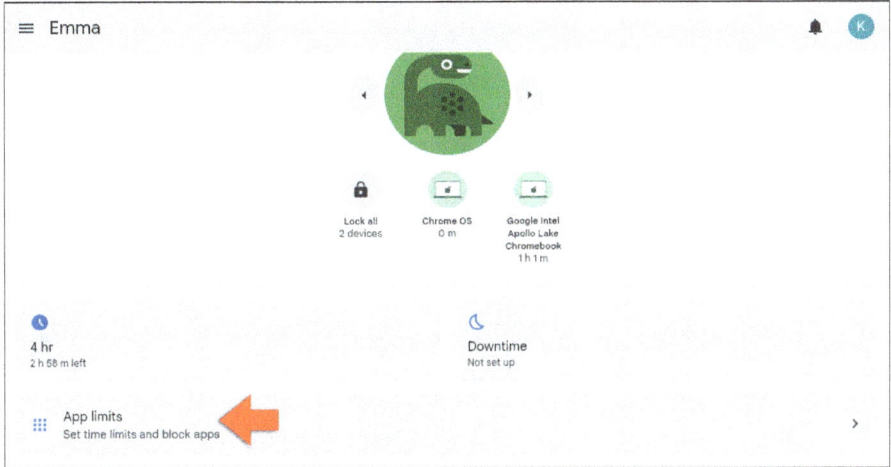

At the bottom of the screen, you'll see a list of apps your child has been using. To block and app or set a time limit, click on the app's icon.

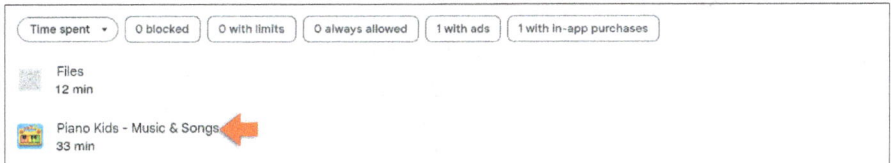

To block/unblock the app click on 'block' or 'unblock'. To set a time limit, click 'set limit' then enter the amount of time.

Click 'done'.

71

Chapter 2: Setting up your Chromebook

Manage Websites

Select 'controls' from the three options along the bottom of the screen.

Highlights	Controls	Location

Scroll down, select 'content restrictions'.

⠿	**App limits** Set time limits and block apps	>
▽	**Content restrictions** Manage search results, block sites	>

Select 'Google Chrome'

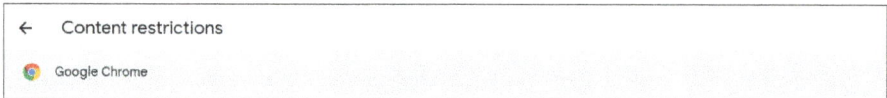

←	Content restrictions
🌐	Google Chrome

Here, you'll be able to block explicit sites.

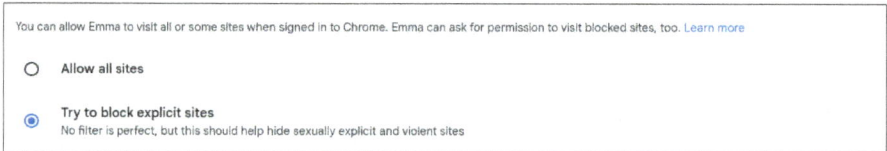

You can allow Emma to visit all or some sites when signed in to Chrome. Emma can ask for permission to visit blocked sites, too. Learn more

○ **Allow all sites**

◉ **Try to block explicit sites**
No filter is perfect, but this should help hide sexually explicit and violent sites

To block a particular website, scroll down click on 'blocked sites' under the 'managed sites' section, then click 'add site'.

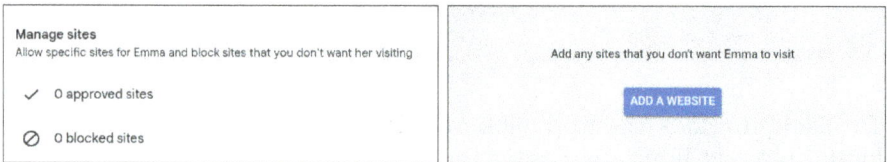

Manage sites
Allow specific sites for Emma and block sites that you don't want her visiting

✓ 0 approved sites

⊘ 0 blocked sites

Add any sites that you don't want Emma to visit

ADD A WEBSITE

Enter the website address to block. Click 'block'.

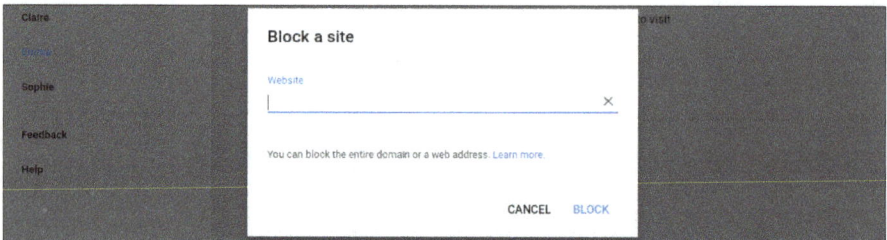

Block a site

Website
_____ ✕

You can block the entire domain or a web address. Learn more.

CANCEL   BLOCK

Configuring System Settings

To change settings on your Chromebook, click the clock on the bottom right to open the system tray, then click the 'settings' icon.

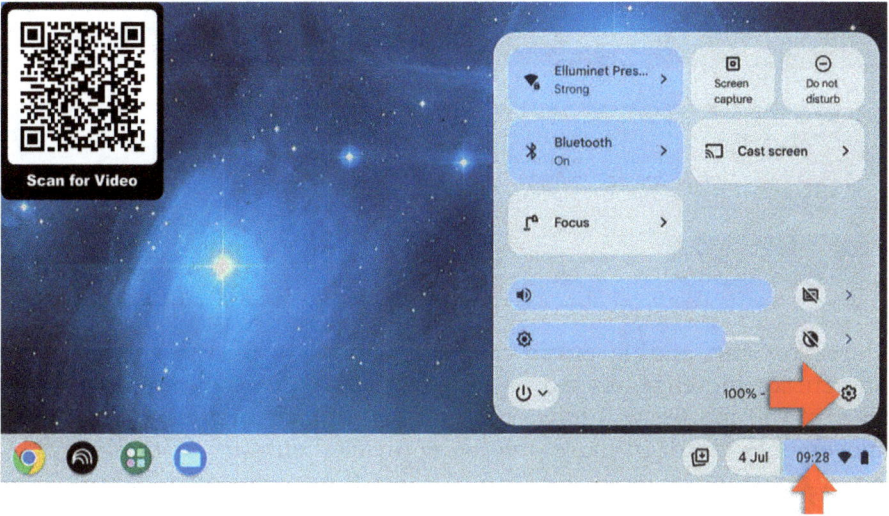

From here, you can configure settings. Settings are divided into categories which you'll find listed down the left hand side of the window. Select one of these to jump to the settings.

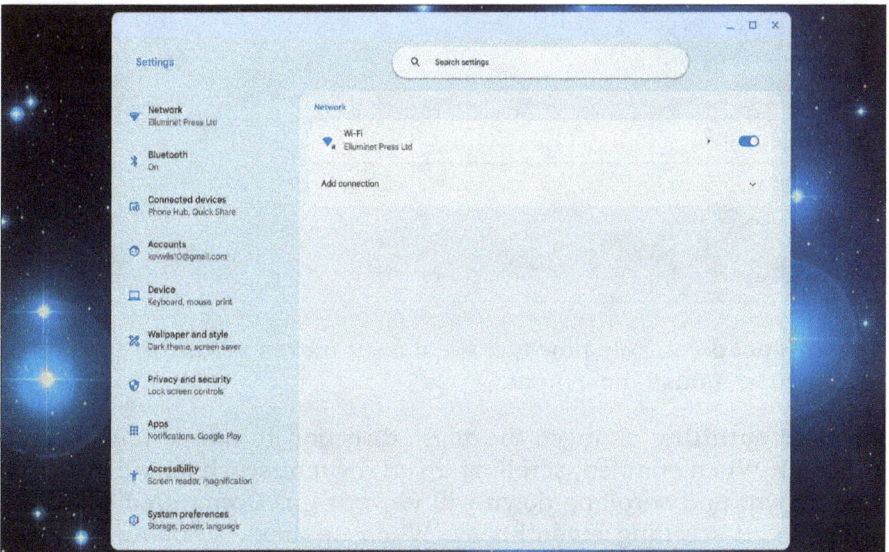

You can also search for a setting. To do this, type the name of the setting into the 'search settings' field on the top of the screen.

Chapter 2: Setting up your Chromebook

Mouse

To configure your mouse settings, select 'device' from the list on the left hand side of the settings window. Then click on 'mouse'.

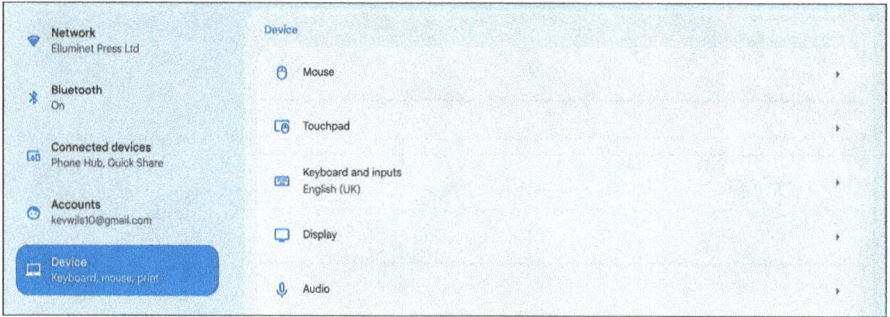

Here you can enable cursor acceleration. This means the speed of the cursor increases based on how fast you move the mouse. A quick flick of the mouse will move the cursor a longer distance, while slow movements result in more precise, controlled cursor positioning.

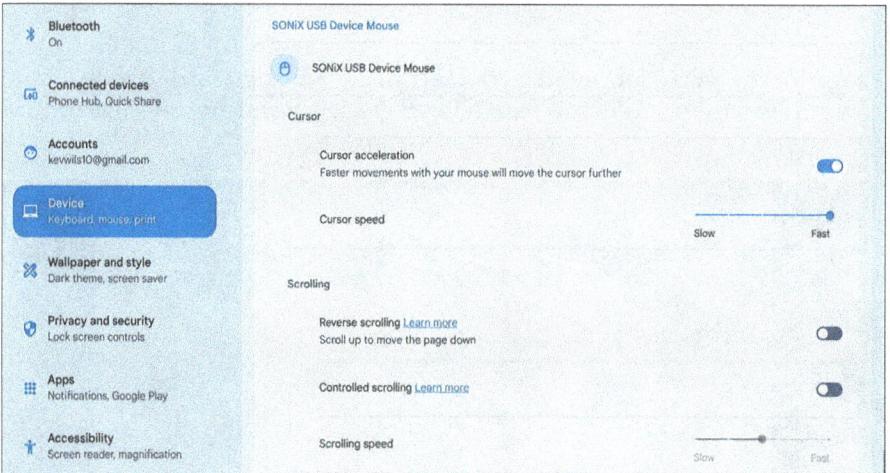

Cursor speed controls how fast the cursor moves across the screen in response to mouse movement.

Reverse scrolling changes the scroll direction to mimic touchscreen behavior. When enabled, scrolling up on the mouse wheel will move the page down, and scrolling down will move it up. **Controlled scrolling** adjusts the scrolling smoothness. When enabled, scrolling becomes more gradual and fluid rather than jumping abruptly by several lines at once. **Scrolling speed** controls how fast the page scrolls when using the scroll wheel.

Touchpad

To configure your touchpad settings, select 'device' from the list on the left hand side of the settings window. Then click on 'touchpad'.

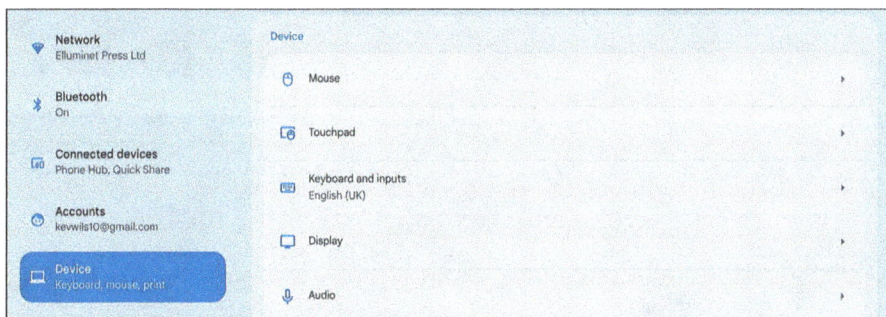

Here, you can enable **tap to click**. This allows you to tap lightly on the touchpad to perform a left-click, rather than physically pressing down on the pad.

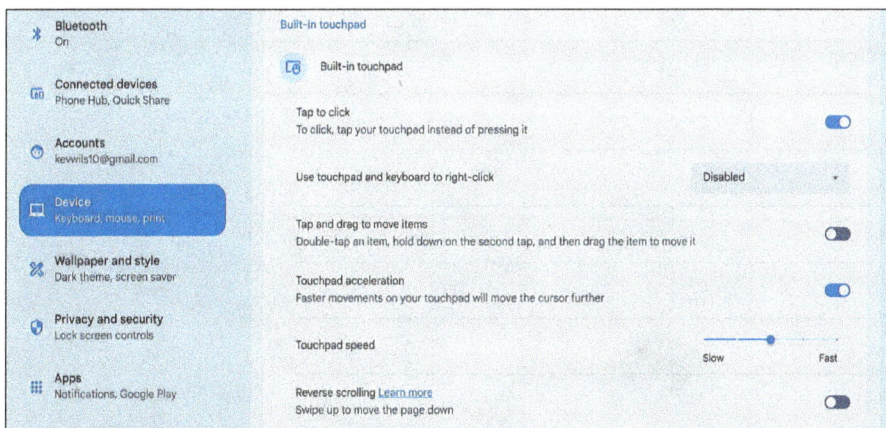

Use touchpad and keyboard to right-click enables an alternative way to right-click by combining the touchpad with a keyboard shortcut such as Alt.

Tap and drag to move items lets you move objects using a tap-and-drag gesture. You double-tap an item, keep your finger on the pad on the second tap, and drag it to a new location.

Touchpad acceleration moves the cursor farther if you swipe faster on the touchpad.

Touchpad speed adjusts the sensitivity of the touchpad and Reverse scrolling controls the scroll direction.

Chapter 2: Setting up your Chromebook

Internal Display Settings

Select 'devices' from the list on the left hand side of the settings window, then select 'display'.

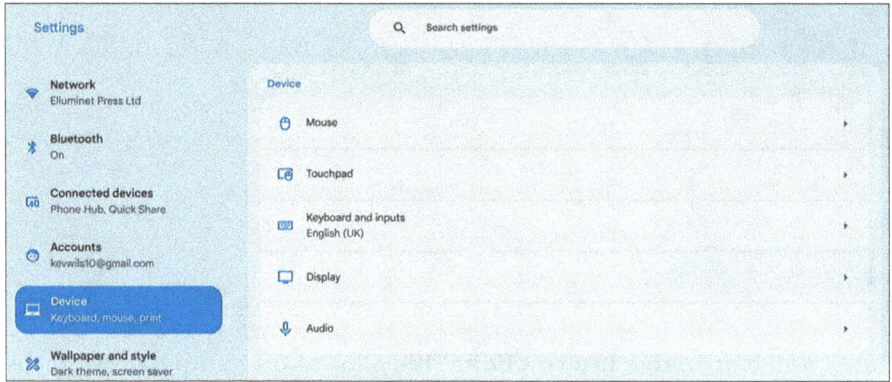

To adjust your Chromebook screen, select 'internal display'.

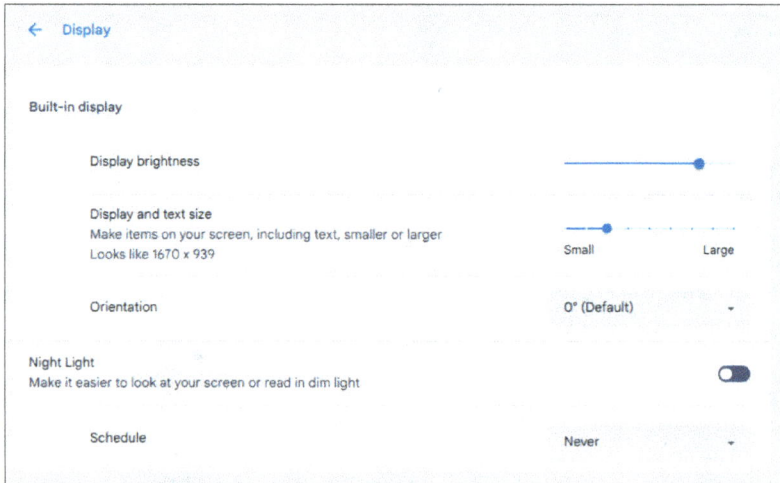

Use the 'display size' slider to make items on your screen smaller or larger. Use the 'orientation' drop down menu to rotate your screen. You can also toggle between the rotations by pressing ctrl, shift and refresh on your keyboard.

You can also turn on the night light. This reduces the amount of blue light coming from your screen. Click the slider switch next to 'night light' to enable/disable.

You can also schedule this, click the drop down menu next to 'schedule'. Select 'sunset to sunrise' to automatically turn it on at night. Click 'customise' to select a time to turn it on and a time to turn it off.

External Display Settings

An external display could be a TV, monitor, or projector. Your Chromebook usually does a good job at detecting the correct resolution for a display. To configure an external screen, open your settings.

Select 'devices' from the list on the left hand side, then select 'displays'.

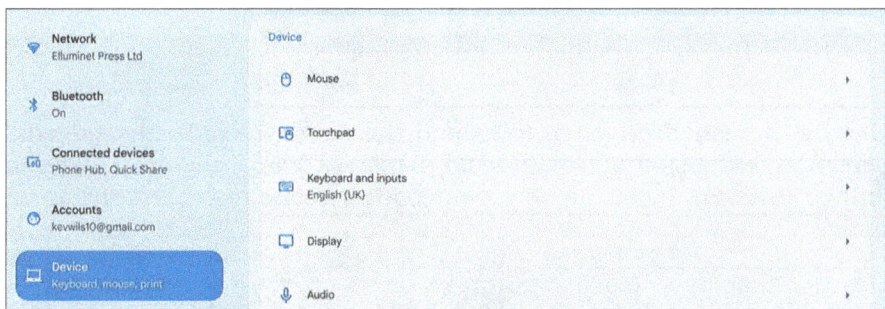

Under the 'arrangement' section, arrange the displays so the external screen extends the left or right side of your internal display.

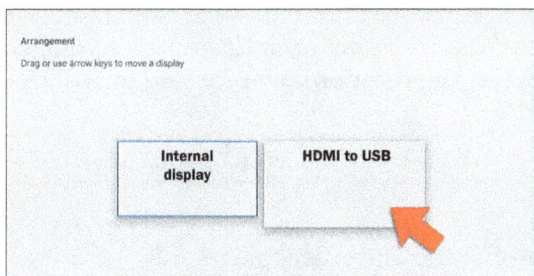

It's best to mirror your setup. If your external screen is on the right of your Chromebook, move the rectangle to the right of the 'internal display' as shown below.

To adjust an external screen, select the screen name.

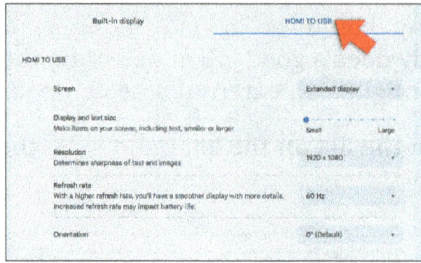

Use the 'screen' drop down to extend the display - make the external screen an extension of the internal display. Change the drop down to 'mirror internal display' if you want both screens to project the same image.

Use the 'display size' slider to make items on your screen smaller or larger.

Use the 'resolution' drop down to change the external screen's resolution (eg 1920x1080 is HD).

Use the 'orientation' drop down menu to rotate your screen. You can also toggle between the rotations by pressing ctrl, shift and refresh on your keyboard.

Time Zone

The time zone on your Chromebook usually sets itself according to your location. If you need to change it, you'll find the option in the settings. Click 'system preferences' on the left hand side, then click 'time zone'.

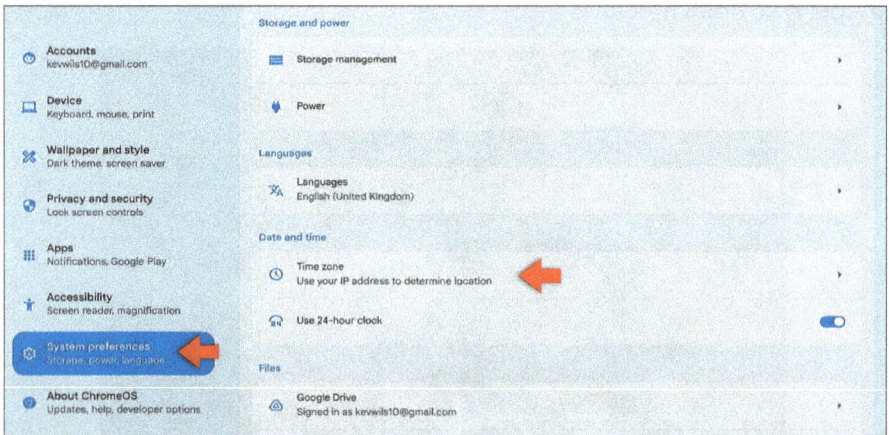

Select 'choose from list', select a time zone from the drop down menu.

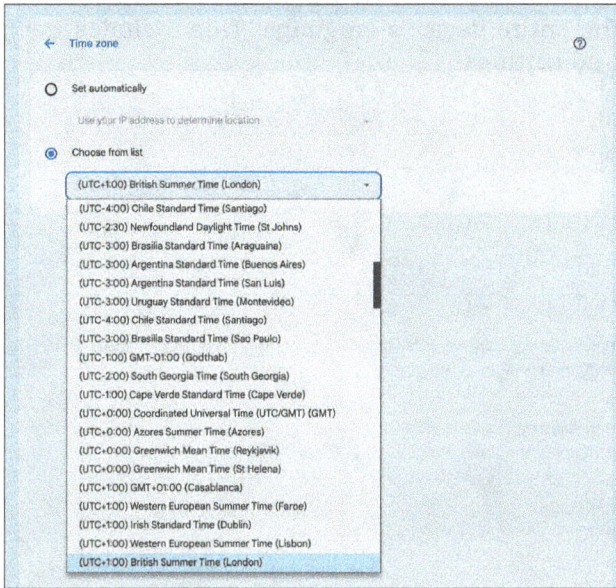

Change Language

You can change the display language from the settings. To do this open the settings window, select 'system preferences', then click 'languages'.

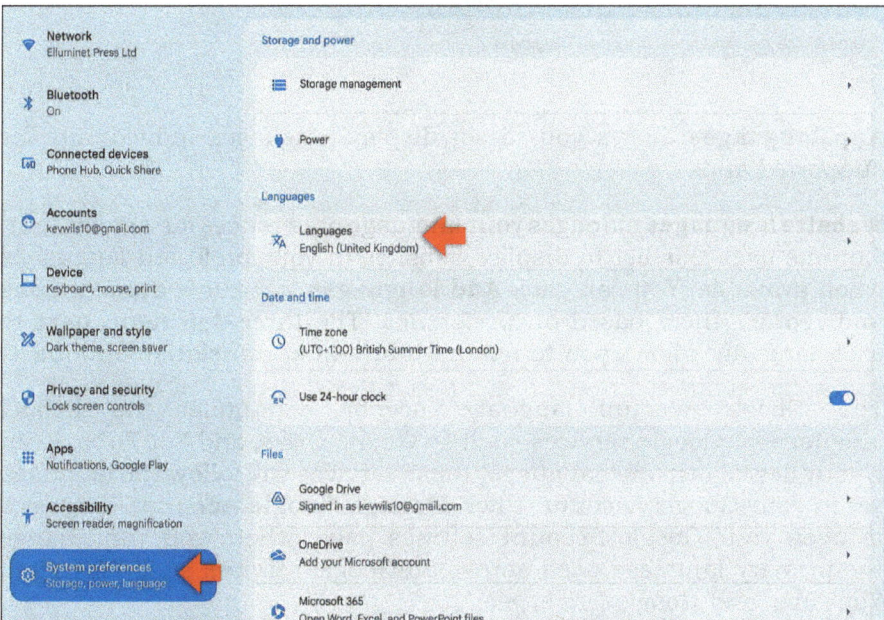

Chapter 2: Setting up your Chromebook

Here, you can change language settings. **Device language** displays the language currently used by the system interface. Click "Change" to change the entire device's language. This includes menus, system messages, and settings.

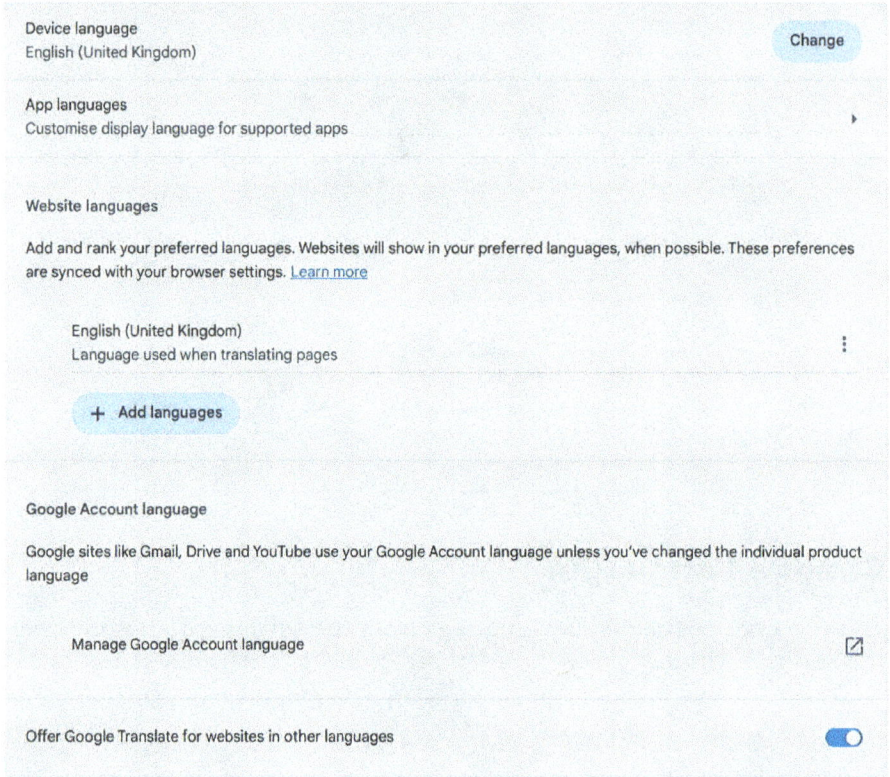

Device language
English (United Kingdom)   Change

App languages
Customise display language for supported apps   ▸

Website languages

Add and rank your preferred languages. Websites will show in your preferred languages, when possible. These preferences are synced with your browser settings. Learn more

English (United Kingdom)
Language used when translating pages   ⋮

+ Add languages

Google Account language

Google sites like Gmail, Drive and YouTube use your Google Account language unless you've changed the individual product language

Manage Google Account language   ⧉

Offer Google Translate for websites in other languages   🔵

App languages allows you to set display languages individually for supported apps.

Website languages manages your language preferences for web content. Chrome uses this list to display websites in your preferred languages when available. You can click **Add languages** to include more options and reorder them based on preference. The three-dot menu next to each language allows you to remove it or adjust translation options.

The "Google Account language" section determines the display language for Google services such as Gmail, Drive, and YouTube. Even if your device is in one language, these services will follow the language set in your Google Account. Click **Manage Google Account language** to open your Google Account settings page, where you can change the primary language used across all Google services such as Gmail, YouTube, and Google Drive.

Offer Google Translate for websites in other languages controls whether Chrome prompts you to translate pages that aren't in your preferred language. When this toggle is turned on, Chrome will automatically offer to translate foreign-language web content.

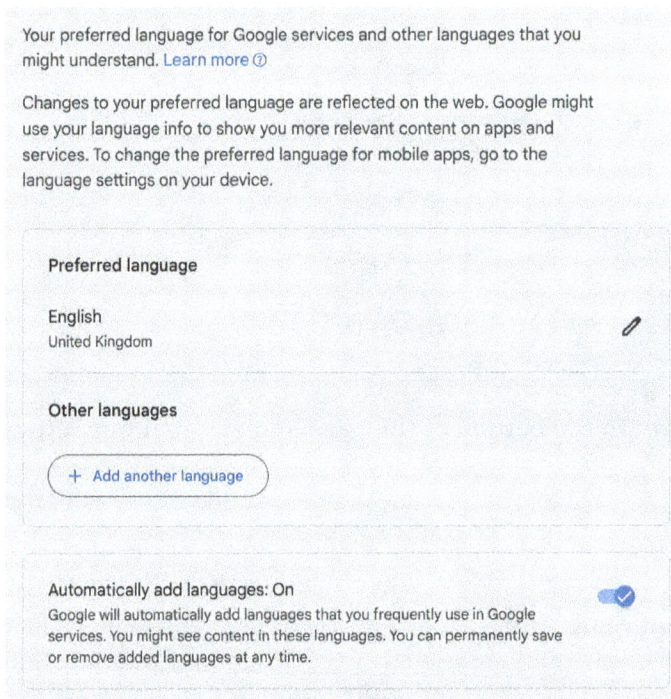

Your preferred language for Google services and other languages that you might understand. Learn more ⓘ

Changes to your preferred language are reflected on the web. Google might use your language info to show you more relevant content on apps and services. To change the preferred language for mobile apps, go to the language settings on your device.

Preferred language

English
United Kingdom

Other languages

+ Add another language

Automatically add languages: On
Google will automatically add languages that you frequently use in Google services. You might see content in these languages. You can permanently save or remove added languages at any time.

The **Preferred language** section shows the language that Google services will use for menus, buttons, and other interface elements. Next to it is a pencil icon, which allows you to edit this setting and choose a different preferred language.

The **Other languages** section lets you add additional languages that you understand. Google uses these languages to deliver content in those languages across its services. For example, if a website, search result, video, or news article is available in one of your additional languages, Google will display it in that language instead of automatically translating it or defaulting to your primary language. This helps provide more accurate, native-language content and reduces unnecessary translations.

Automatically add languages means Google will automatically add languages to your account based on your activity across its services— for example, if you frequently search or view content in another language. You can choose to keep or remove these added languages at any time.

Chapter 2: Setting up your Chromebook

Keyboard Layout

You can change the keyboard layout from the settings. To do this open the settings window and select 'device', then click 'inputs and keyboards'.

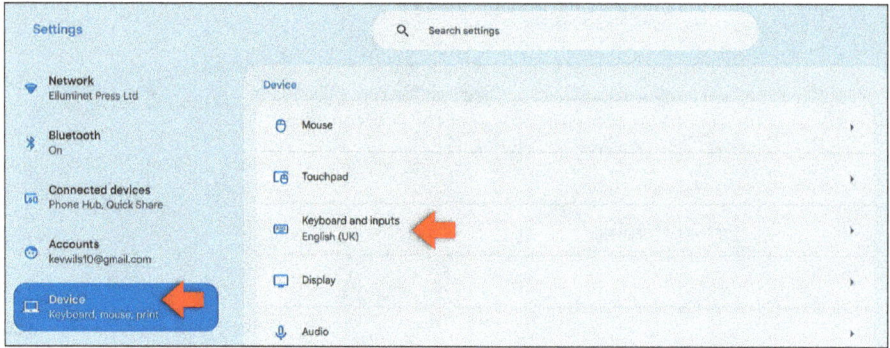

Scroll down to the bottom of the page and select 'input settings'.

Under the input methods section, you can add additional keyboard layouts or input methods, such as US English, Dvorak, handwriting input, voice typing, or non-Latin character systems (e.g., Chinese, Arabic). To do this, click 'add input methods'.

Browse or search through the list of available input options. Select the ones you want and click "Add" to enable them.

Once added, you can switch between input methods using the keyboard shortcut Ctrl + Space.

You can remove any input method by clicking the X icon next to it in the list under 'input methods'.

Keyboard Settings

You can configure various keyboard settings such as key functions, repeat rate, accent marks, and accessibility options.

Open the settings window and select 'device', then click 'languages and input'.

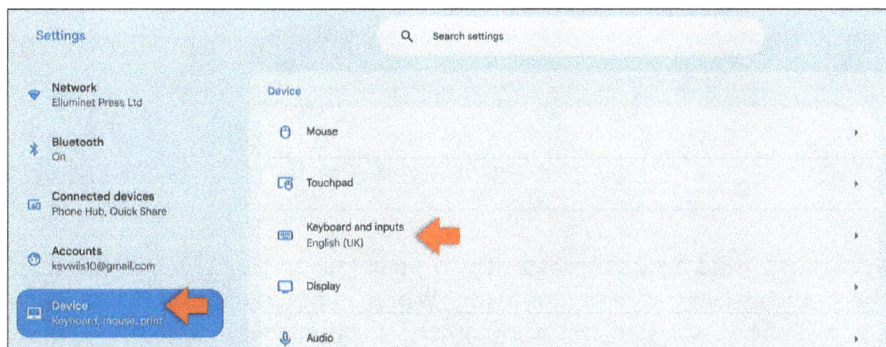

Treat top-row keys as function keys determines how the top row of your keyboard behaves. By default, these keys perform special actions like adjusting brightness, controlling volume, or refreshing the page. When this option is turned on, the top-row keys instead behave as traditional function keys (F1 through F12).

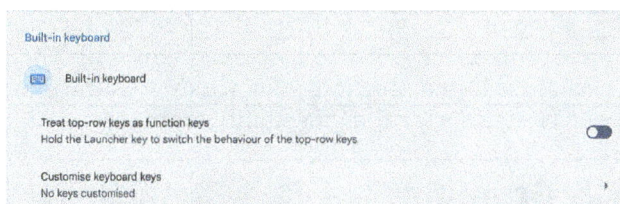

Customise keyboard keys allows you to reassign specific keys, such as the Search (Launcher) key, Ctrl, Alt, Caps Lock, Escape, and Backspace. To do this, click on "Customise keyboard keys" then on the next page that opens, select the desired function from the drop down menu for each key.

Show accent marks and special characters allows you to press and hold letter keys to reveal accent mark options. For example, holding e would display é, è, ê, and other accented versions.

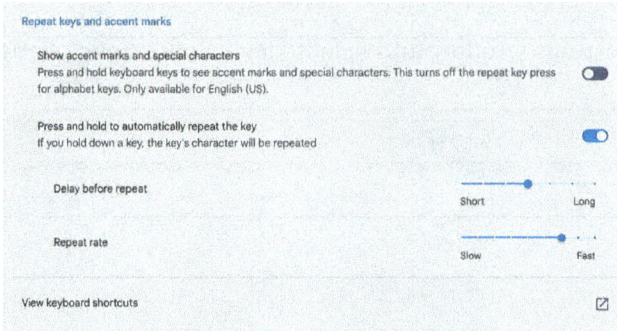

Press and hold to automatically repeat the key enables or disables the standard key repeat behavior. When enabled, holding down any key will cause it to continuously repeat its character after a brief delay. If disabled, holding a key will only produce a single character. You can configure this using the two sliders underneath. **Delay before repeat** slider adjusts how long you must hold down a key before it starts repeating. **Repeat rate** determines how quickly a key repeats after the initial delay.

View keyboard shortcuts opens a full list of available keyboard shortcuts for ChromeOS. It is a helpful reference for users looking to increase productivity or become more efficient with the ChromeOS interface. The list includes shortcuts for window management, virtual desks, browser functions, and accessibility features.

Spelling & Grammar

To change spelling and grammar settings. These control how ChromeOS detects and corrects spelling and grammar as you type in supported applications (e.g., Google Docs, web forms, text fields).

Open the settings window and select 'device', then click 'languages and input'.

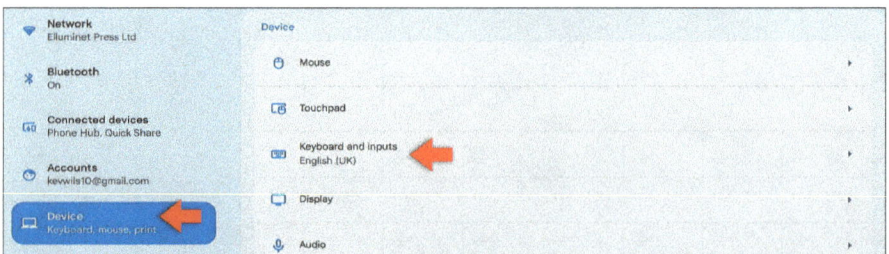

Scroll down to the bottom of the page and select 'input settings'.

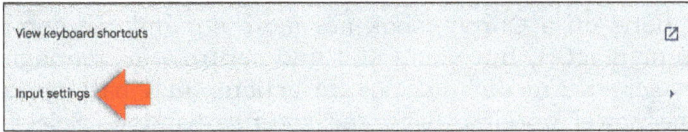

View keyboard shortcuts	☑
Input settings	›

Scroll down to 'spelling and grammar check'. Use the toggle switch next to **Spelling and Grammar check** to turn the feature on or off. Note: At the time of writing, grammar checking is only available in English.

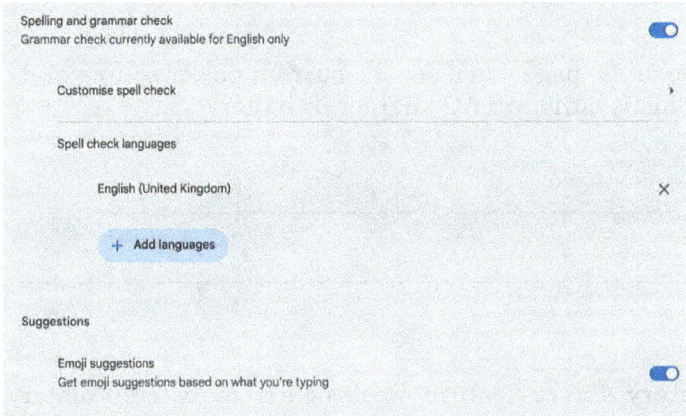

Spelling and grammar check
Grammar check currently available for English only

Customise spell check

Spell check languages

English (United Kingdom)

+ Add languages

Suggestions

Emoji suggestions
Get emoji suggestions based on what you're typing

Customise spell check opens a personal dictionary where you can add custom words that you don't want flagged as spelling errors. Type the word in the field, then click 'add word'. You can also review and delete words you've added. To delete a word, click the x icon next to the word you want to delete.

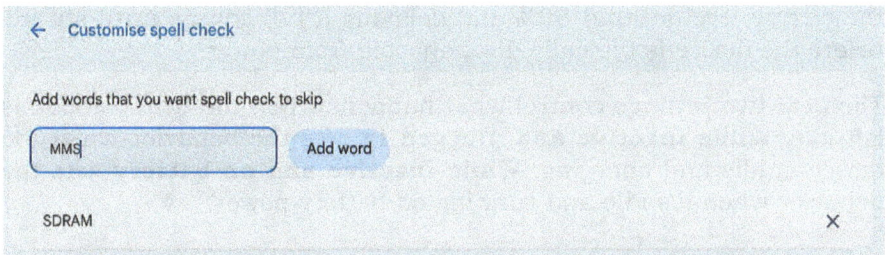

← Customise spell check

Add words that you want spell check to skip

MMS   Add word

SDRAM   ✕

Under **Spell check languages**, you'll see the currently active spell check language(s). To include additional languages, click **Add languages** then select a language from the list.

Emoji suggestions enables emoji prediction based on what you type. For example, typing "happy" will suggest a happy emoji.

85

Power Options

Power options on a Chromebook are more streamlined compared to Windows or macOS, but you'll still find controls for managing sleep behavior, screen timeout, lid closure actions, and battery usage. To adjust the power options, open the settings window. Select 'system preferences', then click on 'power'.

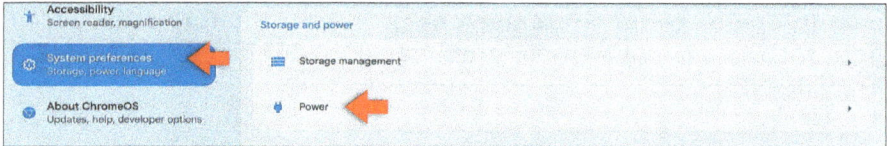

At the top of the page you'll see the current power source and charging status. This is either an AC adapter or battery.

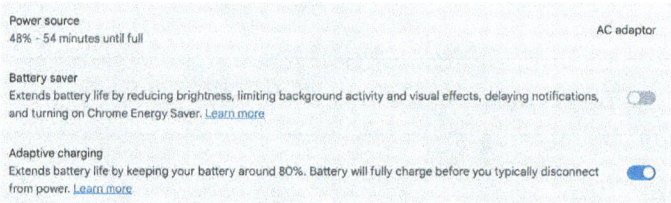

The **Battery Saver** feature is designed to extend battery life by reducing screen brightness, limiting background activity and visual effects. It is particularly useful when running on battery and trying to conserve power during long usage sessions. Note that Battery Saver mode reduces system performance in exchange for improved power efficiency.

Adaptive Charging helps preserve long-term battery health by keeping the charge level around 80% and delaying a full charge until shortly before the device is typically disconnected from power.

The next two settings control what happens when the Chromebook is left idle. **While inactive and plugged in** sets the behavior when the device is idle and charging. **While inactive and on battery** sets the behavior when it's idle and running on battery power.

For each of these, you can choose from three options. **Sleep** puts the device into low-power mode to conserve energy, **Turn off display** keeps the system running while turning off the screen.

Keep display on prevents both the screen and system from sleeping, ensuring everything stays active.

Sleep when lid is closed	⬤

At the bottom, **sleep when lid is closed** determines whether the Chromebook automatically enters sleep mode when you close the lid. When enabled, closing the lid puts the device to sleep.

Audio Settings

Audio settings allow you to manage input and output devices such as microphones, headphones and speakers. You can adjust volume levels, and control microphone and speaker behavior. To adjust the audio settings, open the settings window. Select 'device', then click on 'audio'.

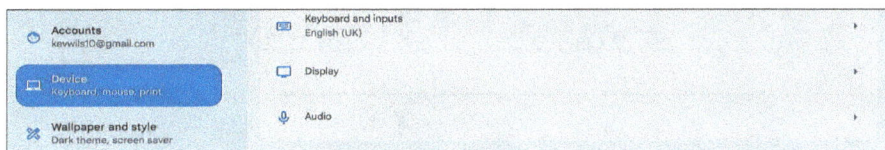

Accounts kewwils10@gmail.com	Keyboard and inputs English (UK)	›
Device Keyboard, mouse, print	Display	›
Wallpaper and style Dark theme, screen saver	Audio	›

Here, the **speaker** dropdown allows you to choose the current audio output device. In this case, it is set to Speaker (internal), which means sound will play through the Chromebook's built-in speakers. If headphones, Bluetooth speakers, or HDMI audio devices are connected, they would appear in this list as alternative options. The **volume** slider controls the master output volume for the selected speaker.

Output

Speaker	Speaker (internal) ▾
Volume	🔊 ————————●

This microphone dropdown shows the currently selected microphone input. If an external USB, Bluetooth, or headset mic is connected, you can select it here. The **volume** slider adjusts the microphone sensitivity (input gain).

Input

Microphone	Microphone (internal) ▾
Volume	🎤 ————————●

Underneath, the **Studio-style mic** toggle enables audio enhancements, such as noise cancellation and other signal processing improvements designed to produce clearer voice recordings. It's turned off in the screenshot. When enabled, it improves microphone quality by filtering out background noise and echo.

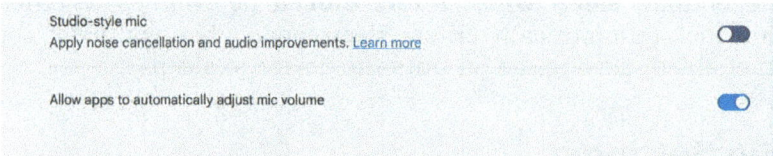

Studio-style mic
Apply noise cancellation and audio improvements. Learn more

Allow apps to automatically adjust mic volume

Allow apps to automatically adjust mic volume lets apps like Zoom, Google Meet, or recording software control the microphone volume automatically based on your speaking level.

The Device sounds section at the bottom of the page controls whether your Chromebook plays certain system notification sounds.

Device sounds

Low battery sound

Charging sounds

Device start-up sound

Low battery sound will play a warning tone when the battery reaches a critically low level and needs charging.

Charging sounds will play a sound when it is connected to or disconnected from power.

Device start-up sound controls whether your Chromebook plays a sound when it powers on or boots up. When enabled, you'll hear a startup chime similar to those on macOS or Windows devices.

These settings are designed for user feedback and accessibility. They help bring your attention to important power-related cues even when they aren't actively looking at the screen.

Network Settings

Once you are connected to a WiFi network, you can change settings such as DNS servers, assign static IP addresses, connect to proxy servers and VPNs.

Open the settings window and select 'network'.

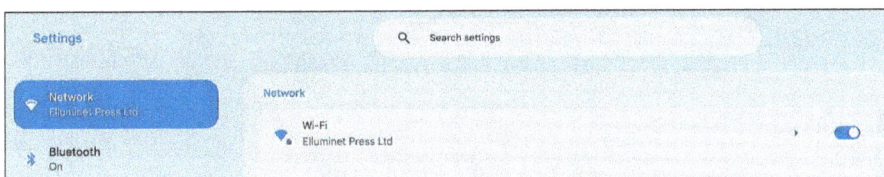

Select your network from the list.

Basic Settings

At the top, the network status is shown as "Connected," indicating that the device is currently using this Wi-Fi connection for internet access. The **Forget** button allows you to remove this network from the Chromebook's saved list, which means you would need to re-enter the password if you reconnect later. The **Disconnect** button simply ends the current connection without erasing the saved configuration, allowing for quick reconnection.

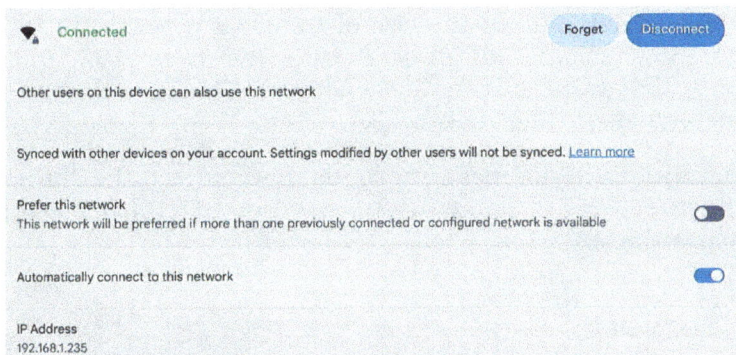

Prefer this network lets you prioritize this Wi-Fi connection over others. If enabled, the Chromebook will favor this network when multiple known networks are available.

Automatically connect to this network means the Chromebook will automatically reconnect to this network whenever it is in range.

Underneath you'll see the currently assigned IP address for the device on the network. The IP address is a unique address that identifies you on your home/business/school network or the internet.

IP Addresses

Most of the time IP addresses are assigned automatically when you join a WiFi network. However, in some circumstances, you might need to assign a static IP address.

To set a static IP address, open the network section. From here click the switch next to 'configure IP address automatically' to turn it off. This will allow you to enter an IP address, subnet mask, and gateway/router IP into the fields. The **IP address** specifies the unique address assigned to the Chromebook on the local network.

Configure IP address automatically

IP address

192.168.1.235

Subnet mask

255.255.255.0

Gateway

192.168.1.1

The **subnet mask** defines the size of the local network. In this case 255.255.255.0 means all devices with IPs from 192.168.1.1 to 192.168.1.254 are on the same local network. This is a common setting for home and small office networks.

The **gateway** is the IP address of the router that connects the Chromebook to the internet. This is usually 192.168.1.1 or 192.168.1.254 for most home networks.

DNS Servers

A DNS server (Domain Name System server) is a service that helps your device find websites on the internet. When you type something like google.com into your browser, the DNS server translates that name into a set of numbers called an IP address which your computer uses to connect to the website. It's like a phone book that matches website names to their correct locations online.

To adjust the DNS servers, from the network settings page open the network section. Go down to 'name servers'. Select one of the options.

Name servers

⊙ Automatic name servers

1.1.1.3, 1.0.0.3

○ Google name servers Learn more

Automatic name servers means your Chromebook is using DNS servers assigned automatically by your router or ISP.

Google name servers uses Google's public DNS servers (8.8.8.8 and 8.8.4.4). These are fast, reliable, and widely used for general web browsing, with no content filtering by default.

Custom name servers allow you to manually enter your own DNS servers. This is useful for advanced configurations, content filtering, or when connecting to a network that requires specific DNS settings—such as in a school or workplace.

⊙ Custom name servers

1.1.1.3

1.0.0.3

0.0.0.0

0.0.0.0

For example, you can enter Cloudflare's DNS servers: 1.1.1.3 and 1.0.0.3. These servers include built-in malware protection and content filtering, helping to block access to harmful or unwanted websites.

Proxy Servers

A proxy server is an intermediary server that sits between your device and the internet. When you use a proxy, your internet traffic is routed through that server and is useful when you want to control, monitor, filter, or reroute your internet traffic for specific purposes.

To change the proxy server settings, from the network settings page open the network section. Go down to 'proxy'.

Chapter 2: Setting up your Chromebook

From here the toggle controls whether proxy settings can be used on shared networks, such as public Wi-Fi or networks shared between multiple users or devices.

Allow proxies for shared networks is a setting that controls whether proxy configurations are applied when you're connected to a shared or public network, such as school Wi-Fi, office networks, or public hotspots. When this setting is turned off, your Chromebook will ignore proxy settings and connect directly to the internet.

Turn Allow proxies for shared networks on. Then from the connection type drop down choose an option.

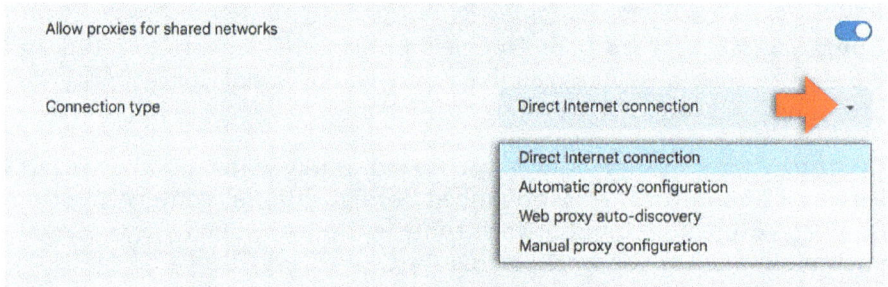

Allow proxies for shared networks	
Connection type	Direct Internet connection
	Direct Internet connection
	Automatic proxy configuration
	Web proxy auto-discovery
	Manual proxy configuration

Automatic proxy configuration allows you to enter a PAC (Proxy Auto-Configuration) file URL. A PAC file contains rules that tell the Chromebook when and how to use a proxy server based on the web address being accessed. It's often used in enterprise or school networks.

Web proxy auto-discovery, also known as WPAD (Web Proxy Auto-Discovery Protocol) allows your Chromebook to automatically detect proxy settings on the network, if the network provides them. It's commonly used in managed or corporate environments.

Manual proxy configuration lets you manually enter specific proxy server details for HTTP, HTTPS, FTP, and bypass lists (e.g. `proxy.example.com`, port `8080`). Choose this if you're given specific proxy details by your school, workplace, or network administrator.

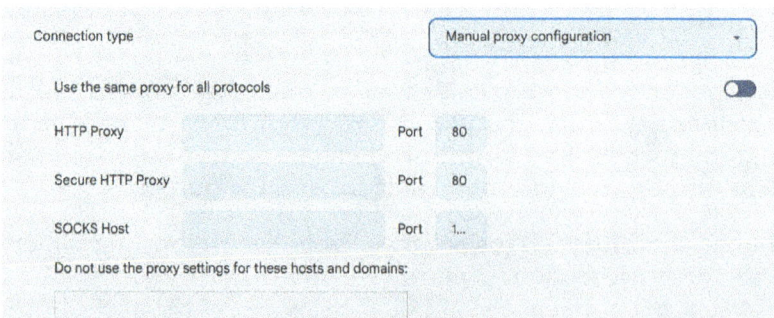

Connection type	Manual proxy configuration		
Use the same proxy for all protocols			
HTTP Proxy		Port	80
Secure HTTP Proxy		Port	80
SOCKS Host		Port	1...
Do not use the proxy settings for these hosts and domains:			

Remote Desktop

You can access another computer remotely such as your Windows PC, or Mac from your Chromebook. First you need to set it up.

In this demo, I'm going to set up my Windows laptop (shown below on the left) so I can access it remotely from my Chromebook (shown below on the right).

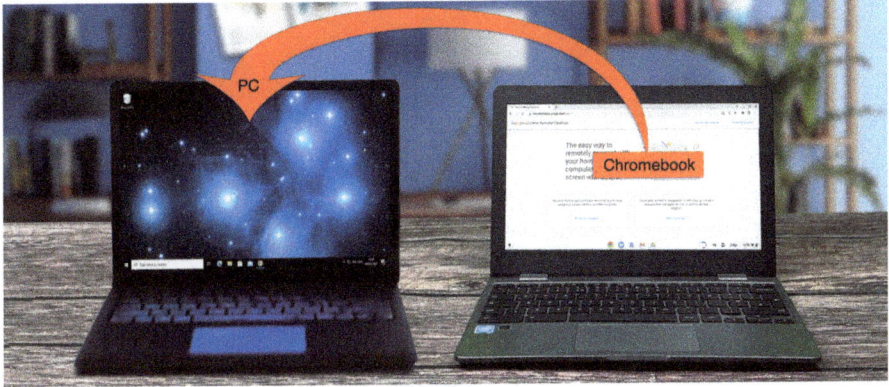

Setup Access to your Computer

On the machine you want to access remotely (eg the Windows laptop), open the chrome browser, navigate to the Google Chrome Web Store

`chrome.google.com/webstore`

On the top left search for

`remote desktop`

Click on 'chrome remote desktop'

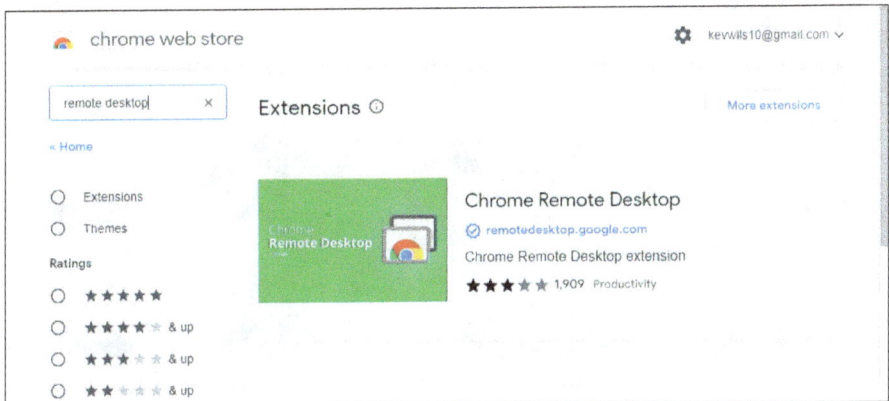

Chapter 2: Setting up your Chromebook

Click 'add to chrome'. Then click 'add extension'

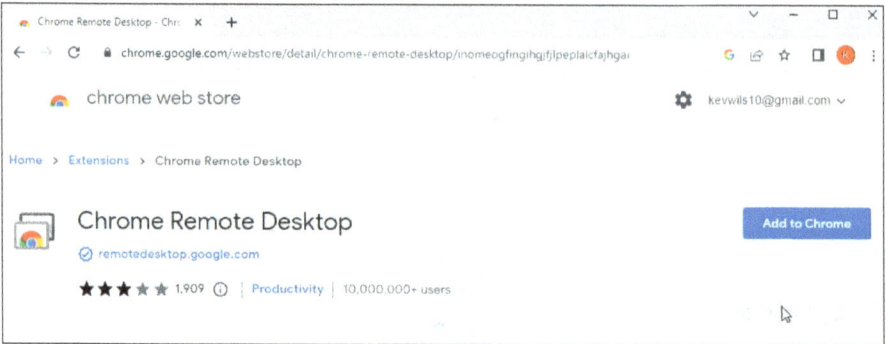

Now open the chrome browser and navigate to the following website:

remotedesktop.google.com/access

Sign in with your Google Account email address and password if prompted.

Click 'install & accept'

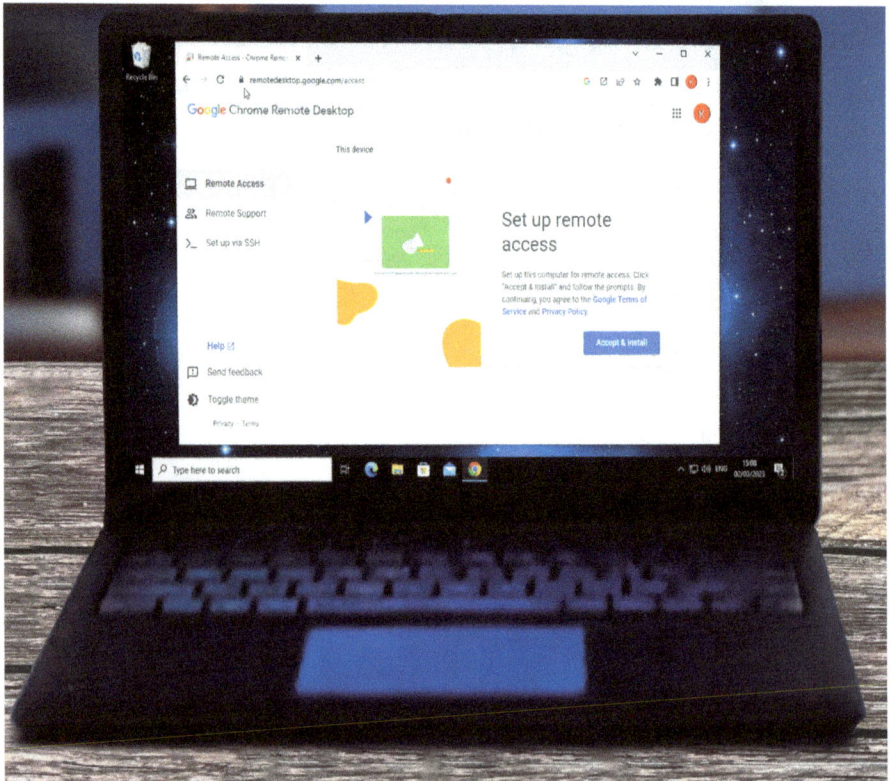

When the installer file is downloaded, you'll find it in your downloads folder. When file explorer pop-ups up, double click on chromeremovedesktophost.msi

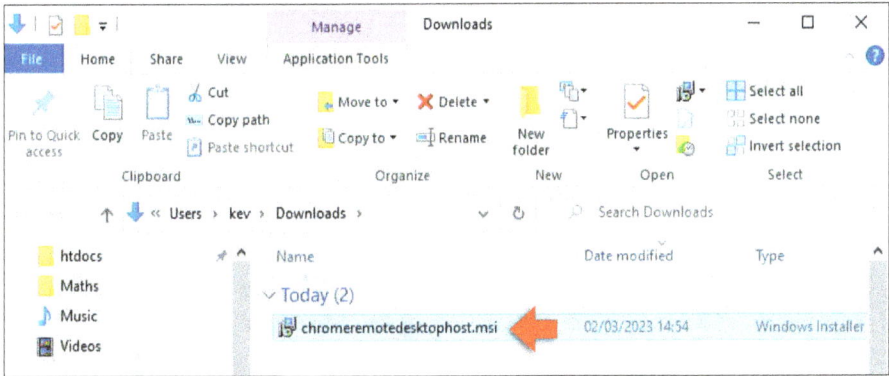

Run through the setup. Choose a meaningful name for this laptop. For example, I'm going to call this one LAPTOP.

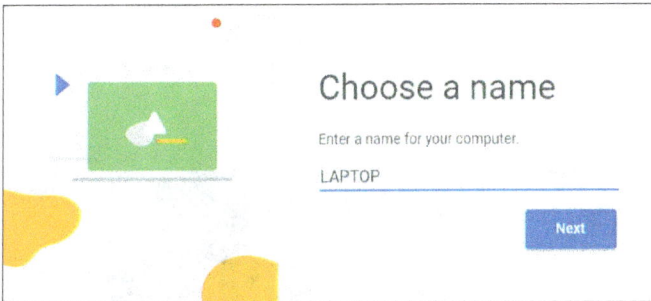

Enter a PIN. This is the code you'll need to connect to this device. Click 'start'.

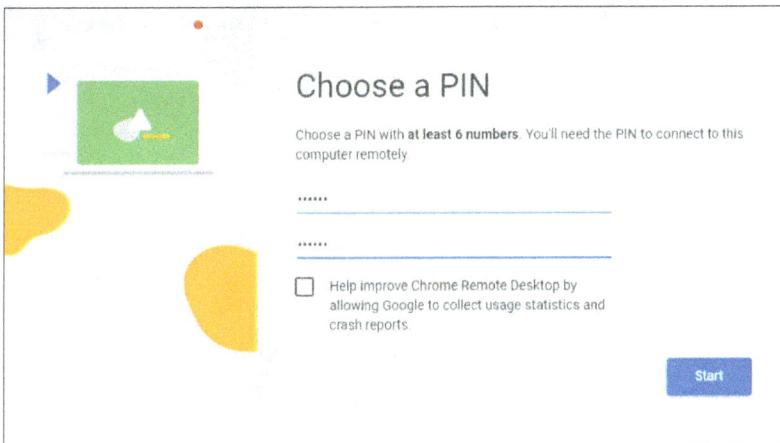

Chapter 2: Setting up your Chromebook

Connecting

Note the machine you're connecting to will need to remain on for this to work.

On your Chromebook, open the Chrome browser, then navigate to the following website and sign in:

`remotedesktop.google.com/access`

At the top of the page, you'll see your computers that have remote desktop enabled. Click on the one you want to use.

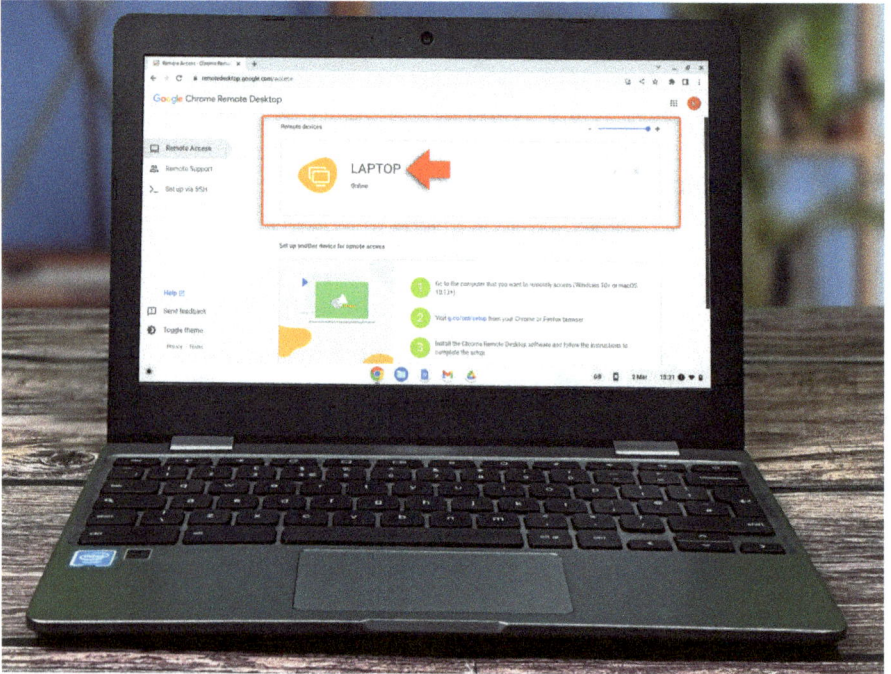

Enter the PIN code you created earlier.

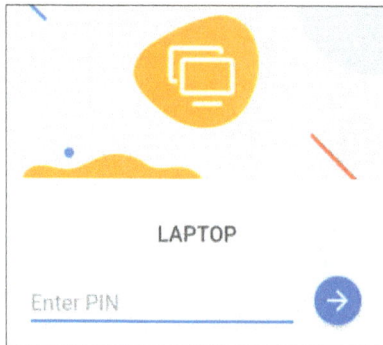

Now you can use your PC on your Chromebook. Here in the demo below, we can see the windows laptop's screen on the chromebook on the right.

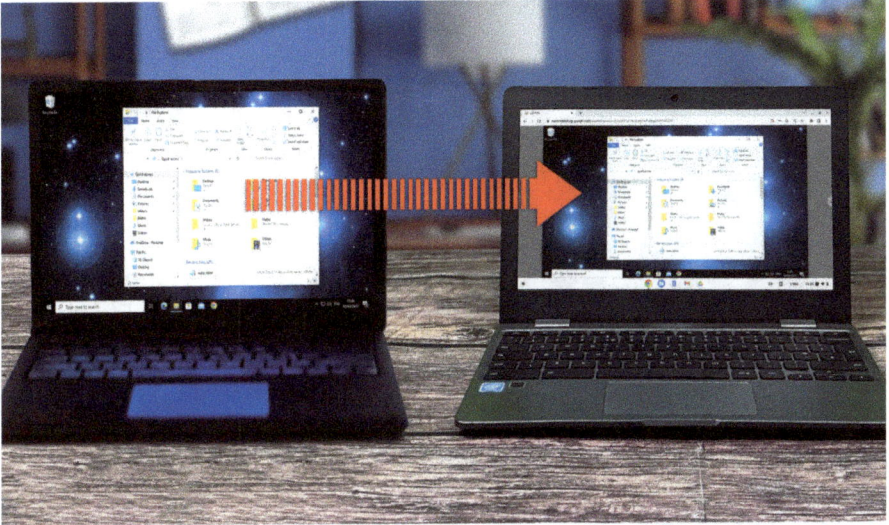

Turn off Sharing

If you want to stop sharing or turn off access to your machine, eg on your windows laptop. Navigate to the following website:

remotedesktop.google.com/access

Sign in with your Google Account email address and password if prompted. Next to the machine name, click the small bin icon to the right

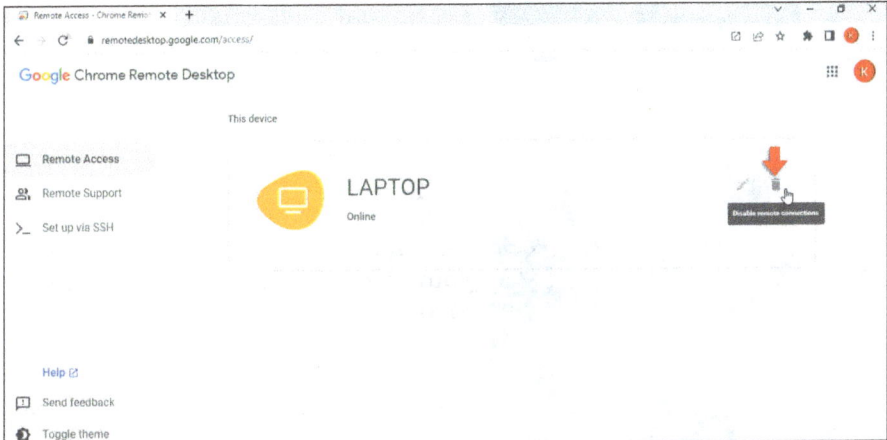

3

Getting around Chromebook

Chromebooks are very easy to navigate. If you're familiar with browsing the web, you'll be able to use your Chromebook with little difficulty.

In this chapter, we'll take a look at:

- Power Up & Power Down
- The Login Screen
- The Touch Pad & Keyboard
- Chromebook Task Manager
- Desktop and the App Shelf
- System Tray
- Notifications
- Calendar
- Phone Hub
- Pinned Files & Holding Space
- Virtual Desktops
- App Launcher
- File Management
- Quick Share
- Screen Capture

Take a look at the video demos. Open your web browser and navigate to the following website:

e l l u m i n e t p r e s s . c o m /
chromebook-nav

Power Up & Power Down

To power up your Chromebook, press the power key on the top right hand side of the keyboard. The Chrome logo will appear on the screen while the system starts.

To shut down your Chromebook, hold the power button for 1 second, you'll see three options pop up onto the screen.

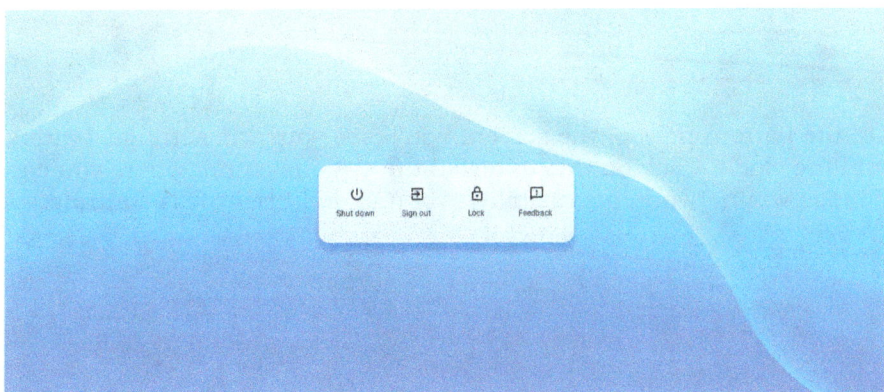

Click 'power off' to shut down your Chromebook. Click 'sign out' to sign out of your account and return to the login screen. Click 'lock screen' to lock your screen - useful if you are working on something and need to quickly lock your screen if you need to leave your Chromebook for a few minutes without having to sign out completely.

If your Chromebook has frozen or crashed, hold the power key until the screen goes blank. Wait a few seconds, then press the power key again to start up your Chromebook

The Login Screen

The login screen, sometimes called the lock screen, is the first screen you'll see when you turn on your Chromebook. Along the bar on the bottom left, you'll see a few icons. From here, you can shut your Chromebook down, allow someone to browse as a guest (without a Google Account) and add a new user with a Google Account to your Chromebook.

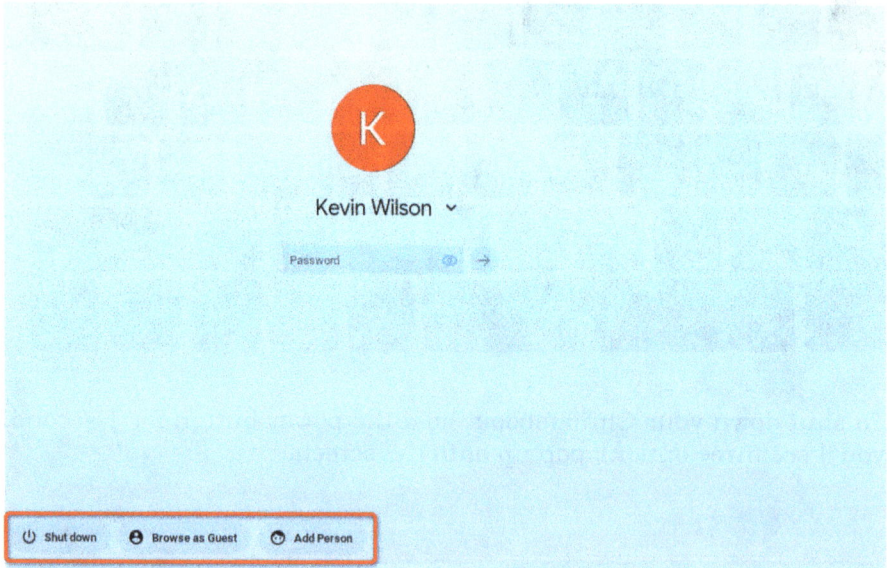

On the bottom right of the screen, you'll see your wifi settings, battery and the clock. Click on this to reveal the options menu, where you can change wifi network, accessibility, volume and brightness controls.

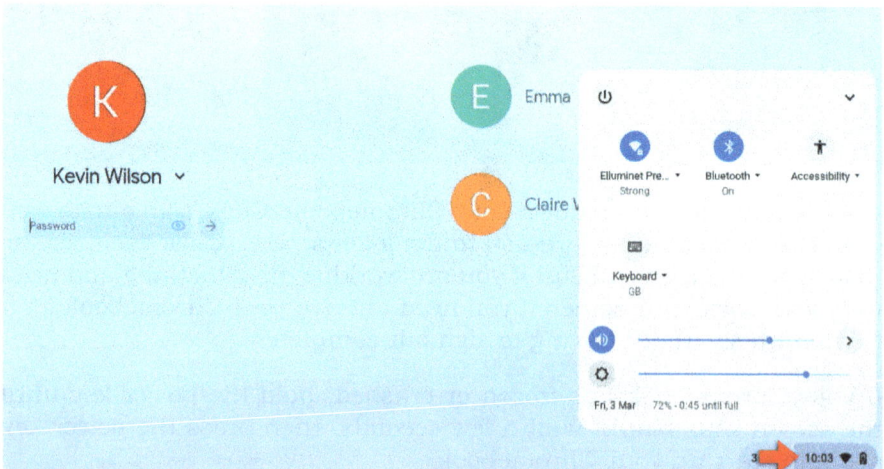

You'll also see a popup calendar if you click on the date.

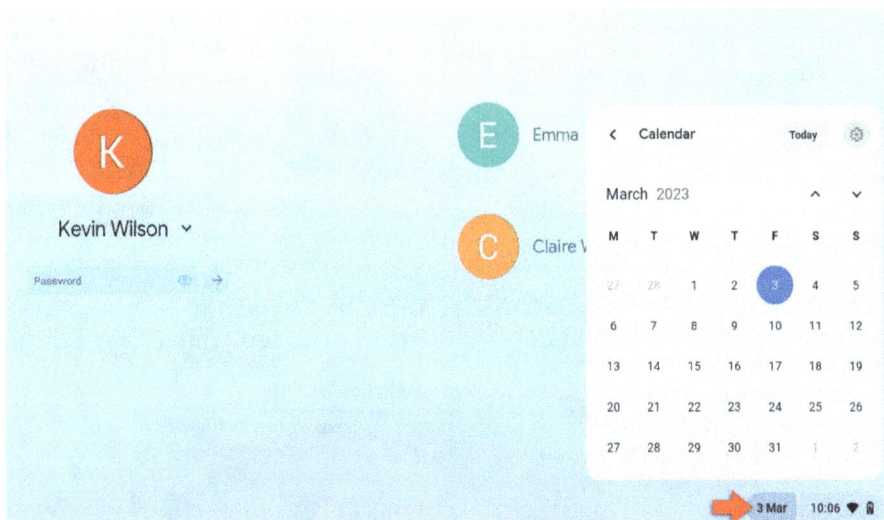

In the centre of the screen, you'll see your user account you registered when you set up your Chromebook, as well as any other user accounts registered on your Chromebook. Click on the correct user, then enter the password to log in.

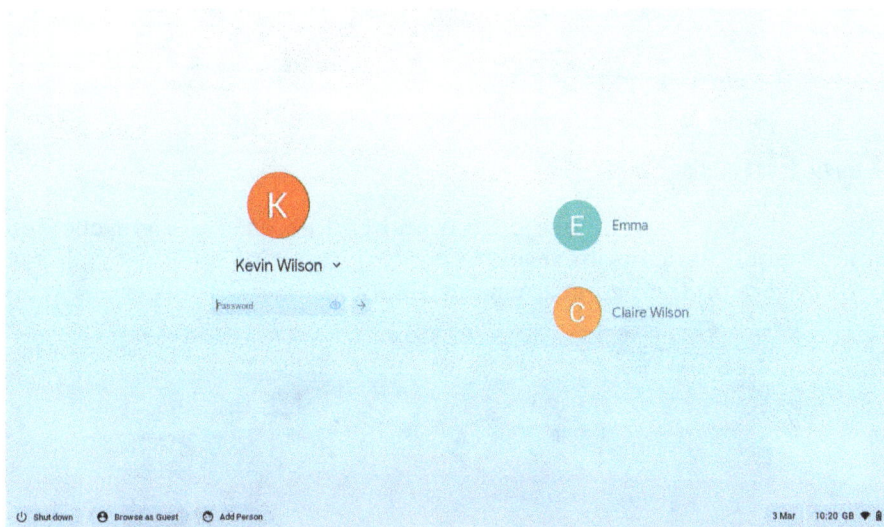

Once your Chromebook is set up, you will need to log in with your Google Account, so on the login screen, enter your password.

Before we go any further, lets take a look at some navigation features we can use to get around the user interface of your Chromebook.

The Touch Pad

If you have used a laptop before, then you'll be familiar with the touch pad or track pad.

You can use your fingers to move your pointer around the screen using what are called touch gestures.

Scan for Video

One Finger Tap

This is like your left mouse button and can be used to select objects such as icons or text fields on the screen. Just tap your finger on the pad.

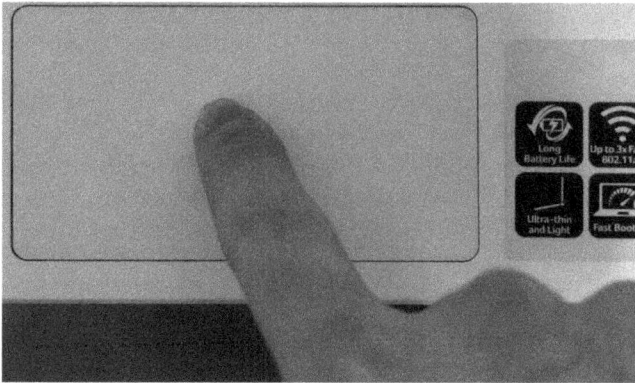

Two Finger Tap

This is like the right mouse button and can be used to right click on objects such as icons to reveal a context menu of options. Just tap both fingers on the pad at the same time.

One Finger Click and Drag

Position your pointer on to an object such as window title bar, or image on your screen, then press your finger on the touch pad until you hear a click, then without releasing your finger, drag across the track pad to move the object.

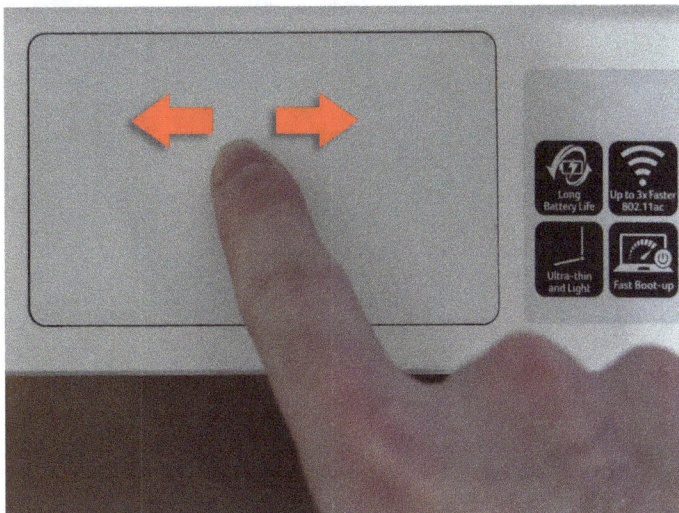

Two Finger Scroll

You can use two fingers on the track pad to scroll up and down windows, web pages, maps and so on.

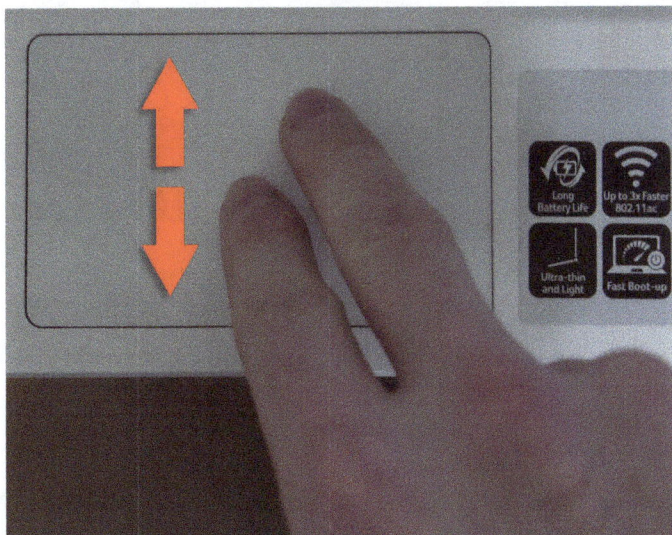

Two Finger Swipe

While you are browsing the web, you can go back to a previous page by swiping your two fingers to the left on the track pad and advance forward a page you have visited by swiping to the right.

Three Finger Swipe

You can quickly display all your open apps by swiping your three fingers downwards on the track pad.

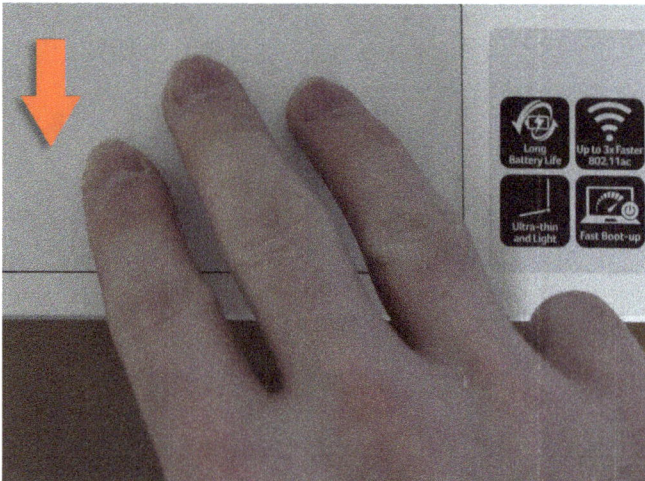

You'll see any open apps show up as thumbnail previews. You can click on these to open them or close them down.

The Keyboard

Here is a typical Chromebook keyboard. It looks like a conventional keyboard you'll find on any computer, but it's worth noting the keys along the top.

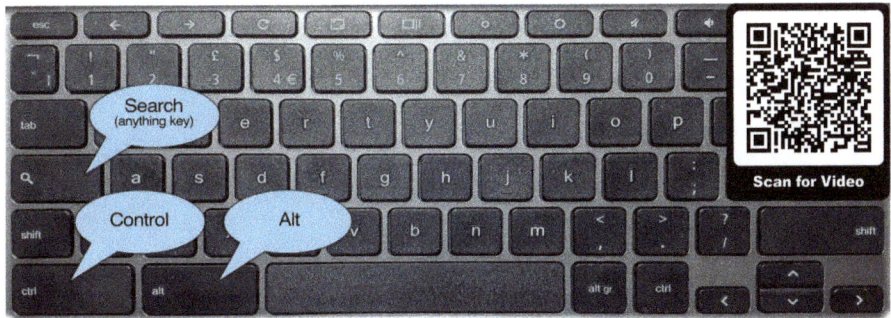

Along the top of your keyboard, you'll see some special keys. These help when using the Chrome web browser.

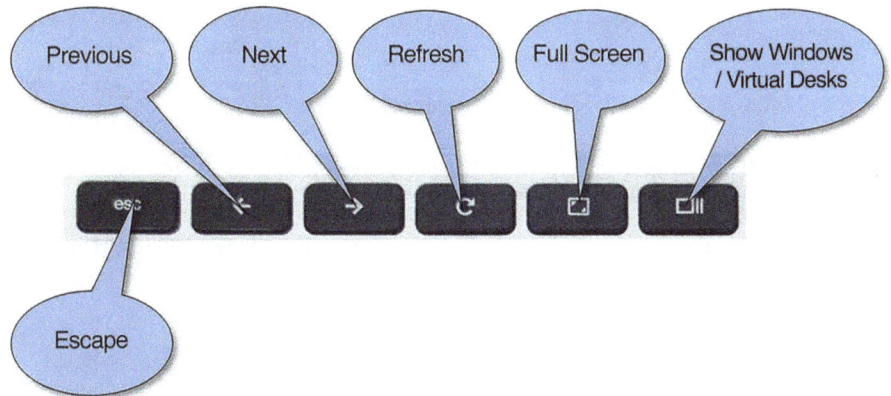

Towards the right hand side of the row, you'll see some keys that allow you to change the brightness of the screen and adjust audio volume.

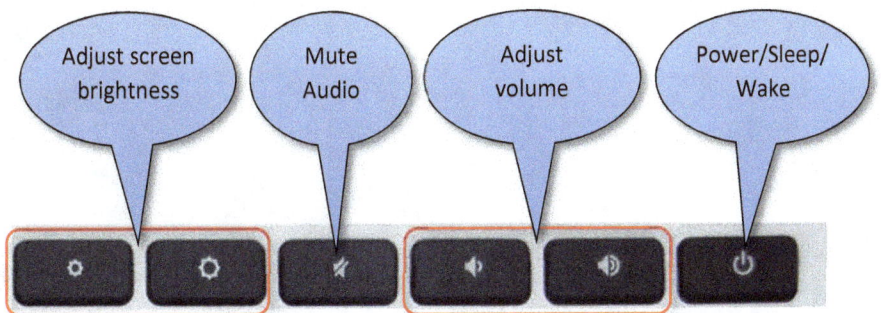

On-screen Keyboard Help

Your Chromebook contains a help screen that shows you all the keyboard shortcuts available. Press **ctrl alt ?** to reveal the help screen.

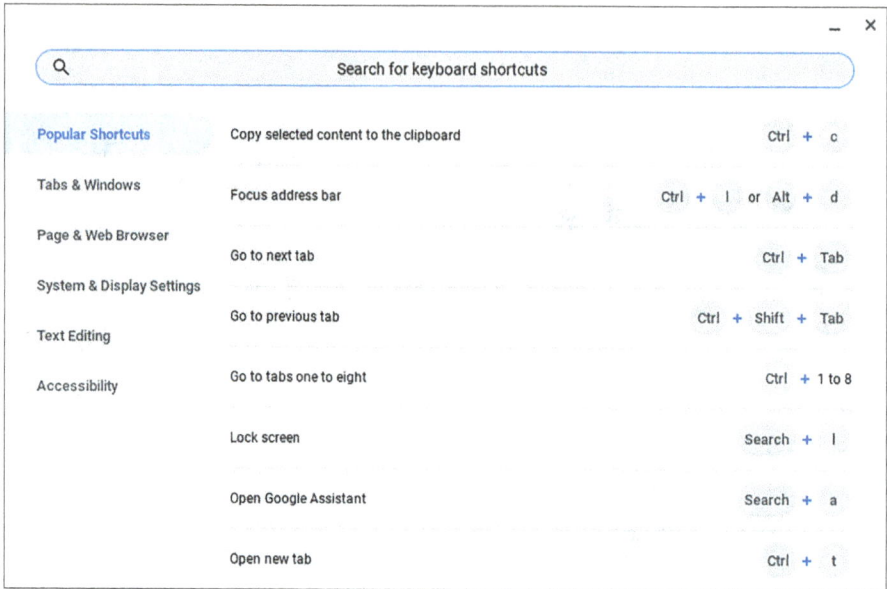

Scroll through the keyboard shortcuts. You can also browse through the categories on the left hand side.

Or you can search for keyboard shortcuts using the search field on the top of the screen.

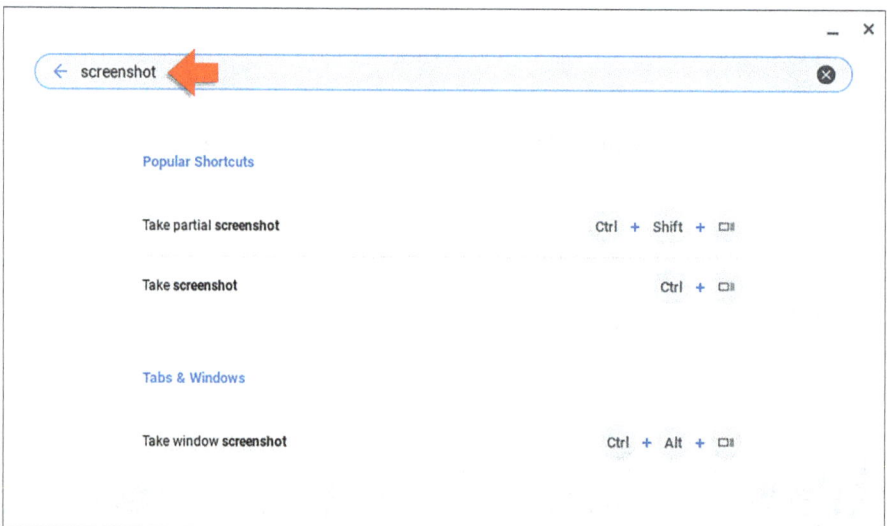

Chromebook Task Manager

Hold down the **search** key, then tap **escape**. The search key looks like a small magnifying glass, you'll find it on the left hand side of your keyboard. On the old Chromebooks press shift-escape.

You'll see a window pop up with a list of tasks (apps) that are currently running, as well as how much memory and cpu time they're using.

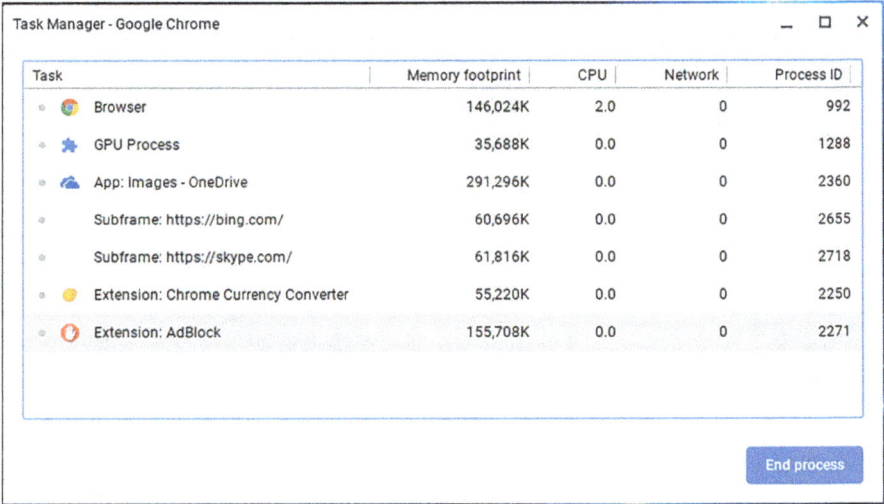

The task manager is useful if an app is not responding or has crashed.

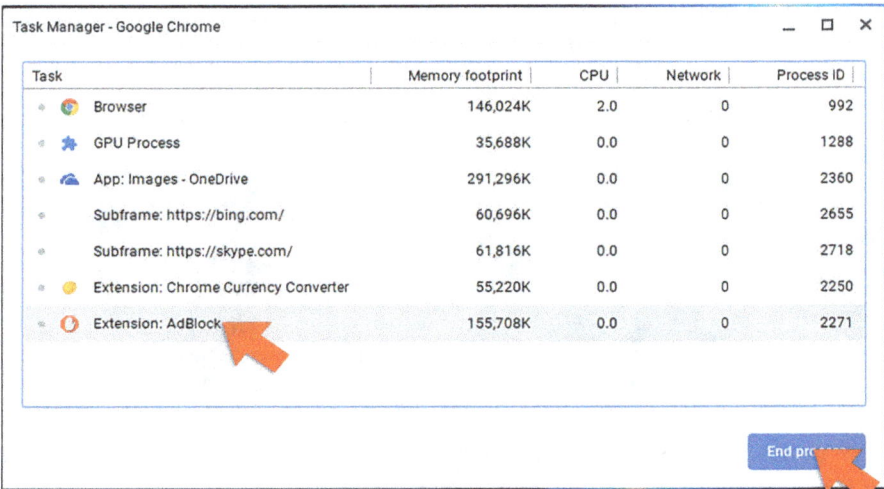

Just click on the task (app) in the list, then click 'end process'. The non-responsive app is usually labelled 'not responding'.

Desktop and the App Shelf

The desktop looks similar to a lot of operating systems out there, you have a background image or wallpaper and along the bottom you have what Google calls the Shelf. This is very much like the task bar found in Windows 10/11 or the App Dock found on a Mac.

Scan for Video

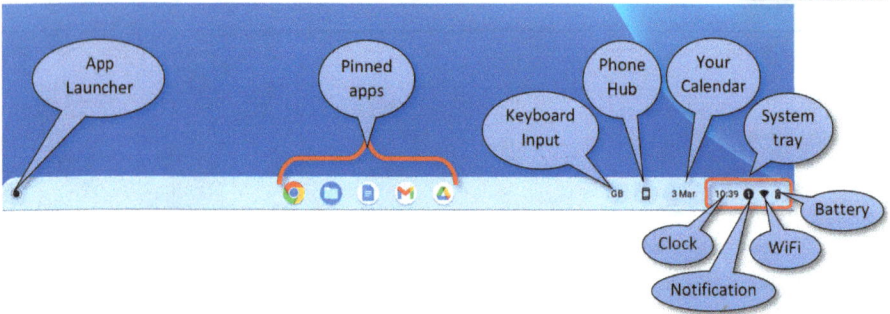

On the left hand side of the app shelf you have what looks like a dot. This is your App Launcher and allows you to open any app that has been added to your Chromebook, as well as searching the web.

The space in the middle of the shelf shows apps that are running - these are indicated with a line under the icon. You can also pin other apps to this section for quick access. For example, you could add, Google Photos, Gmail, Google Drive, word processing apps and so on.

On the right hand side of the app shelf you will find a few small icons.

The first shows the keyboard input - this allows you to change your keyboard language and layout. Next, you'll see the phone hub - this appears when you link your Android phone to your Chromebook. The next icon will reveal your calendar. The final set of icons is known as the system tray.

System Tray

The system tray (or status area) contains all your controls to connect to a WiFi network, pair a bluetooth device such as a mouse, change audio volume, screen brightness, sign in & out, shut down Chromebook, as well as access the system settings.

To reveal the system tray, click on the clock status icon on the bottom right of your screen.

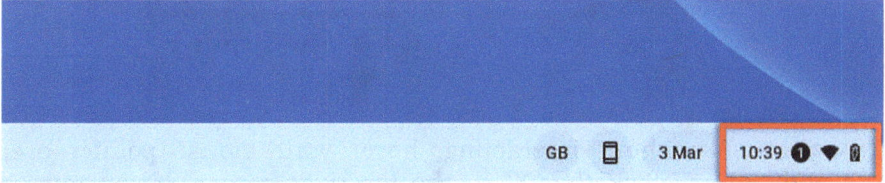

Along the top of the system tray, you'll see your system icons. Click on them to select.

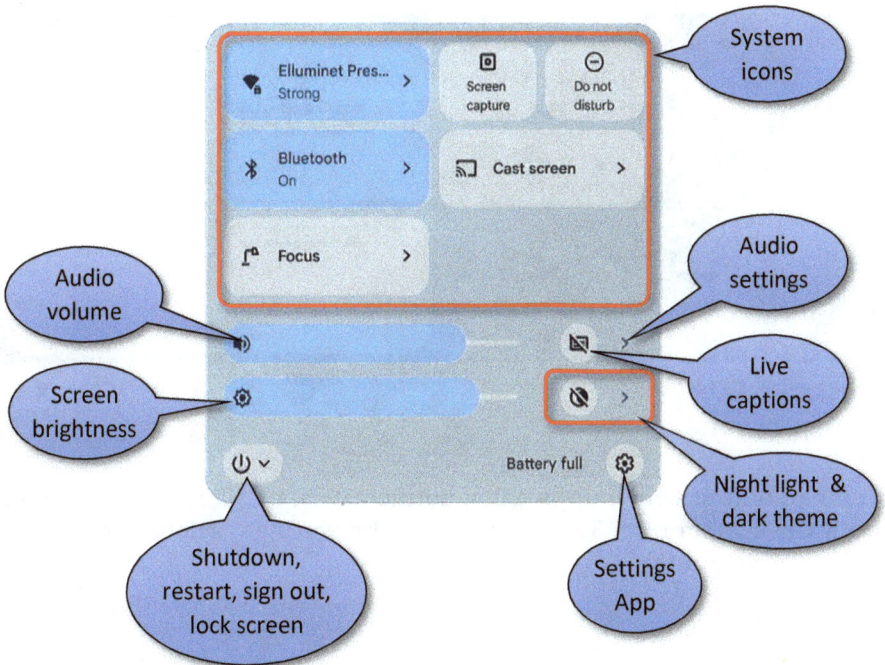

Underneath you'll see your system controls. Here you can sign out, lock your screen or shut down your Chromebook, as well as connect to WiFi networks, bluetooth devices, control the brightness and volume and access system settings.

109

Notifications

Notifications appear on the right side of the screen. When a notification appears, you can click it to open the related app.

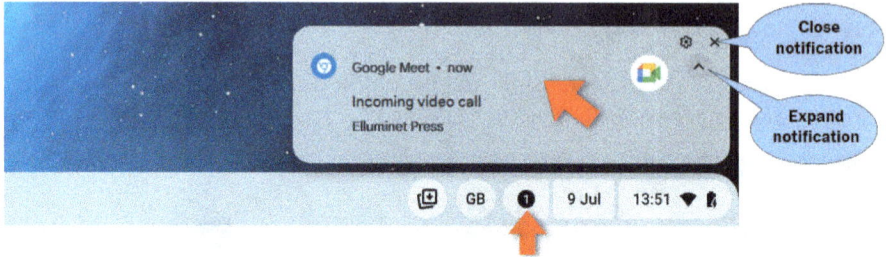

To remove it without interacting, hover your mouse pointer over the notification, click the "X" in the top-right corner. If you miss a notification, click the notifications icon on the bottom-right corner of the screen. From there, you can clear individual alerts or click "Clear all" to dismiss everything.

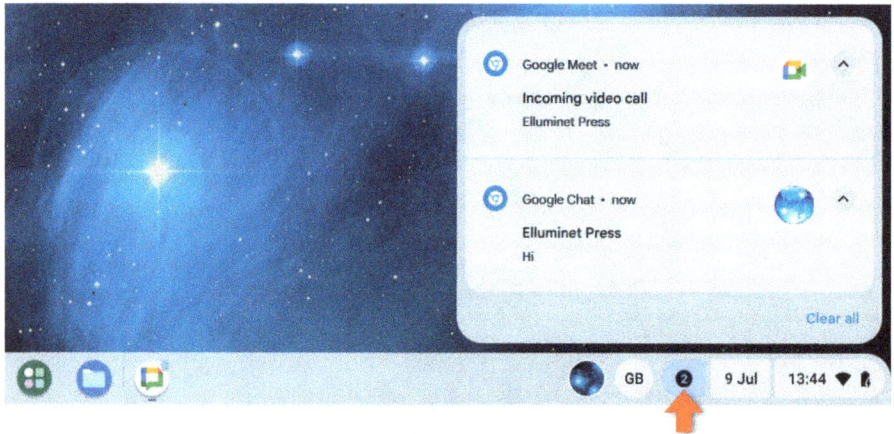

You can adjust which apps show notifications, or silence notifications from the system tray. To do this, open the settings, select 'apps', then click 'notifications'.

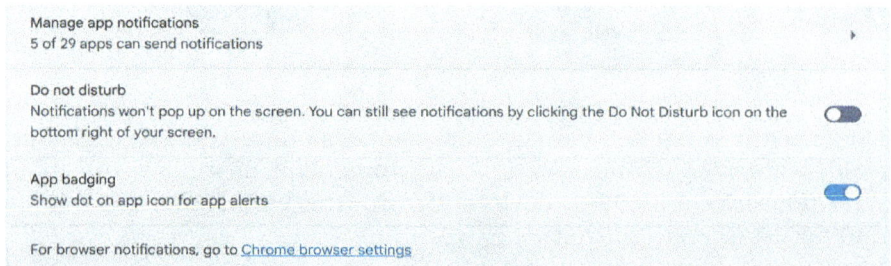

Manage app notifications option allows you to choose which installed apps are allowed to send you notifications.

Here, you can enable or disable notifications for individual apps using the toggle switches.

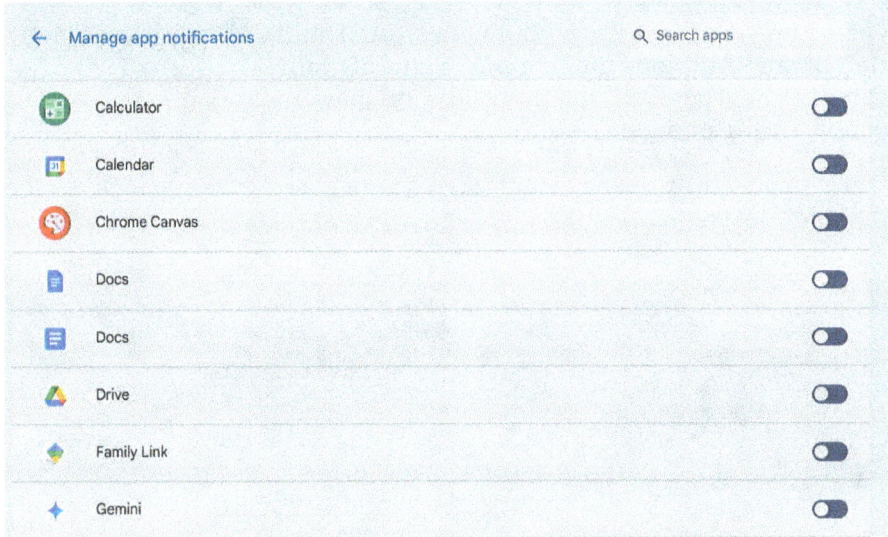

Do not disturb option silences all pop-up notifications on your screen, but you can still view them later by clicking the Do Not Disturb icon in the system tray.

App badging controls whether small alert dots appear on app icons when there are unread or pending notifications.

Chrome browser settings opens Chrome's site notification controls, where you can manage which websites are allowed to show browser-based notifications.

Calendar

You'll find a quick view of your calendar on the bottom right hand side. Just click on the date.

Click on a day in the calendar to see events, or to open the day in the calendar app. See page 211 for information on how to use the app.

Click on 'open in Google calendar' or, click on the name of the appointment/event to open.

Phone Hub

Phone Hub is an extension of your Android phone, and allows you to see phone notifications, browser tabs and sites you've visited on your phone, or access photos from your phone.

Once you've connected your phone, you'll find the phone hub on the bottom right of your screen. See page 51 for more info on how to connect your phone.

Once phone hub opens, you'll see a panel. Let's take a look at the different parts.

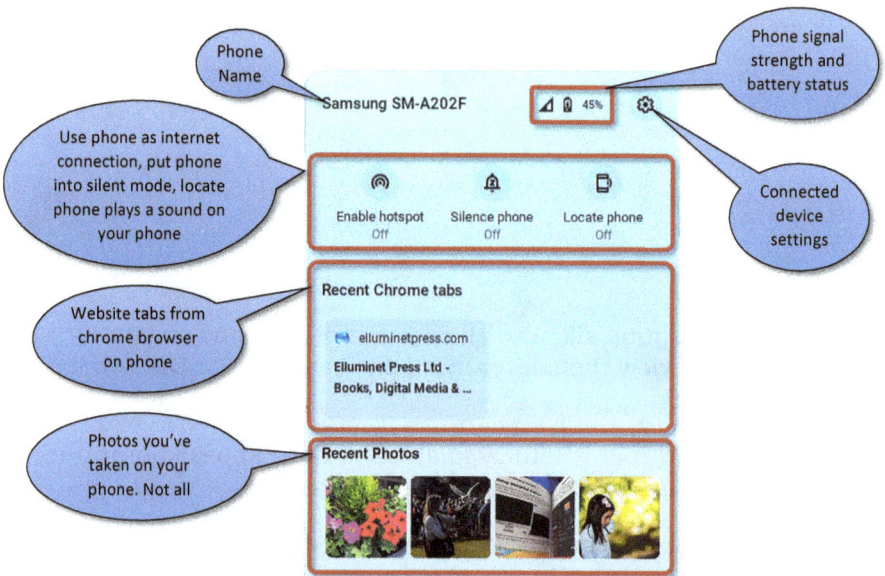

Along the top, you'll see your phone's name, followed by some status icons for signal strength and battery capacity. On the top right of the panel, you can open the 'connected devices' settings.

Underneath you'll see a bar of three icons. You can use a hotspot to use your phone to connect your Chromebook to the internet, you can use silence phone to put your phone into silent mode, and you can use 'locate phone' to play a sound to make it easier to find your phone if you've happen to misplace it someone in the house.

Next, you'll see a list of any websites you've been browsing on your phone in the Chrome browser. Click on any of these to open them up.

At the bottom, you'll also see any recent photos you've taken, or messages that have come in on your phone.

Pinned Files & Holding Space

You can pin files such as documents or pictures to the app shelf from the files app. You'll also see screenshots, screen captures, and files you've downloaded.

You'll find the holding space on the bottom right of your screen. Click on this icon to open it up

Files that have been pinned to your shelf will show up on the bottom right of your screen.

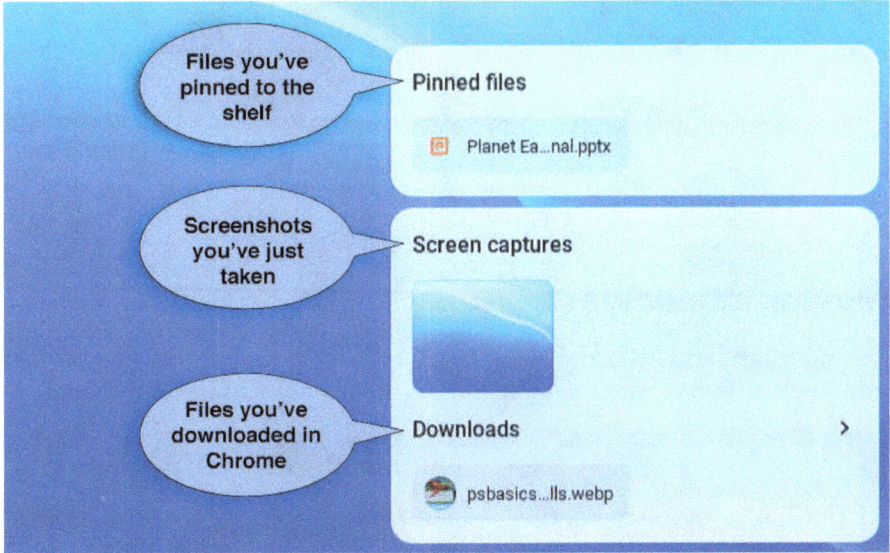

To pin a file to the holding space, right click on the file icon in the files app, select 'pin to shelf'

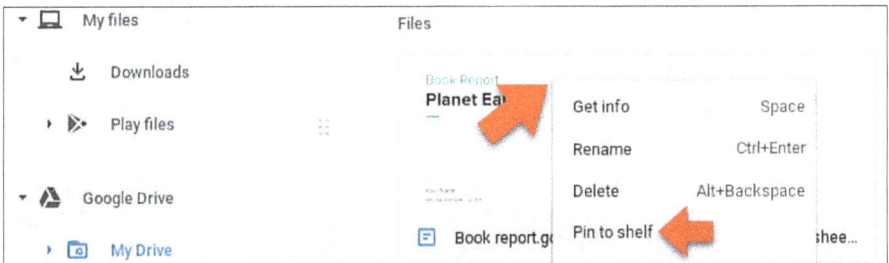

113

Window Management

ChromeOS provides a windowed interface that allows you to organize app windows by moving them freely around the screen, resizing them, or snapping them side-by-side.

Minimize, Maximise & Close

On the top right of the window, you'll see three icons. The minimize icon (a small horizontal line) hides the window from view and sends it to the shelf, allowing the app to continue running in the background. The maximize icon toggles the window between full-screen and its previous size. Clicking it when the window is not maximized will expand it to fill the screen; clicking it again restores it to its original dimensions. The close icon closes the window entirely, which also quits the app.

Moving Windows

To move an app window, click and hold the mouse button on the window's title bar, then drag it to your desired position on the screen.

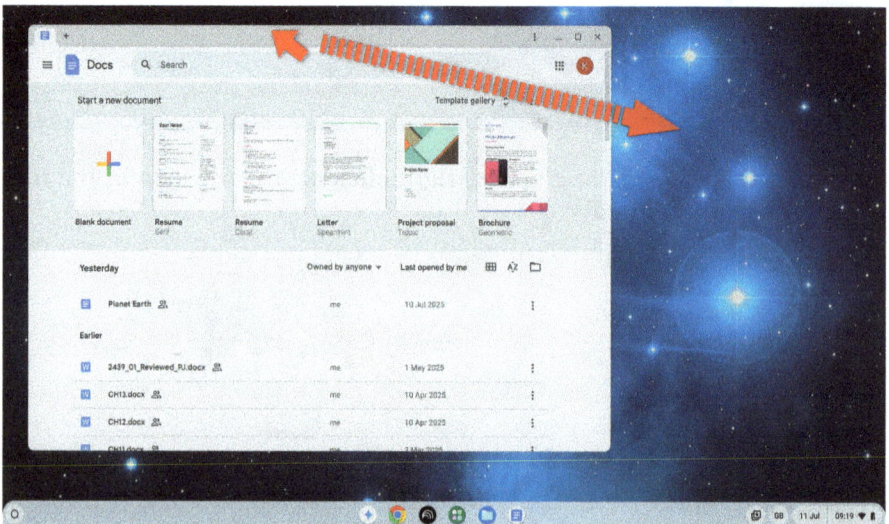

Resizing Windows

You can resize windows to better fit your screen. Move your mouse pointer to the edge or corner of any open app window until it changes to a double-headed arrow.

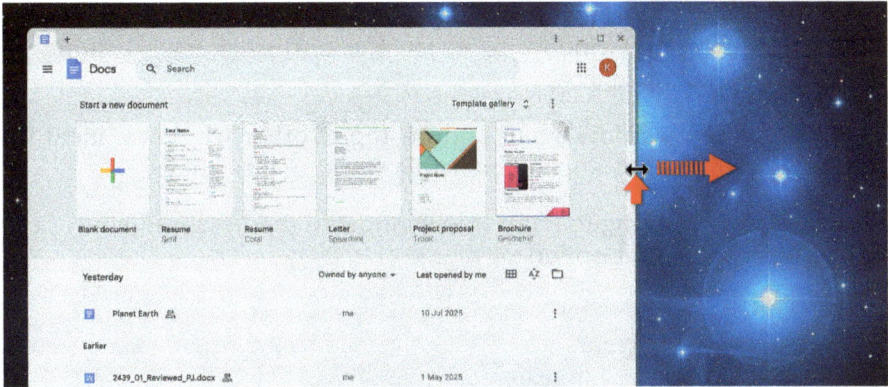

Click and drag to adjust the window's width and height.

Snap Windows

ChromeOS supports Snap Windows, often referred to as Split Screen or Split View, allowing you to quickly position windows side by side. This makes multitasking easier—such as working in a document while referencing a webpage.

To snap a window into position, hover your mouse pointer over the maximize icon. A small layout menu will appear showing options to snap the window to the left or right half of the screen.

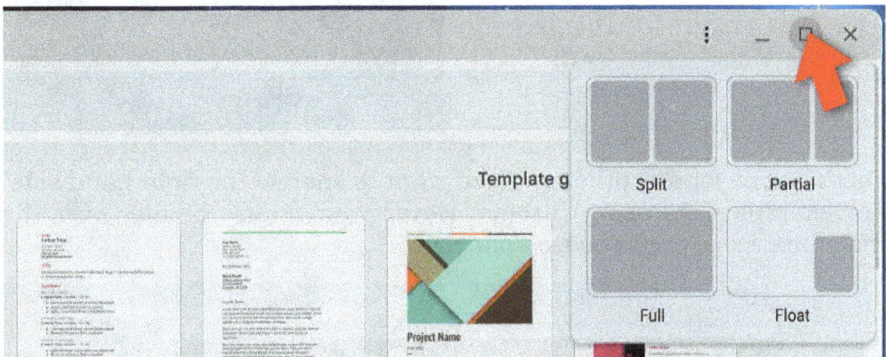

Each option in the layout menu allows you to snap the current window into a specific position on the screen.

115

Split places the window on the left or right half of the screen. Ideal for side-by-side multitasking.

Partial snaps the window to take up one-third or two-thirds of the screen. This is useful when working with apps that don't require full width.

Full maximizes the window to cover the entire screen — same as clicking the maximize icon.

Float keeps the window small and on top of other windows, ideal for keeping a tool or chat app visible while working elsewhere.

For example, I'm going to snap this window to the left hand side of the screen using the split option

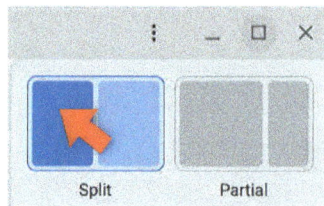

You'll see the window snap into position.

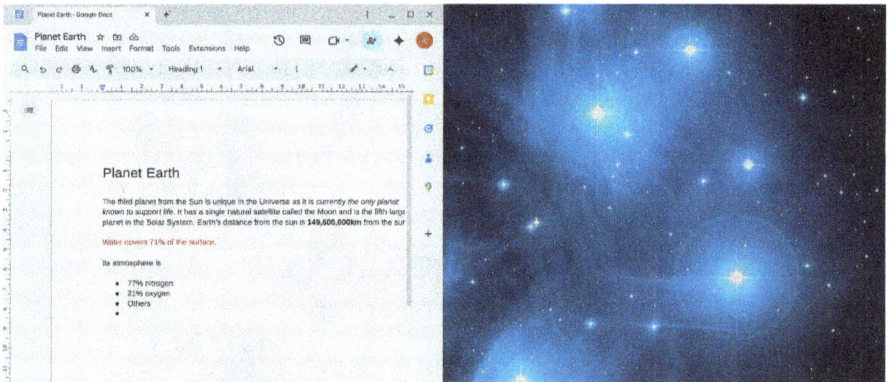

Do the same for any other app you want to snap to the right hand side. For example, lets open Chrome. Hover your mouse pointer over the maximize icon, then choose split right.

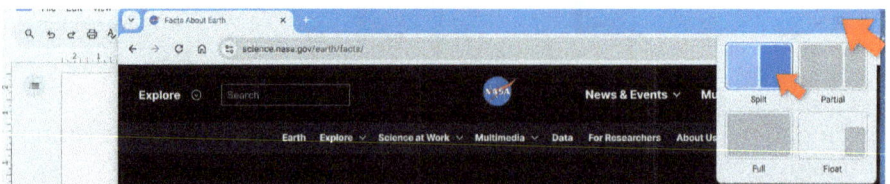

Now we have the two app windows side by side.

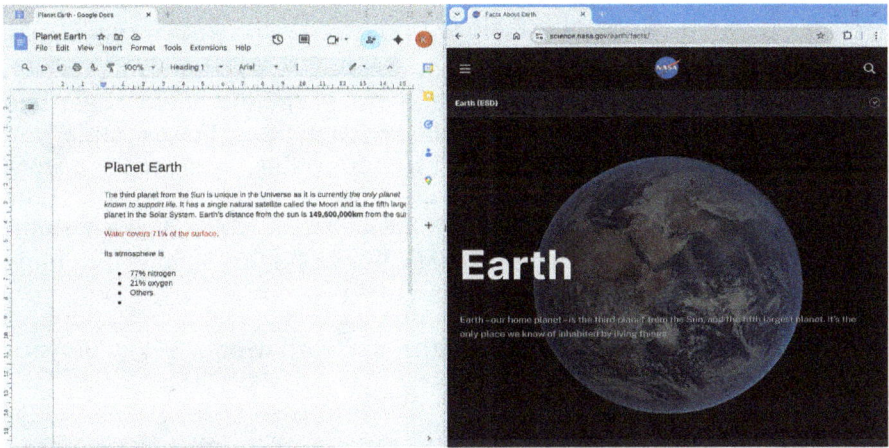

You can also press **Alt + [** to snap a window to the left and **Alt +]** to snap a window to the right.

Overview Mode

Overview Mode lets you see and manage all open windows and virtual desks at a glance. To activate Overview Mode, press the show all windows key on your keyboard.

This shows all open app windows in a single view, making it easy to find and switch to the window you need.

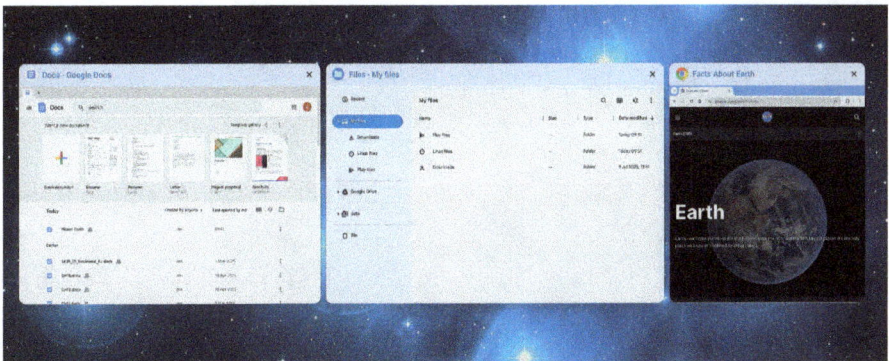

Just click on the app you want to switch to.

Virtual Desktops

Virtual Desks, also known as virtual desktops, is a feature in ChromeOS that allows you to create multiple workspaces, each containing its own set of open apps and windows. This helps keep your tasks organized and reduces clutter by separating different activities. For example, you might create one desk for email and web browsing, another for a work project with Google Docs and Google Sheets, and a third for photo editing or creative tools. You can quickly switch between desks without minimizing or closing any apps. As of ChromeOS 2025, you can create up to eight Virtual Desks at the same time.

To create a new virtual desk, press the 'show all windows' key on your keyboard.

You'll see a toolbar appear along the top of the screen. Select 'new desk'.

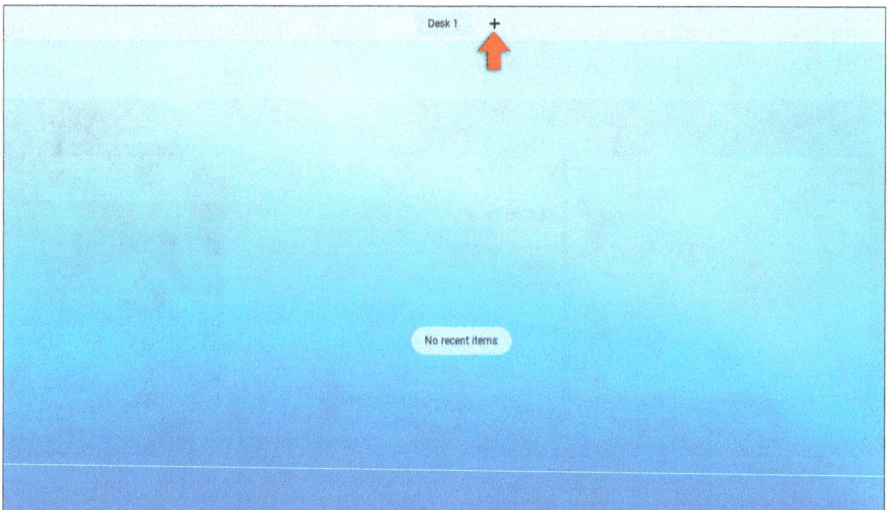

Give the desk a name.

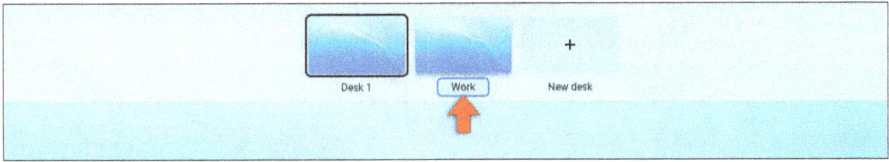

Select the new desk to switch to it.

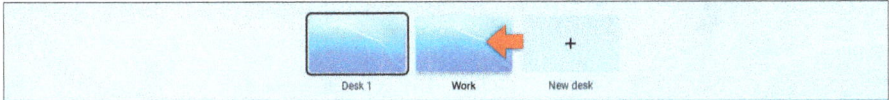

Now you can open the apps to lay out on this desk. In this demo, I'm going to open my work apps such as Google Docs and Google Sheets. These will open on the desk created in the previous step.

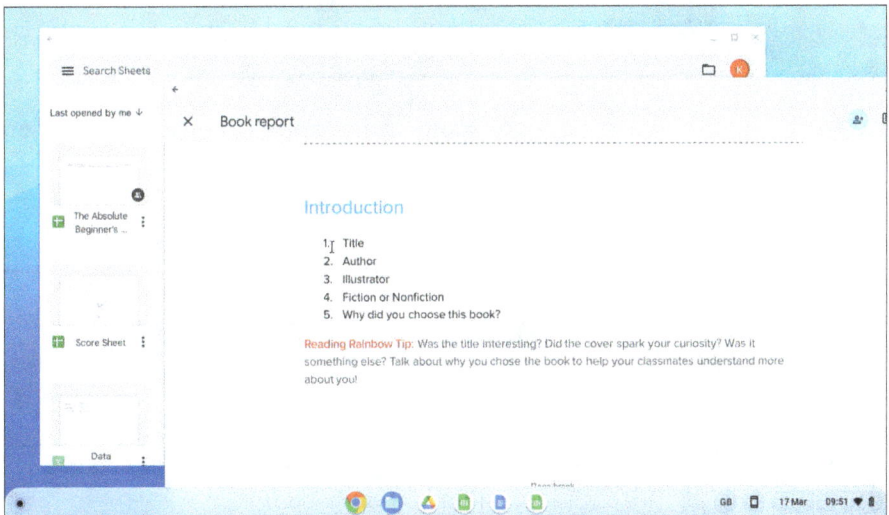

To switch to another desk, press the 'show windows' key on your keyboard.

Chapter 3: Getting around Chromebook

Here in the main window you'll see the apps open on the current desk. Along the top you'll see thumbnail icons of your desks. Click on one to switch. Eg 'Desk 1'.

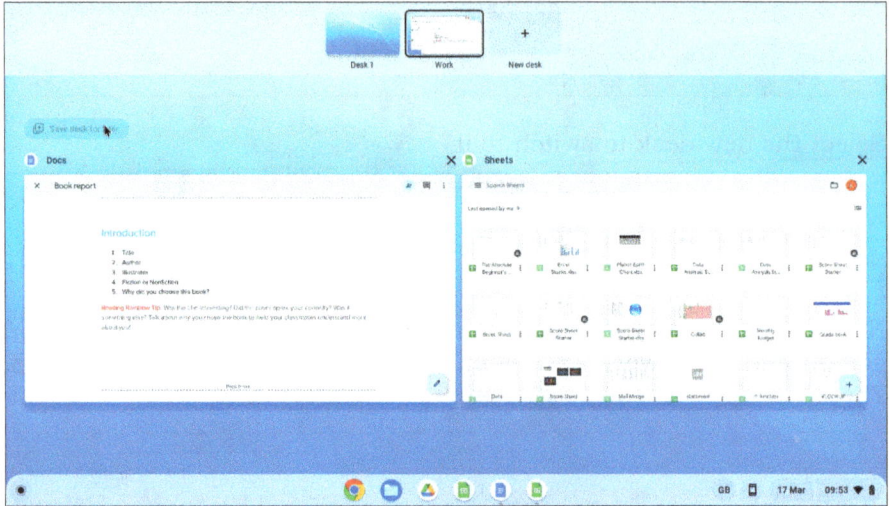

Now on Desk 1, we can open some other apps, for example a web browser.

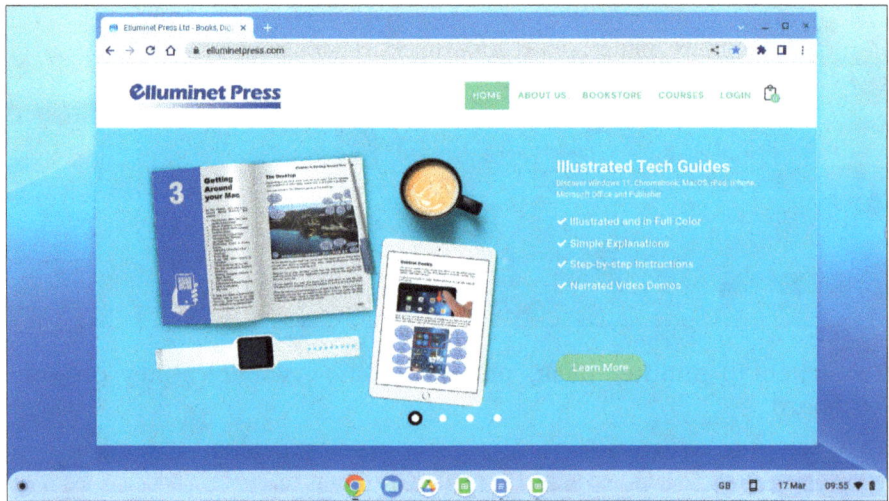

To switch to, or create another desk, press the 'show windows' key on your keyboard.

Now select the desk you want to switch to. Or click 'new desk' to create a new one.

You can also save a desk for later. For example if you're working on something and want to save the apps you have open and the layout. To do click 'save desk for later'.

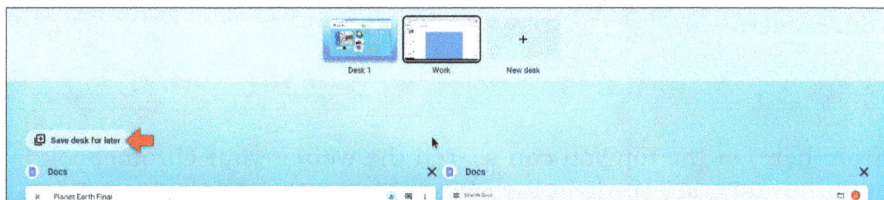

Give the desk a name.

To return to the desk, press the 'show windows' key on your keyboard. Select 'saved for later' from the top toolbar. Underneath you'll see all your saved desks.

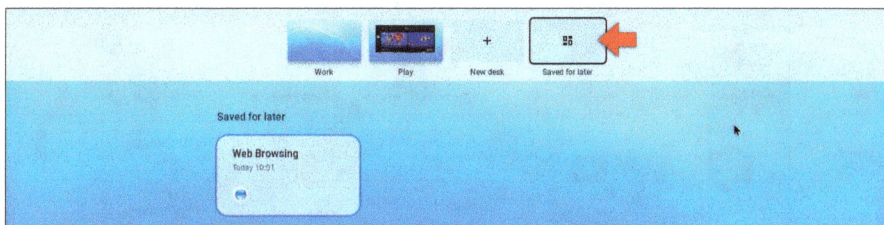

To remove any desks, just hover your mouse over the icon, then click the trash can icon that appears.

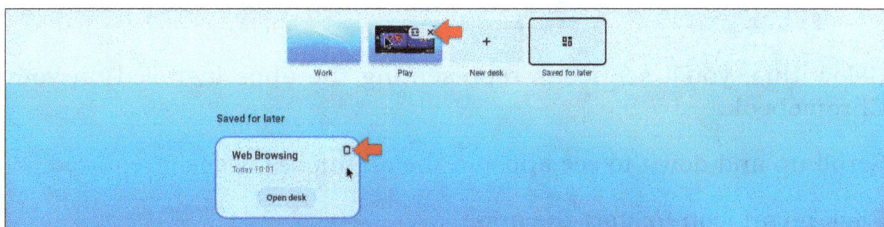

App Launcher

The App Launcher is very much like the start menu in Windows and is where you will find all the apps that have been installed on your Chromebook.

Opening

To reveal the App Launcher, click the circle icon on the bottom left of your screen.

From here, at the top you can search the web or your chromebook by entering some keywords in the search bar.

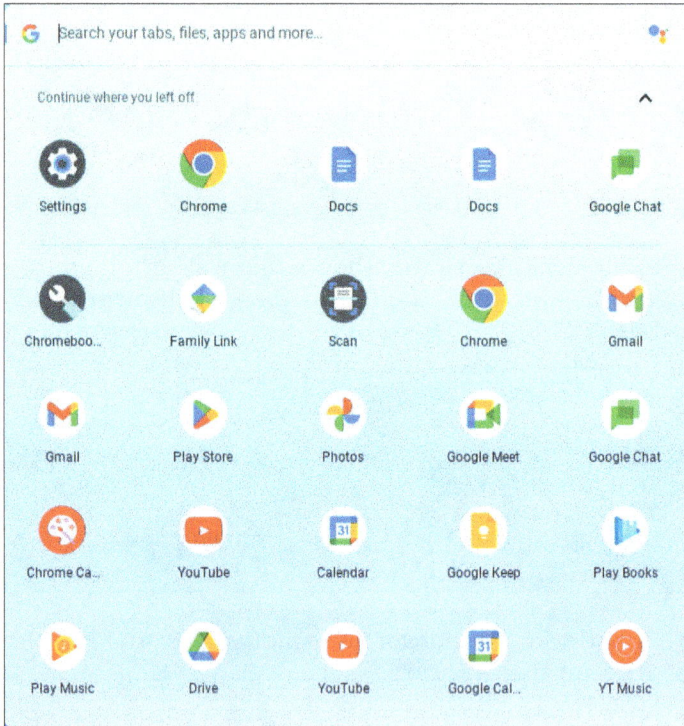

Below this, you'll see icons representing the apps installed on your Chromebook.

Scroll up and down to see apps on the additional pages if required.

Click on an icon to start the app.

Anatomy

Lets take a closer look at the launcher. Here, below you can see the main sections.

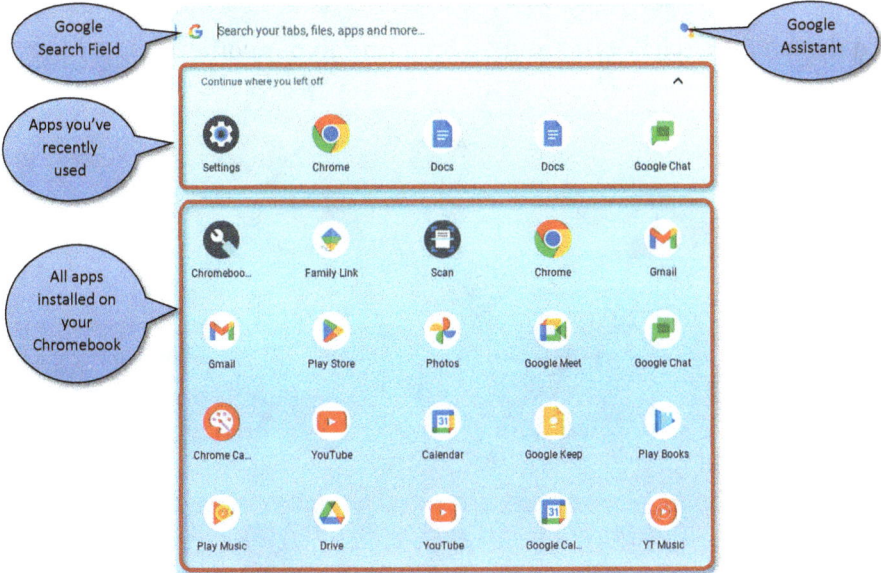

Google Search Field

Google Assistant

Apps you've recently used

All apps installed on your Chromebook

Along the top, you'll see a search bar.

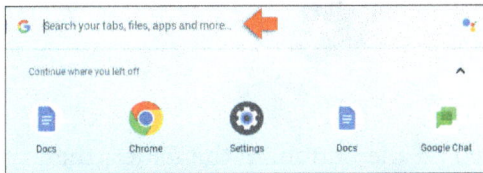

Here, you can use Google to search the web. You can also search for apps, files, documents, or photos on your Chromebook.

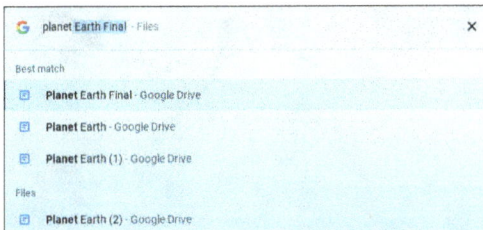

When you start typing a keyword into the search field, you'll see some suggested apps, and a list of previous searches and files. Click on a suggestion to open it up.

123

Create App Folders

You can group your apps into folders on your app launcher. The idea is to group apps that are of the same type. For example, you can group all your productivity apps together, eg Docs, Sheets, Slides.

To do this, just click and drag an icon on top of another.

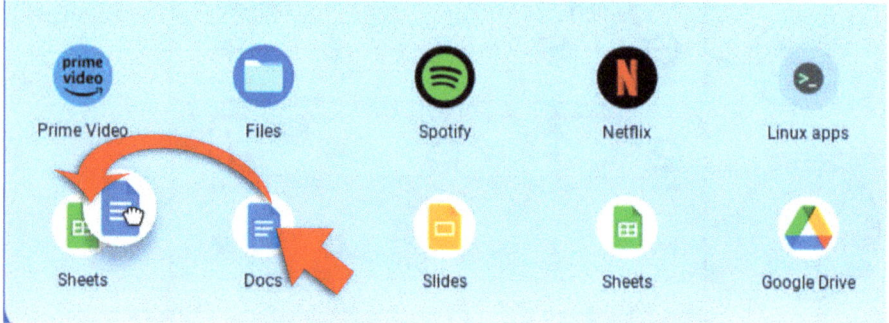

Click on the new folder to open it up.

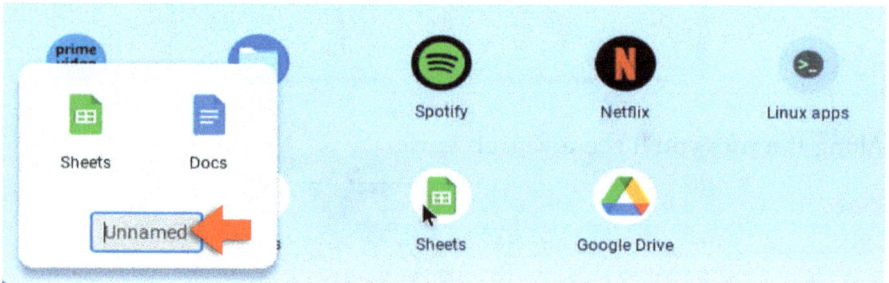

Click on 'unnamed' at the bottom of the folder, then type a meaningful name. Press enter on your keyboard. You can now drag any other apps to this folder.

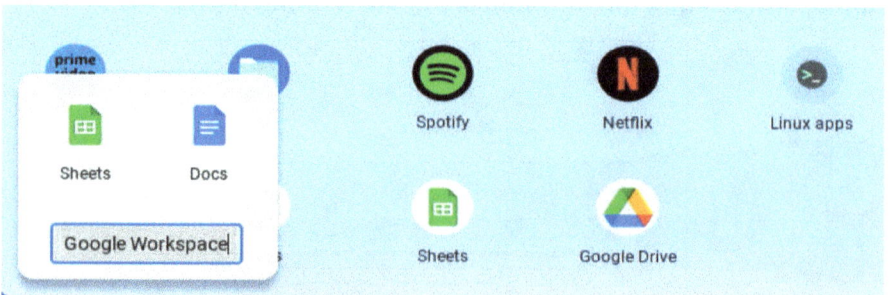

If you want to remove an app from the app folder, just open up the folder, then drag the app icon back onto the app launcher.

124

Pin Apps to your App Shelf

The app shelf is similar to the task bar in Windows 10 and you can pin app icons to this shelf for quick access. So you can add all your most used apps to this shelf and click them when you need them.

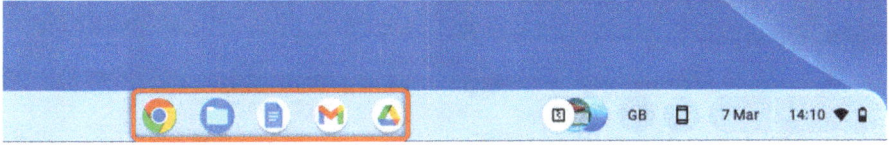

To do this, open up your App Launcher

Right click on the app icon you want to pin to your shelf.

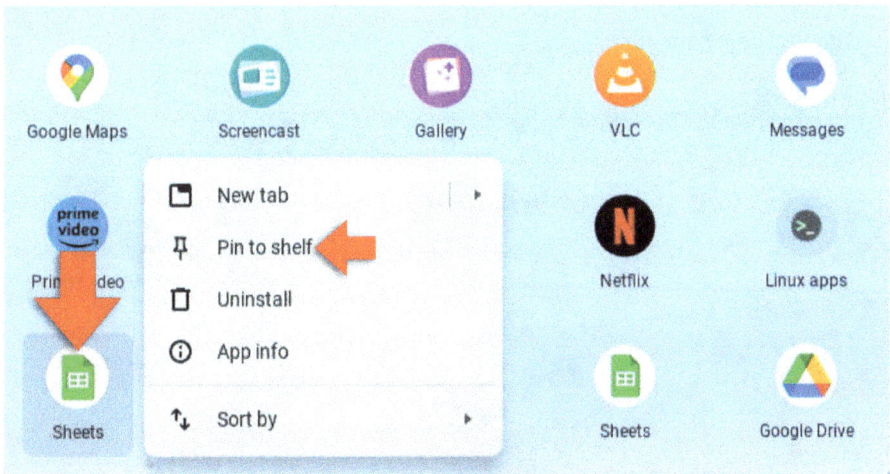

From the popup menu, click on 'pin to shelf'. You will see the app icon appear on the shelf at the bottom left of the screen, as shown below.

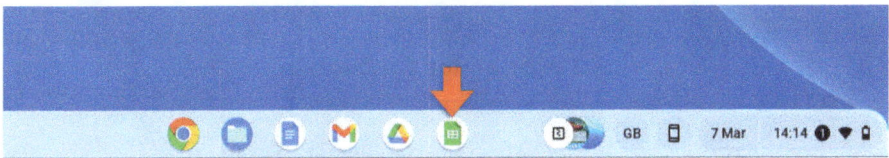

You can do this for all your most used apps, allowing you to quickly launch an app directly from the app shelf.

To remove an app from the shelf, right click on the app icon, then select 'unpin'.

File Management

There are many different types of file types; files for photos, videos, documents, speadsheets, presentations and so on. You can access these files using the Files App. You'll find the Files App on your app launcher.

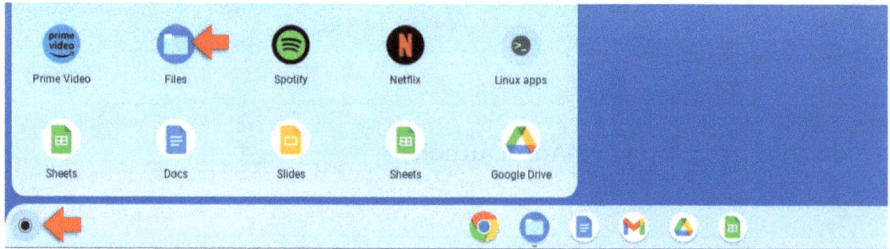

Along the left hand panel in the Files App, you'll see some folders.

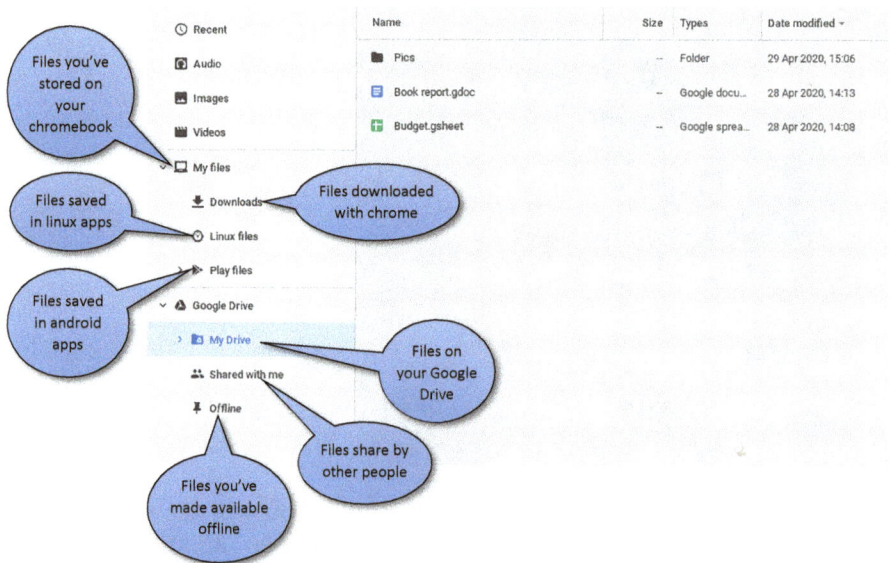

Along the top of the window you'll see some icons. These sometimes change depending what file or folder you've selected.

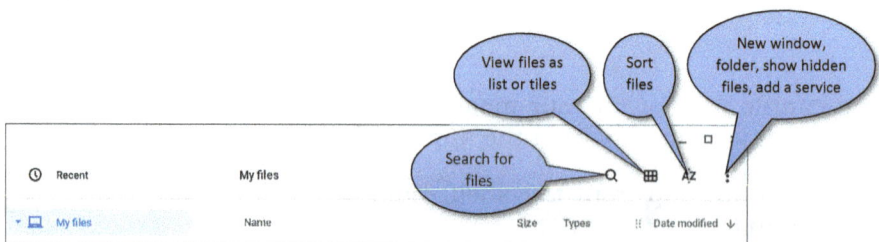

126

List View vs Thumbnail View

You can show your files as a list or as a thumbnail view. List view is ideal for a list of documents or other files. Thumbnail view is ideal for photographs and illustrations, as the thumbnail gives you a small preview of that the file is. To change this view, click on the view icon on the top right of the window.

Below we can see list view on the left and thumbnail view on the right.

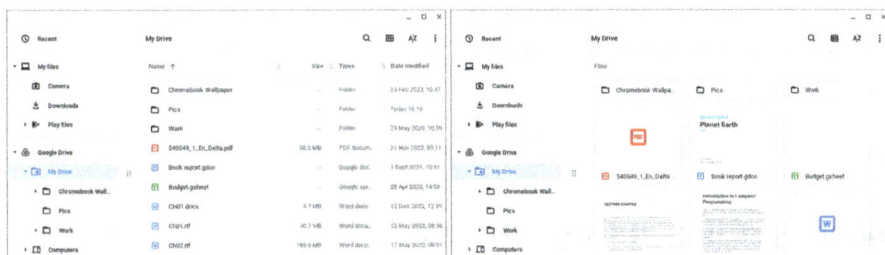

Creating Folders

To create new folders, navigate to the folder you want to create a new folder in using the panel on the left. Eg on google drive in 'my drive'.

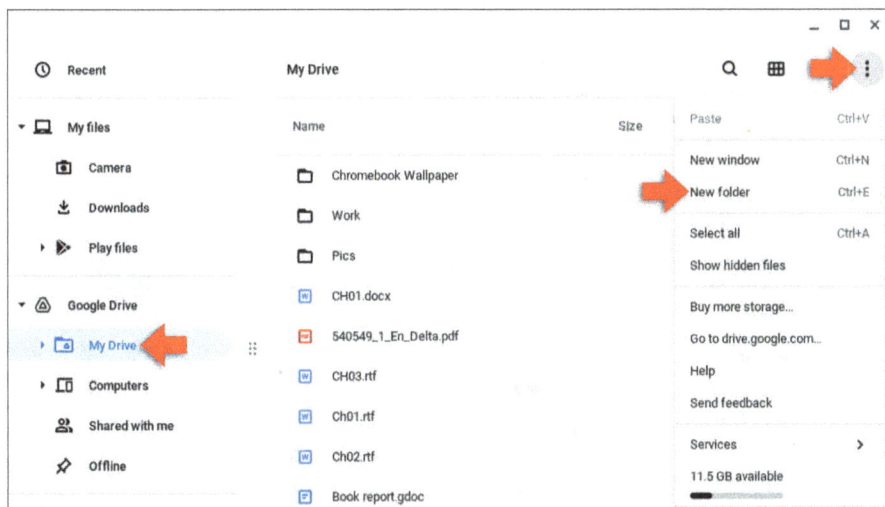

Click the three dots icon on the top right of the screen, then select 'new folder'.

127

Give the folder a meaningful name. Eg, 'work'.

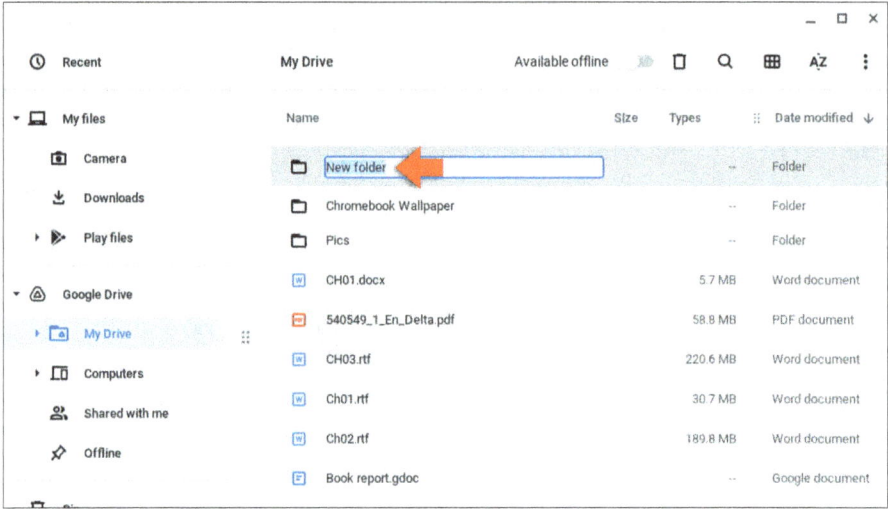

Moving Files using Drag & Drop

Select the files you want to move. Click the file icons to select multiple files, or click the tick box on the top left of the file thumbnail if you're viewing your files in thumbnail view.

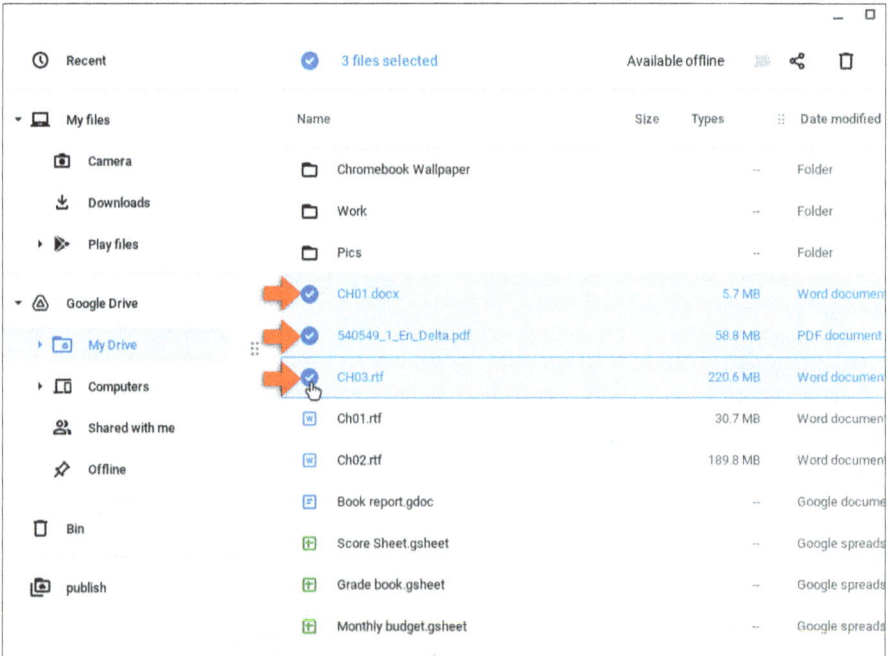

Click and drag the selection to the folder you want to move them to. In this example I'm moving my two files to the 'work' folder I created in the previous section.

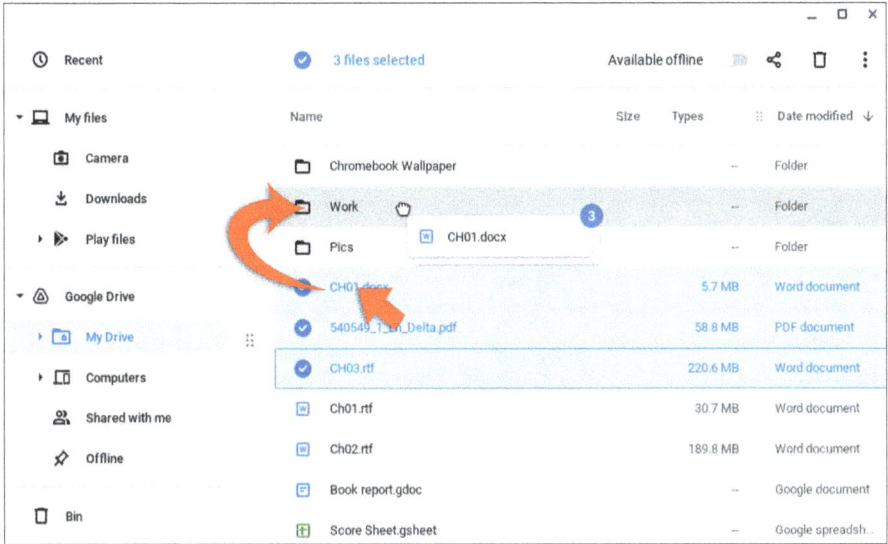

Moving & Copying Files with Cut, Copy & Paste

In the left hand pane, click the folder where the file you want to copy, is saved. For example, in the 'downloads' folder. Then click on the file(s) you want to copy to select them. Click on the name of the file, you'll see a blue tick appear on the file. Do the same for any other files you want to copy. Then click on the three dots icon on the top right, select 'copy' if you want to copy the file, select 'cut' if you want to move the file.

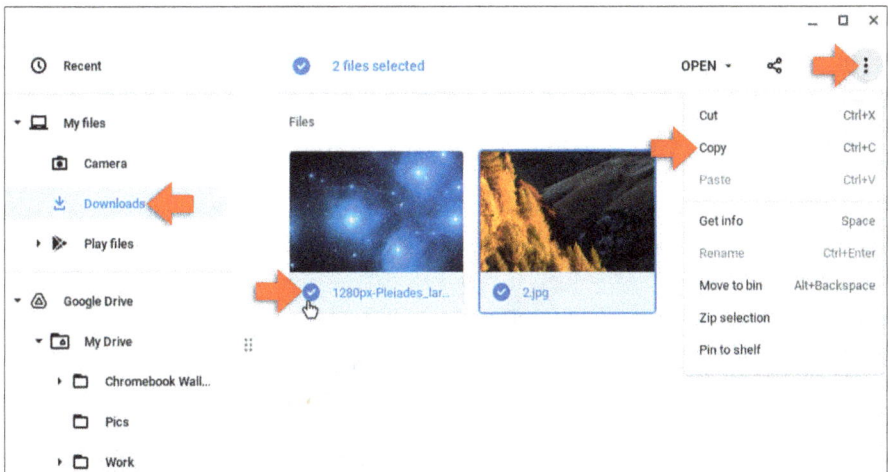

129

Chapter 3: Getting around Chromebook

Using the left hand pane, navigate to the folder you want to copy the file to, eg Google drive in 'my drive'.

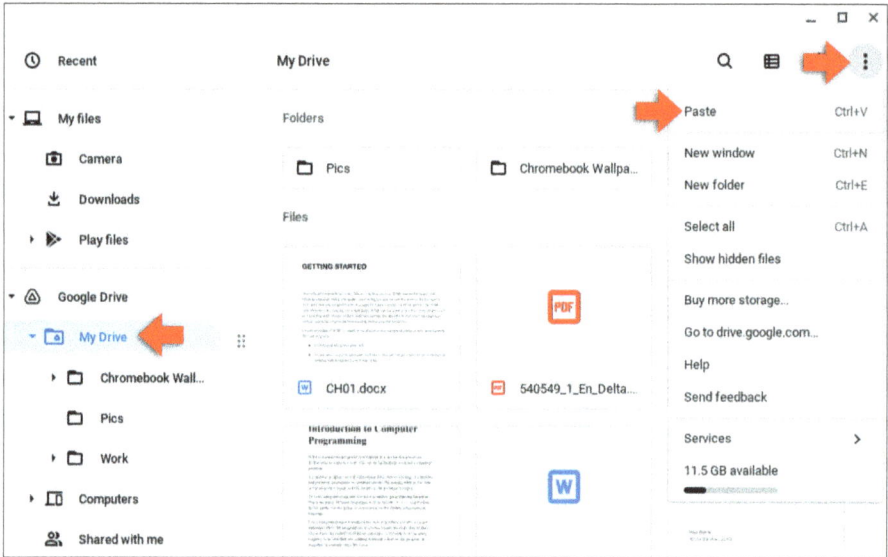

Click the three dots icon on the top right, select 'paste' from the drop down menu.

Renaming Files

Navigate to the folder your file is saved in. In this demo it's in Google Drive. Right click on the file you want to rename, then select 'rename' from the popup menu.

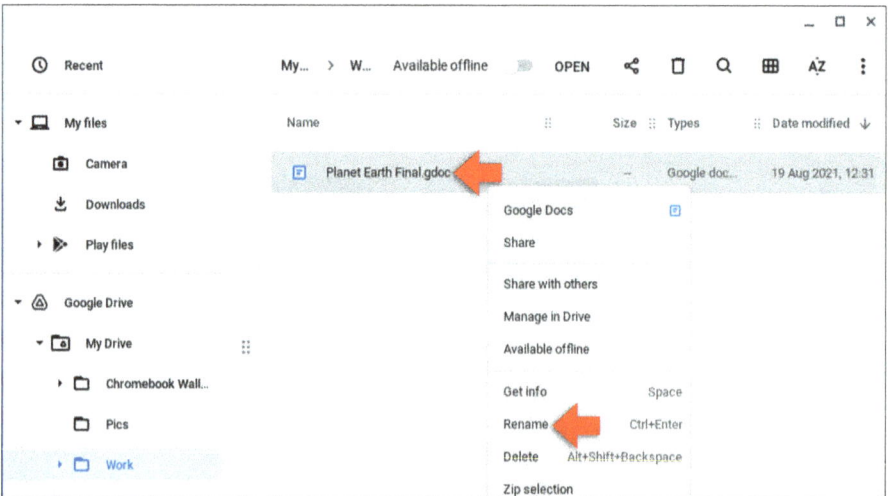

You'll see the name of the file highlighted in blue.

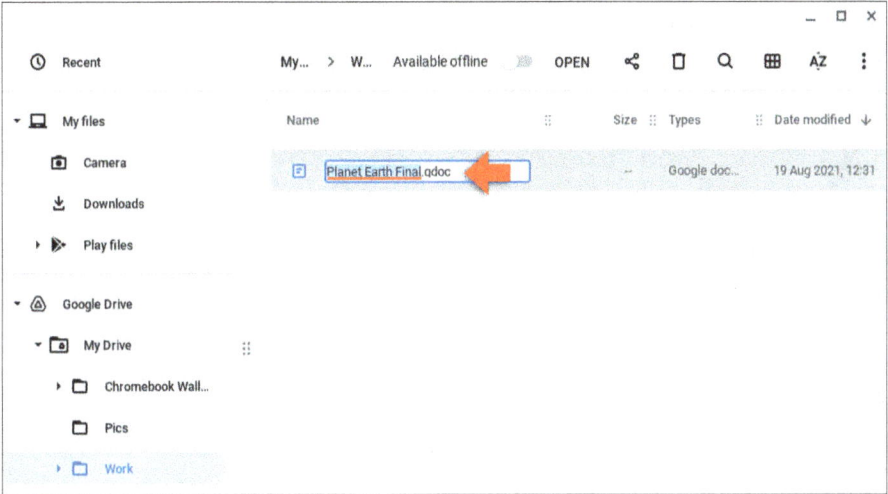

Now type in a meaningful name for the file. Press 'enter' on your keyboard when you're done.

Sorting Files

Within the files app, you can sort files alphabetically by name, or by size and date created. This makes it easier to find files especially when you have a lot of them in one folder. To sort your files, select the folder from the left hand side of the files app, eg, 'Google Drive'.

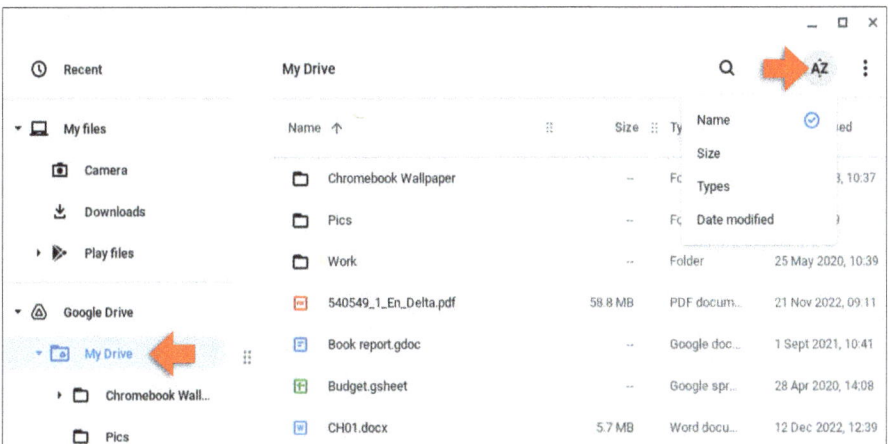

Click the sort icon on the top right. Here, you can sort the files alphabetically by name, by size, by type (doc, jpeg, etc), and by date modified.

131

Chapter 3: Getting around Chromebook

If you're using list view, you can sort your files using the column headings (see page 127 for more info on list view). For example, if you want to sort the files by name, click 'name'. To sort by file size click 'size', by file type click 'types', and by date modified click 'date modified'.

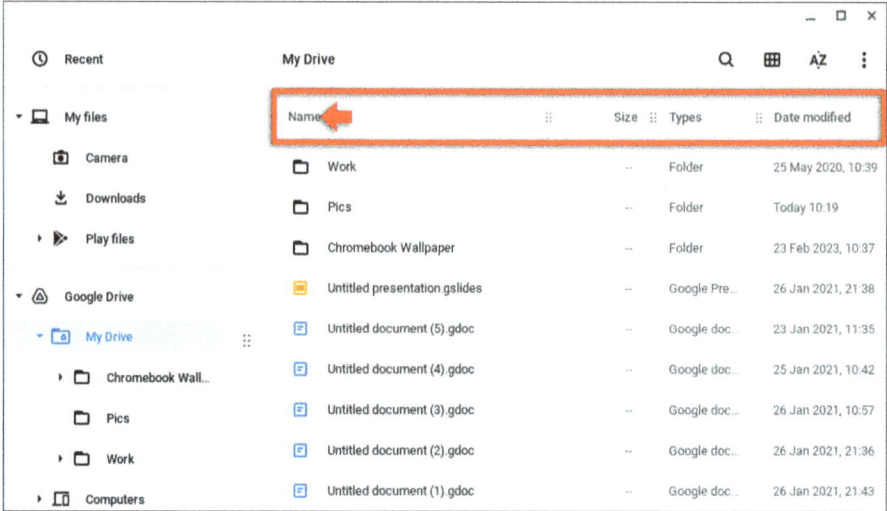

Searching for Files

You can search for files within the files app using the search icon on the top right of the window. First, select the location to search from, eg Google Drive.

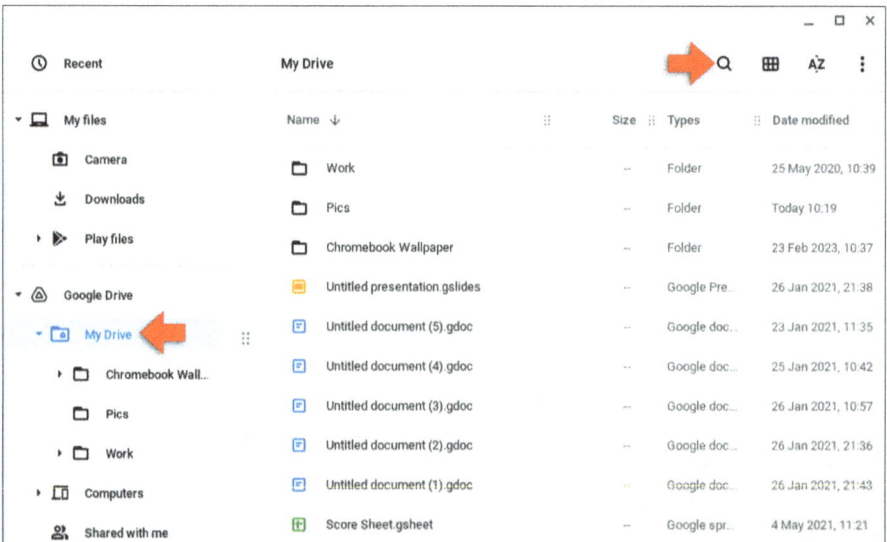

Click the search icon on the top right, then type your search keywords into the search field. You'll see a list of suggestions appear, to select, click on one in the list.

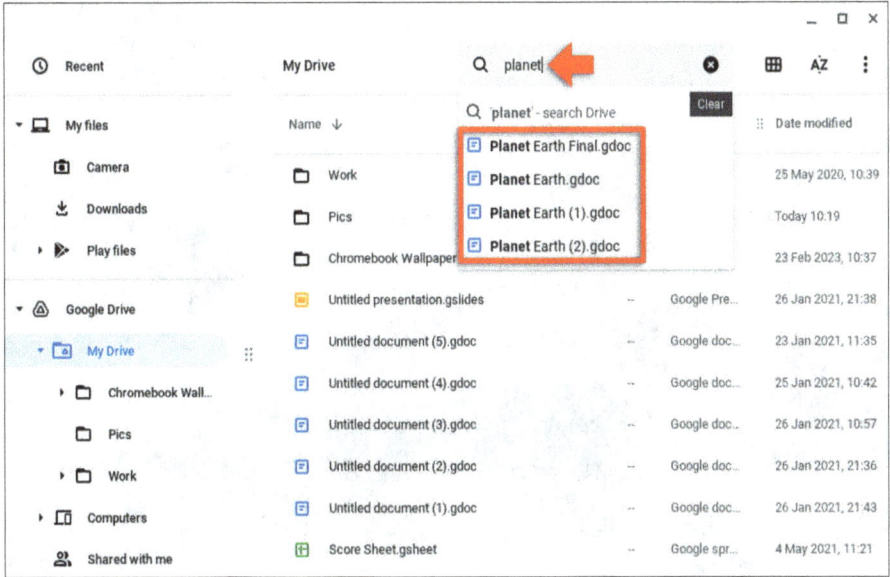

Select a file from the suggestions, or press enter on your keyboard to show all files.

External Drives

You can attach storage devices to your computer. The most common ones are memory sticks - also called usb keys, usb sticks, flash drives or thumb drives. The other type is the portable hard drive.

Memory sticks are usually smaller in capacity ranging from 1GB all the way up to 256GB. Portable hard drives can be larger than 1TB.

133

Chapter 3: Getting around Chromebook

To read the drive, plug the device into a USB port on your Chromebook, then select file explorer from the task bar.

To access the drive, open your files app. Your drive will show up in the panel on the left hand side of the screen. Click on the drive to view any files or folders on the drive.

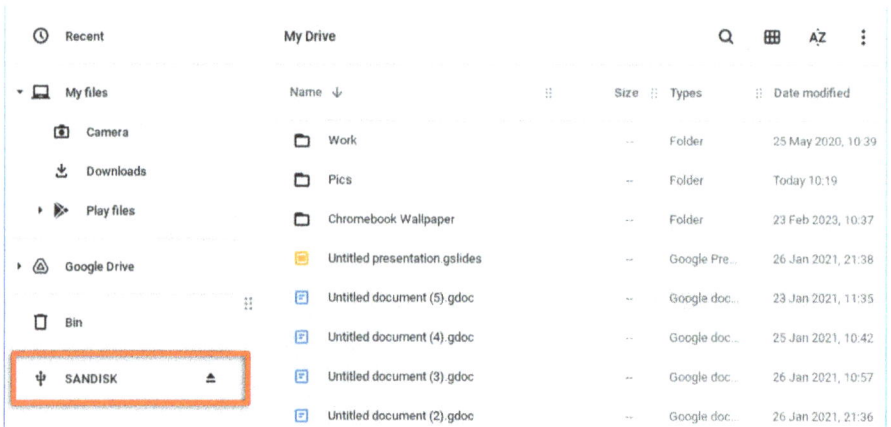

You can drag and drop files to and from your external drive. See moving and copying files on page 128.

Formatting External Drives

To format an external drive on your Chromebook, open the Files app. In the left-hand panel, right-click on the name of the drive you want to format, then select "Format device" from the context menu.

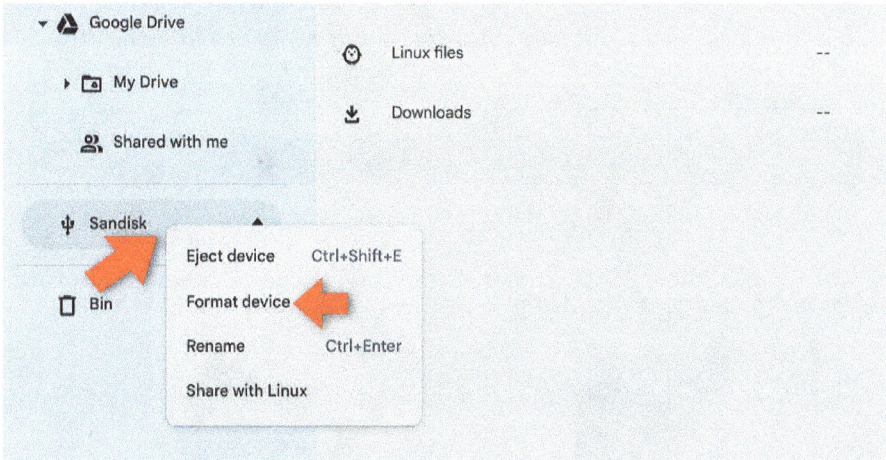

In the format dialog, enter a name for the device. Then choose the file system format.

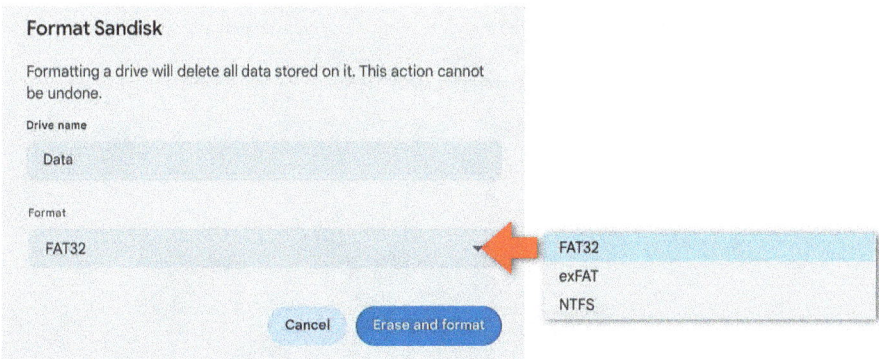

The file system format is the method used by an operating system to organize and manage data on a storage device. **FAT32** is an older, widely supported file system compatible with most devices, but it cannot store individual files larger than 4 GB. It's a good choice if you need maximum compatibility with older hardware.

exFAT is a modern file system designed for compatibility across ChromeOS, Windows, and macOS, and it supports large files over 4 GB. This is the recommended format for most users, especially if you plan to use the drive across different platforms.

NTFS is a Windows-native file system that ChromeOS can read but not write to without additional tools. Don't use this option if you're using the external drive with a Chromebook.

SD Cards

You can expand your internal storage using an SD card. Find the SD card slot on your Chromebook - usually on one of the side panels. This particular Chromebook has a MicroSD card reader.

If you have a MicroSD card slot, then you'll need to insert a MicroSD card. Push the card in until it clicks in place.

Standard SD   Micro SD   SD Card Adapter

Your SD card will show up in your files app.

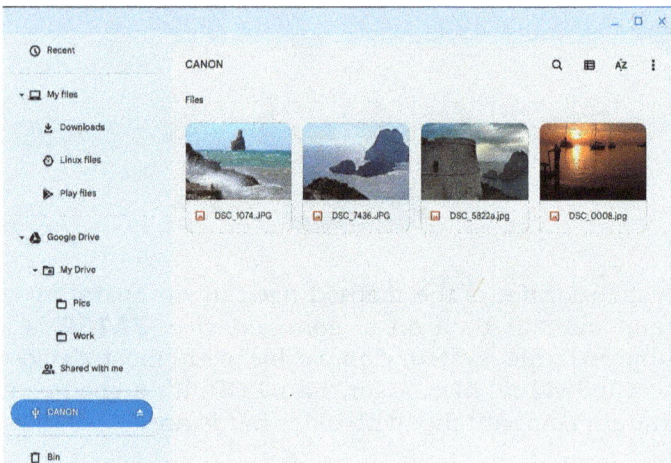

You can format the drive in the same way as any external drive. "Formatting External Drives" on page 135.

To move or copy files see page 128 and page 129.

Quick Share

Quick Share (formerly Nearby Share) is a feature that uses Bluetooth and Wi-Fi to wirelessly transfer files between Android devices and Chromebooks.

Setup on Chromebook

Click the clock on the bottom right, then select the settings icon.

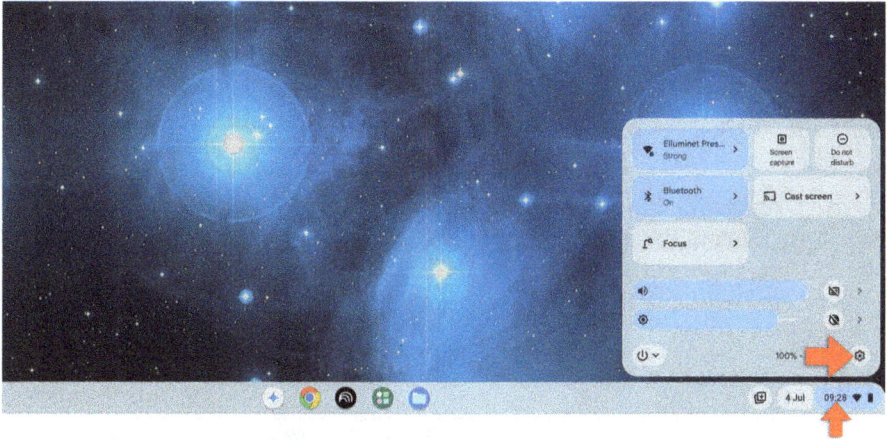

From the list on the left, select 'connected devices'. Scroll down to 'quick share', then turn on the toggle switch.

When prompted, give your device a name. This helps you identify your device when sharing.

137

Click 'all contacts' under 'device visibility'. Choose who can see your Chromebook and share files with you.

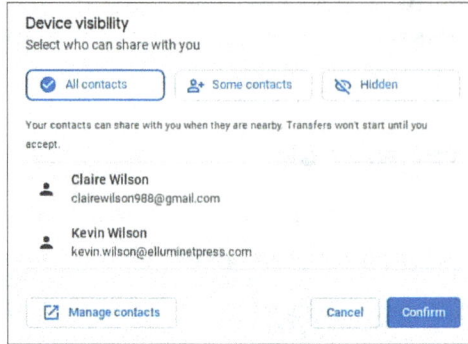

All Contacts. This means all of your contacts on your contacts list will be able to see your Chromebook.

Some Contacts. This means you choose which contacts will be able to see your Chromebook. To choose contacts, select 'some contacts' from the buttons along the top of the dialog box, then turn on the contacts you want to use. To add more contacts to your contacts list, select 'manage contacts'.

Hidden. No will be able to see your Chromebook.

For this demo, I'm going to select 'all contacts'. Click 'confirm' when you're done.

Setup on an Android Device

To set up quick share on an android device, open the settings then select 'Google'. Select 'devices and sharing'.

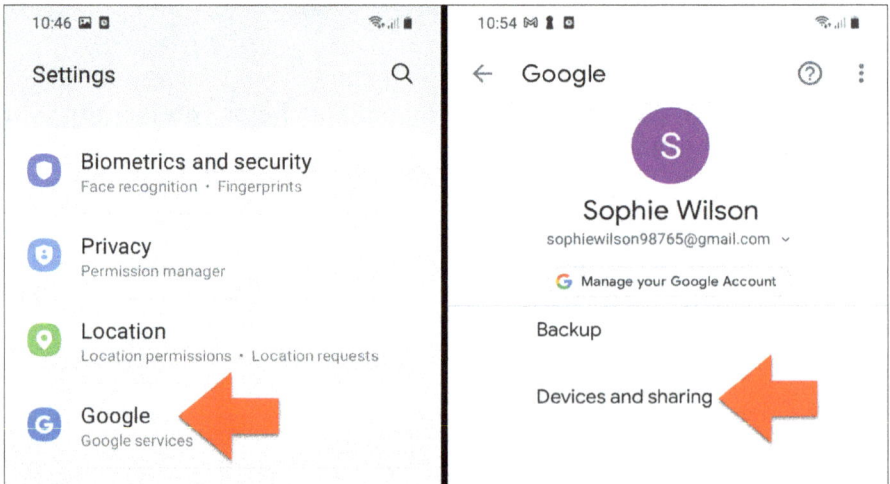

Select 'quick share'. Click the switch to turn on the feature. Then underneath, click 'device name' to give the device a name so people can identify your device when they want to share something with you.

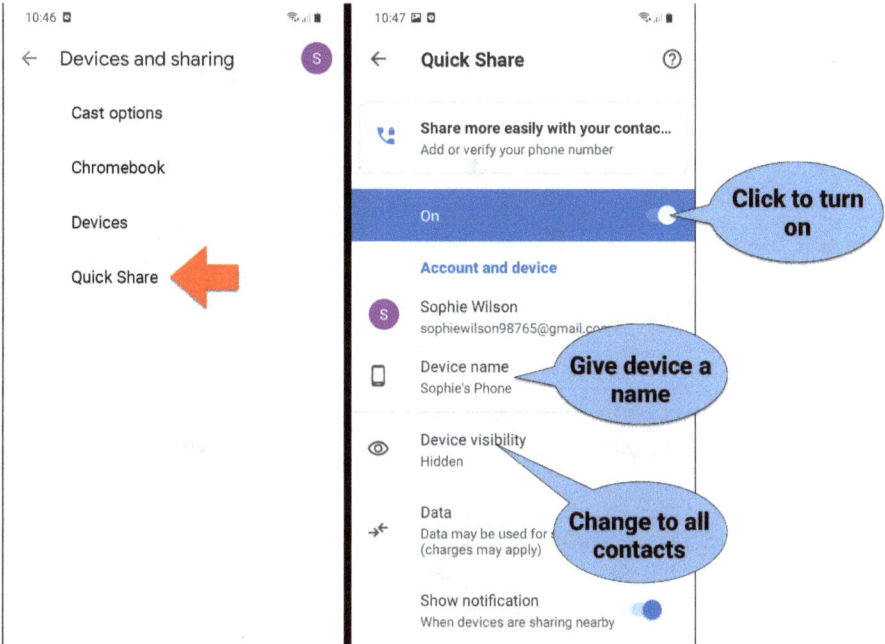

Next, click 'device visibility'. Choose who can see your Chromebook and share files with you.

All Contacts. This means all of your contacts on your contacts list will be able to see your device.

Some Contacts. This means you choose which contacts will be able to see your device. To choose contacts, select 'some contacts' from the buttons along the top of the dialog box, then turn on the contacts you want to use.

Hidden. No will be able to see your device. For this demo, I'm going to select 'all contacts'.

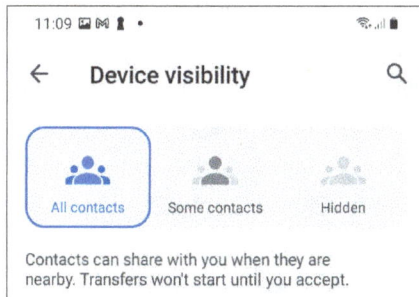

Sharing a File

To share a file, click on the app launcher on the bottom left, then select the files app.

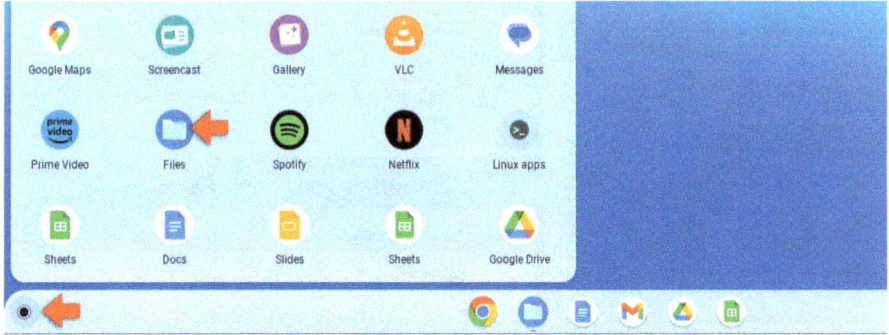

Select a file, then click the share icon on the top right of the window. Here, I'm going to share a file from my Google Drive folder on my Chromebook.

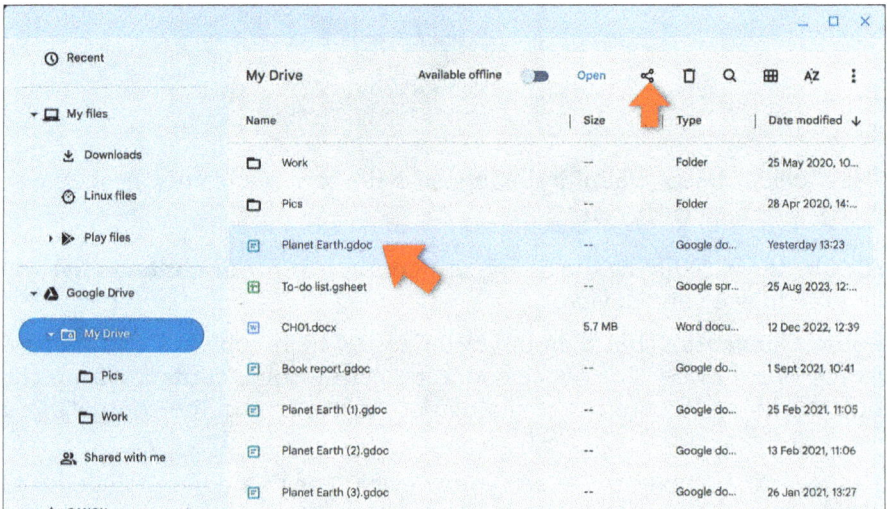

Select 'quick share' from the share dialog box.

Your Chromebook will scan for nearby devices. Select the person's device from the list, click 'next'.

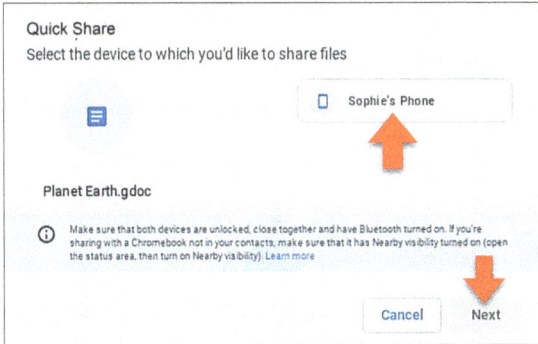

Make sure both devices are unlocked. Also make sure bluetooth is enabled on both devices.

The other person will get a prompt asking them to accept the transfer. They may also get a prompt asking them to "become visible" - tap on the prompt.

Once they tap 'accept', the file will send.

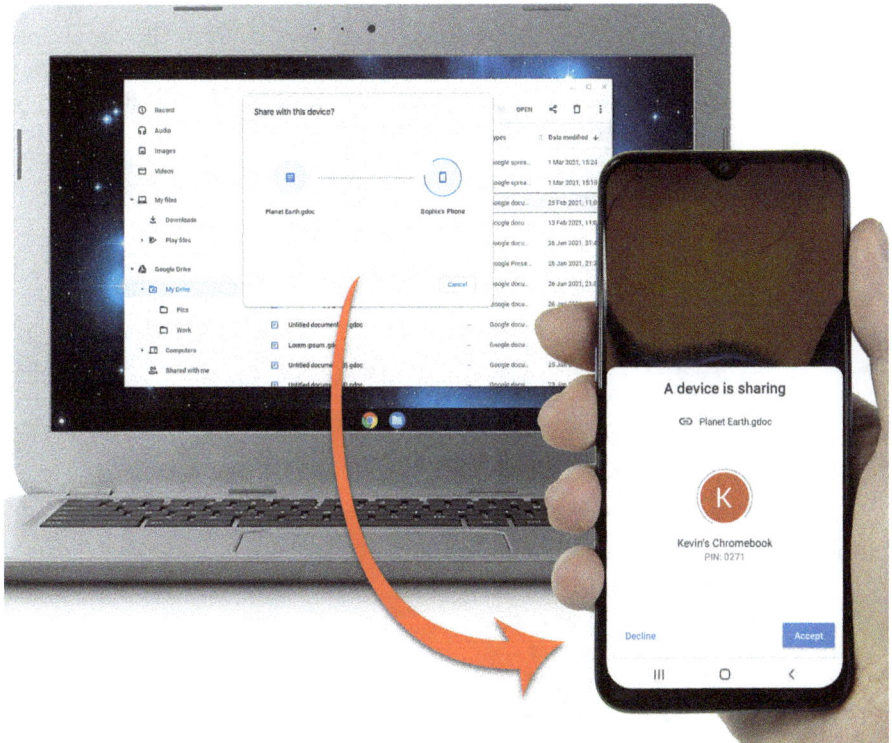

Settings

You'll find the quick share settings in the settings app. Click the clock on the bottom right, then select the settings icon.

Select 'connected devices' from the list on the left, then click on 'quick share'.

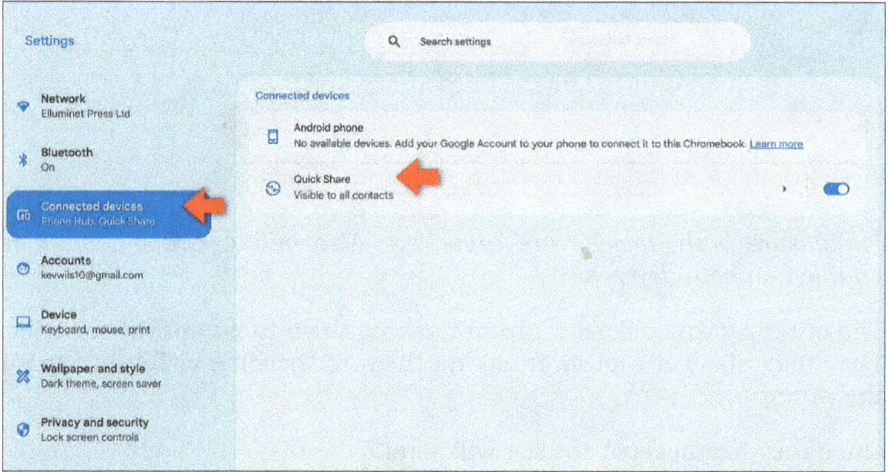

Here, you can change the quick share settings on your Chromebook. The master switch on the top right turns Quick Share on or off. When enabled, your Chromebook can send and receive files with nearby devices using Bluetooth and Wi-Fi.

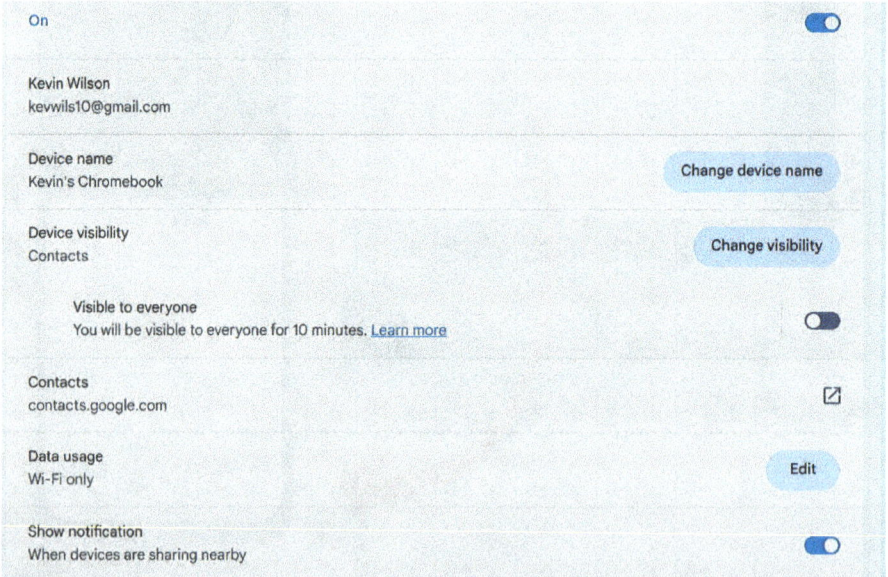

Account Info is displayed at the top. This is the Google Account currently signed in to Quick Share. This is the identity associated with shared files and device visibility.

Device Name is the name that nearby devices will see when your Chromebook is discoverable. Clicking "Change device name" lets you rename it to something more recognizable.

Device Visibility shows who can discover your Chromebook via Quick Share. In the screenshot it is currently set to 'contacts'. To change the visibility, click **Change visibility**.

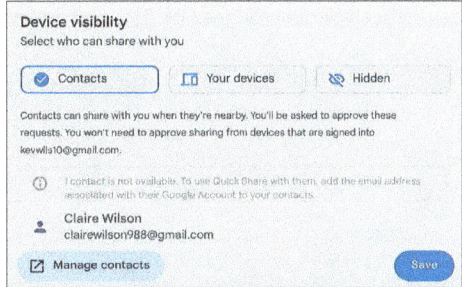

Select an option from the dialog box.

- **Your devices** means only devices signed in with your Google Account can discover and share files with your Chromebook.

- **Contacts** means people saved in your Google Contacts can share files.

- **Hidden** means your Chromebook isn't visible to share files.

Click **manage contacts** to open your Google contacts to add or remove a contact.

Back on the quick share settings, next is **visible to everyone**. This makes your device visible to everyone for 10 minutes. This is helpful for quick sharing without being permanently discoverable.

Contacts links to your Google Contacts. People in your contact list can discover your device when visibility is set to Contacts in Quick Share.

Data Usage determines what type of connection your Chromebook can use to transfer files. To change click **Edit**, then select an option. **Wi-Fi only** means transfers are sent over your local Wi-Fi network or through direct Wi-Fi. **Mobile Data** allows file transfers to use your mobile data connection if needed, which may incur charges depending on your plan. **Without Internet** means files are shared entirely offline using direct peer-to-peer connections.

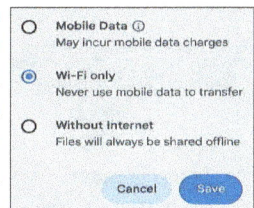

Show Notification enables notifications when nearby devices are sharing content. It alerts you when someone nearby is attempting to send a file using Quick Share.

Screen Capture

You can take a screenshot or record your Chromebook's screen. You can then view, edit, and share the screen captures.

Screenshots

To take a screenshot, click the clock on the bottom right of the screen.

Select 'screen capture' from the options.

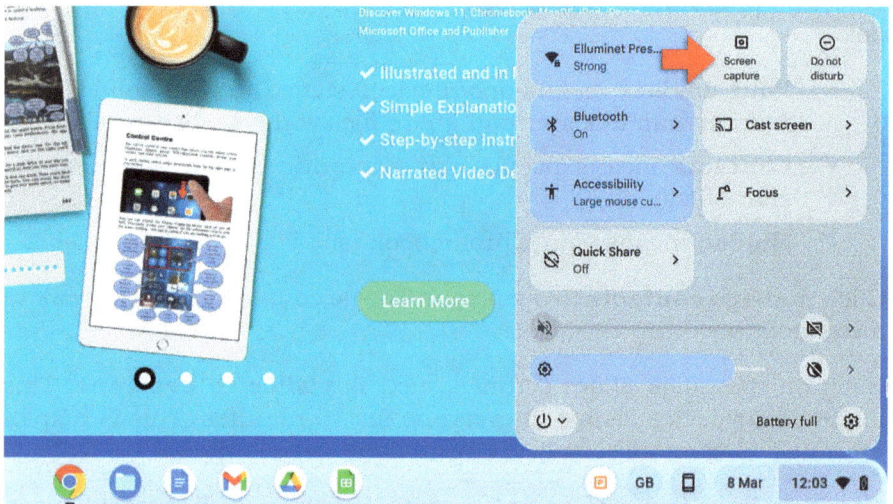

You'll see the screen capture controls appear along the bottom of the screen.

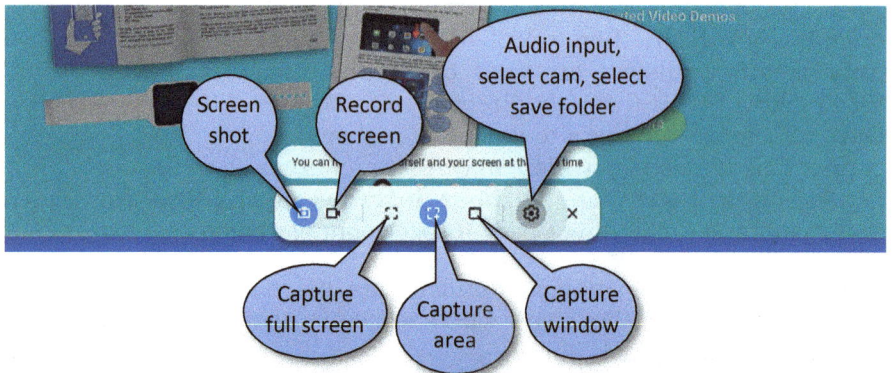

From the screen capture controls, select 'screen shot', then click 'full screen', if you want to take a screenshot of the whole screen.

Click 'capture area' if you want to take a screenshot of a part of the screen. Drag the selection box around the part of the screen you want.

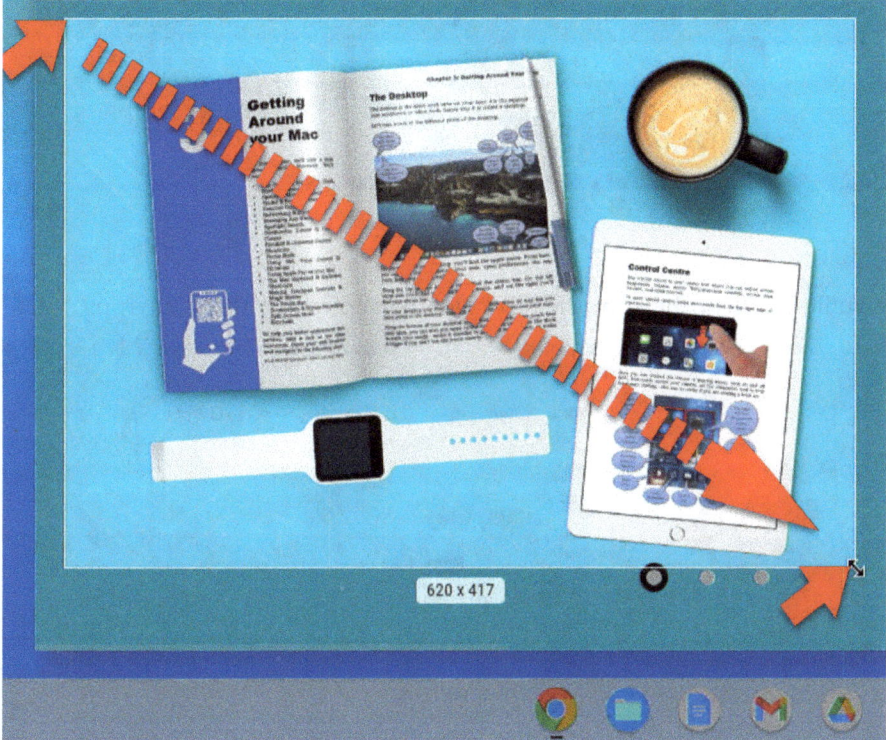

Click the 'capture' button that appears in the center of the selection.

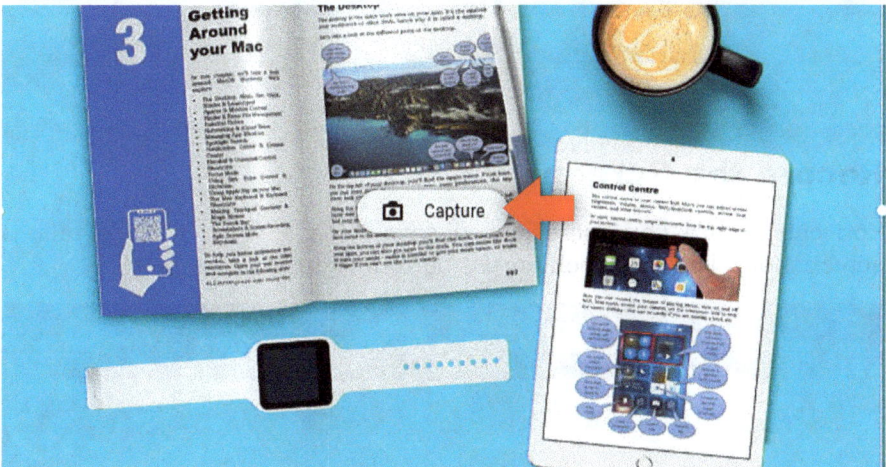

The screenshot will appear in the 'pinned files' on the bottom right of the screen.

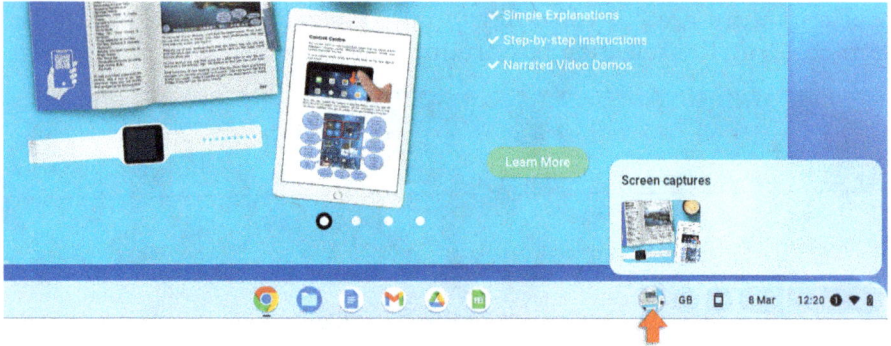

You'll also find them in the 'downloads' section in the files app.

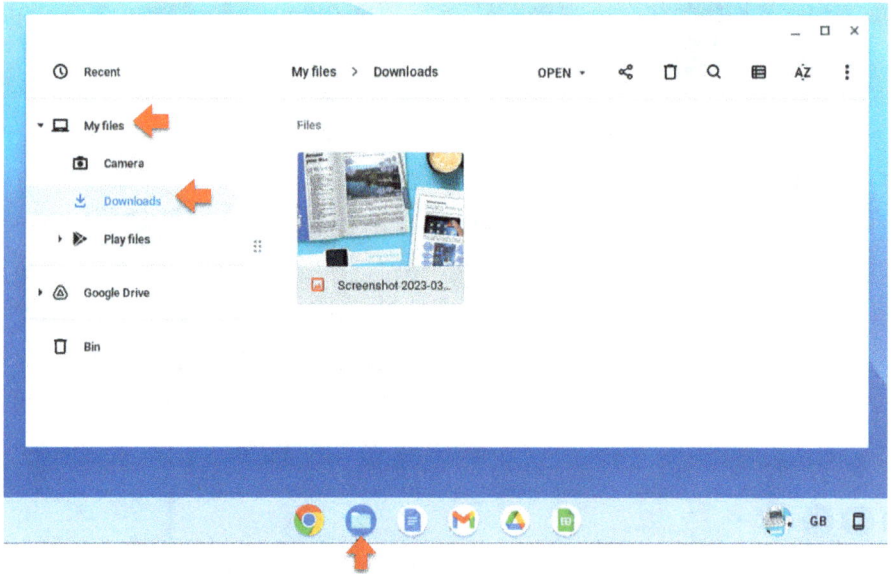

Record the Screen

You can record your screen and save it as a video file. To take a screenshot, click the clock on the bottom right of the screen.

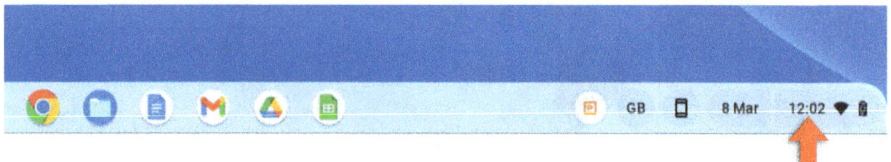

Select 'screen capture' from the options.

Select the record screen icon and the full screen icon from the screen capture controls.

Click anywhere on the screen to being recording. You'll see a 3 second countdown.

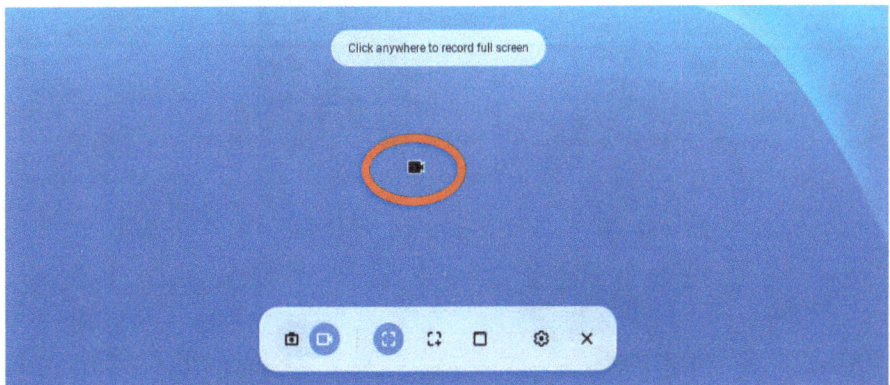

To stop recording, click the stop icon on the bottom right of the screen.

You'll find the recording in the 'downloads' section in the files app.

Google Gemini

As of March 2025, Google officially replaced Google Assistant with Gemini as the default AI assistant on Chromebooks. Built on Google's latest generation of AI models, Gemini offers a more advanced and versatile experience — capable of helping you with writing, coding, summarising, research, and even image generation. Unlike the voice-focused Assistant, Gemini provides a chat-based interface that allows you to interact using natural language.

Using the App

To access the Gemini App, open the Launcher by clicking the circle icon in the bottom-left corner of the screen. Click on the "Gemini" icon.

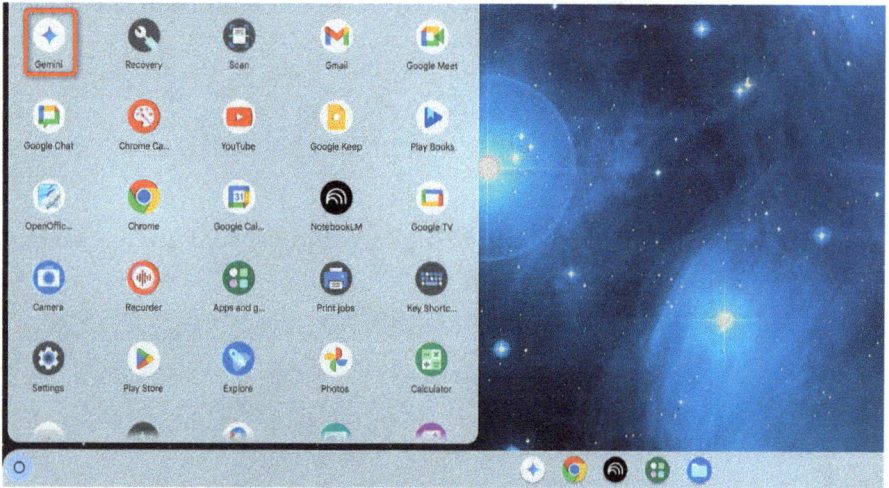

You can also access Gemini through the Chrome Web Browser. Go to gemini.google.com

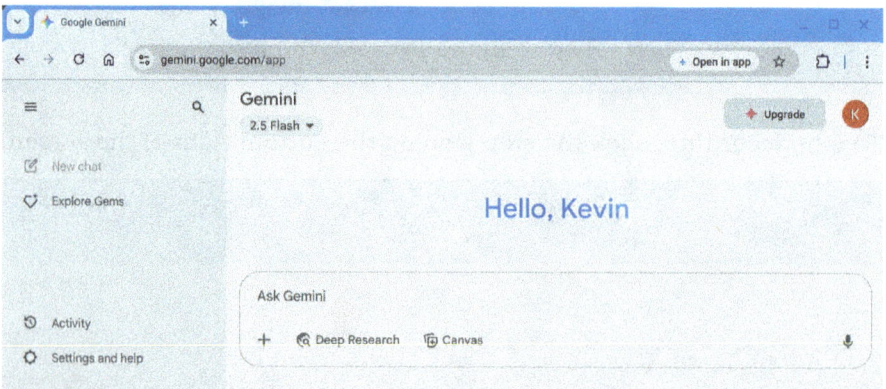

Once opened, you'll see a chat-style interface.

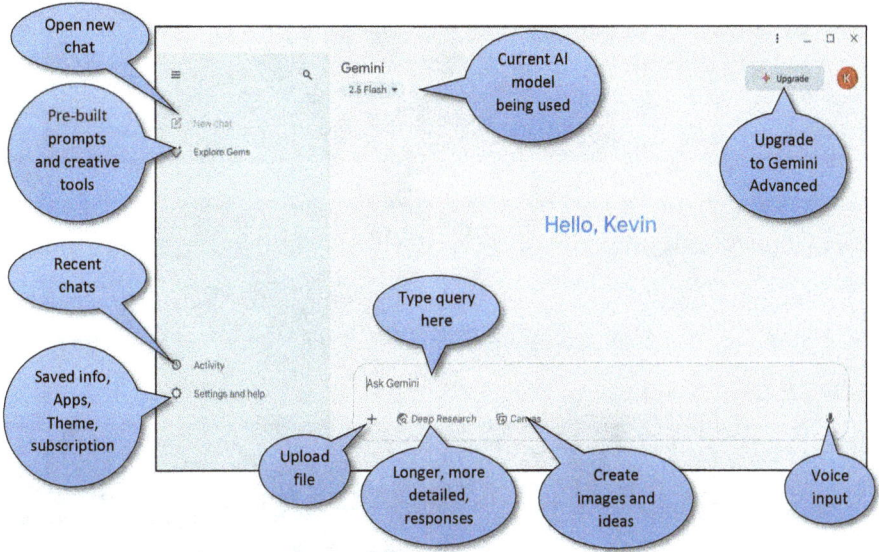

Type your query into the text field, or click the microphone icon to speak your query.

Once you enter your query, Gemini will generate a response. Note that the technology isn't perfect and can make factual errors, so always check the responses.

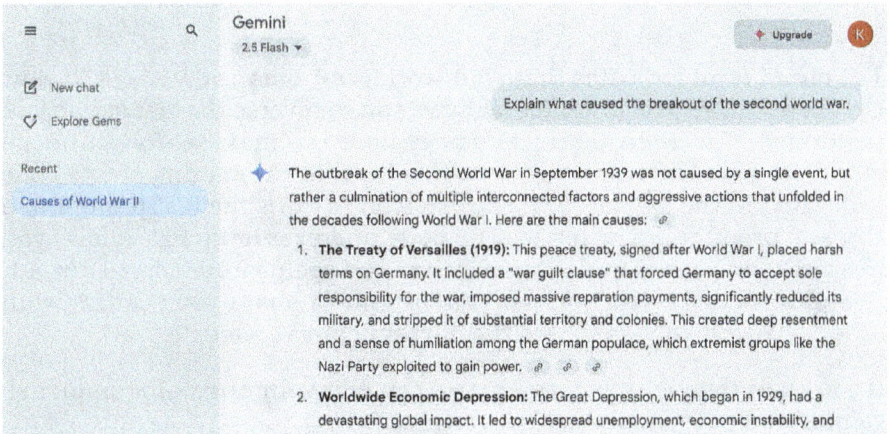

Chapter 3: Getting around Chromebook

You can also generate images from text using Canvas. Select 'canvas', then type in your request. Click the submit icon on the bottom right.

Once Gemini generates the request, it will show up in the main window.

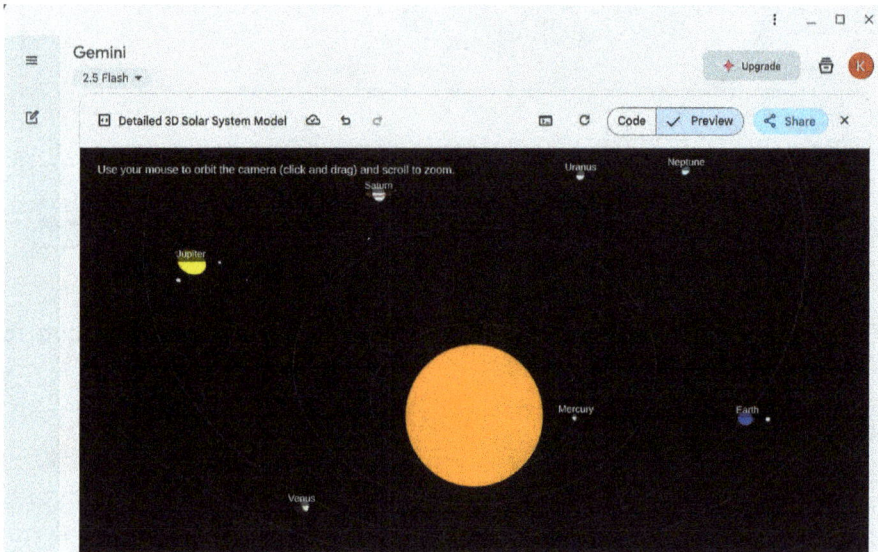

Here, at the top of the window, the project title displays the name of your current canvas; you can click on it to rename your project.

The **cloud icon** indicates that your work is automatically saved to your Google account. The **undo icon** allows you to reverse the last action you performed. The **redo icon** lets you restore the most recently undone step. The **preview icon** is used to display a live rendering of any code generated in the canvas. The **refresh** icon re-runs the last prompt in a block to produce a new result. The **code** and **preview** toggle allows you to switch between viewing the raw code and seeing its rendered output. The **share** button lets you generate a link to share your canvas with others. The **close** icon closes the current canvas window

If you want to make any tweaks, you can edit your original prompt, ask Gemini to revise or expand the response.

150

If you want to save the generated image, right click on the image, select 'save image as'.

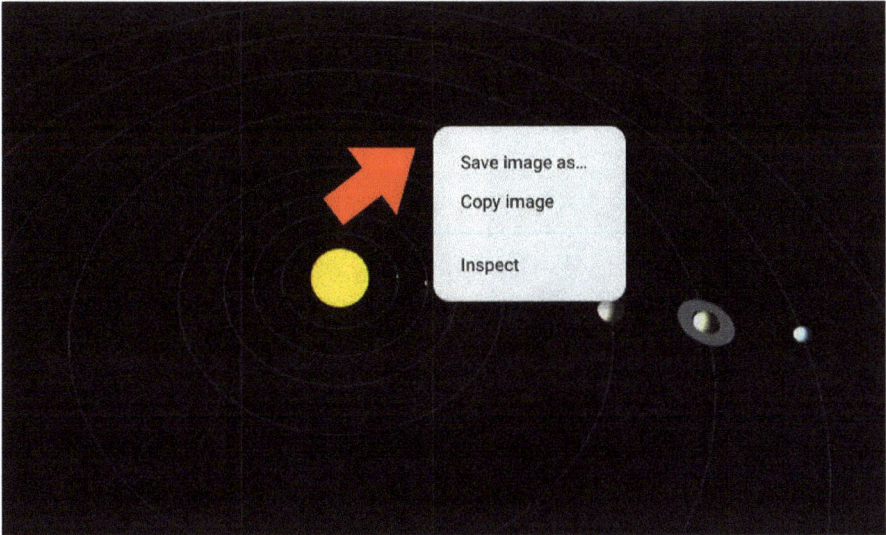

Choose where you want to save the image. For example, I'm going to save the image in my 'pics' folder on my Google Drive. Enter a meaningful name for the file.

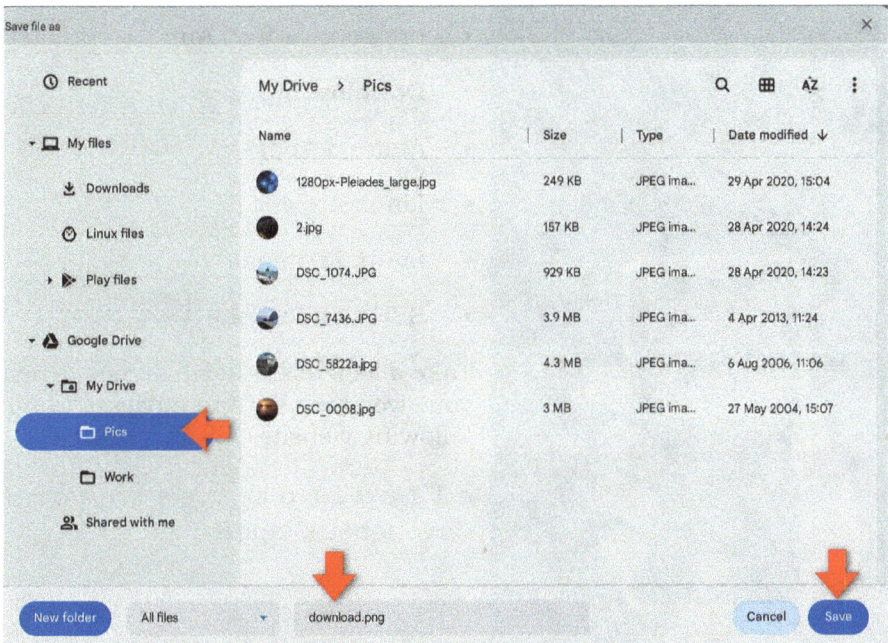

Click 'save' when you're done.

4

Using Apps

Apps are a core part of the Chromebook experience. There are various different types of apps available for your chromebook. You can use web apps, progressive web apps, Android apps and Linux apps.

In this chapter, we'll take a look at:

- Introduction to Apps

- Types of Apps

- Useful Web Apps

- Progressive Web App

- Downloading Apps

- Android Apps

- Linux Apps

- Linux Terminal

- SSH Connections

Take a look at the video demos. Open your web browser and navigate to the following website

e l l u m i n e t p r e s s . c o m /
chromebook-apps

Types of Apps

Chromebooks support four main types of apps, each designed for different use cases. Understanding these will help you choose the best app for your task, avoid redundancy, and get the most out of your Chromebook.

Scan for Video

A web app is simply a website that functions like an app. For example Gmail, and Google Docs run inside the Chrome browser and require no installation.

Many modern web apps are built as Progressive Web Apps (PWAs). These are websites that look and behave like regular apps you might install on your device. They open in their own window, can be added to your Chromebook, work offline, send notifications, and run through the browser—without needing to download them from the Google Play Store.

The above two are the recommended types of apps to use with your Chromebook.

You can also install Android apps through the Google Play Store, allowing you to run the same apps used on Android phones and tablets. However, they're not always ideal for Chromebooks, as many are designed for smaller screens and may not scale well to larger displays or work efficiently without a touchscreen interface. Android apps run in a dedicated Android environment on your Chromebook and can be useful when there is no equivalent web or PWA version. This includes apps like WhatsApp, Instagram, Snapchat, and certain mobile games, which are often only fully functional through their Android versions.

Many modern Chromebooks include support for Linux apps through a feature called the Linux development environment. This creates a virtualized Linux container on your Chromebook, allowing you to install and run full desktop Linux apps and command-line tools. While originally aimed at developers, Linux support has become useful for power users, educators, students, and anyone needing access to open-source or more advanced software. You can use it to install programs such as VS Code, GIMP, LibreOffice, or development tools such as Python, Node.js, and Git. Linux apps run in their own windows and integrate cleanly alongside your other ChromeOS apps.

Each type of app has its strengths and ideal use cases. In general, web apps and PWAs are the most efficient, secure, and well-optimized for ChromeOS—they update automatically, require no installation, and integrate tightly with Google services. Android apps are helpful for specific needs, especially when no equivalent web version exists, while Linux apps provide advanced capabilities for coding, design, and professional workflows.

153

Useful Web Apps

Here are some useful apps you can run directly from your Google Chrome web browser—all of which work well on Chromebooks without needing to install anything.

Google Docs. A word processor included as part Google's free web-based office suite and is part of Google Drive.

```
docs.google.com
```

Google Sheets. A spreadsheet program included as part Google's free web-based office suite and is part of Google Drive.

```
sheets.google.com
```

Google Slides. A presentation program included as part Google's free web-based office suite and is part of Google Drive.

```
slides.google.com
```

Google Keep. An online, web based note-taking service developed by Google.

```
keep.google.com
```

Google Drawings. A web-based diagramming program for drawing charts and diagrams such as org-charts, mind maps and flowcharts.

```
drawings.google.com
```

Google Translate. An online translation program designed to translate webpages or text into a given language.

```
translate.google.com
```

Pixlr Editor. A popular online photo editor. According to its author Pixlr supports all common image formats, including JPG, PNG, GIF, BMP, PSD and TIFF.

```
pixlr.com/editor
```

Grammarly. Allows you to check your English text for grammar, spelling, and punctuation errors.

```
www.grammarly.com/grammar-check
```

Microsoft Office. Free online versions of Microsoft Word, Excel, PowerPoint, OneNote, Outlook, and OneDrive. You'll need to sign up for a free Microsoft Account.

```
www.office.com
```

Installing a Progressive Web App

Many web apps can be installed on your Chromebook as Progressive Web Apps (PWAs), allowing them to run in their own window, work offline, and appear alongside your other apps—without needing to download anything from an app store.

First, open the Chrome web browser, then navigate to the web app you want to install. For example, to install the Google Docs Progressive Web App (PWA), go to:

```
docs.google.com
```

If the site supports PWA installation, you'll see an icon on the far right of the address bar.

Click 'install' on the confirmation dialog box.

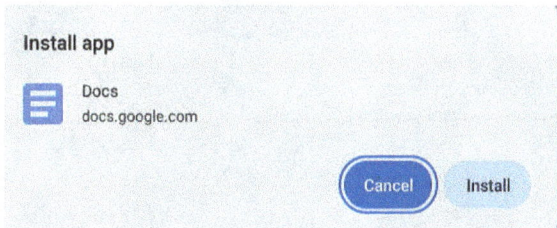

You'll find the app on your app launcher. When you launch the app, you'll notice it opens in its own window, without browser tabs or the address bar—giving it a more app-like experience.

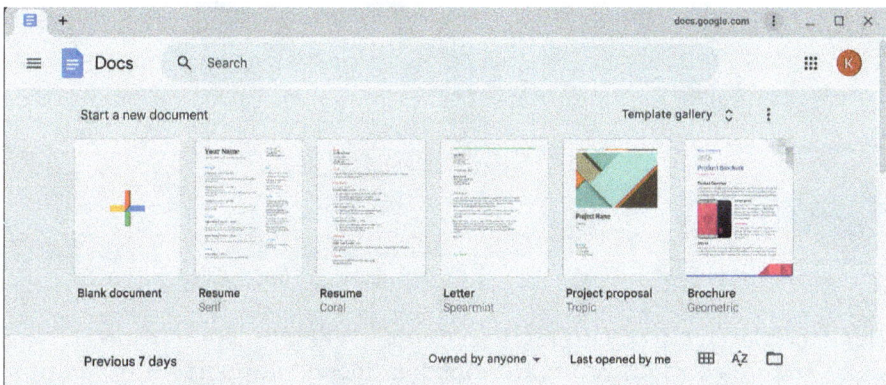

Android Apps

Android apps are available on Chromebooks, but they're not always ideal. Many are designed for small phone and tablet screens, and unless you're using a touchscreen, you're better off using the web or PWA version instead.

Most new Chromebooks come with the Google Play Store already installed so you can download your favourite Android apps. If your Chromebook was released in 2017 or later, then you'll be able to run Android apps.

Enable the Google Play Store

You can install android apps from the Google Play Store directly onto your Chromebook. The Google Play Store is currently only available on certain Chromebooks.

First, you'll need to enable the feature. To do this, open settings.

Select 'apps' from the panel on the left hand side.

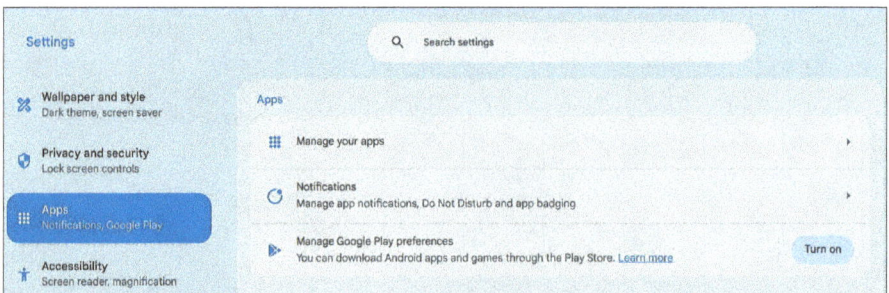

Next to 'Manage Google play Preferences' click 'turn on'. Note: If you don't see this option, your Chromebook doesn't support Android apps.

Click 'more', then 'accept' on the 'Google Play apps and services' screen.

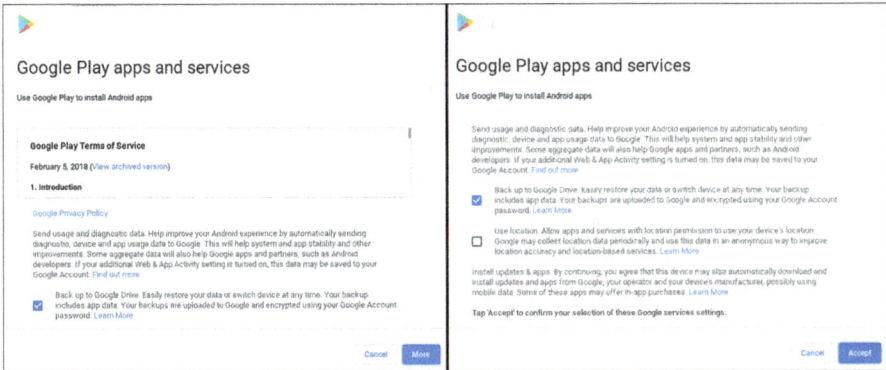

Google Play Store will open when the setup is complete. If not, you'll find the Google Play store on your app launcher. Here, you'll be able to find and install all your favourite android apps.

Google Play Store

Using the Google Play Store, you'll be able to browse, search and download your apps. Open the app launcher, click 'play store'.

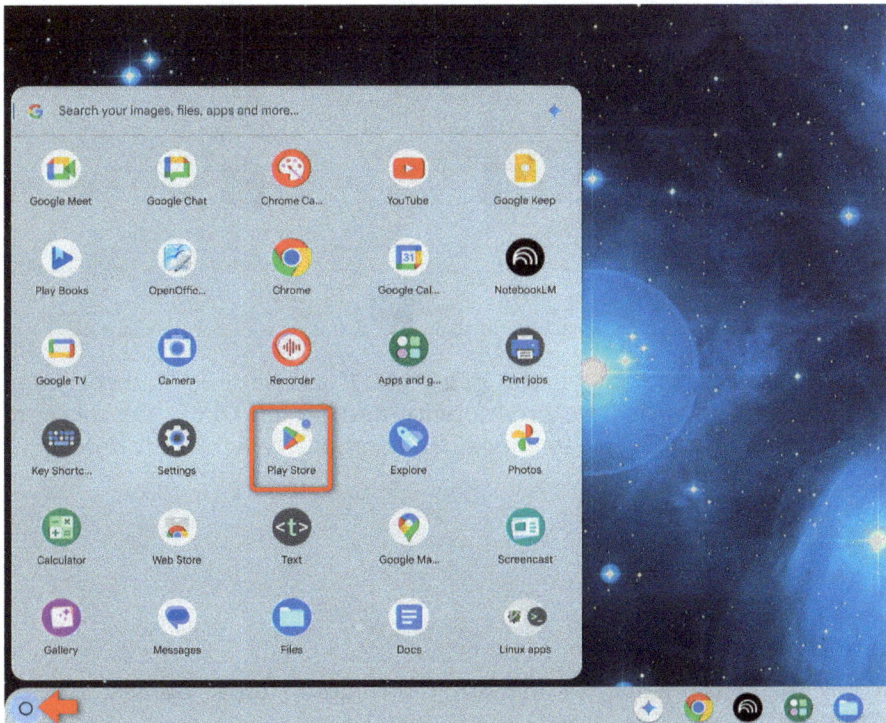

Chapter 4: Using Apps

Browsing the App Store

Down the left-hand side of the Play Store, you'll see a list of navigation tabs such as Games, Apps, Books, Children. These help you browse different sections of the store depending on what you're looking for.

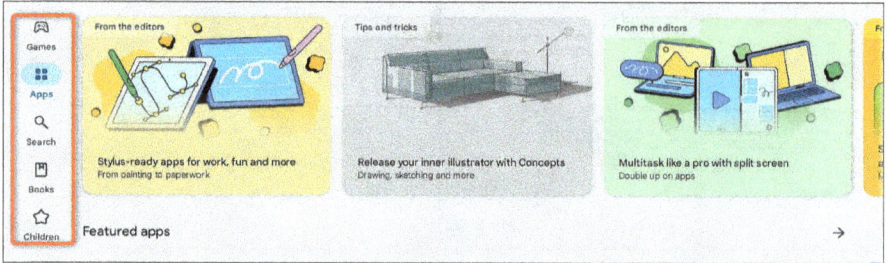

For this example, I'm going to select 'apps' from the list. Here, you can browse apps in 'featured apps', 'top charts', free and paid apps, as well as popular apps in various categories. You'll also find apps that are currently popular and apps that are recommended to you based on your browsing habits.

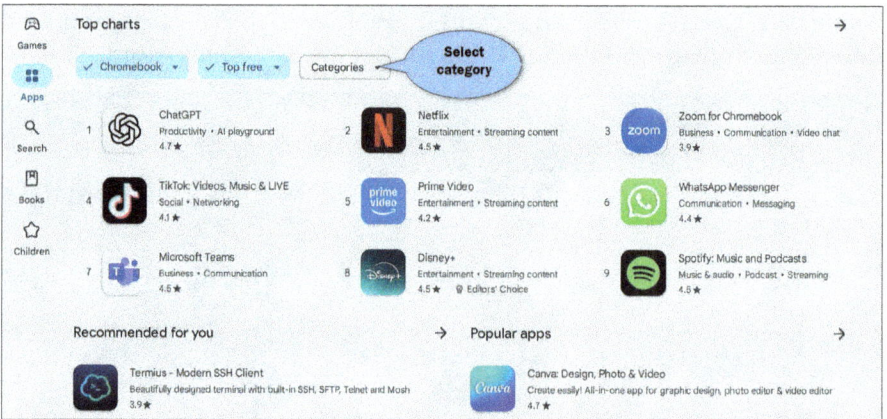

If you scroll further down the page, you'll see various 'categories' of apps such as art design, productivity and so on. Click 'see more' to view the full list of app categories. Click on one to select the category.

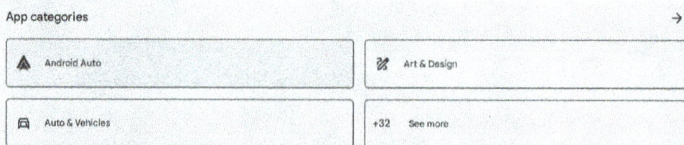

You can do the same for the other navigation tabs: Games, Books, Children.

Have a look through the sections. To install any of the apps, click on the icon.

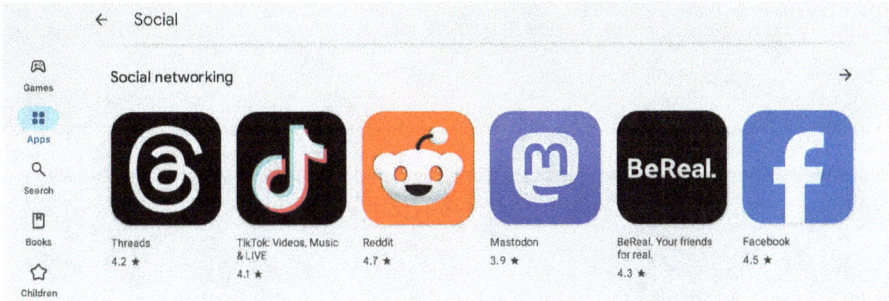

From the app's summary page, click "Install" for free apps, or click the price button if it's a paid app.

Search for Apps

To search for an app, select 'search' from the navigation tabs on the left hand side. Type your search into the field at the top of the window.

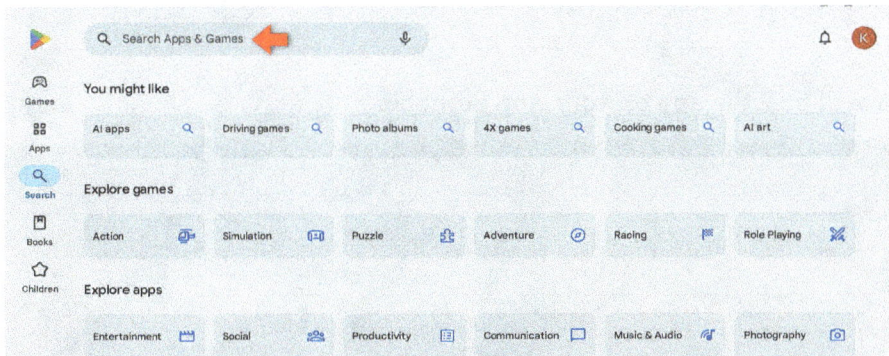

You can also browse through the sections at the bottom. The **You might like** section offers suggested search terms based on trends or your activity. **Explore games** lets you browse games by genre, such as Action or Puzzle, while **Explore apps** organizes non-game apps into categories like Productivity, Social, or Entertainment for easier discovery.

159

Chapter 4: Using Apps

Once you start typing your search, you'll see some matches appear below. Select the closest match.

Then select the app you want from the list. On the app's summary page, click "Install" for free apps, or click the price button if it's a paid app to begin the purchase and installation process.

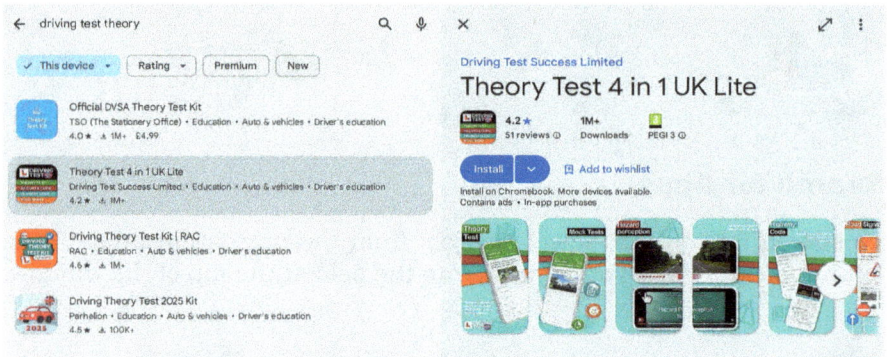

You'll find the app on your app launcher.

Removing Apps

To remove an app, open your app launcher from the bottom left hand side of the screen.

Right click on the app you want to remove.

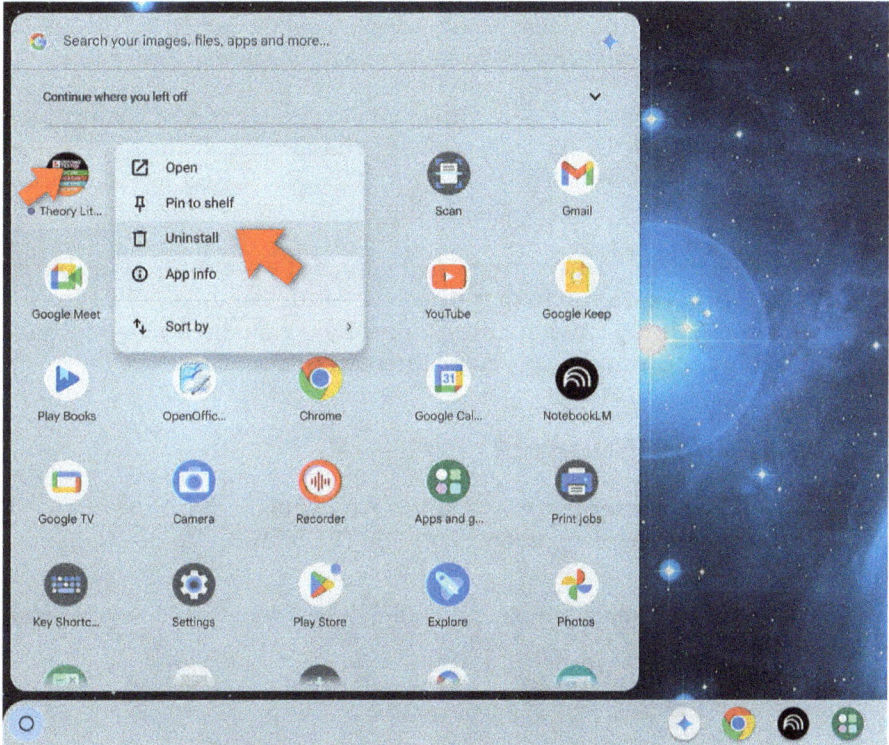

From the popup menu, select 'uninstall'. Click 'uninstall' on the confirmation dialog box.

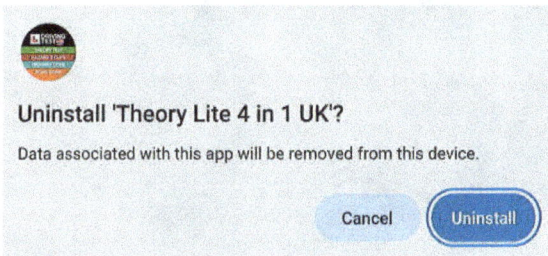

Do this for all the apps you want to remove.

Linux Apps

ChromeOS includes support for Linux apps, giving users access to powerful desktop software and developer tools. This feature, known as the Linux development environment, is available on most modern Chromebooks running the latest stable version of ChromeOS.

Linux is a free, open-source operating system originally created by Linus Torvalds, inspired by Unix. It has since evolved into a flexible, highly customizable platform used across a wide range of devices—from smartphones and laptops to servers and supercomputers.

Linux is typically distributed in different versions called distributions (or "distros"), each with its own package manager and user interface. Common distributions include Ubuntu, Debian, Red Hat, Fedora, SuSE, and Raspberry Pi OS (Raspbian).

On a Chromebook, Linux apps run inside a secure, sandboxed container. This allows you to install and use full desktop applications—such as code editors, image editors, and development tools—without compromising the simplicity and security of ChromeOS.

Enable Linux Support

Linux support is currently only available on certain Chromebooks. To use Linux apps, first you'll need to enable the feature. To do this, open settings.

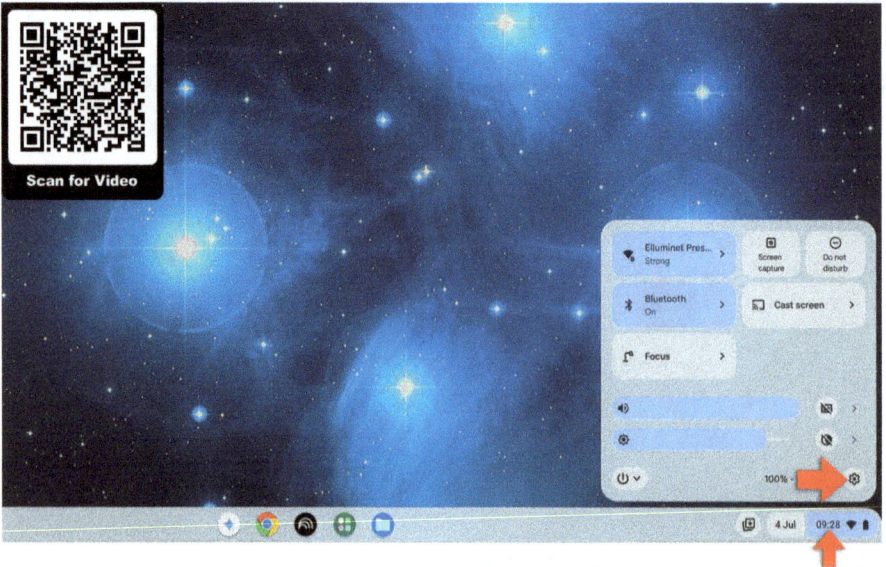

From the list on the left hand side, click 'About ChromeOS'. Scroll down to 'developers', then click 'set up'.

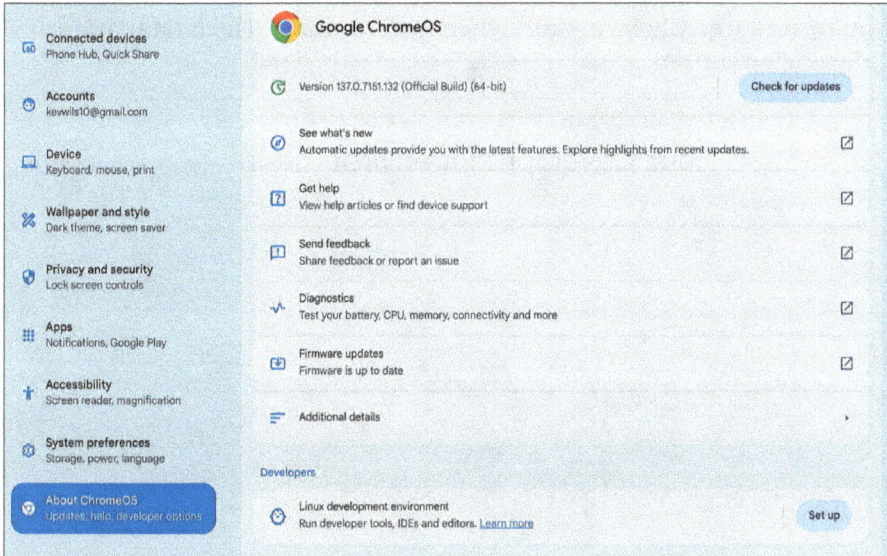

Select 'next' from the 'setup' screen.

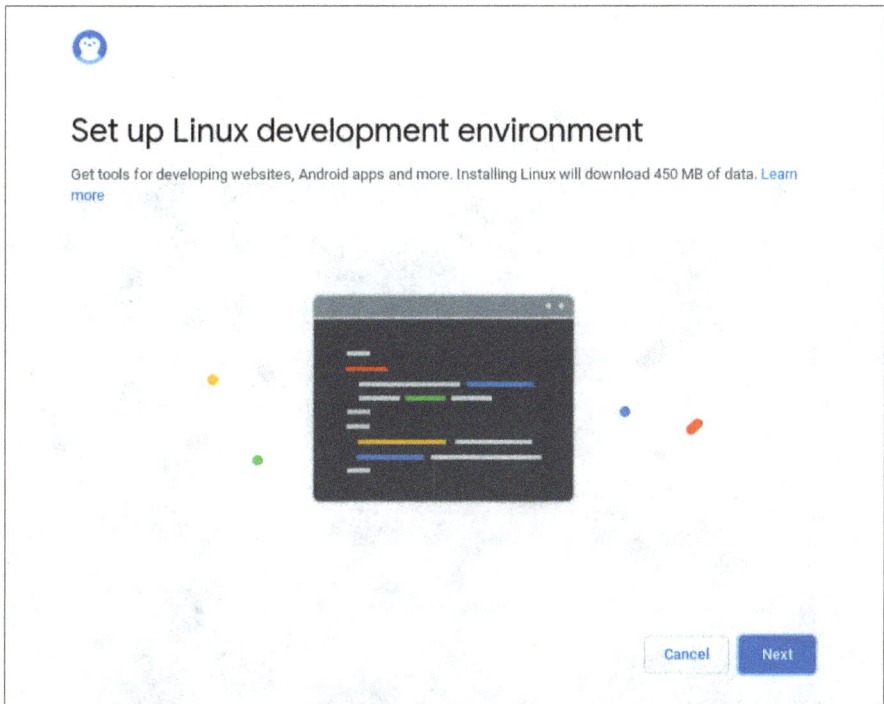

Chapter 4: Using Apps

Enter a Linux username. This will be the username you use within Linux and is separate from your Google Account. Next, select the amount of disk space you want to allocate to Linux. Select 'recommended' if you're unsure. Click 'install' when you're done. The installation will take a few minutes.

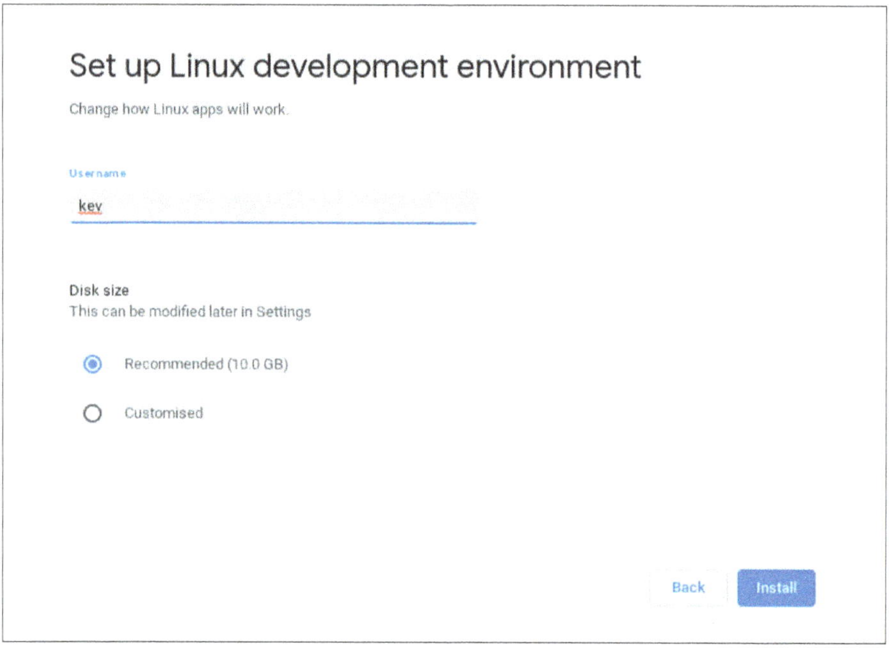

Once Linux is installed, you'll see the terminal window pop up.

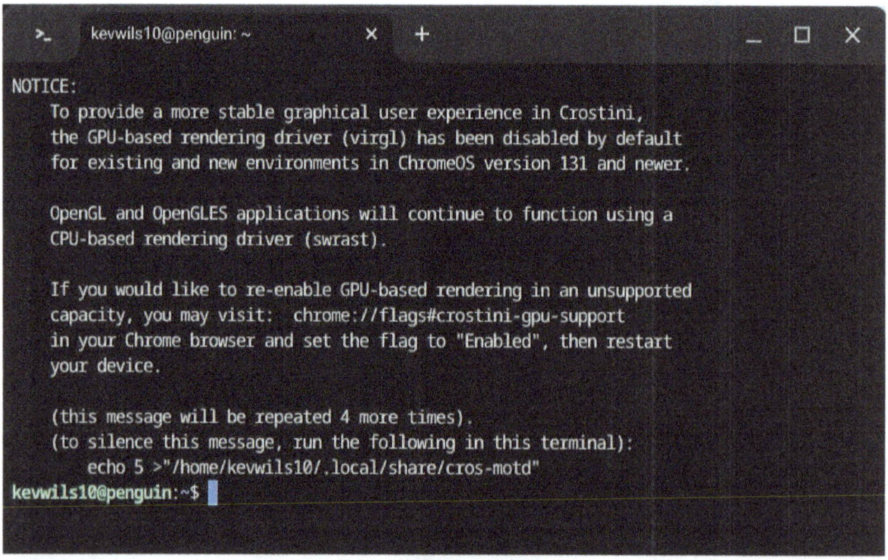

Managing the Linux Environment

To change any settings regarding the Linux development environment, such as disk space. Click on the clock on the bottom right hand side, select the settings icon.

From the list on the left hand side, click 'About ChromeOS'. Scroll down to 'developers', then click 'Linux development environment'.

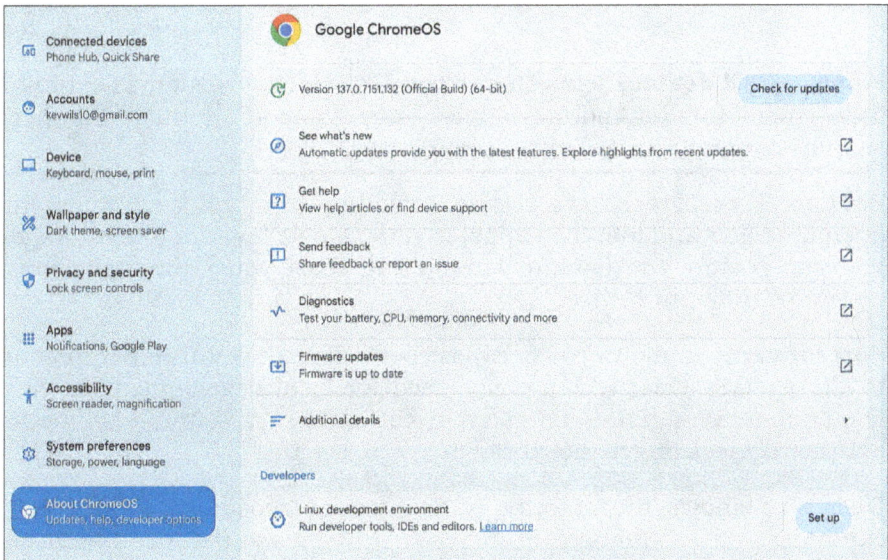

Here you can configure advanced Linux settings, such as sharing folders between ChromeOS and Linux, connecting USB devices, adjusting disk space, managing backups, and enabling access to hardware features like the microphone.

You can also remove the Linux environment entirely if it's no longer needed.

Manage shared folders allows you to choose which ChromeOS folders can be accessed from within the Linux environment. This is useful for sharing files (e.g., documents, downloads, or code projects) between ChromeOS and Linux apps.

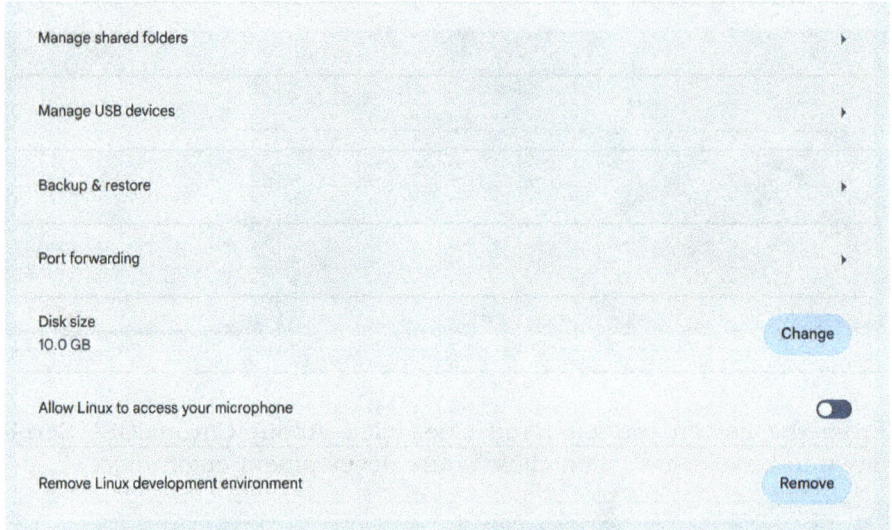

Manage shared folders	▸
Manage USB devices	▸
Backup & restore	▸
Port forwarding	▸
Disk size 10.0 GB	Change
Allow Linux to access your microphone	⬤▭
Remove Linux development environment	Remove

Manage USB devices lets you connect USB devices—such as external drives, cameras, or Android phones—directly to the Linux container, so they can be used by Linux applications.

Backup & restore allows you to back up your Linux environment (including files and installed apps) to your Google Drive or local storage. You can restore the backup later if you reset your Chromebook or move to a different device.

Port forwarding allows you to expose ports from the Linux environment to ChromeOS. This is commonly used for local development servers (e.g., web servers, databases) so they can be accessed from ChromeOS or other devices on the network.

Disk size shows the amount of disk space allocated to the Linux container. Click "Change" to increase or decrease the size based on your usage needs. More space is needed for large packages or media.

Allow Linux to access your microphone allows Linux applications (such as audio recorders or voice-enabled development tools) to access your Chromebook's microphone.

Remove Linux development environment completely deletes the Linux container, removing all Linux apps, packages, and files. Use this if you no longer need Linux or want to reclaim disk space.

166

Using the Linux Terminal

To start using Linux, you'll need to open the Linux terminal. To do this, open your app launcher, scroll down then click the 'Linux apps' group to open.

Click on 'terminal'.

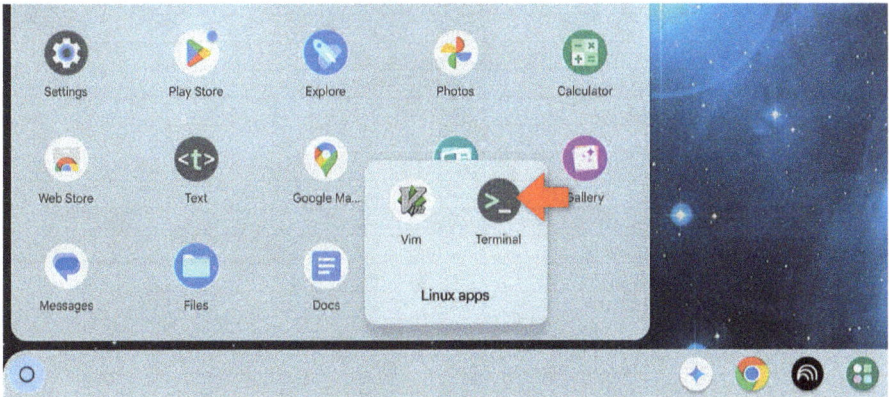

Select 'penguin' from the startup screen.

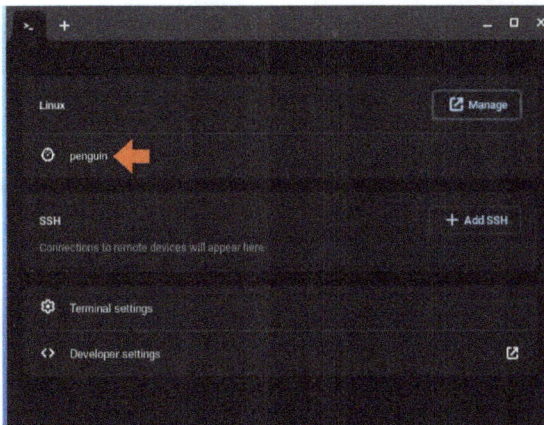

Chapter 4: Using Apps

The Linux terminal will open up in a window with a black background.

```
kev@penguin:~$ uname -r
4.19.98-08076-g24ab33fb8e14
kevw@penguin:~$ whoami
kev
kev@penguin:~$ 
```

This is a command line interface where you type in Linux commands. Here are a few commands you can use...

Command	Function
ls	List files and directories
ls -a	List all files and directories
ls -l	Detailed list of files and directories
mkdir <dir-name>	Create directory
cd <dir-name>	Change to directory
pwd	Display the path of the current dir
cp <file> <destination>	Copy file to destination
mv <file> <destination>	Move file to destination
rm <file>	Delete file
rmdir <dir>	Delete directory
sudo <command>	Execute command with root privileges
su <username>	Switch user
sudo useradd <username>	Add new user
sudo groupadd <groupname>	Add new user group
sudo usermod -g <group> <user>	Change user's group
sudo passwd <username>	Change password of user
whoami	Show user currently logged in
netstat	Displays network state
ping	Check host is online
sftp [user-name]@[server]	Secure ftp connection to server
hostname	Display hostname or machine name
ssh [user-name]@[server]	Open a SSH connection to server

Give them a try...

```
kevwils10@penguin:~$ mkdir work
kevwils10@penguin:~$ ls -l
total 0
drwxr-xr-x 1 kevwils10 kevwils10 0 May 28 13:52 work

kevwils10@penguin:~$ mkdir pictures
kevwils10@penguin:~$ ls -l
total 0
drwxr-xr-x 1 kevwils10 kevwils10 0 May 28 13:52 pictures
drwxr-xr-x 1 kevwils10 kevwils10 0 May 28 13:52 work

kevwils10@penguin:~$ ping www.ell.com
PING www.elluminetpress.com (104.31.92.92) 56(84) bytes of data.
64 bytes from 104.31.92.92 (104.31.92.92): icmp_seq=1 ttl=57 time=8.30 ms
64 bytes from 104.31.92.92 (104.31.92.92): icmp_seq=2 ttl=57 time=9.31 ms
64 bytes from 104.31.92.92 (104.31.92.92): icmp_seq=3 ttl=57 time=9.07 ms
```

Terminal Settings

This area provides customization options for the ChromeOS terminal itself. Open the terminal, then click on the home tab on the top left hand corner. Then select 'terminal settings'.

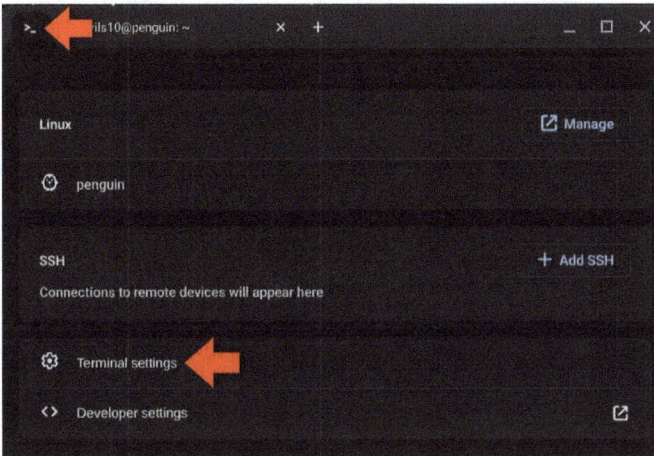

Here in the **Appearance tab** you customize the visual style of the terminal. You can choose from several predefined themes. You can also set a custom background color using a hex code, or add a background image by clicking "Select" then choosing an image

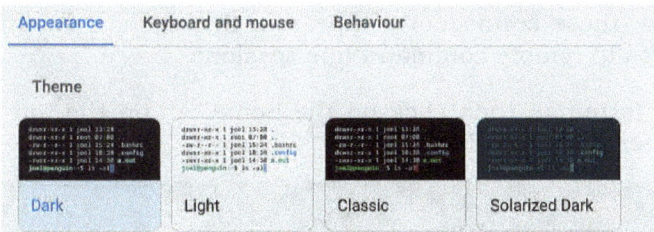

In the **Keyboard and mouse tab**, you can adjust how input behaves in the terminal. This includes remapping keys, modifying how Ctrl behaves (such as using Ctrl+C to copy or to interrupt a running command), and changing how right-click actions work—either opening a context menu or sending the click directly to the Linux environment

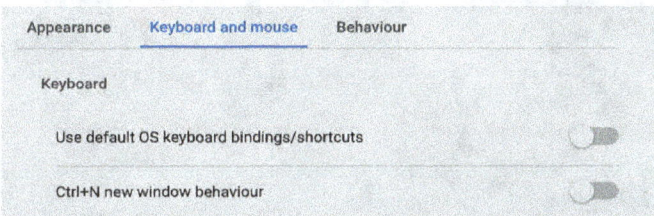

Chapter 4: Using Apps

The **Behaviour tab** controls how the terminal functions. You can change the cursor style (block, underline, or beam), enable or disable cursor blinking, and set the default shell or command to run at startup. You can also adjust font size here for readability or accessibility.

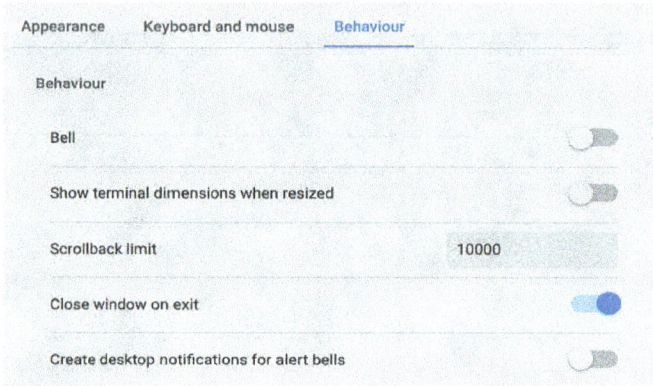

Appearance   Keyboard and mouse   Behaviour

Behaviour

Bell

Show terminal dimensions when resized

Scrollback limit   10000

Close window on exit

Create desktop notifications for alert bells

SSH

The SSH (Secure Shell) section allows you to connect securely to remote servers and devices using the SSH protocol. This is especially useful for developers, system administrators, or users managing headless systems like Raspberry Pi. By clicking Add SSH, you can save connection profiles to frequently accessed remote machines. Once configured, these connections appear in this section for quick, one-click access to remote command-line sessions.

Open the terminal, then click on the home tab on the top left hand corner. Then select 'Add SSH'.

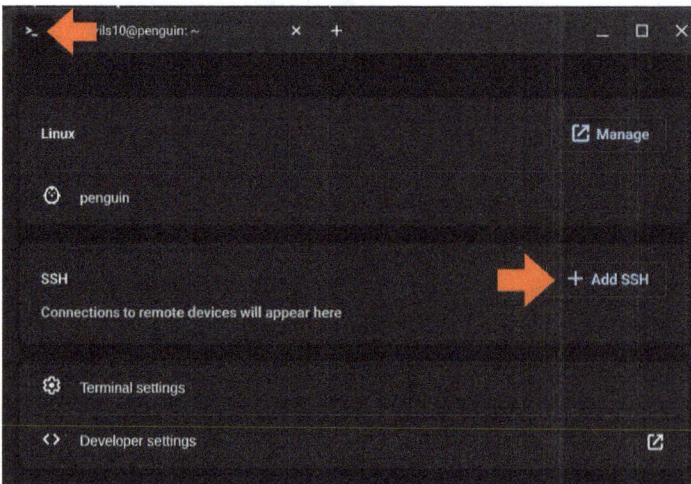

In the first field, enter the SSH command used to connect to your remote server.

Identity sets the SSH key used for authentication. If you haven't imported a specific key, it defaults to the Chromebook's built-in identity. If your server uses key-based authentication, you may need to click **Import** and upload your private SSH key file to match the one authorized on the remote server.

SSH relay server options is an optional field typically left blank for standard direct SSH connections. It's used in enterprise environments where an intermediate relay server is required to reach the destination.

Mount Path by default is the remote user's home directory—e.g., /home/kevwils on the remote server. This is where the SSH session will start when connected. You can leave this as-is unless you have a specific directory you want to use as the mount point.

Click 'save' when you're done.

The new connection will appear on the home tab.

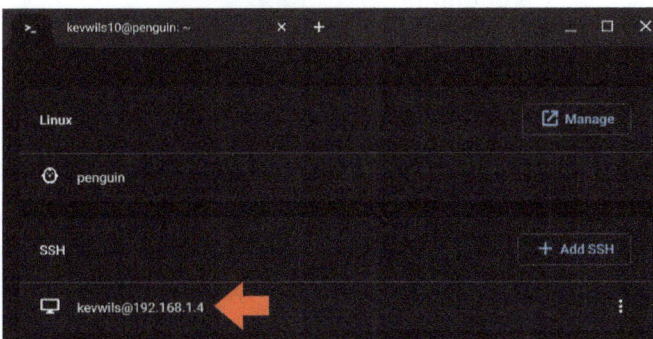

Chapter 4: Using Apps

Click on the connection name to begin. The Terminal will open and attempt to connect. If the remote server uses password authentication, you'll be prompted to enter your password, then press Enter to log in.

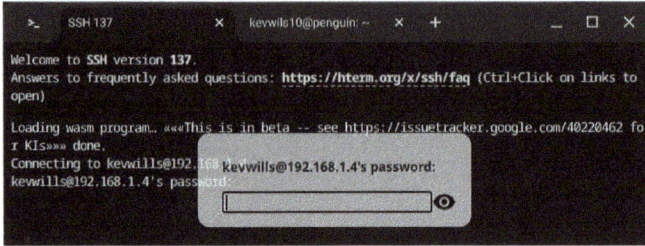

You'll land on a command prompt inside the remote server where you can type commands.

Install a Linux App

First make sure you're using the latest version of apt-get. To check type:

```
sudo apt-get update
```

To install programs on Linux you need to type a command into the Linux terminal.

```
sudo apt-get install [app-name]
```

Finding Apps

You can find a full list of Linux packages at the following website.

```
packages.debian.org/stable/
```

Select a category (eg 'development'), then note the app-name in bold (eg if we wanted to install 'idle3'). This is the name you use in the `sudo apt-get install` command.

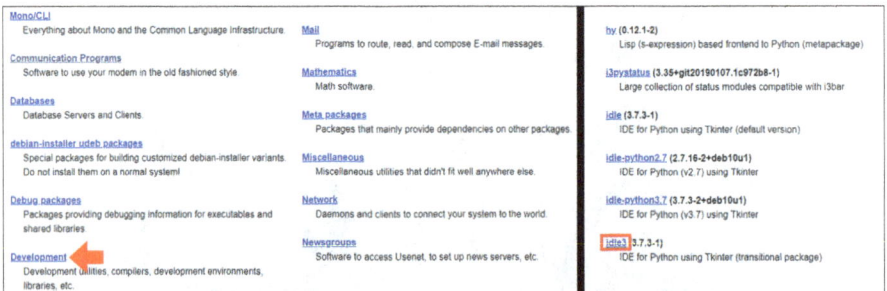

So in the example above, we insert the name 'idle3' in place of app-name. So...

```
sudo apt-get install [app-name]
```

Becomes...

```
sudo apt-get install idle3
```

Install FileZilla FTP

FileZilla is a free FTP program for transferring files using FTP or sFTP and is useful for uploading files to a web server. To install FileZilla, open the terminal window and type

```
sudo apt-get install filezilla
```

Install Audacity

Audacity is a free audio recording and manipulation program. To install Audacity, open the terminal window and type

```
sudo apt-get install audacity
```

Install Gimp Image Editor

Gimp is a free graphics program for image retouching and editing. To install Gimp, open the terminal window and type:

```
sudo apt-get install gimp
```

Install Libre Office

Libre Office is a free office package similar to Microsoft Office. To install Libre Office, open the terminal window and type:

```
sudo apt install libreoffice
```

Install Python

Python is an interpreted, high-level, general-purpose programming language. To install the python interpreter, open the terminal window and type:

```
sudo apt-get install python3.6
```

To install the integrated development environment, type:

```
sudo apt-get install idle3
```

Remove Linux Apps

To uninstall a Linux app on your Chromebook, open the Linux terminal and use the following command:

```
sudo apt-get remove [app-name]
```

For example, to remove the IDLE Python editor, you would enter:

```
sudo apt-get remove idle3
```

You'll be prompted to confirm the removal. Type Y and press Enter to proceed. You can also use `sudo apt-get purge [app-name]` to remove the app and its configuration files.

Running Linux Apps

You'll find installed Linux apps on your app launcher. Open your app launcher. Select 'Linux apps'.

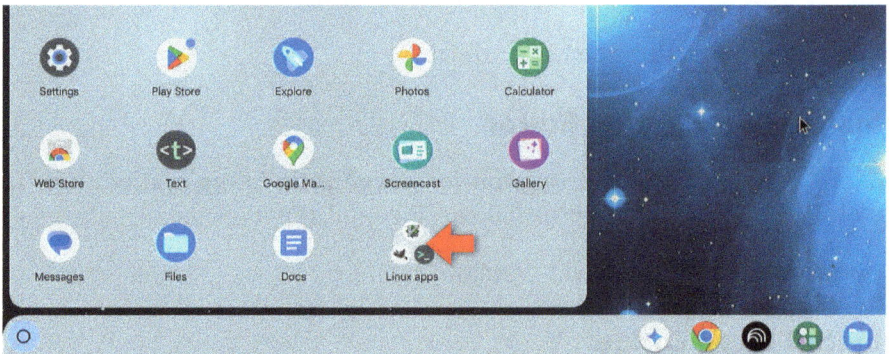

All the Linux apps you install will appear in this group. Click on one of the icons to start the app.

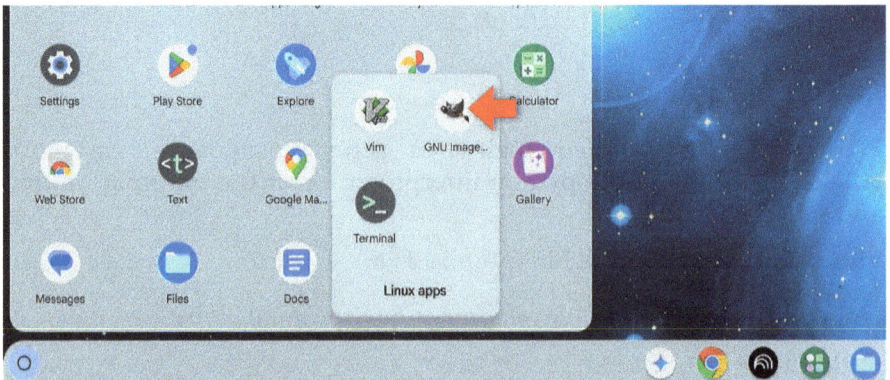

Here, I've started Gimp.

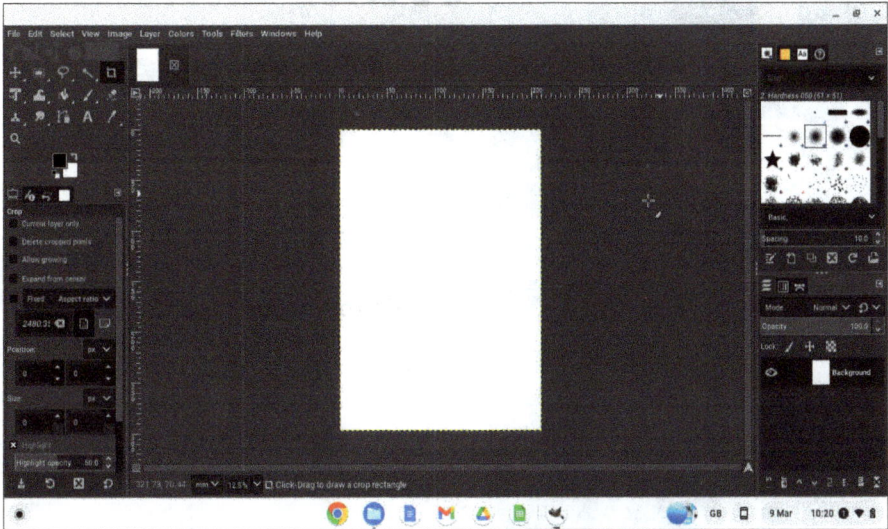

Note that when you save your files in a Linux app, they are saved to the 'Linux files' directory.

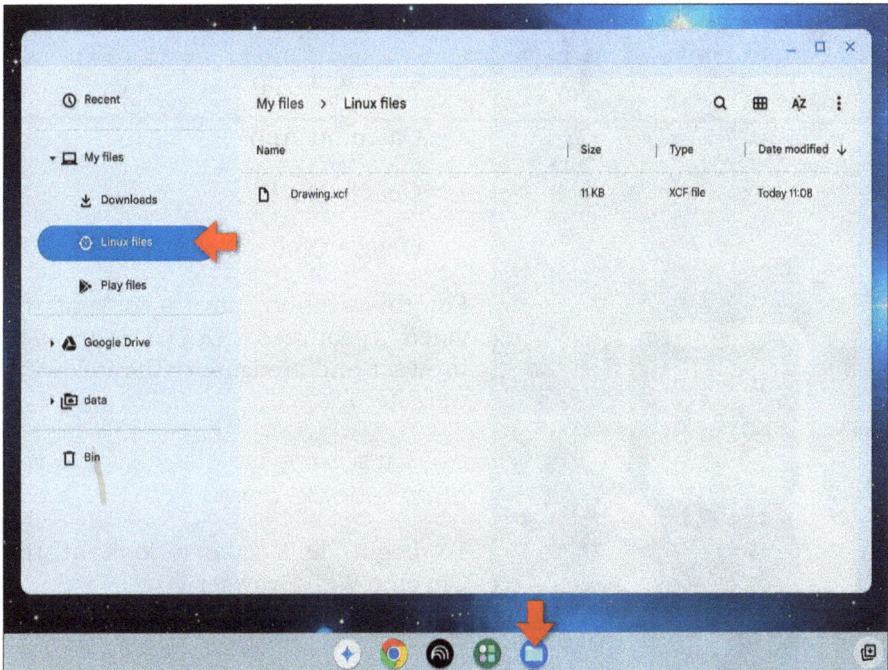

You'll find them in the files app under 'Linux files' in the 'My Files' section on the left hand side.

5

Web, Email & Comms

The Chromebook includes several communication tools, such as Gmail for email, Google Meet for video calls, and Google Chat for messaging, along with the Google Chrome browser for accessing websites and online services.

In this chapter, we'll take a look at:

- Google Chrome

- Gmail App

- Contacts App

- Calendar App

- Google Meet

- Google Chat

For this section, have a look at the video resources. Open your web browser and navigate to the following website:

elluminetpress.com/ chromebook-comms

To begin, let's take a look at the Chrome Web Browser.

Google Chrome

Google Chrome is the web browser built into your Chromebook, and is the app you use to browse the internet, open websites, and web apps. You'll find Google Chrome on the app launcher.

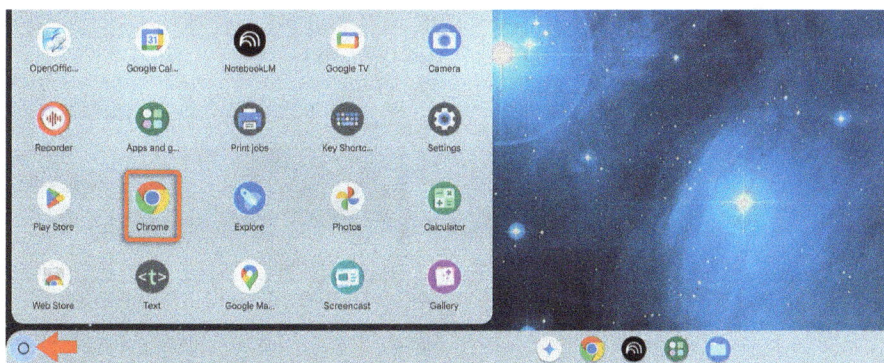

You'll also find Chrome on the app shelf along the bottom of your screen.

Once Chrome starts up, you'll see the main screen similar to the one below.

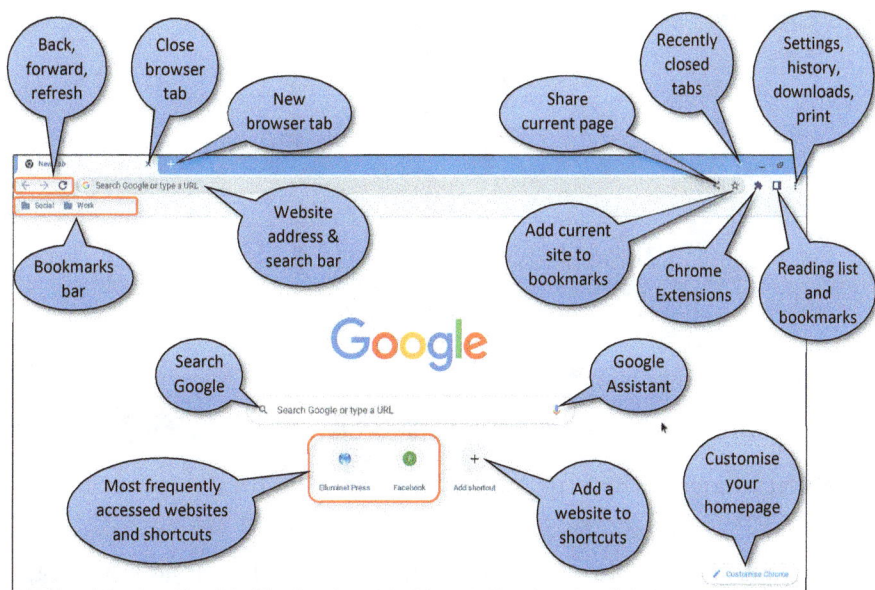

Browser Tabs

Browser tabs help you to keep track of websites you have open instead of having multiple browser windows open at the same time. This makes it easier to see what sites are open and switch between them.

You'll find your browser tabs along the top of the screen. In this example there are three different websites open in three different tabs.

When you want to open a new website, click on the new tab icon.

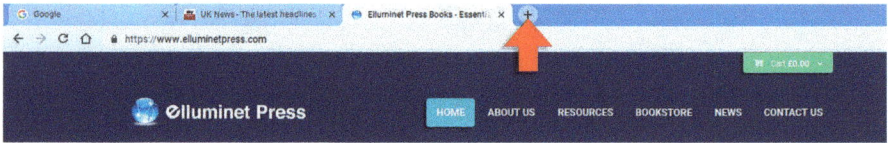

Enter the website address or Google search. You can also select one of your shortcuts under the Google search bar, or select a bookmark from the bookmarks bar along the top.

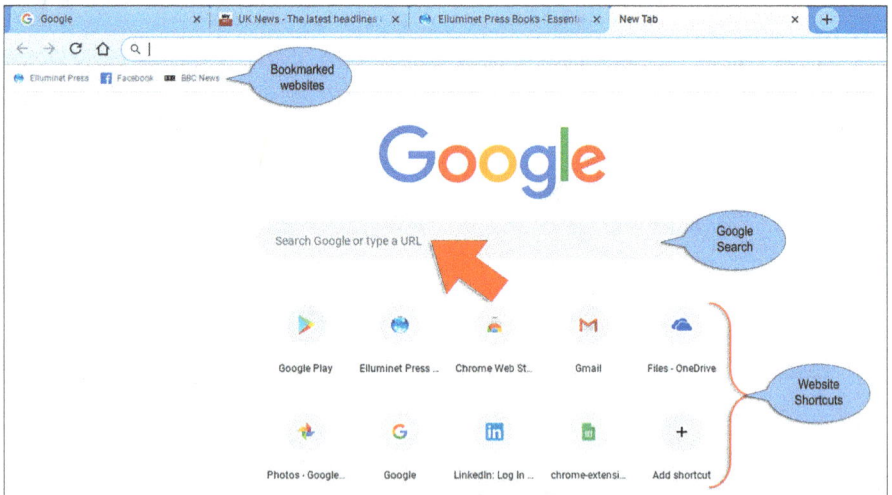

To return to any of the other websites, just click on the tab at the top of the screen.

To close a tab, just click the small x on the right hand side of the tab you want to close.

Browse Incognito

This mode is useful if you don't want Google Chrome on your Chromebook to record your browsing activity, such as website history, cookies, site data, or information entered into forms. This mode doesn't hide your activity from your ISP, school/college, or employer.

To open an incognito tab, click the three dots icon on the top right of your screen

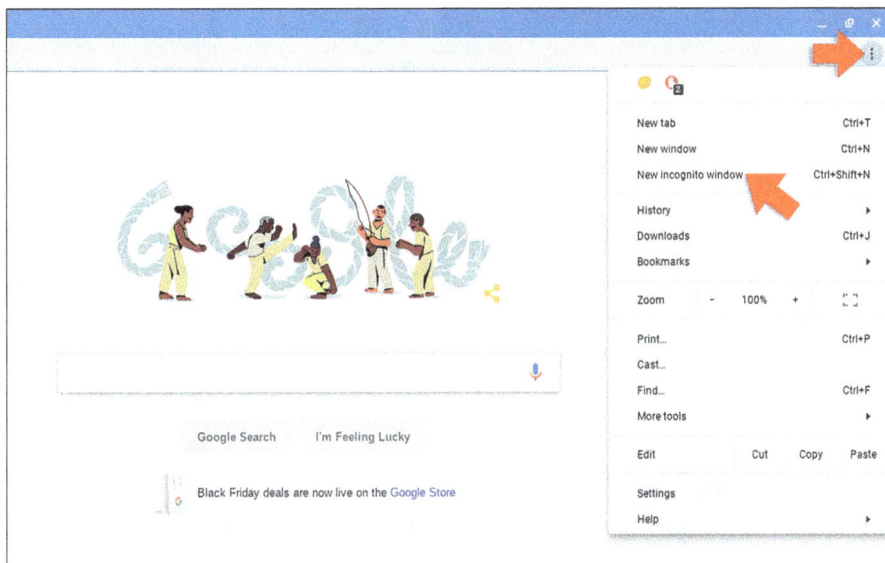

A new window will popup telling you you've gone icognito.

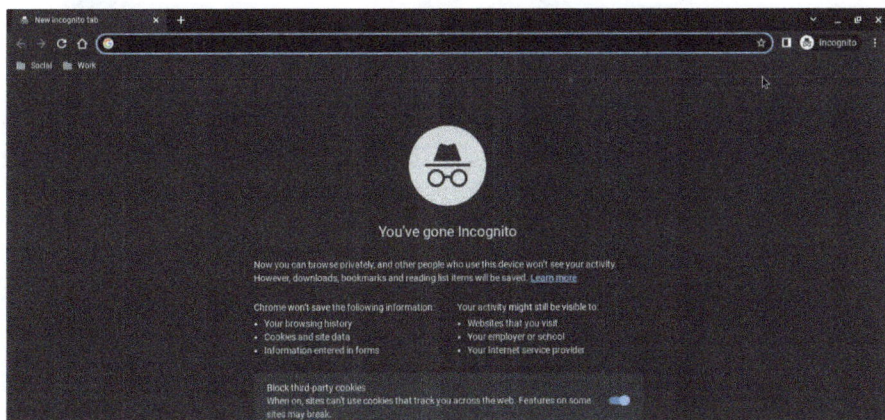

Type the web address of the site you want to visit, or a Google search into the field at the top of the screen.

Chapter 5: Web, Email & Communication

Browsing History

The browsing history keeps a list of all the websites you've visited with Google Chrome. To find your browser history, click the three dots icon on the top right of your screen and select 'history' from the drop down menu.

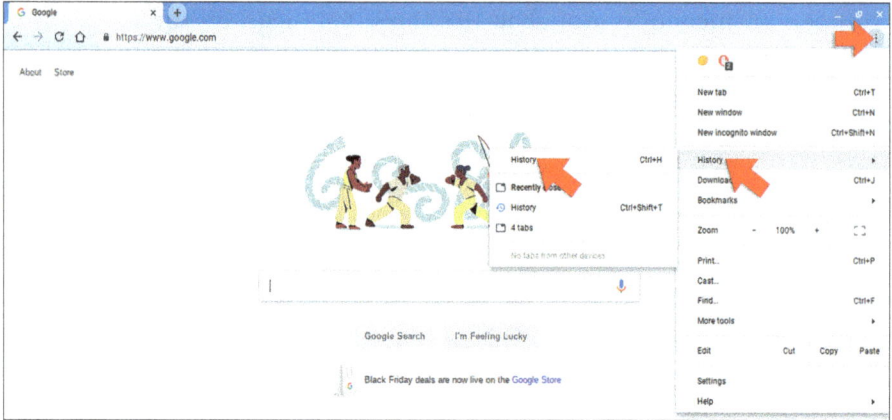

A new tab will pop up. From here, you can scroll down and click any site to revisit.

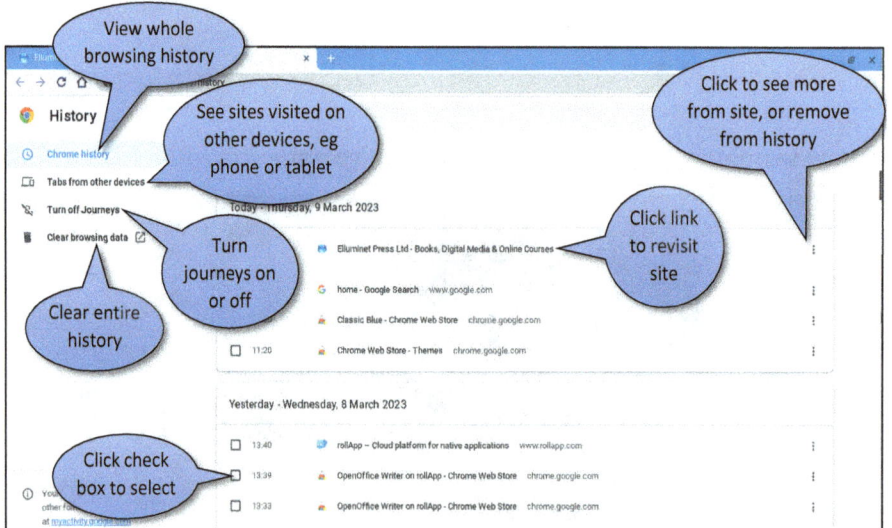

To delete a site from the history, click the tick box next to the website in the list, then click 'delete' on the top right.

Click 'clear history' to clear the list of visited websites, cache, cookies, and other site data.

Bookmarking a Site

It is useful to bookmark, or favourite a site you visit frequently. To do this, navigate to the website you want to bookmark, then click the small star icon to the right of the address bar at the top of your window.

Enter a meaningful name in the 'name' field, if there isn't one. Add your bookmark to the bookmarks bar along the top of your screen. Or select a folder to add your bookmark to. Click 'done' when you're finished.

To view your bookmarks, open the side panel on the right hand side. To do this, click the sidebar icon on the right hand side of the toolbar.

From the drop down menu at the top, select 'bookmarks'.

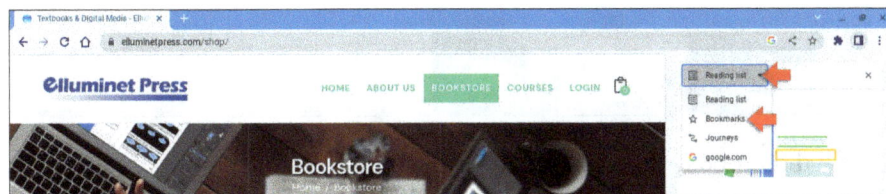

Here, you'll see your website listed. Click on the site to revisit.

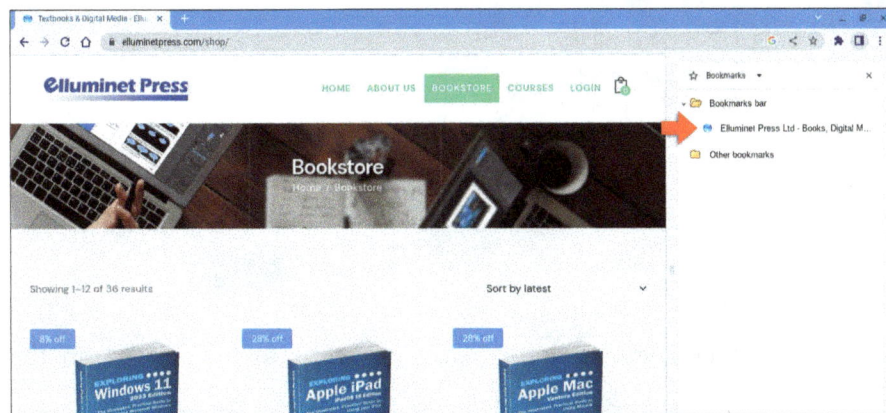

Bookmark Folders

If you have a lot of bookmarked sites, the side bar can become very cluttered. To get around this, you can create folders on the bar to make it easier to find your websites. To do this, open the sidebar, then select 'bookmarks' from the drop down menu if it isn't already selected.

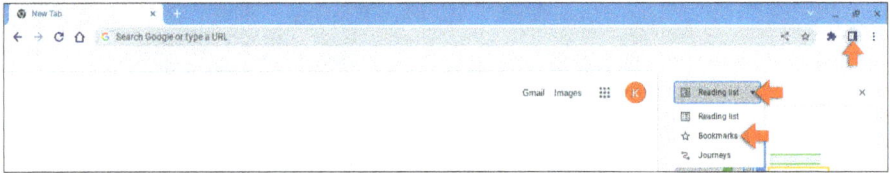

Right click on the 'bookmarks bar', select 'add folder' from the popup menu.

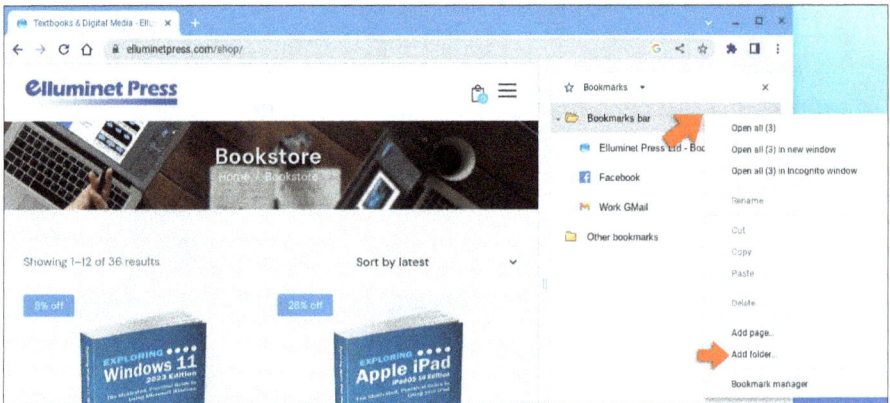

In the dialog box, type in the name of the folder and select 'bookmarks bar'.

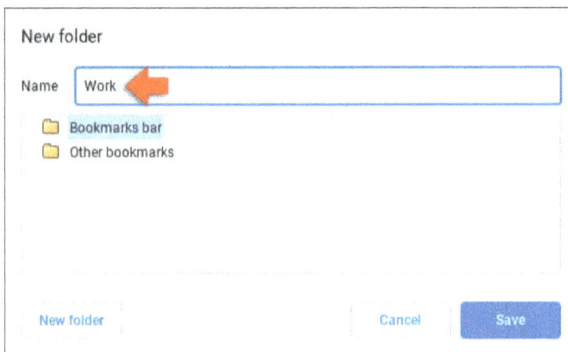

Click 'save' when you're done. You'll see your folder appear on the bookmarks bar.

Now you can drag and drop the bookmarks you want to put in this folder. For example, I'm going to add 'Elluminet Press Ltd' to the 'work' folder. So I would click and drag 'Elluminet Press Ltd' to 'work'.

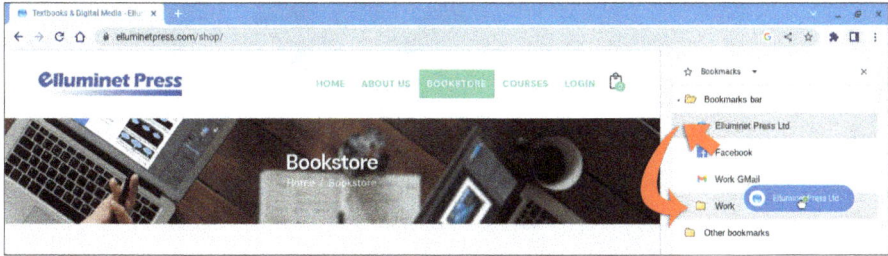

Bookmarks Bar

You can show your bookmarks on the bookmarks bar along the top of the screen. This makes it easier to find the sites you use most often. To add the bookmarks bar to your browser, click on the three dots icon on the top right of the screen, go down to 'bookmarks', then select 'show bookmarks bar'.

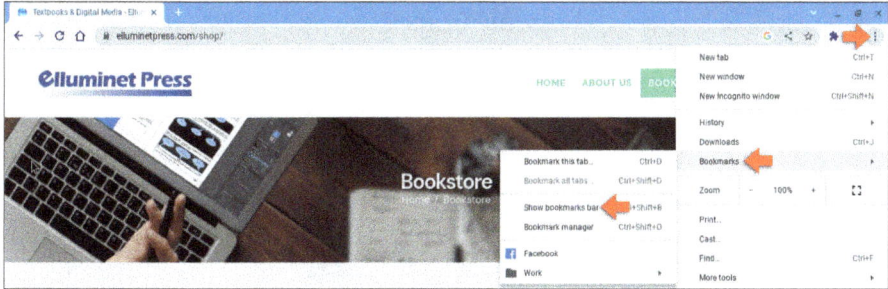

All the bookmarks you've added to the bookmarks bar will show up on this bar.

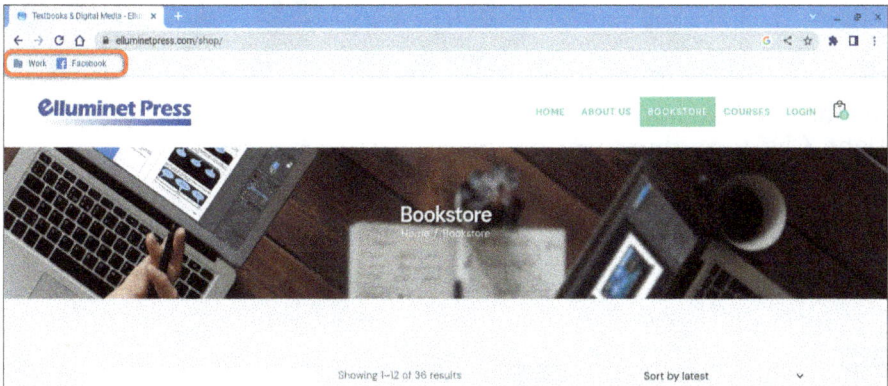

Site Shortcuts

Site shortcuts appear on your home page - the page that appears when you open Chrome or when you open a new tab.

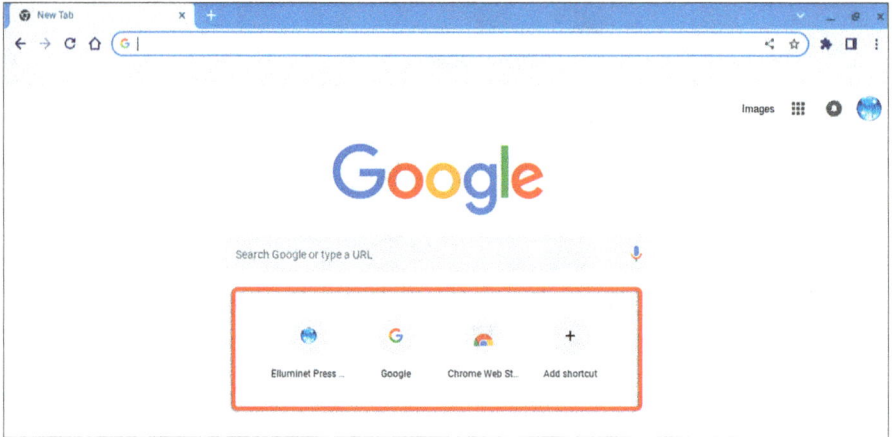

To add a shortcut, you need to know the websites address or URL. For example, I want to add the Elluminet Press website to the shortcuts. To do this, click 'add shortcut' from Chrome's home screen. In the dialog box that appears, type in the website's name and address.

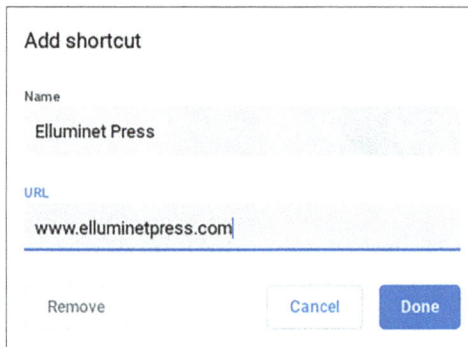

To delete a shortcut, hover your mouse pointer over the shortcut's icon on the Chrome home screen. You'll see three dots appear on the top right. Click on this icon.

From the popup, click 'remove'.

Journeys

A Google Journey groups pages you've visited from a Google search. For example, if you were researching your latest vacation spot, Google Journeys will remember all of the sites you visited that had to do with that research. Such as the initial Google Search, then pages visited from there, and so on. All this information kept together in order to help you revisit any of those pages and continue where you left off.

In this demo, I've been browsing the web searching for **"windows 11 book"**. I have visited various different websites and looked at a few different books. This is called a journey.

To see all your journeys, open Google Chrome, click on the three dots icon on the top right of the menu bar. Go down to history, then select 'history' from the slideout menu.

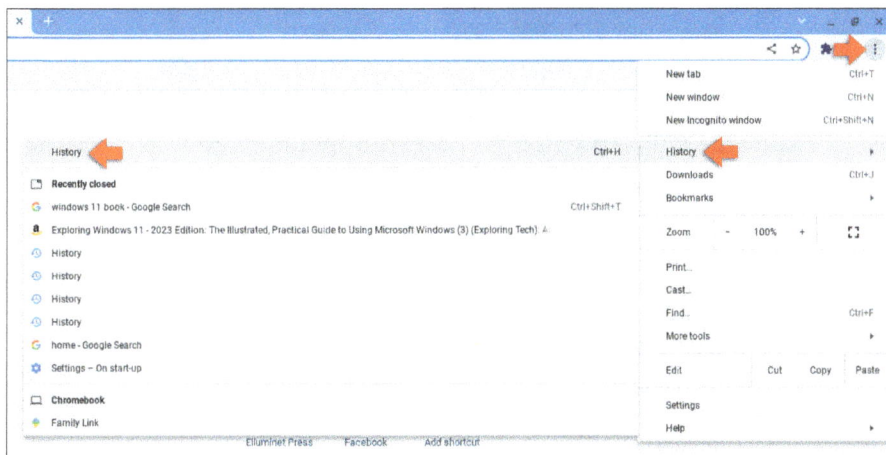

Select 'journeys' from the two options at the top of the screen in the middle.

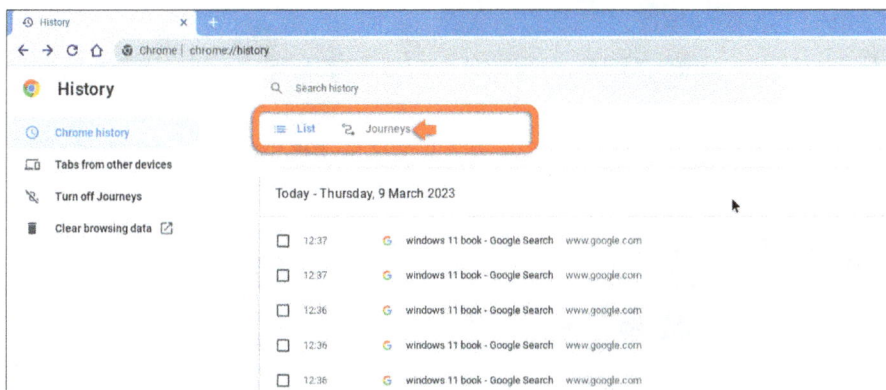

Chapter 5: Web, Email & Communication

You'll see a list of all your web search journeys grouped together under the search keywords you used to search. Here in the screenshot below, we can see the 'windows 11 book' search journey I made a few minutes ago. You'll see a list of all the websites you've visited with this search. Just click on a website to revisit.

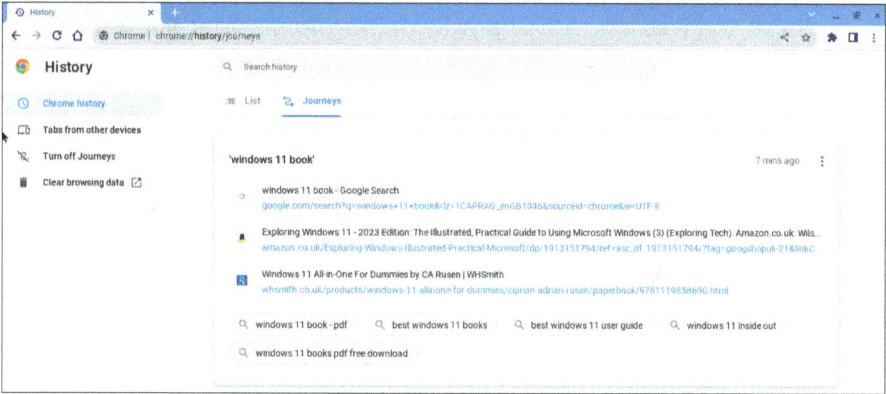

When you search for the exact same search keywords you used earlier, Google Chrome will ask you if you want to resume a previous journey

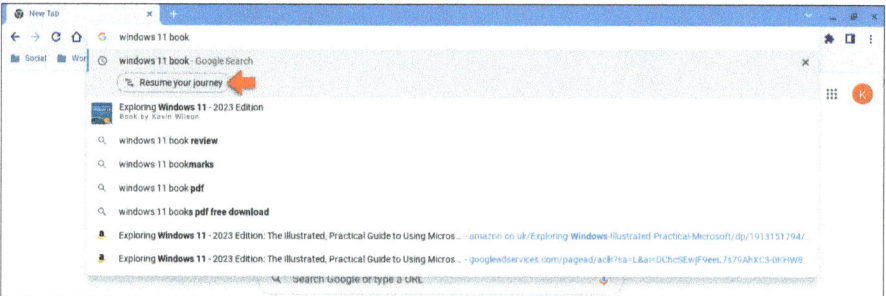

Your journey will open up in the sidebar on the right hand side. From here you can select a site to revisit. You'll also see some relevant search terms underneath.

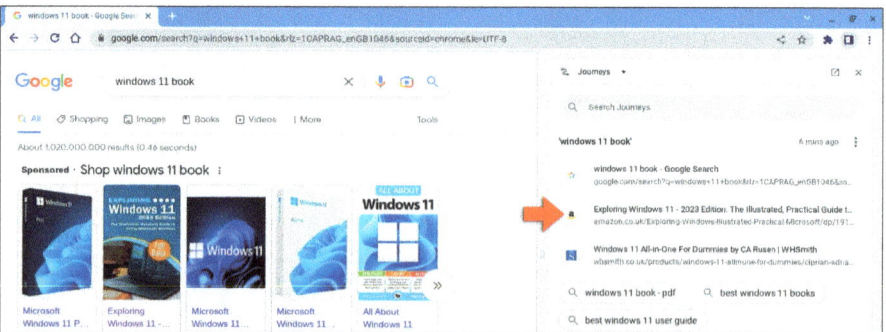

Downloads

If you have downloaded photos, files, or web pages for offline viewing, you'll find them here in the downloads folder. To get to your downloads, click the '3 dots' icon on the top right. From the menu that appears, select 'downloads'.

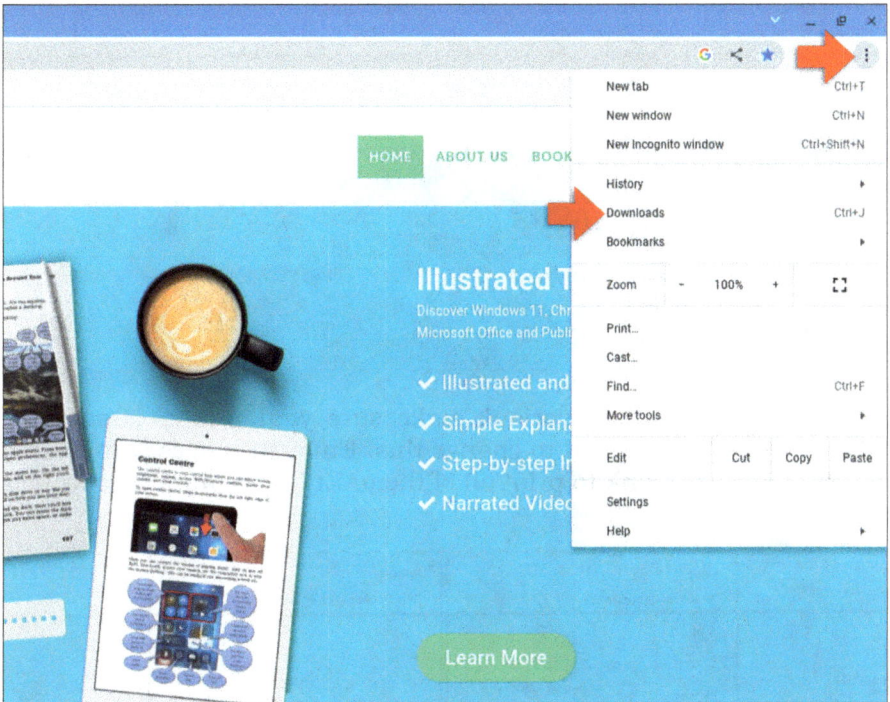

Here you'll see a reverse chronological list of items you've downloaded.

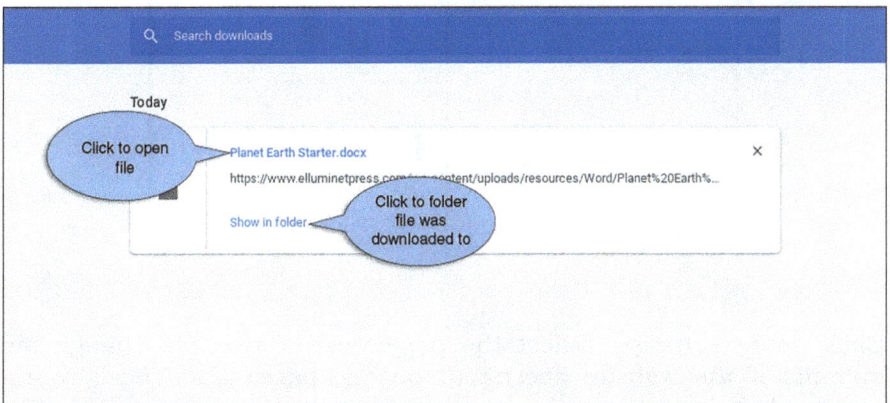

Click on an item in the list to open it up.

Printing a Webpage

To print a webpage in Chrome, click the three dots icon on the top right of your screen, then from the drop down menu, select 'print'.

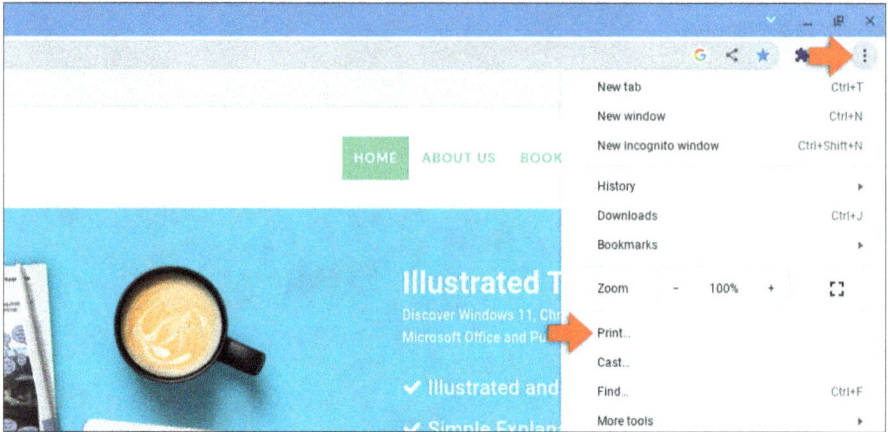

Check the printer 'destination', make sure your printer is selected. Click 'change' if you need to change this. Enter the pages you want to print, or leave it blank to print all of them. Enter the number of copies you want.

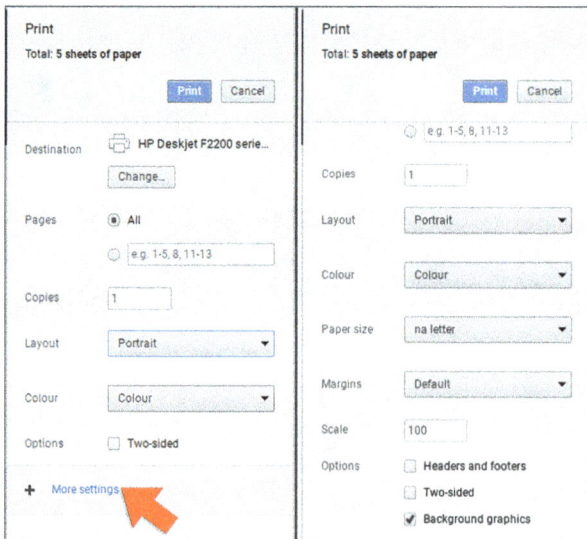

Click 'more settings'. Select the paper size if needed. Change the margins if the website doesn't fit on the page. Click 'background graphics' - this ensures all the graphics will print.

Click 'print' when you're done.

Saving Passwords

When you sign into a website or for the first time, you will receive a prompt asking you whether you want to save your login details.

Sign in - enter your username and password. Once you sign in successfully, Chrome will prompt you to save the password. If this prompt doesn't show up, click the small 'key' icon on the top right of your screen.

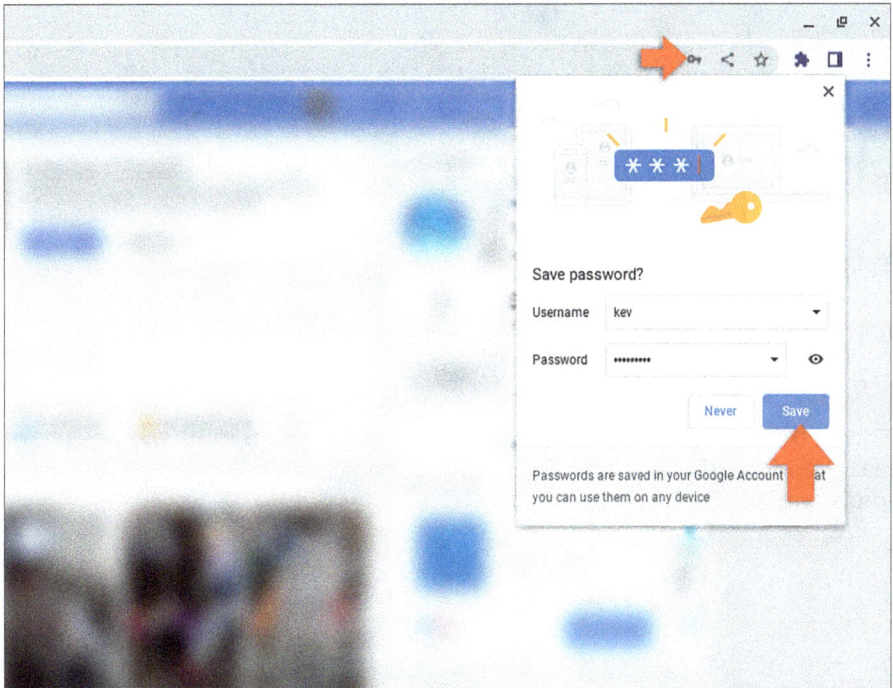

Click 'save'. This will save your password so you don't have to type it in each time.

To sign in the next time, just click in the username or password field.

Select the username from the drop down list, click 'log in' or 'sign in'.

Chapter 5: Web, Email & Communication

Managing Passwords

You can save passwords to your password list from various different websites so you don't have to remember them all. Top open password manager, click the three dots icon on the top right. From the drop down menu, click 'settings'.

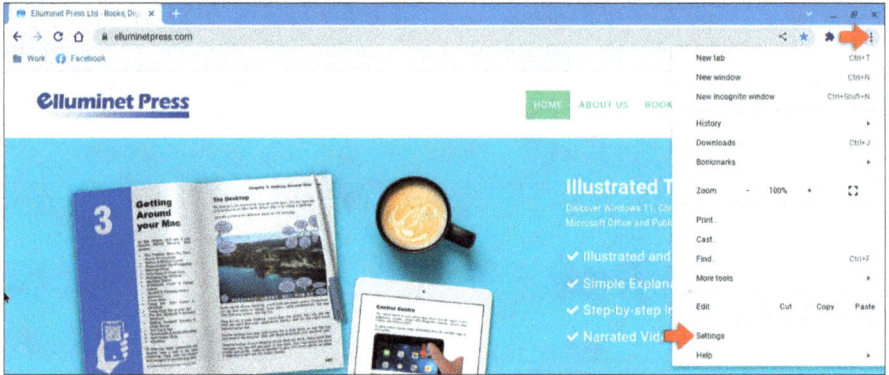

Scroll down to the 'auto fill' section, then click 'passwords'.

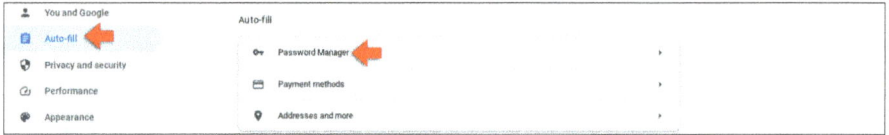

Along the top section you can turn on/off auto sign in or the password save option. If you turn these off, Chrome will no longer save your passwords.

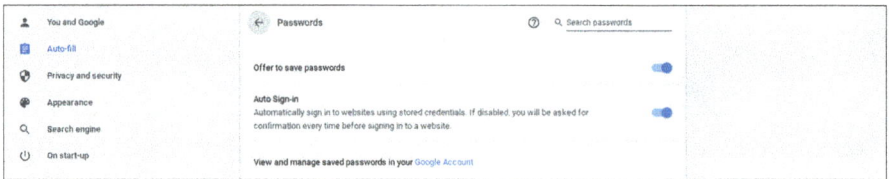

Underneath, you'll see a section called 'saved passwords'. This is the list of all sites you've allowed Chrome to save the password. Click the various icons indicated below to manage your passwords.

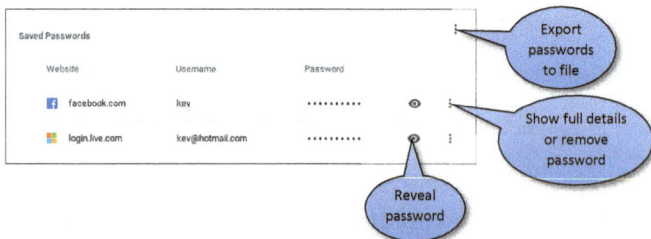

Generate Automatic Strong Passwords

Strong passwords are a must these days. To help you generate good passwords, chrome can automatically generate them for you when you use it to sign up or open an account on any website - whether it's Facebook, Google, Microsoft, yahoo and so on.

To start, go to a website where you where you want to sign up for an account. In this example I'm going to sign up to Facebook.

Fill in the 'create account' form with your details. Click in the password field. You'll see a drop down menu appear.

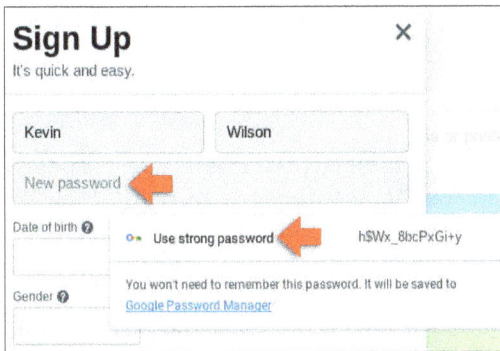

Click 'Use Strong Password'. Chrome will automatically generate a strong password for you. Chrome will also prompt you to save the password. If this doesn't appear, click the key icon on the top right of the address bar. This will allow you to save the username and password you used to sign up with the website. Click 'ok' to save.

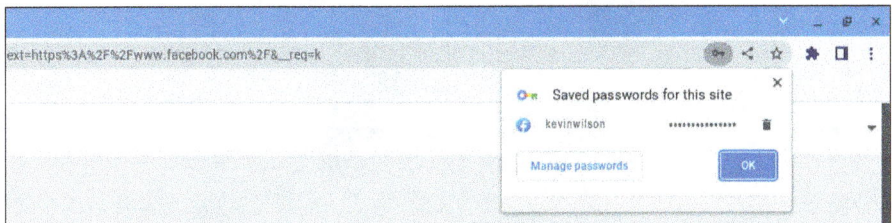

The next time you need to sign into the site, just click in the username or password field, then select the username & password for that site.

Chrome Security

In Chrome, click the three dots icon on the top right, then select 'settings' from the menu.

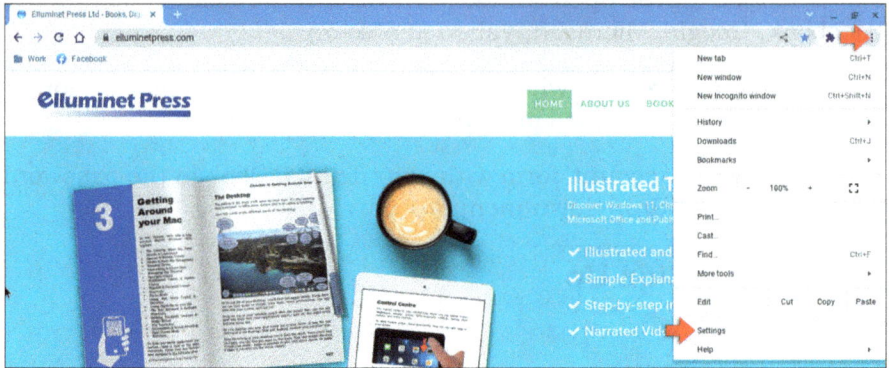

Scroll down to 'privacy & security'. Here, you can clear your browsing data such as the cache, cookies, history and so on. You can run through the 'privacy guide' which takes you through a series of steps allowing you to configure your privacy and security settings according to Google's recommendations. You can adjust 'cookies and other data' for specific websites allowing you to block or allow cookies. Using the 'security' option you can change between standard security or enhanced security. These are presets that configure Chrome's security settings automatically to help block fraudulent sites, and other unsafe content.

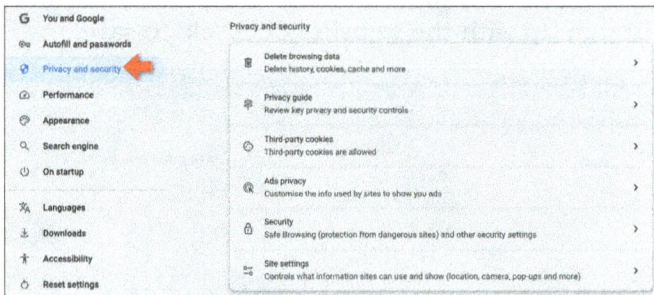

Click 'site settings'. Here you can adjust security permissions for websites. You can allow or deny permission to your location, camera, as well as cookies and other site data.

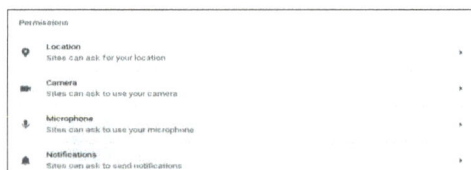

Scroll down the list, select from the list to change the settings. You can view cookies and other site data, enable/disable javascript. Sites usually use javascript to display interactive features so disabling it may cause problems. You can change image behavior to show images or not on particular websites.

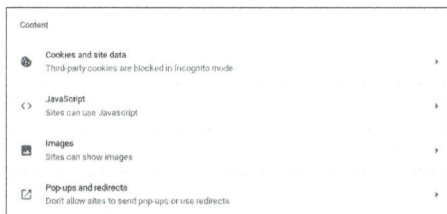

You can also block popups and other redirects what appear on some websites. For example, If you wanted to block irritating ads on websites click 'popup ads and redirects' On the following page, turn the switch on the right to blocked.

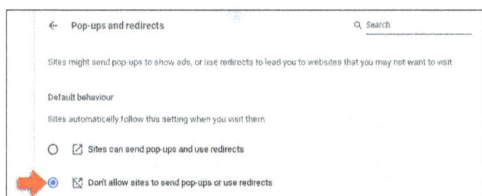

Gmail App

Gmail is Google's email service, and you can access it on your Chromebook in two main ways: through the web app or the Android app. The web app is the recommended version to use on Chromebook and opens in Google Chrome with the full Gmail interface and all standard features. To open Gmail, open app launcher, then select 'Gmail'.

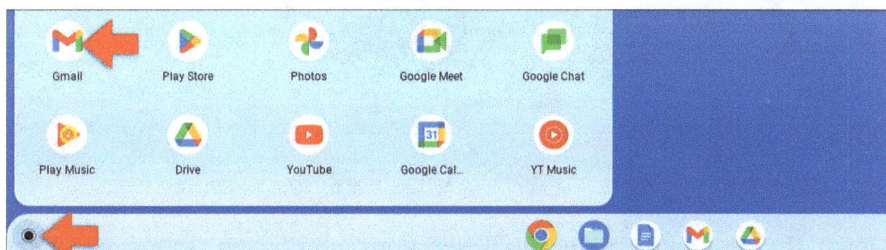

Or, open the Chrome browser and navigate to:

```
mail.google.com
```

Chapter 5: Web, Email & Communication

Once Gmail opens, you'll be able to see the email messages sent to your Google Account email address. On the far left, you'll see the side panel.

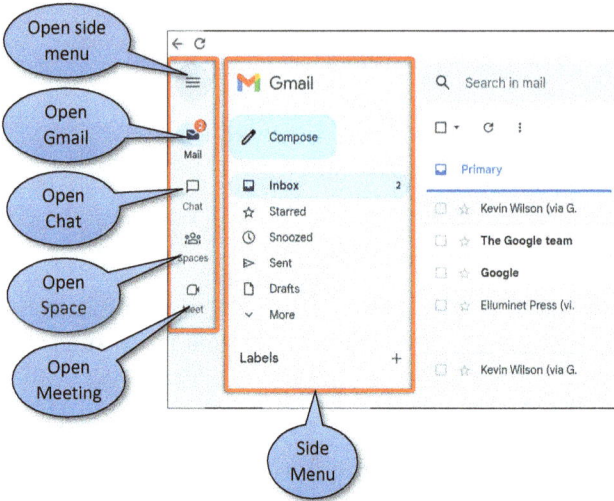

Let's take a look at the rest of the main screen.

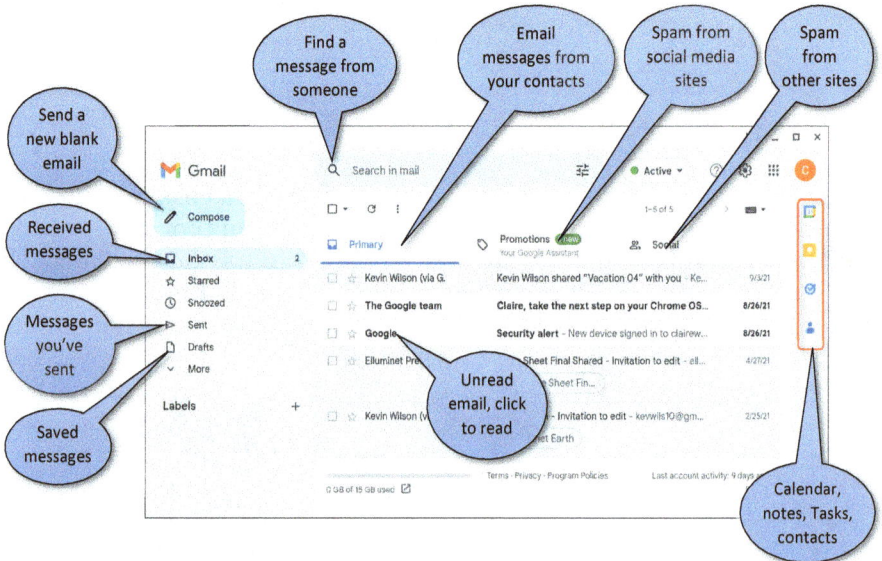

Down the lest hand side you'll see your mailboxes. Inbox is where all your new messages will appear. Starred messages are messages you've marked as important. Snoozed messages are you don't want to be notified about. Spam is what Google detects as spam or junk email.

Reading Mail

When you open Gmail it will check for email, any new messages will appear in your inbox. Click on the message in your inbox.

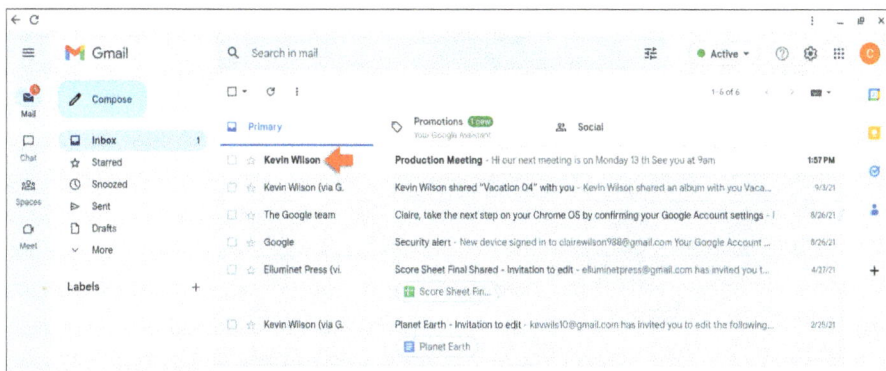

The contents will be displayed in the main window. Along the top of the message, you'll see some icons. Let's take a look:

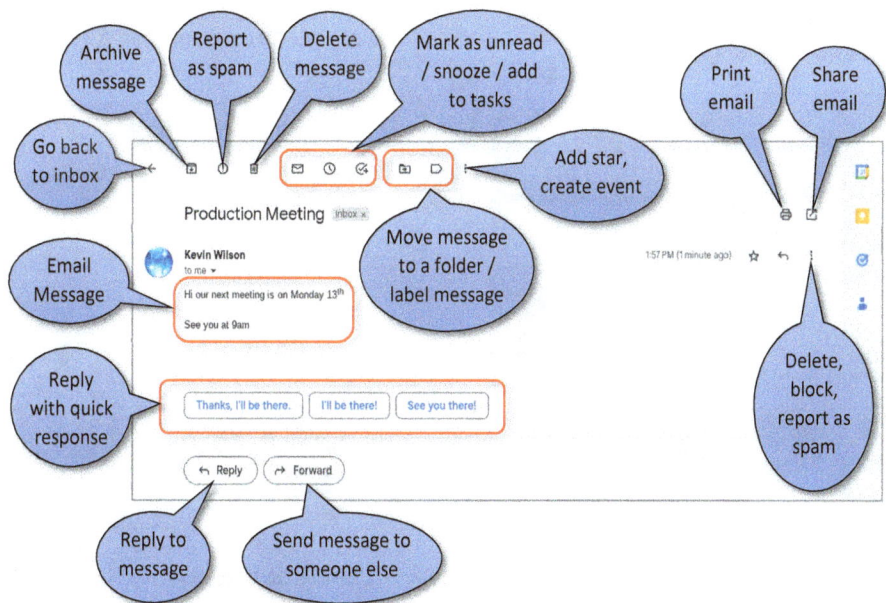

At the bottom of the message, you can use the quick reply to send a standard response to the email message. Google automatically generates these responses according to what your email is about.

To reply to the message, click 'reply' at the bottom. If you want to forward the message to someone else, click 'forward'.

Writing a New Message

To start a new message, click 'compose' on the top left hand side of the main screen.

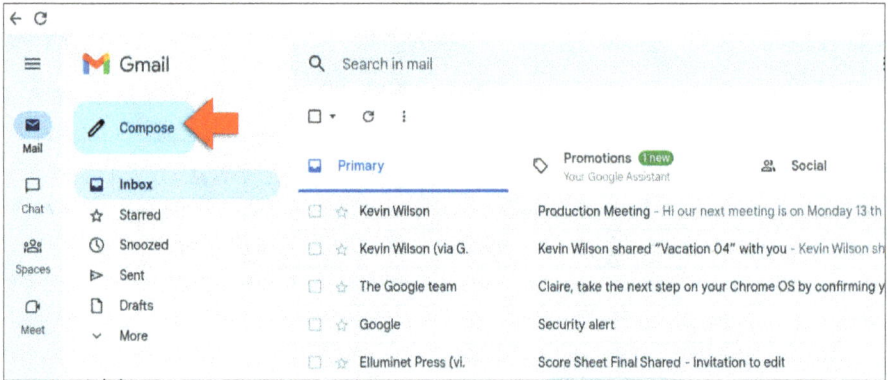

In the message popup window, you will need to enter the person's email address in the 'To' field.

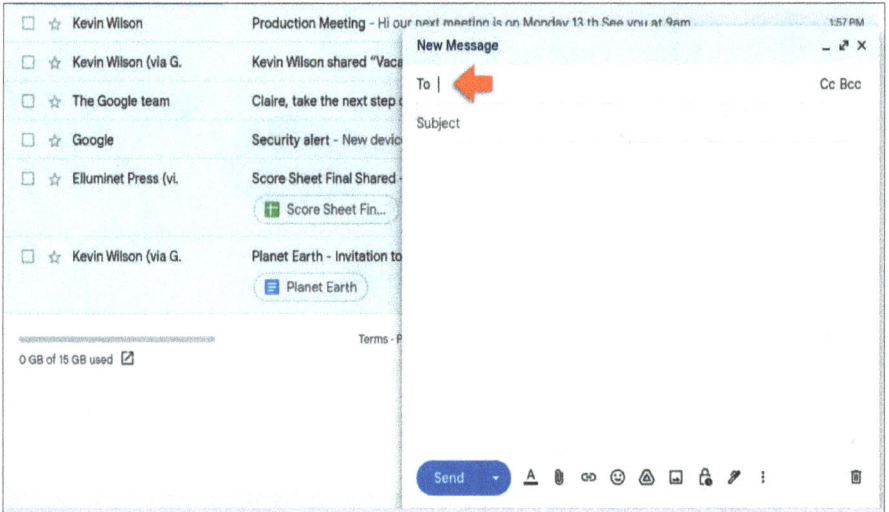

Add a subject, then type your message in the body section.

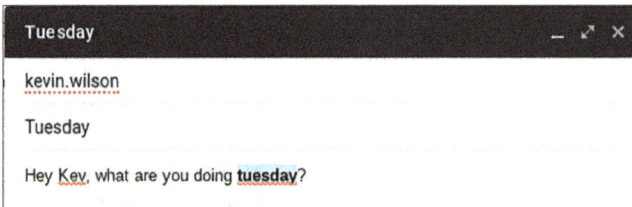

In the body section, you can use the normal text formatting tools such as bold, change the font colour or size and so on, using the format tool bar as you can see below.

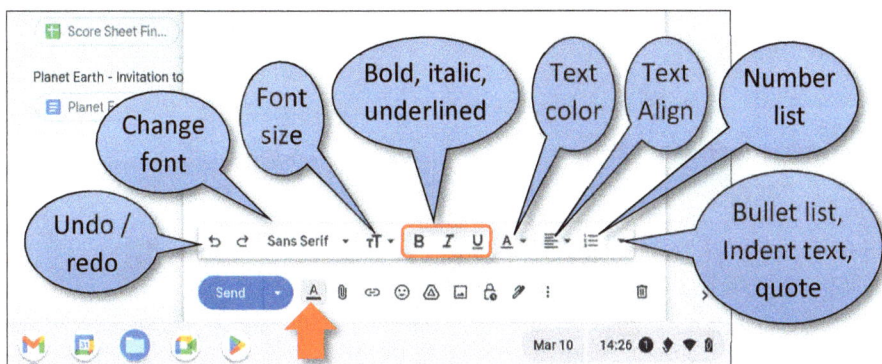

Hit 'send' on bottom left to send your message.

Reply to a Message

First select the message in the inbox to open it up. To reply, you can either use one of the quick reply messages, or to write your own reply, click 'reply' at the bottom of the email.

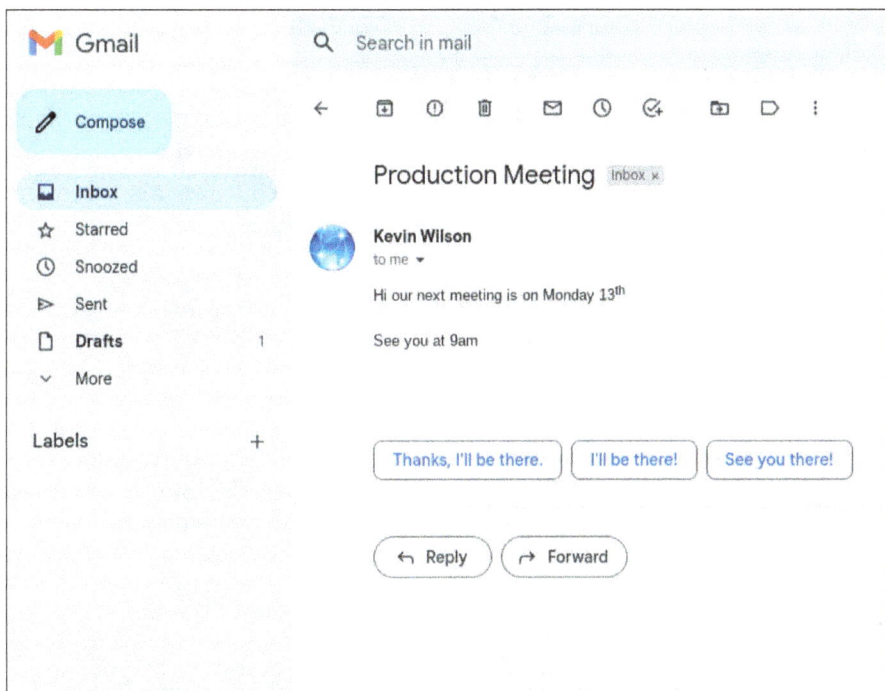

Chapter 5: Web, Email & Communication

You'll see a screen that looks a bit like a word processor. Here you can type in your message. Your message will appear under the message you're replying to, as shown below.

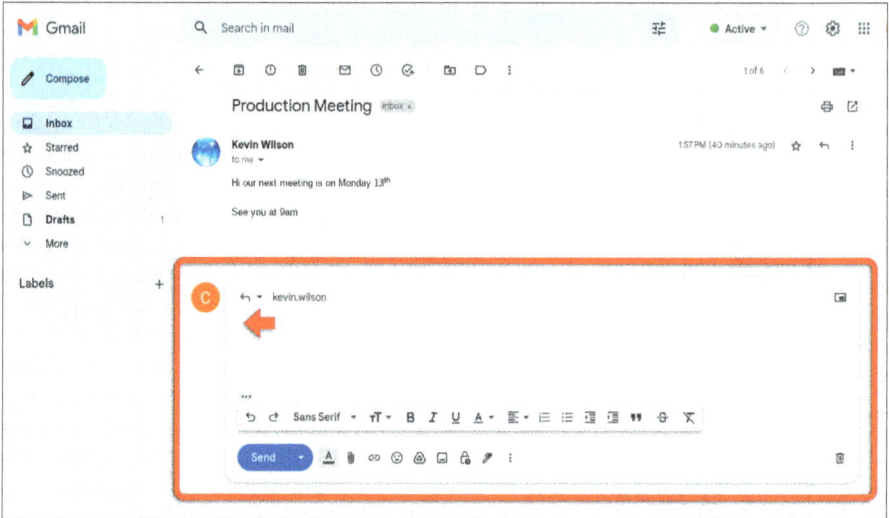

You can use the basic formatting tools.

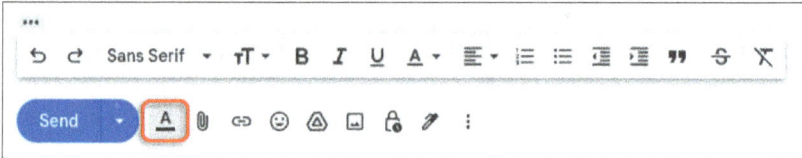

You can make text bold - select the text and click the 'A' icon next to the 'send' button to open the formatting bar. You can also use the formatting bar to change the font size, typeface, text indent, and add bullet or numbered lists.

Click 'send' if you're ready to send the message.

Adding Attachments

To attach a file, click the paperclip icon along the bottom of your message. Use this option to attach files such as documents, videos, music, or multiple photos.

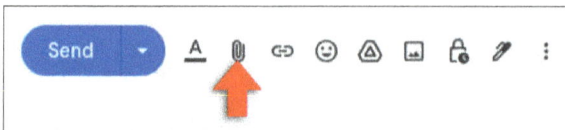

Select your file from the dialog box. Click the tick box on the top left of the images to select multiple files. Click 'open' when you're done.

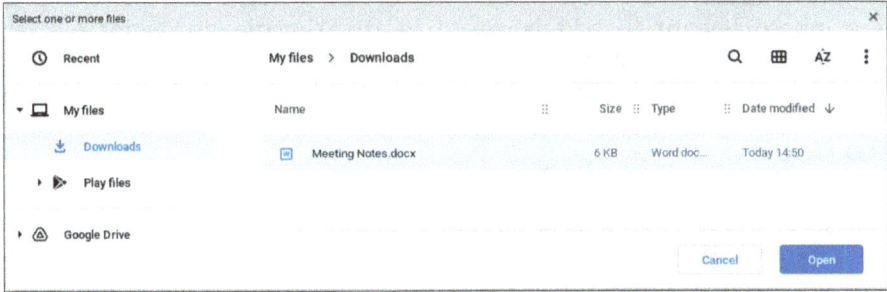

These attachments will be added to the end of the email.

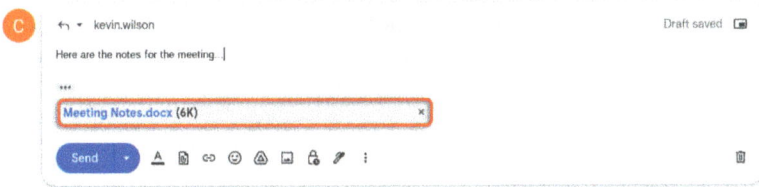

Once you are done, click 'send' on the bottom left.

Inserting Images

Inserting images is a little different from adding an attachment. When you insert an image, you insert it into the body of the email message so it appears inline with the text.

In your email message, click the images icon from the bottom of your message.

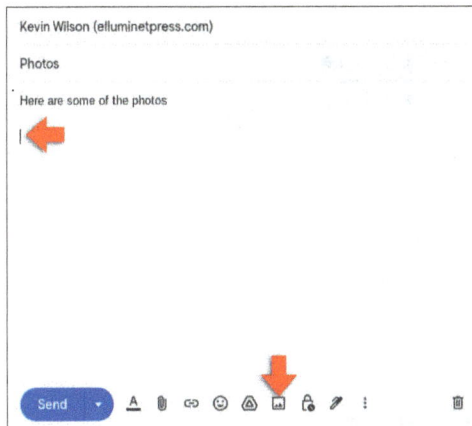

Chapter 5: Web, Email & Communication

Now select where the photo is saved. This could be on your Chromebook itself in which case click 'upload', or it could be saved on Google Photos if you've taken the photo with your phone or chromebook camera. The photo I want to add is saved in the 'downloads' folder on my Chromebook so I'd click 'upload'. Select 'inline' from the two options on the bottom right of the window.

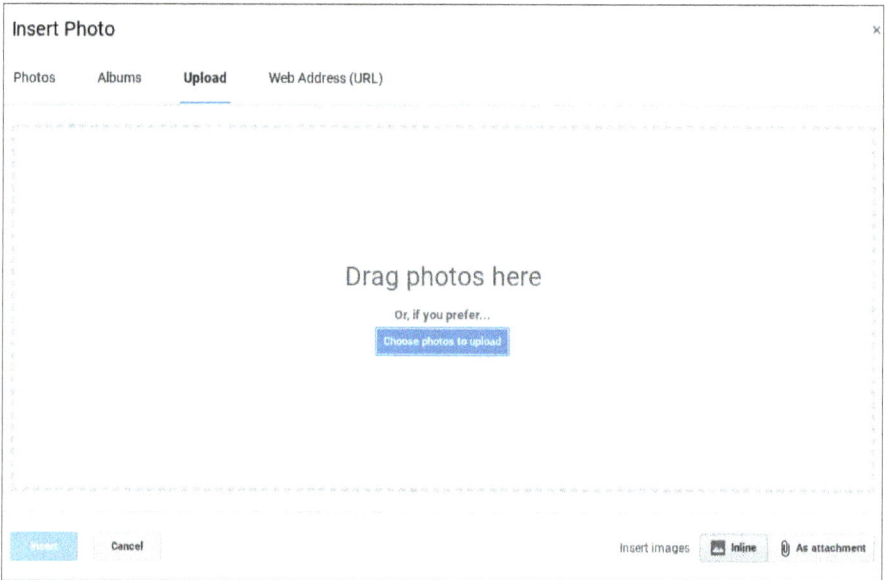

Click 'choose photos to upload'. Select your file from the dialog box. Click the tick box on the top left of the images to select multiple files. Click 'open' when you're done.

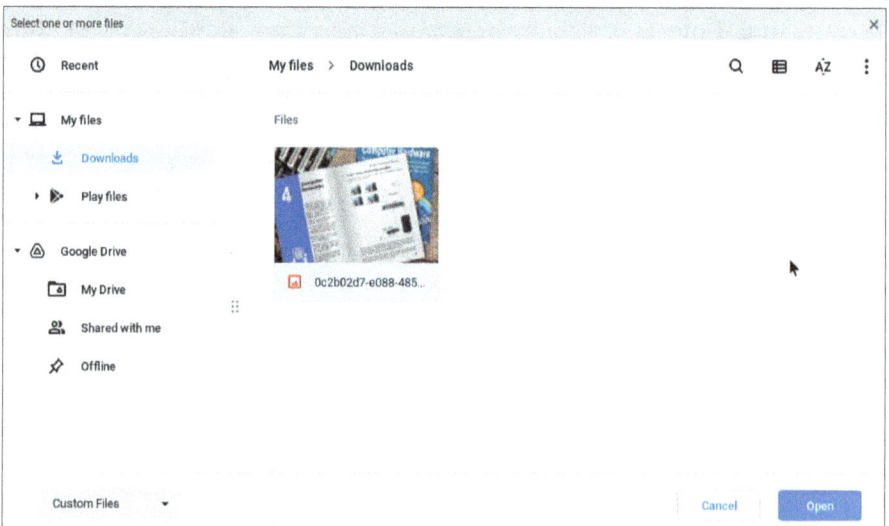

Notice the photo has been inserted within the text body of your email, rather than just attached to the end as an attachment. Click on the picture to resize - drag one of the four corners of the image to resize, or select from 'small', 'best fit', or 'original size'.

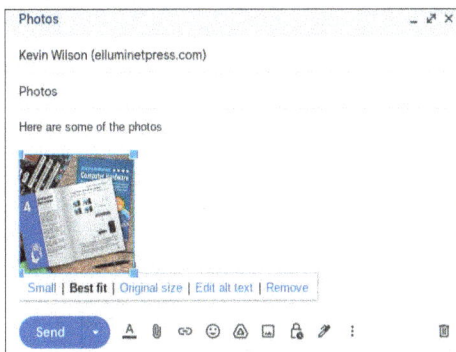

Click the 'send' icon on the top right when you're done.

Sending Money

You can send money to someone using Google Pay. To use this feature, you'll need to have a payment method set up on your Google Account.

To send money, click the $ or £ icon on the bottom of your message.

Enter the amount you want to send and choose a payment method or add a new one.

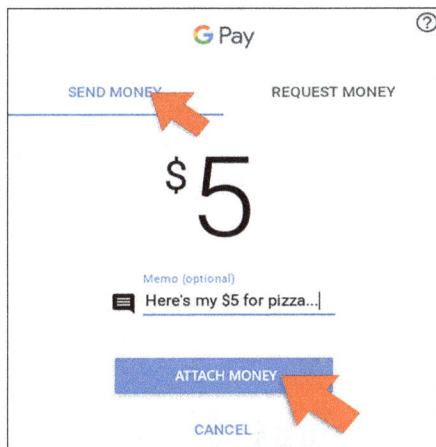

Click 'attach money'.

If you don't have a payment method set up on your Google Account, click 'add debit card' then enter your card details.

X   Add debit card

Card number

|

Cardholder name

Claire Wilson

Billing address

By continuing, you create a Google Payments account and agree to the Google Payments Terms of Service, Privacy Notice and Electronic Communications Policy

CANCEL   SAVE

You'll see the Google Pay attachment at the bottom of your email. Click 'send' on the bottom left to send the message.

Production Meeting   _ ⟋ ×

To: Kevin Wilson

Production Meeting

Here's my $5 for pizza...

Claire.

G Pay
                                        🔒 Claire Wilson
                              Clairewilson977@gmail.com

	Pay to	Amount
	Kevin Wilson	$5.00
	lm21@gmail.com	

Now, when the recipient checks their email, they'll get a message like this in their inbox.

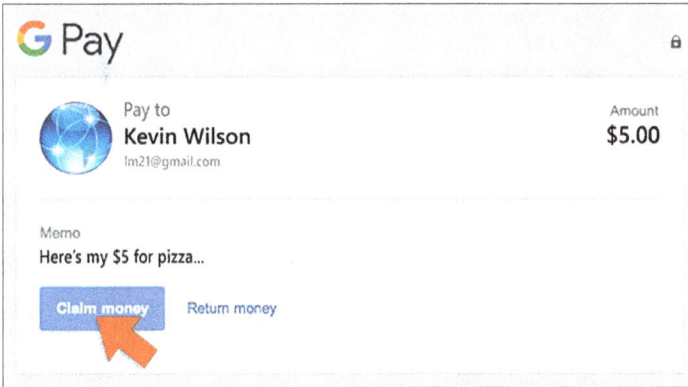

To claim the money, click 'claim money' at the bottom of the message.

Once you've claimed your money, it will be available in your Google Pay Balance. Go to

`pay.google.com`

From here you'll be able to send money to other people, transfer to your bank account, or use it on the Google Play Store.

Confidential Mode

Confidential mode protects sensitive information from unauthorized or accidental sharing. Confidential mode messages don't have options to forward, copy, print, or download messages or attachments. You can also set an expiration date for the message - meaning the message will be deleted after this date. Note that emails are send unencrypted.

To send a message using confidential mode, open a new message as normal. To activate confidential mode, click the lock icon on the toolbar along the bottom.

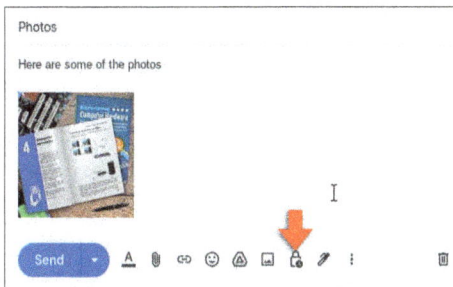

From 'set expiration' select how long you want the message to be available before it's automatically deleted.

Confidential mode

Recipients won't have the option to forward, copy, print, or download this email. Learn more

SET EXPIRATION

Expires in 1 day ▾   Tue, Mar 14, 2023

REQUIRE PASSCODE

All passcodes will be generated by Google. ⑦

◉ No SMS passcode   ○ SMS passcode

Cancel   Save

Under 'require passcode', select 'no SMS passcode' if the recipient uses Gmail. If your recipient uses any other email service, select 'SMS passcode' then enter the recipient's phone number. This will send the recipient a code to their phone that they'll need to unlock the message.

Click 'save'.

Adding Other Email Accounts

In the top right, click the 'settings' icon, then select 'see all settings' from the side panel.

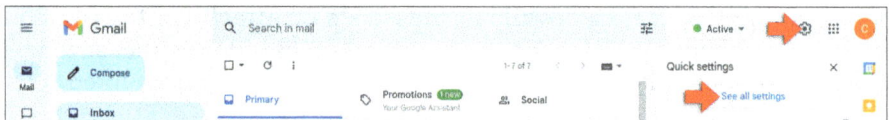

Click 'accounts and import', then select 'add an email account'.

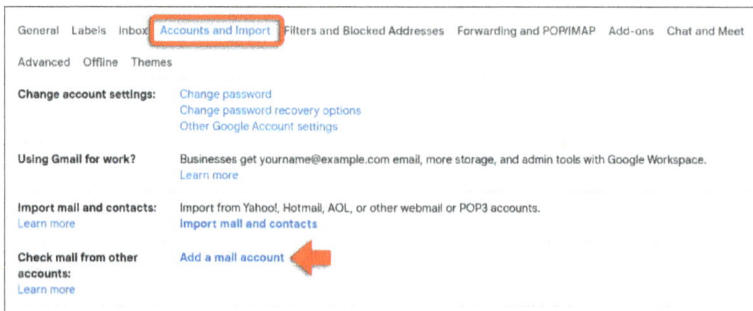

In the dialog box that appears, enter the email address of the account you want to add.

Add an email account

Enter the email address that you would like to add.

Email address: clairewilson98@hotmail.com

Cancel   Next »

Click 'next'.

Select 'link accounts with Gmailify' if available, then click 'next'.

Add an email account

You can either import emails from clairewilson98@hotmail.com to your Gmail inbox, or link the accounts using Gmailify. With Gmailify, you keep both email addresses but can manage emails from both using your Gmail inbox. More about Gmailify

● Link accounts with Gmailify
○ Import emails from my other account (POP3)

Cancel   « Back   Next »

Sign in with the password for the account you're adding.

Chrome - Sign in to your Microsoft account   _ □ ×

🔒 https://login.live.com/oauth20_authorize.srf?response_type=code&client_j...   ⚷

■■ Microsoft

clairewilson98@hotmail.com

Enter password

••••••••

☐ Keep me signed in

Forgotten my password

Sign in

Click 'yes' to grant access to the email account you're adding.

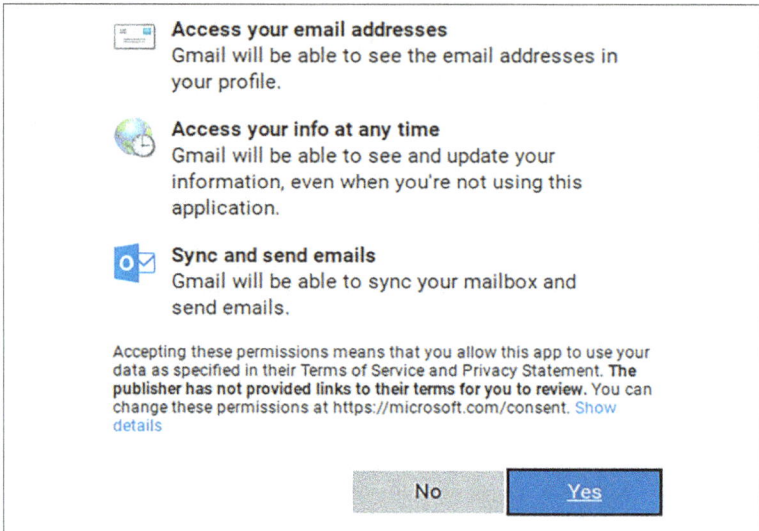

Access your email addresses
Gmail will be able to see the email addresses in your profile.

Access your info at any time
Gmail will be able to see and update your information, even when you're not using this application.

Sync and send emails
Gmail will be able to sync your mailbox and send emails.

Accepting these permissions means that you allow this app to use your data as specified in their Terms of Service and Privacy Statement. **The publisher has not provided links to their terms for you to review.** You can change these permissions at https://microsoft.com/consent. Show details

No   Yes

Click 'close' on the last dialog box, and you're done.

Contacts App

The contacts app is your address book and contains your contact's email addresses, phone numbers and addresses.

Open the Chrome browser, then navigate to the following website

`contacts.google.com`

You'll land on the contacts home page.

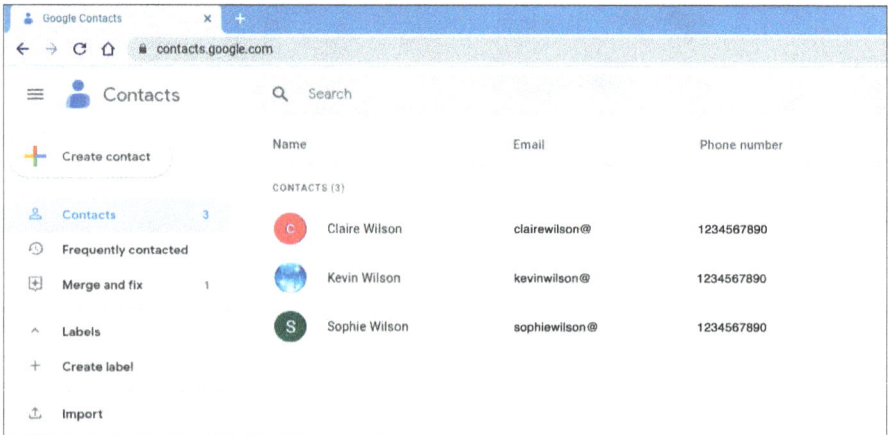

Name	Email	Phone number
Claire Wilson	clairewilson@	1234567890
Kevin Wilson	kevinwilson@	1234567890
Sophie Wilson	sophiewilson@	1234567890

View Contact Details

Once the contacts app opens, you'll see a list of all the people you have contact information for. Click on one of the names to view or edit the details for that person. I'm going to click on my contact 'Sophie' in the list.

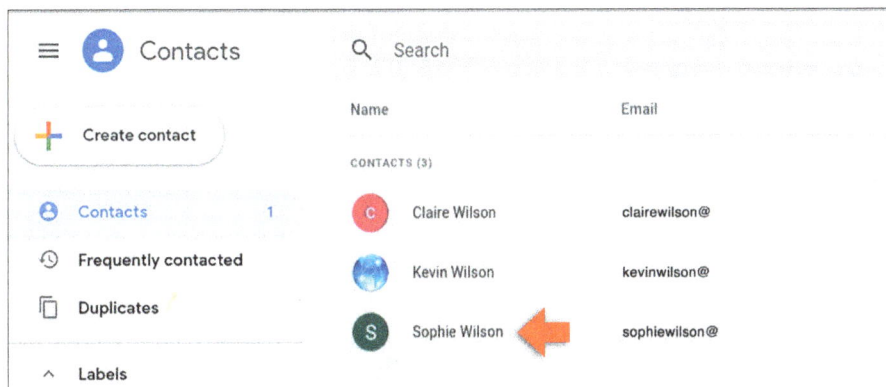

The person's details will open up on your screen. Let's take a look. At the top you'll see the person's name and profile photo if they have one. You can also use the quick icons to send a message to this person, schedule an event involving this person, send this person a message or chat invitation.

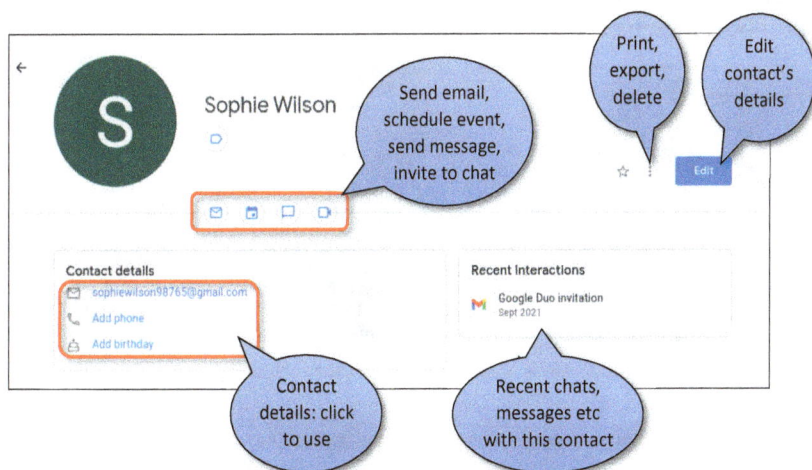

At the bottom you'll see their contact details. Click on the email address to send this person an email, or click on the phone number to contact them. Use the three dots icon on the right to open the drop down options menu. Here you can delete the contact, export, hide, or print the details.

Edit Details

Click on the name of the person in the list whose details you want to change.

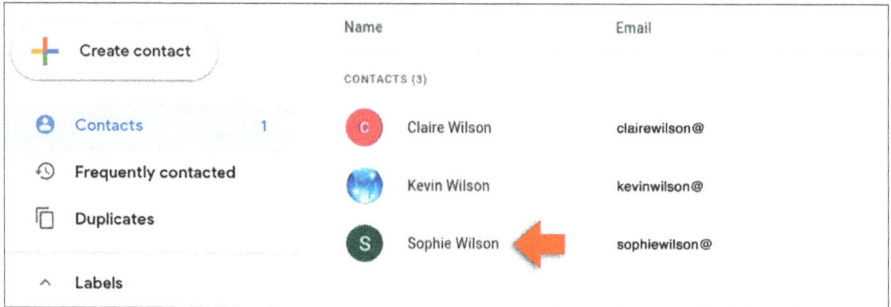

Click the 'edit' on the top right of the contact details box.

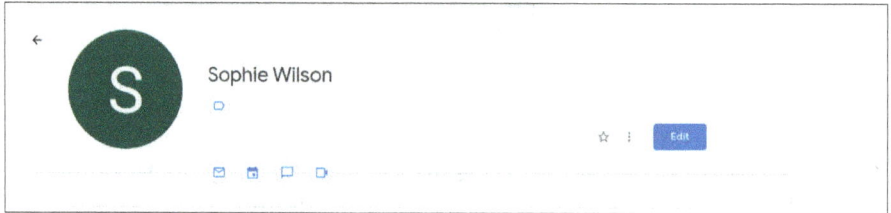

Click on the field you want to change. In this example I'm adding a mobile phone number.

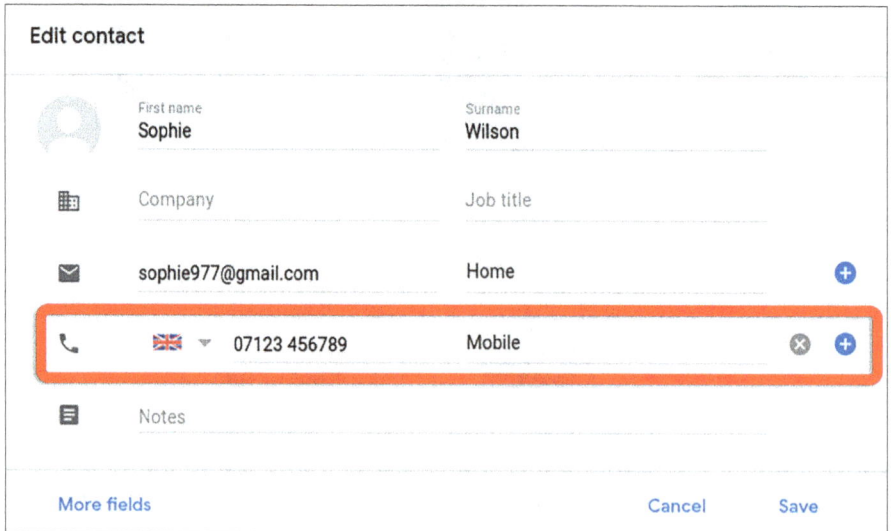

Make any other changes you need to, then click 'save'.

Add New Contact

You can add a new contact from scratch using the contacts app. To do this, click 'create contact' on the top left of your screen. Select 'create a contact' from the popup.

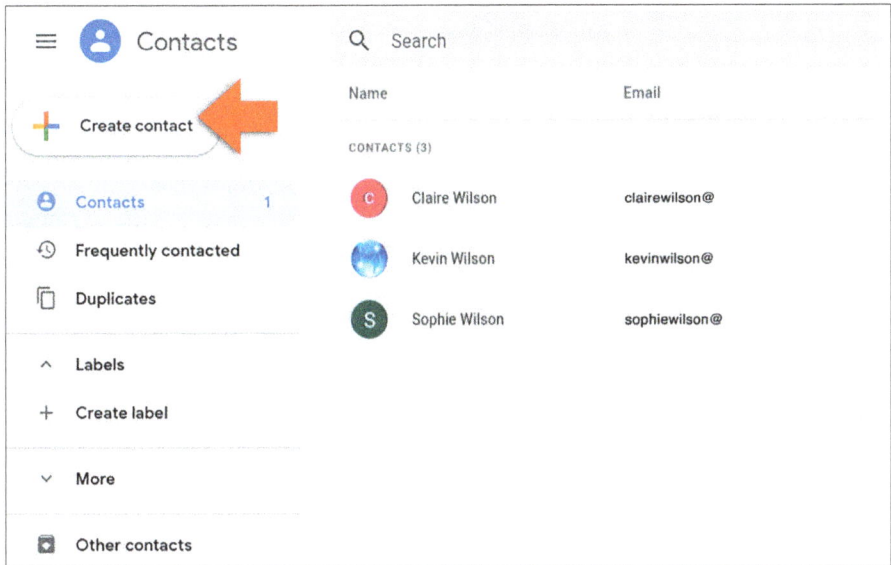

Enter the details into the appropriate fields, as shown below.

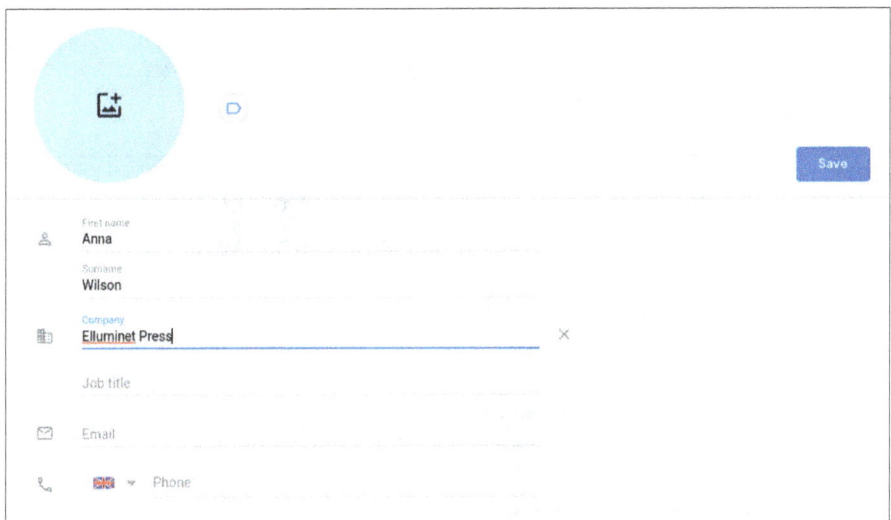

Click on the image on the top left to add a profile picture.

Click 'save' when you're done.

Add Contact from Message

To add a new contact from the Gmail App, first open the email message.

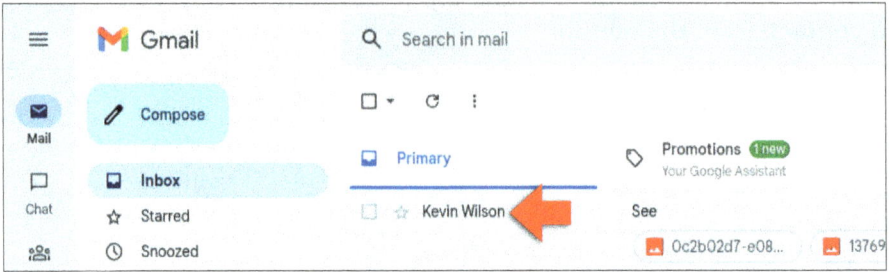

Click on the contacts icon on the far right of your email message, then select 'add ... to contacts list'.

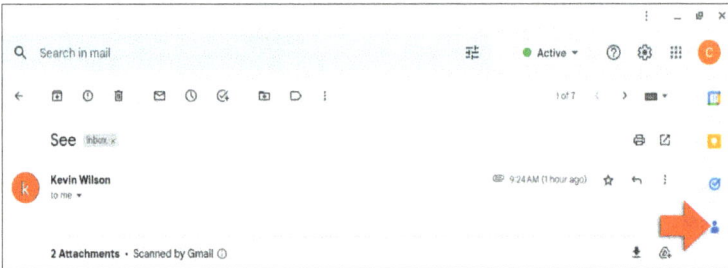

Select the email address from the list

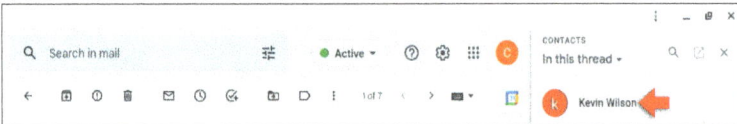

Click the 'add to contacts' icon on the top right of the card.

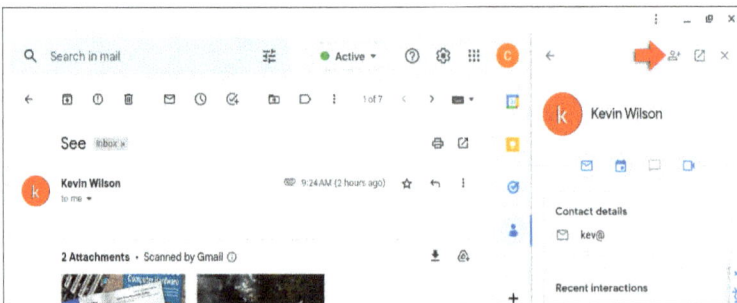

The email address and the person's name will be added to your contacts. Click on the contact's name in your contacts app to edit any details.

Calendar App

The calendar app allows you to keep track of events and appointments. You can add reminders, create appointments and events, so you never miss anything. To open the app click on the google calendar icon on the app launcher.

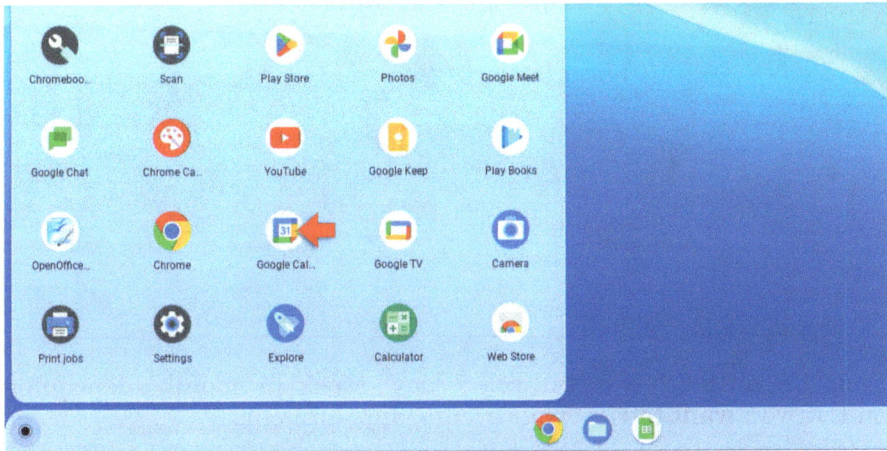

Or open the Chrome browser and navigate to the following website

calendar.google.com

Calendar View

You can change the calendar view to show appointments and events by month, week or day - as shown below.

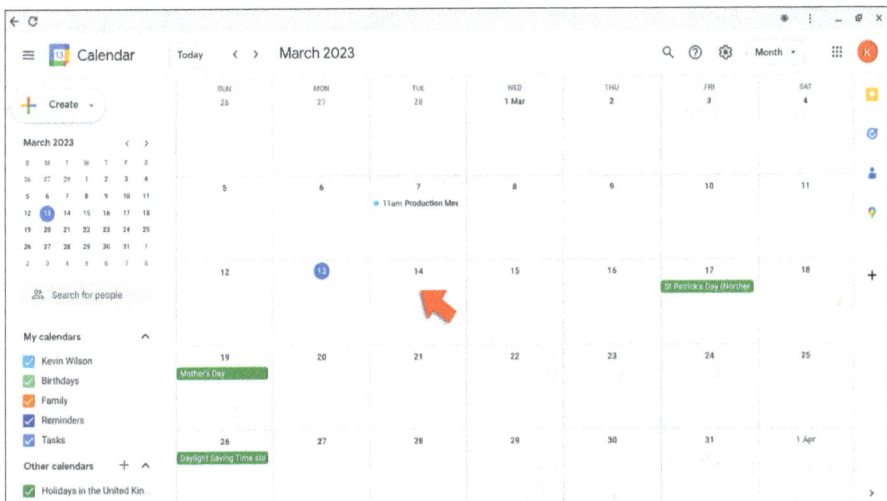

Chapter 5: Web, Email & Communication

To do this, click the icon on the top right of the screen.

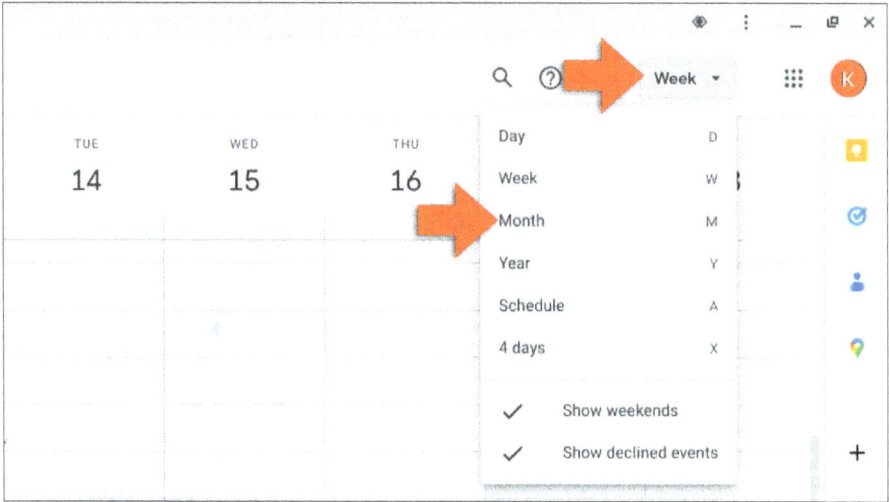

From the drop down menu, select 'day', 'week' or 'month', depending on how you want to view your events/appointments.

Add Event

To add a new event, reminder or appointment, in month view, click on the day the appointment falls on.

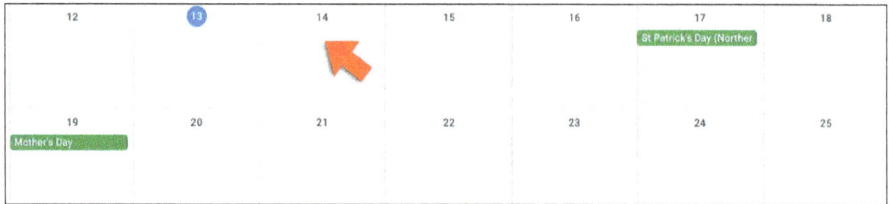

In the popup box, start typing in the name of the event or appointment in the field at the top. Eg "production meeting", "coffee with claire", and so on. Select 'event', then click 'more options'.

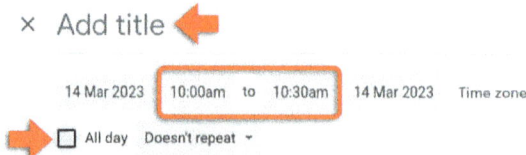

Remove the tick from 'all day' and enter the start and finish times of the event. Eg 10am to 10:30am

If this event repeats, for example, a weekly meeting, click where it says 'doesn't repeat'. From the drop down, select how often the event repeats. This event occurs every week, so I'm going to select 'weekly'.

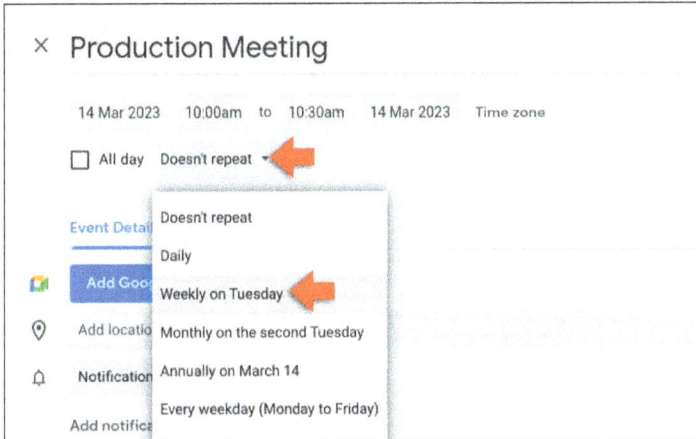

Now select where the event/appointment will be held. If it's a virtual meeting, click 'add google meet video conferencing'. This will send all your participants an invitation.

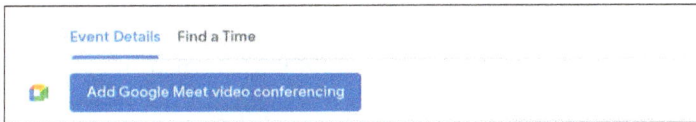

If it's not a virtual meeting, type in the location.

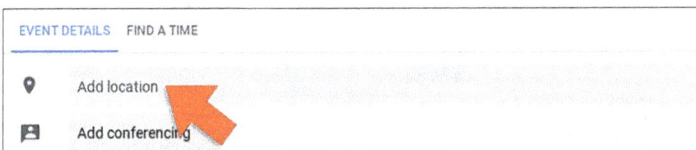

Google will search for places you've been, go to frequently, or places nearby. Click on one of these. So if we were meeting at the Valley Centre, I'd click on 'valley centre' in the list.

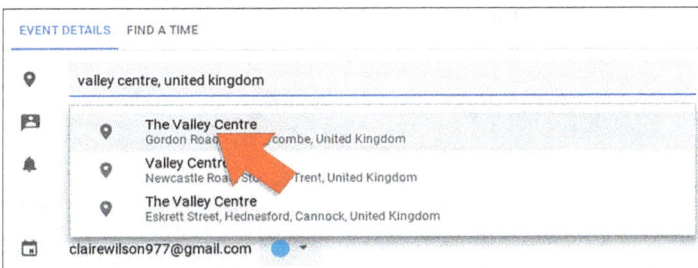

You'll see a summary of the appointment. Here you can amend any details, set a reminder - where it says 'notification', change the times - select how far in advance you want to be reminded. In this example, I've set it to remind me a day before. You can also set it to 30 mins before, an hour before, and so on.

Now we need to say who we are meeting. Over on the right, click where it says 'add guests' on the right hand side.

Start typing in the names of the people you want to send an invite to. You'll see a list of your contacts - select their name.

Underneath where it says 'guests can', remove the ticks from the permissions to prevent your guests from making changes to the event invitation. You can allow them to 'see the guest list' so they can see who is attending.

At the bottom left, where it says 'add description'. Add a message, and any attachments, or documents needed for the event. These could be minutes, meeting notes, programmes, and so on.

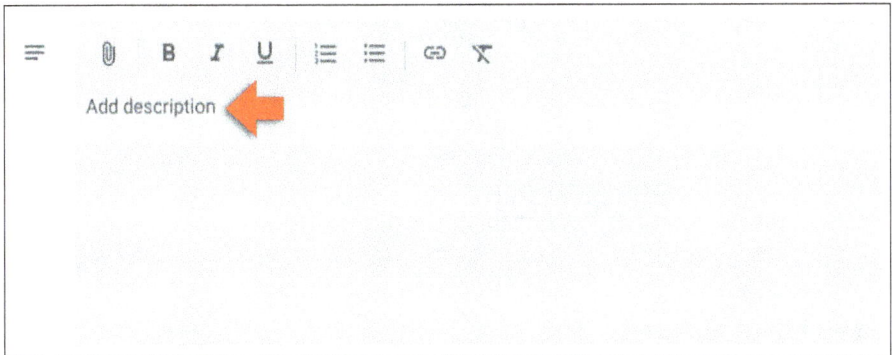

To add an attachment, click the paper-clip icon, then select a file to attach.

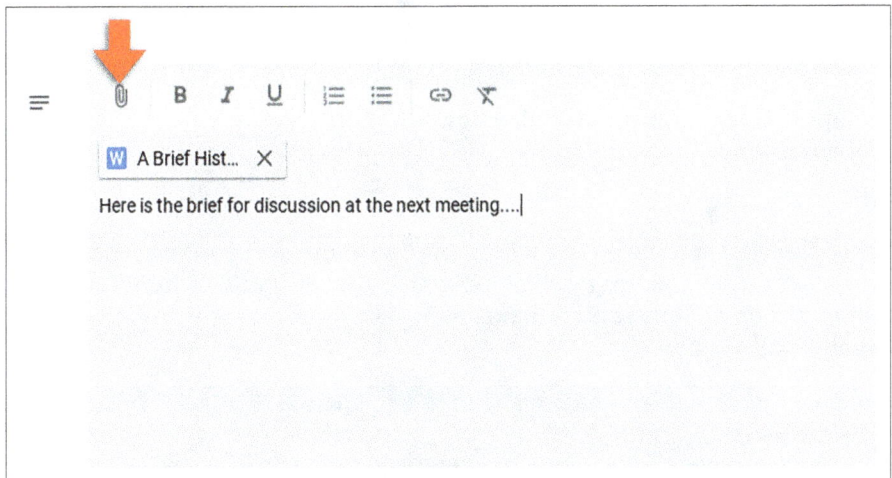

Click the blue 'save' button on the top right when you're done.

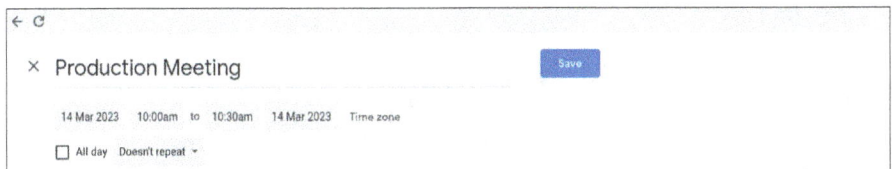

Click 'send' to send the invitations to your attendees if you added any guests.

Click 'invite' to allow your attendees to access any files you attached.

Google Meet

Google Meet is a video-communication service where you can host meetings, share your desktop, and presentations with friends, colleagues, large groups, and customers.

The free version of Google Meet allows 1 to 1 meetings up to 24 hours, and group meetings with three or more participants for up to 1 hour at a time. You can purchase Google Workspace Individual or Google Workspace Enterprise depending on your needs. Go to the following website for more up to date information.

`apps.google.com/meet/pricing`

Starting Google Meet

You can open the Google Meet app on your app launcher. *If you don't see it, go to the Google Play store and download it.*

Or open Google Chrome Web Browser then navigate to the following website:

`meet.google.com`

Once the app loads up, you'll land on the home screen. From here, you can start a new meeting - click 'new meeting' or you can join a meeting using a code or link someone has sent you - just paste it into the 'enter a code or link' box.

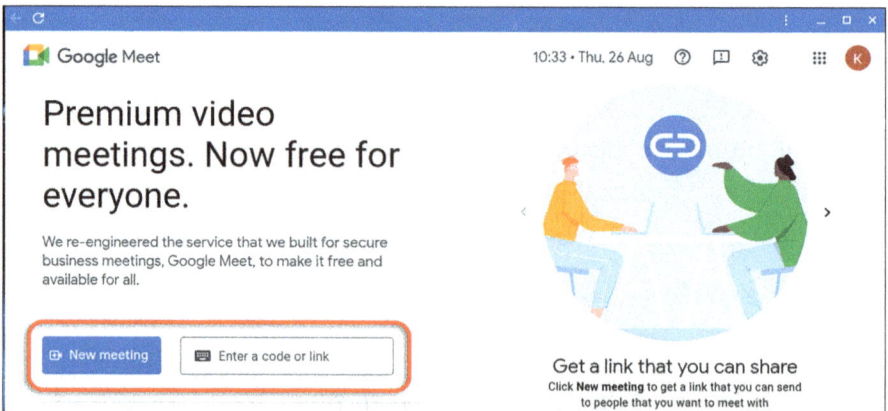

From the settings icon on the top right, you can setup your camera, speakers, and microphone.

Create Meeting for Later

Create a meeting for later sets up a meeting and generates a link you can send to other people. No meeting is actually scheduled.

To create a meeting for later, click 'new meeting', then select 'create meeting for later' from the drop down menu.

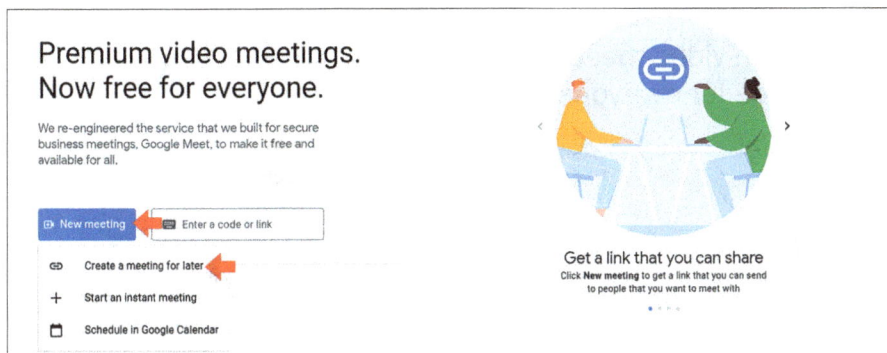

A popup box with a link will appear. Click the clipboard icon on the right to copy the link.

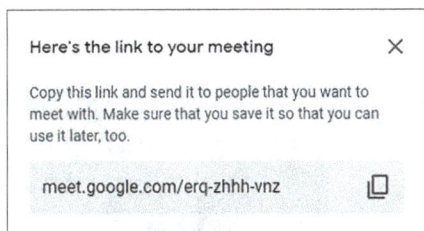

Now you can paste the link into an email or text message.

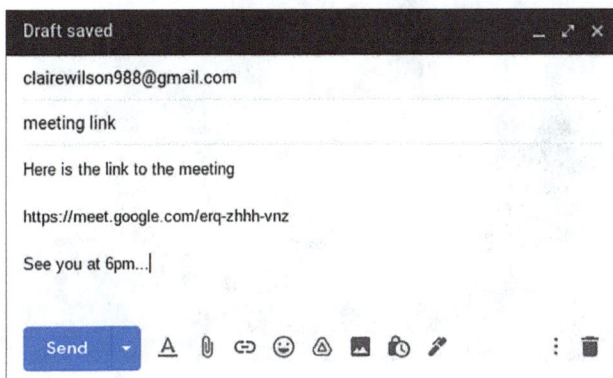

Make sure you keep a copy of that link so you can join the meeting too. A good way to do this is send yourself a copy of the email.

Start Instant Meeting

Start an instant meeting sets up a meeting room for you and opens it up. It then generates a link you can use to invite other people.

To start an instant meeting, click 'new meeting', then select 'start an instant meeting' from the drop down menu.

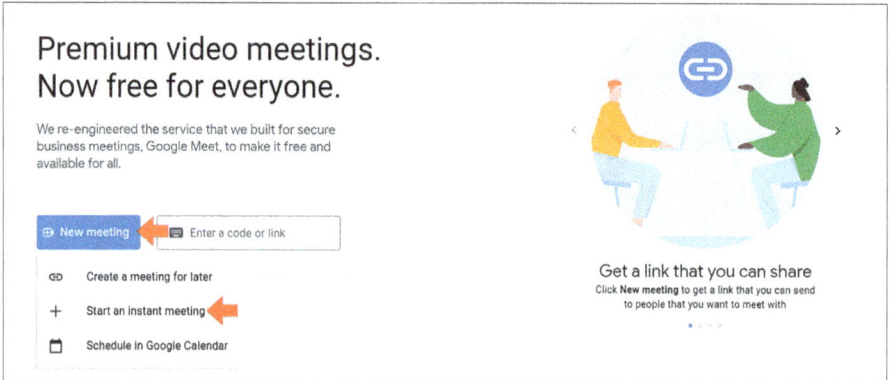

Your meeting will open up in the in call chat window. Allow access to your cam and mic if prompted. On the top right of the screen, you'll see and invite box.

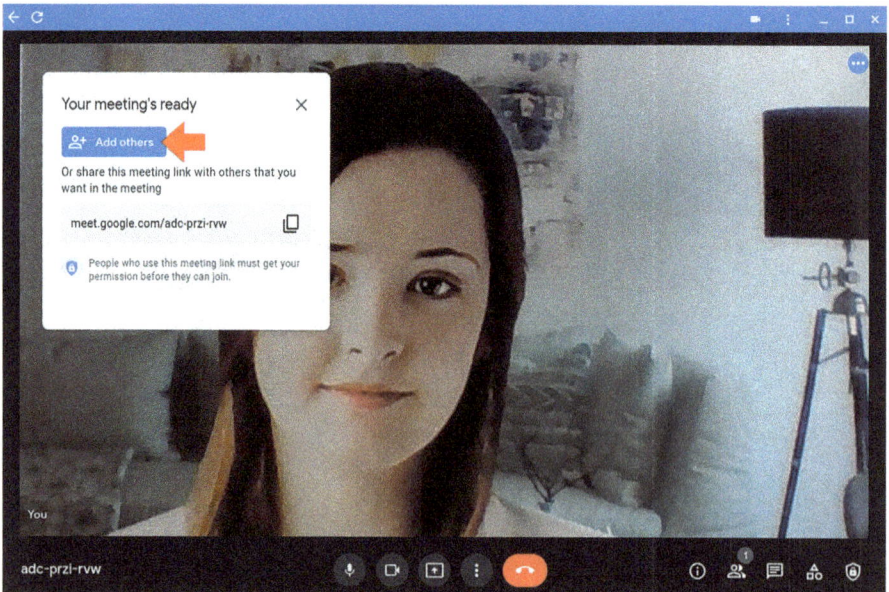

Click 'add others' to invite someone to the meeting you just created. You can also copy the link at the bottom of the invite box and send it to the person you want to invite.

Add the email addresses in the field at the top. If you want to type more than one email address, separate them with a comma. Then click 'send' when you're done.

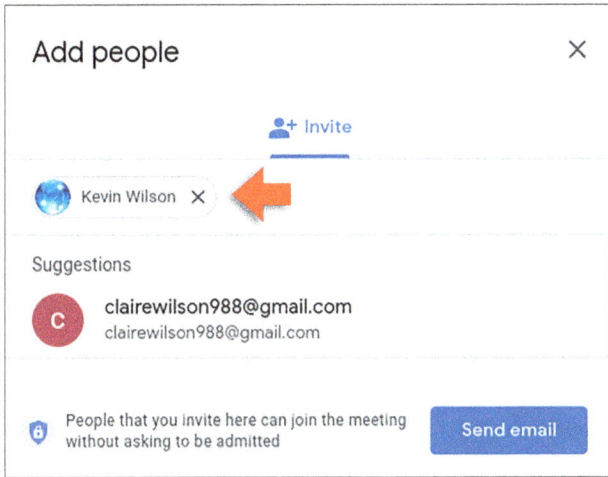

The other person will receive an email with a link.

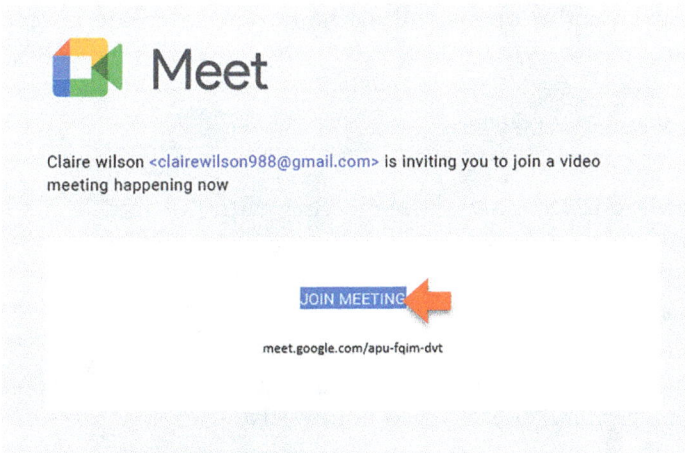

Once they click the link, you'll get a notification allowing you to admit the person to your meeting.

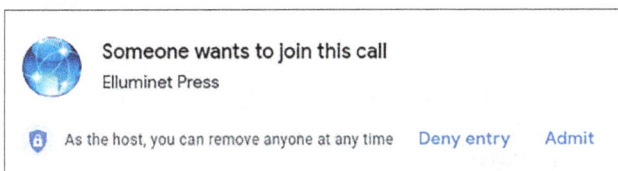

Click 'admit' to let them in.

219

Chapter 5: Web, Email & Communication

Schedule Meeting in Calendar

Schedule a meeting allows you to open up your calendar app and schedule a meeting at a later date. Google Meet also generates an email with a link you can use to invite people to the meeting.

To schedule a meeting, click 'new meeting', then select 'schedule in Google calendar' from the drop down menu.

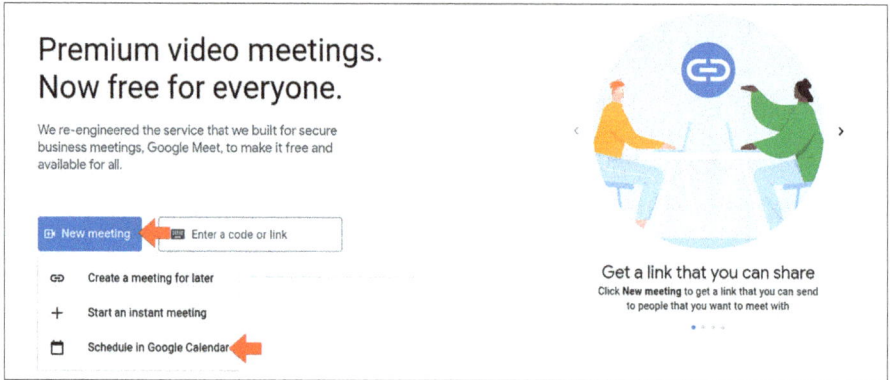

When your calendar opens, fill in the details to create an event. Add the meeting name at the top.

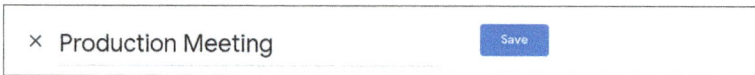

Underneath, add the date of the meeting, with the start and end times.

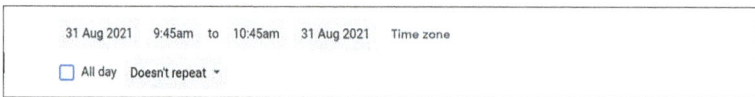

Under 'event details' add a location if required. This could be a street address, or venue if the meeting is held elsewhere.

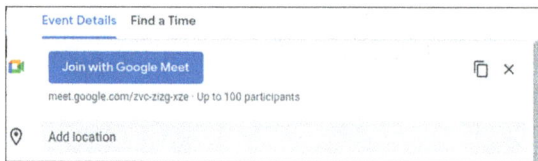

Click 'add notification' to add a reminder notification, if you want to be reminded of the event. Select how long before the event you want the notification to appear.

Select which calendar to add it to if you have more than one, then select a highlight colour. This is the colour the event is marked as on your calendar. Next, select if you want your calendar to show you as busy or free during the event, and the visibility (public or private). Add a message to include in the invite to your participants.

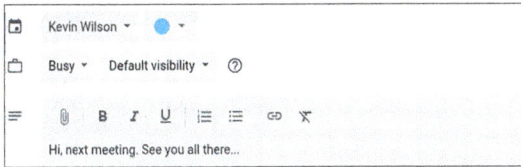

To invite participants to the meeting, click 'add guests' on the right hand side of the screen.

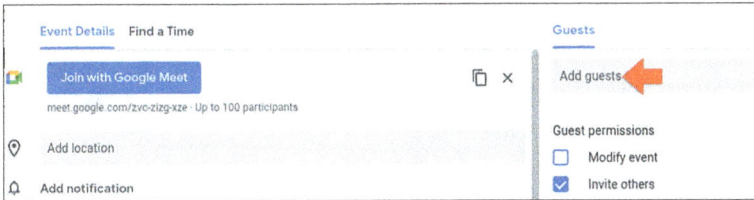

Enter the names or email addresses of the people that you want to invite - these are your participants. Click 'save' when you're done.

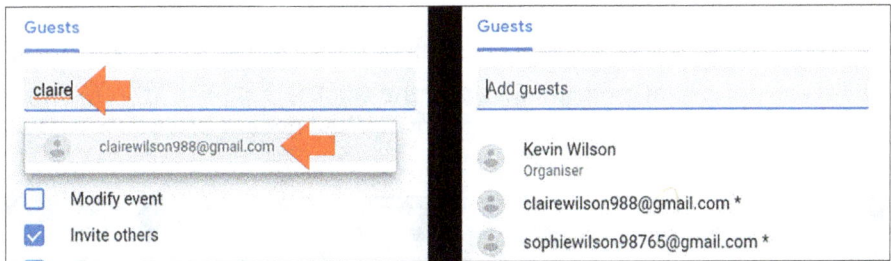

Click 'save' on the top right of the screen.

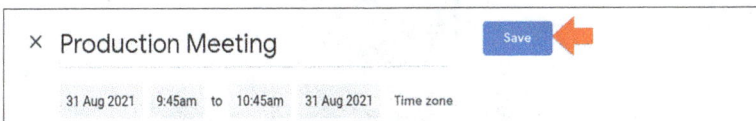

Then click 'send' to email the notification to your participants.

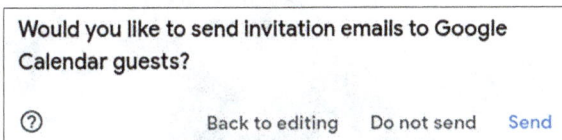

Joining a Meeting

If someone has sent you a meeting link in an email, click the link to join the meeting.

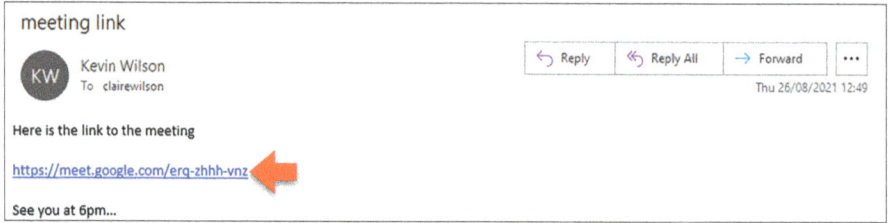

meeting link			
KW **Kevin Wilson** To clairewilson	↩ Reply ↩ Reply All → Forward •••		Thu 26/08/2021 12:49

Here is the link to the meeting

https://meet.google.com/erq-zhhh-vnz ⬅

See you at 6pm...

If someone has sent you a code such as `erq-zhhh-vns`, open Google Meet, then type or paste the code into the 'enter a code or link' box, click 'join'.

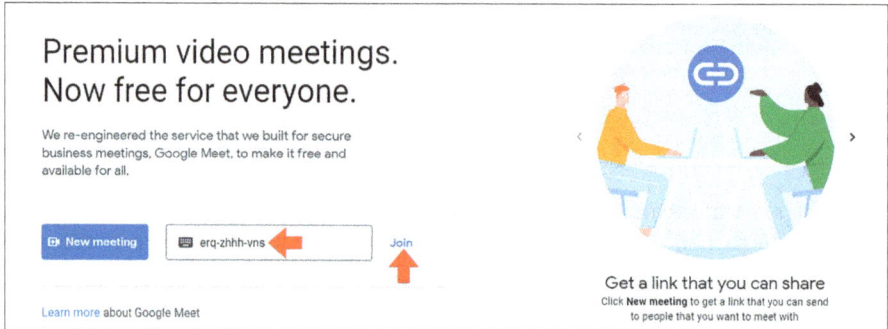

Premium video meetings.
Now free for everyone.

We re-engineered the service that we built for secure business meetings, Google Meet, to make it free and available for all.

[➕ New meeting]   [🖮 erq-zhhh-vns ⬅]   Join ⬆

Learn more about Google Meet

Get a link that you can share
Click **New meeting** to get a link that you can send to people that you want to meet with

Click 'ask to join' if prompted. Once the host lets you in, the meeting will open up in the in call chat window. Allow access to your cam and mic if prompted.

Claire Wilson

erq-zhhh-vns

In Call Options

When you're in a call, you'll see the other participants tiled along the top of your screen. At the bottom, you'll see your own camera. In the screenshot below, you can see our friend Nadia chatting to Sophie and Claire. Let's take a look around the window.

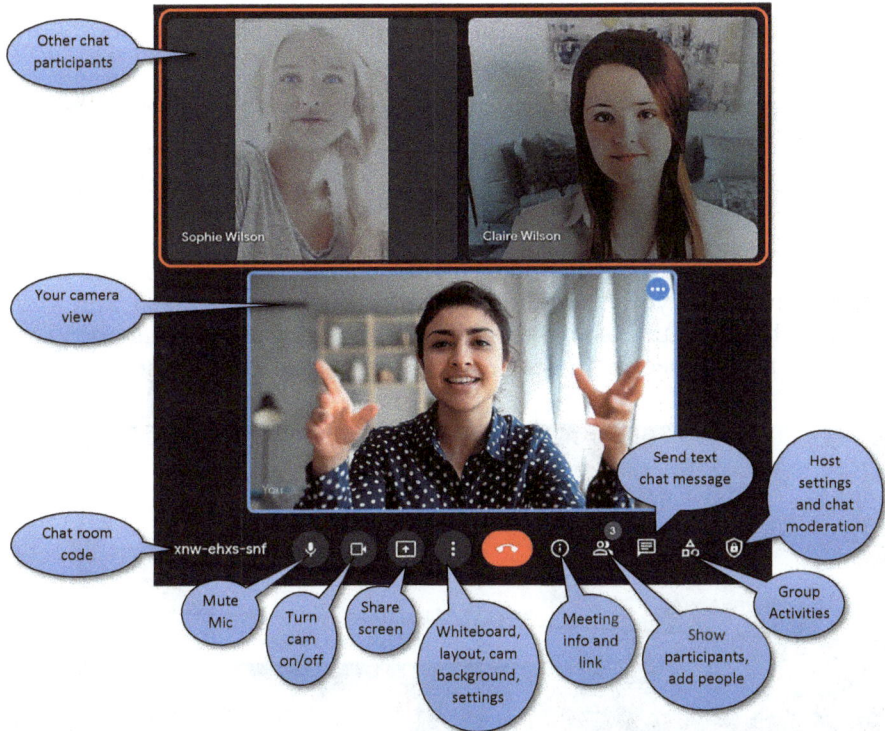

Along the bottom of the window, you'll see some tools and options. Here, you can mute your mic and turn off your camera.

The third icon from the left allows you to share your screen, a window, or a browser tab. With the next icon, the three dots, you can open whiteboard, change your cam background or the screen layout.

The large red icon in the middle hangs up your call - click this when you're finished your meeting.

The next icon shows you meeting info, here you'll find the meeting link you can use to invite others to your meeting. With the show participants icon, you can view a list of all the people participating in your meeting. You can also mute all, add people, search for people, and turn on/off host controls (allow people to share their screen or send messages).

Host settings allows you to allow/disallow any of your participants to share their own screens or send chat messages. You'll only see these options if you are hosting the meeting.

Chapter 5: Web, Email & Communication

Present & Share Desktop

You can share your whole screen with your participants, or you can share an app (in a window), or a browser tab. This is useful if you want to show your participants something such as a presentation, a website, or a video.

To share your desktop, select the 'present' icon from the toolbar along the bottom of the 'in call' screen.

Select 'a window' from the popup menu. You can also share your entire screen, however your participants will see every app open and your desktop background, so make sure you haven't got anything open that you don't want people to see. You can also share a browser tab from Chrome.

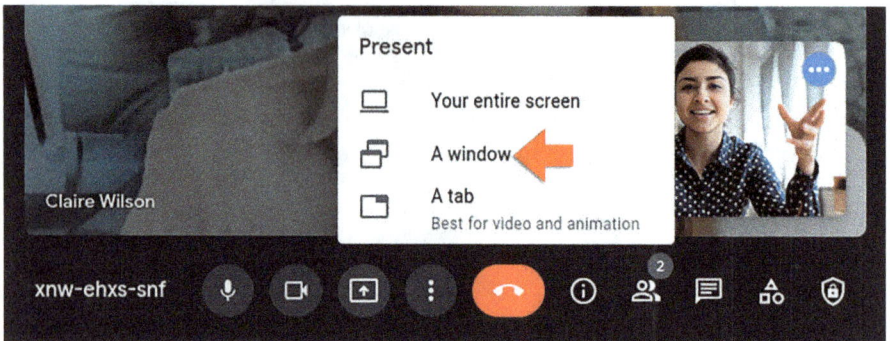

Open the app you want to present, if you haven't already done so. You can do this using the app launcher. Here, I've opened Google Chrome as I want to show a website.

Click on the Google Meet icon on the app shelf along the bottom to switch back to the app.

224

Select the app from the 'share application window', then click 'share'.

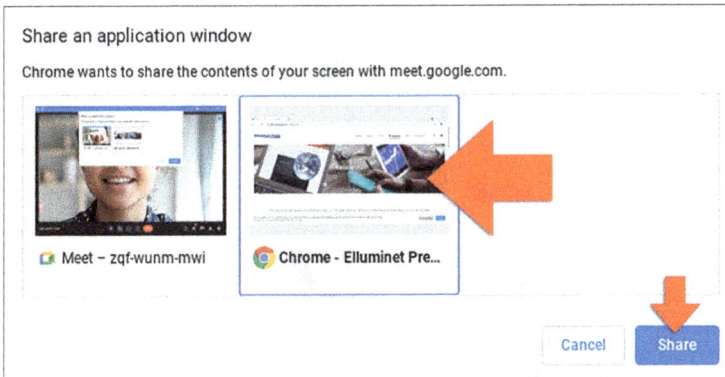

Now, the other participants in your meeting will be able to see the app your just shared. You can use it to show what you want to show.

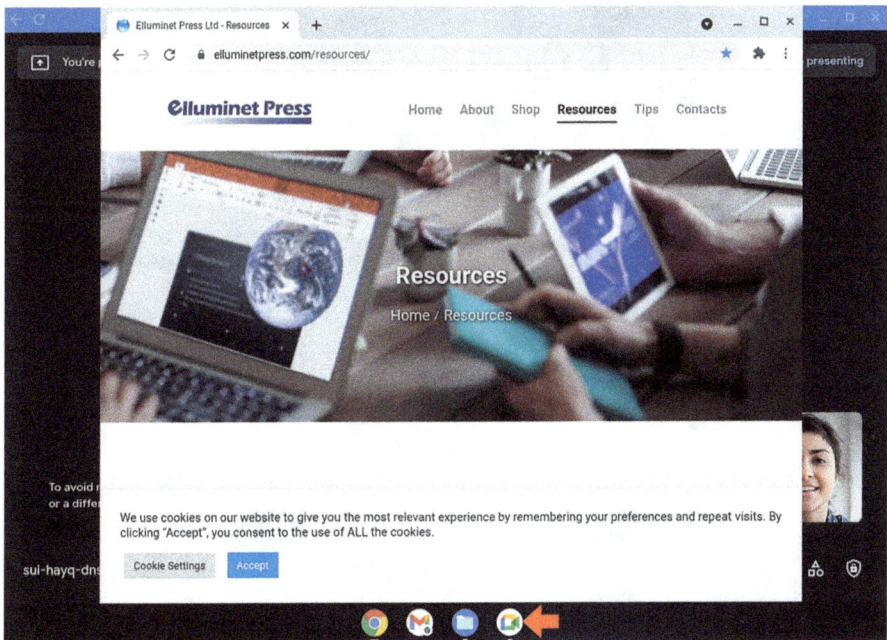

To stop sharing your screen, click on the Google Meet icon on the app shelf along the bottom. Select 'stop presenting' on the top right of Google Meet 'in call' window.

Whiteboard

You can open a whiteboard and share it with your participants. This is useful if you want to illustrate something. This feature works best if you are using Google Meet on a Chromebook or tablet with a touchscreen where you can use a pen.

To open your whiteboard, click the three dots icon in the middle, then select 'whiteboard' from the popup menu.

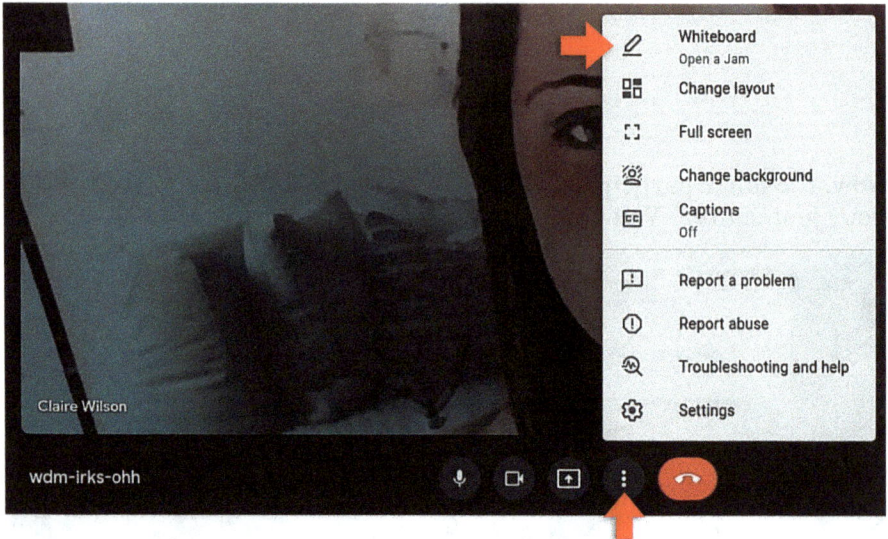

Click 'choose from drive' to load a saved whiteboard from Google Drive, or click 'start a new whiteboard' to create a blank board.

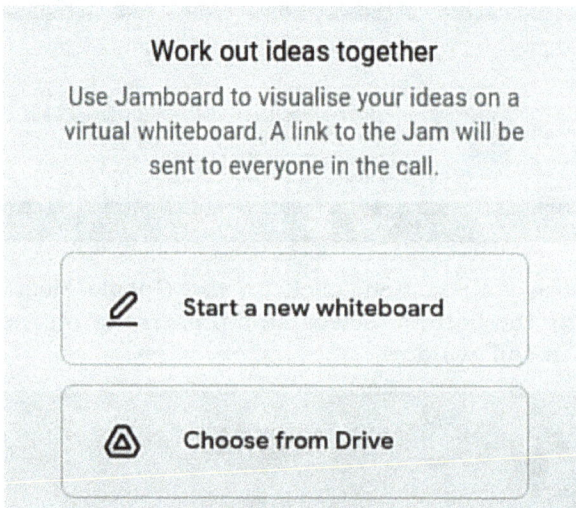

Click 'send' to send the access invitation to the person.

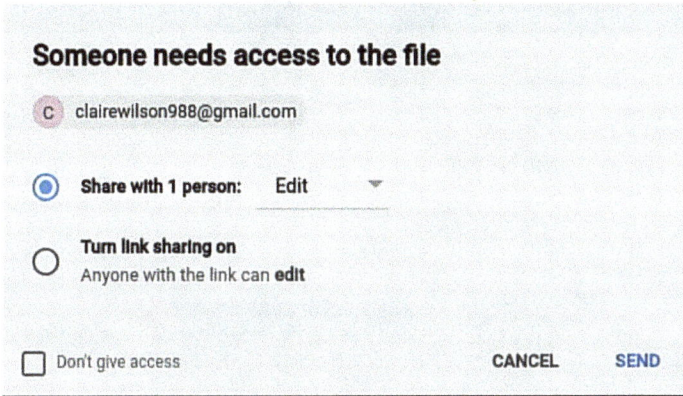

When your whiteboard opens, select a pen from the icons on the left, then choose a colour. If you have a touchscreen on your Chromebook, or you're running Google Meet on a tablet, use your pen to write on the whiteboard.

To present your whiteboard to your team, click the present icon on the toolbar at the top of the screen.

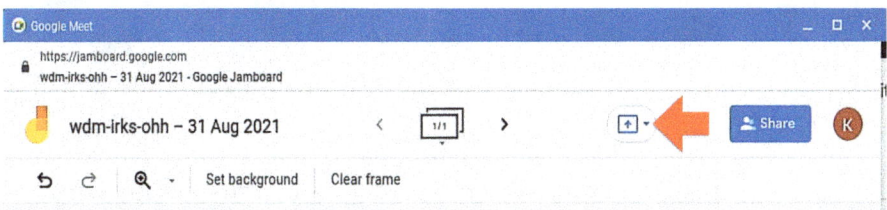

Chapter 5: Web, Email & Communication

Select 'present tab to meeting' from the drop down menu.

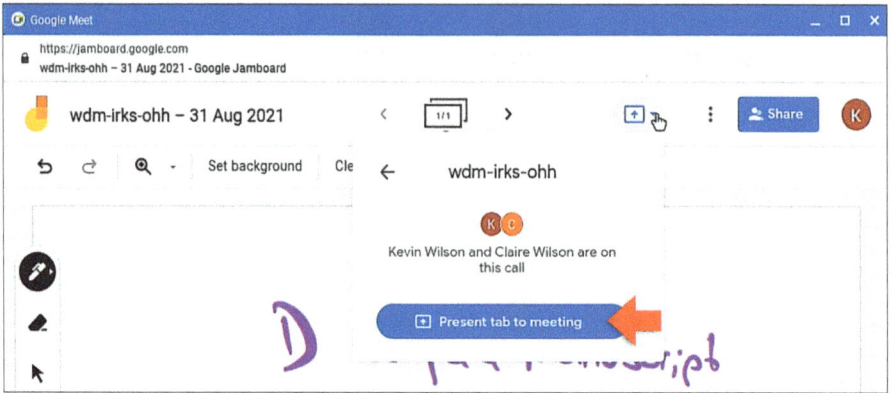

Select the whiteboard under 'this tab' from the share options. Click 'share'.

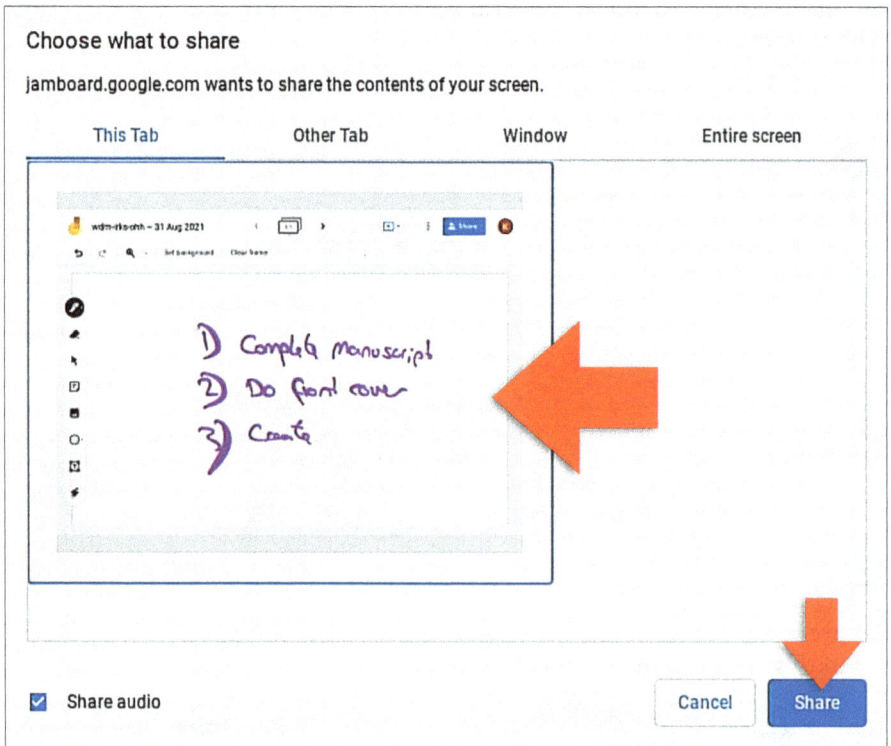

Now, your participants will be able to see the whiteboard. You can draw more ideas on your board as your meeting progresses.

To stop sharing, click 'stop' at the top of the whiteboard window.

Change Background

To change the background, click the three dots icon, then select 'change background' from the popup menu.

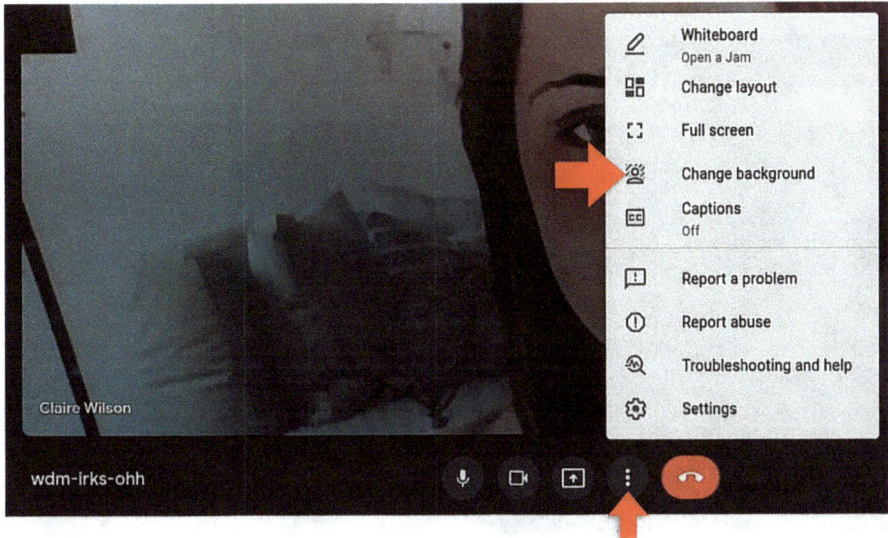

Choose a background from the pre-designs or click the + icon to add an image of your own as a background.

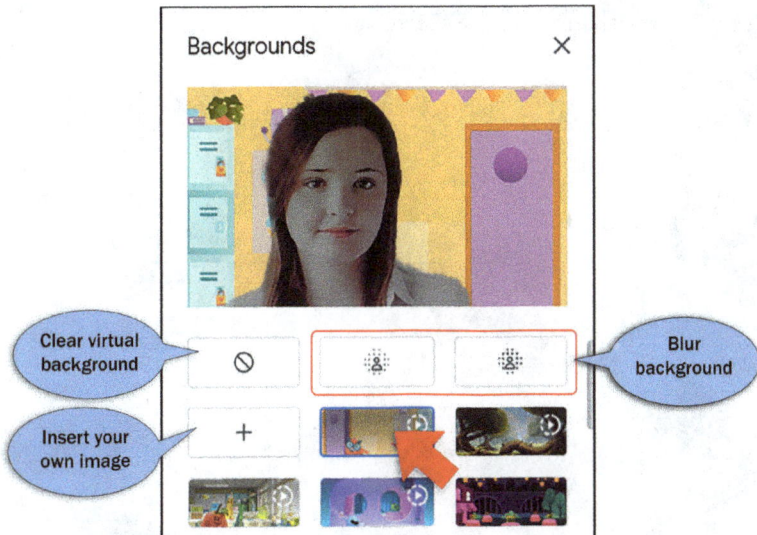

For best results, make sure you sit in-front of a plain background in a well lit room for the effect to work

Captions

Captions are useful if you happen to be hard of hearing have no sound. To turn them on, click the three dots icon in the middle, select 'captions' from the popup menu.

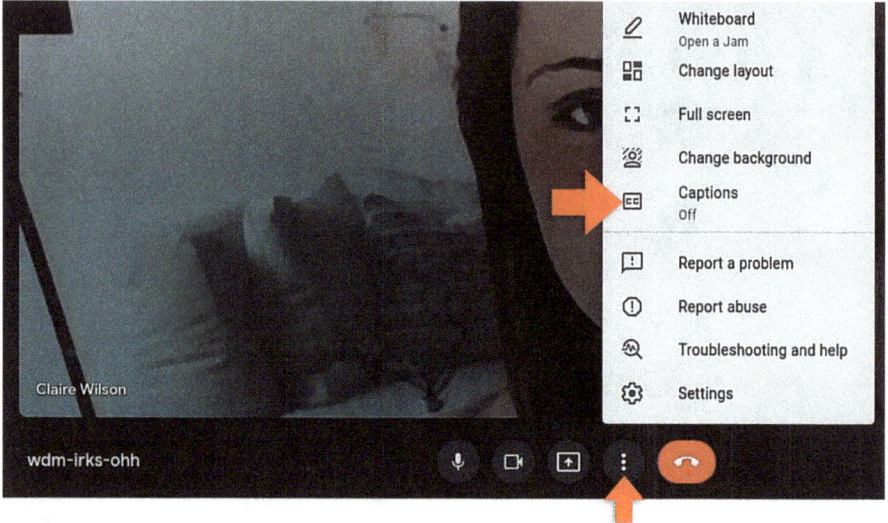

Choose your language from the list.

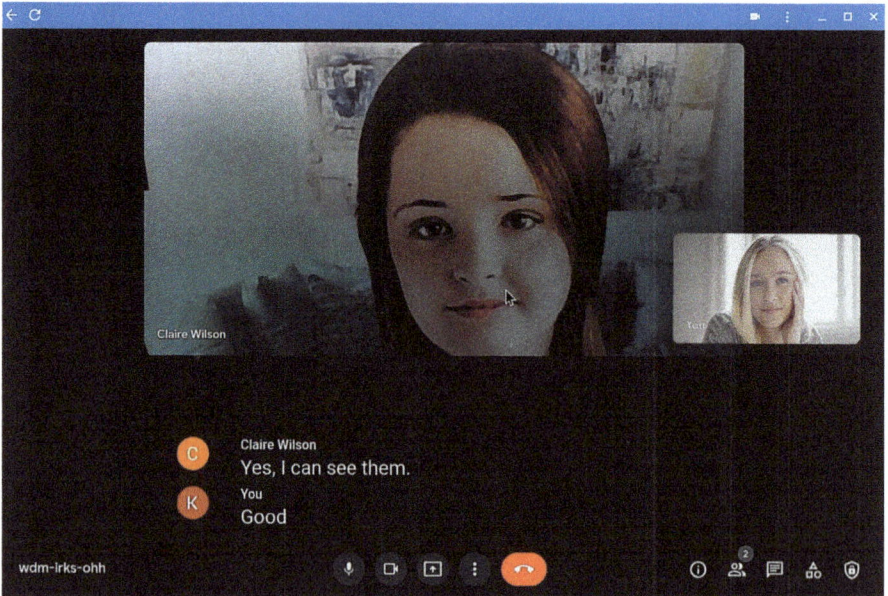

You'll see auto generated captions appear at the bottom of your window.

Google Chat

Google Chat makes it easy to collaborate with your team, colleagues, friends or family. You can create chat rooms, send messages, share files in Google Docs, Sheets, and Slides. Google Chat does not have video/audio calling or screen sharing options, however you can link with Google Meet for this.

Starting Google Chat

You can open the Google Chat app on your app launcher. *If you don't see it, go to the Google Play store and download it.*

Or open Google Chrome Web Browser then navigate to the following website:

`chat.google.com`

Once the app loads up, you'll land on the home screen. From here, you can start a group conversation or create a chat room.

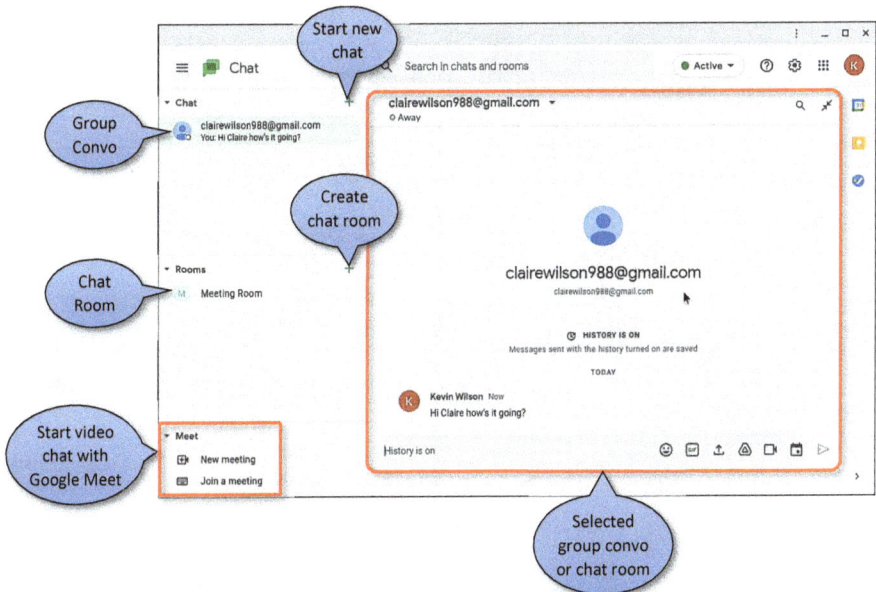

On the left hand side, under 'chat', you'll see all your previous or current group conversations. When you select a conversation, it will open up in the main window on the right. Same with 'rooms' - lists your chat rooms.

231

Chapter 5: Web, Email & Communication

Group Conversations

To create a group chat conversation, click the '+' icon next to 'chat' on the left hand side of the screen. Select 'start group conversation' from the popup menu.

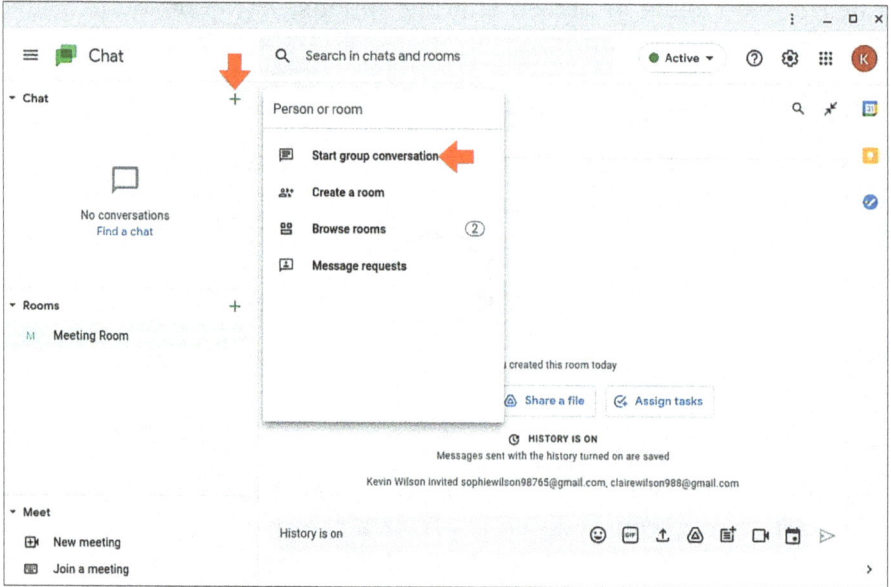

Enter the email addresses of the people you want to invite. Click the blue tick icon when you're done.

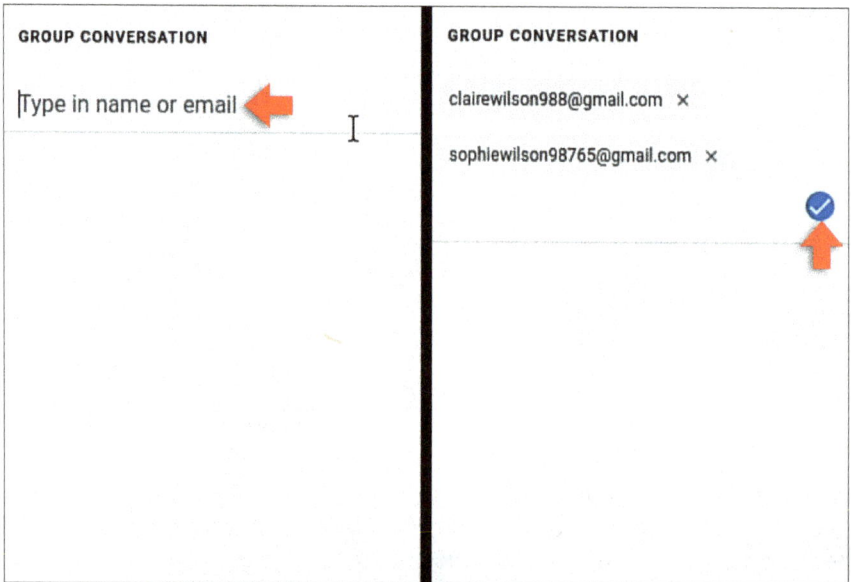

Once your participants accept the invite, they'll enter your group conversation.

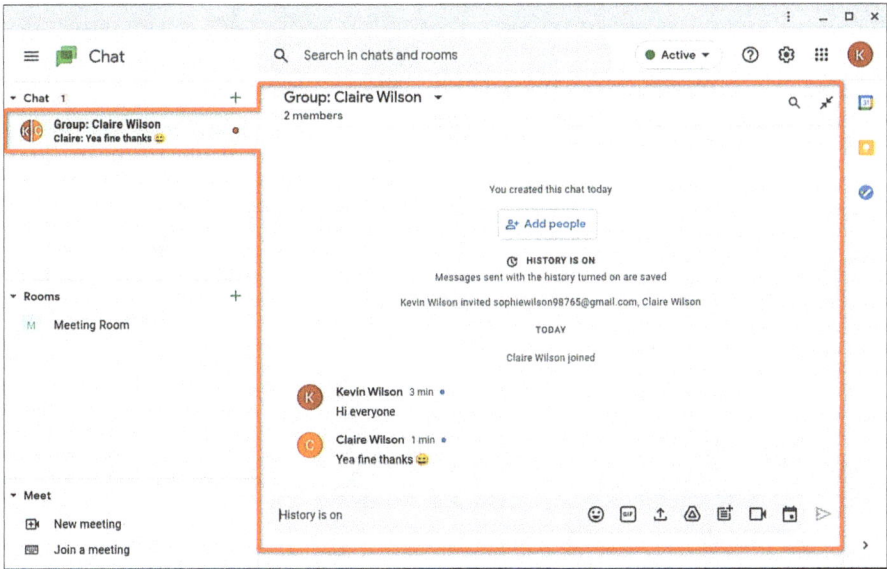

You'll see messages from your participants appear in the main chat window. In the grey bar along the bottom of the window, you can type your message. Press enter to send.

To the right on the grey bar, you'll see some icons. Lets take a look at what these icons do.

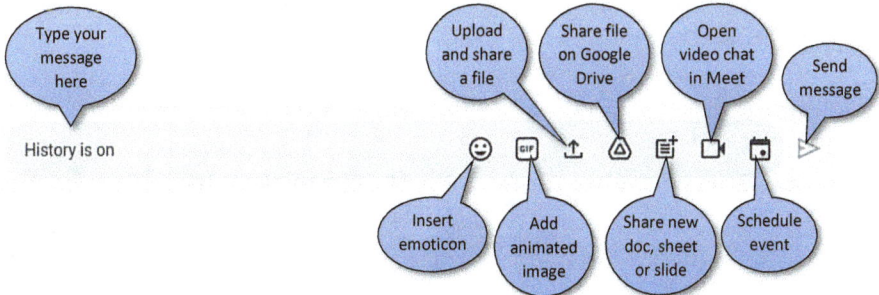

You can use these to insert emoticons such as smileys, and animated gifs - little animated images you can send to people. You can upload a file from your device or Google Drive and share it with the group.

You can also create a new Google Docs document, spreadsheet or slide to share with the group.

Finally, you can open a chat in Google Meet or schedule an event.

Chat Rooms

Chat rooms are similar to group conversations, except you can post files and assign tasks to participants. Chat rooms are better suited to long term collaboration or meetings and has separate sections for chat, files shared, and tasks assigned.

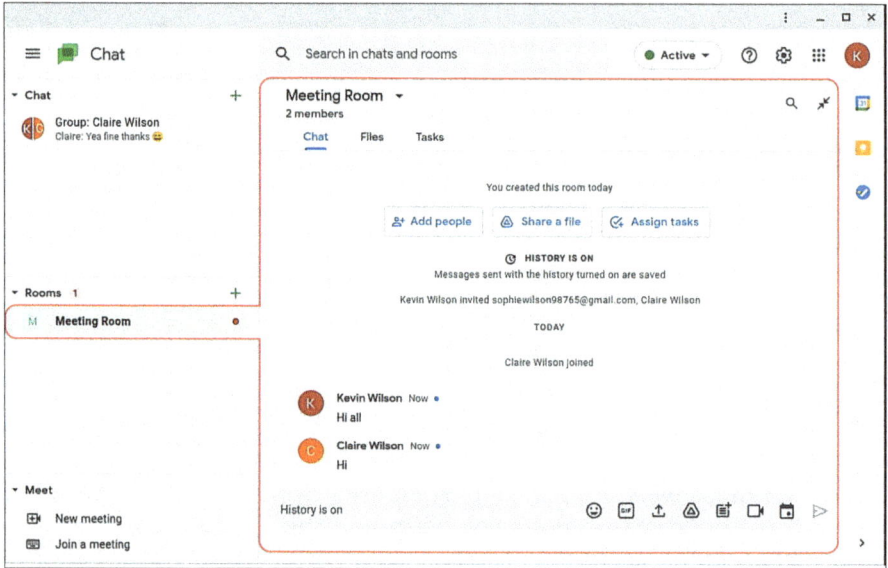

Creating a Room & Chatting

To create a room, click the '+' icon on the top right under the 'rooms' section. Select 'create a room' from the popup menu.

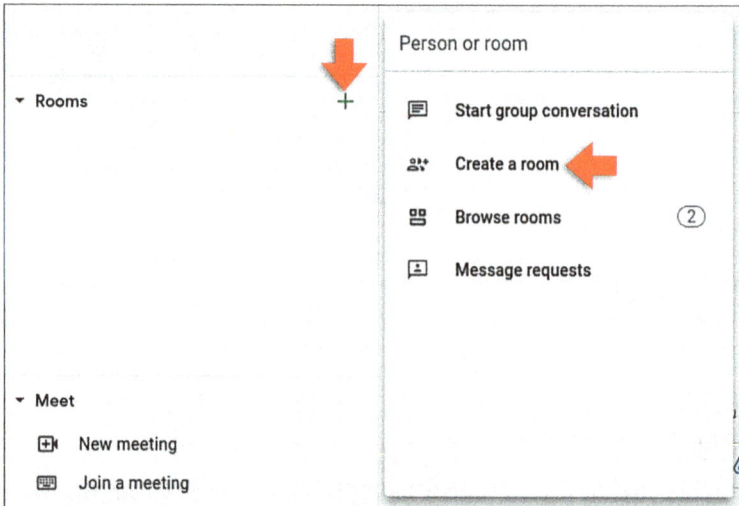

Add a name in the top field. Then enter the email addresses of the people you want to invite. Click 'create' when you're done.

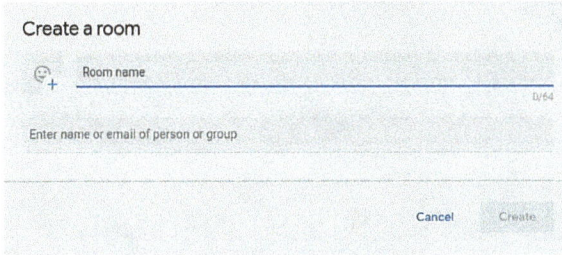

Create a room

Room name

0/64

Enter name or email of person or group

Cancel   Create

You'll see your new room appear under 'rooms' on the bottom left of the screen. Let's take a look around the room.

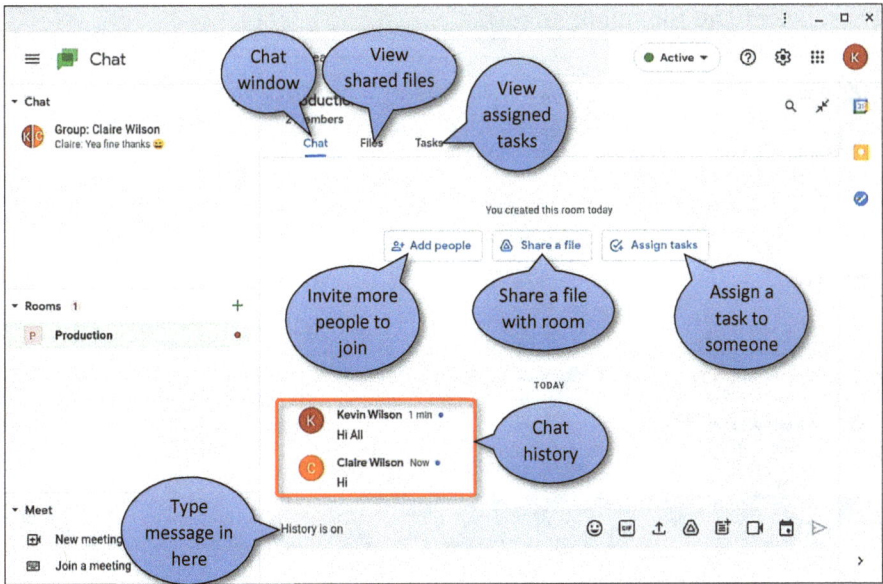

To the right on the grey bar at the bottom of the screen, you'll see some icons. Lets take a look at what these icons do.

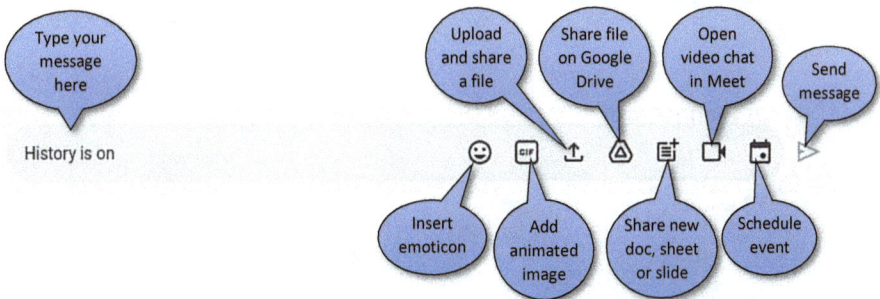

Chapter 5: Web, Email & Communication

Share a File

To share a file, select the 'files' tab along the top of the room window. Click 'add file'

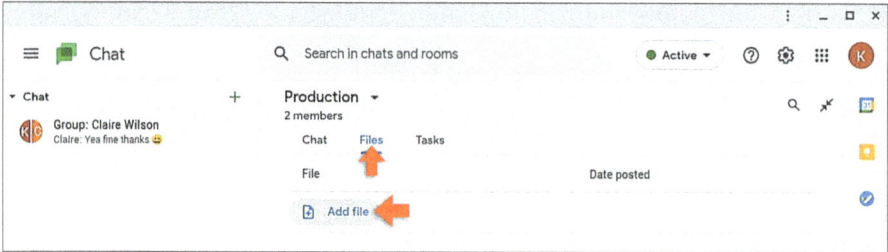

Select where the file is saved - your device (upload), or Google Drive. Then select the file, click 'insert'.

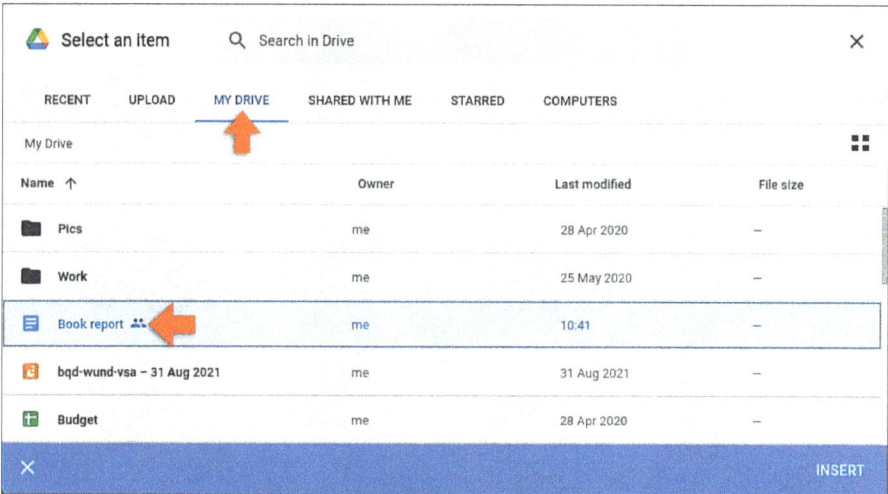

Click the send icon to share with the room.

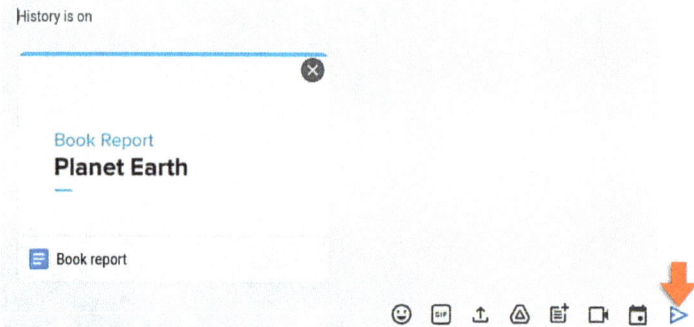

Assign a Task

To share a task with the room, select the 'tasks' tab along the top of the room window.

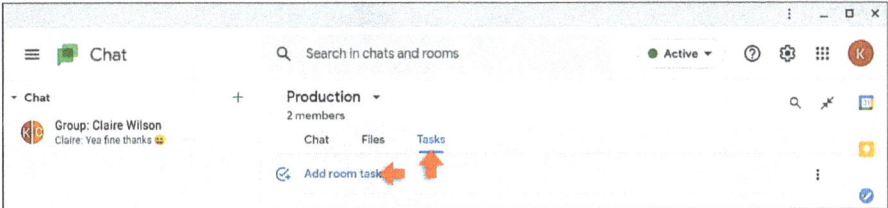

Enter the task title, the date task is to be completed by.

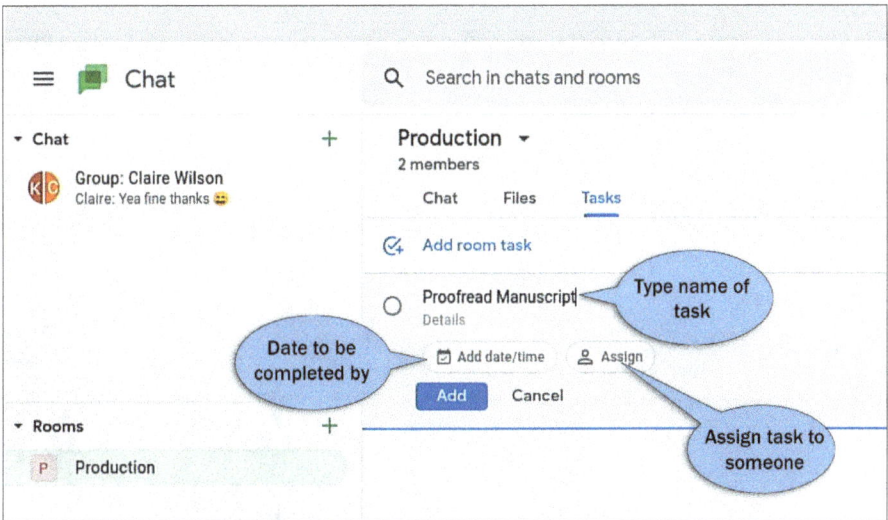

To assign the task to someone, click 'assign' then select the name of the person. Click 'add' when you're done.

Tasks will appear in the 'tasks' tab. When the person has completed the task, they can click on the circle to the left of the task. This marks the task as complete.

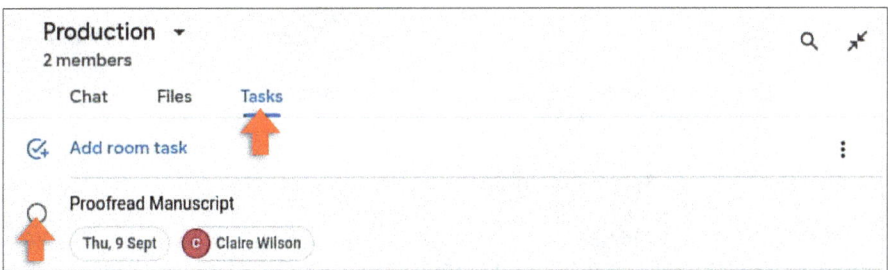

Google Duo

Google Duo has been discontinued and merged into Google Meet, which now includes Duo's features for one-on-one and group video calls.

Starting Google Duo

You can open the Google Duo app on your app launcher. *If you don't see it, go to the Google Play store and download the app.*

Or open Google Chrome Web Browser then navigate to the following website:

`duo.google.com`

Once the app loads up, you'll land on the home screen. Lets take a look around the screen.

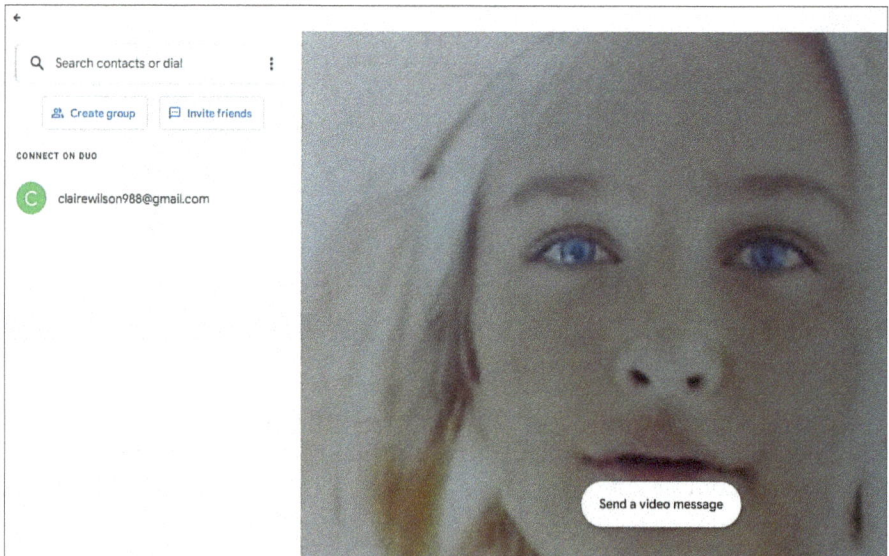

On the left hand side of the screen, you can search for contacts, create a chat group and invite friends.

Under that, you'll see a list of people you've been in contact with.

On the right hand side, you'll see a preview of your camera, where you can also record and send a video message.

Setup

Open the app from your app launcher. Sign in with your Google Account if prompted, then click 'give access' to your microphone and camera.

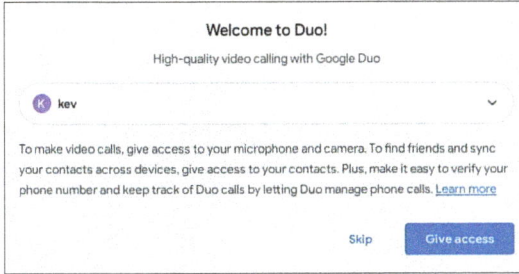

Click 'allow' on any access prompts for contacts, mic and camera you may get.

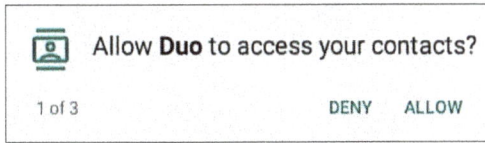

Click 'add phone number'. Enter your phone number.

Check your phone for a text/sms message. Type in the code you receive.

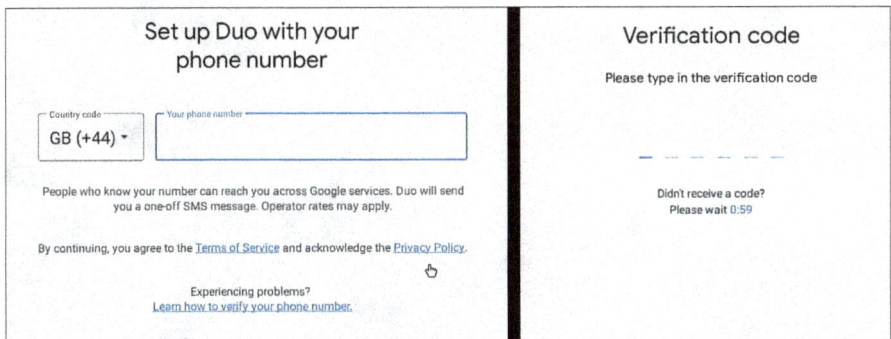

Start a Conversation

From the main screen select a contact to call from the list on the left. You'll see your recent calls at the top. If you don't see their name, type their Google Account email address or phone number into the search field at the top of the screen.

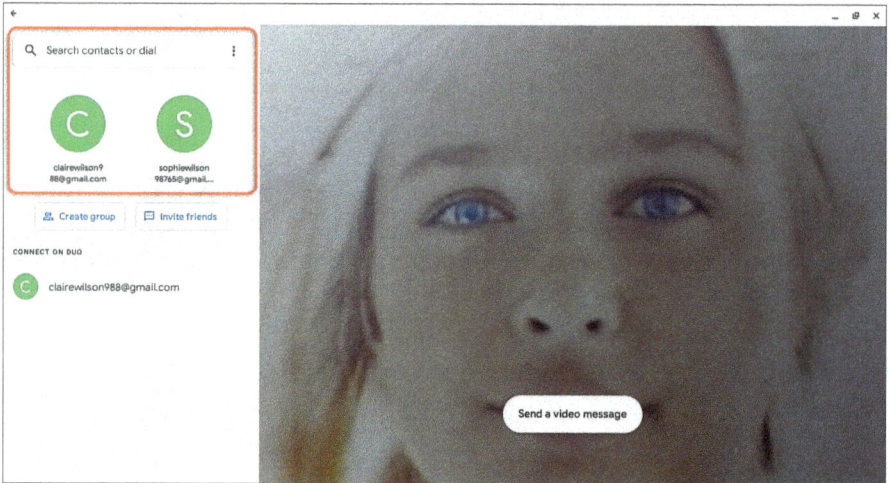

Select 'video call' at the bottom of the screen, then wait for the other person to answer.

Once the other person answers, you'll see their camera in the main view. You'll also see your own camera on the bottom left.

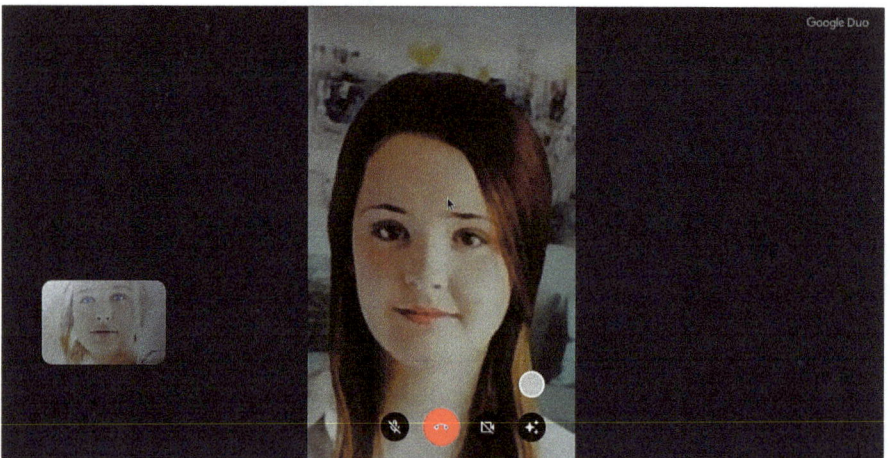

Group Conversations

To create a group, click 'create group'.

Add the participant's email addresses or phone numbers. Type these into the search field at the top of the window. Click 'done' when you're finished.

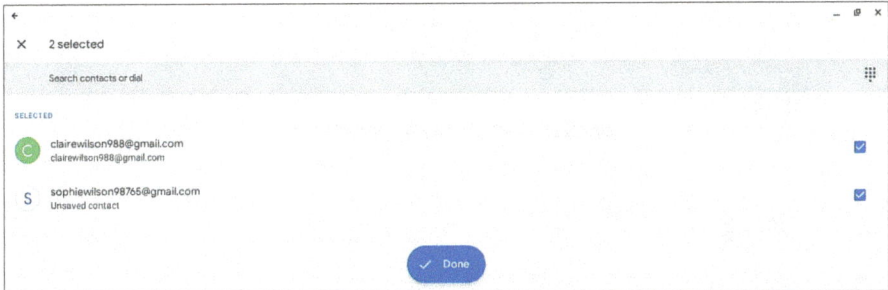

Wait for your participants to join the group.

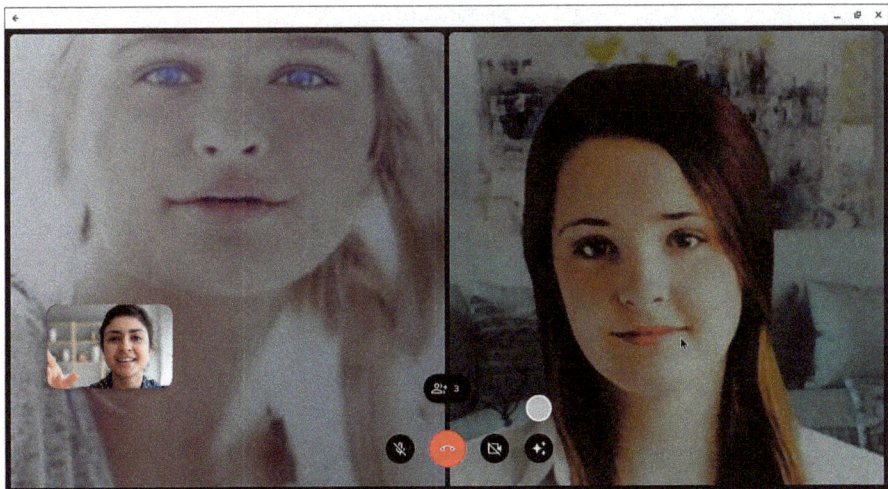

Chapter 5: Web, Email & Communication

Invite Friends

To invite people to Duo, click 'invite friends' on the top left of the screen.

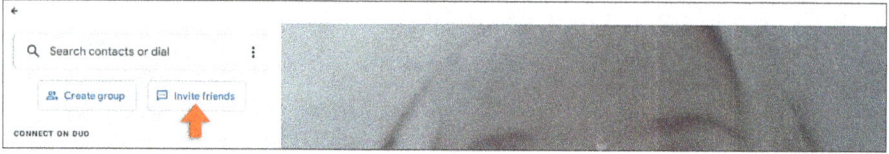

Type in the person's Google Account email address, or the person's phone number.

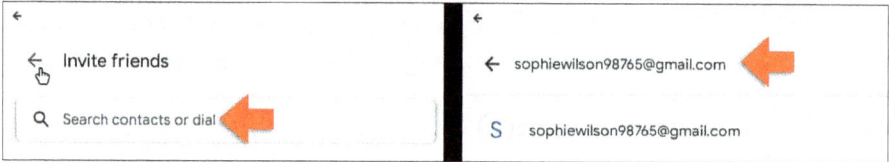

Click compose invitation

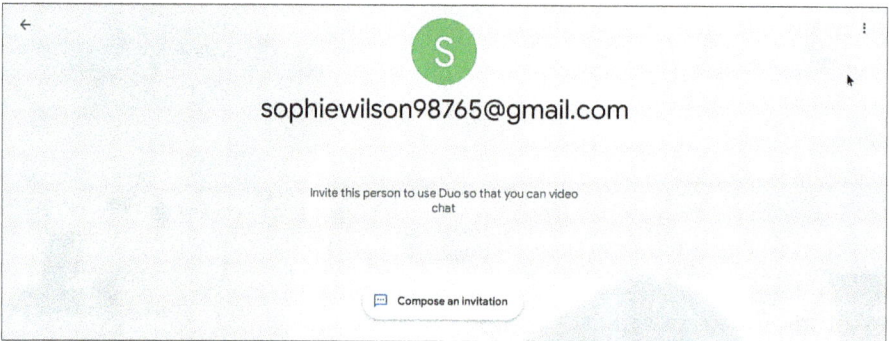

Select the app you want to use to send the invitation eg Mail.

Type in a message, click the send icon on the top right.

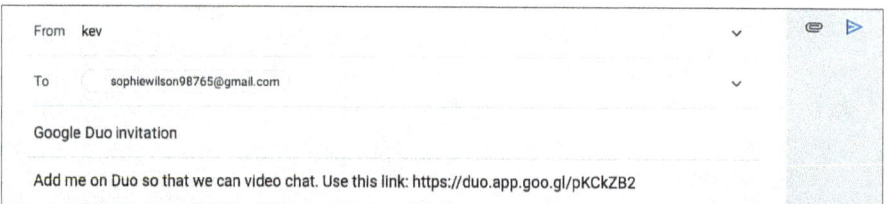

Google Hangouts

Google hangouts has now been discontinued and has been replaced with Google Chat and Google Meet.

You can call anyone on a tablet, Chromebook, laptop, phone or pc that has Google hangouts and a webcam on the device. You can also send instant messages, photographs and videos.

To start the Google hangouts, open Google Chrome and navigate to:

```
hangouts.google.com
```

When hangouts opens up, you'll see a list of contacts you've been in contact with listed down the left hand side.

If you use hangouts a lot, you'll find all your most recent contacts listed here. Click on the names to see the conversations you've had with these contacts.

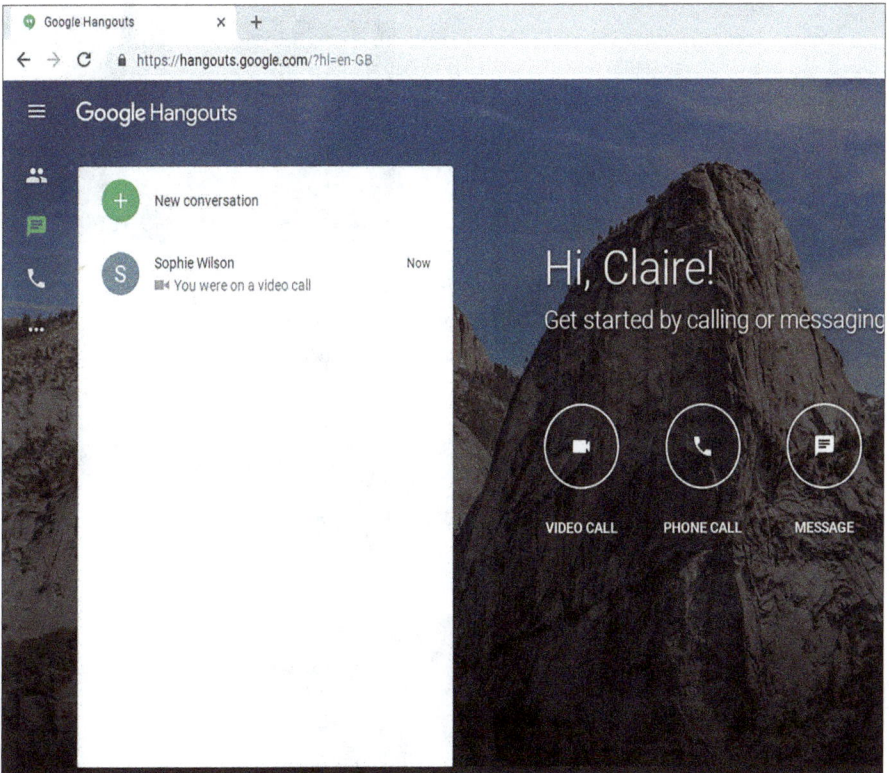

In the middle of the screen, you'll see three buttons. Here you can make a video call, a phone call, or send an instant message.

Messaging New Contacts

To contact someone new, click 'new conversation' on the top left of your screen.

Type the person's name in the field, then select from the contact list that appears.

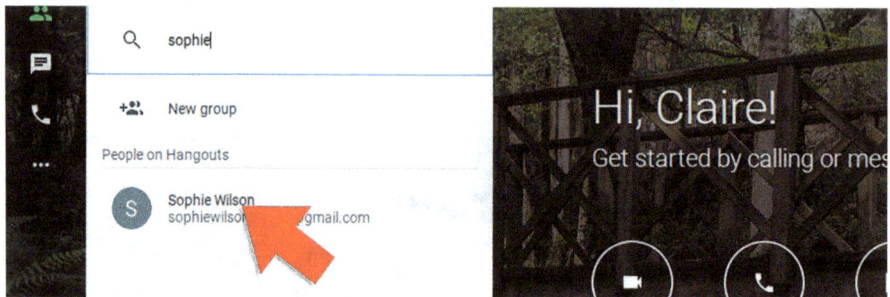

You'll see an instant message window pop up on the right hand side of your screen. Here, you can send instant text messages, as well as start video and audio chats. Just type your message in using the field at the bottom of the window.

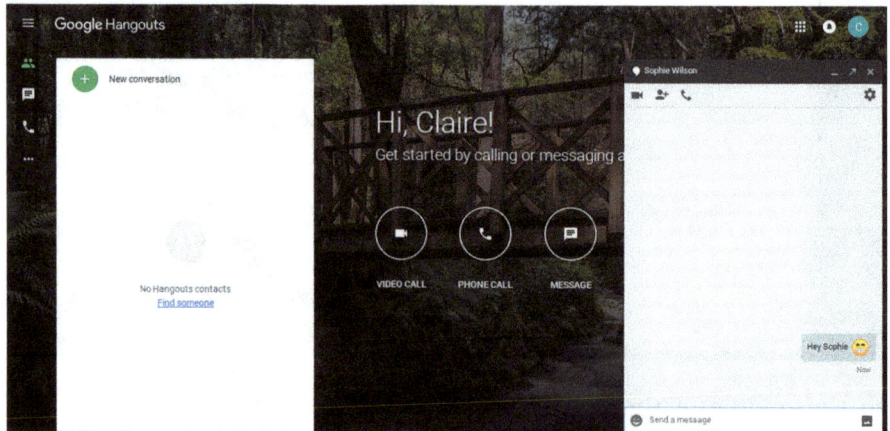

Calling Someone New

To place a new video call, click the video icon in the middle of the screen.

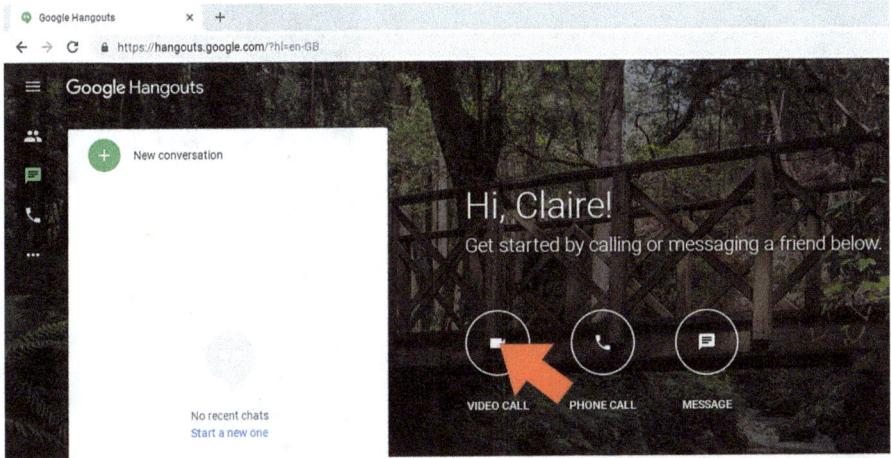

Enter the name or Gmail address of the person you're calling. Click the correct name from the drop down list.

Click 'invite'.

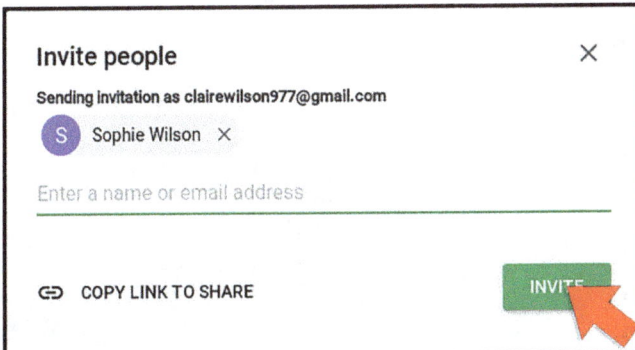

The other person will get a prompt on their hangouts window.

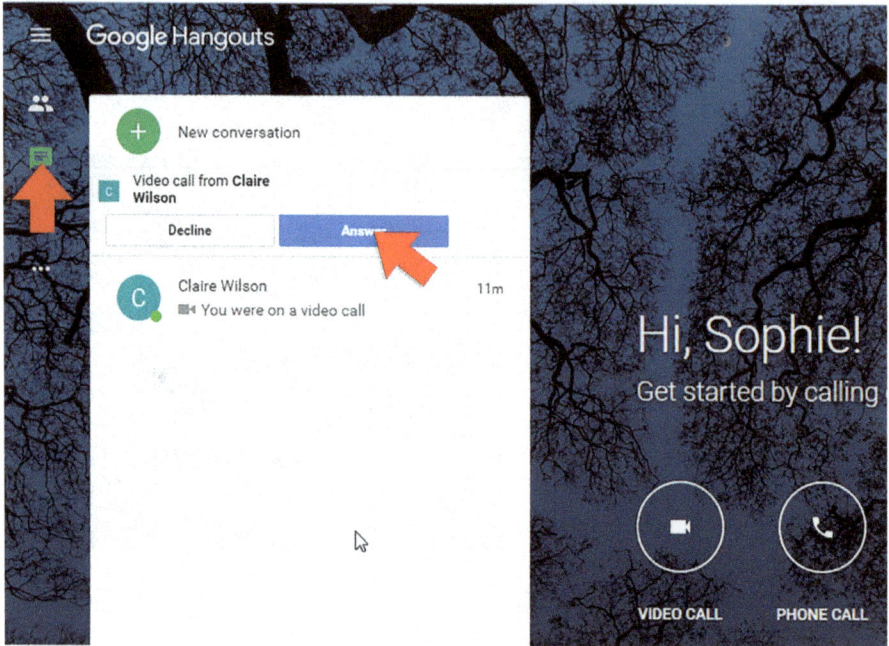

Now you can have a video conversation with that person.

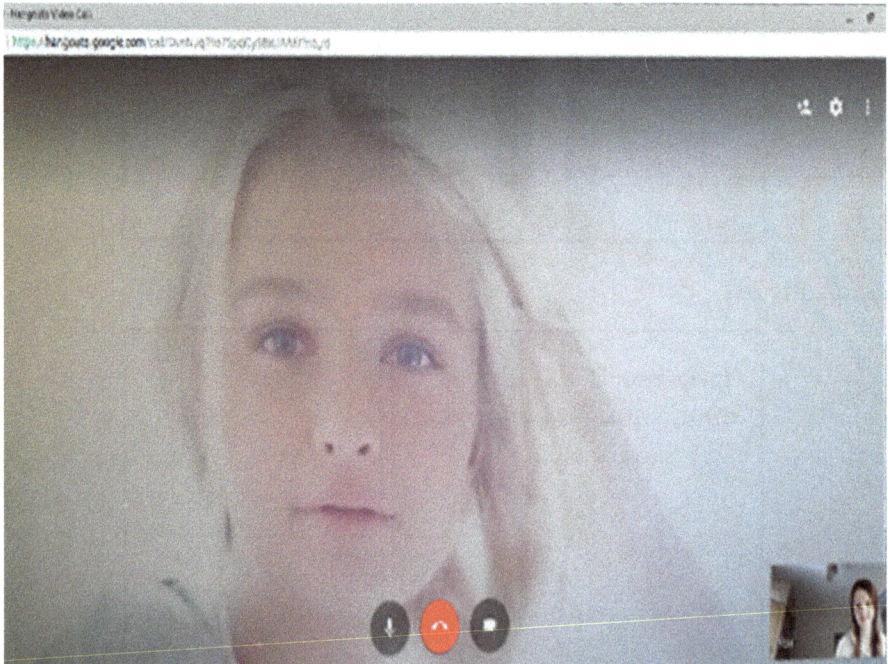

Calling Someone in Conversation Window

If you've had a conversation with someone before, you'll see their name listed in the recent contacts list when you open hangouts. Click on one of these names to see the conversations you've had.

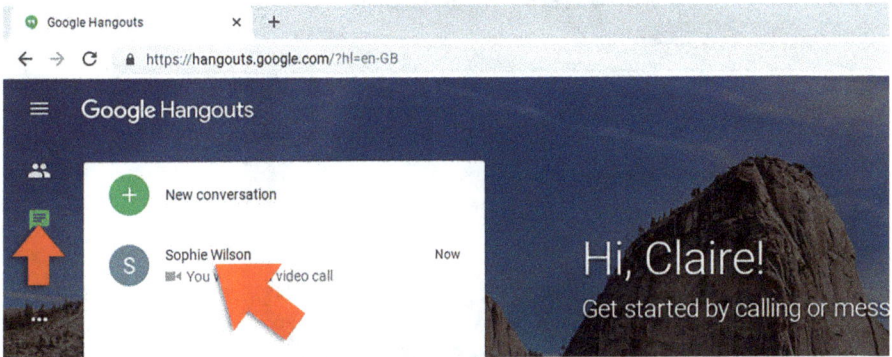

This will open up your conversation window with that person. To place a video call, click the small camera icon on the top left.

When you place the call, you'll see an image of your webcam in the main viewer while you are waiting for the other person to answer.

The other person will get a prompt allowing them to either answer or decline the call.

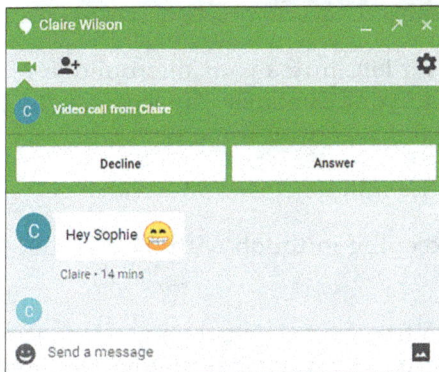

To answer, just select 'answer' from the prompt.

Chapter 5: Web, Email & Communication

When the other person answers, you'll see their webcam in your main viewer. You'll also see a preview of your own camera on the bottom right of your screen, as you can see below.

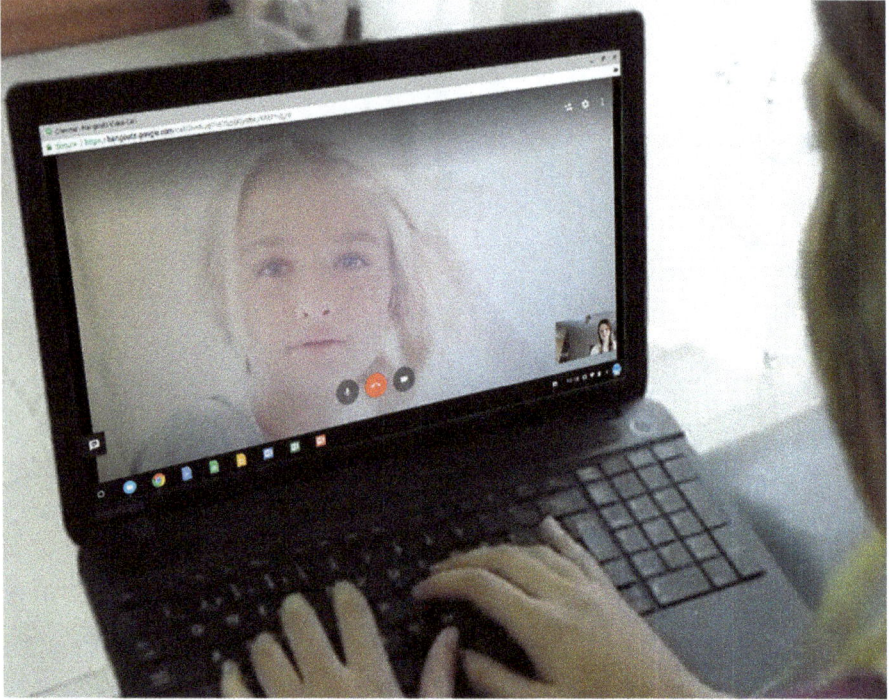

Along the bottom of your screen, you'll also see three buttons. These usually disappear during a call - just click the screen to bring them up.

The button on the far left mutes your microphone so the person you're talking to can't hear you. Similarly the icon on the far right turns off your camera. Useful if you want a moment's privacy.

The red button in the middle closes your video call.

This is useful for keeping in touch with friends and family all over the world.

These calls are also free to make and you can chat as long as you like - you'll still have to pay for your internet connection though, whether that is through cable, broadband, wifi or cellular depending on your service provider.

Sending Images

You can send files such as photos using the conversation window.

To send an image, click the image icon on the bottom right of the conversation window.

Select 'upload photos'. Then click 'select a photo from your computer'.

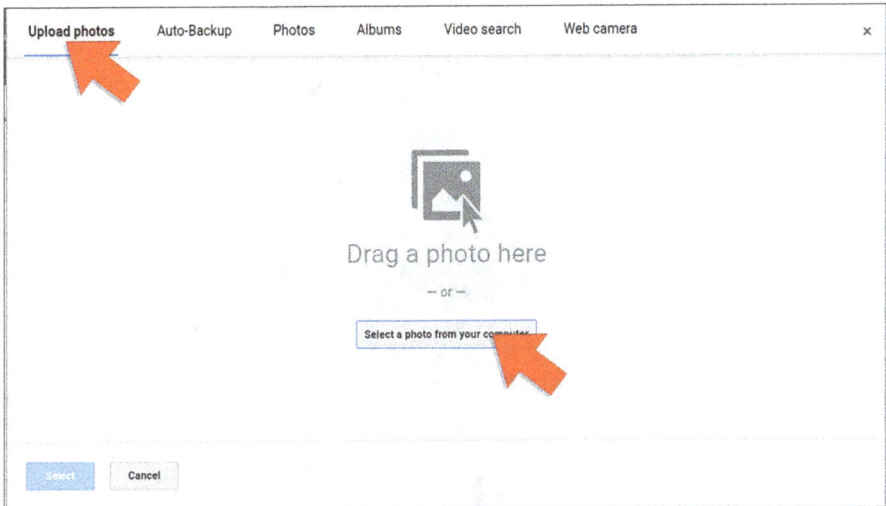

You can also send photos from Google Photos, albums, video search on the web, or the web cam on your Chromebook.

Select 'Google Drive', or 'My Files', depending on where the image you want to upload is stored.

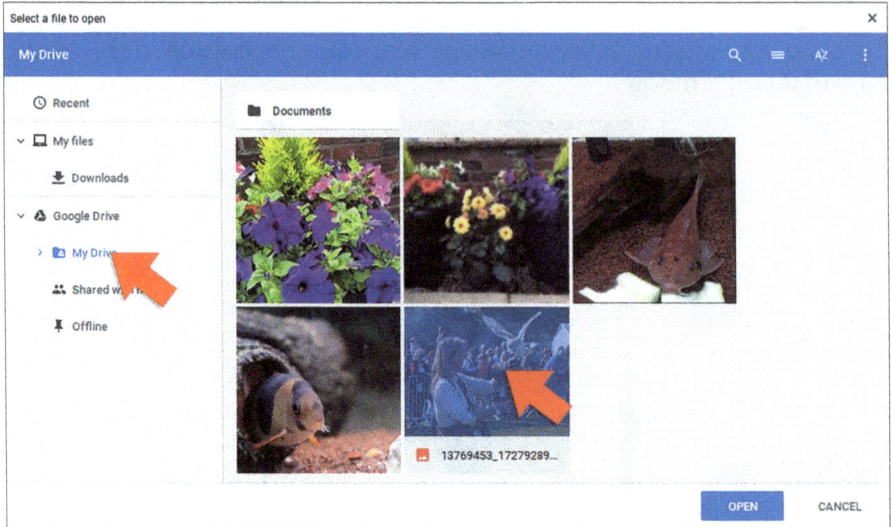

Click 'open', when you're done.

You'll see a preview of the image in the conversation window. Click the 'send' icon in the middle of the image to send.

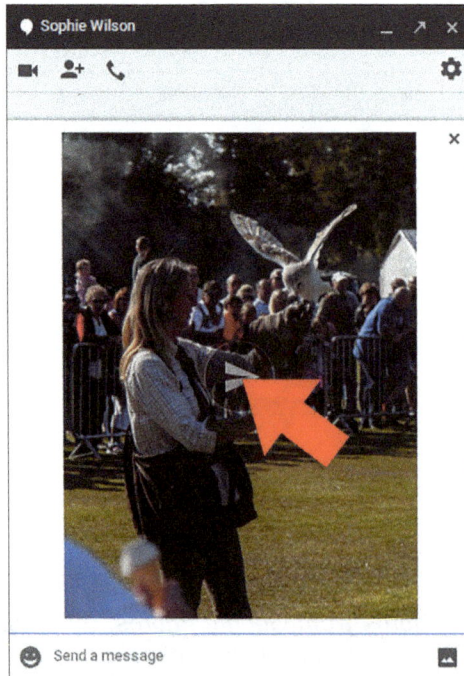

Sending Emoticons

You can send smilies and all sorts of other emotes in the conversation window.

To do this, click the smiley face icon on the bottom left hand side of the window.

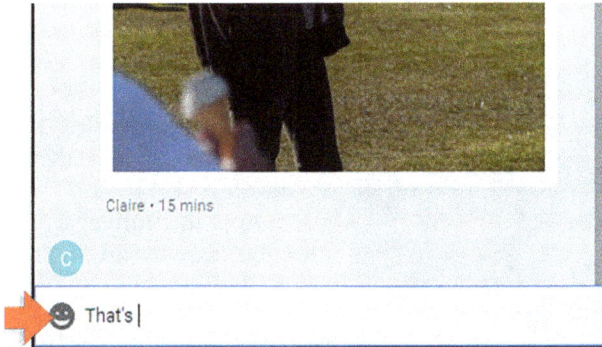

Select a category of emoticons or stickers using the row of icons along the top.

Then click an emoticon or sticker from the list, to send or insert into your message.

6

Entertainment

Your ChromeBook has a large collection of multimedia apps available. You'll find these apps on your app launcher, and many more can be downloaded from the play store.

In this chapter, we'll take a look at:

- Google Play Store

- Google Photos

- Spotify

- YouTube Music

- YouTube

- Google TV

- Netflix

- Prime Video

- Projectors & TVs

- Google Play Books

For this section, have a look at the video resources. Open your web browser and navigate to the following website:

elluminetpress.com/chromebook-mm

Google Play Store

Google Play allows you to search for and download digital media such as music, books, movies, and television programs, as well as apps and games.

You'll find the play store on your app launcher. Click the play store icon to start the app.

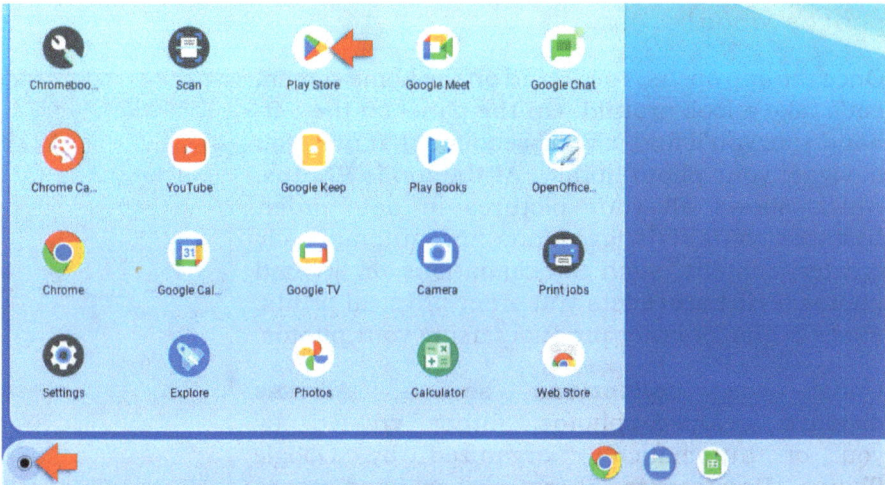

The play store will open. Along the left hand side of the screen, you can search for apps, games, books and apps suitable for kids.

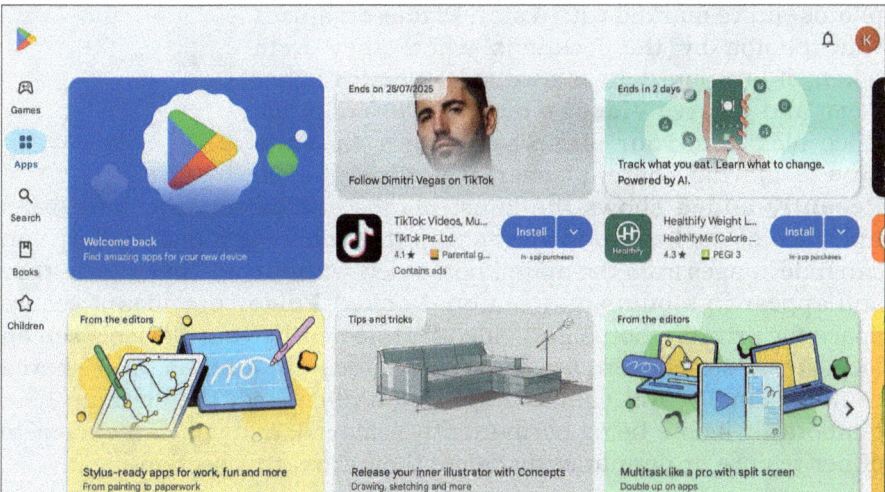

See page 157 for more info on how to download apps from the Google Play Store.

Chapter 6: Entertainment

Google Photos

With the photos app you can manage, store and enhance the photographs you take with your camera. You can also share photos on social media, or send them to friends and family. On a Chromebook, the web version is far better than the android app on the app launcher. To open Google Photos, open the Chrome browser then navigate to the following website.

`photos.google.com`

Once the app opens, you'll land on the home screen. Let's take a look around. On the panel on the left-hand side you'll find several sections that help you navigate your photo library. At the top is **Photos**, which shows all your pictures in date order. **Updates** contains suggestions and automatically created content, such as animations or stylized photos. **Print store** lets you order physical prints, photo books, or other products using your photos.

Under the **Collections** section, **Albums** displays grouped photos, either created by you or automatically organized by Google Photos. **Documents** filters out scanned pages or photographed paperwork. **Screenshots and recordings** shows images captured from your screen or screen recordings. **Favourites** are any photos you've marked with a star. **Places** organizes your photos by the locations where they were taken, if location data is available. Scroll further down and you see **Videos** which displays only the video files from your library, making it easier to browse moving content separately from photos.

Recently added shows the latest photos and videos that have been uploaded or backed up to your account. **Archive** is a place where you can hide images from the main Photos view without deleting them—they still appear in albums and search. **Locked Folder** provides a secure space for private photos and videos, protected by your device's screen lock; items stored here are hidden from search, albums, and shared content. Finally, **Bin** contains items you've deleted; they remain here temporarily before being permanently removed, and you can choose to either restore or permanently delete them from this section.

In the middle of the screen, you'll see the photos or options from whatever tab you have selected in the left hand panel. Click on any of these to open them up.

254

Viewing Photos

To browse through all your photos, click the photos icon on the left hand side.

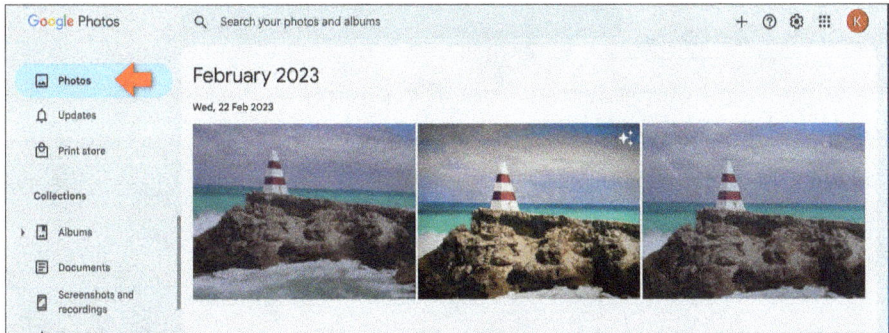

Scroll up and down, you'll see your photos listed in reverse chronological order. Click on one of the thumbnails to view the image in full.

Search

Google Photos uses an intelligent image recognition search that scans your photos for recognisable patterns, shapes and objects. To search for photos, type your keywords into the search field at the top of the screen.

In this example, I'm searching for all photos taken by the sea.

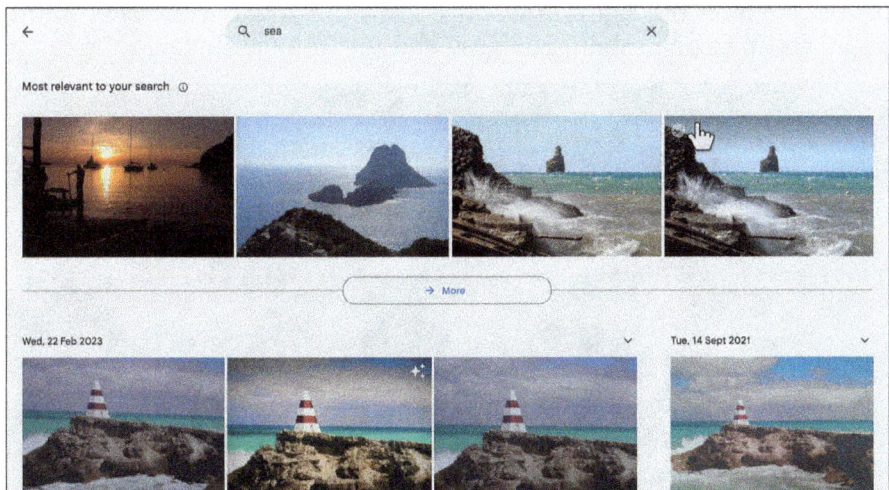

Adjusting Photos

You can adjust the brightness, contrast, bring up detail in shadows or highlights, as well as crop, and straighten up photos.

Open a Photo

To adjust a photo, select it from the photos section or album. The photo will open up.

Select the edit icon from the icons along the top right of the screen.

Brightness & Contrast

To change the brightness, contrast, shadows, highlights and so on, open the photo as shown above, then select the 'adjust' icon from top of the panel on the right hand side. Click the small arrow next to the 'light' group to open the brightness and contrast settings.

You'll see a whole list of adjustments you can make. Scroll down the list, click and drag the slider left or right to make the adjustments.

Lets take a look at what each adjustment does:

- **Brightness** changes the overall brightness of the image. You can make the whole photo lighter or darker.

- **Contrast** is the difference between the dark and light parts of the image. Increasing the contrast can make parts of your image stand out.

- **White Point** adjust the brightest part of the image such as objects that appear mostly white.

- **Highlights** adjust the bright parts of the image. Eg you could darken the sky in a photo if it's too bright.

- **Shadows** adjust the dark parts of the image. Eg you could lighten up the shadows of a photo.

- **Black Point** adjusts the darkest part of the image such as objects that are mostly black.

- **Saturation** adjusts the intensity of the colours. For example, if you turn up the saturation, the colours become darker and more intense.

- **Warmth** adjusts the colour cast of the image. If you increase the 'warmth' the photo becomes more orange, and if you decrease the warmth, the photo becomes more blue. This is useful if your photographs have come out too orange or too blue. If you photo is too orange (ie too warm), just turn the 'warm' slider towards the left.

- **Tint** adjusts how much white is added to the photo

- **Skin Tone** enhances 'skin colours' in the photograph. This can help make people look a bit more natural in the photo.

- **Blue Tone**, is useful for oceans, skies, and anything that is blue.

- **Pop** makes the image stand out more by enhancing the edges of objects.

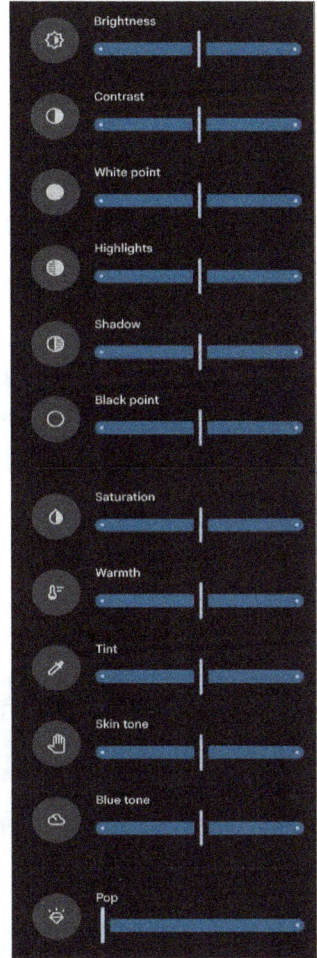

In this example, I'm going to decrease the shadows. To make your adjustment, drag the shadow slider. As you drag the slider, you'll see the image change. Click 'done' at the top when you're finished.

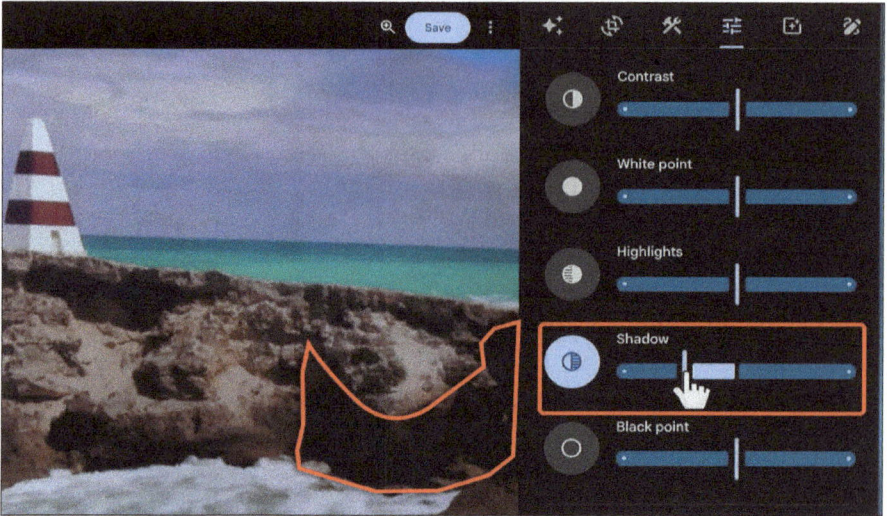

Crop & Rotate

To crop, open the photo, click the 'edit' icon, then select the 'crop' icon from the list along the top of the sidebar on the right.

To crop the image, drag the small white circles around the part of the image you want to keep.

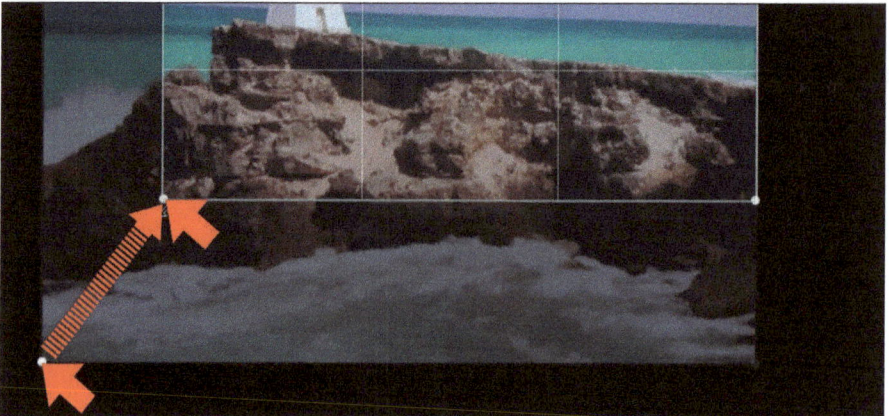

You can also crop to a preset size. To do this, select a preset from the panel on the right. For example 16:9

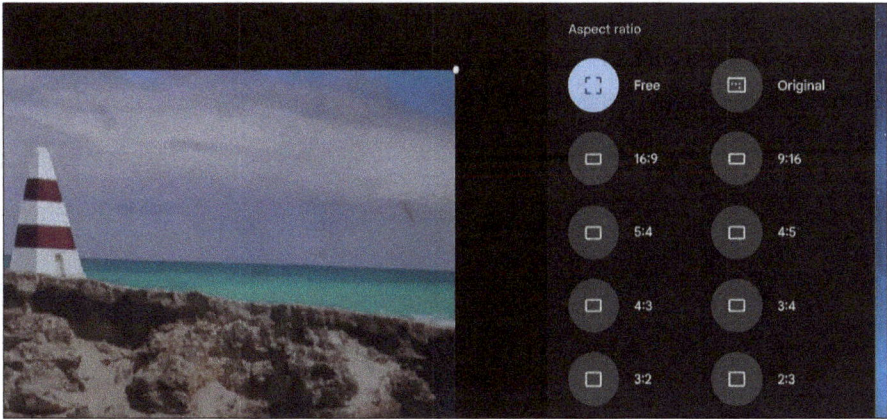

Click and drag the image so it fits inside the crop box.

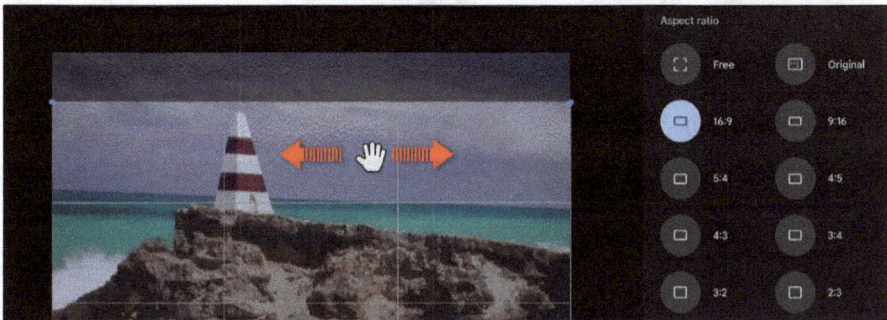

If you want to rotate the image. Click the rotate icon on the bottom left Each click will rotate the image 90° counter-clockwise.

Click 'save' on the top right when you're finished, then click the back arrow on the top left to go back to your photos.

To go back to your photos, click the back arrow on the top left of the screen.

Chapter 6: Entertainment

Straighten

To straighten the photo, first open the photo, click the 'edit' icon on the top right, then select the 'crop' icon from the list along the top of the sidebar on the right.

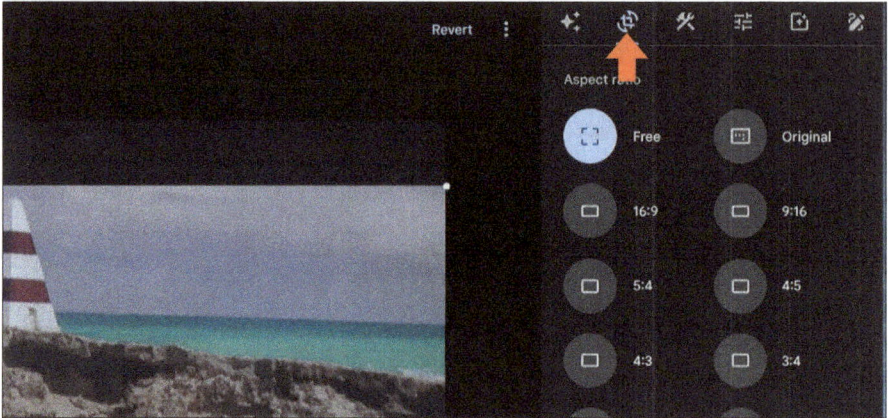

Use the dial on the right of the screen. Drag the marker up or down to rotate the image a number of degrees. Here in the demo below I'm straightening up the horizon so it is parallel to the horizontal grid line.

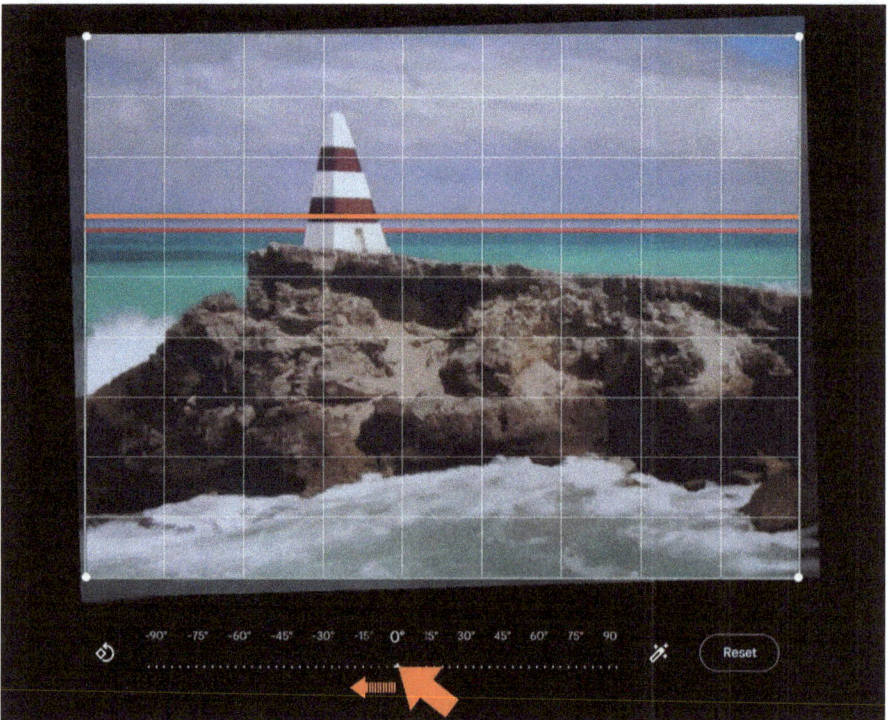

Photo Albums & Collages

You can create albums to keep your photos together, create collages and share them with people.

Creating

Select 'photos' from the panel on the left, then select the photos you want to add to your album - click the 'tick' icon on the top right of the photo. Click the '+' icon on the top right, then select 'album' from the popup menu.

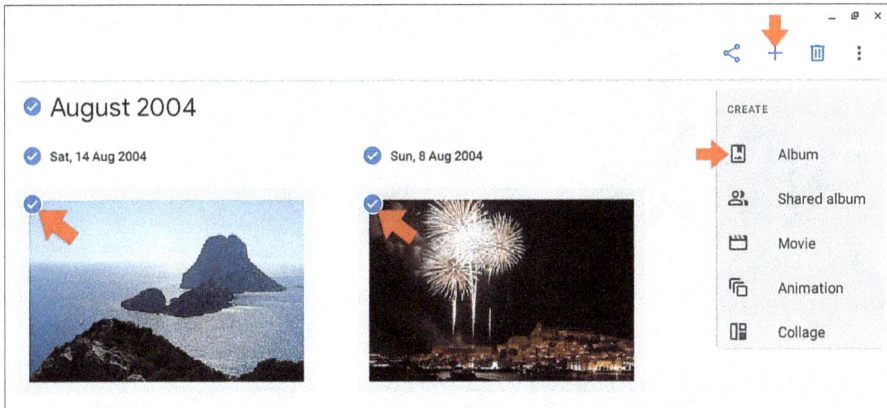

Click 'new album'. Give your album a name, then click the blue 'tick' icon on the top left of the screen.

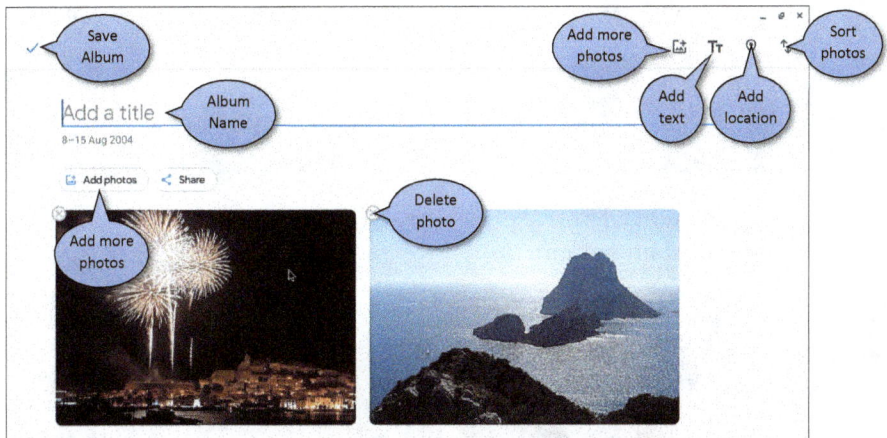

You'll find all your albums in your 'album' section of Google Photos. Select 'library' from the panel on the left hand side of the screen.

Chapter 6: Entertainment

Collage

A photo collage is a composition made up of various different photographs assembled together. These are useful for posting to social media.

To create a collage, select 'photos' from the panel on the left, then select the photos you want to use. Choose six good ones. Click the '+' icon on the top right of the screen. From the drop down menu select 'collage'.

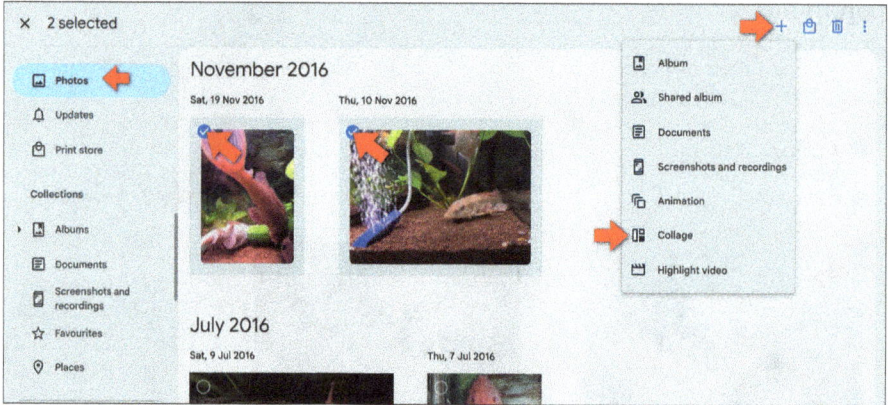

Click the adjustments icon to add a filter, or adjust the colour and brightness.

Click the share icon at the top to post your collage to social media, or send to a friend using email.

You'll find all collages you have created in your albums section.

Sharing Photos

To create a collage, select 'photos' from the panel on the left, then select the photo(s) you want to share from the photos section in Google Photos. Select the 'share' icon on the toolbar along the top of the screen.

Type in the person's email address or select a name you want to share the photos with. The person receiving the photos must have a Google account email address and password. If you want to send the photos to more than one person, click 'new group', then select the people from the list.

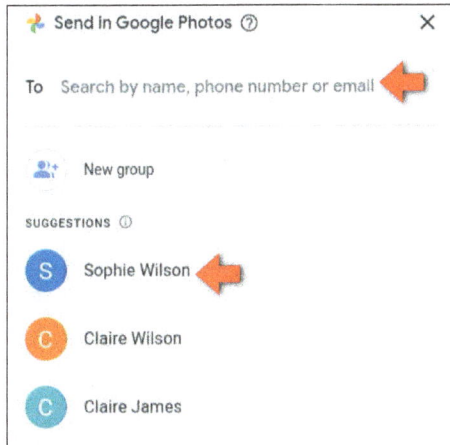

Add a message then click the 'send' icon.

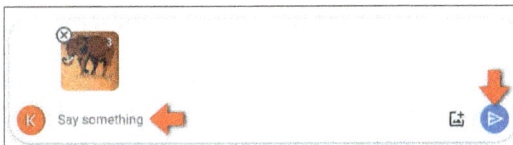

Sending a Link

If you want to send a link to the shared photos, select 'photos' from the panel on the left, then select the photo(s) you want to share from the photos section in Google Photos. Select the 'share' icon on the toolbar along the top of the screen.

At the bottom of the If you want to send to anyone else click 'create link'.

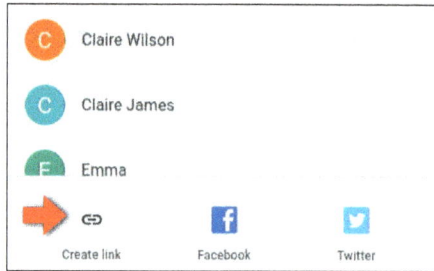

From the popup dialog box, click 'create link'

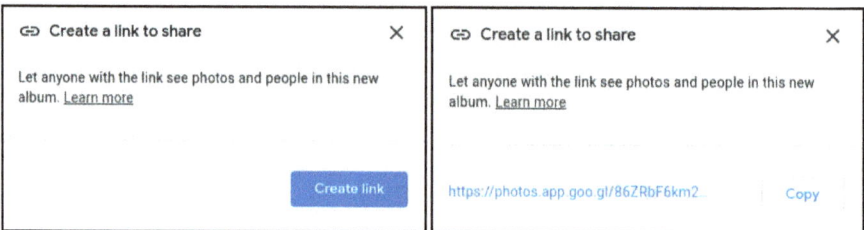

Click 'copy', then paste the link into an email or message.

Similarly if you want to post on facebook or twitter, click on the links and follow the instructions on screen.

Sharing Albums

You can share an album on social media such as facebook or via email. To do this, select 'library' from the icons on the left hand side of the screen. Select the album you want to share.

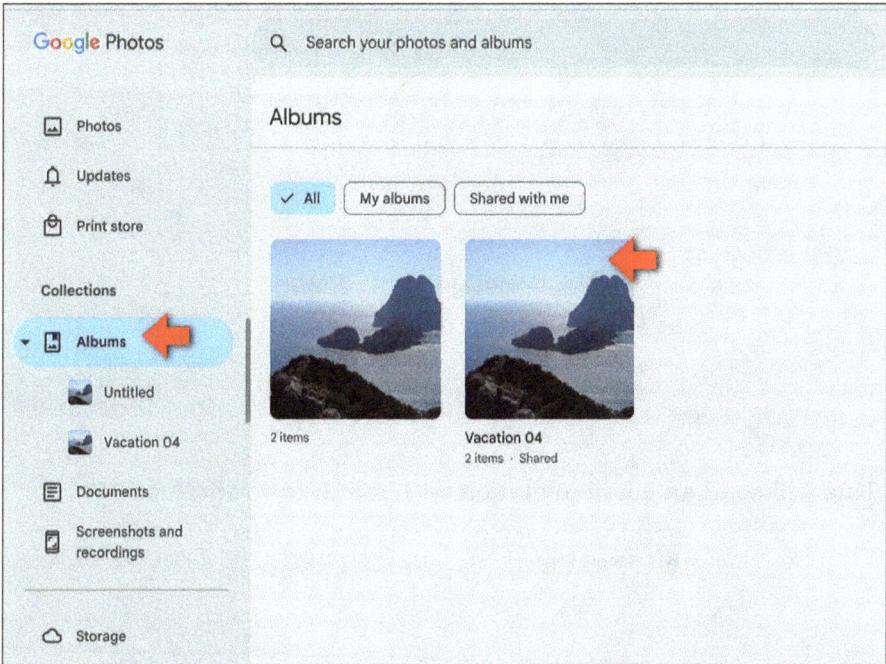

Click 'share'.

Select the people or person you want to share your album with from your contact list, or enter their email address. Click 'send' icon on the top right.

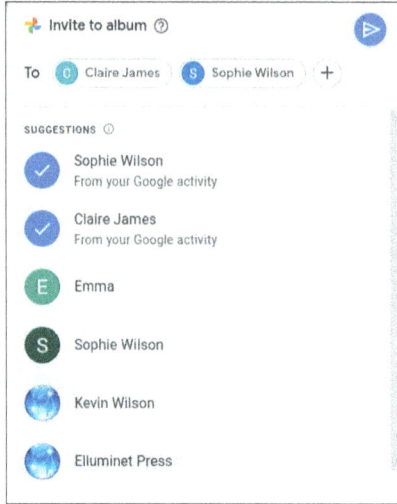

This will send an email invitation with a link to your album.

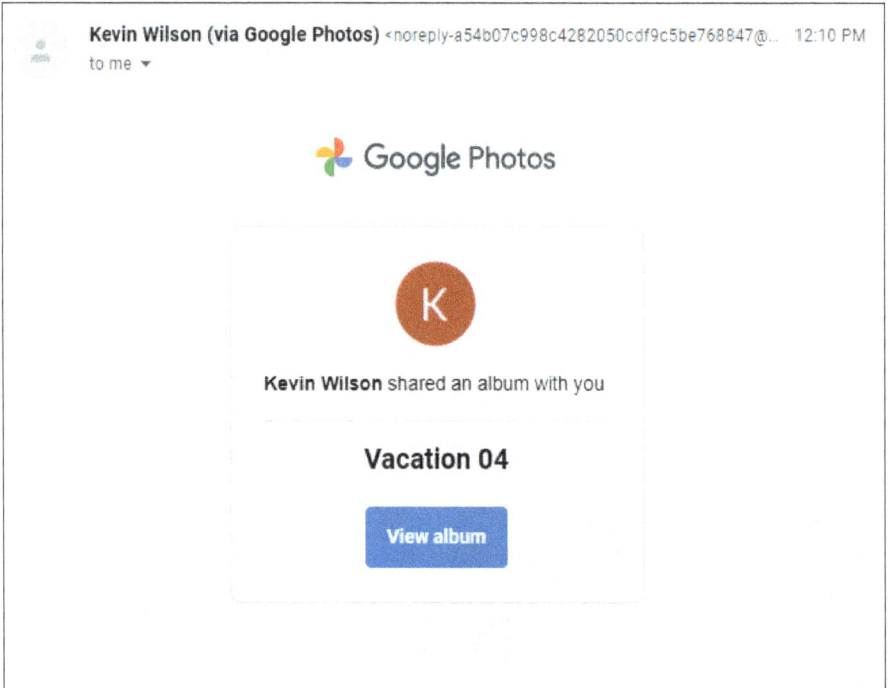

Just click 'view album'

Printing Photos

Within Google photos you can order hard copy prints of your photographs. You can print the photos as individual prints of various sizes such as 4x6, 5x7 and so on. You can also create photo albums with all your photos in, as well as create canvas prints of special photos you'd like to display on your wall. Here's a summary below.

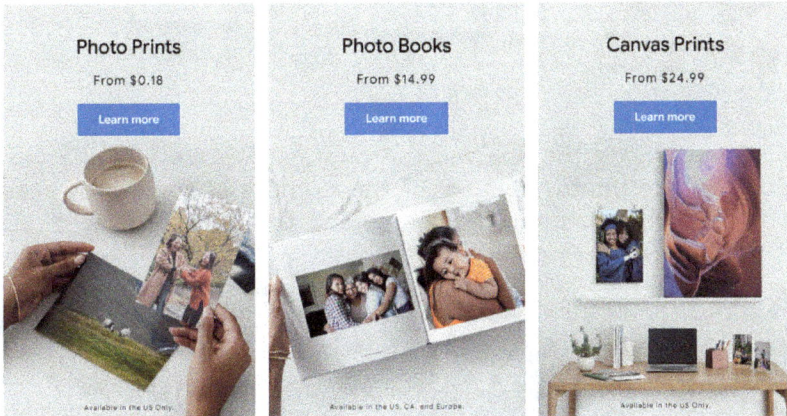

First select 'print store' from the panel on the left hand side. Select 'order prints' if you want individual photos.

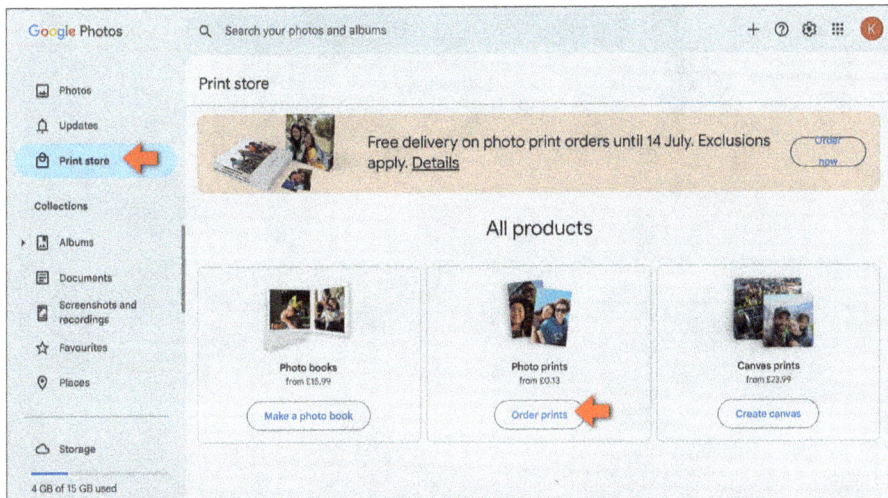

If you want to create a photo album or print book, select 'make a photo book'. If you want to print the photo on a large canvas to put on your wall click 'create canvas'.

In this demo, I'm going to select 'order prints'.

Chapter 6: Entertainment

Select the photos you want to print. Click the 'tick' on the top left of each of the photos you want to include. Click 'done' on the top right when you're finished.

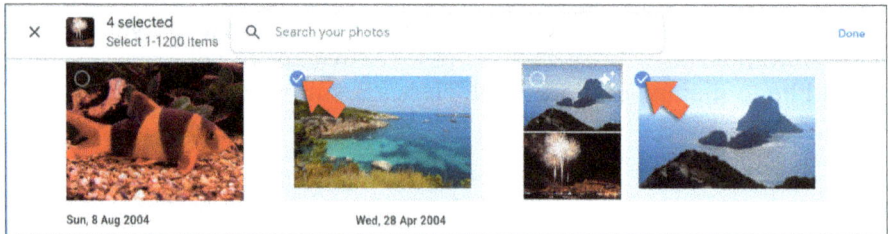

Scroll down, check the sizes of the photos. You can also adjust the crop or edit the photo. Also select the number of copies you want of each photo. Do this using the bar along the bottom of each photo. Click 'next'.

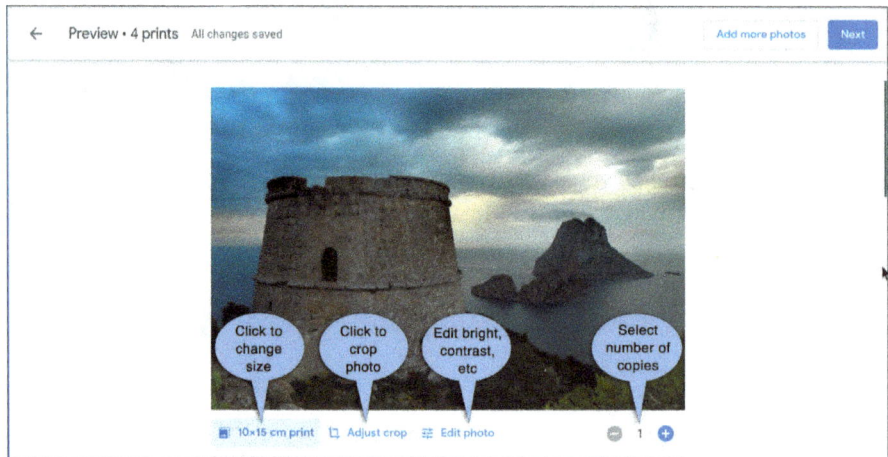

Enter payment details, then scroll down click 'save changes'.

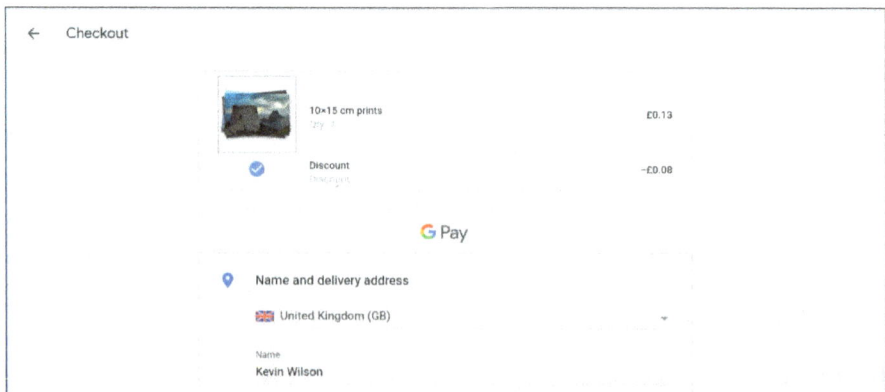

Spotify

Spotify is a popular digital music and podcast streaming service where you can access millions of songs and audio content from artists around the world. Spotify allows you to stream music on demand, create custom playlists, discover new tracks through personalized recommendations, and follow their favorite artists. It offers both a free, ad-supported version and a premium subscription with additional features such as offline listening and ad-free playback.

To get started, you'll need to download the app from the Google Play Store. Open the Play Store and search for 'Spotify'. Select 'Spotify' from the search results.

Click 'install'.

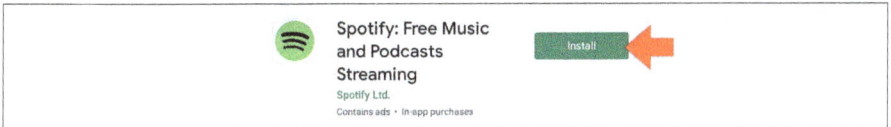

Once downloaded and installed, you can start the Spotify app from your app launcher. You'll need to sign up for a free account. Click 'sign up for free' and fill in your details. If you already use Spotify, click 'log in'.

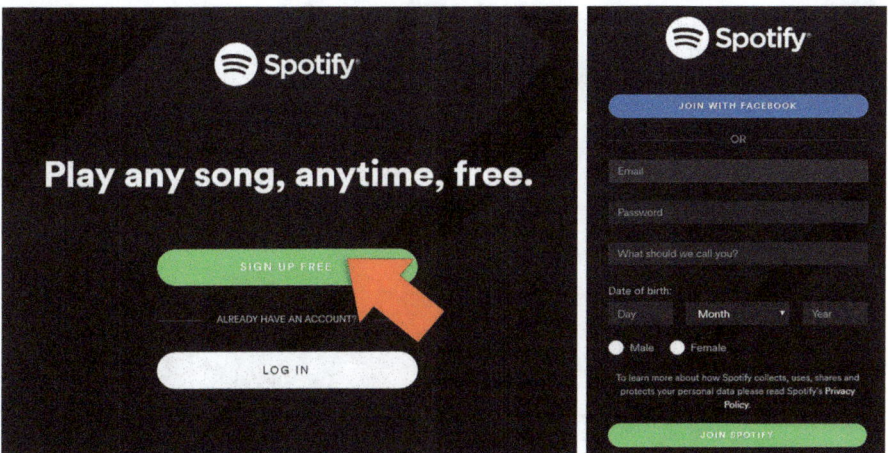

Click 'join Spotify' when you're finished.

Chapter 6: Entertainment

With Spotify, you can search for any song, album or artist you like. Just type it into the search field at the top of the screen.

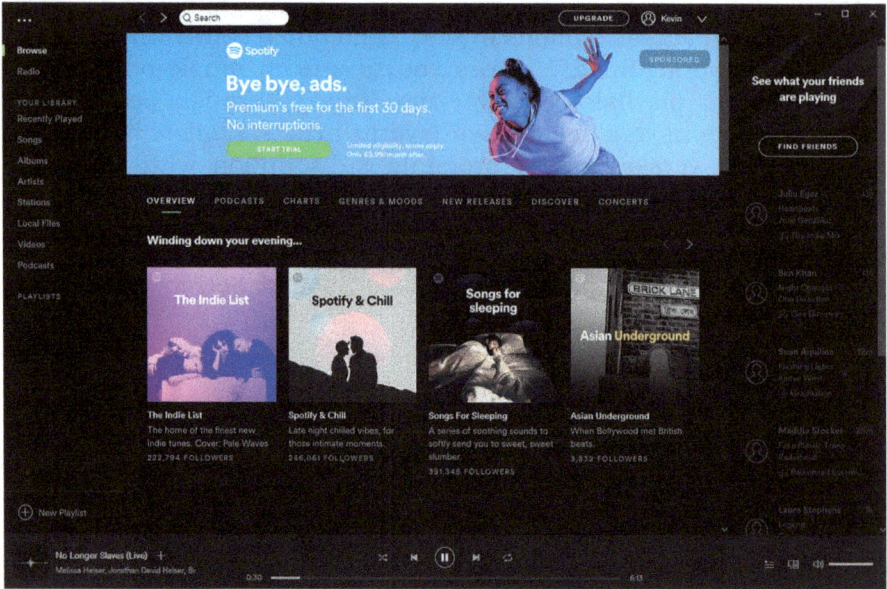

You can scroll down the main page and browse through the genres. Once you've found a song, either by searching or browsing through your favourite genres, you can add them to your library. To do this, click the '+' sign to the left of the track name.

You'll find the tracks in your library on the top left of the main screen

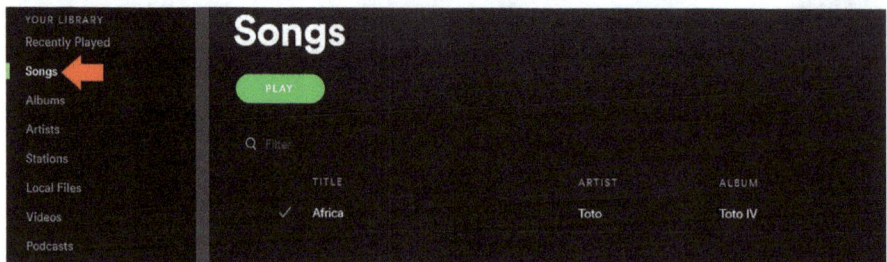

Click on the track to play.

YouTube Music

YouTube Music is free to download and use, however viewers can also subscribe to a premium membership to get an ad-free experience that also allows them to download music to listen offline or without video.

You'll find the app on your app launcher.

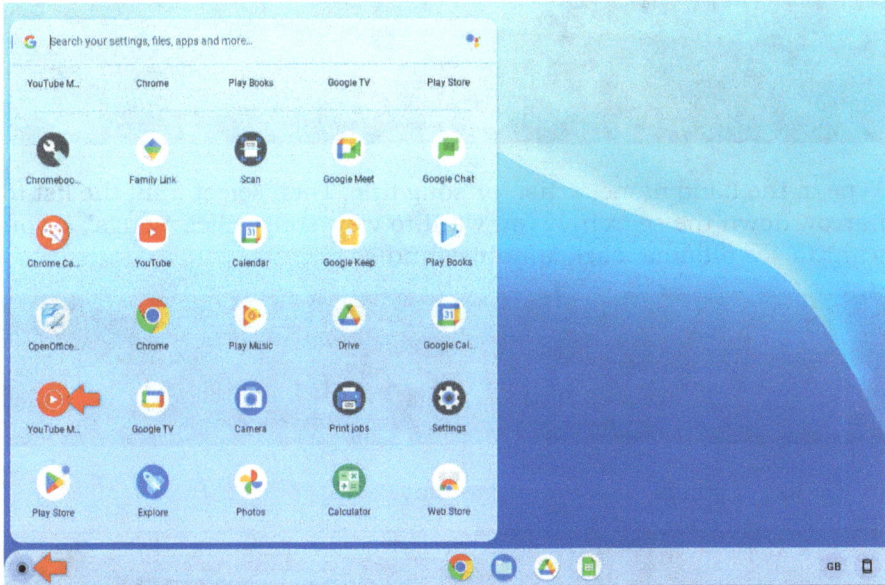

Once you start the app, you'll land on the home screen. Let's take a look.

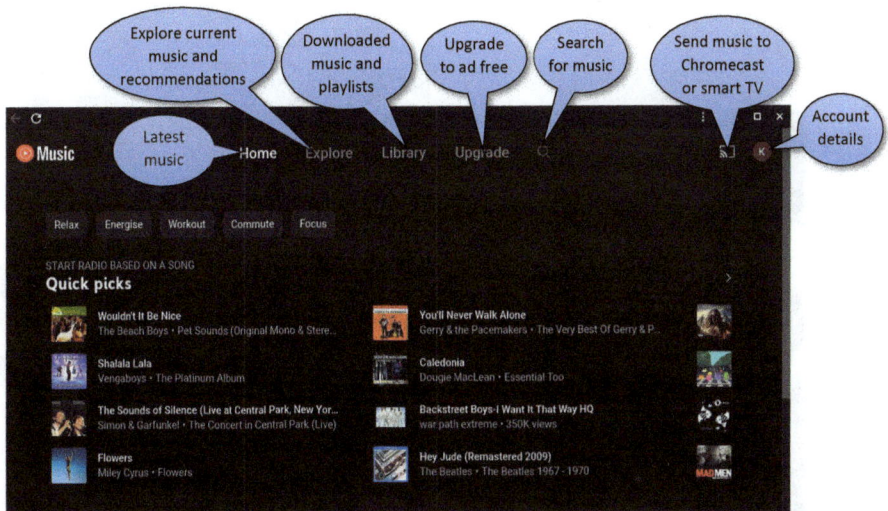

Chapter 6: Entertainment

Listening to Music

The easiest way to find music you like is to search for it.

Search

To do this, click the search icon on the top right of the screen.

Type in the band name, artist, or song title. Then select from the list to narrow down the search. If you want to view songs click 'songs', if you want to see albums, click 'albums', and so on.

In the list of songs click on one to play.

You'll see the play screen appear.

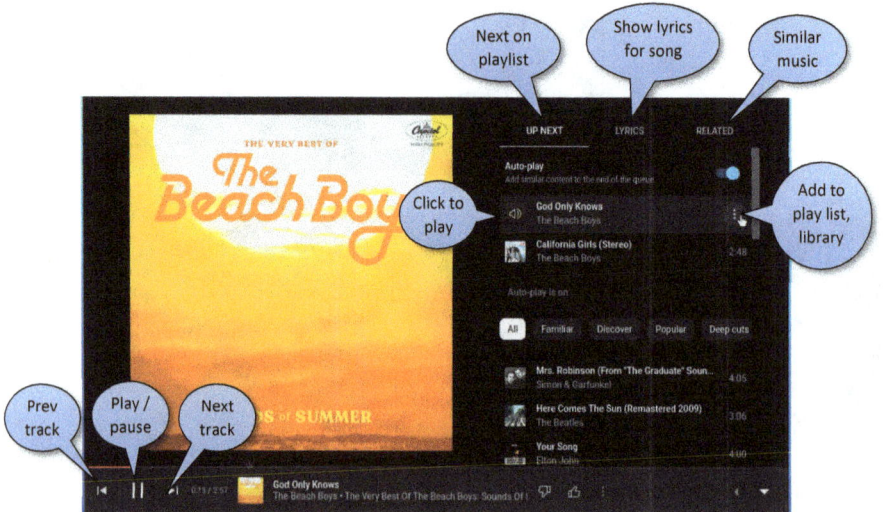

Add to Playlist

You can create your own playlists. You can create private playlists - ones only you can see, or you can create public playlists you can share with others.

To add a song to a playlist, hover your mouse over the track, click the three dots icon that appears on the right hand side. Select 'add to playlist'.

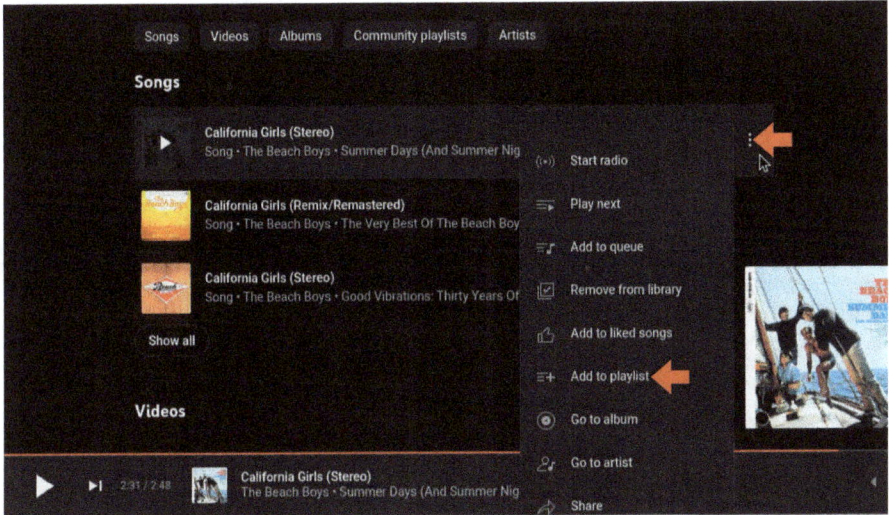

Select the playlist you want to add the song to. If there is no playlist, click 'new playlist'.

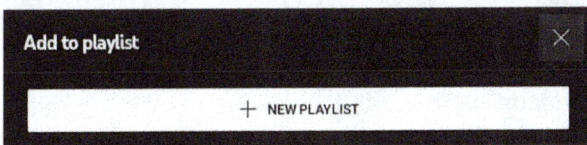

Add a name, then select your privacy settings. If you just want to listen to the songs yourself, click private. If you want to share with others, select public.

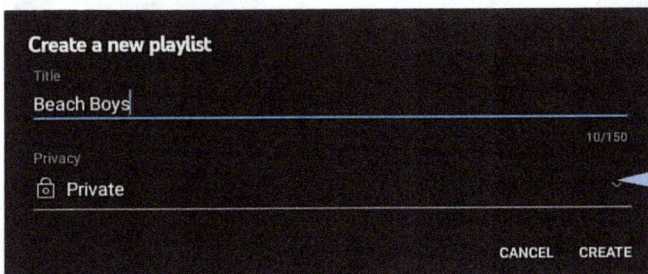

Chapter 6: Entertainment

Open Playlist

You'll find your playlists in your library. Click the 'library' icon at the top of the screen.

Select 'playlists'

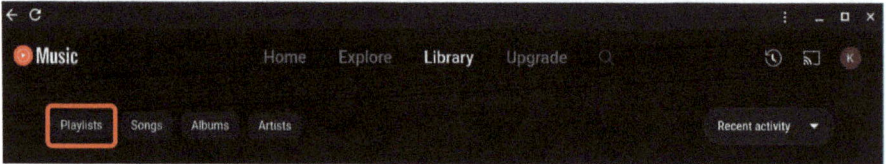

Click on the playlist you want to listen to.

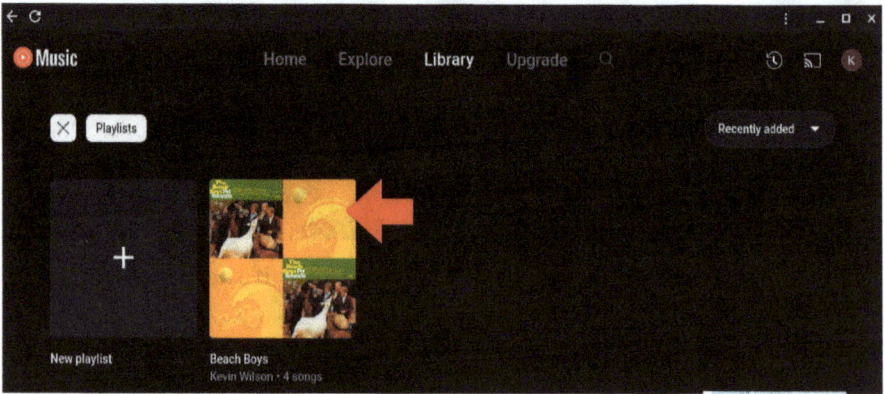

Click the 'play' icon next to the track.

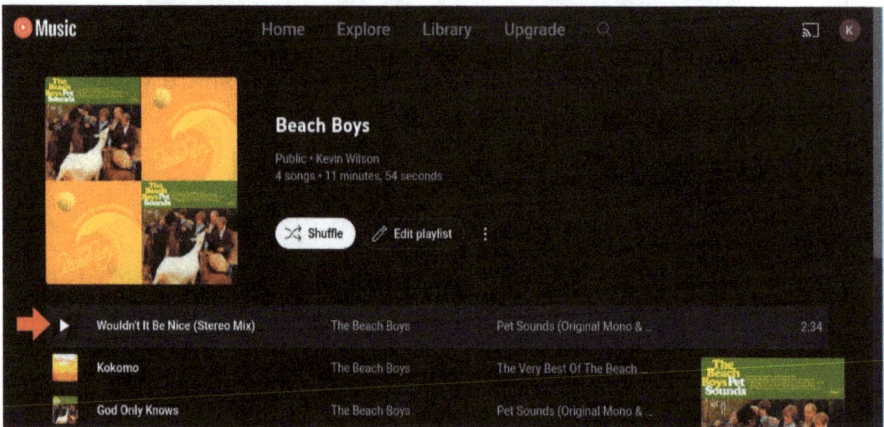

Share a Playlist

If you set your playlist privacy to public, you can share the playlist with other people.

Open your playlist, from the library as shown in the previous section. Click the three dots icon underneath the playlist title. Select 'share' from the menu.

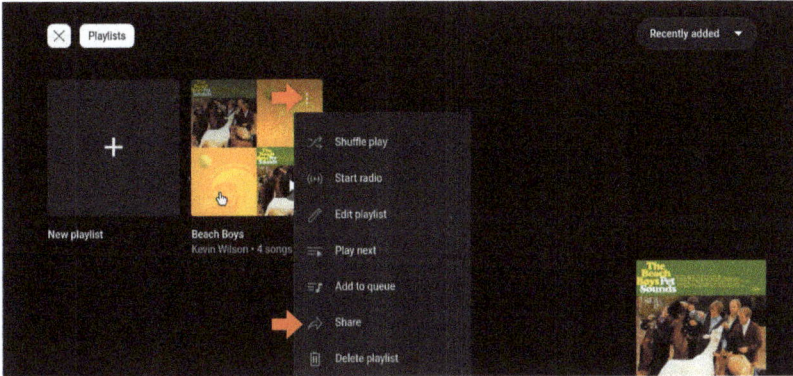

Select the app you want to use to send the link, eg email.

Type the person's email address in Gmail, click send.

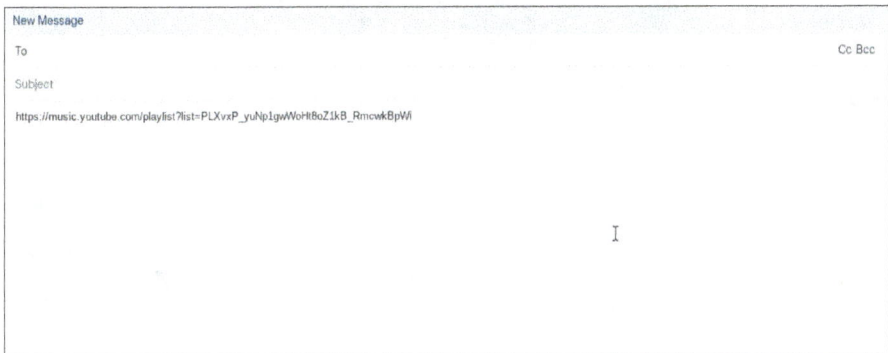

YouTube

YouTube is an online video sharing and streaming website that allows users to upload, view, share and comment on videos. It offers a wide variety of user-generated content as well as content from TV channels and other corporate media. You'll be able to search for video clips, music videos, movie trailers, live streams, video blogs, short original videos, educational videos, self help and how-to videos.

You'll find the YouTube app on the app launcher.

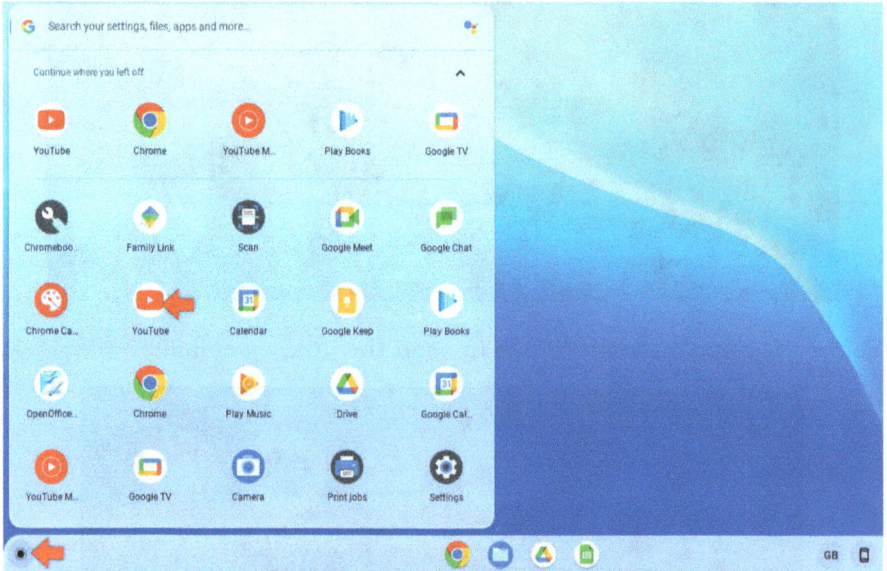

You can browse through the video content on the main page.

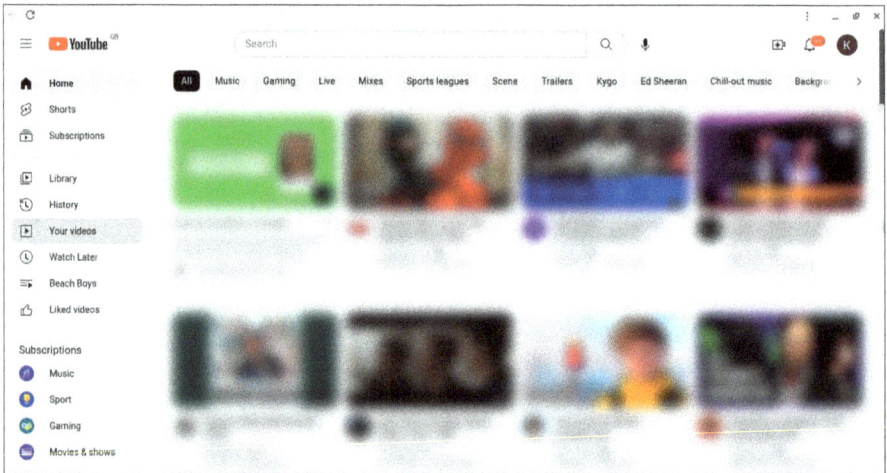

Search for any content you want to watch. Type in your search using the search bar along the top of the screen.

In the search results, click on the thumbnail to view.

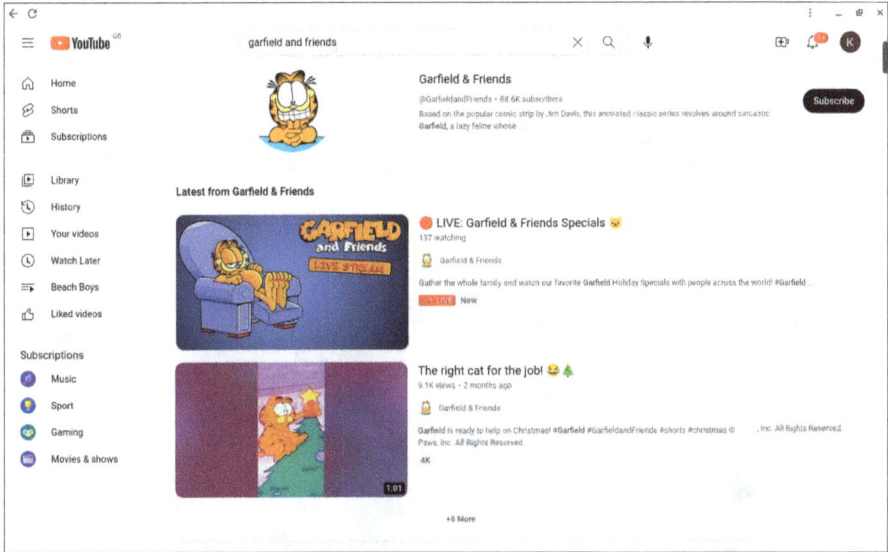

The video will automatically start playing.

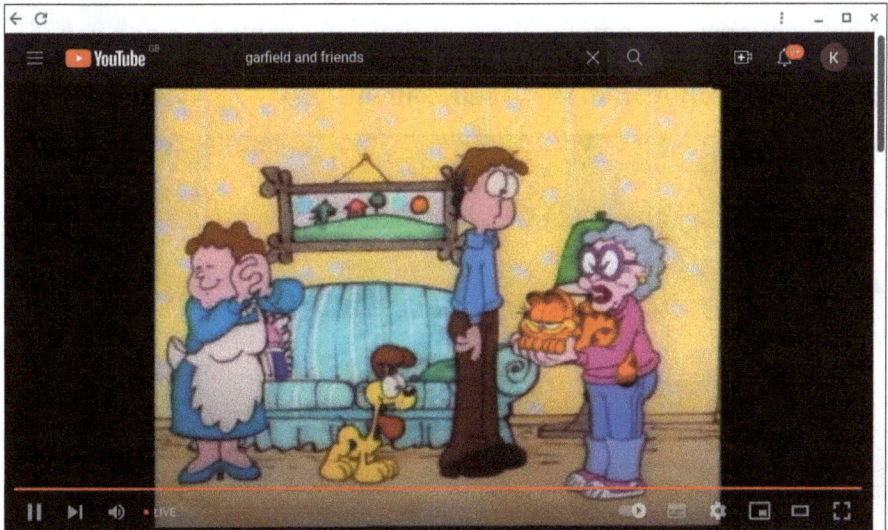

If not, click play icon.

Google TV

Google TV is an app that aggregates TV shows, movies, live TV, and YouTube videos from services such as Netflix, Disney+, Prime Video, YouTube TV, and various others—depending on your subscriptions and region. You can browse personalized recommendations, manage your watchlist, and even buy or rent movies directly through the Google TV app.

To begin, open the app launcher icon on the bottom left, then select the Google TV icon.

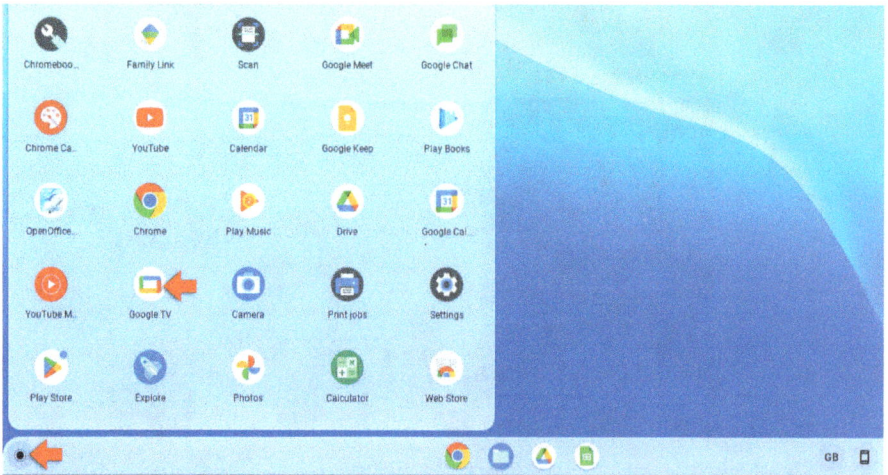

When you open the app for the first time, you can select any services you're interested in. Keep in mind that most of these will require a separate subscription to view their content.

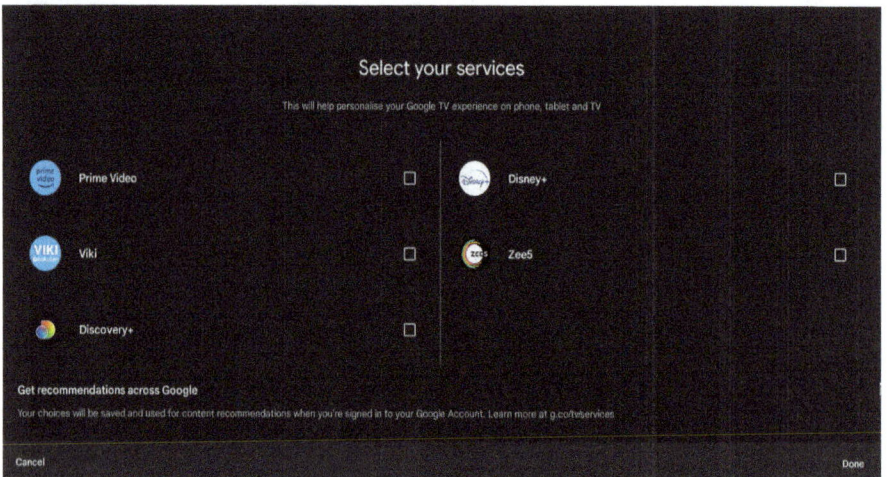

Google TV app will open. Here you'll see any movies or tv programmes you have downloaded, as well as the latest movies and tv shows for you to rent or buy. Let's take a look around

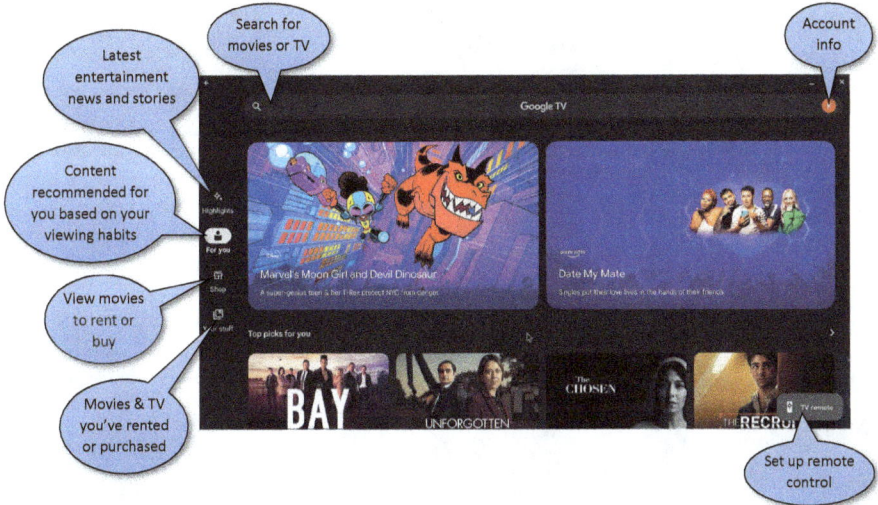

Browsing the Store

To get new movies, you'll need to go the home screen. Here, you can browse through latest releases. You can browse movies, or tv programmes. You can also browse movies or TV programmes that are available to rent or buy. To do this, select 'shop' from the sidebar.

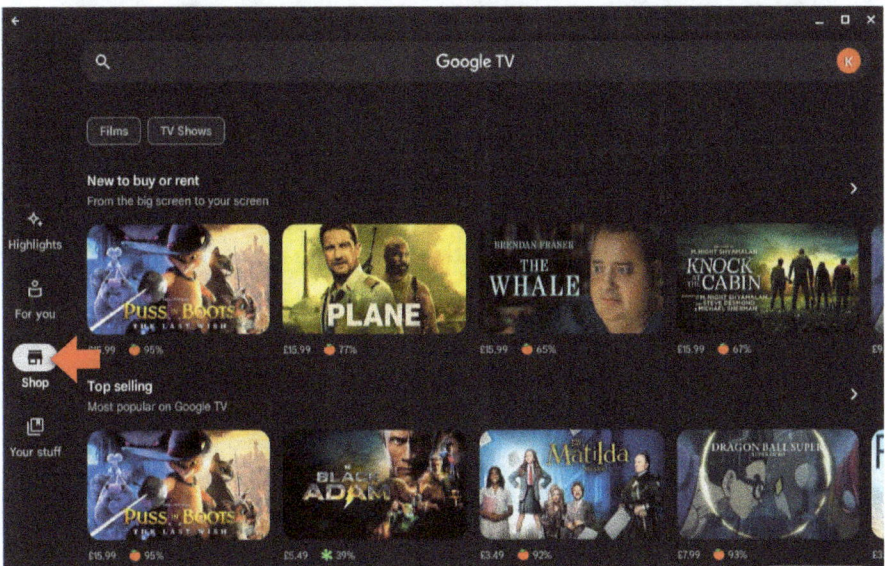

Chapter 6: Entertainment

Click on one of the movies, or TV programmes to view details.

Here, you can watch a trailer, view a write up of the movie. To rent the movie, click 'rent', to buy it click 'buy'. You'll need to add a payment method to do this.

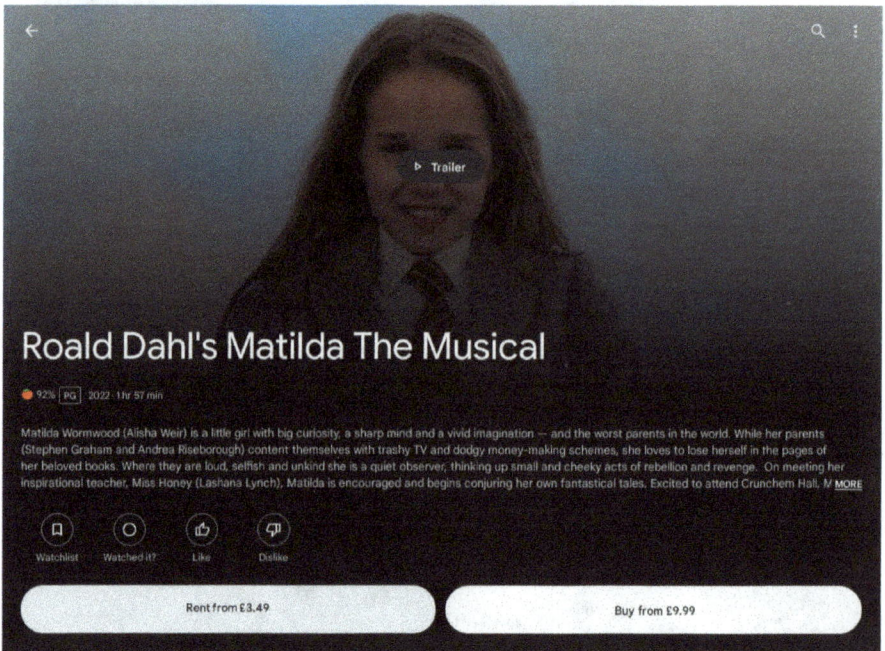

Select the quality you want. If your Chromebook can play back HD quality, or you intend to watch the movie on an external screen or projector then Choose HD. If not, choose SD.

Searching for Movies or TV Programmes

To search for movies or TV programmes, use the search field at the top of the screen.

Type in the name of the movie, TV programme, or actor. Select the movie from the search results.

Here, you can watch a trailer, view a write up of the movie.

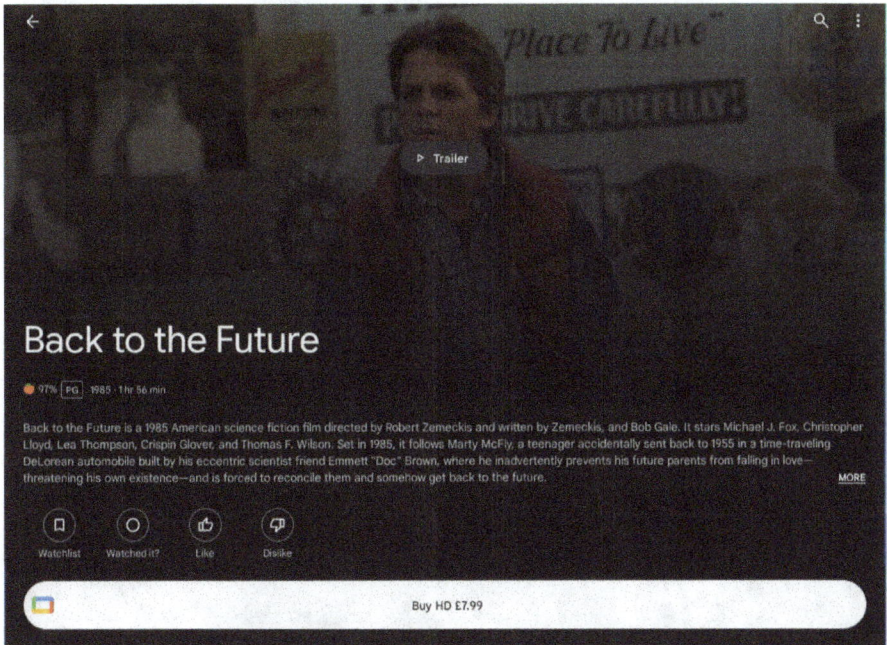

To rent the movie, click 'rent', to buy it click 'buy'. You'll need to add a payment method to do this.

Chapter 6: Entertainment

Select the quality you want. If your Chromebook can play back HD quality, or you intend to watch the movie on an external screen or projector then Choose HD. If not, choose SD. Then enter your payment details.

You'll find your movie in the 'your stuff' library.

Watching Movies

Once you've rented or purchased your content, you'll find it in the 'your stuff' section of the app.

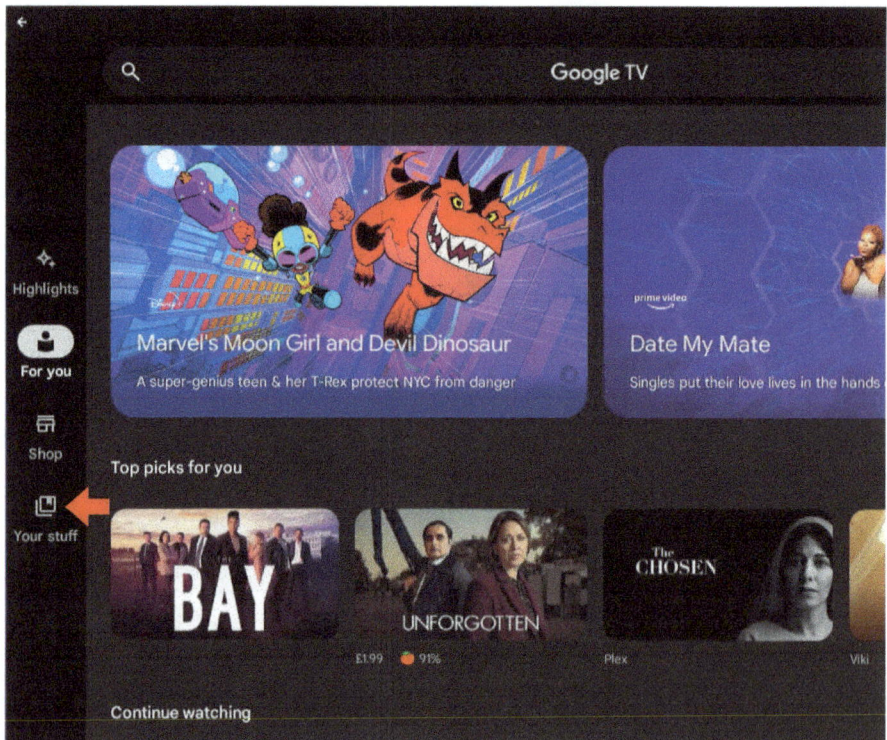

Click the thumbnail cover of the movie you want to watch.

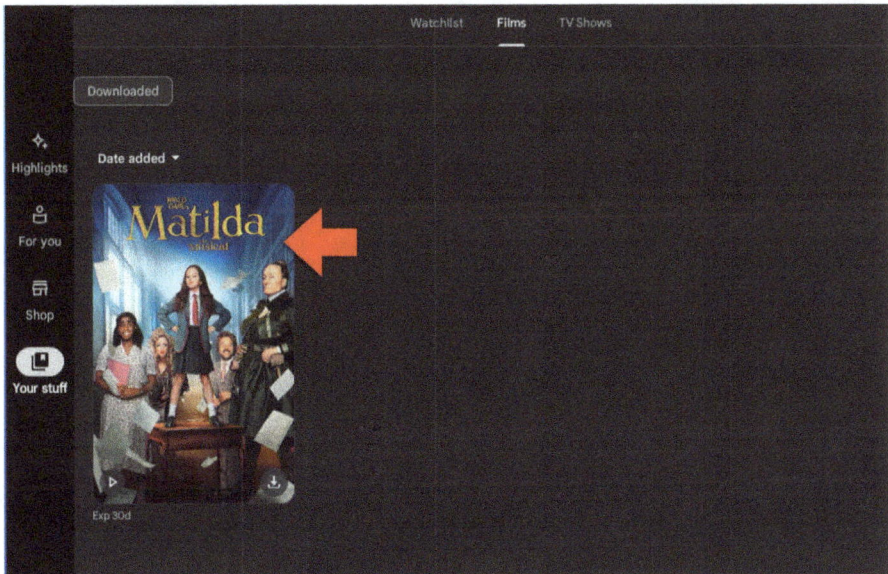

On the movie details page, click 'watch' to start your movie.

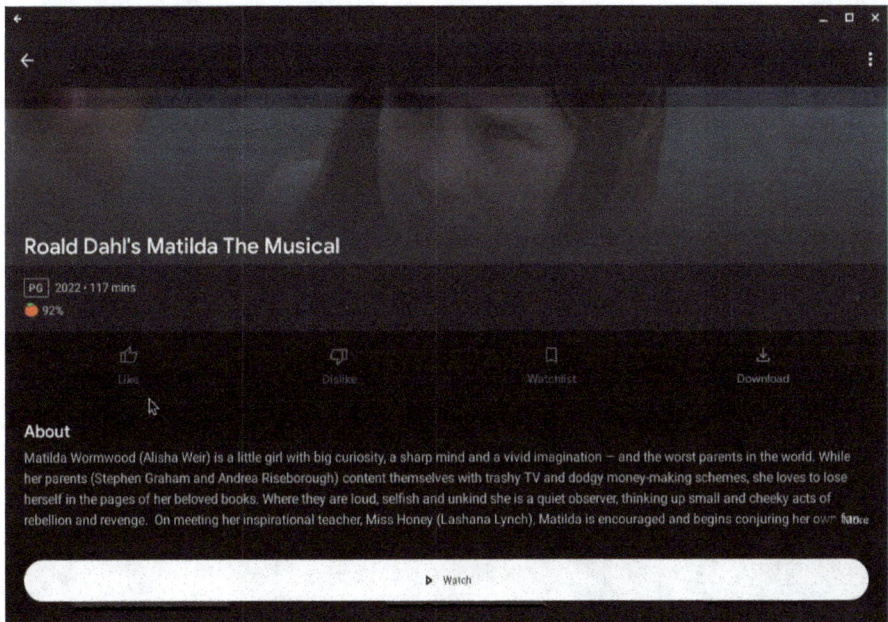

To watch the movie, you'll need a good internet connection. If your connection isn't that good or if you want to watch the movie offline, click 'download'.

Chapter 6: Entertainment

Press the full screen button on the keyboard, then enjoy your movie.

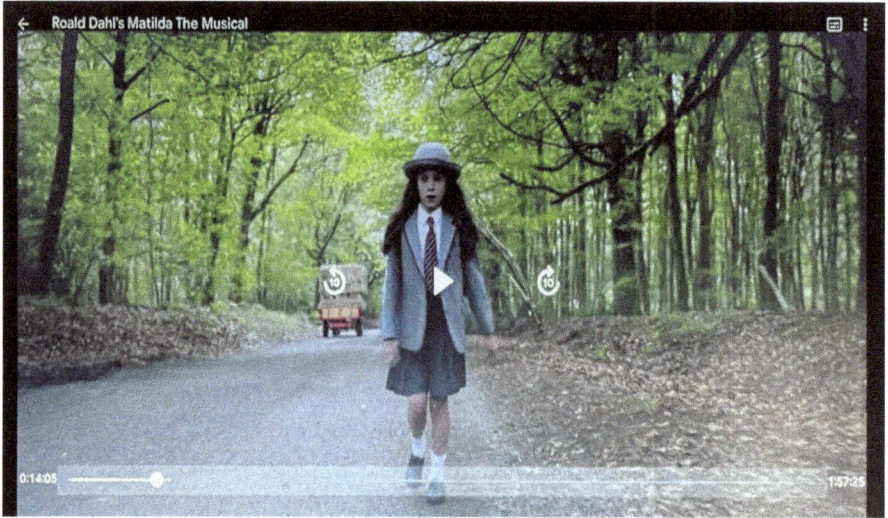

You can also watch your movie to a TV or Projector, you can connect to it using an HDMI cable, and watch your movie on a big screen.

Netflix

Netflix is a subscription-based streaming service that offers an online library of films and television programs. A free trial is available but you'll need to sign up and subscribe to the service for £8.99 a month.

Open the Play Store and search for 'netflix'. Select 'netflix' from the search results.

Click 'install'

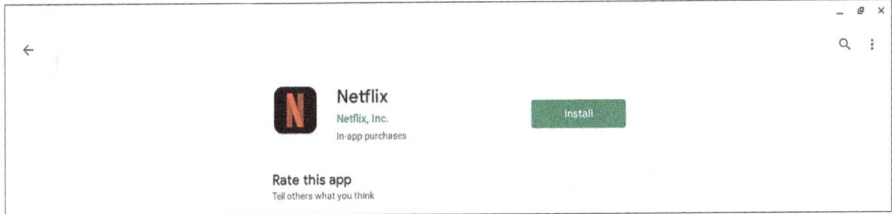

Once downloaded and installed, you can start the netflix app from your app launcher.

When you start netflix, you'll need to either sign up for an account or log in with an existing account.

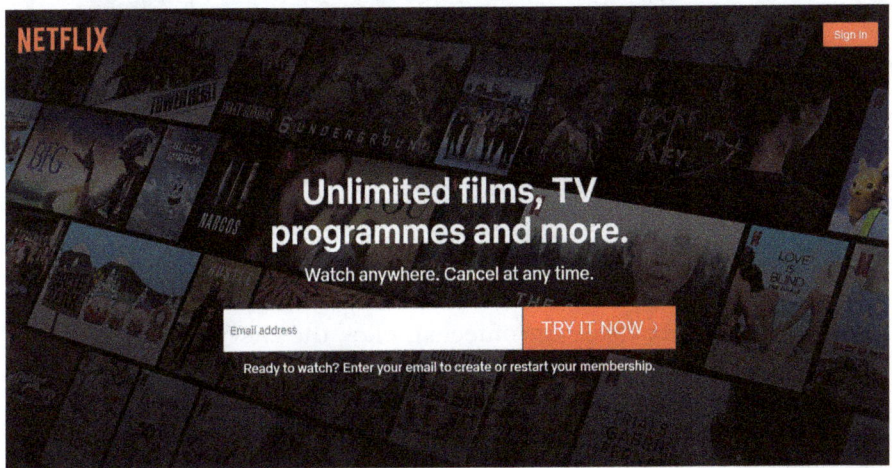

To sign up, click 'try it now', then follow the instructions on the screen to open your account.

Chapter 6: Entertainment

You can browse through TV Shows and Films. Use the categories along the top of the screen, scroll down the home page to view latest films and TV shows. Click the one you want to watch.

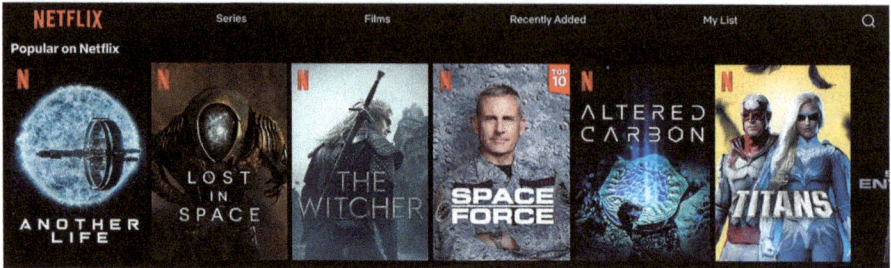

You can also search for content using the search icon on the top right.

Type in your search. Click on a TV show or movie in the search results.

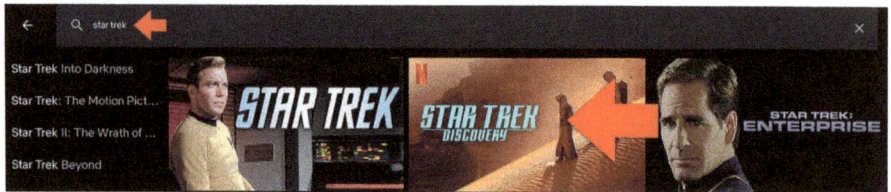

Here, you'll see details of the show or movie. Select an episode, click the play button to play.

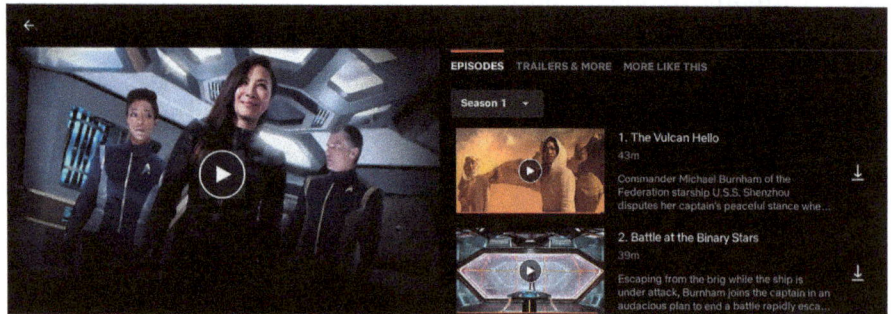

If you have a smart TV or Chromecast, click the cast icon to watch the film on your TV.

Prime Video

Prime Video is a streaming video service provided by Amazon and is included with an Amazon Prime membership.

Open the Play Store and search for 'prime video'. Select 'prime video' from the search results. Click 'install'.

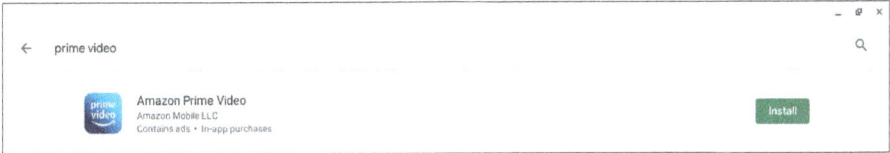

Once downloaded and installed, you can start the amazon prime video app from your app launcher.

Sign in with your amazon account.

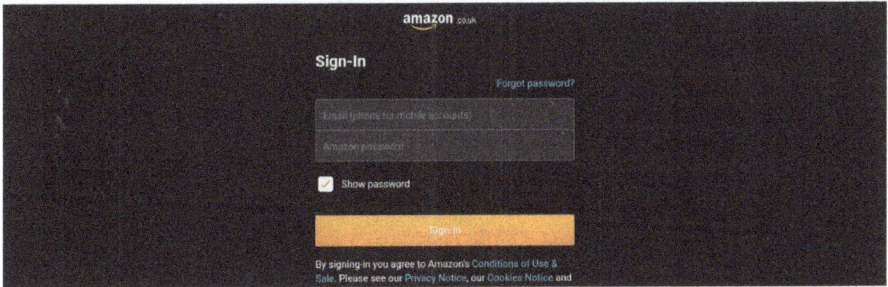

Here, you can rent movies, watch TV shows, just select what you want to watch.

Projectors & TVs

You can hook your ChromeBook up to a digital projector or television. You can also cast your video wirelessly to a ChromeCast device plugged into your TV or projector.

HDMI

Your ChromeBook has an HDMI port on the side that will enable you to connect to a TV or projector. Most modern TVs & projectors will have at least 1 HDMI port on the back.

You can buy an HDMI cable from most electronic stores and online. An HDMI cable looks like the one below.

Plug one end into an HDMI port on your TV or projector, then plug the other end into the HDMI port on your ChromeBook.

ChromeCast

To use ChromeCast, first you'll need to buy a ChromeCast device, and plug it into an HDMI port on your TV or projector.

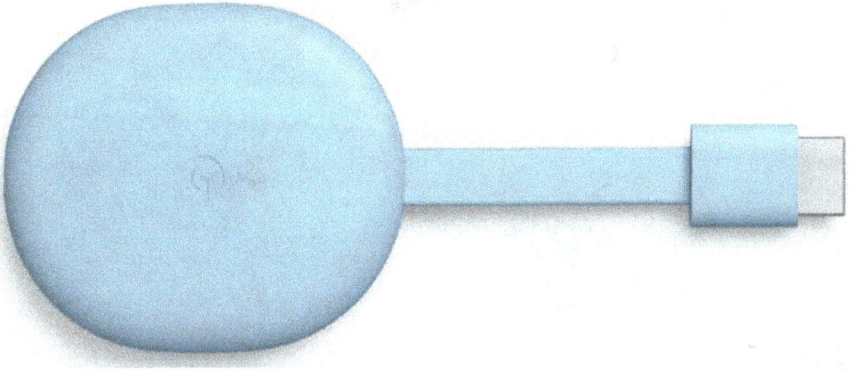

With ChromeCast you can stream from Netflix and YouTube, as well as any movie, TV show, or app from the Google Play Store. You can also use it to stream anything from Chrome browser on your ChromeBook.

Both your ChromeCast device and your ChromeBook will need to be on the same wifi network for it to work.

To cast a video, open the Google TV app.

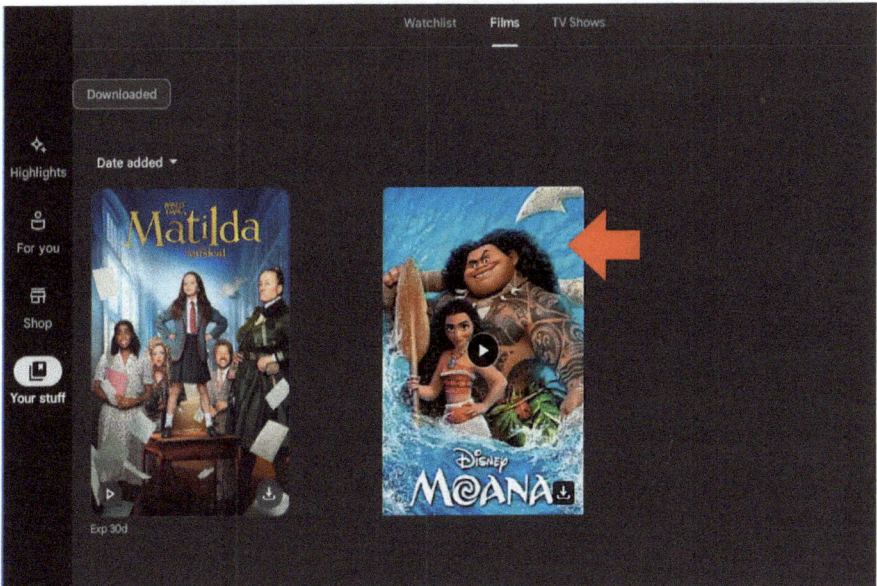

Select the movie you want to watch.

Chapter 6: Entertainment

Click 'watch' on the summary screen.

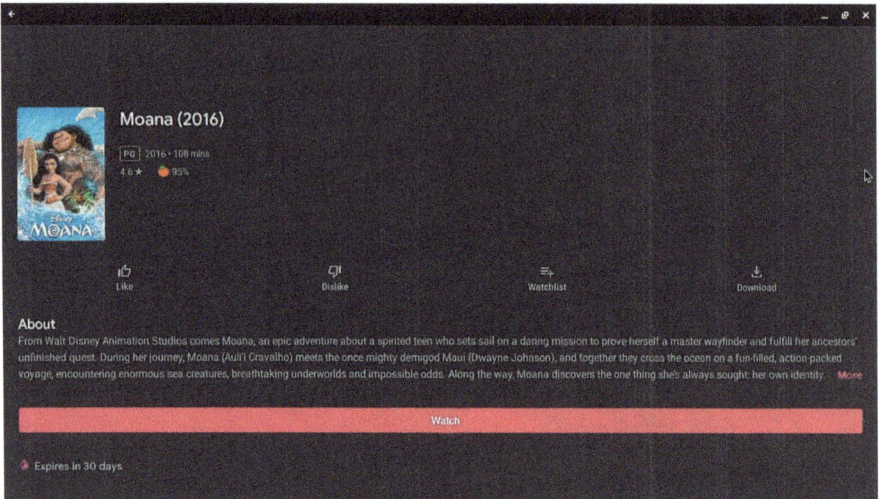

As you hover your mouse over the video, you'll see some icons. Tap the 'cast' icon on the top right hand side of the screen, then select your Chromecast device from the device list.

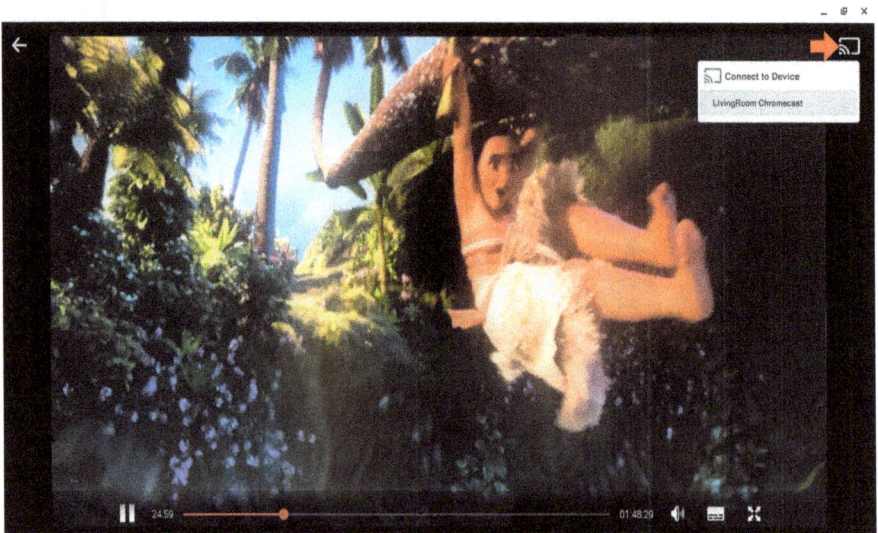

You can do the same for any movie or TV show you have downloaded from the Google Play Store.

The cast icon will only appear if your Chromecast device is plugged in, powered on, and connected to the same wifi network as your Chromebook.

Google Play Books

With the books app you can buy and read ebooks in a wide variety of different genres from the play store.

Click the app launcher icon on the bottom left, then click on the Google play books icon.

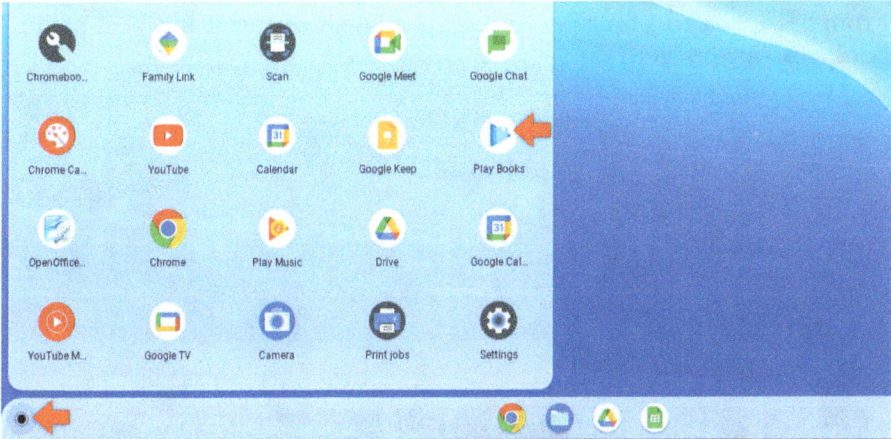

Google play books will open up on the main screen.

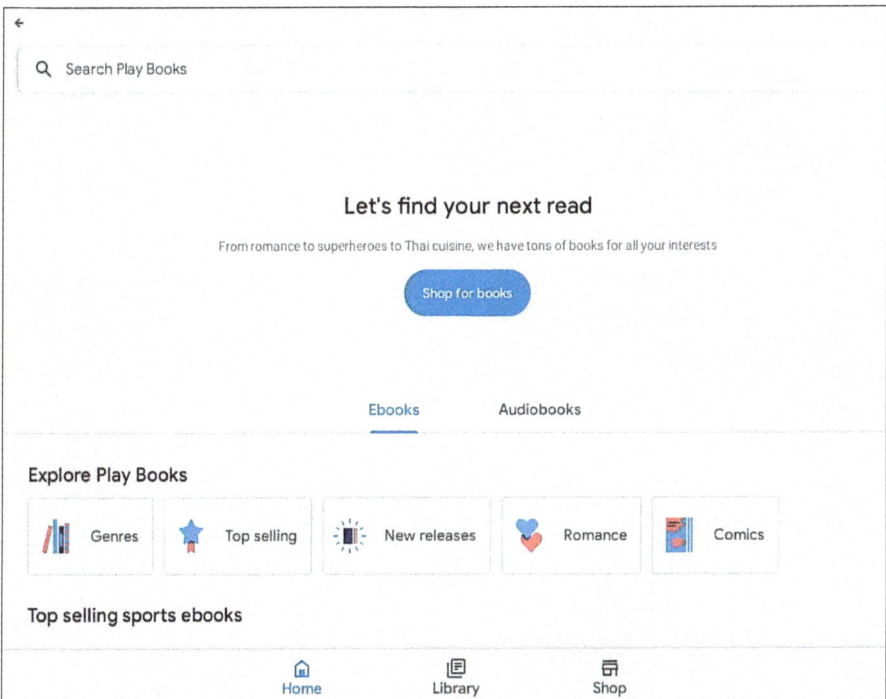

Chapter 6: Entertainment

Downloading eBooks

To download new eBooks, click 'shop' on the bottom right of the screen.

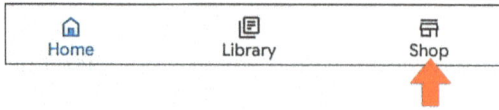

From here, you can browse through the latest releases and best selling books in various genres.

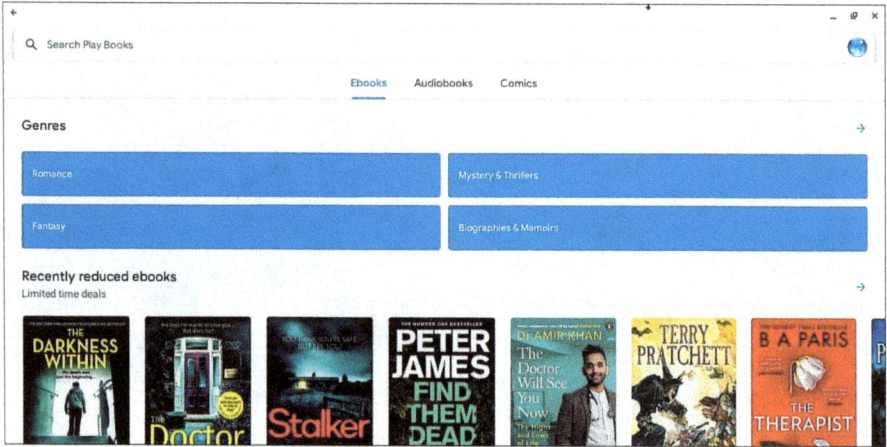

You can also use the search field at the top of the screen to find book titles or authors you want. Press enter on your keyboard to execute the search.

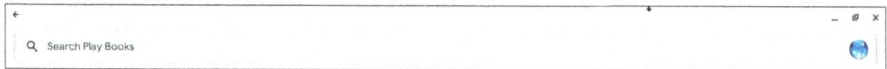

Browse through the search results, click on a book cover thumbnail to view details of the book.

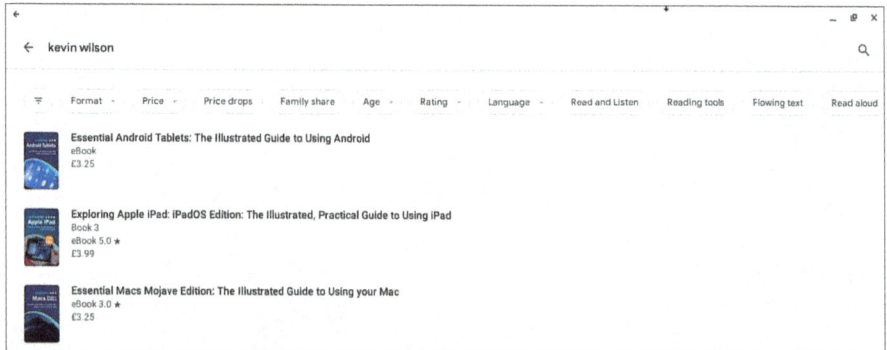

From here you'll be able to read a write up of the book, see reviews and other technical information. Click 'free sample' to read a sample of the book, or click the price tag, to buy and download the book.

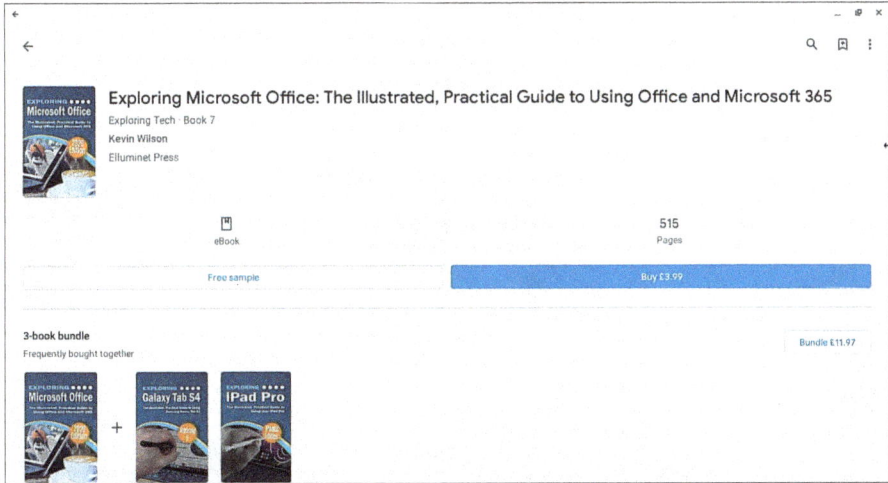

Select your payment method if needed, then click 'buy ebook' to confirm.

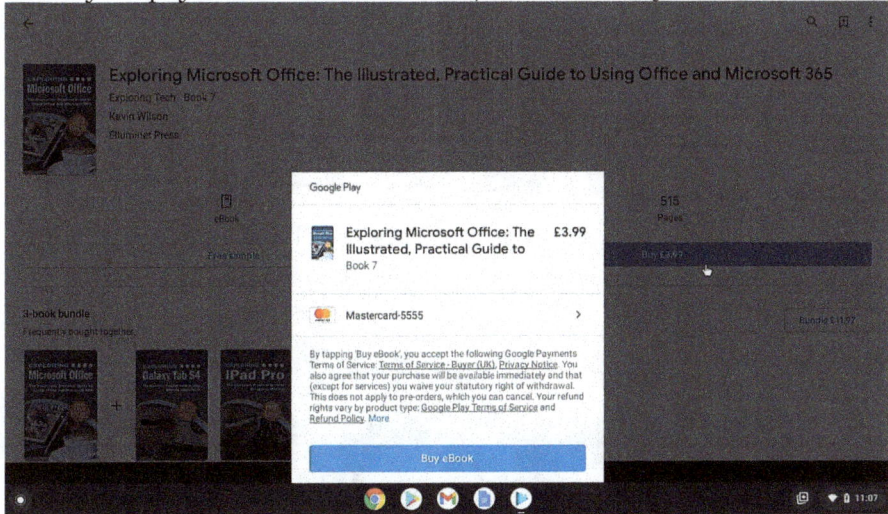

Click 'read' to start reading your book

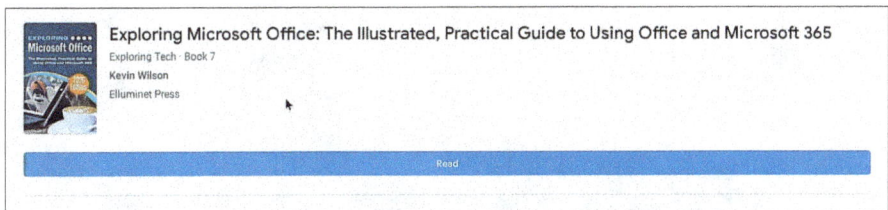

Chapter 6: Entertainment

Library

Open Google Play Books if you haven't already done so, click 'library' on the bottom of the screen.

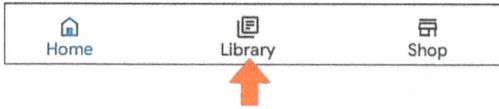

Here, you'll find the books you've downloaded. Click on the book cover to open it up.

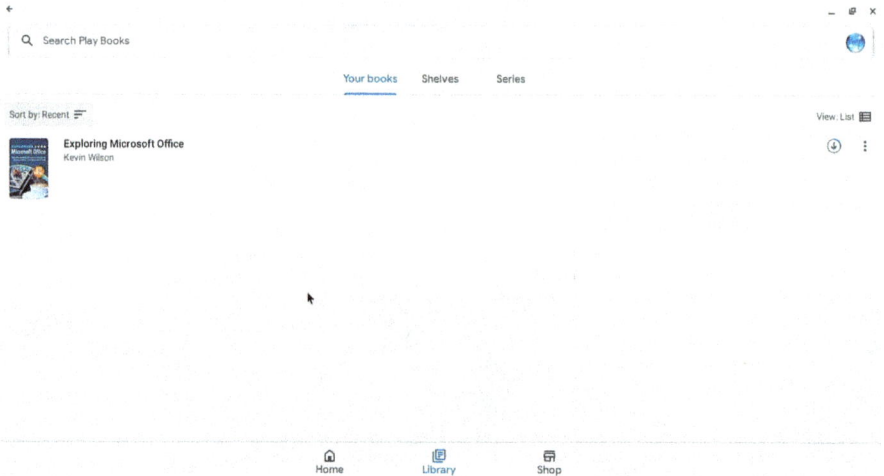

Swipe with two fingers left or right on the touchpad to turn the pages.

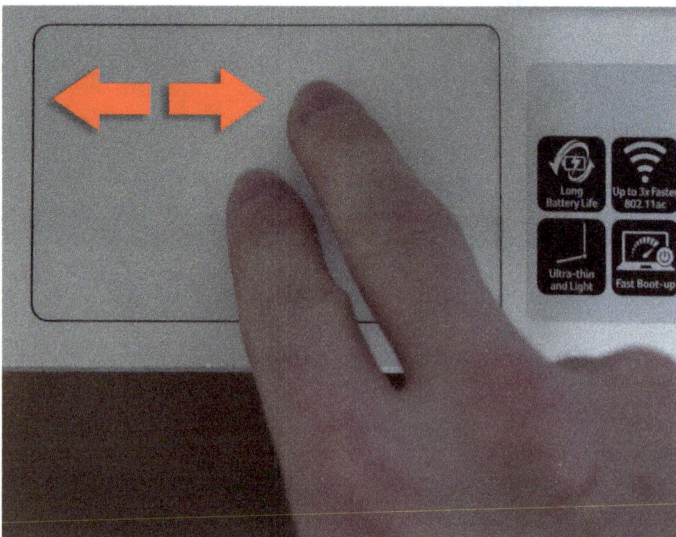

Click on a page to open up the options. On the top right, you can search for keyboards, or change the text size.

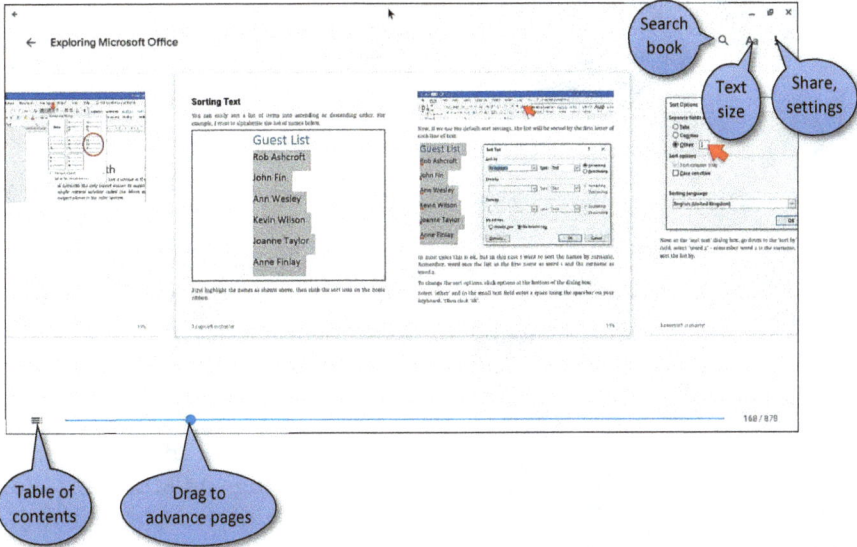

On the bottom left, you can open up the table of contents, bookmarks or notes. You can drag the blue slider to advance pages.

Right click on a word, here you can add a note, translate the word, search the book for the word, or highlight the word in a colour.

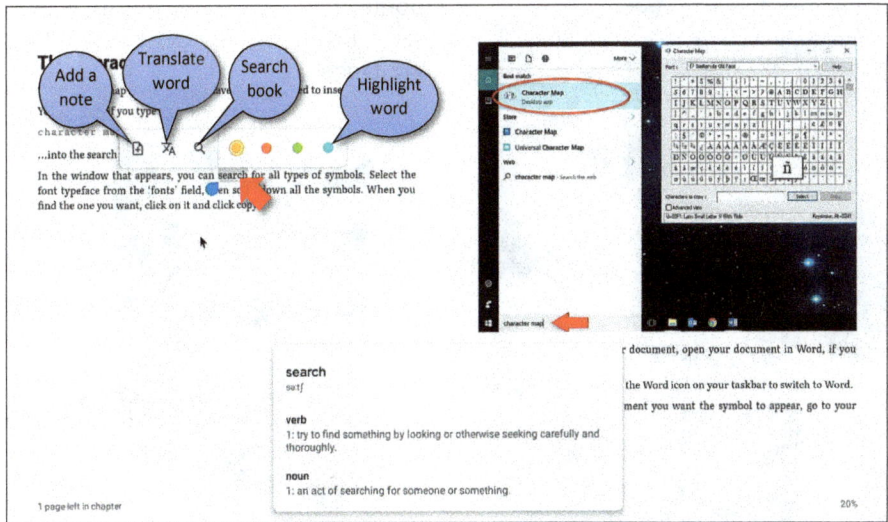

Underneath you'll see a definition of the word you've selected. You'll find a list of all your notes in the notes section of the table of contents.

7

Google Docs

Google Docs is an online word processor much like Microsoft Word and is included as part of a free, web-based office suite developed by Google.

Google Docs allows you to do many of the same things as Microsoft Word but lacks some of the more advanced features.

However, Google Docs is a great alternative and works well on a Chromebook.

In this section, we'll take a brief look at Google Docs. For more detail, check out our other book 'Understanding Google Docs'.

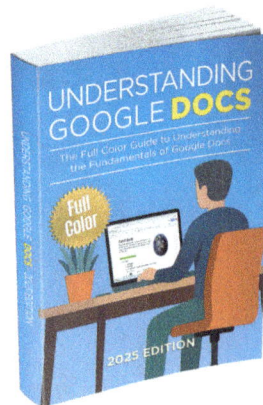

ISBN: 9781917945011

Getting Around Google Docs

I find the best version of Google Docs to use is the web based version rather than the Android Version you might find on your Chromebook. To start the web based version of Google Docs, open your app launcher, then click on Google Chrome.

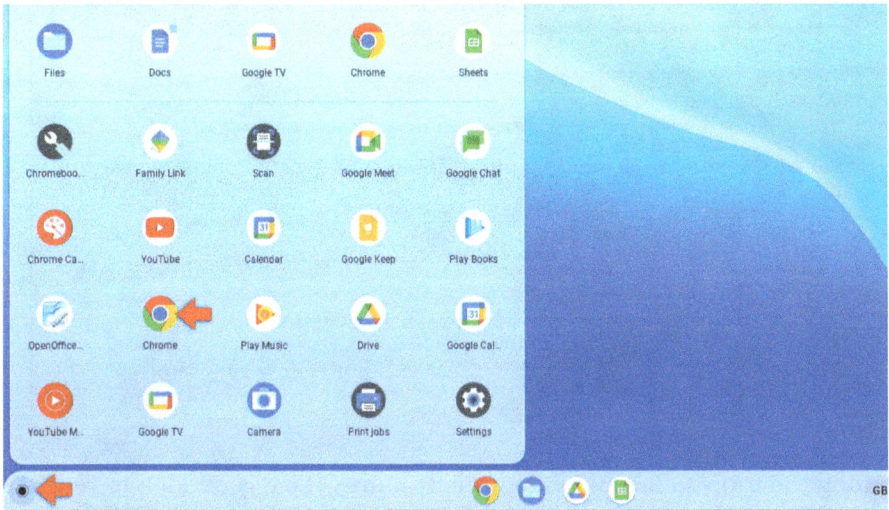

Navigate to the following website:

docs.google.com

When Google Docs opens, you'll see the documents you have been working on recently. You can click any of these to re-open them. To create a new document, click blank on the top left of the screen.

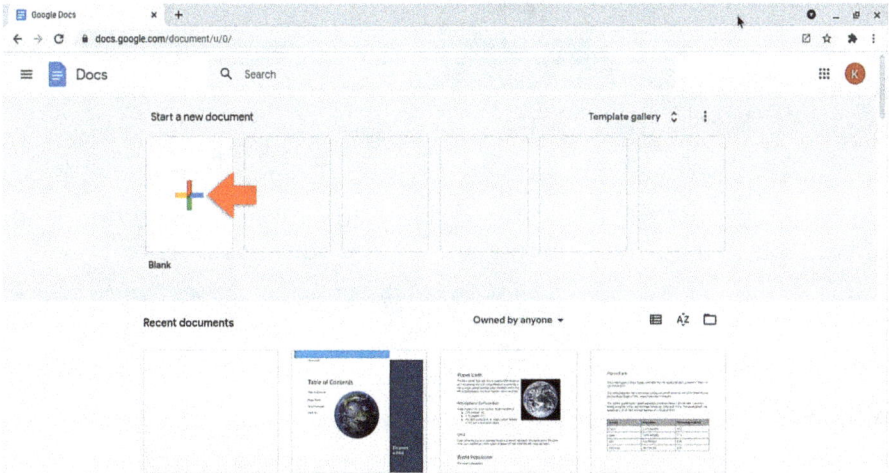

Chapter 7: Google Docs

Google Docs will open the main window where you can create your document.

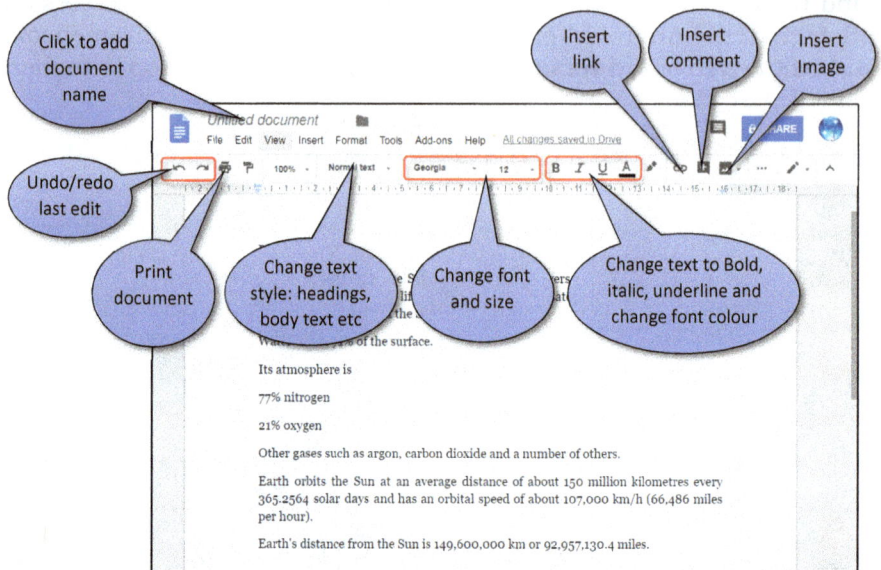

Along the top you'll see the document name. It's a good idea to rename this to something more meaningful that 'untitled document'. Click on the text and type in a name.

Underneath are the menus. This is where you'll find tools that are not represented as icons on the toolbar.

Under the menus you'll see the toolbar. This is where you'll find most of the tools you'll need to create and format your documents.

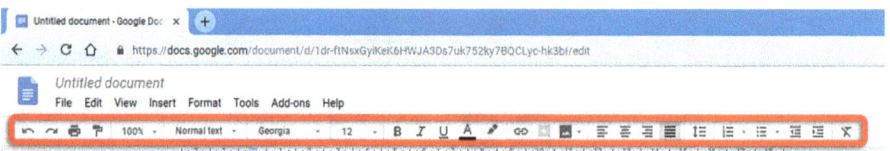

Using Paragraph Styles

Google Docs has several paragraph styles that are useful for keeping your formatting consistent.

For example you can set a font style, size and colour for a heading or title style...

Headings

To set the styles for a heading or paragraph, just highlight it with your mouse and click the drop down box 'normal text'.

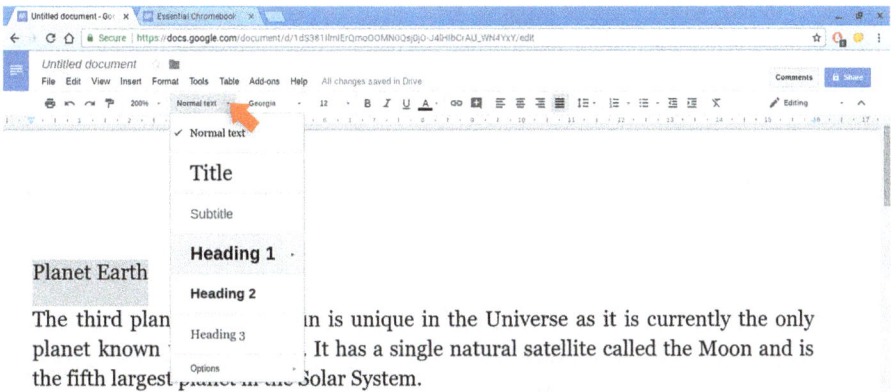

Bold, Italic, Underlined

To make text **bold**, *italic,* or underlined, highlight the text with your mouse and select the bold, italic, or underline icon from the toolbar.

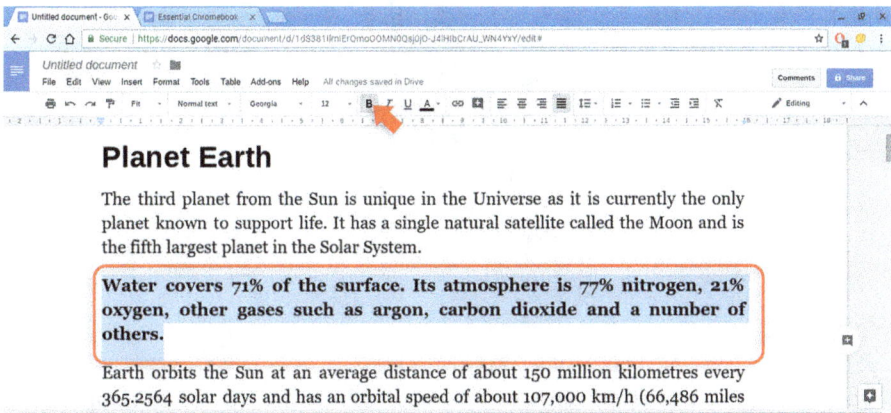

Changing Fonts

Google Docs has a variety of fonts to choose from. To apply a different font to your text, highlight the text, then click the font style drop down box as shown below.

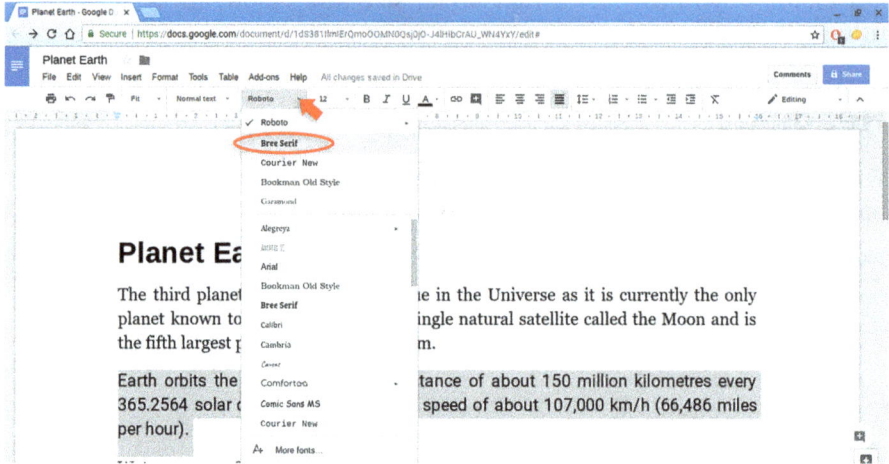

Font Colour

To change the colour of the text, first highlight it with your mouse. In the example below, I want to change the text colour of the second paragraph. To do this, click before the word 'Earth' and drag across the paragraph, to the end after '...miles per hour', to highlight it.

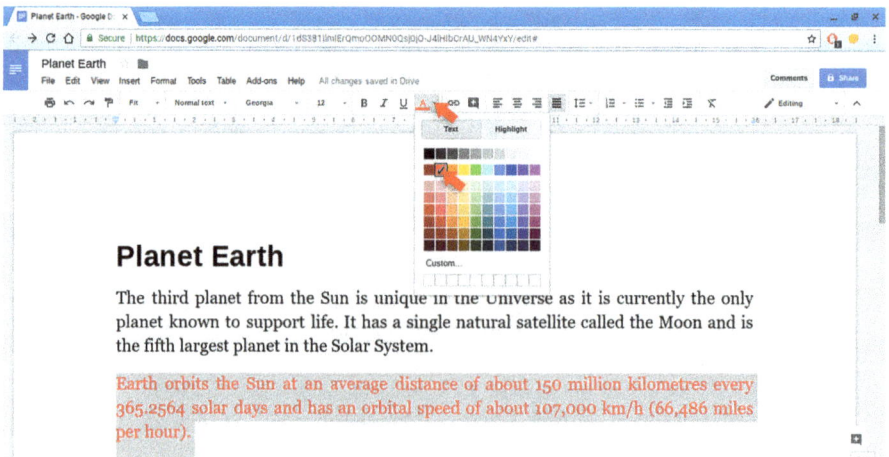

From the toolbar, select the font colour icon and from the drop down choose a colour. In this example I'm using red.

Justify Text

You can align text to different margins: left align, centred, right align, and fully justified.

> The third planet from the Sun is unique in the Universe as it is currently the only planet known to support life. It has a single natural satellite called the Moon and is the fifth largest planet in the Solar System.
>
> The third planet from the Sun is unique in the Universe as it is currently the only planet known to support life. It has a single natural satellite called the Moon and is the fifth largest planet in the Solar System.
>
> The third planet from the Sun is unique in the Universe as it is currently the only planet known to support life. It has a single natural satellite called the Moon and is the fifth largest planet in the Solar System.
>
> The third planet from the Sun is unique in the Universe as it is currently the only planet known to support life. It has a single natural satellite called the Moon and is the fifth largest planet in the Solar System.

In this example, I want right justify the first paragraph. This means the text is aligned to the right hand margin. To do this, click before the word 'The' and drag across the paragraph, to the end after '...solar system as shown above to highlight it.

> The third planet from the Sun is unique in the Universe as it is currently the only planet known to support life. It has a single natural satellite called the Moon and is the fifth largest planet in the Solar System.

Select the right align icon from the toolbar.

The selected text will move to the right hand margin.

> The third planet from the Sun is unique in the Universe as it is currently the only planet known to support life. It has a single natural satellite called the Moon and is the fifth largest planet in the Solar System.

Bullets Lists

Select the text using your mouse as shown below.

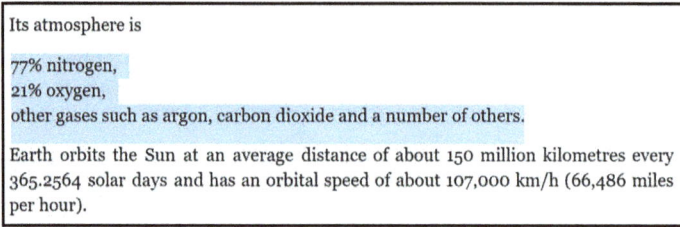

> Its atmosphere is
>
> 77% nitrogen,
> 21% oxygen,
> other gases such as argon, carbon dioxide and a number of others.
>
> Earth orbits the Sun at an average distance of about 150 million kilometres every 365.2564 solar days and has an orbital speed of about 107,000 km/h (66,486 miles per hour).

Then from the toolbar, click the bullet points icon on the right hand side.

You can also have different styles of bullets such as ticks, stars and so on. To get the drop down menu, click the small down arrow next to the bullet icon.

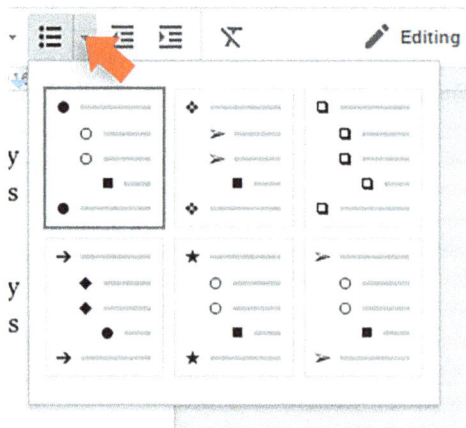

Bullet points will be added to the selected text.

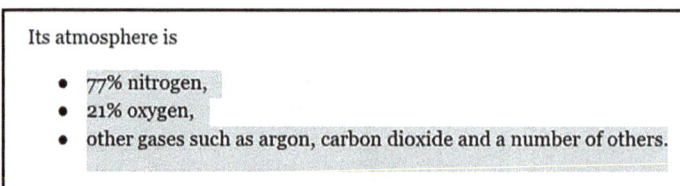

> Its atmosphere is
>
> • 77% nitrogen,
> • 21% oxygen,
> • other gases such as argon, carbon dioxide and a number of others.

Numbered Lists

Select the text using your mouse as shown below.

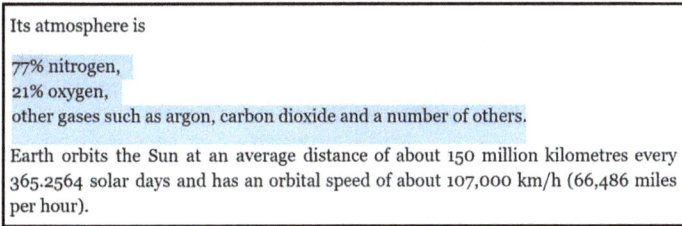

> Its atmosphere is
>
> 77% nitrogen,
> 21% oxygen,
> other gases such as argon, carbon dioxide and a number of others.
>
> Earth orbits the Sun at an average distance of about 150 million kilometres every 365.2564 solar days and has an orbital speed of about 107,000 km/h (66,486 miles per hour).

Then from the toolbar, click the numbered points icon on the right hand side.

You can also have different styles of numbers such as roman numerals, letters, and so on. To get the drop down menu, click the small down arrow next to the numbered icon.

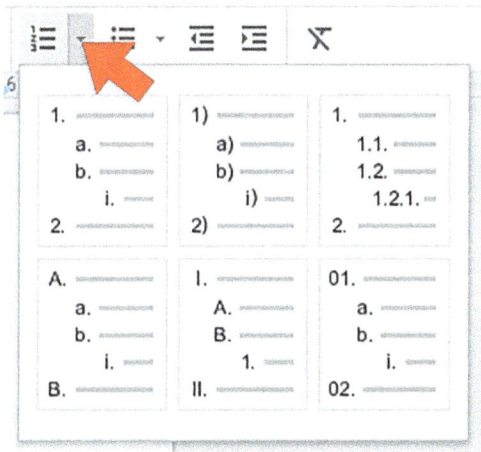

Numbers will be added to the selected text.

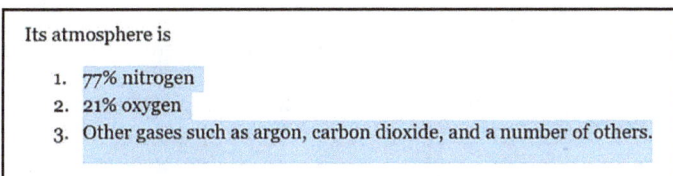

> Its atmosphere is
>
> 1. 77% nitrogen
> 2. 21% oxygen
> 3. Other gases such as argon, carbon dioxide, and a number of others.

Cut, Copy & Paste

To ease editing documents, you can use copy, cut, and paste to move paragraphs or pictures around on different parts of your document.

First select the paragraph you want to cut or copy with your mouse. I'm going to cut the last paragraph in the document below.

Click before the word 'Earth', and dragging your mouse across the line towards the end of the line, as shown below.

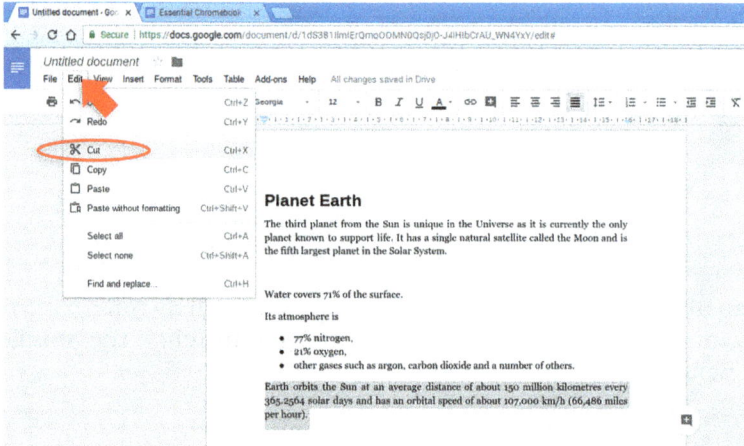

From the edit menu, select 'cut'. Now click on the position in the document you want the paragraph you just cut out to be inserted.

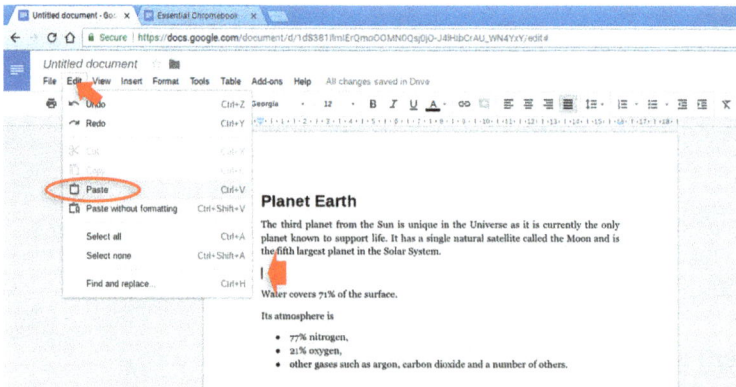

Once you have done that, click the 'edit' menu and select 'paste'.

If you wanted to copy something ie make a duplicate of the text, then use the same procedure except select 'copy' instead of 'cut' from the edit menu.

Adding Images

You can insert images from your Chromebook, from the web, Google Drive, your Photos App or directly from the onboard camera.

From your Chromebook

Click on the line in your document where you want your photograph or image to appear.

Go to your insert menu and click on 'image'. From the slideout menu select 'upload from computer'.

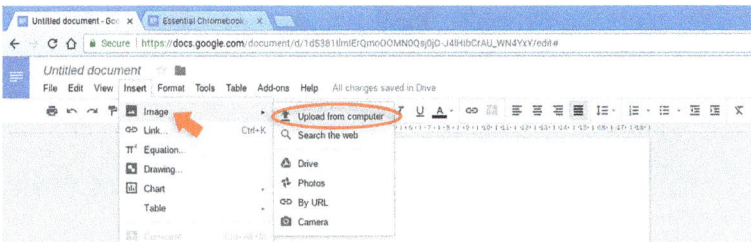

Choose the picture or photo you want on your Google Drive, from the dialog box that appears.

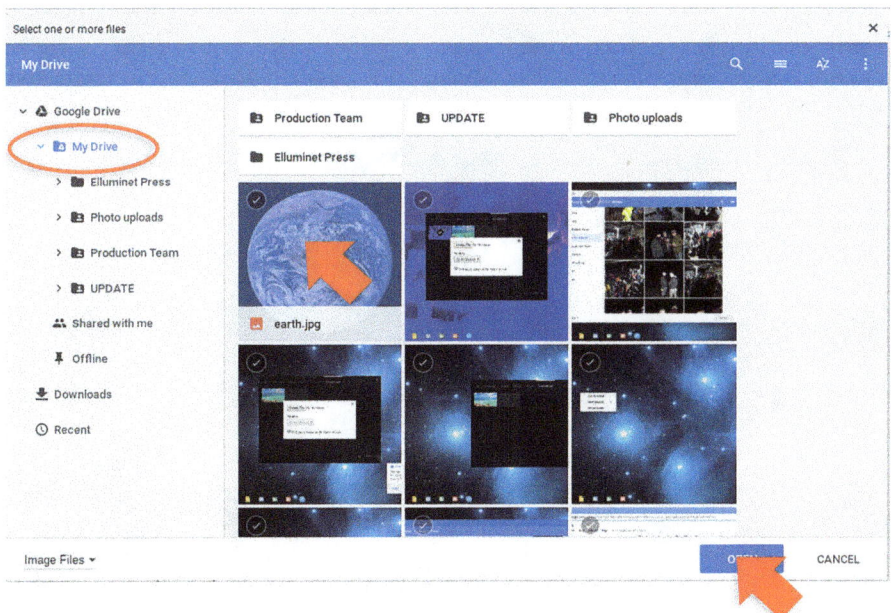

Click 'open' to insert the image.

From the web

You can add images from a Google Image search. To do this, click the 'insert' menu, then select 'image'. From the slideout select 'search the web'.

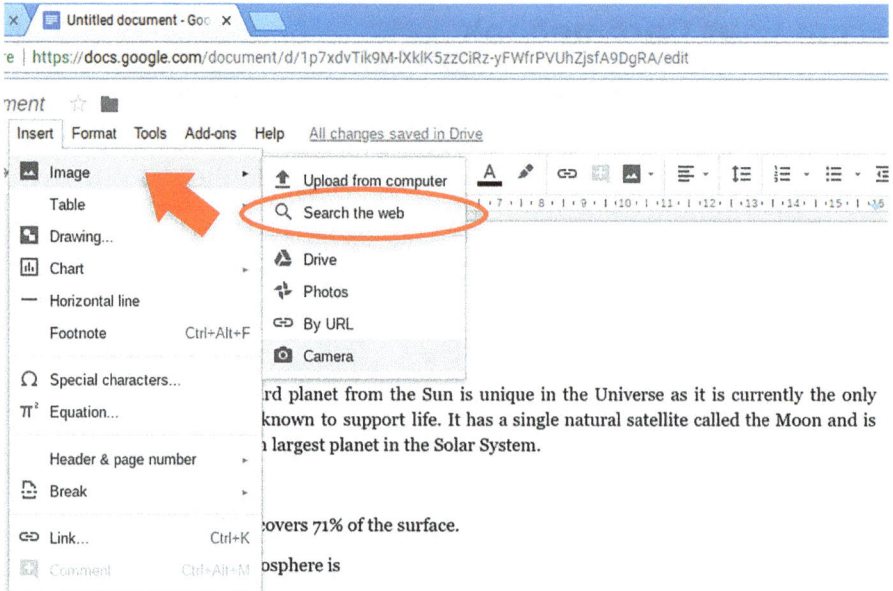

You'll see a search box appear on the right hand side of the screen. Type in the name of what you're searching for. In this example I need an image of the earth, so I'm going to type in 'planet earth'.

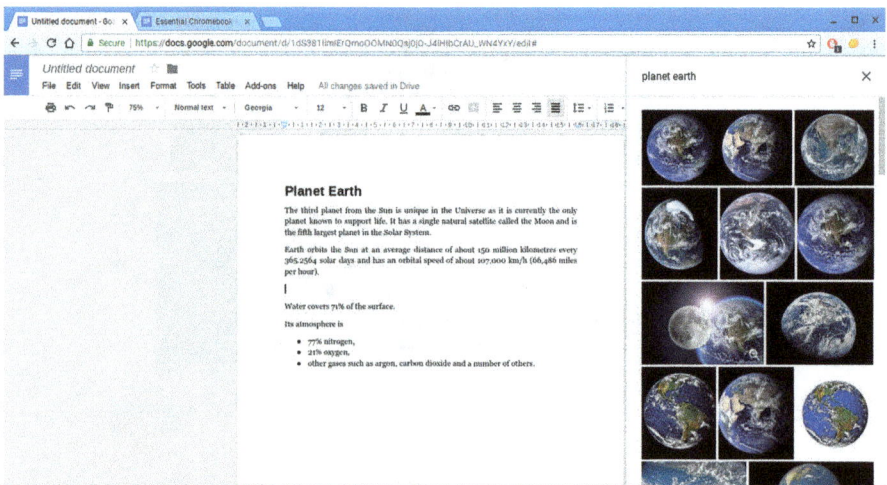

Click on one of the images to insert it into your document.

From your Photos

You can add images from your Google Photos App. To do this, click the 'insert' menu, then select 'image'. From the slideout select 'photos'.

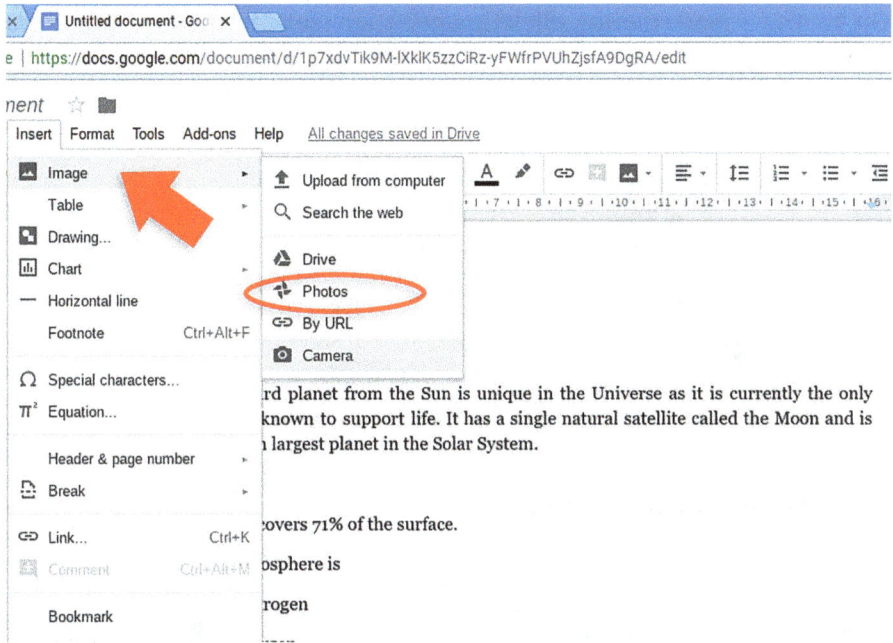

You'll see the Google Photos Panel appear on the right hand side of the screen.

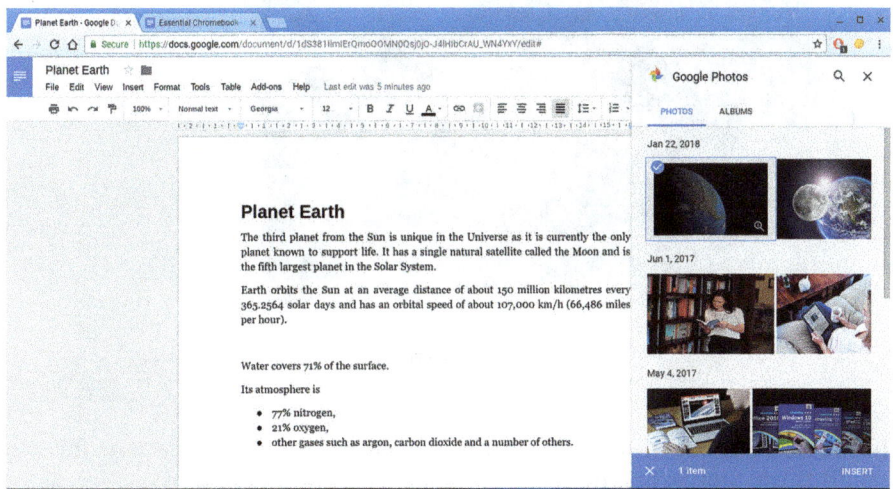

Browse through the photos and select the one you want to insert.

From your Camera

Probably works better on an android tablet, but can still be achieved using the onboard camera that comes with your Chromebook.

Go to the insert menu, click image, then select 'camera' from the slideout.

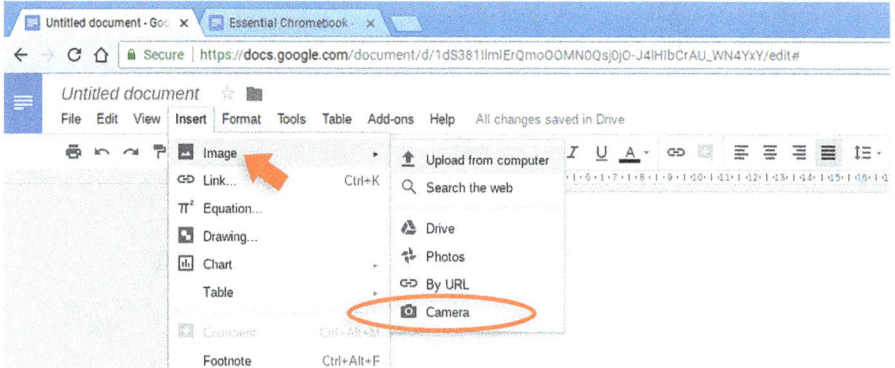

Click the yellow camera icon to take the photo.

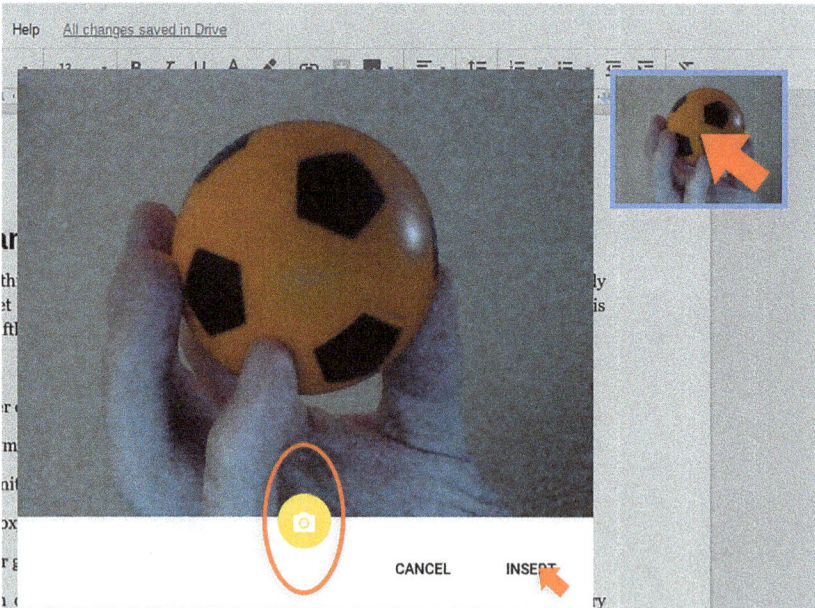

If you took more than one photo, select the one you want from the small thumbnails on the right.

Click 'insert' to add the image to your document.

308

Formatting Images

Right click on your image and select 'image options' from the popup menu.

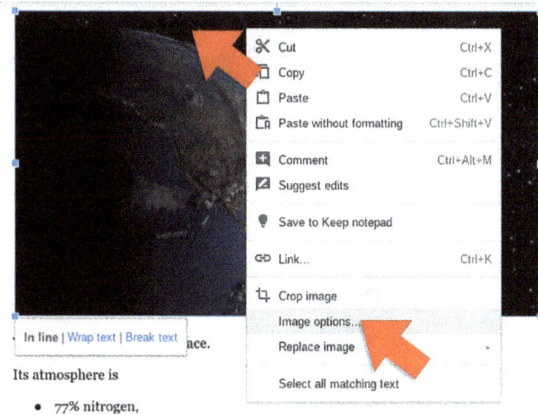

On the right hand side of the screen, you'll see the image options panel open up. From here you can recolour the image - that is give it a red, blue, green, or yellow hue, or turn it into black and white.

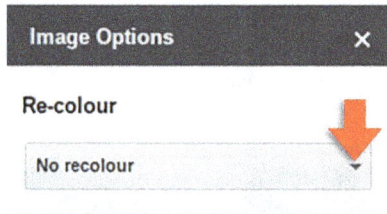

You can adjust the transparency of the image, as well as the brightness and contrast of the image using the sliders.

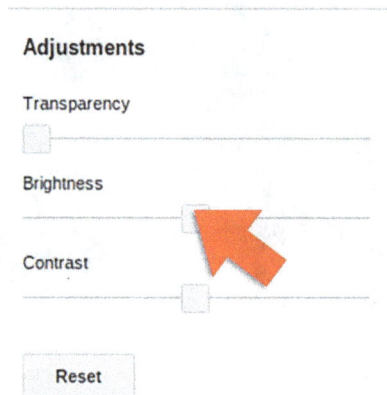

Cropping Images

To crop an image, right click on it and from the popup menu, select 'crop image'.

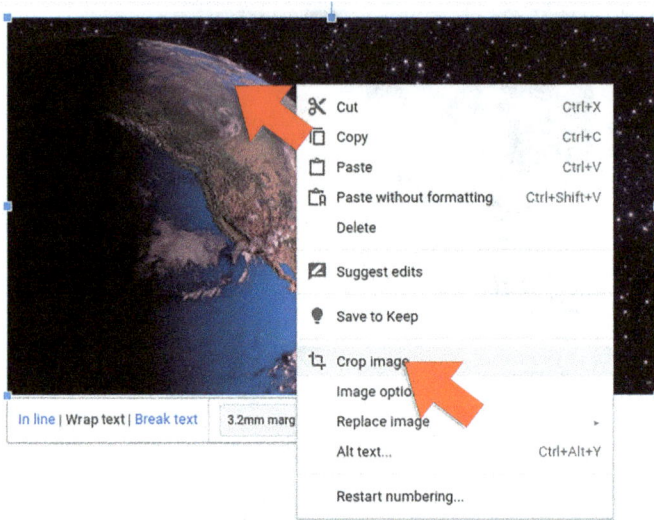

You'll see black crop handles appear on the corners and sides of the image. Click and drag these inwards, around the part of the image you want to keep as illustrated below.

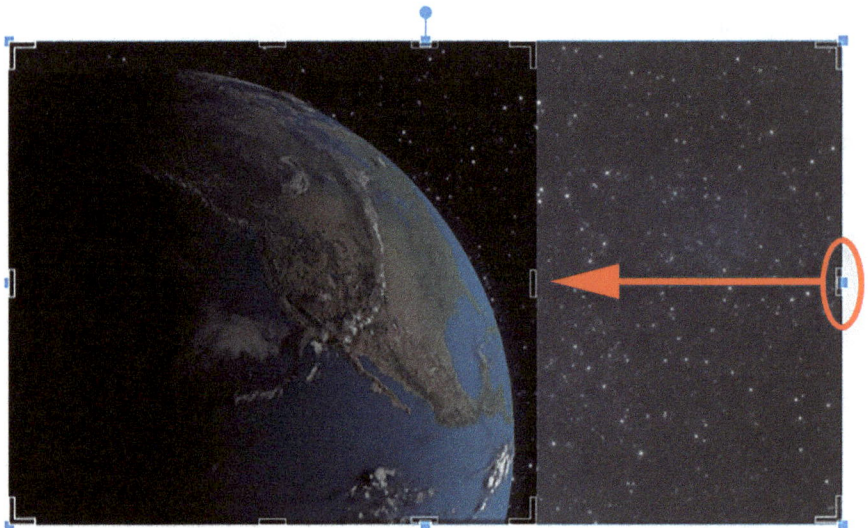

Click anywhere outside the image to execute the crop.

310

Adding Tables

First click the position in the document you want the table to appear.

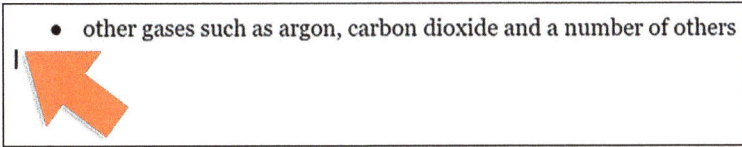

To add a table, click the 'table' menu and select 'insert table'. From the slideout, select how many rows and columns you want in your table.

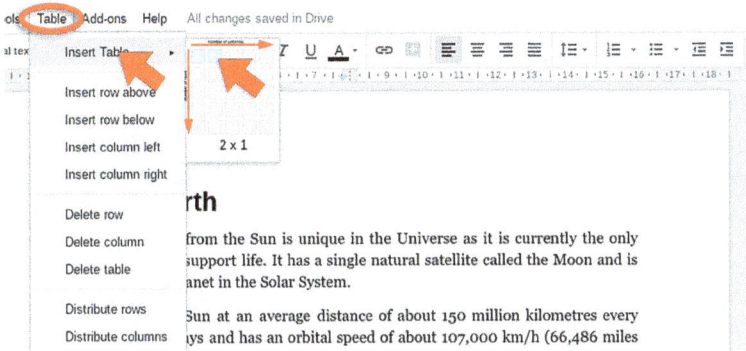

Inserting Rows & Columns

To insert a row or column, right click on the position in the table where you want to insert the row or column.

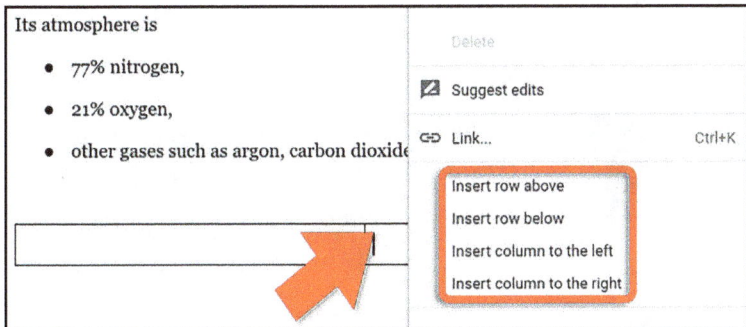

If you want to insert a row below the row selected, click 'insert row below'.

If you want to insert a column after the column selected, click 'insert column to the right'.

Saving Documents

Documents are automatically saved to your Google Drive. Make sure you give your document a name. You will see the document name on the top left of the screen. If you haven't given your document a name you'll see "untitled document" in the title.

Click on this title and type in a name for the document.

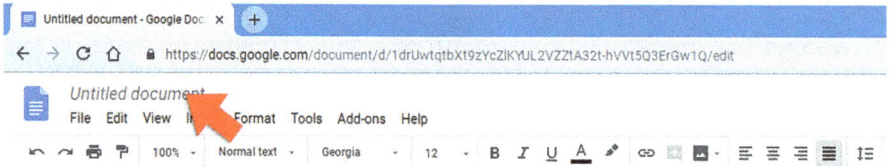

This will save it in Google Drive. To save in another folder on Google Drive, click 'my drive' then select the folder you want to save in.

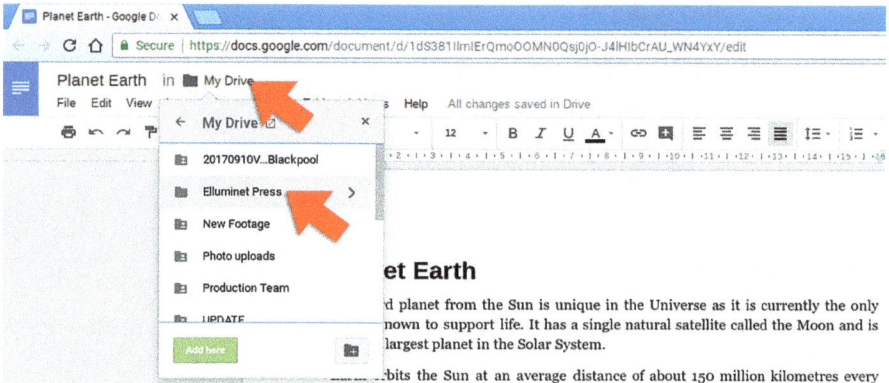

If you want to create a new folder, click the 'new folder' icon on the bottom right of the drop down.

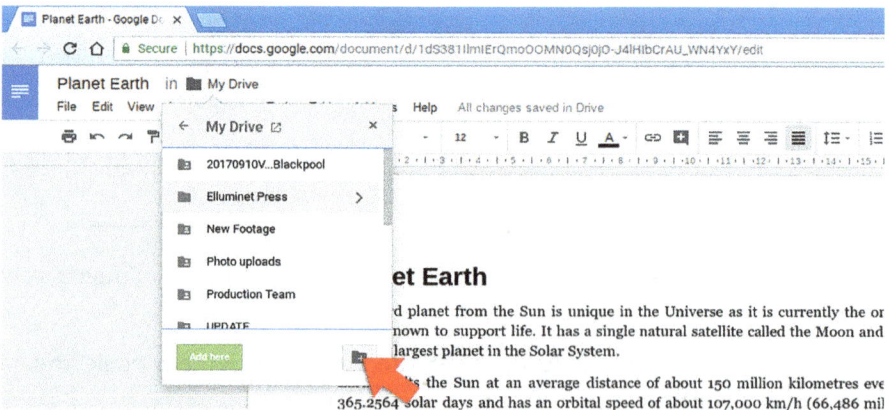

Opening Saved Documents

To open a document from Google Drive, double click on the document.

When you open Google Docs, you'll see a list of documents you've recently opened. Click on one of these to open it up.

To open a document within Google Docs, click the file menu, then select 'open'.

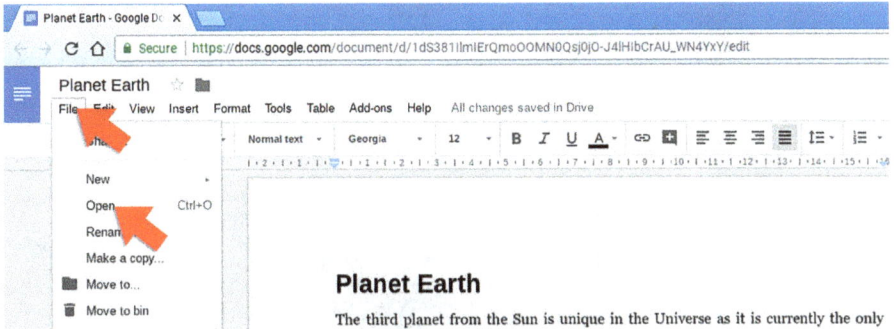

From the dialog box, select the file you want to open. Select 'my drive' to open a file saved on your Google Drive. Click 'shared with me' to open files other users have shared with you. Click 'recent' to open a file you've recently worked on.

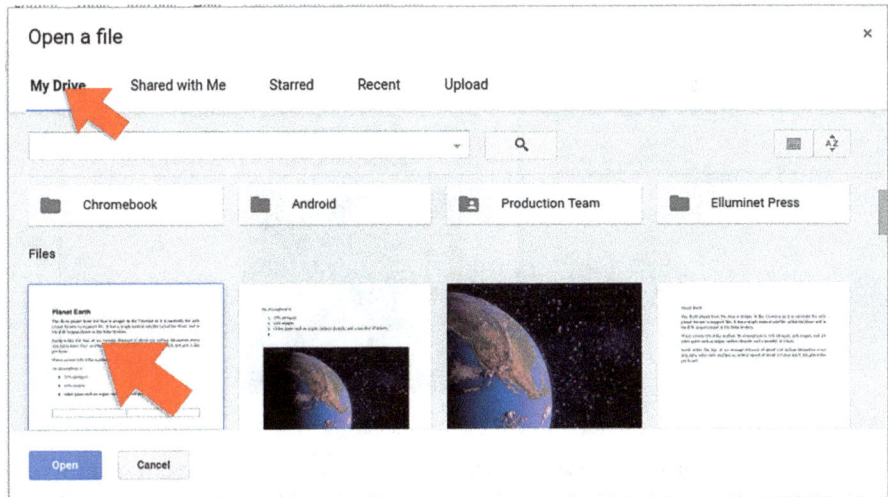

You can also search for the file using the search field at the top of the screen.

Click on a file to select it, then click 'open'.

Printing Documents

To print a document from within Google Docs, click the file menu, then select 'print'.

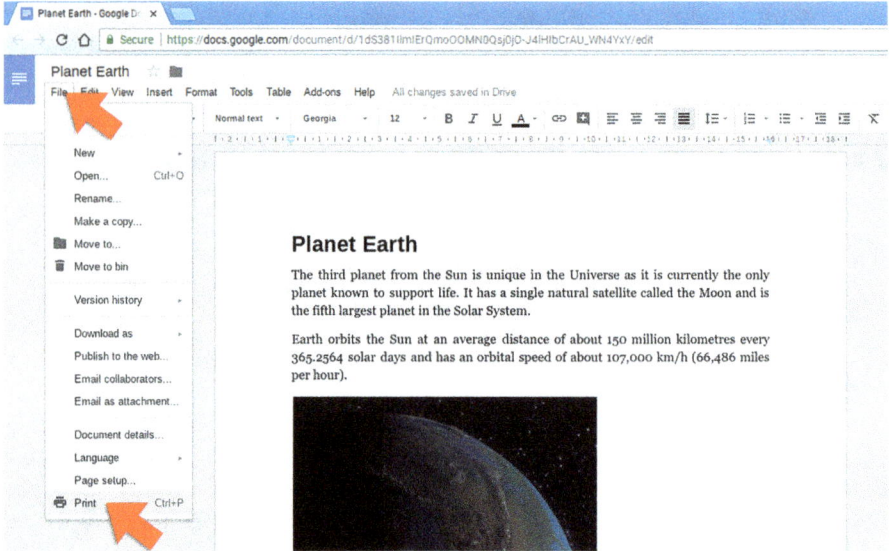

From the dialog box, select the printer you want to print to. To do this click 'change', then select a destination.

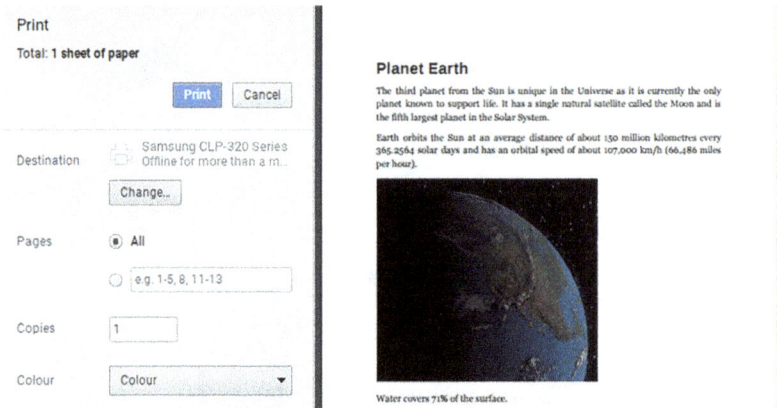

Enter which pages you want printed, or leave the option on 'all' if you want the whole document.

If you want the document in black and white, click 'colour', then change the setting to 'black and white'.

To print the document click 'print' at the top of the dialog box.

314

Sharing Documents

You can share your document using email and Google Drive's collaboration features.

To do this, click the 'share' icon on the top right of the screen.

Enter the names of the people you want to grant access to in the 'add more people' field.

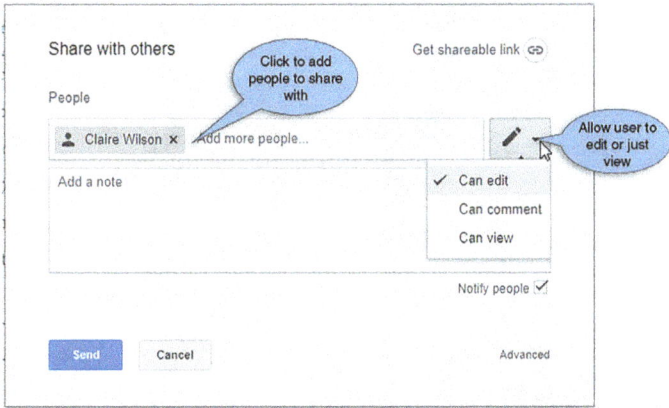

Click the pencil icon to the right of the field and select 'can edit' if you want these people to be able to edit your document, if not select 'can view'.

Click 'send' when you're done.

If you just want a link to the document, click 'get shareable link'.

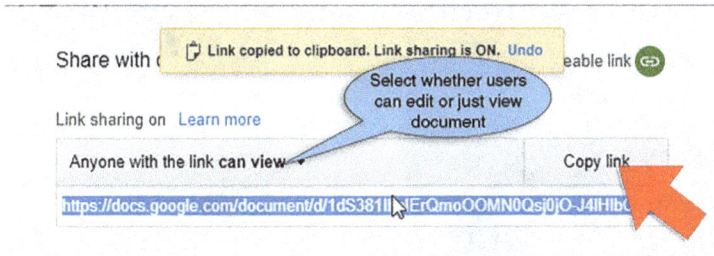

The link will be copied to your clipboard. From here you can paste into an email or another document.

8

Google Sheets

Google Sheets is an online spreadsheet programme much like Microsoft Google Sheets and is included as part of a free, web-based office suite developed by Google.

Google Sheets allows you to do many of the same things as Microsoft Excel but lacks some of the more advanced features.

However, Google Sheets is a great alternative and works well on a Chromebook.

In this section, we'll take a brief look at Google Sheets. For more detail, check out our other book 'Understanding Google Sheets'.

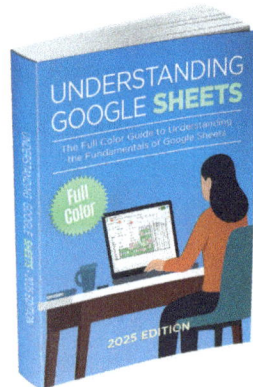

ISBN: 9781917945028

What is a Spreadsheet

A spreadsheet is made up of cells each identified by a reference. The reference is made up by using the column, eg D, and the row, eg 10. So for a particular cell, you look to see what column it's in (D), then what row it's in (10). Put them together and you get the cell reference for that cell.

[COLUMN] [ROW]

So the highlighted cell in the illustration below would be D10.

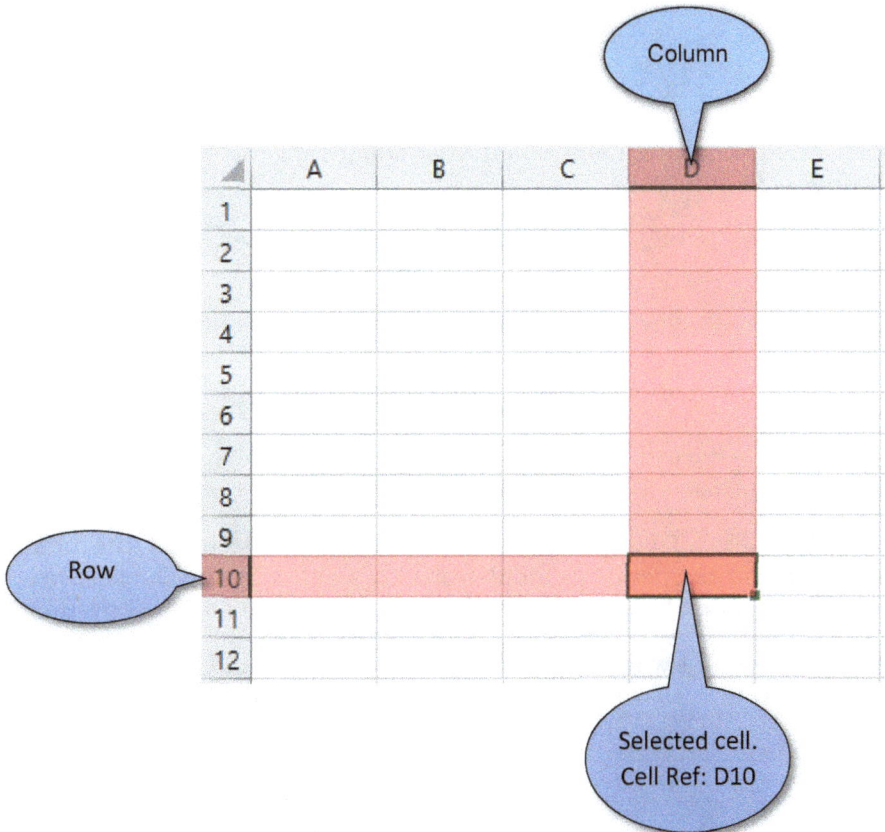

You can also select multiple cells at the same time. A group of cells is called as a cell range. You can refer to a cell range, using the cell reference of the first cell and the last cell in the range, separated by a colon.

[FIRST CELL in RANGE] : [LAST CELL in RANGE]

Chapter 8: Google Sheets

For example, this cell range would be A1:D10 (firstcell : lastcell).

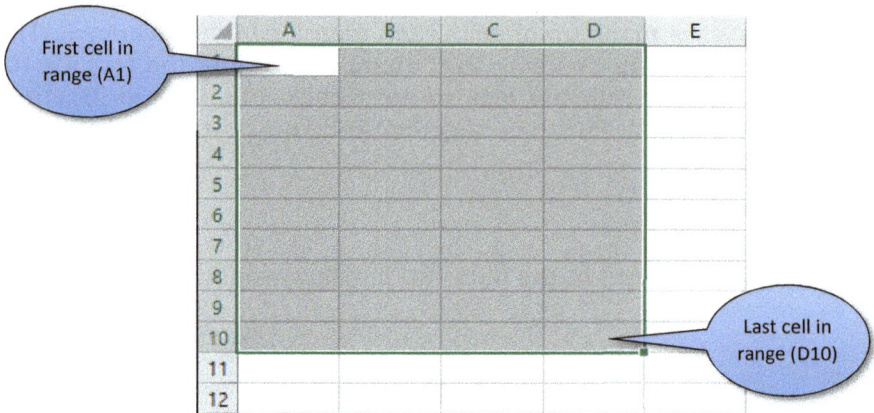

Cell references are used when you start applying functions to the numbers in your cells.

In the example below, to add two numbers together, you can enter a formula into cell C1.

Instead of typing in **=5+5** you would enter **=A1+B1**.

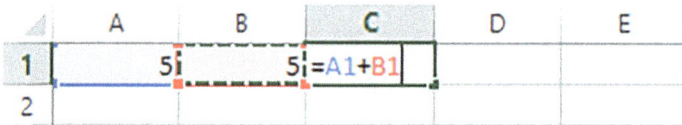

The theory is, if you enter the cell reference instead of the actual number, you can perform calculations automatically and Google Sheets will recalculate all the numbers for you should you change anything.

For example, if I wanted to change it to **5+6**, I would just change the number in cell B1 without rewriting the formula in C1.

Now you can type any number in either cell A1 or B1 and it will add them up automatically.

This is a very basic example but forms the building blocks of a spreadsheet. You can use these concepts to build spreadsheets to analyse and manipulate data, as well as allow changes to the individual data and other parts of the spreadsheet without constantly changing formulas and functions.

Now that we understand the basics of what a spreadsheet is, lets take a look at Google Sheets.

Getting Around Google Sheets

I find the best version of Google Sheets to use is the web based version rather than the Android Version you might find on your Chromebook. To start the web based version of Google Sheets, open your app launcher, then click on Google Chrome.

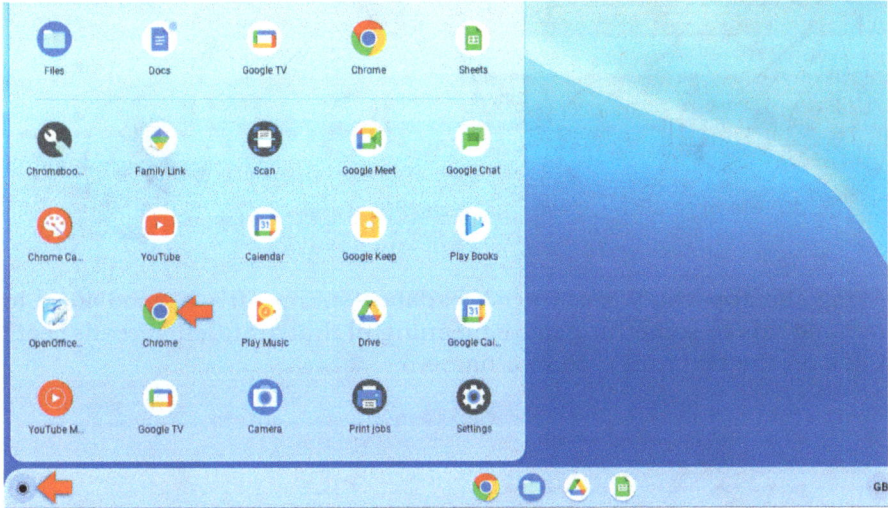

Navigate to the following website:

`sheets.google.com`

When Google Sheets opens, you'll see the sheets you have been working on recently. You can click any of these to re-open them. To create a new sheet, click 'blank' on the top left of the screen.

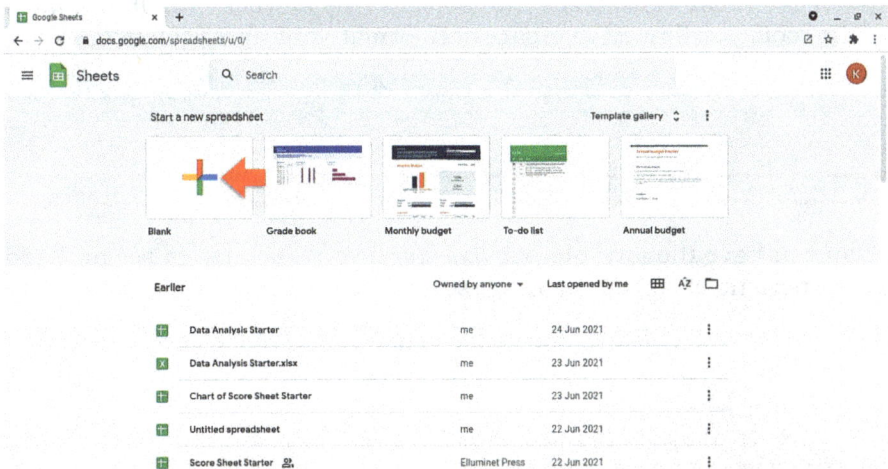

Chapter 8: Google Sheets

Google Sheets will open the main window where you can create your spreadsheet.

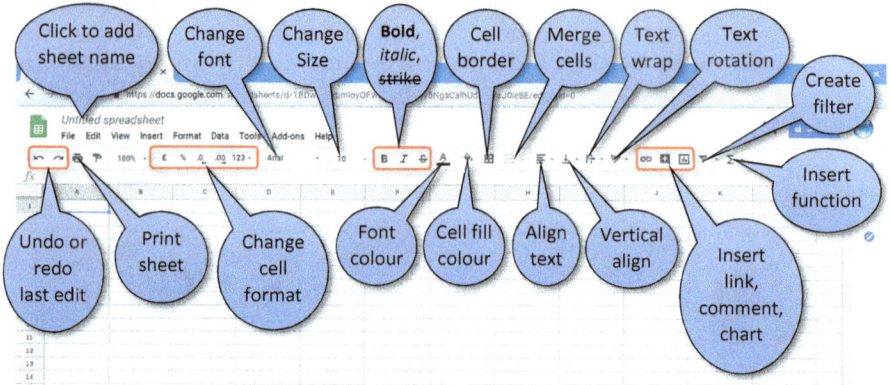

Along the top you'll see the spreadsheet name. It's a good idea to rename this to something more meaningful that 'untitled spreadsheet'. Click on the text and type in a name.

Underneath are the menus. This is where you'll find tools that are not represented as icons on the toolbar.

Under the menus you'll see the toolbar. This is where you'll find most of the tools you'll need to create and format your spreadsheets.

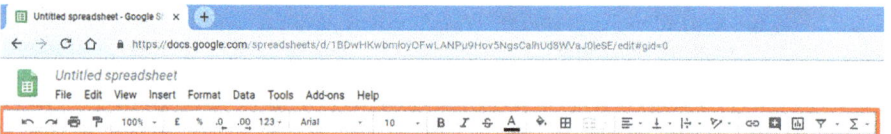

Then you have the formula bar *(fx)*. Here, you'll be able to see and add any functions or formulas in the selected cell.

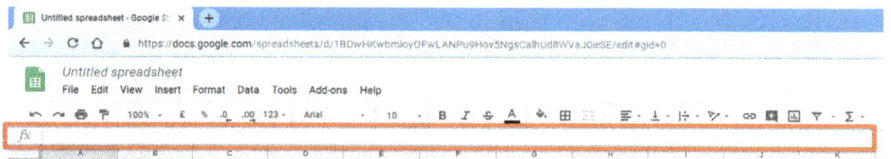

Simple Text Formatting

In this example we are doing a basic scoring sheet. Enter the sample data into the spreadsheet as shown below.

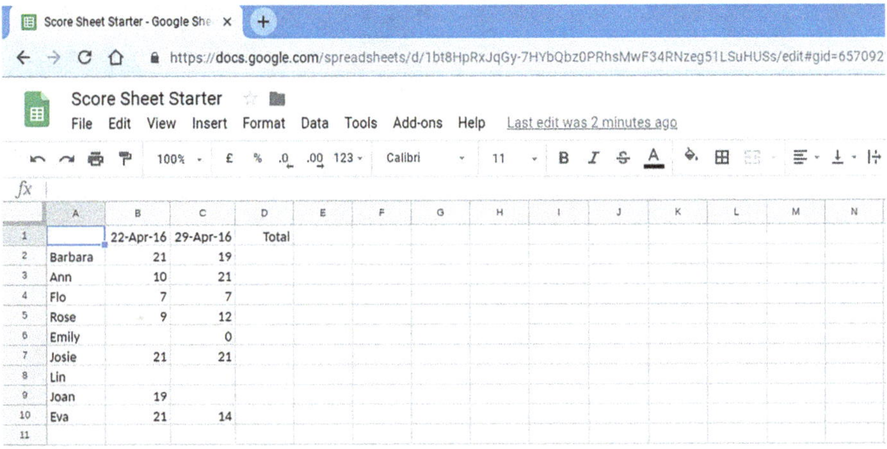

Bold, Italic, Strike & Underlined

Sometimes it improves the readability of your spreadsheet to format the data in the cells.

For example, we could make the column headings and the player's names bold.

First, select the cells you want to apply the formatting to, click the bold icon from the toolbar.

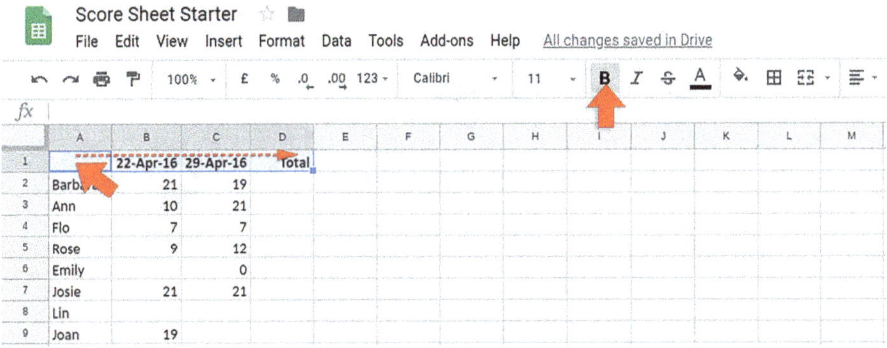

If you want *italic* text, click the 'I' icon on the toolbar. If you want ~~strike~~ text, click the 'S' icon. If you want <u>underlined</u> text, you'll need to go to the format menu and select 'underlined'.

Changing Fonts

First, select the cells you want to apply the formatting to.

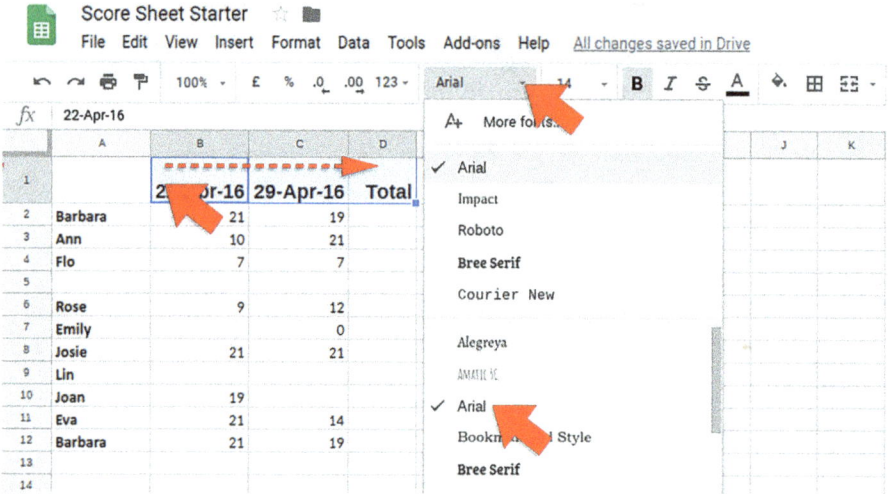

Click the font selector from the toolbar, and select a font from the drop down box.

Font Size

First, select the cells you want to apply the formatting to.

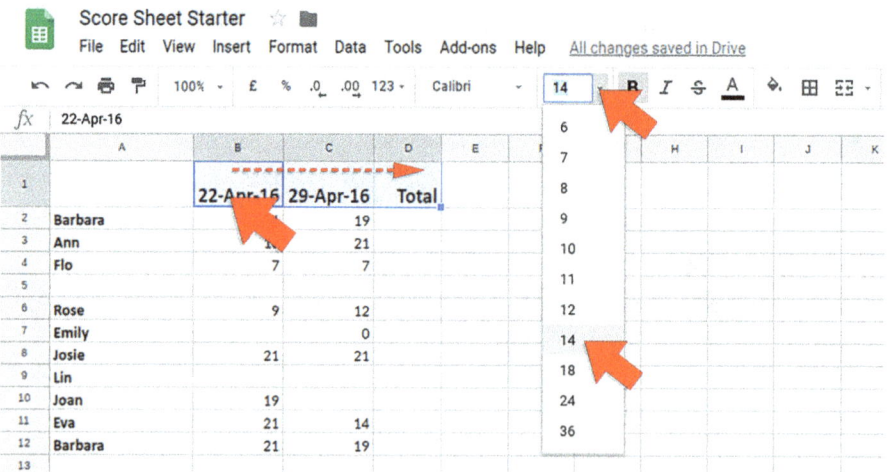

Click the font size selector from the toolbar, and select a size from the drop down box.

322

Cut, Copy & Paste

You can copy and paste a cell or cell range and paste it into another worksheet or in a different location on the same worksheet.

To perform a basic copy, select the cells you want to copy.

	A	B	C	D	E	F	G	H	I	J
1		22-Apr-16	29-Apr-16	Total						
2	Barbara	21	19							
3	Ann	10	21							
4	Flo	7	7							
5	Rose	9	12							

Right click on the selection, then select 'copy' from the popup menu.

	A	B	C	D	E	F	G	H	I	J
1		22-Apr-16	29-Apr-16	Total						
2	Barbara	21								
3	Ann	10		✂ Cut			Ctrl+X			
4	Flo	7	7							
5	Rose	9	12	⧉ Copy			Ctrl+C			
6	Emily		0	📋 Paste			Ctrl+V			
7	Josie	21	21	Paste special			▸			
8	Lin									

Right click the cell where you want the cells to be copied to. I'm going to paste the cells at the end of the table. From the popup menu, select 'paste'.

	A	B	C	D	E	F	G	H	I	J
1		22-Apr-16	29-Apr-16	Total						
2	Barbara	21	19							
3	Ann	10	21							
4	Flo	7	7							
5	Rose	9	12							
6	Emily		0							
7	Josie	21	21							
8	Lin									
9	Joan	19								
10	Eva	21	14							
11			✂ Cut			Ctrl+X				
12										
13		⧉ Copy			Ctrl+C					
14		📋 Paste			Ctrl+V					
15										
16		Paste special			▸					
17										

Do the same for 'cut', except choose 'cut' from the menu instead of 'copy'.

Resizing Rows and Columns

You can resize a column or row by clicking and dragging the column or row divider lines as shown below.

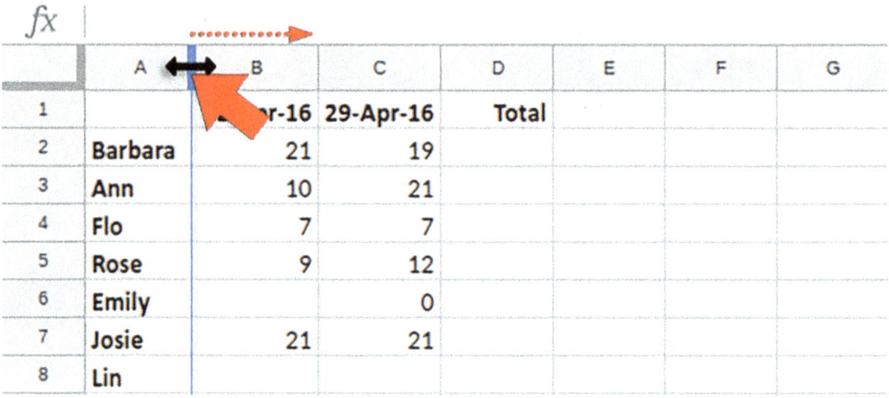

You can also double click on these lines to automatically size the row or column to the data that is in the cell.

Inserting Rows & Columns

To insert a row between Flo and Rose, right click your mouse on the row 'Rose' is in. In this case row 5

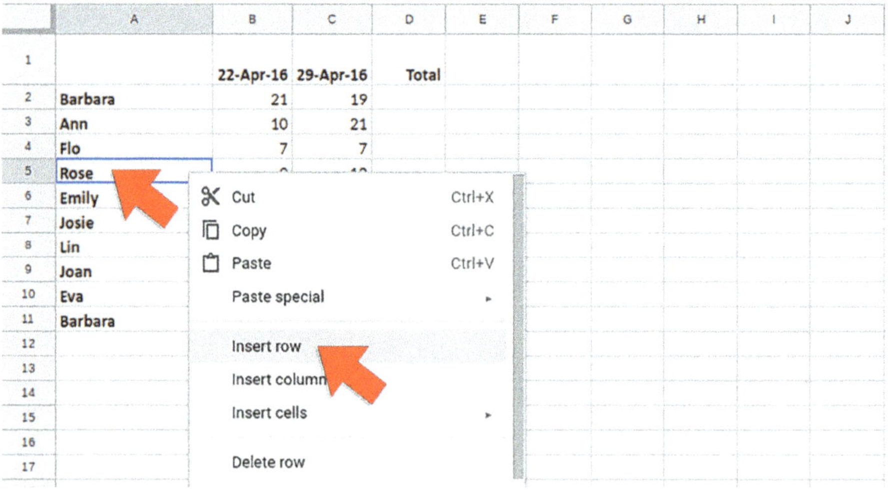

Remember, Google Sheets always adds a row or column before the one you've selected.

Cell Alignment

This helps to align your data inside your cells and make it easier to read. You can align data in the cells to the left, center, or right of the cell.

To do this highlight the cells you want to apply the alignment to, then select the alignment icon on the toolbar. From the drop down box, click the centre icon to align everything to the centre of the cell, click the right hand icon to align everything to the right of the cell.

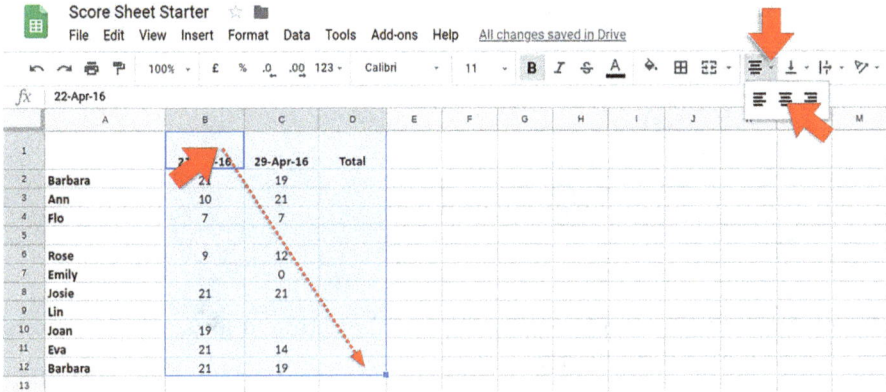

You can also align data vertically in the cell: top, middle, bottom. To do this highlight the cells you want to apply the alignment to, then select the vertical alignment icon on the toolbar.

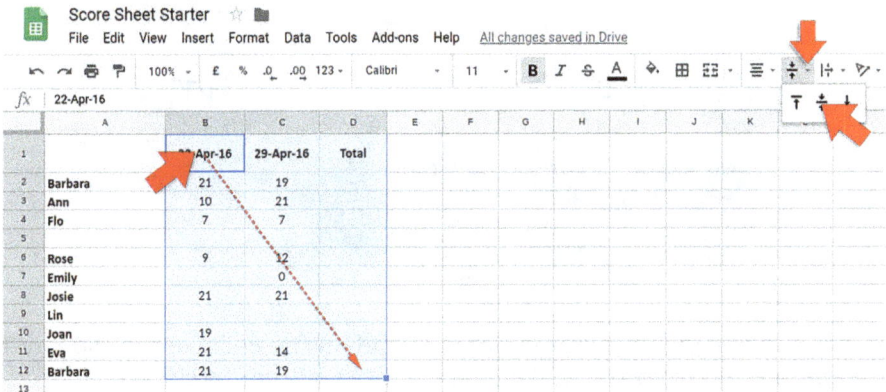

From the drop down box, click the left icon to align everything to the top of the cell, click the centre icon to align everything to the middle, and click the right hand icon to align everything to the bottom of the cell.

Cell Borders

To apply borders to your spreadsheet, with your mouse select the cells you want to format. In this case, I am going to do the whole table.

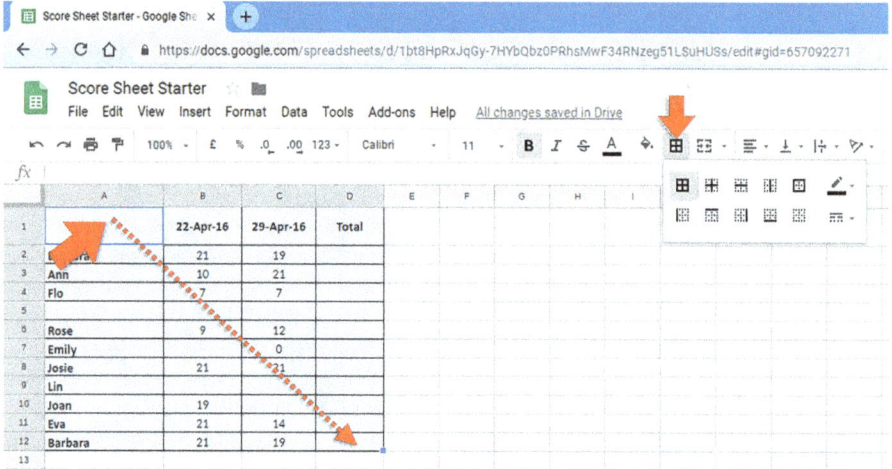

Select the borders icon from the toolbar. Lets take a look at the options on the borders drop down box.

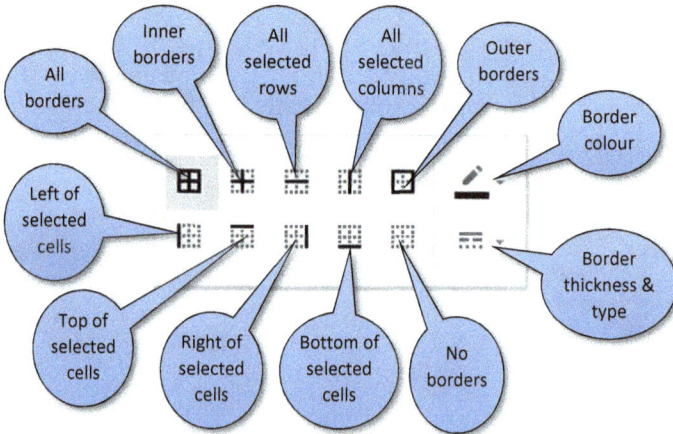

In the example, I want the borders around all the cells both inside and the outline. So from the dialog box click the 'all borders' icon.

To change the thickness, click the 'border thickness & style' icon and select an option.

To change the colour of the border, click the 'border colour' icon, and select a colour.

Using Formulas

If I wanted to add up all the scores in my score sheet, I could add another column called total and enter a formula to add up the scores for the two weeks the player has played.

To do this, I need to find the cell references for Barbara's scores.

Her scores are in row 2 and columns B and C circled below.

Enter formula in this cell

So the cell references are B2 for her score of 21, and C2 for her score of 19.

So we enter into the cell under the heading 'total'

= B2+C2

Remember all formulas must start with an equals sign **(=)**.

To save you entering the formula for each row, you can replicate it instead.

If you click on the cell D2, where you entered the formula above, you will notice on the bottom right of the box, a small square handle.

I've enlarged the image so you can see it clearly.

Drag this handle down the rest of the column to replicate the formula.

327

Using Functions

A function is a pre-defined formula. Google Sheets has hundreds of different functions all designed to make analysing your data easier.

Count

Say I wanted to count the number of games played automatically. I could do this with a function.

Insert a new column after "29 Apr" into the spreadsheet and call it "Played". To do this, right click on the D column (the 'Total' column) and from the menu click 'insert column'.

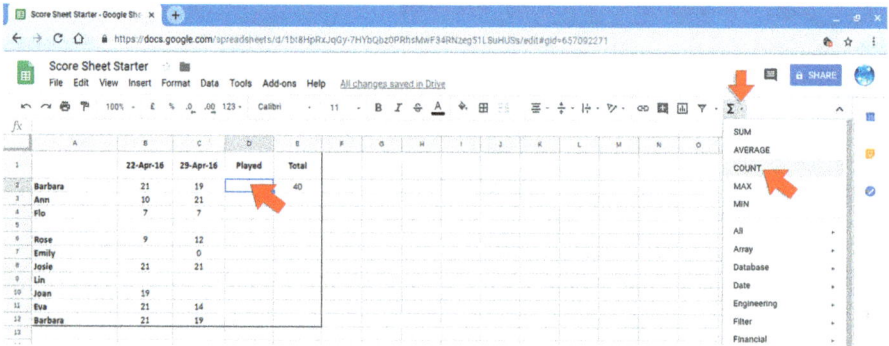

Make sure you have selected the cell you want the formula to appear in, then click 'insert function' icon on the toolbar.

Now, click and drag across the row of cells you want to apply the function to. In this example, I want to count the number of games a player has played, so I'd drag the selection box across the two scores in cells B2 to C2.

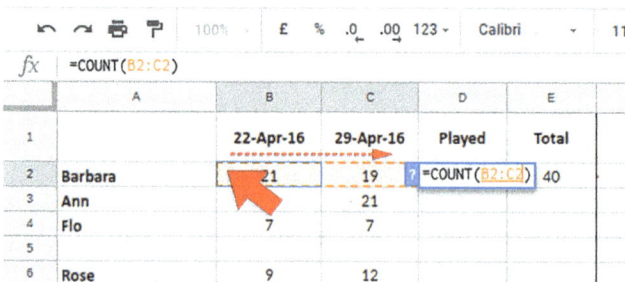

Press the enter key on your keyboard to execute the function. Drag the handle, down to replicate the formula down the column as normal, as shown in the previous example.

Auto Sum

Auto sum, as its name suggests, adds up all the values in a row or column.

To add up a row, click on the cell you want the total to appear in.

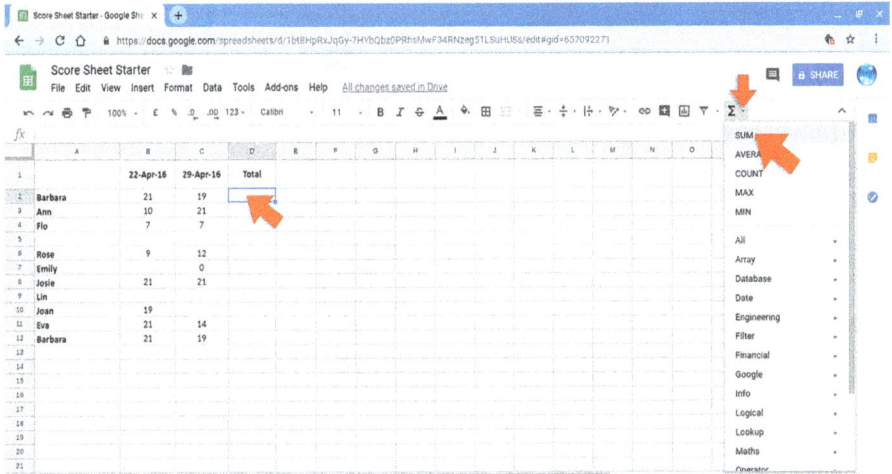

Now, click and drag across the row of cells you want to apply the function to. In this example, I want to add up the scores for each player, so I'd drag the selection box across the two scores in cells B2 to C2.

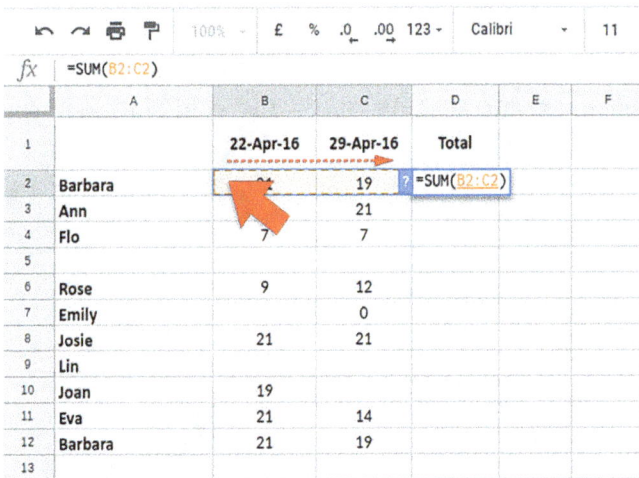

Press the enter key on your keyboard to execute the function. Drag the handle, down to replicate the formula down the column as normal, as shown in the previous example.

Types of Data

There are several different types of data you will come across while using Google Sheets. These data can be numeric such as whole numbers called integers (eg 10), numbers with decimal points (eg 29.93), currencies (eg £4.67 or $43.76), as well as date and time, text and so on.

Going back to our scoring spreadsheet, we need another column for the average scores. Insert a new column and type the heading 'Average' as shown below.

	A	B	C	D	E	F	G	H	I
1	Name	22-Apr-16	29-Apr-16	Played	Total	Average			
2	Barbara	21	19	2	40				

We are going to work out the average scores over the number of games the players have played. In the Cell F2 enter the formula

```
Average = Total Score / Total number of Games Played
```

The total score is in E2 and the total number of games played is in D2.

So we enter into F2:

```
= E2 / D2
```

Replicate the formula down the column as we did previously in the example.

Now we need to change the data type of the average to a number with two decimal places. To do this, select the values in the column, then click the data type icon from the toolbar.

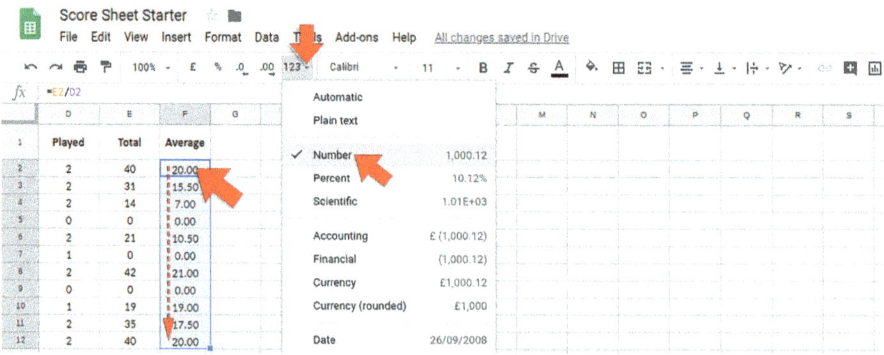

Select 'number' from the drop down menu.

It would be the same for recording the fees paid by the players. Insert another column and call it 'fee'. Say the fees are 4.50. When we enter 4.5 into the cell, Google Sheets thinks it's just a number, so we need to tell Google Sheets that it is currency.

Select all the data in the fee column. You don't need to include the heading row.

	B 22-Apr	C 29-Apr	D Played	E Total	F Average	G Fee
2	21	19	2	40	20.00	4.5
3	10	21	2	31	15.50	4.5
4	7	7	2	14	7.00	4.5
5	9	12	2	21	10.50	4.5
6		0	1	0	0.00	4.5
7	21	21	2	42	21.00	4.5
8			0	0	0.00	4.5
9	19		1	19	19.00	4.5
10	21	14	2	35	17.50	4.5

Click the data type icon on the toolbar.

From the drop down menu click currency. This will format all the numbers as a currency.

Adding a Chart

There are many different types of charts to choose from, here are a few examples of some common ones.

First select all the names in the first column. This will be the X-Axis on the chart.

Now hold down the control key (ctrl) on your keyboard. This allows you to multi-select. While holding down control, select the data in the total column with your mouse. This will be the Y-Axis on the chart. Note the data in the names column is still highlighted.

Click the chart icon on the toolbar.

From the chart editor that appears on the right hand side, select the chart type you want. You can change it to a line chart, bar chart, column chart, pie chart, and so on.

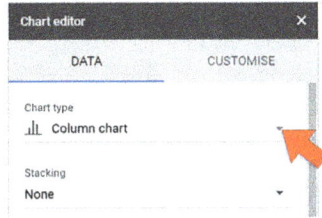

To edit the chart title, click the title on the chart and type in a name. On the chart editor on the right hand side, you can change font, size, and alignment using the controls.

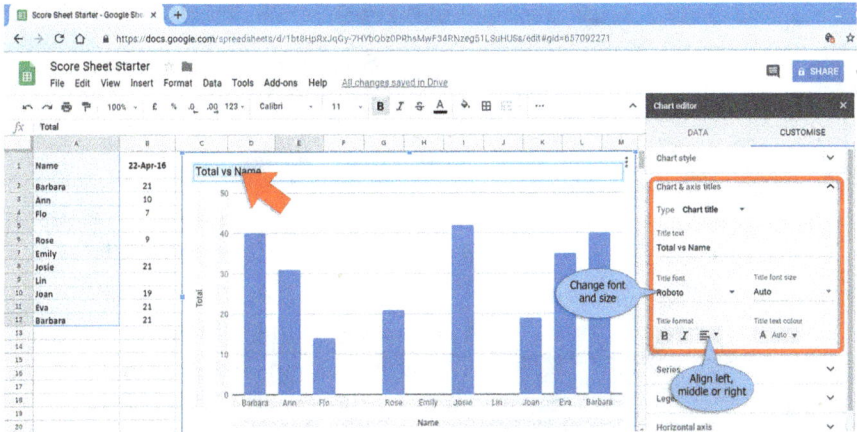

To change the x and y axis labels. Click the label on the chart.

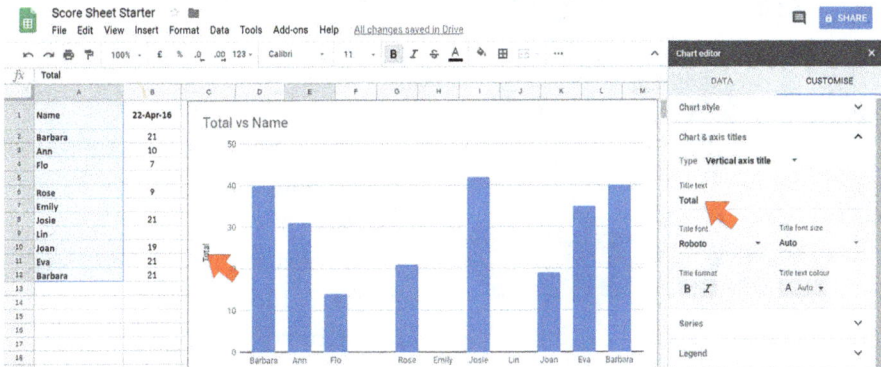

In the chart editor that appears on the right hand side, click 'title text' and type in a label.

9

Google Slides

Google Slides is an online presentation programme much like Microsoft PowerPoint or Apple Keynote and is included as part of a free, web-based office suite developed by Google.

Google Slides allows you to do many of the same things as Microsoft PowerPoint but lacks some of the more advanced features.

However, Google Slides is a great alternative and works well on a Chromebook.

You can also connect your Chromebook to a projector or TV screen to give your presentation.

In this chapter, we'll take a look at:

- Designing a Slide
- Add, resize, and crop an Image
- Add a Video
- Slide Layer Arrangement
- Add a New Slide
- Change Slide Layout
- Slide Masters
- Slide Transitions & Animations
- Insert a Table
- Add a Chart
- Printing Presentations
- Giving your Presentation
- Present with ChromeCast

Getting Around Google Slides

I find the best version of Google Slides to use is the web based version rather than the Android Version you might find on your Chromebook. To start the web based version of Google Slides, open your app launcher, then click on Google Chrome.

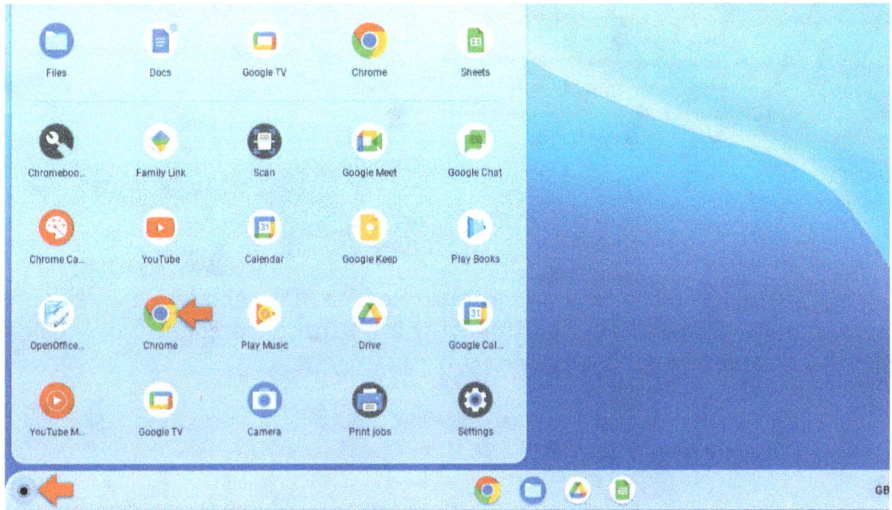

Navigate to the following website:

`slides.google.com`

When Google Slides opens, you'll see the presentations you have been working on recently. You can click any of these to re-open them. To create a new presentation, click blank on the top left of the screen.

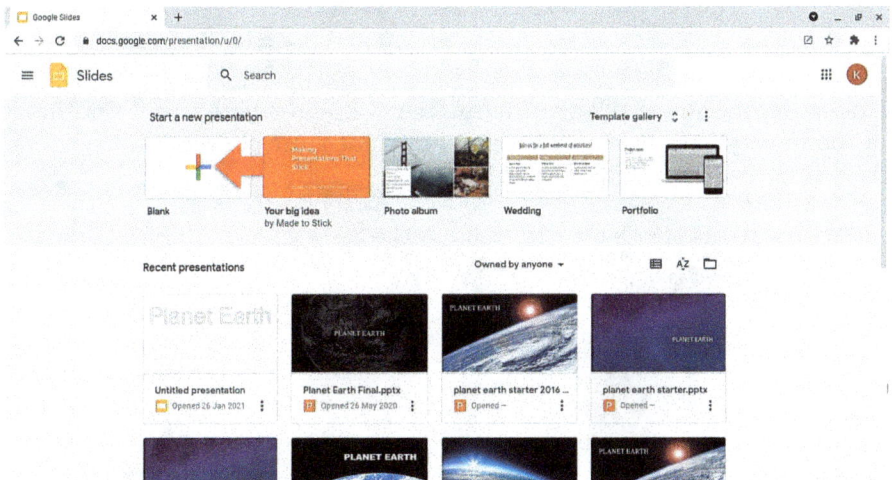

Chapter 9: Google Slides

Google Slides will open the main window where you can create your presentation.

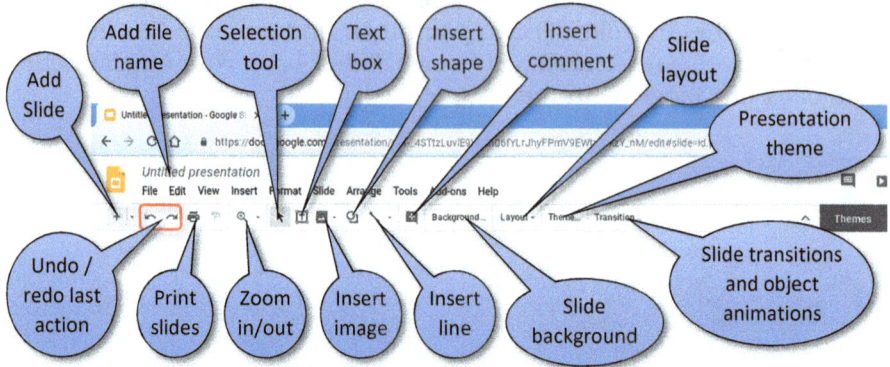

Along the top you'll see the presentation name. It's a good idea to rename this to something more meaningful than 'untitled presentation'. Click on the text and type in a name.

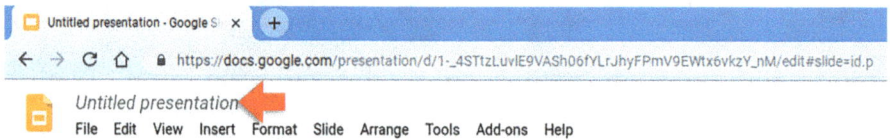

Underneath are the menus. This is where you'll find tools that are not represented as icons on the toolbar.

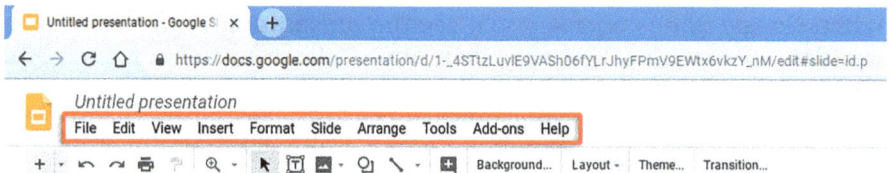

Under the menus you'll see the toolbar. This is where you'll find most of the tools you'll need to create and format your presentations.

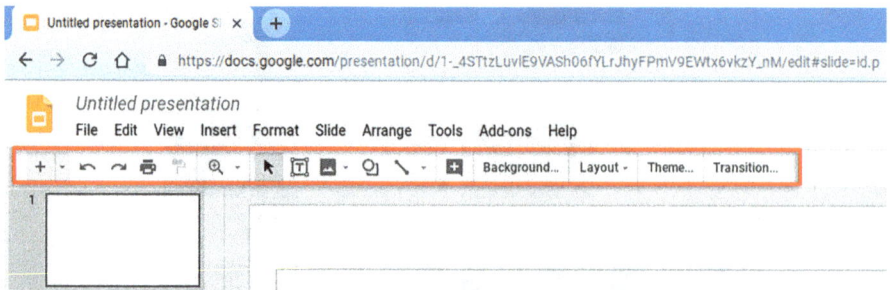

Designing a Slide

Let's begin by adding the title to our first slide. First, select a theme from the templates on the right hand themes panel. Once you have selected a theme, click the white cross on the top left of the panel to close it.

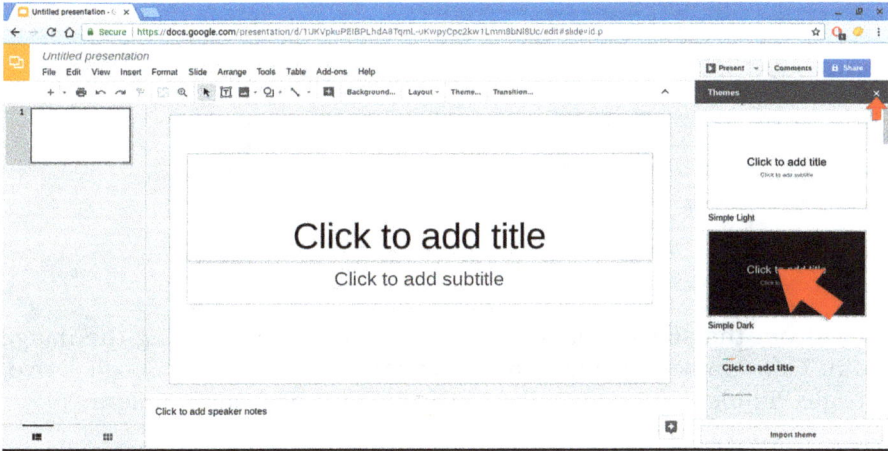

On your slide, click where it says 'click to add title'. This is a place holder for you to enter a title.

Enter the title 'Planet Earth'.

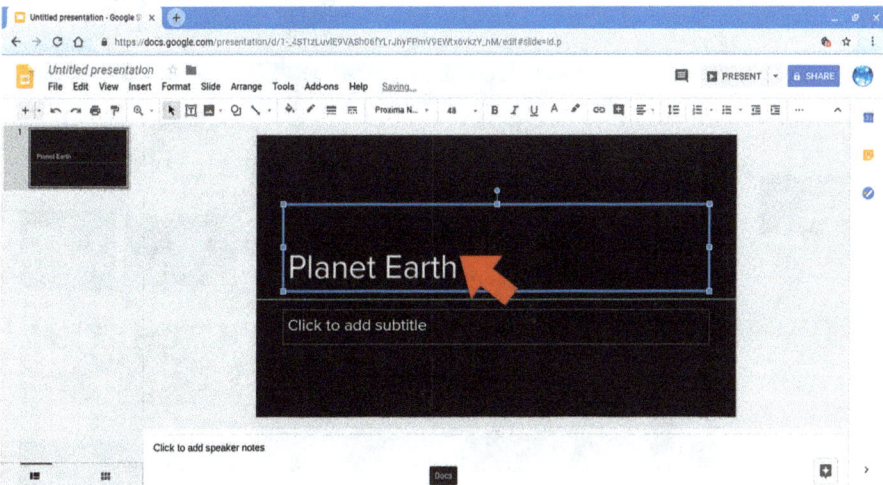

In this example, we won't be adding a subtitle, but you can add one if you want to.

Lets add some images to spice our title slide up a bit.

Add an Image

To add an image, select the slide you want to add the image to using the slide selector on the left hand side. Go to the insert menu then select 'image'.

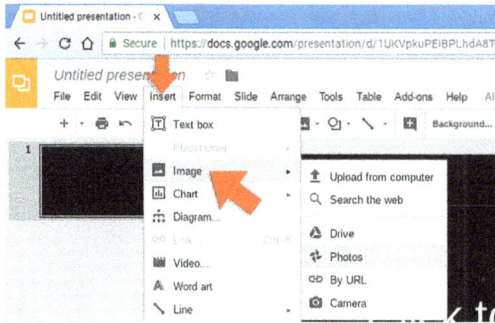

Now, from the slideout menu, select where you are adding the image from. This can be uploaded from your computer, the web, Google Drive, Google Photos, a direct weblink, or from your on-board camera.

From Photos

To add an image from Google Photos, select 'photos' from the image slideout menu. Google Photos contains photos you've taken with your android phone, or any other tablet you've signed into with your Google Account.

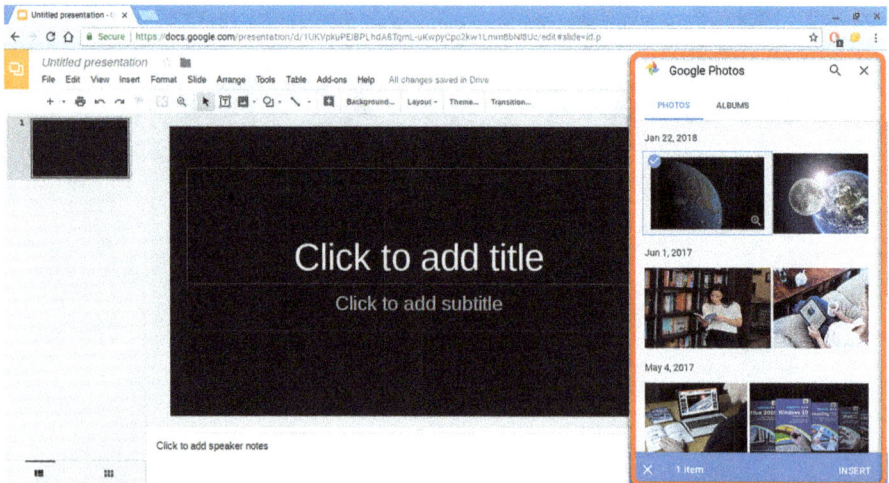

Google Photos will open in a panel on the right hand side, scroll through, click a photo then click 'insert'.

From the Web

To add an image from the web, select 'the web' from the image slideout menu. Google Search will open up in the panel on the right hand side. Type in your search into the field at the top

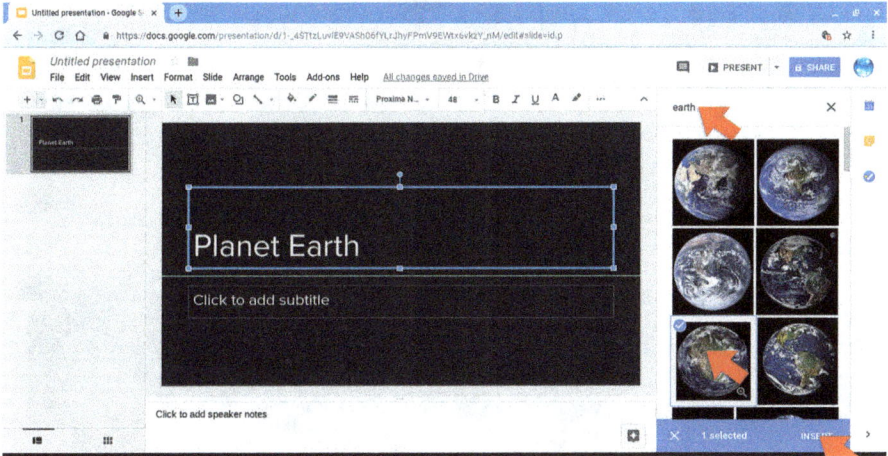

Click on the image you want then click 'insert'.

From your Google Drive

To add an image from your Google Drive, select 'Drive' from the image slideout menu. In the panel on the right hand side click 'my drive'. Any images stored on your Google Drive will open up in the panel on the left hand side.

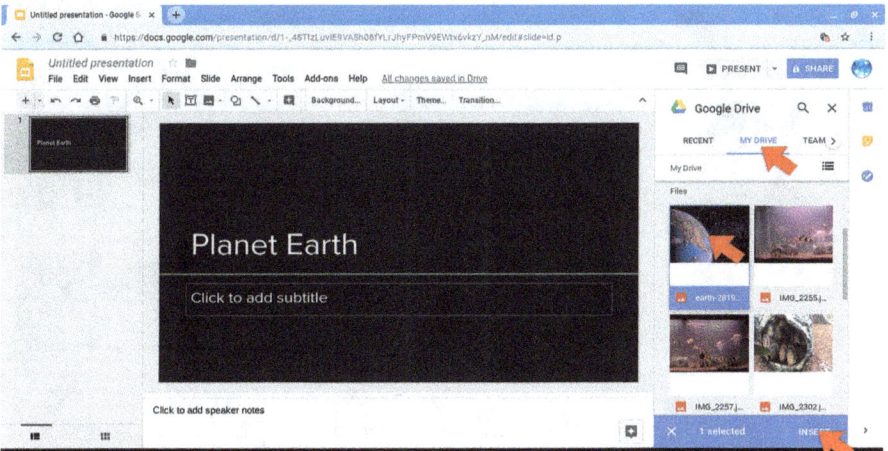

Click on the image you want then click 'insert'.

Resize an Image

When you click on an image on your slide, you'll see some resize handles appear around each corner.

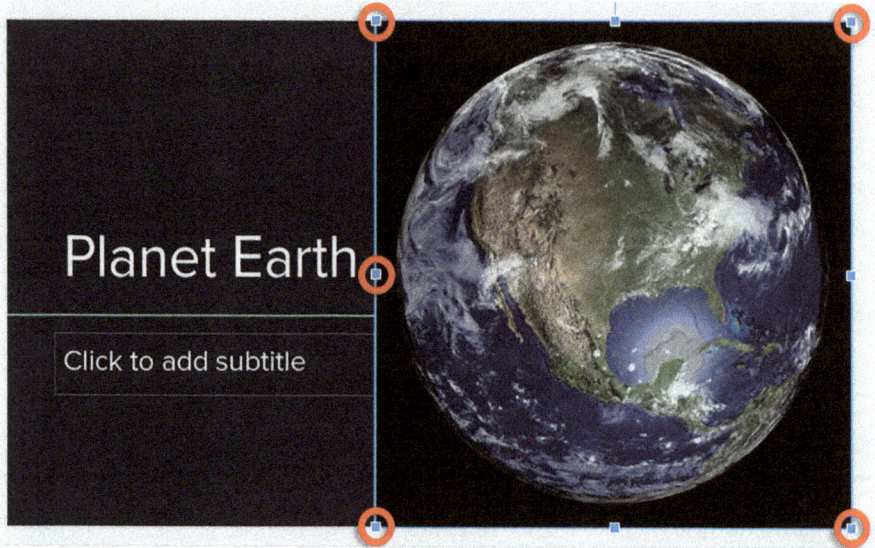

Click and drag these resize handles to resize the image.

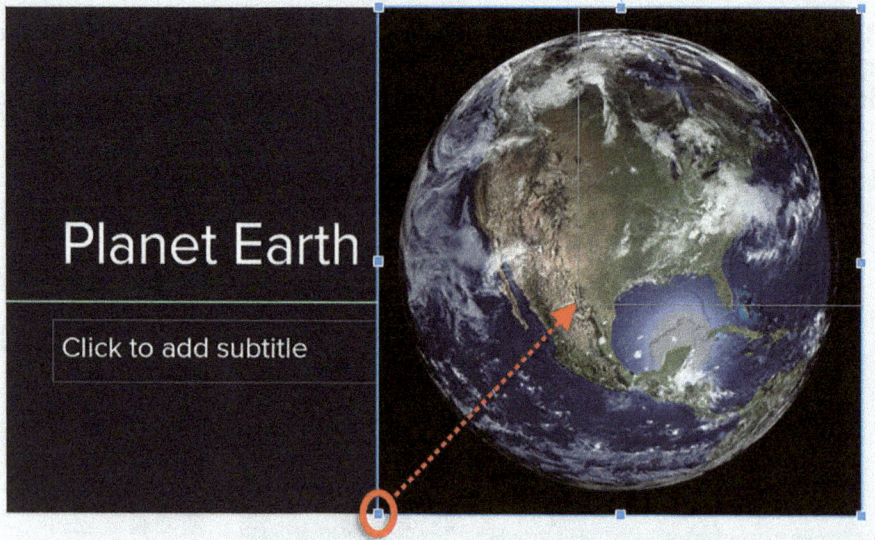

You may need to move the image into position. To do this, click and drag the image into position.

Crop an Image

Click on the image you want to crop, then from the toolbar, select the 'crop' icon.

You'll see some crop handles appear around each corner.

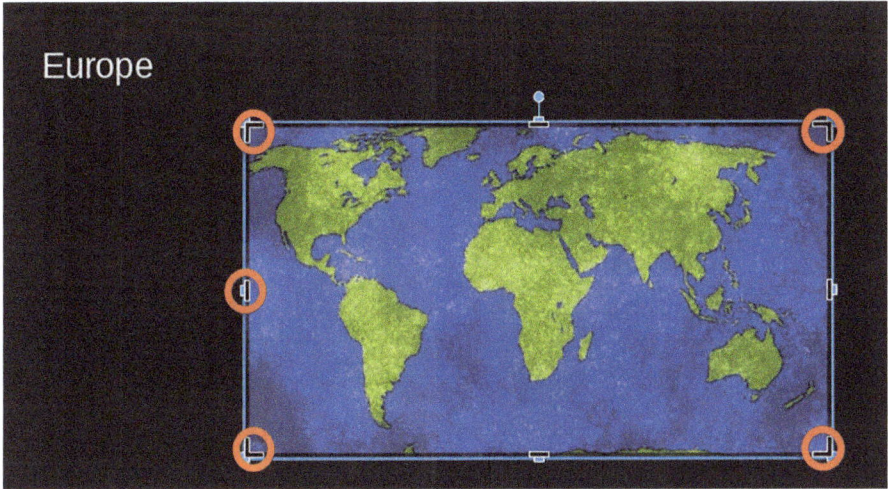

Click and drag these crop handles around the part of the image you want to keep. In this example, I only want to highlight Europe on this map.

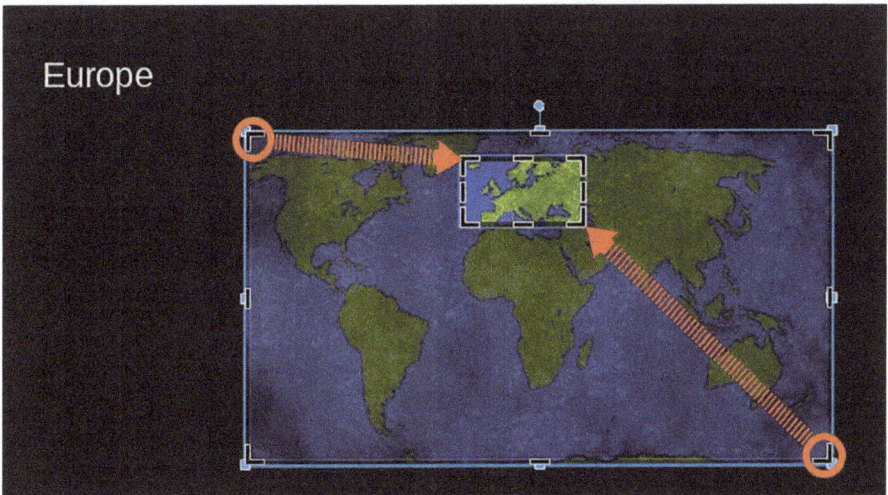

You may need to move the image into position. To do this, click and drag the image into position. Resize the image if needed.

Add a Video

You can add YouTube videos, or your own videos stored on Google Drive.

To do this, select the slide you want to add your video to, from the slide selector on the left hand side. From the insert menu, select 'video'.

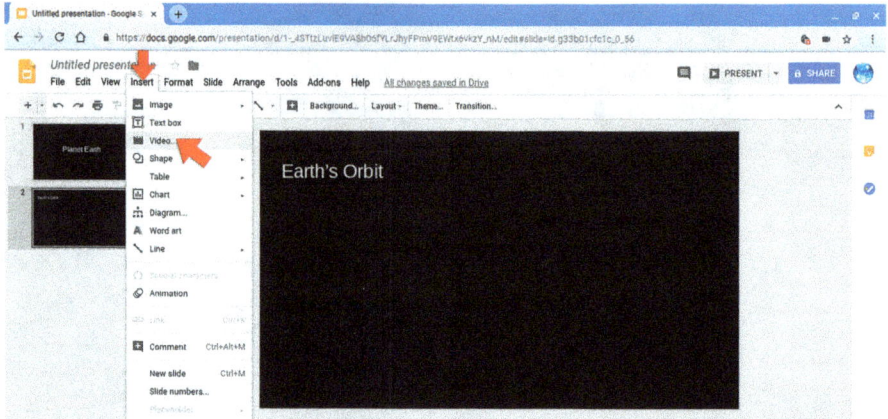

From the dialog box that appears, select 'search' to search the web for a YouTube video, or click 'Google Drive' to use one of your own videos.

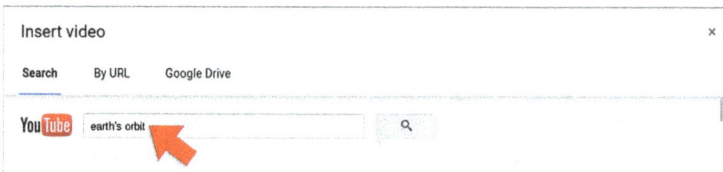

In the search field at the top of the screen, type in your search and press the enter key on your keyboard.

From the search results, select the video you want to insert, then click 'insert'.

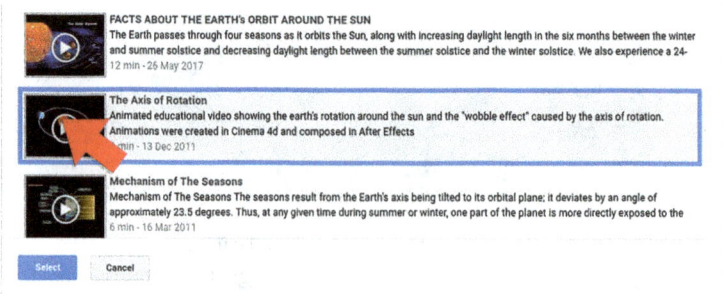

Videos on YouTube have a lot of rubbish in them that you don't need. You can trim the beginning and end of the video, so it starts and ends exactly in the right place. To do this, right click on the video on the slide. From the popup menu, select 'format options'.

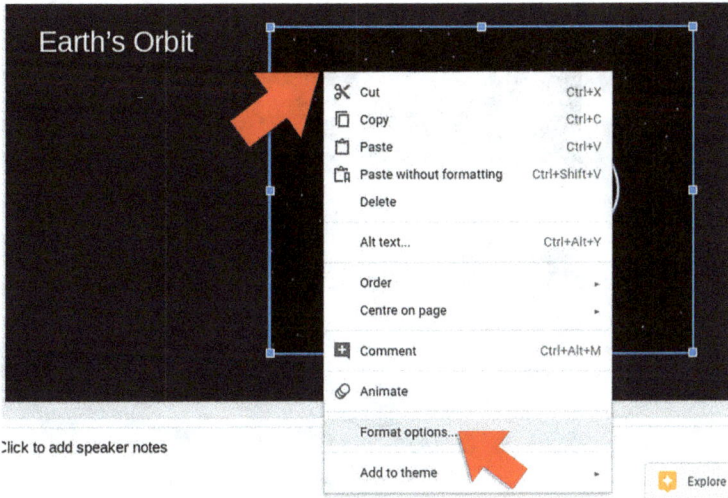

The 'format options' panel will open on the right hand side of the screen. From here hover your mouse over the video progress bar and you'll see a silent preview of the video. Click on the position you want the video to start.

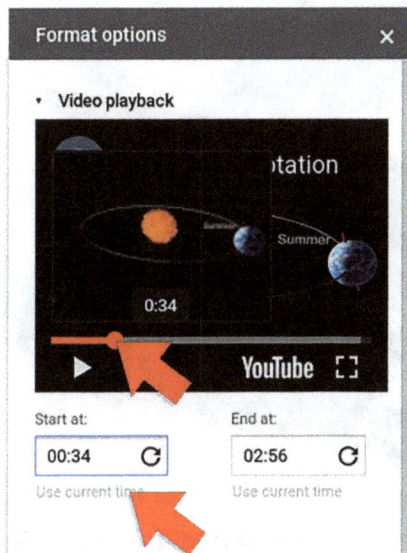

Click 'use current time' to trim the start time to the position in the video. Repeat the procedure for the end times.

Slide Layer Arrangement

In the example below, I've added an image to the title slide.

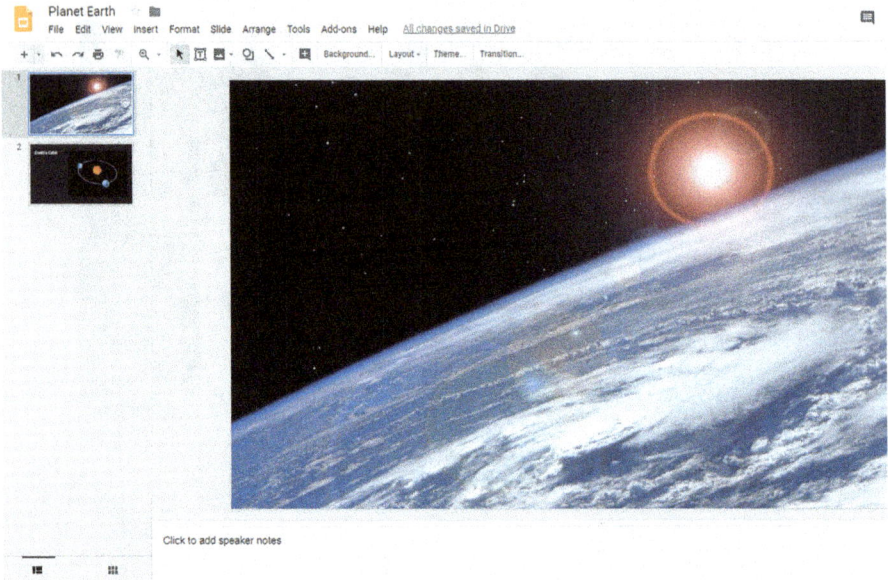

You'll notice when you add an image, video, or other object, it covers the title or another object. This is because Google Slides constructs slides using layers. So the title "Planet Earth" will be on one layer, and the image will be on another layer.

Now, because the image was inserted after the title, the image layer is on top of the title layer. We want the title layer on top. We need to send the image to the back layer.

344

To do this, right click on the image or object, then from the popup menu, select 'order'. From the slideout, select 'send to back'.

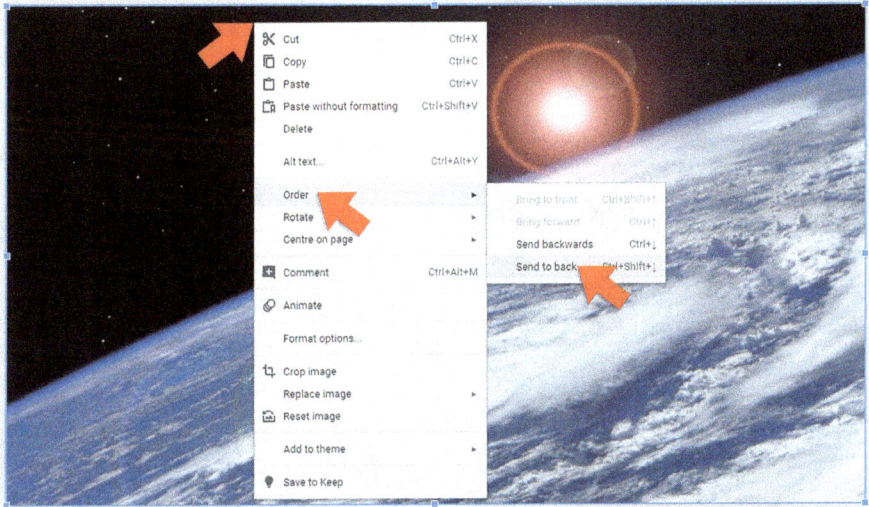

This will put the image in the background. Now you can see the title, and you can drag it into position on the slide.

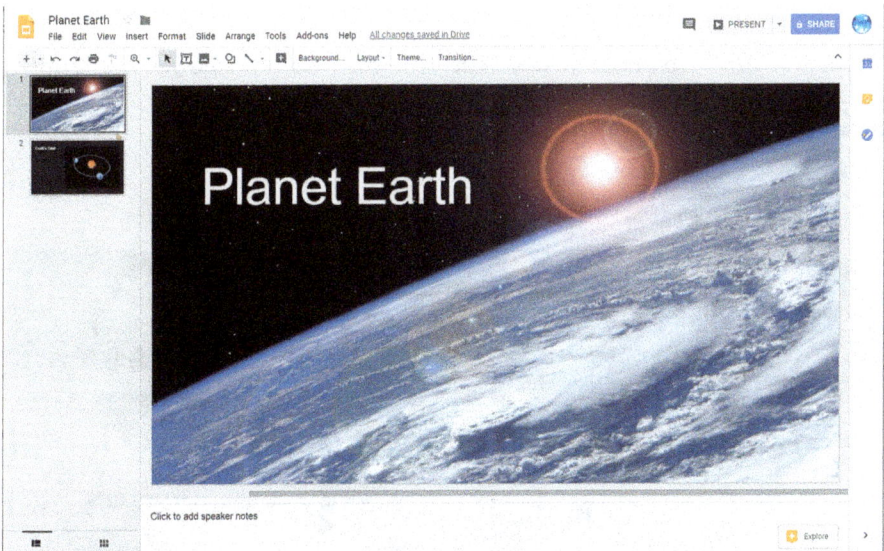

Add a New Slide

To continue building our presentation we need additional slides to show our information. To add a new slide, click the small down arrow next to the 'New Slide' icon.

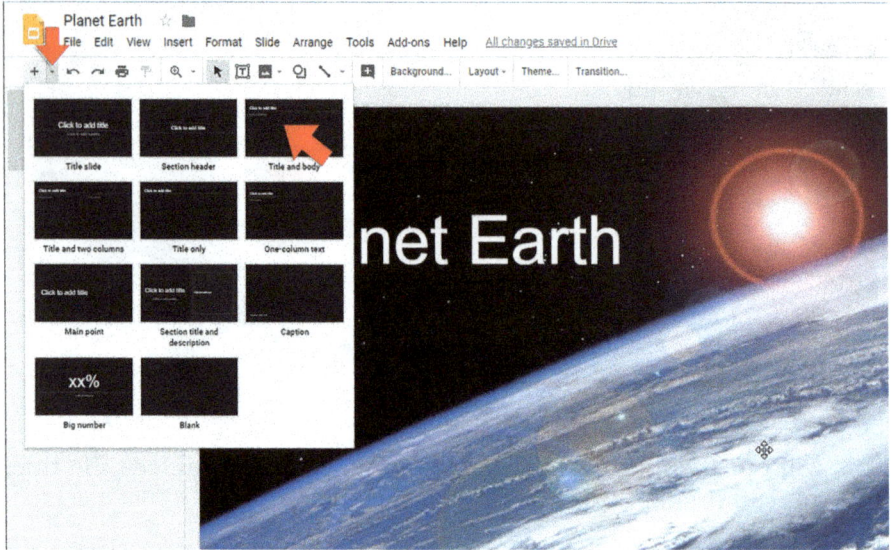

From the drop down menu, select 'title and body' because we want a title on the slide but also we want to add some information in bullet points.

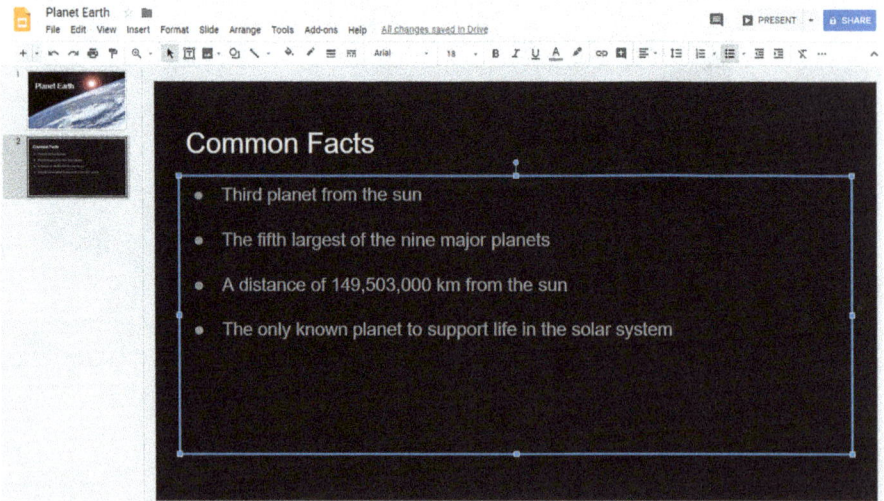

Now enter the data into your new slide.

Change Slide Layout

Select the slide whose layout you want to change. Then go to the 'slide' menu and select 'apply layout'.

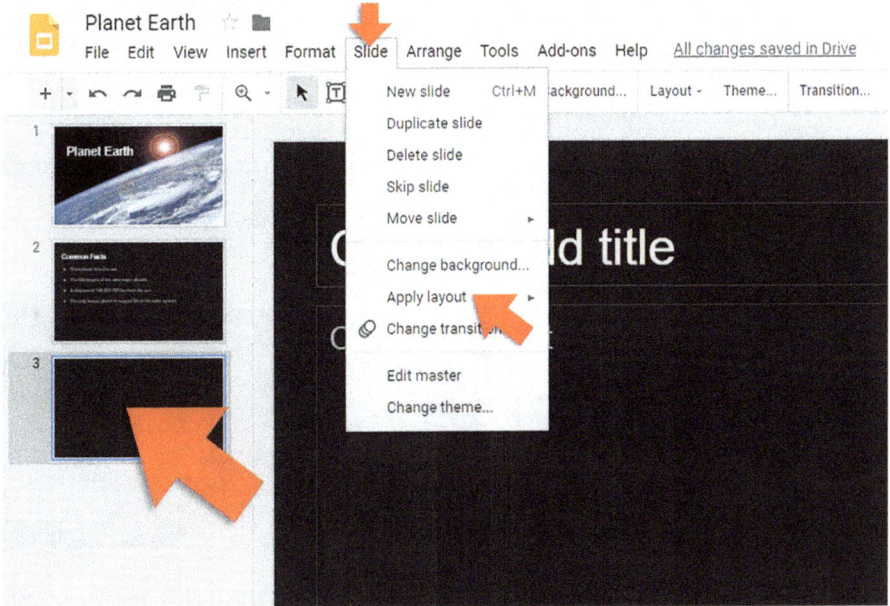

From the slideout menu, select a template from the options.

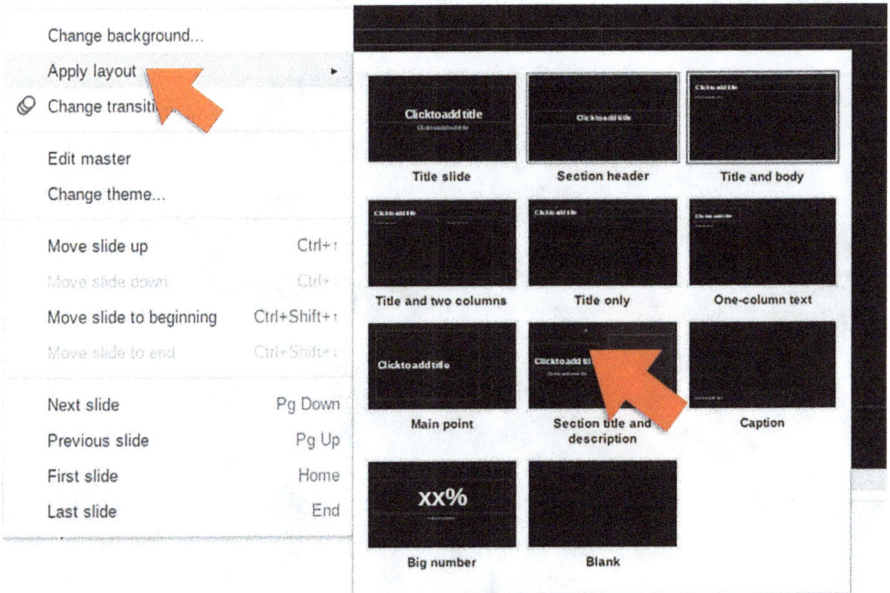

Slide Masters

Slide masters allow you to create layouts and templates that are common to all your slides, so you don't have to make those changes to each slide.

Say you are creating a presentation and want a company logo on the bottom, you can add it to your slide master and the logo will appear on every slide you create.

To edit your slide masters, go to the slide menu and click 'edit master'.

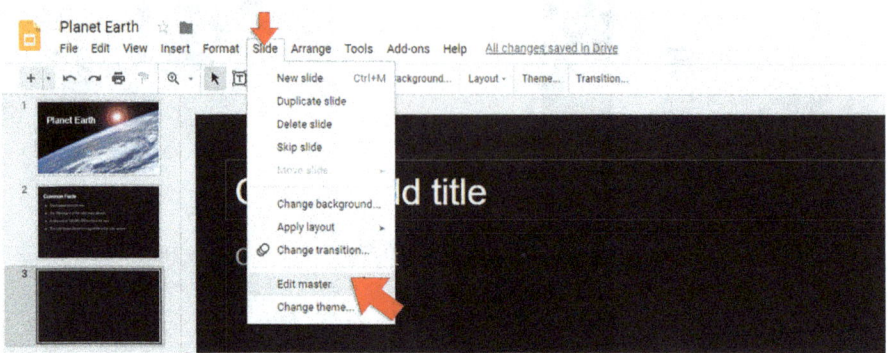

The larger slide listed down the left hand side is your master for all slides. The ones below are masters for individual slide templates such as 'title slides' or 'title and body' slides. These appear in the 'new slide' drop down menu. You can split them up so you can create templates for specific slides.

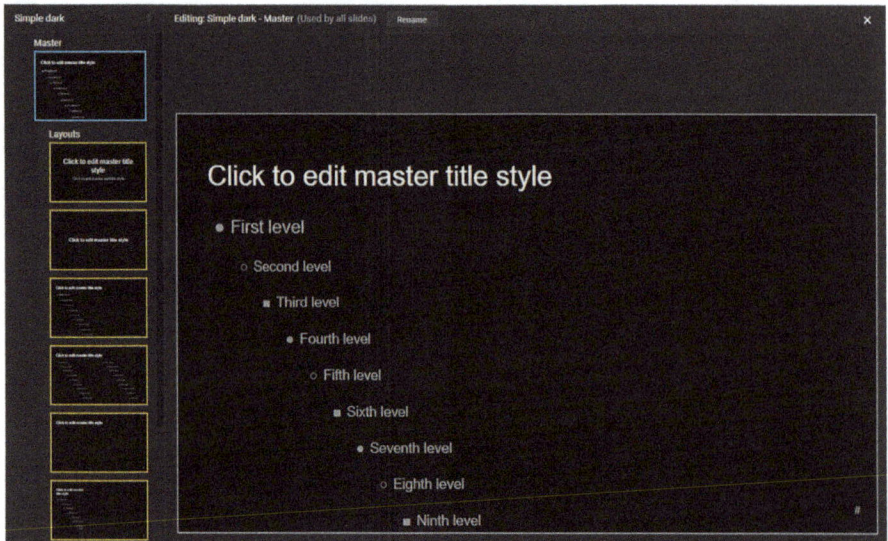

In this simple example, I am going to add the company logo to the bottom right of every slide. To do this, click on the larger master slide in the list on the left hand side.

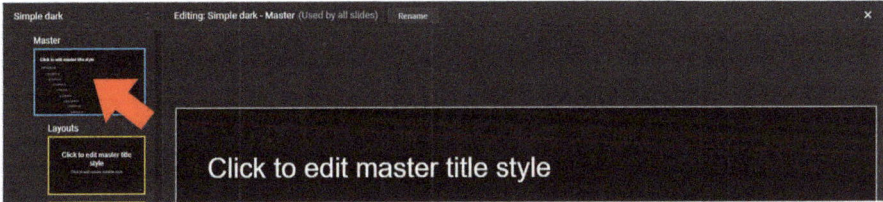

Open your file explorer and navigate to your Google Drive folder, or the folder where the picture you want is saved. Click and drag your image onto the master slide.

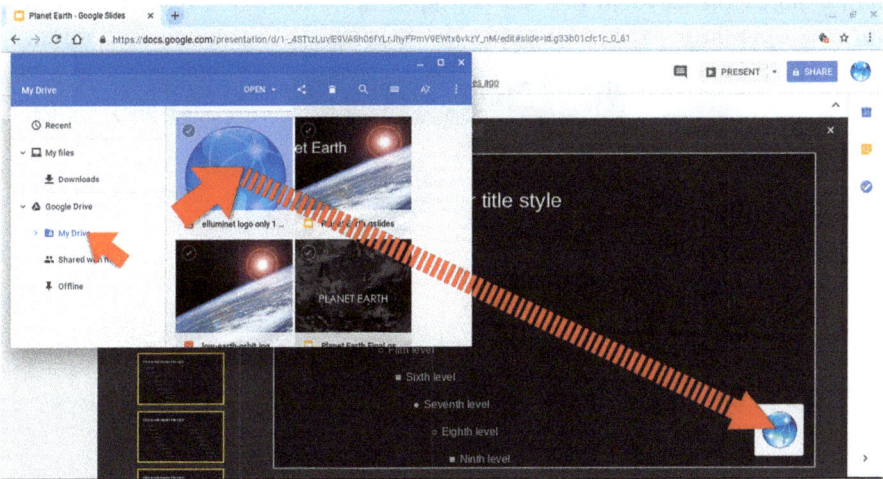

Notice, the logo we just added appears on all the slides.

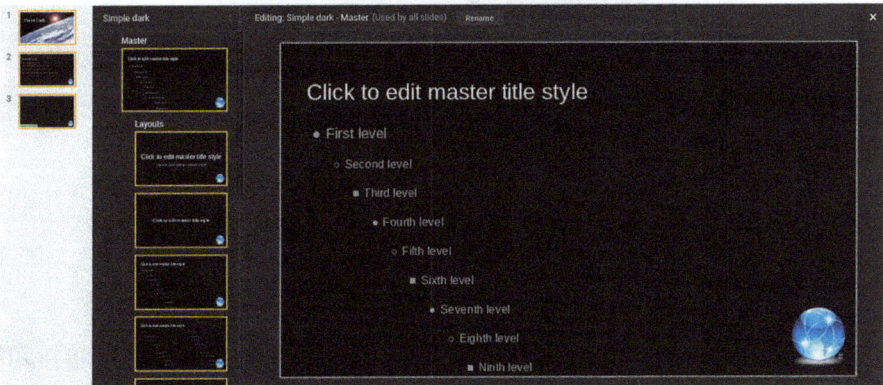

Click the small white x on the top right to close the masters.

Chapter 9: Google Slides

Slide Transitions

A slide transition is an animation or effect that is displayed when you move from one slide to the next.

To add transitions to your slides, click the slide you want to add the transition to, then click 'transition'.

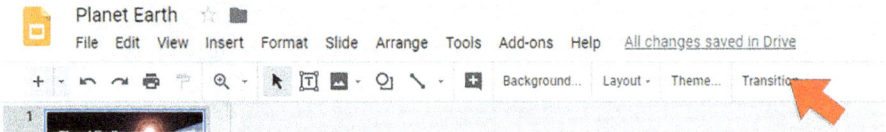

From the animations panel on the right hand side of the screen, you can select from several pre set transitions. If you click on a transition, for example 'fade', this will apply the transition to the selected slide.

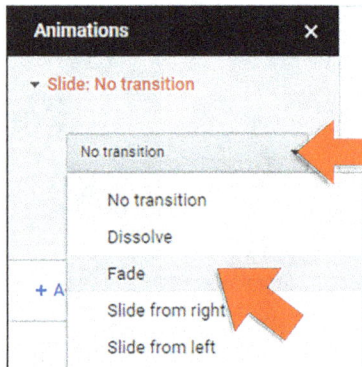

Select how fast you want the slides to transition, using the slider.

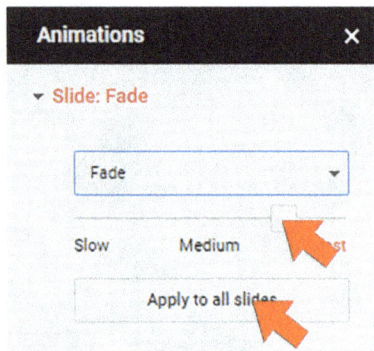

By default, the transition is only applied to the slide you have selected. Click 'apply to all slides' if you want to apply the same transition to all the slides you have added to your presentation

350

Slide Animations

You can add animations to slides to move text boxes, make bullet points appear, animate shapes and so on. This can help to make your presentation flow so objects and text appear at the right time while you're presenting. Animation effects can also help to emphasise certain points.

Effects

Looking at the slide below, say you wanted each bullet point to appear one at a time, instead of all at once.

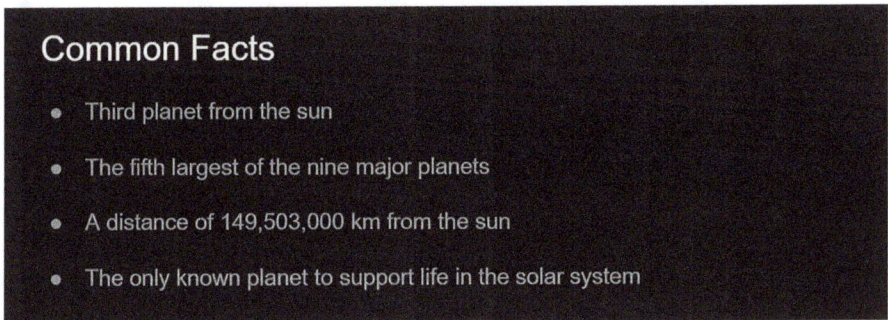

To add an animation effect to the bullet points, click 'transition' on the right hand side of the toolbar.

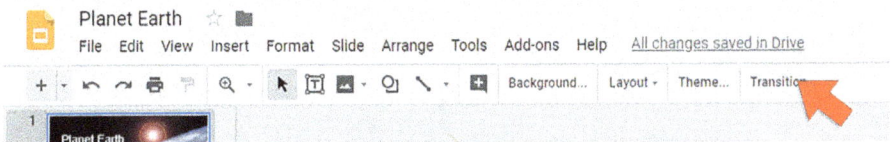

This will open up the 'animations' panel on the right hand side of your screen.

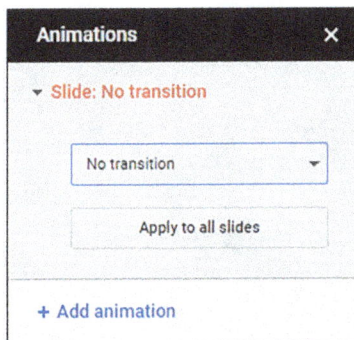

Chapter 9: Google Slides

First, select the object you want to add an animation to. In this case the textbox with the bullet points in.

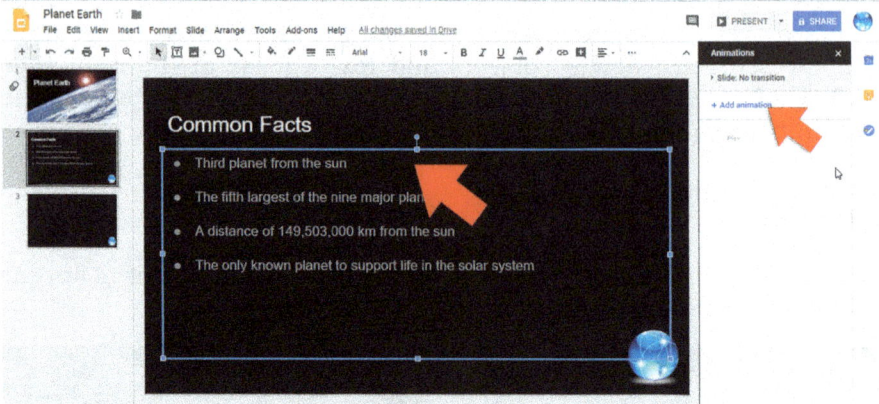

In the first drop down box, select the animation preset you want, eg 'fade in'.

In the second drop down box, select 'on click' - meaning you click the mouse to show the next point.

Select 'by paragraph'. This means a 'paragraph' will appear at a time. A new paragraph is created each time you press return when typing in your slide information into the text box.

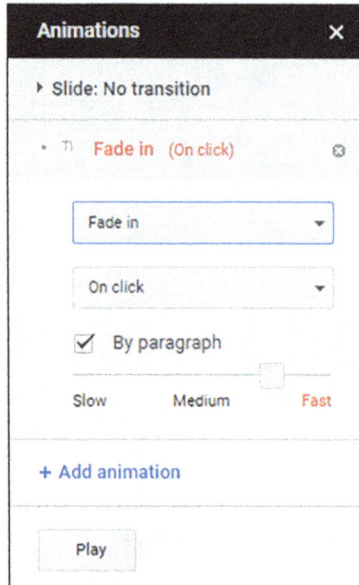

Click 'play' to preview the animation.

Insert a Table

We are going to add a table to a new slide. In this example I have added a new slide with 'title only'.

To add a table to this slide, go to the 'insert' menu and select 'table'. From the slideout, select the number of columns and rows. This table is going to have 2 columns.

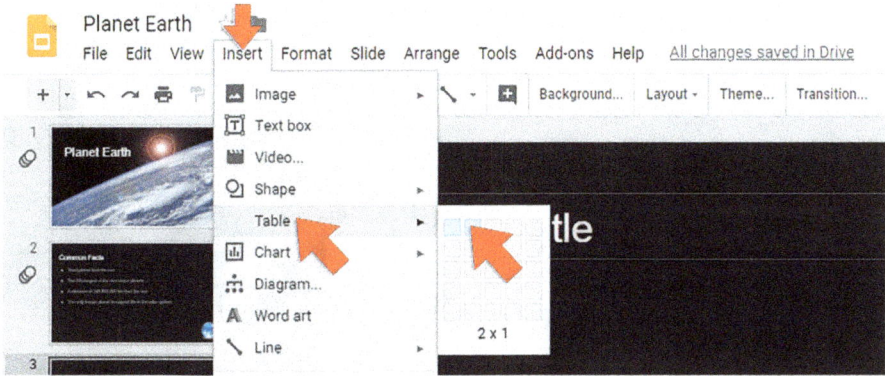

Your table will appear in the centre of the slide. You can type in your data.

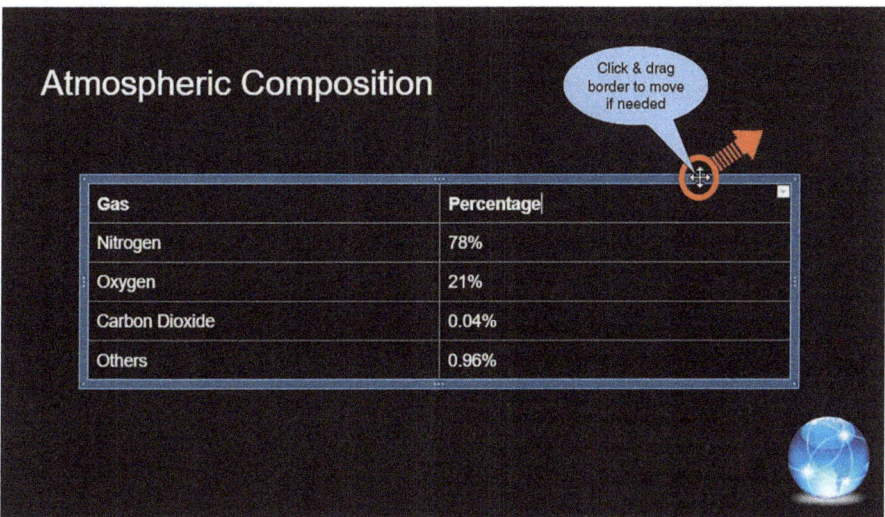

Press the tab key on your keyboard to insert a new row, when you get to the end.

Click & drag the solid double blue border to move the table into position on your slide.

Add a Chart

We are going to add a chart to a new slide. In this example I have added a new slide with 'title only'

Click the 'insert' menu, then select 'chart'. From the slideout, select the type of chart you want. In this example, I am going to use a nice pie chart.

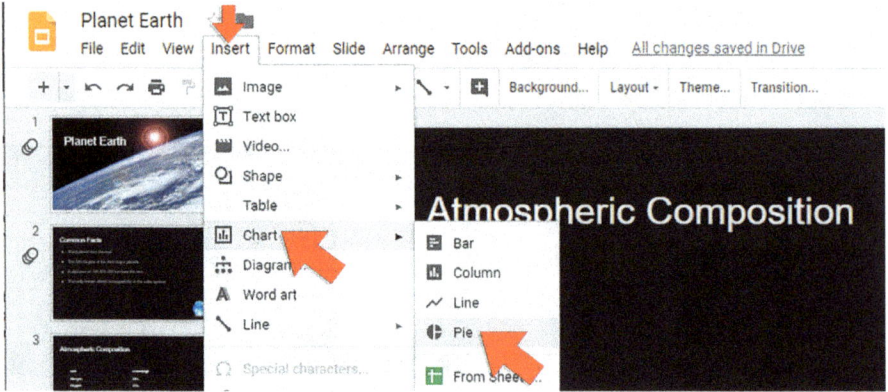

Google Slides will insert a default chart. To enter your own data, click the down arrow on the top right of the chart and select 'open source'.

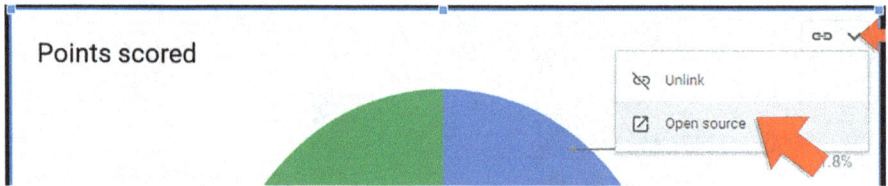

In the spreadsheet that opens, enter your data in the first two columns.

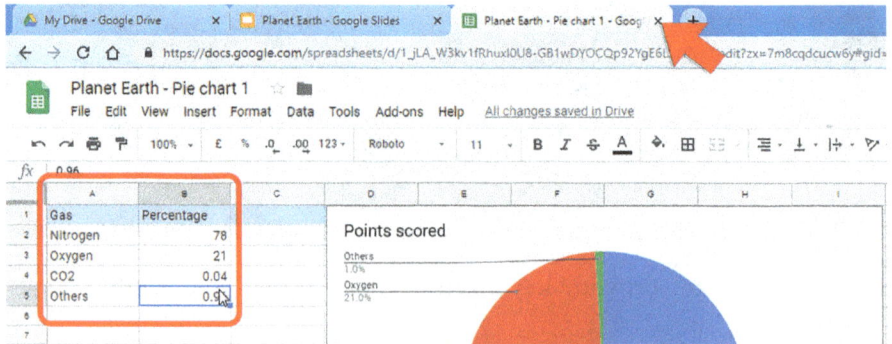

Click the x on the tab at the top of the screen to close and return to Google Slides.

Printing Presentations

To print your slides, click the 'file menu', then select 'print settings and preview.

Click '1 slide with notes' - the second icon along the toolbar at the top, then from the drop down menu, select how many slides you want on each page. For handouts to give to your audience, select 6 slides per page. This will print 6 small slides on each page, leaving them some room to take notes. Click 'print'.

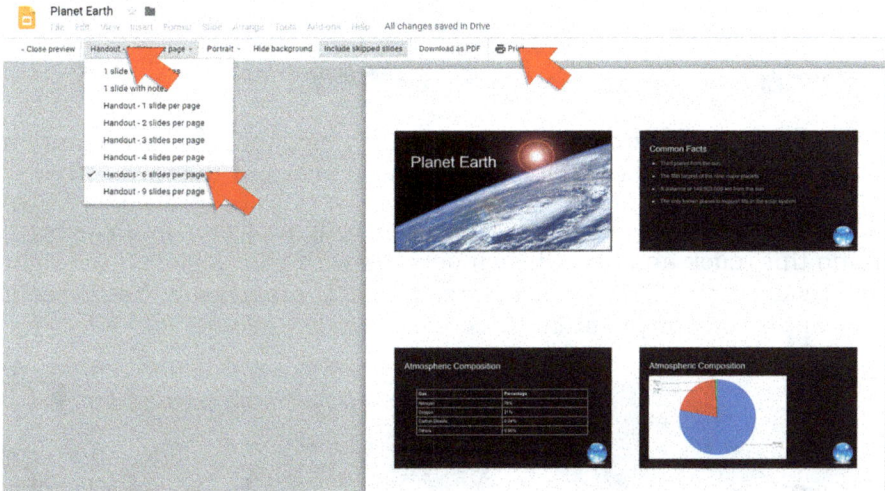

Select the printer you want to print to, and the number of copies you want.

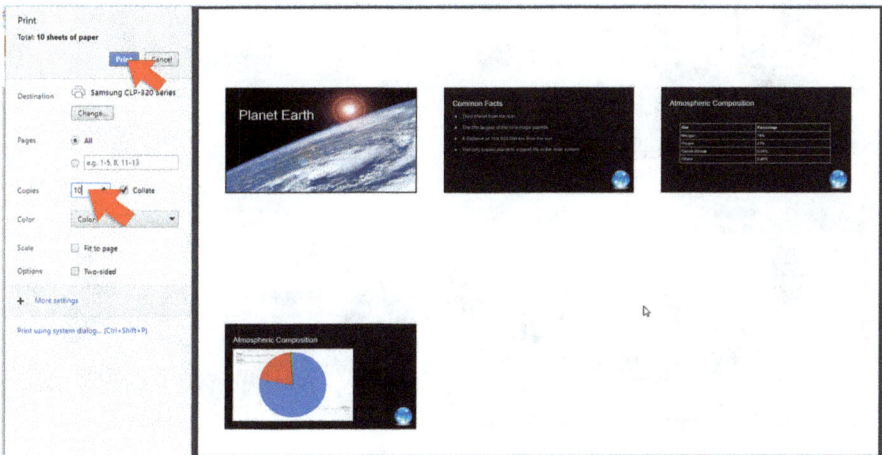

Click 'print' when you're done.

Giving your Presentation

First connect your Chromebook to your projector or TV. When you do this your Chromebook will extend its desktop onto the projector or TV. This enables you to have a presenter view on your Chromebook screen with presenter notes, slide lists and other tools, while the audience see just the presentation.

Open your presentation, then click the small arrow next to 'present' on the toolbar on the right hand side.

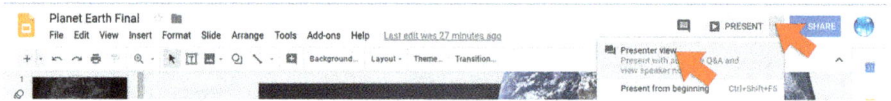

Two windows will pop up, your presenter view, and your presentation view. You may need to drag your presenter view out the way.

Now, move your presentation view onto your projector or TV screen. To do this, click and drag the window tab with your slide, off the right hand side of the Chromebook screen until it disappears. You'll see it appear on your projector or TV screen.

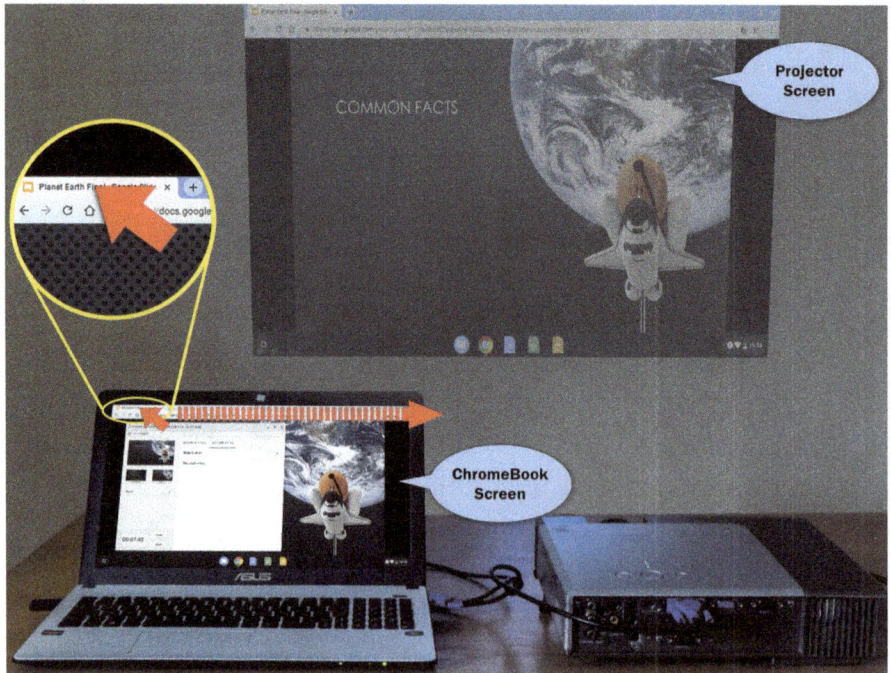

Some Chromebooks you'll need to drag if off the left hand side of the screen - try this if it doesn't work.

On the projector or TV screen (move your mouse pointer to the right until it appears on the projector/tv screen), click the three dots icon on the top right, then click the 'full screen' icon.

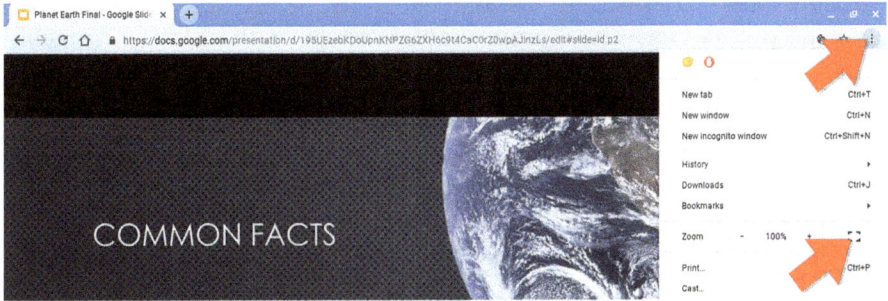

Now, maximise the presenter display on your Chromebook screen.

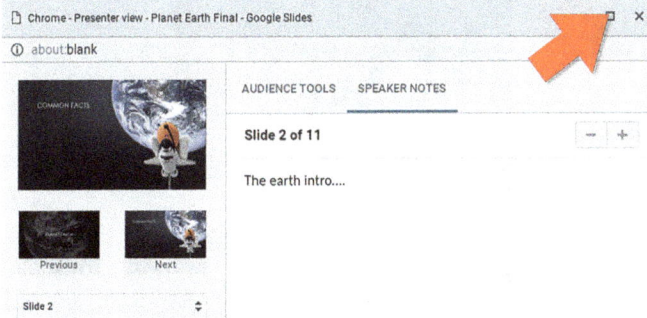

You'll end up with something like this. You'll be able to control your Google Slides presentation using the presenter view on your Chromebook.

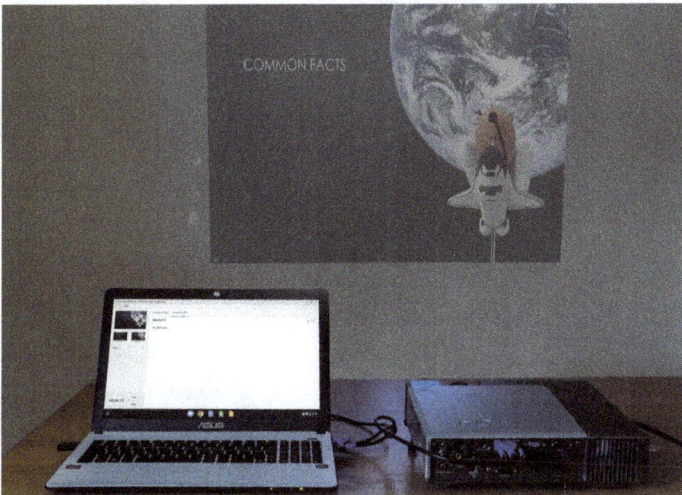

Present with ChromeCast

To be able to cast your presentation to a ChromeCast device, your Chromebook will need to be on the same Wi-Fi network as your ChromeCast device. The ChromeCast device can be plugged into a TV or a projector.

Open your Google Slides presentation, then click the small down arrow next to the 'present' icon. From the drop down menu, select 'present on another screen'. If it's greyed out, check your wifi settings on your ChromeCast device and Chromebook.

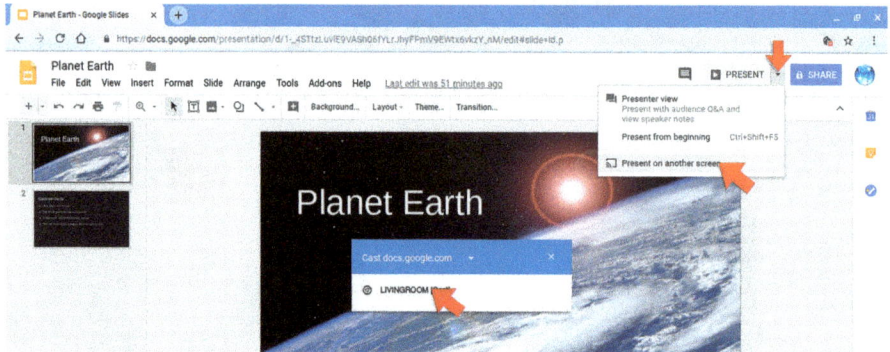

From the popup box that appears, select your ChromeCast device. Your presentation will appear on your TV or projector screen.

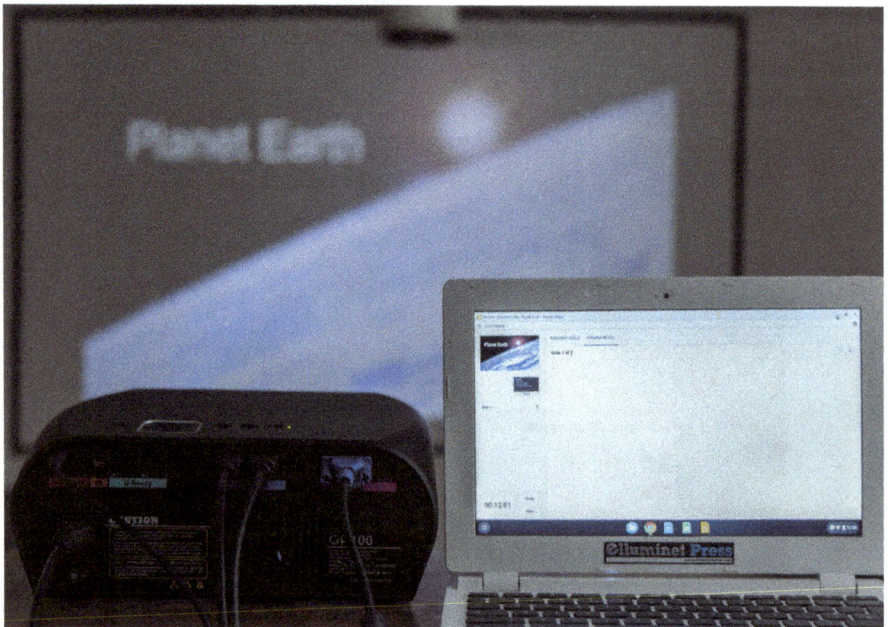

Now that your Chromebook is completely wireless, you can give your presentation.

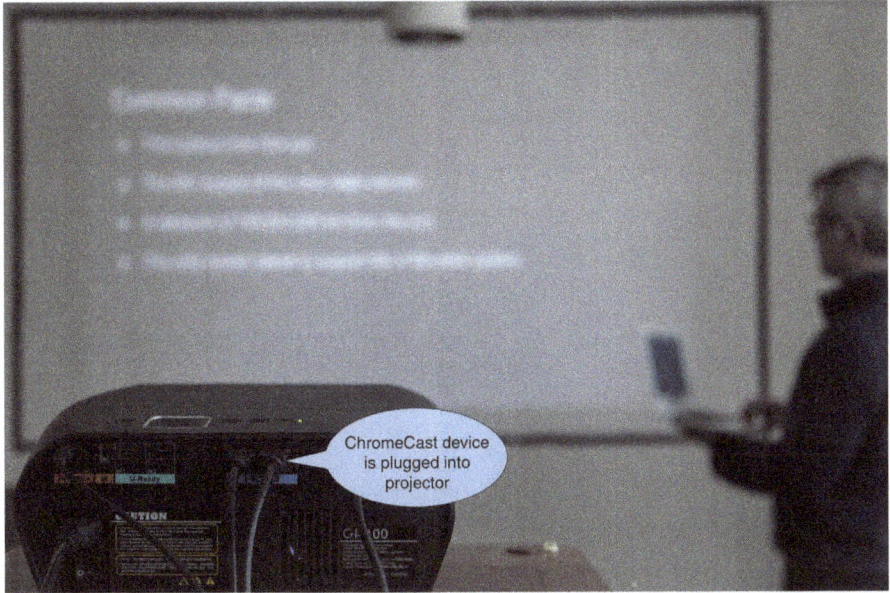

ChromeCast device is plugged into projector

On your Chromebook you can use a laser pointer, see your presenter notes, as well as advancing and selecting slides to show. You'll see a control bar popup when you move your mouse pointer to the bottom of the screen.

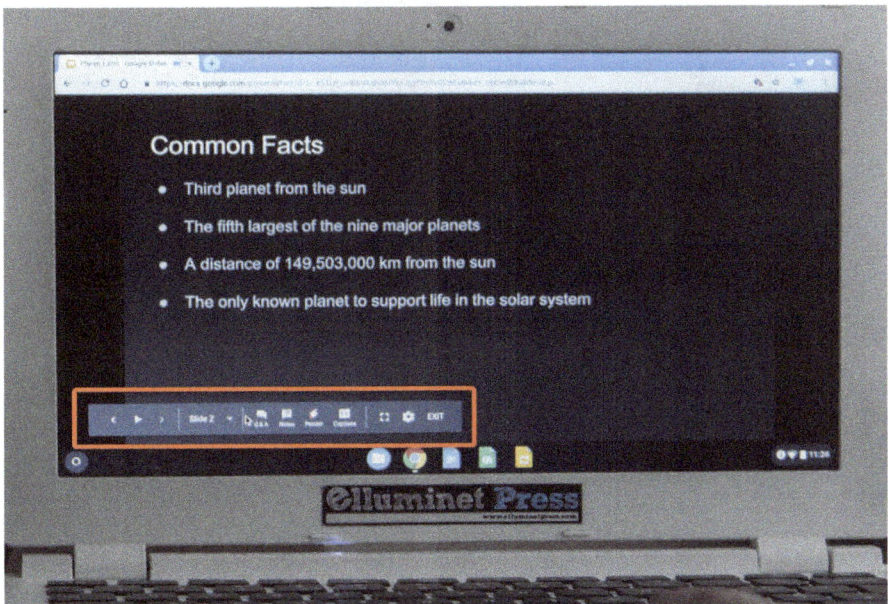

10

Google Drive

Google Drive is a cloud-based storage service by Google that lets you store and manage files online—documents, images, videos, and PDFs.

On a Chromebook, Google Drive acts as a central hub for all your files, seamlessly integrating with Google Workspace apps like Docs, Sheets, and Slides as well as various other apps.

You get 15 GB of free storage, shared across Google services (including Gmail and Photos), with additional storage available via Google One subscriptions.

In this chapter we'll take a look at:

- Google Drive
- Integration with Chromebook
- Opening Google Drive
- Search and Filters
- Offline Access
- Sharing and Collaboration
- Google One & Storage Management

Take a look at the video demos. Open your web browser and navigate to the following website:

elluminetpress.com/ chromebook-nav

Integration with Chromebook

Chromebooks are designed with Google Drive at their core. Anything you create with Google Docs, Sheets, or Slides is automatically saved to Google Drive.

Your Chromebook treats Google Drive as a native part of its file system, allowing you to access files directly from the Files app, just like local files.

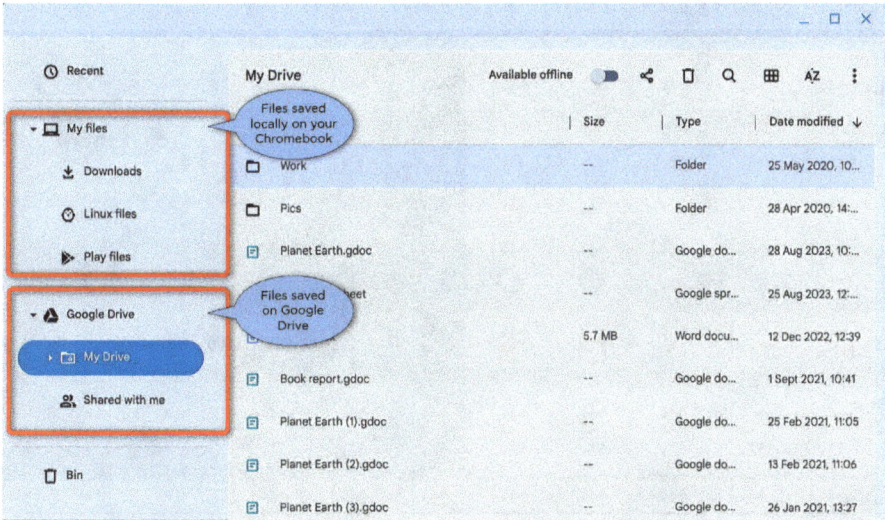

This means you can browse your Google Drive files as if they were stored locally on your device. You can create new folders, upload files from other sources, rename and organize your documents, and move items between local storage and Google Drive with a simple drag-and-drop action.

You can create, view, and organize folders and documents; open files that have been shared with you; and enable offline access by marking selected files for use without an internet connection.

This tight integration means that your files are always available—even if you switch devices—provided you're signed in with your Google Account.

So whether you're logging in from a another machine, or accessing files from your phone or tablet, your work is always accessible from anywhere.

Opening Google Drive

You can access Google Drive using the files app on your Chromebook, or from the Google Drive App on a tablet or phone.

On your Chromebook

Click on the Launcher at the bottom-left corner of your screen, then find and click on the "Files" app.

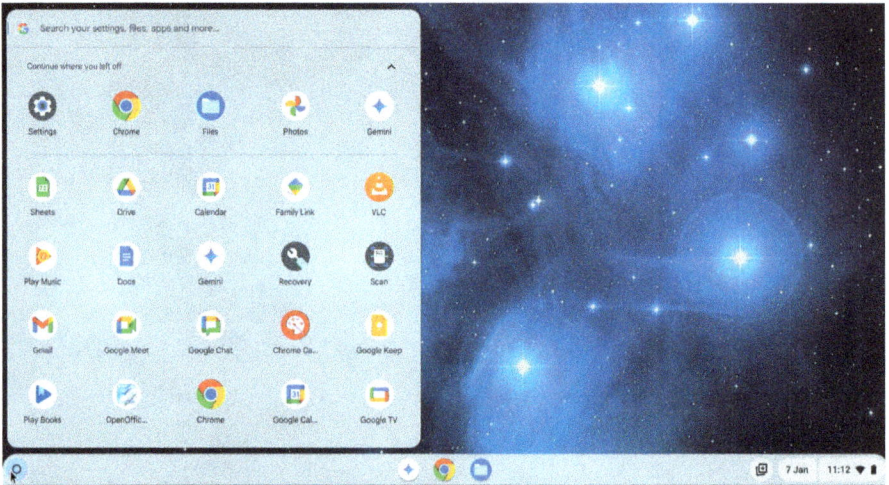

In the Files app, you'll see a section on the left sidebar for Google Drive. Click on it to view all the folders and files stored in your Drive.

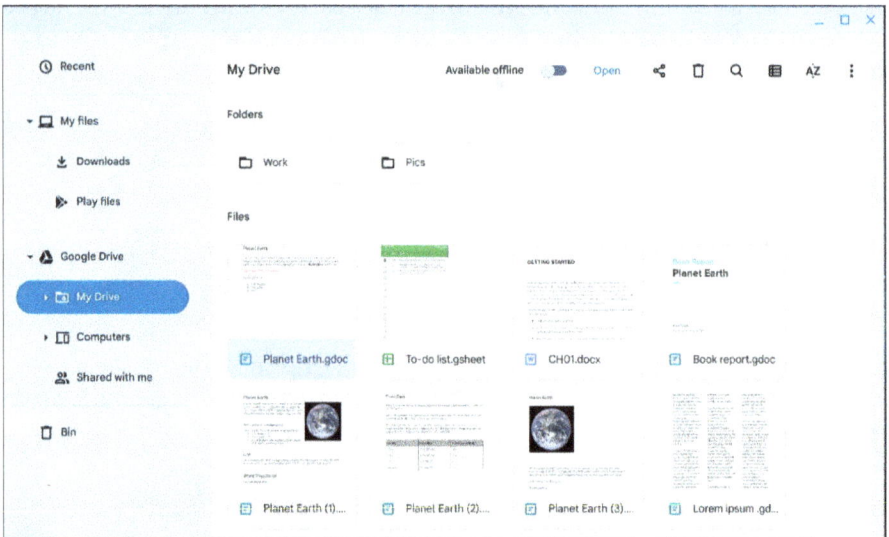

On the Web

To access Google Drive on the web, open your web browser, then navigate to the following website.

`drive.google.com`

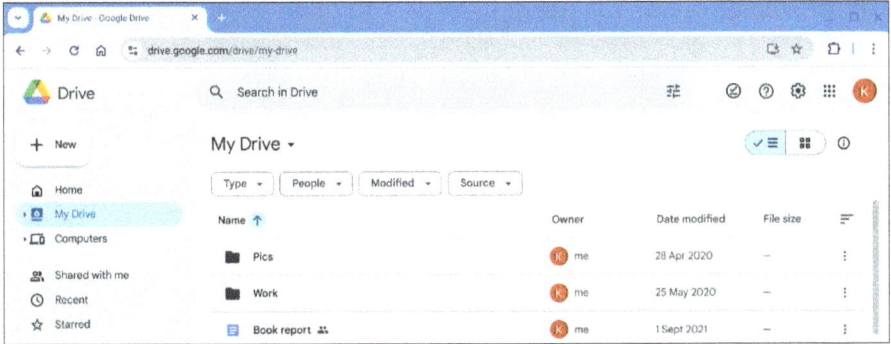

The App

If you're using Google Drive on a tablet or phone, open the app store then download Google Drive if you haven't already done so.

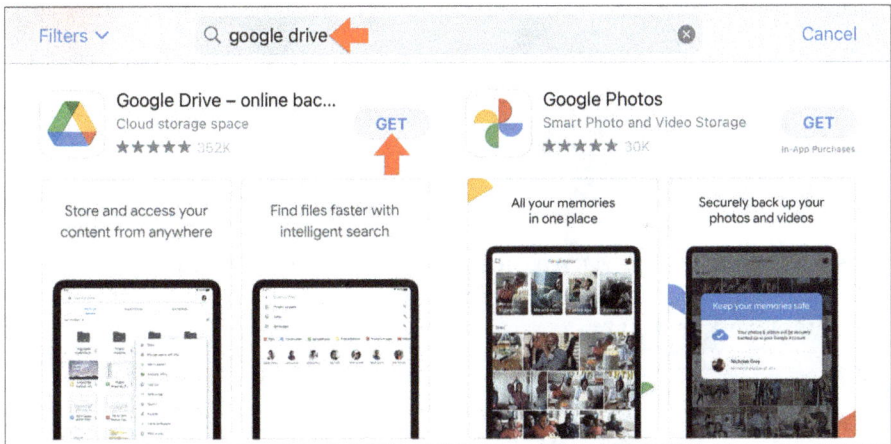

You'll find the Google Drive app on your home screen. Just tap on the icon to start the app.

Getting Around Google Drive

The Files app on Chromebook provides an intuitive interface for navigating Google Drive. When you open the Files app from the Launcher, the left-hand sidebar displays various storage locations. Among them, Google Drive appears as a separate section labelled "My Drive." Clicking on this section reveals your folders and files stored in the on Google Drive in the cloud. You can navigate to folders by clicking on them, and open files with a double-click.

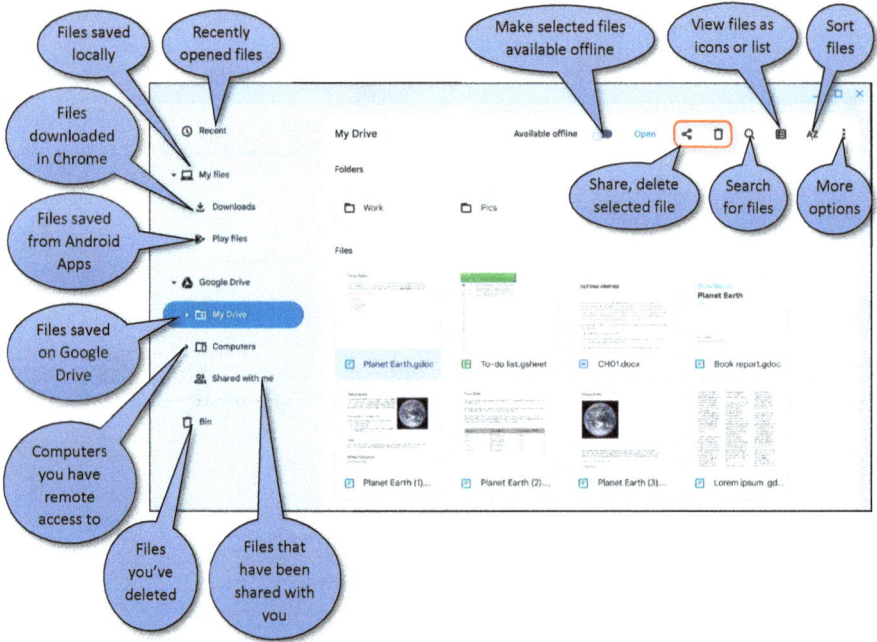

When you Select My Drive, folders appear first in the list or grid, followed by individual files. Here in the example below, we can see the files displayed as a list.

Name		Size	Type	Date modified ↓
📁	Work	--	Folder	25 May 2020, 10:...
📁	Pics	--	Folder	28 Apr 2020, 14:...
📄	Planet Earth.gdoc	--	Google do...	28 Aug 2023, 10:...
📊	To-do list.gsheet	--	Google spr...	25 Aug 2023, 12:...

To open a file, double-click it. Depending on the file type, it will either open in a web-based Google app—such as Docs, Sheets, or Slides—or in a compatible Android or web application if available.

My Drive	Available offline	Open						
Name		Size		Type		Date modified ↓		
📁 Work		--		Folder		25 May 2020, 10...		
📁 Pics		--		Folder		28 Apr 2020, 14:...		
📄 Planet Earth.gdoc		--		Google do...		28 Aug 2023, 10:...		
📊 To-do list.gsheet		--		Google spr...		25 Aug 2023, 12:...		
📄 CH01.docx		5.7 MB		Word docu...		12 Dec 2022, 12:39		

Right-clicking on a file or folder brings up a menu that allows you to rename, delete, move, copy, share, or download the item. You can also make a file available offline directly from this menu.

My Drive	Available offline	Open					
Name				Type		Date modified ↓	
	Google Docs	📄					
📁 Work	Share			Folder		25 May 2020, 10...	
📁 Pics				Folder		28 Apr 2020, 14:...	
	Manage in Drive						
📄 Planet Earth.gdoc	Available offline			Google do...		28 Aug 2023, 10:...	
📊 ...do list.gsheet				Google spr...		25 Aug 2023, 12:...	
	Cut	Ctrl+X					
📄 CH01.docx	Copy	Ctrl+C		Word docu...		12 Dec 2022, 12:39	
	Paste	Ctrl+V					
📄 Book report.gdoc				Google do...		1 Sept 2021, 10:41	
	Get info	Space					
📄 Planet Earth (1).gdoc	Rename	Ctrl+Enter		Google do...		25 Feb 2021, 11:05	
📄 Planet Earth (2).gdoc	Delete	Alt+Shift+Backspace		Google do...		13 Feb 2021, 11:06	
📄 Planet Earth (3).gdoc	ZIP			Google do...		26 Jan 2021, 13:27	
	Pin to shelf						
📄 Lorem ipsum .gdoc				Google do...		26 Jan 2021, 10:35	
📄 Untitled document (3).gdoc	New folder	Ctrl+E		Google do...		25 Jan 2021, 10:42	

Chapter 10: Google Drive

You can change how files are displayed within My Drive using the view toggle located in the toolbar at the top-right corner of the window. This switch lets you alternate between a list view, which shows detailed information about each file, and a thumbnail grid view, which may be more helpful when browsing photos or videos.

In list view you can sort your files by clicking on any of the column headings. For example, clicking on the "Name" column will sort files alphabetically; clicking it again will reverse the order. Similarly, selecting "Date modified" sorts files by the most recent or oldest edits.

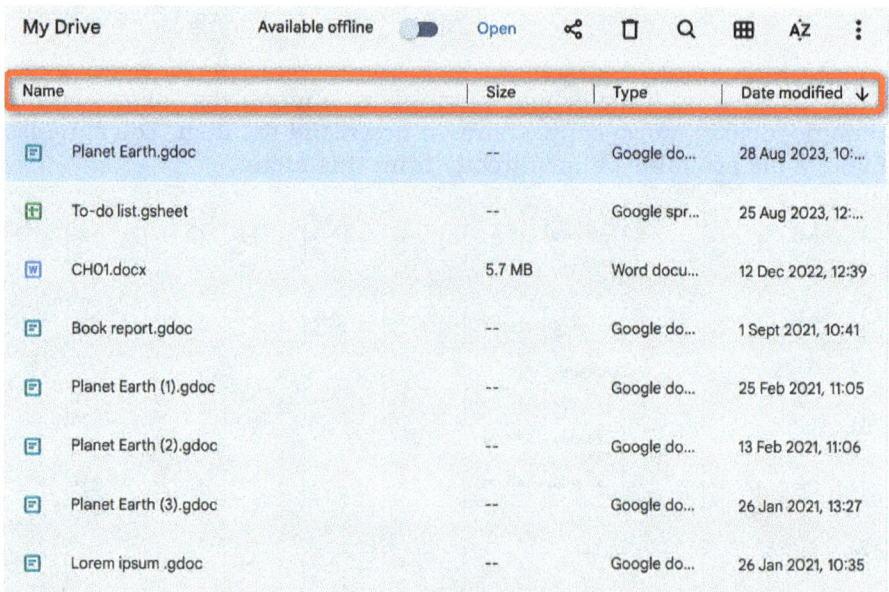

You can also sort the contents of the current folder by name, date modified, file type, or size using the sort icon on the toolbar.

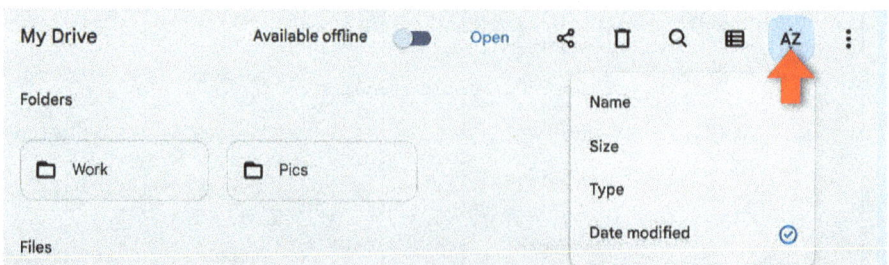

Search and Filters

Google Drive includes a search feature that helps locate files quickly. Select the magnifying glass icon from the toolbar on the top left.

You can type the name of a file, a keyword, or a phrase from within a document into the search bar.

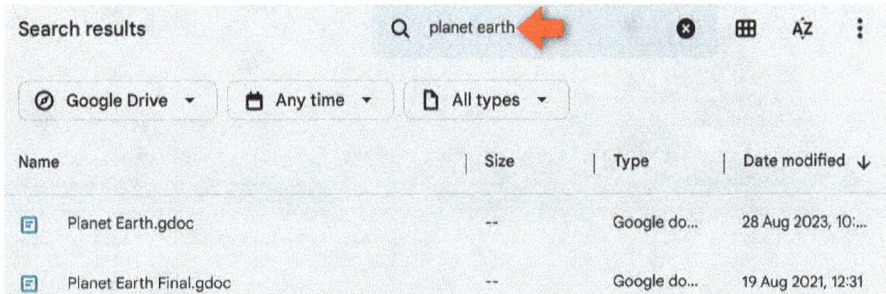

To narrow results, use the advanced search options accessible by clicking the filter drop down options.

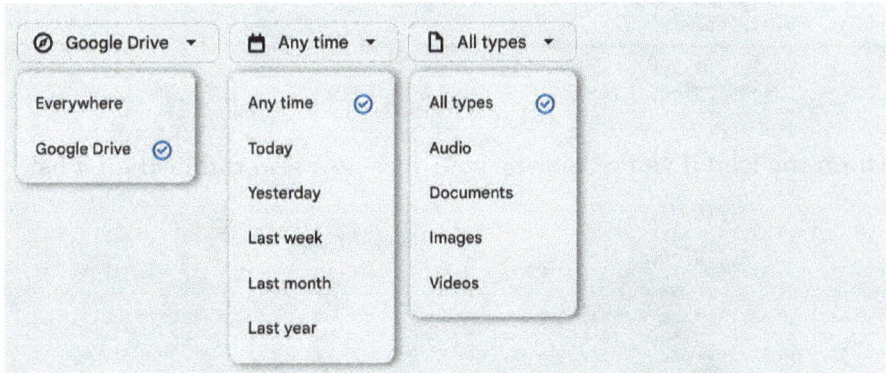

The first **Google Drive** menu, you can choose to search either Everywhere—which includes all files your account can access—or restrict the search to just Google Drive. The **Any time** menu and allows you to limit results by modification date. You can choose from common time ranges such as Today, Yesterday, Last week, Last month, or Last year. **All types** menu allows you to filter by file format. This is useful when searching within folders that contain a mix of media, documents, and other content.

Offline Access

Offline access allows you to work with files on your Chromebook even when you're not connected to the internet. To make a file available offline, select the files you want to make available. Click the "available offline" switch. Hold down control on your keyboard while you click to select multiple files.

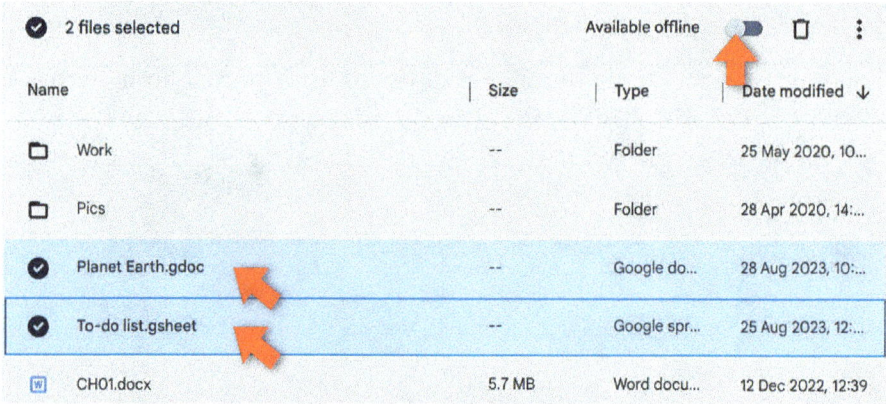

The file is then downloaded and stored locally. You can open and edit it using the appropriate app—Docs, Sheets, or Slides. You'll see a small offline icon next to the file you've made available offline

Or on the icon if you're viewing your files as a grid rather than a list.

Once your device reconnects to the internet, any changes made offline are automatically synced to the cloud. This is useful for users who travel or experience unreliable network connections and want continuous access to their work.

Sharing and Collaboration

Files and folders in Google Drive can be shared with other users for collaboration.

To share a file, right-click on it and choose the "Share" option.

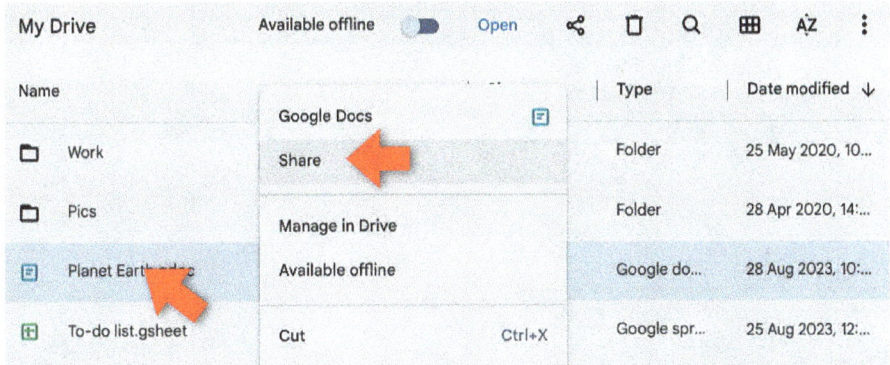

Select "share with others"

You can enter email addresses of individuals or groups.

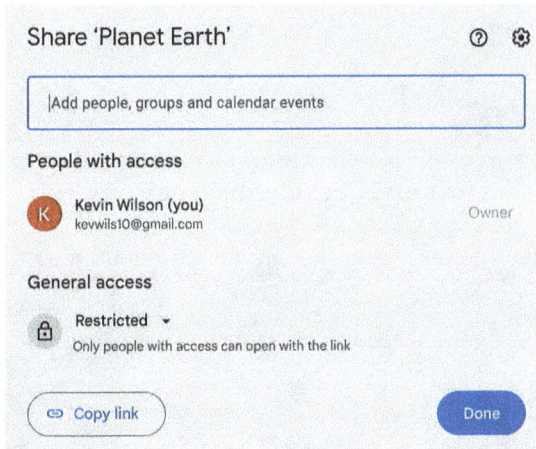

Chapter 10: Google Drive

Specify the level of access they should have: viewer, commenter, or editor

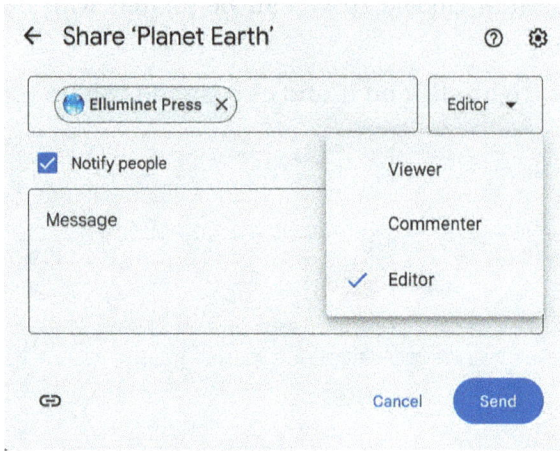

Multiple users can work on a file at the same time, with changes synced automatically and shown live. Here in the example below, we can see Elluminet Press editing the document

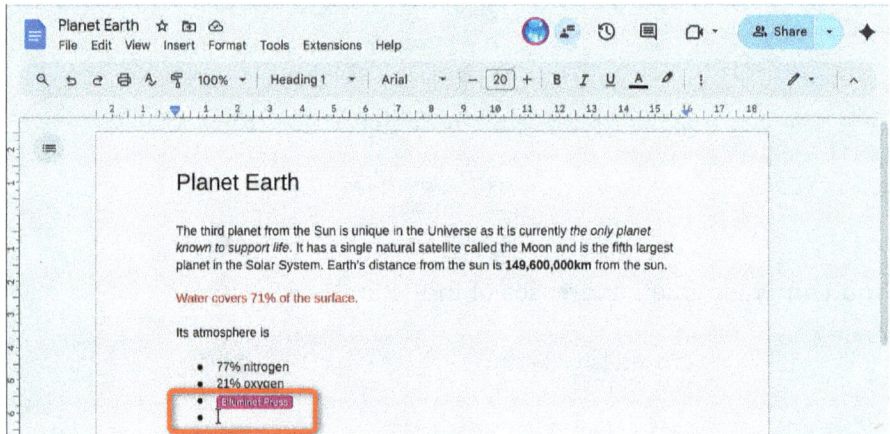

Editors' cursors are visible in the document, and comments can be added by selecting text and clicking the comment icon.

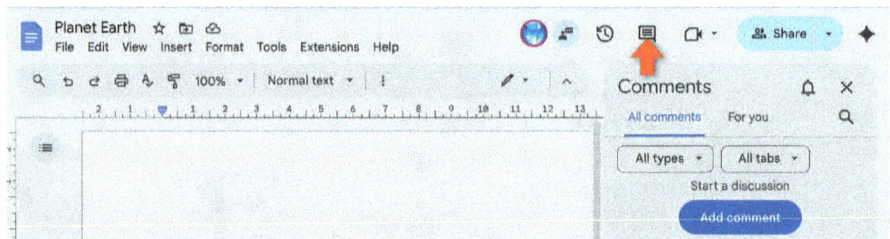

You can also bring up the group chat if you want to talk to the other collaborators.

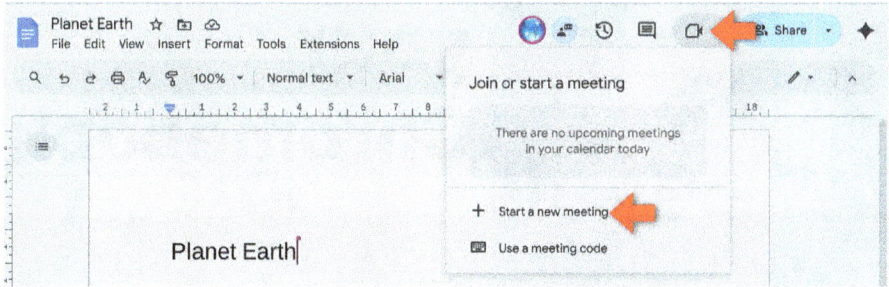

This functionality makes Google Drive a practical solution for team projects, reviews, and educational tasks.

Google One & Storage Management

Google Drive includes 15 GB of free cloud storage, shared across Drive, Gmail, and Google Photos. This space can fill up quickly due to large email attachments, high-resolution photos, or sizable files stored in Drive. You can check your current storage usage by visiting drive. google.com click 'storage' on the bottom left. From there, you can review which services use the most space and delete unnecessary items.

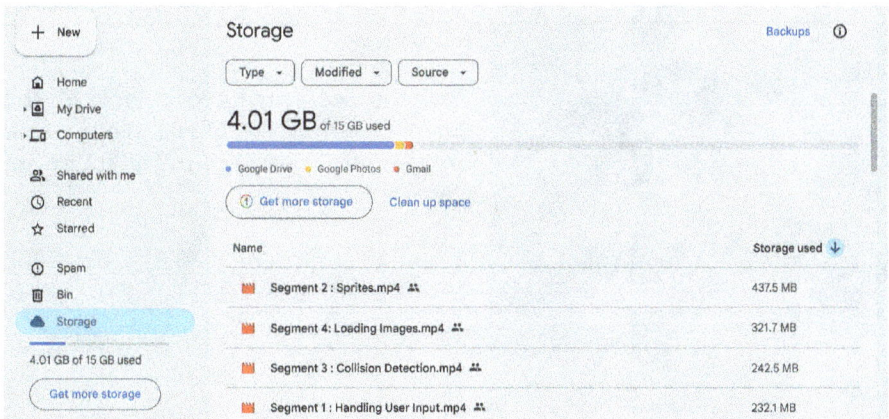

If more space is needed, click 'Get more storage' in the storage summary at the bottom left of Google Drive. This opens the Google One upgrade options. Available plans increase your total storage and apply across all Google services linked to your account. A monthly fee is charged based on the plan you choose.

11 Maintaining your Chromebook

Chromebooks require very little maintenance. However, it is crucial to keep your Chromebook up to date to make sure you have the most recent security updates.

In this chapter, we'll take a look at:

- Diagnostics

- Updating ChromeOS

- Powerwash

- Chromebook Recovery

- App Info

- VPNs

For this section, have a look at the video resources. Open your web browser and navigate to the following website

elluminetpress.com/
chromebook-sys

Diagnostics

Diagnostics is a somewhat useless app that checks your Chromebook for hardware problems such as battery, CPU or memory issues.

To run the diagnostics, click on the clock on the bottom right, then select settings.

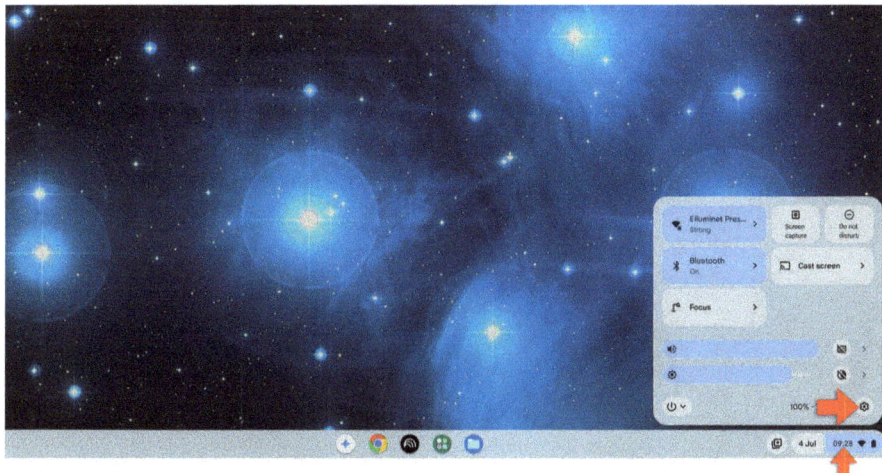

Select 'about chrome OS', then click 'diagnostics'.

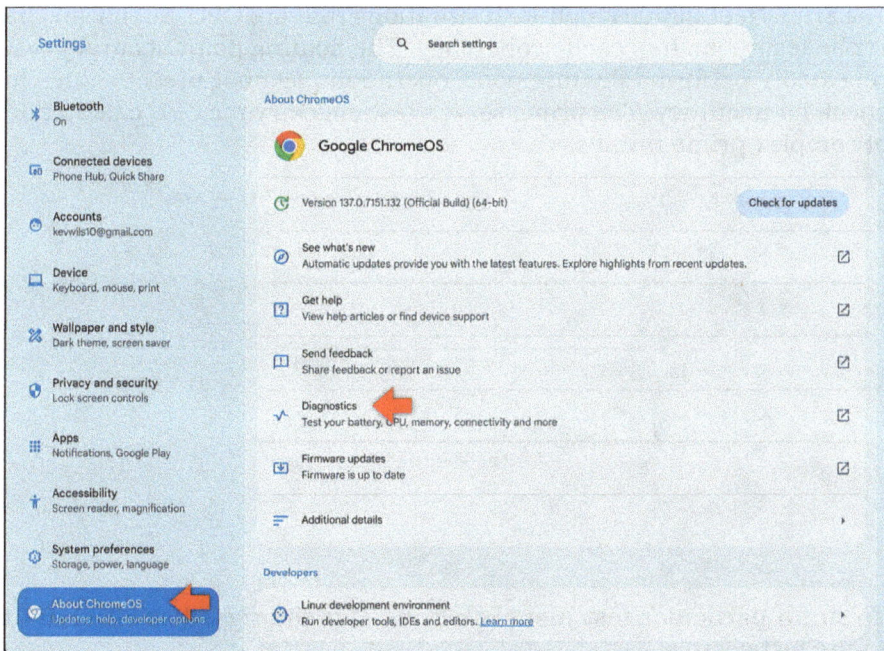

Chapter 11: Maintaining your Chromebook

On the diagnostics screen you can run various tests. On the top left, you can select system tests, connectivity tests and keyboard tests.

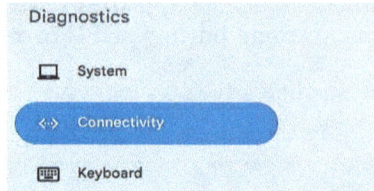

Diagnostics

System

Connectivity

Keyboard

In system tests, you can run a battery discharge test. This test measures the rate of charge and discharge over a fixed period of time for your Chromebook. If the rate of charge and discharge is very low, there may be a problem with the battery or charging port.

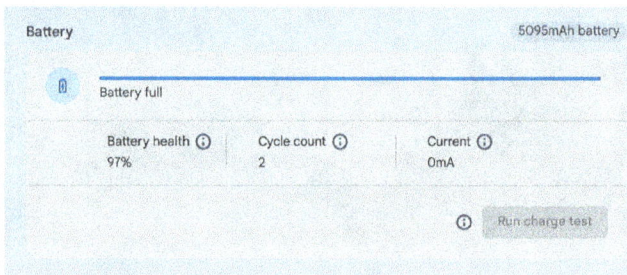

Battery   5095mAh battery

Battery full

Battery health ⓘ   Cycle count ⓘ   Current ⓘ
97%   2   0mA

ⓘ   Run charge test

You can run a CPU test. The test will consist of various different test. The stress test mimics high-load situations that are CPU-intensive. The cache test measures cache coherency. The floating point accuracy test repeatedly performs floating point operations against preset values to check for accuracy. The prime search test checks your CPU calculation of complex prime numbers.

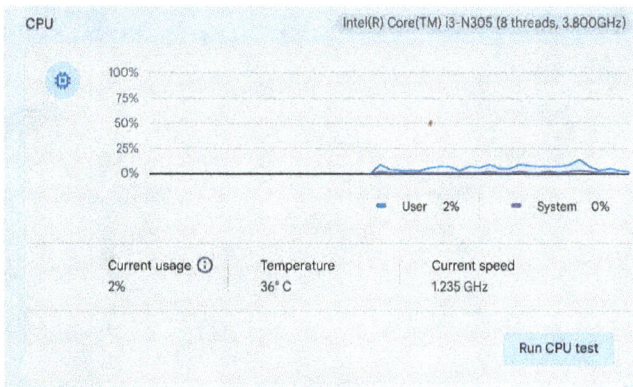

CPU   Intel(R) Core(TM) i3-N305 (8 threads, 3.800GHz)

100%
75%
50%
25%
0%

— User   2%   — System   0%

Current usage ⓘ   Temperature   Current speed
2%   36° C   1.235 GHz

Run CPU test

To run a particular test just click 'run...' on the right hand side next to the test section.

Updating ChromeOS

Google release updates to ChromeOS all the time. To make sure you're using the latest release, open your settings then click the hamburger icon on the top left.

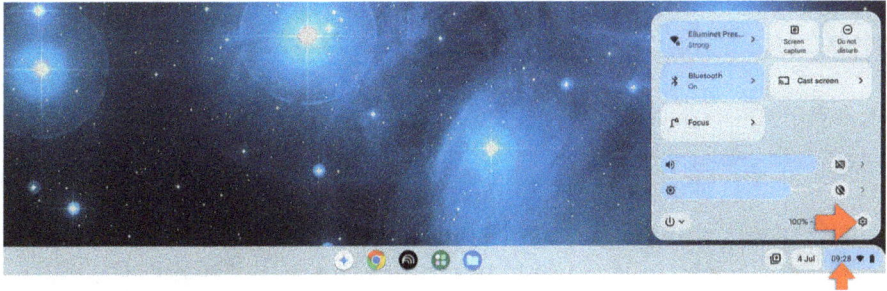

From the side panel that opens up, scroll down the list and select 'about chromeOS'.

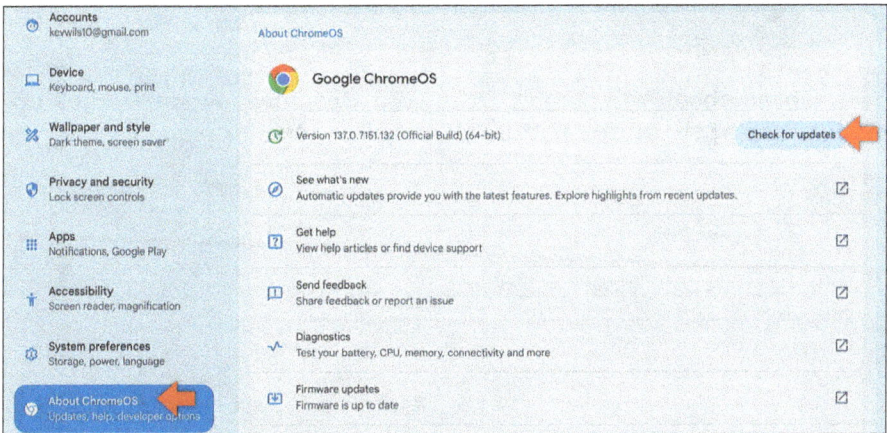

Click 'check for updates'.

Powerwash

Powerwash is a feature that resets your Chromebook to its factory settings. If you want to clear your personal data, accounts, and settings from the device—such as before selling it, giving it away, or starting fresh—you can use Powerwash to erase everything and return the Chromebook to its original state.

Note this process removes **all** user profiles and files stored locally on your device. It does not affect anything stored in your Google Account, Google Drive or Gmail.

To use Powerwash, open settings. Scroll down to 'system preferences'. Next to 'Powerwash', click 'Reset'.

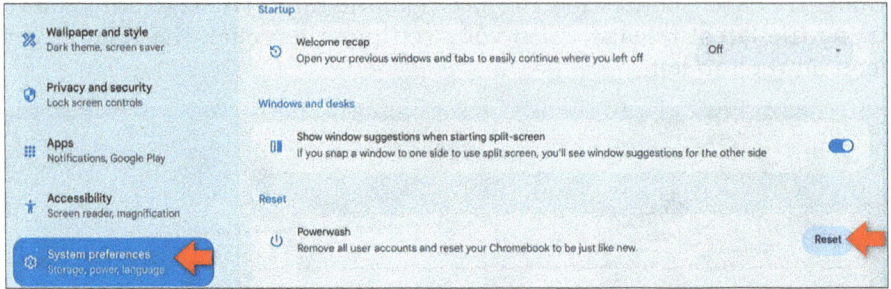

Click 'restart' on the confirmation dialog box.

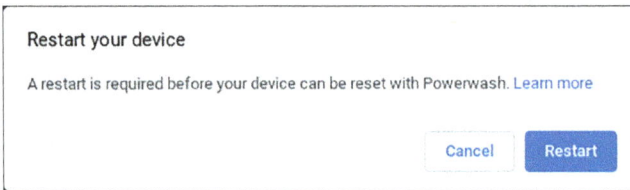

Your Chromebook will restart. Once your Chromebook starts back up, click 'powerwash' on the bottom right of the 'reset' screen.

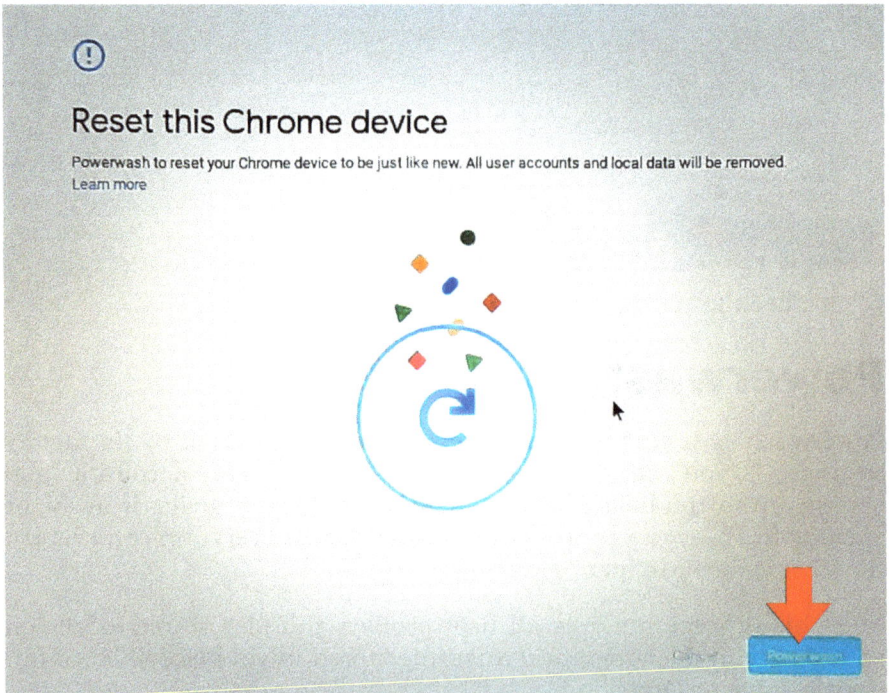

Click 'continue' on the confirmation dialog.

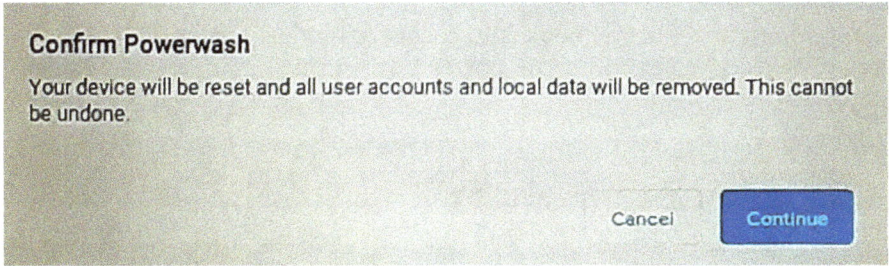

Confirm Powerwash

Your device will be reset and all user accounts and local data will be removed. This cannot be undone.

Cancel   Continue

Your Chromebook will reset.

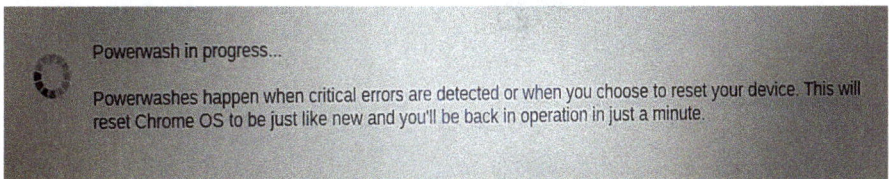

Powerwash in progress...

Powerwashes happen when critical errors are detected or when you choose to reset your device. This will reset Chrome OS to be just like new and you'll be back in operation in just a minute.

Once power wash has finished, you'll need to go through the initial setup again. See "Initial Setup" on page 26.

Safety Reset

Safety Reset is non-destructive reset that restores system and network settings to their defaults without deleting user accounts or personal files. This is useful for fixing issues like persistent pop-ups, browser hijackers, extension problems, or connectivity errors — without wiping your entire device with Powerwash.

Open the settings, select 'system preferences' then click 'safety reset' at the bottom of the page.

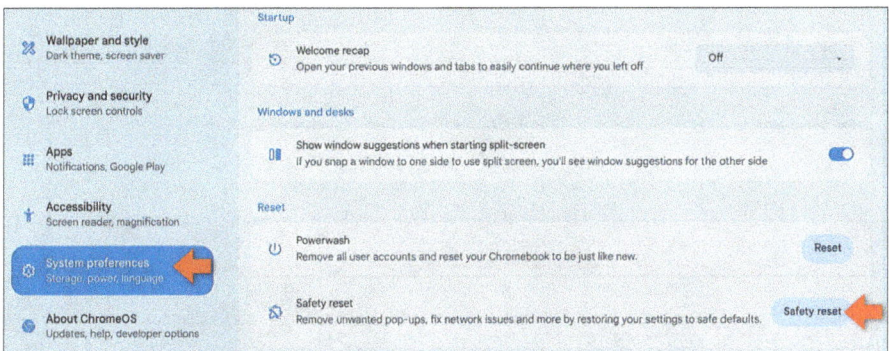

Run through the on screen prompts.

Chromebook Recovery

First, boot your Chromebook into recovery mode. Turn it off, then hold down escape, refresh and the power button until you see the recovery screen.

Next, you'll need to download the recovery utility. To to this, go to your PC or Mac, open the Chrome Web Browser and search for:

```
chromebook recovery utility
```

Click the link from the Google search results, as shown below.

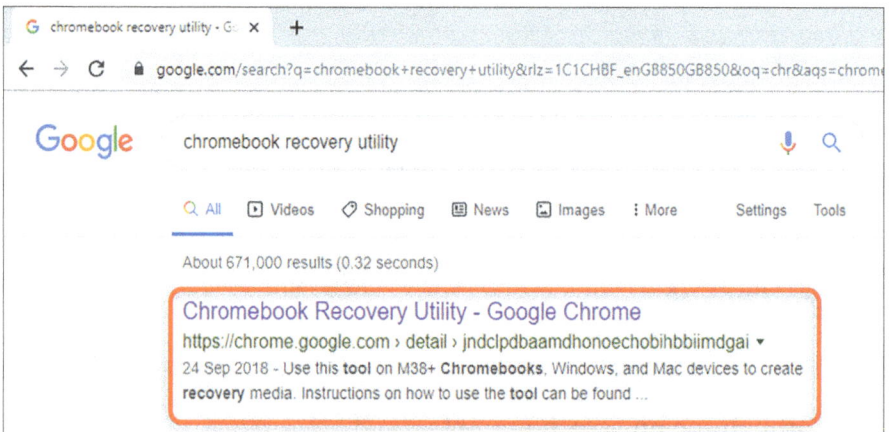

From the recovery utility page, click 'add to chrome', then click 'add app' on the pop up box.

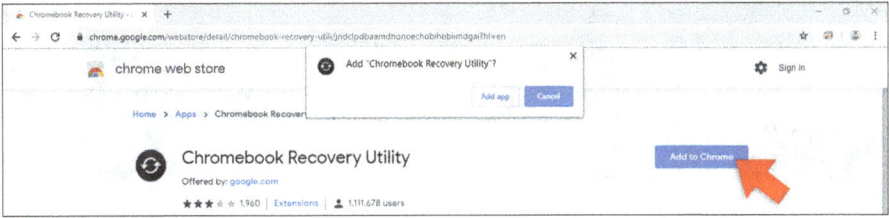

Click 'get started'.

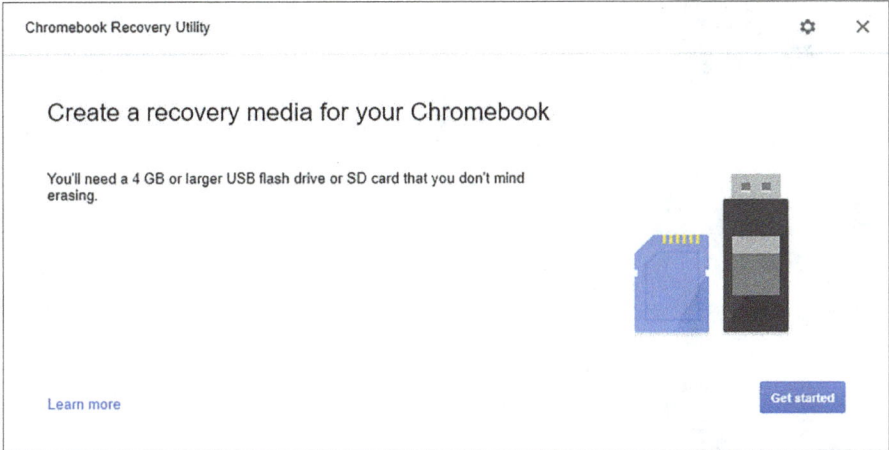

Now, select your Chromebook model.

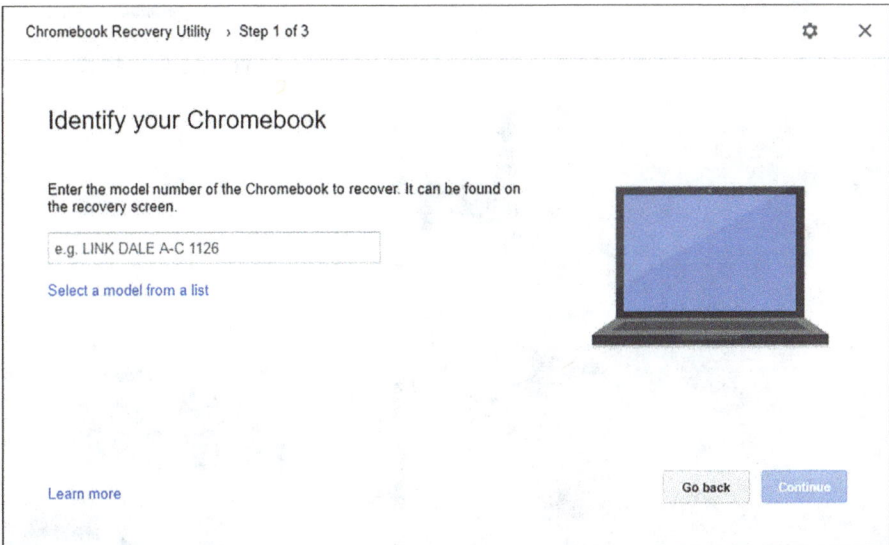

Chapter 11: Maintaining your Chromebook

To do this, type the code on the bottom of the recovery screen shown on your Chromebook, into the text field on the recovery utility. Click 'continue'.

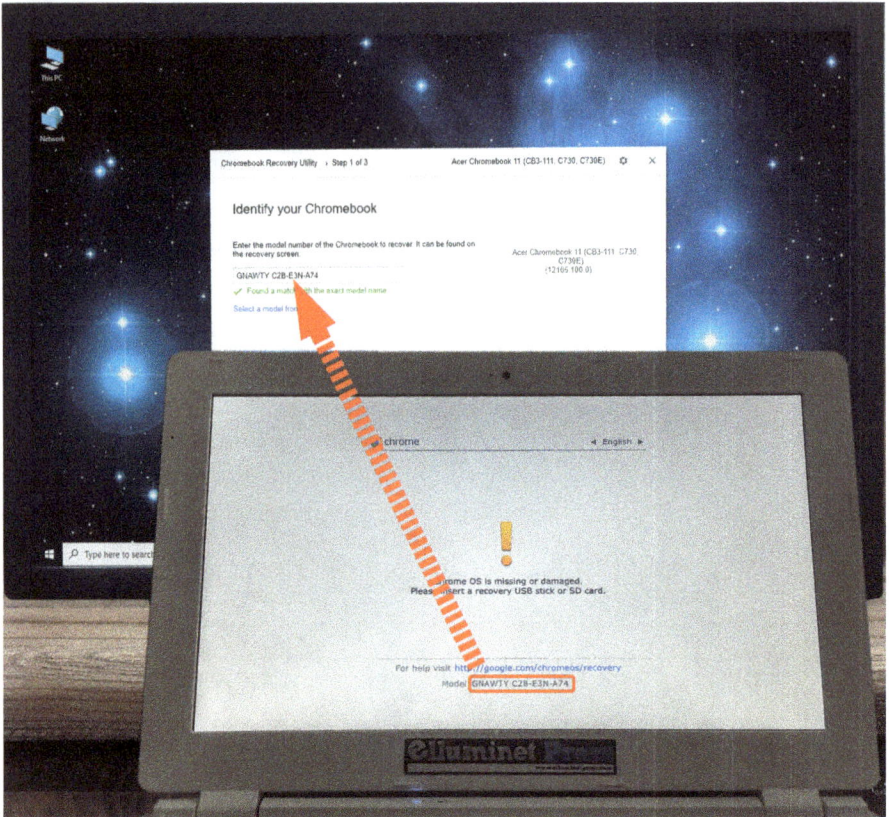

Insert a USB flash drive into a spare USB port on your PC/Mac.

From the drop-down menu, select the USB flash drive you just inserted. *Note that the USB flash drive will be erased.*

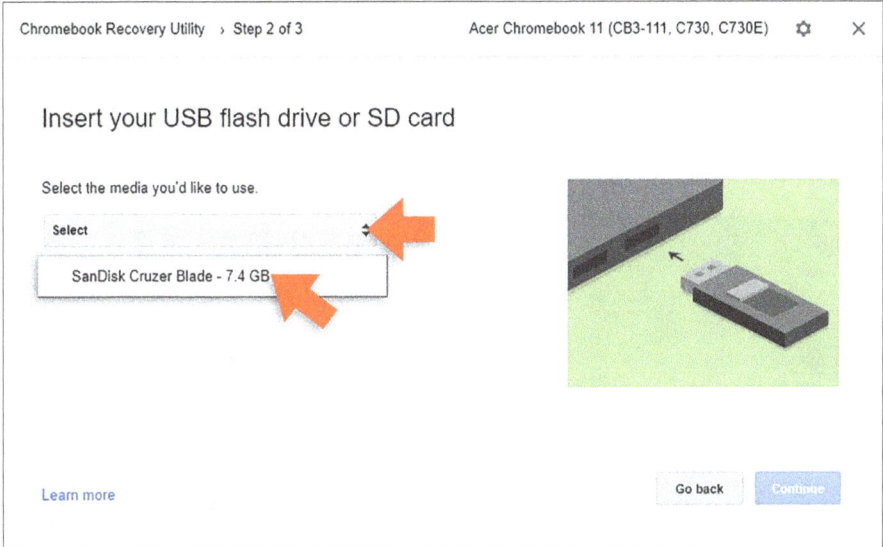

Click 'continue' on the bottom right of the window, then click 'create now' on the next screen. This process will take roughly 15 mins.

Once the process has finished. Remove the USB flash drive, from your PC/Mac, then insert it into a USB port on your Chromebook

Now you can begin the recovery procedure on your Chromebook.

Chapter 11: Maintaining your Chromebook

Once your Chromebook detects the USB flash drive, the recovery procedure will automatically begin.

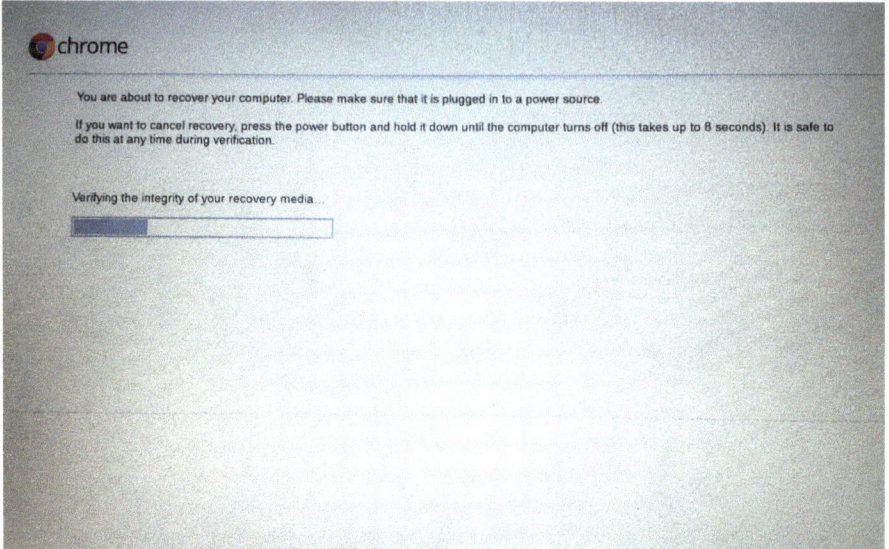

Once the process has finished, remove the USB flash drive, and the system will automatically restart.

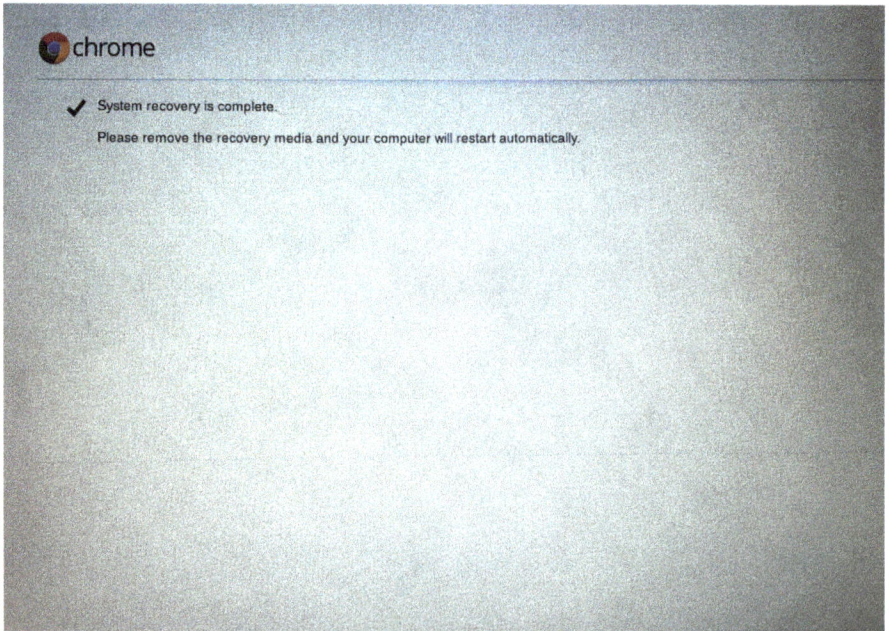

You'll need to go through the initial setup again on page 26.

App Info

The app info screen shows you information about a particular app such as how much space it occupies, permissions, data stored and cache.

To find info in a particular app, right click on the app's icon on the app launcher. Select 'app info' from the popup menu.

From here, you can set permissions that allow the app to access different hardware, or your physical location.

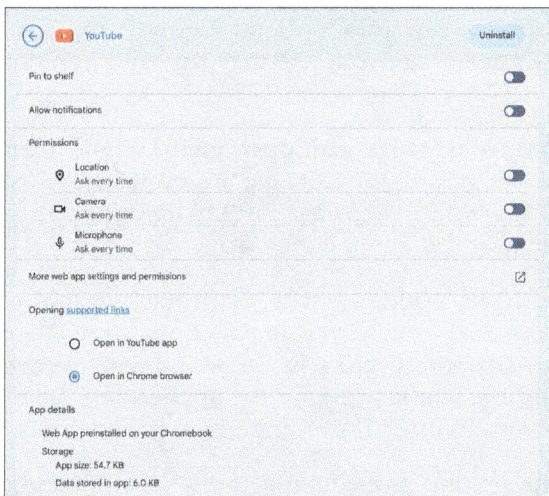

Click the switches on the right to enable or disable the permissions.

Chapter 11: Maintaining your Chromebook

You can click **Uninstall** to uninstall the app. **Pin to shelf** adds a shortcut to the app shelf for easy access. **Allow notifications** lets the app send you alerts and updates.

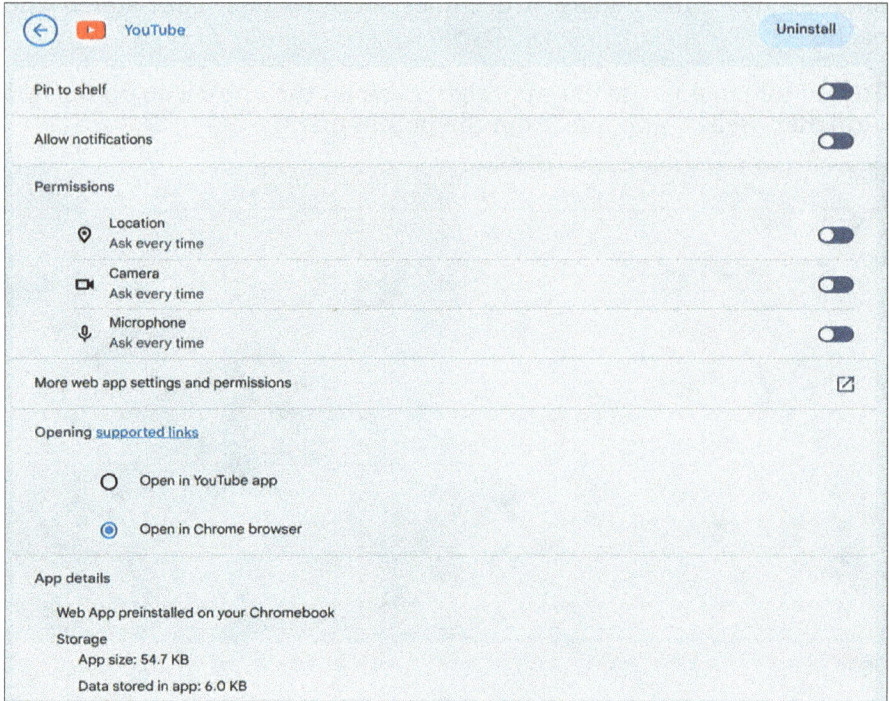

Under permissions, **Location** controls whether the web app can access your Chromebook's physical location using Wi-Fi or IP-based positioning. **Camera** controls whether the web app can access your webcam. **Microphone** controls whether the web app can access your microphone.

The **More web app settings and permissions** link opens the full site settings for the web app in the Chrome browser, where you can manage additional permissions such as notifications, pop-ups, automatic downloads, background sync, clipboard access, etc.

Opening supported links section controls how your Chromebook opens web links associated with this particular app. Choosing **Open in app** will launch supported links in the standalone web app, providing a dedicated window similar to a native application. Selecting **Open in Chrome browser** will open those links in a regular browser tab.

The **App details** section gives details about the app along with app size that shows the total storage space used by the app. Data stored in app indicates how much local data the app has saved on your device.

VPNs

A VPN is short for virtual private network. A VPN masks your IP address and establishes a secure and encrypted connection between you and the VPN service. This provides greater privacy when using the internet on public Wi-Fi hotspots.

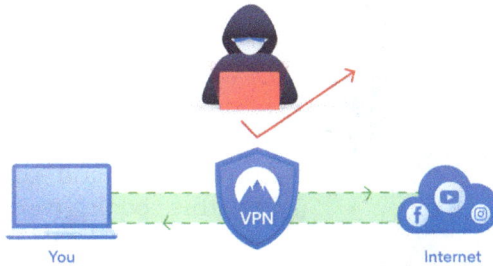

To use a public VPN on your Chromebook, you'll need to download an app from a VPN provider using the Google Play Store. There are various ones to choose from and the best VPN services come at a cost. Avoid the free ones. Some good VPNs are windscribe.com, nordvpn.com, and expressvpn.com. *Windscribe is good, as it gives you 10GB free a month.* Open the Play Store and search for the app.

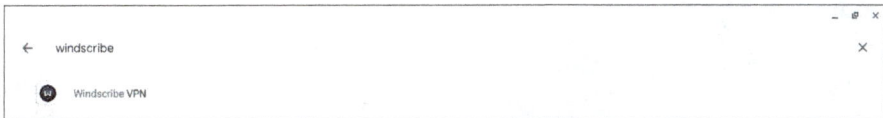

You'll find the app on your app launcher. Once you install and run the app, you'll need to sign up for an account.

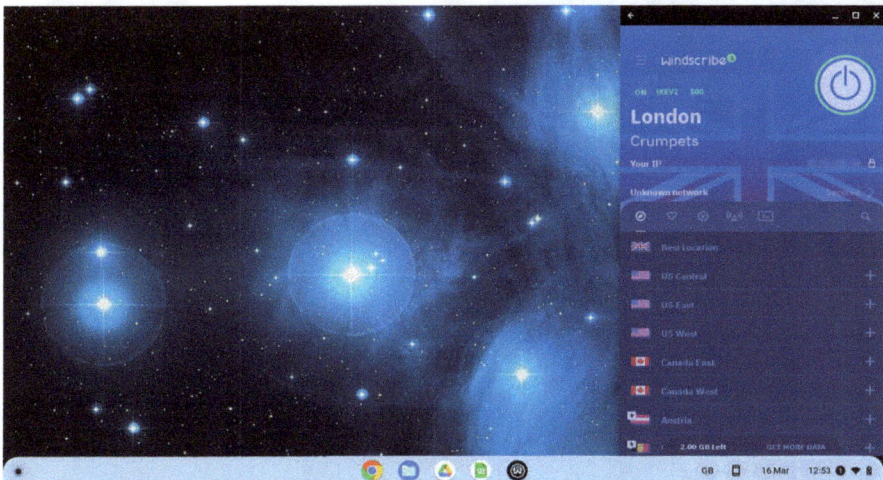

Turn on the VPN.

a Video Resources

To help you understand the procedures and concepts explored in this book, we have developed some video resources and app demos for you to use as you work through the book.

To find the resources, open your web browser and navigate to the following website

elluminetpress.com/chromebook

At the beginning of each chapter, you'll find a website that contains the resources for that chapter.

Using the Videos

Type the website URL into the address bar at the top of your browser. Don't use a search engine.

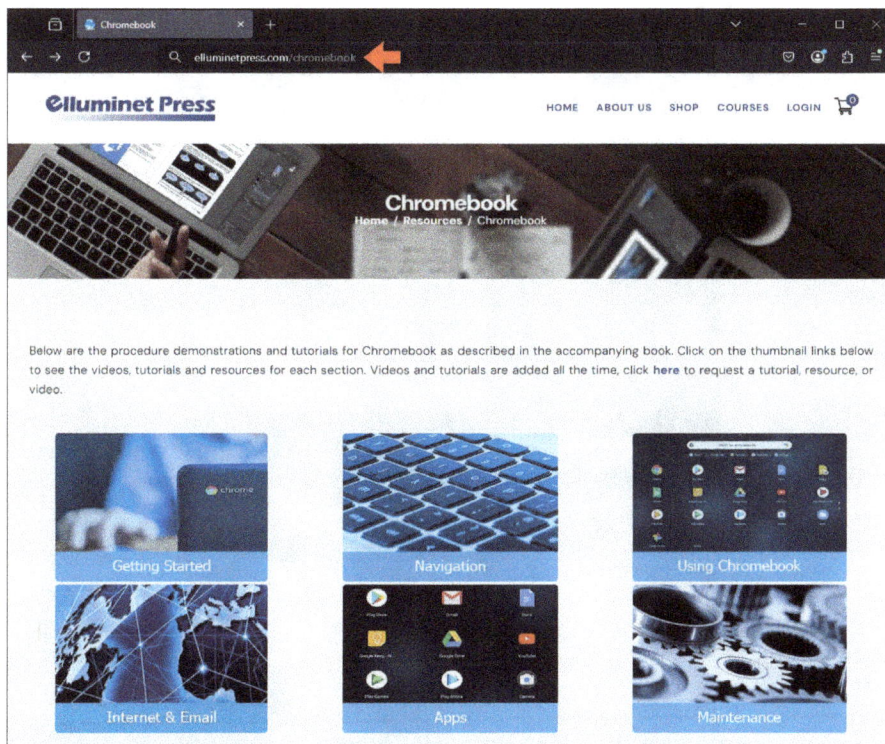

You'll see different categories. Click on these to access the videos.

When you open the link to the video resources, you'll see a thumbnail list at the bottom.

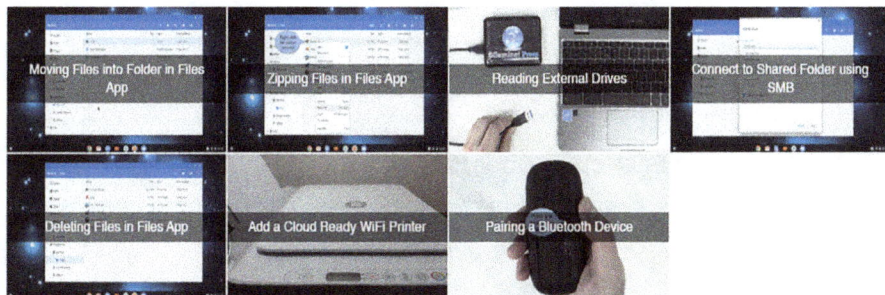

Click on the thumbnail for the particular video you want to watch. Most videos are between 40 and 90 seconds outlining the procedure, others are a bit longer.

387

When the video is playing, hover your mouse over the video and you'll see some controls.

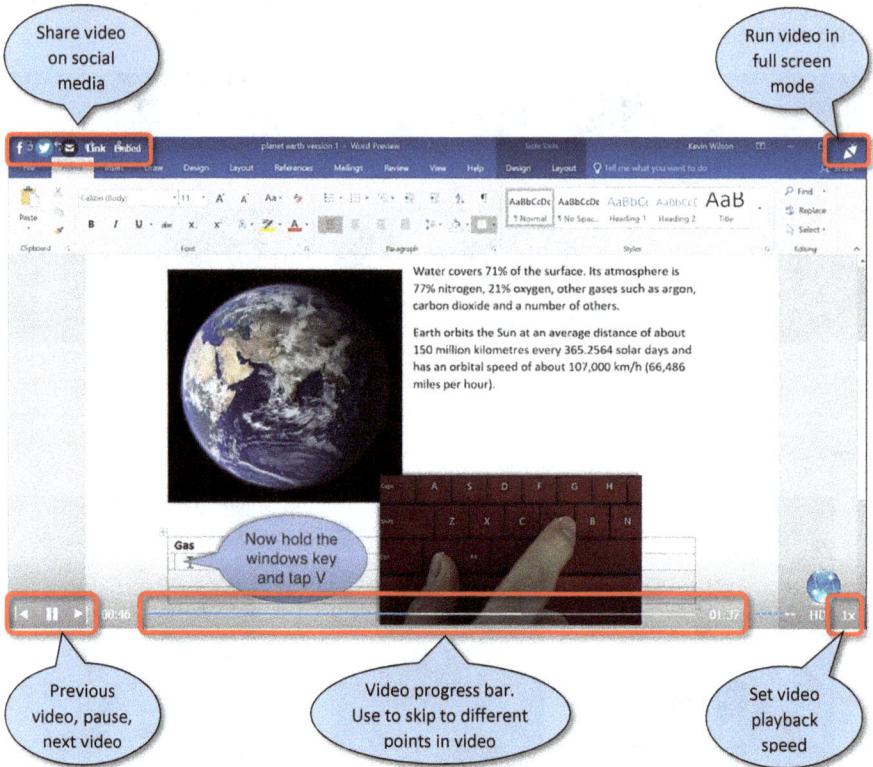

Share video on social media

Run video in full screen mode

Now hold the windows key and tap V

Previous video, pause, next video

Video progress bar. Use to skip to different points in video

Set video playback speed

Here, you can share the video on social media, make it full screen. You can also play/pause the video, jump to a particular part of the video using the progress bar and set the playback speed.

You'll also find cheat sheets.

Keyboard Shortcuts

Tips

Here, you'll find short-cuts, updates and tips.

Keyboard Shortcuts	

We've included some common keyboard shortcuts for your to use while you make your way around

Shortcut	Action
Ctrl + Alt + ?	Show all shortcuts
Shift Esc	Show task manager

You'll also find a tips section. Here, we'll keep you up to date with the latest tips and tricks to help you get the most out of Chromebook.

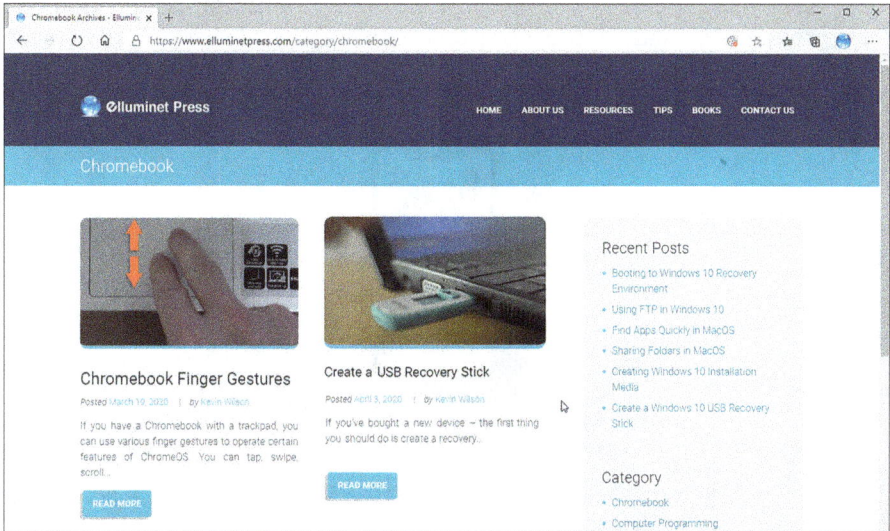

Finally, you'll find a glossary of computing terms.

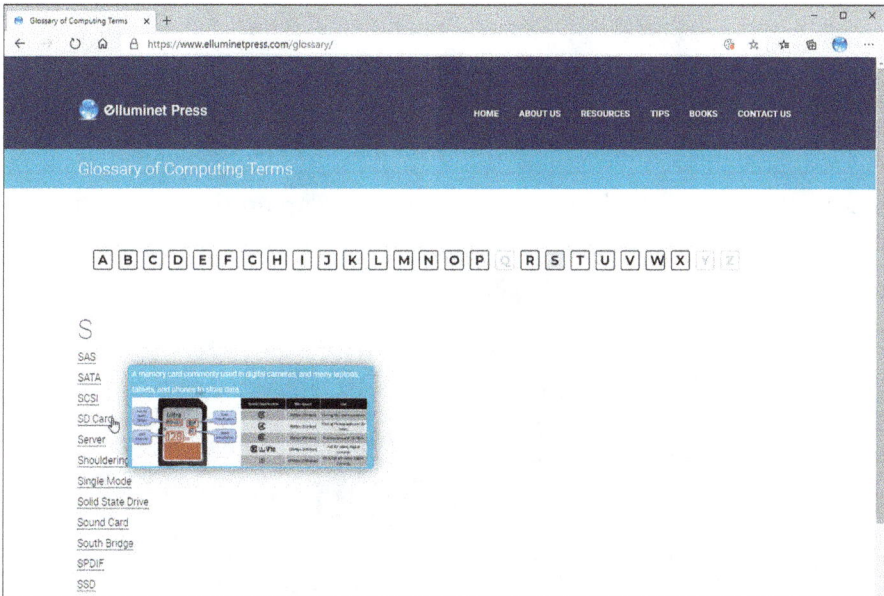

You can find the index here:

`elluminetpress.com/glossary`

This is integrated into the resources section.

Scanning the Codes

QR codes are placed at the beginning of each chapter and alongside key procedures within the chapter. You can scan these codes with your phone to access additional resources, downloadable files, and video demonstrations..

iPhone

To scan the code with your iPhone/iPad, open the camera app.

Frame the code in the middle of the screen. Tap on the website popup at the top.

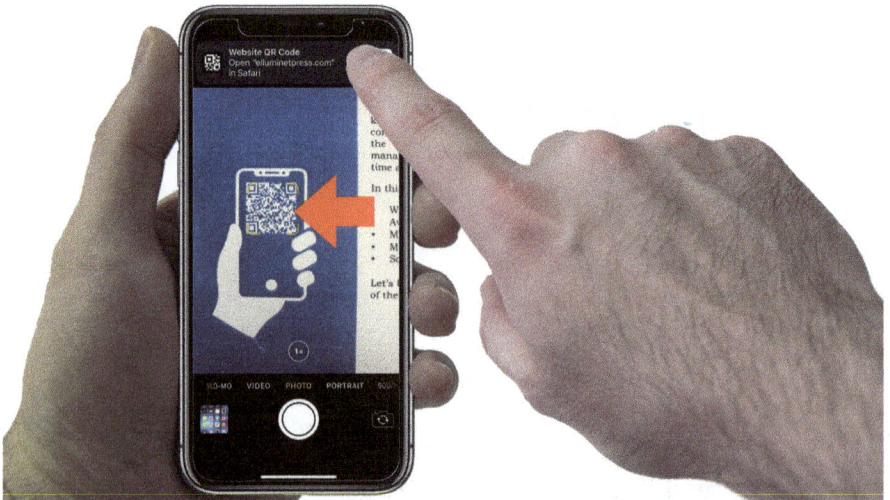

Android

To scan the code with your phone or tablet, open the camera app.

Frame the code in the middle of the screen. Tap on the website popup at the top.

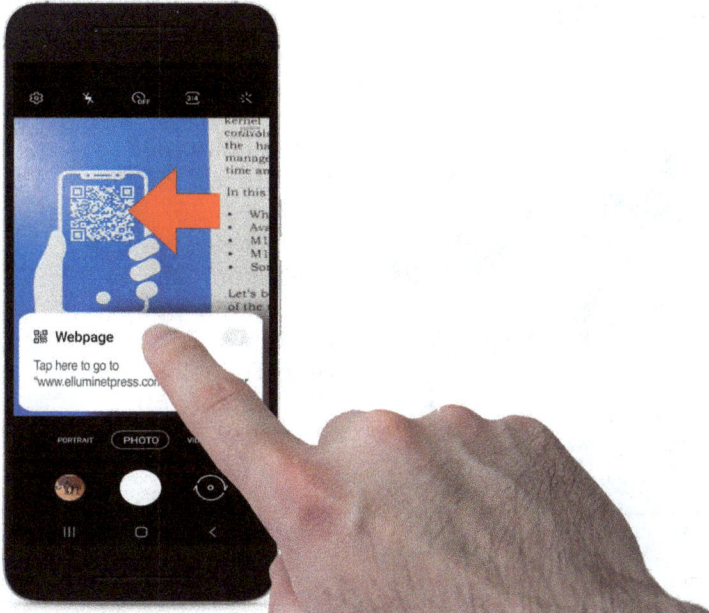

If it doesn't scan, turn on 'Scan QR codes'. To do this, tap the settings icon on the top left. Turn on 'scan QR codes'.

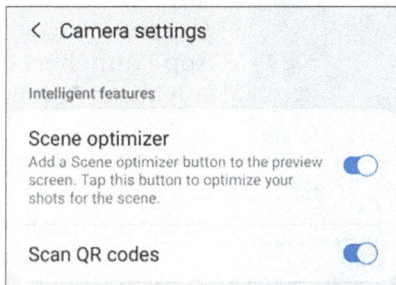

If the setting isn't there, you'll need to download a QR Code scanner. Open the Google Play Store, then search for "QR Code Scanner".

Index

Index

Index

Index

Index

SOMETHING NOT COVERED?

We want to create the best possible resources to help you learn and get things done, so if we've missed anything out, then please get in touch using the links below and let us know. Thanks.

office@elluminetpress.com

elluminetpress.com/feedback